ILLUSIONS OF JUSTICE

HUMAN RIGHTS VIOLATIONS IN THE UNITED STATES

Second Edition Augmented

An adaptation of the Legal Petition submitted to the United Nations on December 11, 1978, the 30th anniversary of the signing of the Universal Declaration of Human Rights by the United Nations, on behalf of Petitioners:

National Conference of Black Lawyers,
National Alliance Against Racist and Political Repression,
Commission on Racial Justice—United Church of Christ.

LENNOX S. HINDS

Attorney for the Petitioners

Hinds, Lennox S.
Illusions of justice.

"An adaptation of the Petition to the United Nations Commission on Human Rights and the Sub-Commission on Prevention of Discrimination and Protection of Minorities—Submitted to the United Nations on December 11, 1978 (the 30th anniversary of the signing of the Universal Declaration of Human Rights by the United Nations) on behalf of Petitioners: National Conference of Black Lawyers, National Alliance Against Racist and Political Repression, Commission on Racial Justice—United Church of Christ."

1. Civil rights – United States. I. Title
JC599.U5H45 323.4'0973 79-19318

First Edition Published in 1979
School of Social Work
University of Iowa
Iowa City, Iowa 52242

University of Iowa
Iowa City, Iowa 52242

Second Edition, printed in 2019

ISBN 9781079520286

TABLE OF CONTENTS

FOREWORD

Ambassador Andrew Young's remark in *Le Matin* on July 12, 1978, that "…there are hundreds, perhaps even thousands, of people I would call political prisoners…in the United States" reverberated throughout the world like a verbal rocket. In this country, it precipitated emotions ranging from appreciation of his candor to moral outrage. According to *The Washington Post,* U.S. Senator Barry Goldwater (R-Arizona) called the remark "lies" and said Young should be fired. Goldwater's reaction was followed by an abortive attempt to impeach Young, led by U.S. Representative Larry McDonald (D-Georgia), a John Birch Society sympathizer.

On the other hand, U.S. Representative John Conyers (D-Michigan) suggested that anyone familiar with the historical experience of Blacks and minorities in the U.S. was not shocked by Young's charge. He said, "Simply by reading the morning paper each day… [one finds] violations of constitutional and civil rights by the nation's highest officials [and] the FBI and the CIA." In the same July 12 edition of *The Washington Post* which carried these congressional reactions to Young's speech, other stories appeared as if to remind readers of the widespread government abuses that took place in response to political dissent in the 1960's. The following are three examples:

1. "Justice Department Vows Swift Probe of FBI Informant's Role" reported that the Justice Department is investigating charges that a paid FBI informant was responsible for the murders of civil rights workers in Alabama in the 1960's.
2. "Testimony Cites Hoover Approval of Black-Bag Jobs" reported that former FBI director Patrick L. Gray and Assistant Director Mark W. Felt were charged with conspiracy to violated the civil rights of family and friends of Weather Underground members. Attorneys for Gray and Felt argued that they were just following orders of J. Edgar Hoover, who personally authorized the series of break-ins and allegedly illegal wiretaps.
3. "Intelligence 'Reform' Sent to Floor" discussed congressional debate over a bill to impose judicial safeguards on the use of wiretapping and bugging.

Contrary to popular belief, however, controversy about political imprisonment in the United States is not only a product of the political activism of the 1960's. According to former U.S. Senator Charles Goodell in his 1973 book, *Political Prisoners in America,* we have always had political prisoners; throughout America's history, political dissenters have been imprisoned.

> In the perennial struggle for political power and in the inevitable conflicts that accompany change, dissenters and government alike have manipulated America's criminal process for political ends. It is through this intercourse of the political and criminal systems that "political prisoners" are born.

This duality of vision concerning the nature of legality in the United States—impartial evenhanded neutrality vs. selective application to dissidents—has characterized the analysis and experience of law and legal process in the United States for all of its history. Ambassador Young's remark, which can be seen as a spontaneous, simple, and undiplomatic response to his own experiences as a Black man and former civil rights activist, merely propelled to the front pages a perception which permeates both scholarly literature and the lives and thoughts of millions of Americans, particularly people of color.

Almost all of the material in this book was included in a Petition filed with the United Nations on December 11, 1978. That Petition, seeking the cleansing light of international scrutiny of the legally sanctioned treatment and conditions of confinement of many thousands in this country, was not a response to Andy Young's remark.

Long before, members of the petitioning organizations (The National Conference of Black Lawyers, the National Alliance Against Racist and Political Repression, and the Commission on Racial Injustice) and individual citizens everywhere had expressed outrage and frustration at their inability to pierce the domestic cocoon of smug, unexamined self-righteousness that shields the American legal system from examination, and encourages increasing and unconscionable abuse.

As a Black lawyer, teacher, and student of history, I could no longer participate without comment in the illusions of justice, in that endless and intricate labyrinth of legal process which holds tantalizing promises of relief, but which in practice merely validates the results of proceedings tainted with racism and political expediency.

The Petition was submitted to the United Nations not only to obtain relief from domestic oppression for the victims discussed, but also to focus national attention on the corrosive effects of manipulated and biased legal processes which subvert national standards of decency and democracy, and encourage an increasing national tolerance of domestic indifference to brutality and injustice under color of law.

As the Petition documents, despite our written Constitution and elaborate procedural mechanisms, despite national reliance on the law as an individual's shield against abusive governmental action, despite First Amendment guarantees of rights to protest and to voice unpopular views, repressive laws can be passed and existing laws used to suppress potentially effective action when those in power perceive real or imagined threats.

> "Civil liberties are thus parceled out to us at the discretion of the authority that we wish to dissent from, alter or destroy. All is on their terms, according to their rules and their application of the rules."[1]

The law is the mechanism by which authority implements its intentions.

For example, the response to anti-war demonstrators was the use of criminal laws to suppress their exercise of the right to assemble. Minority civil rights demonstrators have been prosecuted on criminal charges such as disorderly conduct, loitering, and violation of fire ordinances, because they attempted to realize their constitutional rights.

As dissidents are usually in pursuit of goals at variance with those who formulate and administer the law, those in power can and do use their authority to silence dissent when they perceive a threat to their control. Charging dissidents as criminals can serve to neutralize them by forcing them to spend time and funds needed for a legal defense; if prosecution is successful, it can take them out of civil society. Criminal charges damage the dissident's reputation and legitimacy.

---

1 Richard Quinney, *Critique of Legal Order: Crime Control in Capitalist Society* (Little, Brown & Co., 1973), p. 145.

Political dissidents and racial minorities who protest and demand change too often find that constitutional rights have little meaning as applied to them. In practice, freedom of speech, freedom of assembly, and the right to petition for redress of grievances are made to yield to political expediency under the rubrics of "law and order" or "national security." As shall be demonstrated, racial minorities (whose very economic, social, and political status have been defined historically by the racism which permeates the fabric of every institution in this society) are those who are most often forced into confrontation with the criminal law and the selective application of its sanctions, as a means of social control.

This analysis of the reality and implications of the administration of justice and of the roles of law and legality in the United States for advancing majority political purposes merely applies the same standards to this country as are applied to any other.

In the United States, as in other countries, the laws and administration of justice are not neutral, but rather are political tools for legitimating the exercise of authority by those in power and for suppressing dissent when deemed necessary.

The historical relationship of racial minority groups in America to the law is singularly graphic and illuminative of the selective use of the law to serve political ends. The law was used to strip Native Americans and Mexican-Americans of their property rights. The law enabled Europeans to make chattel goods of Africans. The law ensured the subjugation of minorities, excluded them from participation in the political process, and prevented challenges they might pose to white supremacy.

The political nature of the law is also manifested in the types of activities that are defined as crimes, and by the penalties selectively imposed for crimes committed by the rich and powerful as opposed to those committed by the poor and minorities.

Throughout the history of the United States, law has been the politically motivated instrument of racism. It has been used both overtly and covertly to enforce and legitimize enslavement, segregation, murder, and the theft of land, as well as for the systematic political, social, and economic oppression of minorities. A brief overview of the laws that have shaped the Black, Native American, Mexican-American, and Asian-American experience in the U.S. makes clear the roots of the use of the criminal justice system to victimize and oppress racial minorities. (In addition to citations within the Petition, readers seeking extended analysis of the role of law in perpetuating injustice are referred to Derrick Bell, *Race, Racism and American Law*; Haywood Burns, "Racism and American Law", in *Law Against the People*, Robert Lefcourt, ed.; and Paul Jacobs, Saul Landau, with Eve Pell, *To Serve the Devil*, Vol. 1, *Natives and Slaves,* and Vol. II, *Colonials and Sojourners.*

The first Africans taken forcibly from their homeland to colonial America arrived at Jamestown in August 1619. Within forty years, the Africans brought to America had become a group apart, separated from the rest of the population by law and custom. Legally classified as slaves for their lives, a status inherited by their children, forbidden to contract, learn, or intermarry with whites, deprived of their African traditions, and dispersed among Southern plantations, Blacks in American lost tribal, regional, and family ties. Chattel slavery, as it developed in the United States, laid the foundation for the institutionalized and legally sanctioned oppression discussed at length in the Petition.

Although most of the overtly racist laws have been overturned, and even though Blacks, Native Americans, and Asian-Americans are not longer barred from testifying in court against whites, the legacy of racism lives on through institutions which favor the rich over the poor and which favor white over Black, Brown, Red, or Yellow.

Institutionalized racism is most graphically demonstrated in the processes of the criminal justice system and in the selective enforcement of the laws against minorities as political dissidents and as disposable segments of the citizenry.

It is the contention of the Petition that the application of the law as a means of political control has impacted most heavily and egregiously on minority persons whose overt and expressed opposition and resistance to domestic policy and their oppressed status has placed them in direct confrontation with the majority society. They have opposed the historic use of the law to maintain the *status quo* of the poor and minority people in relation to the economic and social institutions of American society. By virtue of this opposition, they have become targets for criminal prosecution and illegal invasions of their rights through governmental efforts to suppress and control their dissent.

Three types of political prisoners whose treatment is exacerbated by their activism are discussed in the Petition:

1. Political activists who deliberately violate laws they believe to be unjust and immoral. Such political crimes includes a broad range of activities, ranging from non-violent acts of civil disobedience to acts of violence, but share a common intent to make a political statement. Because these are overt political acts, those convicted of them are sentenced far more harshly and severely than those without political intent who are convicted of the same acts.
2. Political activists who have been falsely charged with crimes they did not commit in a concerted effort by government authority to discredit them among their followers and to remove them physically from the arena of political organizing.
3. Prisoners who, after incarceration, articulate political views which prison authorities find threatening and who are therefore labeled as "trouble makers," a characterization which brings beatings and other brutalizing harassment, extended time in solitary confinement and "management control units", and extended prison sentences resulting from confrontations initiated by prison officials.

Finally, we discuss the broad range of prisoners whose race and economic status have made them victims of politically and racially selective application of the criminal law and whose conditions of confinement are brutal and inhumane.

Since the filing of the Petition in December 1978, as is not surprising, international interest in its allegations has far surpassed domestic concern.

The Commission on Human Rights, Sub-commission on Prevention of Discrimination and Protection of Minorities considered the Petition in the course of its agenda at its August 1979 meeting in Geneva. This author was present during the debate and deliberations which caused extensive interest among members of the international community.

Early in August 1979, an internationally representative delegation of jurists and lawyers from Africa, Asia, Europe, South America, and the Caribbean were invited to the United States to review the allegations contained in the Petition and the documentation in support of those allegations. They conducted in-person interviews with named prisoners and observed the conditions complained of so that they, as independent observers, could determine if there were "reasonable grounds to believe that...[the conditions of prisoners in the United States named in the Petition] reveal a consistent pattern of gross and reliably attested violation of human rights and fundamental freedoms including policies of racial discrimination...." To that end, eight jurists were invited to the United States August 3-20, 1979. They attended seminars, visited with prisoners, human rights activists, lawyers, and elected officials to make an independent determination of the reliability of the allegations consistent with the criteria established by ECOSOC Resolutions 1503(XLVIII) 27 May 1970 and Resolution 1(XXIV) 13 August 1971.

The Report and Findings of the International Jurists is included in its entirety as Appendix 1 to this publication of the adaption of the original Petition.

We have added two new chapters to this edition. Chapter Sixteen, entitled "The Death Penalty in the United States: A Consistent Pattern of Gross Violations," discusses the history of court-sanctioned capital punishment in the United States and its relationship in the context of international norms. Chapter Seventeen, entitled "Abuse of Power: Offenders and Offenses beyond the Reach of Law—Police Crimes in the United States," relates the racist and pervasive nature of police misconduct in the United States. Most of the material in Chapter Seventeen was presented at the Sixth United Nations Congress on Prevention of Crime and Treatment of Offenders in 1980 in Caracas, Venezuela.

Like the first edition, this book incorporates the complete text of the Petition filed with Secretary General Kurt Waldheim of the United Nations on December 11, 1978, on the occasion of the thirtieth anniversary of the signing of the Universal Declaration of Human Rights. Many of the appendices to the original Petition, which were filed with the United Nations as a separate volume, have been integrated into the text of the book to facilitate a coherent and comprehensive presentation. Footnotes refer to appendices which have not been included in this edition.

In addition to minor editorial corrections, some supplemental material has been added. Such new material is indicated in the text. The book has been newly divided into sections and chapters to enhance study of its content.

Publication of the Petition in this book form is intended to stimulate, goad, and, we hope, anger all who read it. We want to alert the American people to the growing unbridled use of power being exercised by State and Federal authorities whose very power is financed and authorized by the will of the people. We hope to force societal consideration of the increasing national tolerance for the brutalization of significant segments of the American people. We hope that conspicuous demonstrations of concern by readers of the book will result in some relief from oppression of those whose conditions we describe.

Those who view concern for the human rights of the poor and minority people in the States as a luxury that we can ill afford in times of inflation, international hostility, and an eroding quality of life must ask themselves what relationship the conditions we describe may have to our troubles at home and abroad. We hope that these connections will be made before it is too late.

LENNOX S. HINDS
Bluffton, South Carolina
May, 2019

ACKNOWLEDGMENTS

I want to extend my deep appreciation and gratitude to the following people and organizations for the generous contributions of expertise, energy, time, and money in the drafting, dissemination, and publication of the Petition and this volume.

Karoline Adams
Kay Anderson
Lauren Anderson, Esq.
Dr. John Else
Carol and Ping Ferry
Richard Harvey, Esq.
Shane Haynes
Deborah Jackson, Esq.
Dr. Dale Miller
Leora Mosston, Esq.
Patricia Murray, Esq.
Nathaniel Scott
Robinson-Spangler Carolina Room, Charlotte Mecklenburg Library
DeCourcy Squire

The National Conference of Black Lawyers, Victor Goode, Esq., and staff.
The National Alliance Against Racist and Political Repression, Charlene Mitchell and staff.
The Commission for Racial Justice of the United Church of Christ, Reverend Charles Cobb, and staff.
Disciples for Justice for Rice and Poindexter, Frank and Gladys Clark, and Bob Oberbillig.
I owe a special debt of gratitude to Anne Else for the endless hours of typing, proofreading and editing countless drafts and putting up at times with my unreasonable demands.

And to my brothers and sisters inside the jails and on the streets—solidarity and struggle.

Lennox S. Hinds

UPDATE ON POLITICAL PRISONERS

The information below appeared in the first edition and has been augmented in April 2019 with the latest information known to us about some of the prisoners and events referred to in the text.

American Indian Movement (AIM) Defendants

Dennis Banks. After Gov. Pat Brown of California refused to extradite Dennis Banks by executive order, Mr. Banks was free to live and travel within the confines of that state only, because he was still under indictment in South Dakota. After Gov. Brown left office in 1984, Banks received sanctuary from the Onondaga Nation in upstate New York. In 1985, Banks surrendered to federal law enforcement officials in South Dakota and served 18 months in prison related to the 1973 charges for the Custer riot. He died on October 29, 2017, of complications following heart surgery.

Russell Means. After a slow recovery from his injuries, Means sought parole in April 1979. He was not only denied parole but returned to maximum custody status without explanation to complete his sentence for riot to obstruct justice—under a statute which has since been repealed. He served a year in prison during which time he was stabbed by another prisoner. He died of esophageal cancer on October 22, 2012. It should be noted that *Ted Means*, Russell's brother, was also convicted on the same charge, in the fourth series of trials of the American Indian Movement Defendants. They were prosecuted by William Janklow, who was later elected governor of South Dakota, having built his political reputation on prosecution of AIM leaders.

Leonard Peltier. Peltier remains incarcerated at the U.S. Penitentiary in Coleman, Florida. His next parole hearing is scheduled for 2024 when he will be 80 years old. Mr. Peltier was denied clemency by President Obama in 2017.

Charlotte Three

As in the case of the Wilmington 10, relentless national and international protests focusing on North Carolina's repressive laws forced Gov. Jim Hunt to reduce the draconian sentences of the Charlotte Three and he subsequently commuted their sentences, so they were able to be freed from prison.

Imani (Johnny Harris)

On May 21, 1991, Imani (Johnny Harris) was released from prison after serving more than 20 years behind bars, all of them on death row.

Marion Prison

Bono v Saxbe

This was a lawsuit brought by prisoners held at the federal prison at Marion, IL, in the Behavior Control Unit. The appeal cited the cruel and unusual punishment to which they were subjected by the extreme isolation imposed on them and the unreasonable searches to which they were routinely subjected. Two years after the 1978 decision of the 7th Circuit Court of Appeals, which granted very limited relief, they sued because they contended that the prison was in violation. They lost this appeal, and the case was not heard by the US Supreme Court.

Olympic Prison

In 1978-79 there was organizing against turning the Olympic Village in Lake Placid NY into a prison. A group called STOP (Stop the Olympic Prison) brought a civil suit to try to halt its conversion. Unfortunately the suit failed, and the prison opened as Ray Brook Federal Correctional Institution in 1980. It is a medium security prison which houses about 700-800 male prisoners, serving an average sentence of 10 years.

George Merritt

George Merritt was tried and convicted a third time based on the testimony of the State's only eye-witness, whom the Appellate Court had described as unreliable. In 1980, the U.S. District Court reversed Mr. Merritt's conviction, based upon the finding that the state prosecutor had withheld exculpatory evidence. Mr. Merritt was finally freed after spending over 10 years in prison for a crime he did not commit.

Imari Abubakari Obadele I

Mr. Obadele died on January 18, 2010.

The Puerto Rican Nationalists

Lolita Lebron, Rafael Cancel Miranda, Andres Fugueroa Cordero and Irving Flores spent 25 years in prison and Oscar Collazo spent 29 years in prison, before being pardoned by President Jimmy Carter after their cases were presented by this author in a Petition to the United Nations Human Rights Commission.

David Rice and Edward Poindexter

Although FBI memos from its COINTELPRO program (see Chapter 3) obtained in the late 1970's documented suppression of evidence by the local police in collaboration with the FBI, numerous subsequent appeals utilizing this evidence, as well as raising other issues of irregularities in the judicial process which convicted these two men, were all unsuccessful. David Rice, who took the name Wopashitwe Mondo Eyen we Langa while in prison, died on March 11, 2016 in the Nebraska State Penitentiary; Edward Poindexter remains incarcerated in the Nebraska State Penitentiary. It should be noted that, in the early to mid-1990s, the Nebraska State Parole Board voted unanimously several years consecutively that the life sentences for these two men should be commuted to make them eligible for parole because they did not pose a danger to the community. The Nebraska Pardons Board would not even grant hearings to consider commutation. Instead, Gov. Ben Nelson changed the personnel on the Nebraska Parole Board.

Assata Shakur

In 1979, Assata Shakur escaped from Clinton Reformatory for Women in New Jersey and was subsequently granted political asylum in Cuba, where she still lives. On May 2, 2013, Ms. Shakur was named to the FBI's Most Wanted Terrorists List.

Delbert Tibbs

Tibbs was released from prison in January 1977 and died on November 26, 2013.

Gary Tyler

In 2012, Gary Tyler's sentence was declared unconstitutional. The district attorney agreed to vacate his conviction and Mr. Tyler agreed to plead guilty to manslaughter and receive a maximum sentence of 21 years. Since he had served more than twice that amount of time in Louisiana jails and maximum security prison, he was released at 4:45 p.m. on April 29, 2016.

Wilmington Ten

An opinion was finally handed down on June 19, 1979, on the *Habeas Corpus* petition filed on their behalf in May 1977. It found that their trial was "not constitutionally flawed" even though it recognized certain "problems" during the proceedings.

As a result of protracted national and international protests, after nearly a decade, the Wilmington Ten had their convictions overturned in 1980. Subsequently, a petition drive by the National Conference of Black Lawyers, the National Alliance Against Racist and Political Repression, the United Church of Christ's Commission for Racial Justice, the North Carolina NAACP, and other civil rights groups, Gov. Beverly Perdue formally pardoned the Wilmington Ten.

Helsinki Watch

Helsinki Watch began as a US NGO. It was formed in 1978 to monitor the USSR's compliance with the human rights standards established by the Helsinki Accords. In 1981, to be balanced, it initiated Americas Watch, to monitor human rights violations in the Western Hemisphere. There it focused primarily on human rights abuses in Central America as well as US interventions there. The organization expanded to Watches on other continents. In 1988 all of the Watch organizations were consolidated to form Human Rights Watch. In 1993, in conjunction with the ACLU, it issued a report on US violations of the human rights set forth in the International Covenant on Civil and Political Rights.

SECTION ONE OF THE PETITION
The Legal and Historical Basis for the Petition

Chapter One
The Legal Basis for the Petition

A. Statement of Purpose

As one examines the effects and results of the criminal justice system within the United States, it becomes clear that Blacks, Puerto Ricans, Native Americans, Mexican-Americans, and other minorities are victims of deliberate governmental policies and practices that deny them basic human rights and abridge fundamental freedoms solely on the basis of race, color, descent, or national or ethnic origin. These racist policies and practices are sharply manifest by the plights of the numerous political prisoners incarcerated in the jails and prisons throughout the United States.

When Andrew Young, U.S. Ambassador to the United Nations, stated that, "After all, in our prisons too, there are hundreds, perhaps even thousands, of people whom I would call political prisoners…,"[1] there was immediate and hostile reaction from the majority political structure. In addition to calls for Ambassador Young's resignation, an impeachment resolution was introduced in the House of Representatives. Every major establishment newspaper carried editorials vigorously condemning and denying the validity and implications of this statement. Ambassador Young was not asked to explain or clarify his remarks to the public. These reactions are clearly understood when viewed in the context of the United States foreign policy decision to take upon itself the duty and responsibility of denouncing and monitoring human rights violations in various countries, albeit in a highly selective manner. An examination of the U.S. voting record at the United Nations over the thirty-three years since its establishment is quite instructive on the question of the U.S. government's positions on human rights.[2] Furthermore, the United States has consistently refused to investigate the validity of serious and blatant human rights violations within its own borders, in spite of voluminous documents and petitions that have been filed with the appropriate governmental agencies and departments.

The racially selective and repressive use of the American criminal justice system, in the various states and by the federal government, inculpates the processes of arrest, indictment, trial by judge or jury, conviction, sentencing, and incarceration. Because of the institutionalization of racism in these processes, the United States violated the fundamental principles embodied in the *United States Constitution* as well the basic human rights and fundamental freedoms outlined in the *Universal Declaration of Human Rights*, the *International Convention on the Elimination of All Forms of Racial Discrimination*, the *International Covenant on Civil and Political Rights,* and the *International Covenant on Economic, Social, and Cultural Rights*.

It is because of the continuing racist and political oppression and exploitation visited upon Blacks and other minorities within the United States solely on the basis of their race, color, descent, or national or ethnic origin and political views that the Petitioners—the National Conference of Black Lawyers, the United Church of Christ Commission for Racial Justice, and the National Alliance Against Racist and Political Repression—have filed this petition on behalf of the victims of these racist government policies and practices.

This petition, by highlighting the situations of those individuals whom the Petitioners define as political prisoners within the United States, will provide this forum with instances of the patterns and practices of racism about which Petitioners complain. Political prisoners are defined as

(a) Those persons whose overt and expressed rejection of, opposition and resistance to United States national policies and activities place them in direct confrontation with the majority government and who, thereby, are selected by governmental entities for criminal prosecutions and illegal invasions of their rights as evidenced by the revelations of the COINTELPRO activities of the Federal Bureau of Investigation and other governmental misconduct;[3]

(b) Persons imprisoned initially for convictions of crimes who receive additional and extended sentences and are subjected to harsh and brutal treatment as a result of their political activities within the prison to bring about changes in the dehumanizing conditions and treatment of prisoners in general; and

(c) Persons whose race, ethnic identity, and economic status expose them to politically selective application of the law and make them victims of the criminal justice processes. The treatment of such arbitrarily selected persons during the proceedings of arrest, trial, and sentencing, and during incarceration reflects the callous disregard for human and legal rights which characterizes their conditions in every other phase of American life and is intended to ensure political control of this population.

Petitioners seek to bring to the attention of the Commission on Human Rights and the Sub-Commission on Prevention of Discrimination and Protection of Minorities the consistent pattern of gross, well-documented, and attested violations of human rights and fundamental freedoms prevalent in the United States by the examples of the experiences and conditions of various political prisoners as exemplars of the allegations set forth herein. These named individuals are to be viewed not only on the basis of their particular situation, but also as representatives of the class of persons discussed herein who are victims of racist and oppressive government policies and practices since it is impossible to name each individual in the United States who is similarly situated.

The Petition is presented to the bodies of the United Nations because, as will be demonstrated, the very processes which purport to provide hope of legal and equitable redress are so tainted with the racist and politically repressive conduct complained of by Petitioners on behalf of the class that it is therefore improbable, if not impossible, to obtain relief in the domestic forum.[4]

Because all efforts for domestic inquiry and remedies have failed, petitioners seek assistance from the Commission on Human Rights and the Sub-Commission for Prevention of Discrimination and Protection of Minorities and pray that they will review the allegations herein and take the necessary measures to remedy such gross and consistent patterns of the violations of human rights and fundamental freedoms which exist within the United States of America, as we will establish.

B. Jurisdiction

Jurisdiction to review this Petition is conferred upon the U.N. Commission on Human Rights and the Sub-Commission for Prevention of Discrimination and Protection of Minorities pursuant to three resolutions:

> *Resolution 728 F (XXVIII) of the Economic and Social Council* (hereinafter referred to as ECOSOC) of 30 July 1959, providing for the distribution of communications by the Secretary-General which deal with the principles involved in the promotion of universal respect for, and observance of, human rights.
>
> *ECOSOC Resolution 1503 (XLVII)* of 27 May 1970, authorizing the Sub-Commission on Prevention of Discrimination and Protection of Minorities to consider communications which reveal a consistent pattern of gross and reliably attested violations of human rights and fundamental freedoms and to refer them to the Commission on Human Rights for consideration.
>
> *Resolution I (XXIV) of the Sub-Commission on Prevention of Discrimination and Protection of Minorities* (13 August 1971), delineating the appropriate procedures for the admissibility of communications received pursuant to the aforementioned Resolutions.

These Resolutions, in conjunction with the Charter of the United Nations, vest the power to investigate and define the policy and standards by which evidence of human rights violations in any country should be analyzed by the Commission on Human Rights. The full texts of these Resolutions, which appeared as Appendix Two in the original Petition, are included in total here.

Resolution 728 F (XXVIII) of the Economic and Social Council
Communications Concerning Human Rights

The Economic and Social Council,

Having considered Chapter V of the report of the Commission on Human Rights at its first session, concerning communications, and Chapter IX of the report of the Commission on its fifteenth session,

1. *Approves* the statement that the Commission on Human Rights recognizes that it has no power to take any action in regard to any complaints concerning human rights;

2. *Requests* the Secretary-General:

(a) To compile and distribute to members of the Commission on Human Rights before each session a non-confidential list containing a brief indication of the substance of each communication, however addressed, which deals with the principles involved in the promotion of universal respect for, and observance of, human rights and to divulge the identity of the authors of such communications unless they indicate that they wish their names to remain confidential;

(b) To compile before each session of the Commission a confidential list containing a brief indication of the substance of other communications concerning human rights, however addressed, and to furnish this list to members of the Commission, in private meeting, without divulging the identity of the authors of communications except in cases where the authors state that they have already divulged or intend to divulge their names or that they have no objection to their names being divulged;

(c) To enable the members of the Commission, upon request, to consult the originals of communications dealing with the principles involved in the promotion of universal respect for, and observance of, human rights;

(d) To inform the writers of all communications concerning human rights, however addressed, that their communications will be handled in accordance with this resolution, indicating that the Commission has no power to take any action in regard to any complaint concerning human rights;

(e) To furnish each Member State concerned with a copy of any communication concerning human rights which refers explicitly to that State or to territories under its jurisdiction, without divulging the identity of the author, except as provided for in sub-paragraph *(b)* above;

(f) To ask Governments sending replies to communications brought to their attention in accordance with sub-paragraph (e) whether they wish their replies to be presented to the Commission in summary form or in full;

3. *Resolves* to give members of the Sub-Commission on Prevention of Discrimination and Protection of Minorities, with respect to communications dealing with discrimination and minorities, the same facilities as are enjoyed by members of the Commission on Human Rights under the present resolution;

4. *Suggests* to the Commission on Human Rights that it should at each session appoint an ad hoc committee to meet shortly before its next session for the purpose of reviewing the list of communications prepared by the Secretary-General under paragraph 2(a) above and of recommending which of these communications, in original, should, in accordance with paragraph 2(c) above, be made available to members of the Commission on request.

1088 plenary meeting,
30 July 1959.

Resolution 1503 (XLVIII) of the Economic and Social Council
Procedure for Dealing with Communications Relating to Violations of Human Rights and Fundamental Freedoms

The Economic and Social Council,

Noting Resolutions 7 (XXVI) and 17 (XXV) of the Commission on Human Rights and Resolution 2 (XXI) of the Sub-Commission on Prevention of Discrimination and Protection of Minorities,

1. *Authorizes* the Sub-Commission on Prevention of Discrimination and Protection of Minorities to appoint a working group consisting of not more than five of its members, with due regard to geographic distribution, to meet once a year in private meetings for a period not exceeding ten days immediately before the sessions of the Sub-Commission to consider all communications, including replies of Governments thereon, received by the Secretary-General under Council resolution 728 F (XXVIII) of 30 July 1939 with a view to bringing to the attention of the Sub-Commission those communications, together with replies of Governments, if any, which appear to reveal a consistent pattern of gross and reliably attested violations of human rights and fundamental freedoms within the terms of reference of the Sub-Commission;

2. *Decides* that the Sub-Commission on Prevention of Discrimination and Protection of Minorities should, as the first stage in the implementation of the present resolution, devise at its twenty-third session appropriate procedures for dealing with the question of admissibility of communications received by the Secretary-General under Council resolution 728 F (XXVIII) and in accordance with Council Resolution 1235 (XLII) of 6 June 1967;

3. *Requests* the Secretary-General to prepare a document on the question of admissibility of communications for the Sub-Commission's consideration at its twenty-third session;

4. *Further requests* the Secretary-General:

To furnish to the members of the Sub-Commission every month a list of communications prepared by him in accordance with Council Resolution 728 F (XXVIII) and a brief description of them, together with the text of any replies from Governments;

To make available to the members of the working group at their meetings the originals of such communications listed as they may request, having due regard to the provisions of paragraph 2(b) of Council Resolution 728 F (XXVIII) concerning the divulging of the identity of the authors of communications;

To circulate to the members of the Sub-Commission, in the working languages, the originals of such communications as are referred to the Sub-Commission by the working group;

5. *Requests* the Sub-Commission on Prevention of Discrimination and Protection of Minorities to consider in private meetings, in accordance with paragraph 1 above, the communications brought before it in accordance with the decision of a majority of the members of the working group and any replies of Governments relating thereto and other relevant information, with a view to determining whether to refer to the Commission on Human Rights particular situations which appear to reveal a consistent pattern of gross and reliably attested violations of human rights requiring consideration by the Commission;

6. *Requests* the Commission on Human Rights after it has examined any situation referred to it by the Sub-Commission to determine:

(a) Whether it requires a thorough study by the Commission and a report and recommendations thereon to the Council in accordance with paragraph 3 of Council Resolution 1235 (XLII);

(b) Whether it may be a subject of an investigation by an ad hoc committee to be appointed by the Commission which shall be undertaken only with the express consent of the State concerned and shall be conducted in constant co-operation with that State and under conditions determined by agreement with it. In any event, the investigation may be undertaken only if:

(i) All available means at the national level have been resorted to and exhausted;

(ii) The situation does not relate to a matter which is being dealt with under other procedures prescribed in the constituent instruments of, conventions adopted by, the United Nations and the specialized agencies, or in regional conventions, or which the state concerned wishes to submit to other procedures in accordance with general or special international agreements to which it is a party.

7. *Decides* that if the Commission on Human Rights appoints an ad hoc committee to carry on an investigation with the consent of the State concerned:

(a) The composition of the committee shall be determined by the Commission. The members of the committee shall be independent persons whose competence and impartiality is beyond question. Their appointment shall be subject to the consent of the Government concerned;

(b) The committee shall establish its own rules of procedure. It shall be subject to the quorum rule. It shall have the authority to receive communications and hear witnesses, as necessary. The investigation shall be conducted in co-operation with the Government concerned;

(c) The committee's procedure shall be confidential, its proceedings shall be conducted in private meetings and its communications shall not be publicized in any way;

(d) The committee shall strive for friendly solutions before, during and even after the investigation;

(e) The committee shall report to the Commission on Human Rights with such observations and suggestions as it may deem appropriate;

8. *Decides* that all actions envisaged by the implementation of the present resolution by the Sub-Commission on Prevention of Discrimination and Protection of Minorities or the Commission on Human Rights shall remain confidential until such time as the Commission may decide to make recommendations to the Economic and Social Council;

9. *Decides* to authorize the Secretary-General to provide all facilities which may be required to carry out the present resolution, making use of the existing staff of the Division of Human Rights of the United Nations Secretariat;

10. *Decides* that the procedure set out in the present resolution for dealing with communications relating to violations of human rights and fundamental freedoms should be reviewed if any new organ entitled to deal with such communications should be established within the United Nations or by international government.

1693rd plenary meeting,
27 May 1970.

Resolution 1 (XXIV) of the Sub-Commission on Prevention of Discrimination and Protection of Minorities
Question of the Violation of Human Rights and Fundamental Freedoms, Including Policies of Racial Discrimination and Segregation and of Apartheid in All Countries, with Particular Reference to Colonial and Other Dependent Countries and Territories

The Sub-Commission on Prevention of Discrimination and Protection of Minorities

Considering that the Economic and Social Council, by its Resolution 1503 (XLVIII), decided that the Sub-Commission should devise appropriate procedures for dealing with the question of admissibility of communications received by the Secretary-General under Council Resolution 728 F (XXVIII) of 30 July 1959 and in accordance with Council Resolution 1235 (XLII) of 6 June 1967,

Adopts the following provisional procedures for dealing with the question of admissibility of communications referred to above:

1. Standards and criteria

(a) The object of the communication must not be inconsistent with the relevant principles of the Charter, of the Universal Declaration of Human Rights and of the other applicable instruments in the field of human rights.

(b) Communications shall be admissible only if, after consideration thereof, together with the replies of any of the governments concerned, there are reasonable grounds to believe that they may reveal a consistent pattern of gross and reliably attested violations of human rights and fundamental freedoms, including policies of racial discrimination and segregation and of apartheid in any country, including colonial and other dependent countries and peoples.

2. Source of communications

(a) Admissible communications may originate from a person or group of persons who, it can be reasonably presumed, are victims of the violations referred in subparagraph 1.(b) above, any person or group of persons who have direct and reliable knowledge of those violations, or non-governmental organizations acting in good faith in accordance with recognized principles of human rights, not resorting to politically motivated stands contrary to the provisions of the Charter of the United Nations and having direct and reliable knowledge of such violations.

(b) Anonymous communications shall be inadmissible; subject to the requirements of subparagraph 2.(b) of Resolution 728 F (XXVIII) of the Economic and Social Council, the author of a communication, whether an individual, a group of individuals or an organization, must be clearly identified.

(c) Communications shall not be inadmissible solely because the knowledge of the individual authors is second-hand, provided that they are accompanied by clear evidence.

3. Contents of communications and nature of allegations

(a) The communication must contain a description of the fact and must indicate the purpose of the petition and the rights that have been violated.

(b) Communications shall be inadmissible if their language is essentially abusive and in particular if they contain insulting references to the State against which the complaint is directed. Such communications may be considered if they meet the other criteria for admissibility after deletion of the abusive language.

(c) A communication shall be inadmissible if it has manifestly political motivations and its subject is contrary to the provisions of the Charter of the United Nations.

(d) A communication shall be inadmissible if it appears that it is based exclusively on reports disseminated by mass media.

4. Existence of other remedies

(a) Communications shall be inadmissible if their admission would prejudice the functions of the specialized agencies of the United Nations system.

(b) Communications shall be inadmissible if domestic remedies have not been exhausted, unless it appears that such remedies would be ineffective or unreasonably prolonged. Any failure to exhaust remedies should be satisfactorily established.

(c) Communications relating to cases which have been settled by the State concerned in accordance with the principles set forth in the Universal Declaration of Human Rights and other applicable documents in the field of human rights will not be considered.

5. Timeliness

A communication shall be inadmissible if it is not submitted to the United Nations within a reasonable time after the exhaustion of the domestic remedies as provided above.

627th meeting,
13 August 1971.

C. Statement of Standing

The Petitioner, the National Conference of Black Lawyers (NCBL), in cooperation with the National Alliance Against Racist and Political Repression and the United Church of Christ Commission for Racial Justice, presents the inhumane treatment and conditions of political prisoners within the United States of America before the United Nations Commission on Human Rights and the Sub-Commission on Prevention of Discrimination and Protection of Minorities for consideration in its capacity as a non-governmental organization. Petitioner NCBL brings this petition in good faith and in accordance with recognized principles of human rights and has direct and reliable knowledge of the violations stated herein.

Since its inception in 1968, the **National Conference of Black Lawyers** has been involved in the struggle against the racist oppression visited upon Black, Brown and Native American citizens of the United States of America. The conditions which sparked the founding of NCBL were outlined in a Declaration of Commitment and Concern which was adopted in 1968 as the Preamble to NCBL's Constitution. The Declaration stated in pertinent part:

> "Today, as virtually never before in our history, Black communities across the nation face a crisis of racism which threatens not merely our constitutional rights but our homes, our safety, and our survival.
>
> "Political offices at the highest level are won by those most committed to the cynical campaign cry of law and order, which, in fact, mandates calm in the ghetto through a mobilization of laws and at the sacrifice of justice.
>
> "Investigatory commissions find that white racism is at the core of the nation's most serious domestic problem, and yet society's major

response is acceleration of the police weapons race to the point that the smallest disturbance in the Black area initiates an invasion of police armed with instruments of war and destruction, ready to intimidate, maim, and kill, if necessary, to suppress the Black community.

"The systematic suppression of Black people continues, notwithstanding the plethora of court decisions, civil rights laws, anti-poverty legislation, human relations commissions, enlarged political representation, and the other symbolic promises to Blacks which serve as this society's substitute for true equality...."

Preamble to Constitution of the
National Conference of Black Lawyers

These provisions are as descriptive of the situation and plight of Blacks and other minorities in the United States in 1978 as they were in 1968. It is NCBL's organizational experience that the conditions of racial minorities continue to deteriorate. Over the past ten years, NCBL has established itself as an activist organization of the Black bar, utilizing the professional skills of its membership of approximately 1,000 Black attorneys and jurists and over 5,000 law students to combat racist policies and practices which deny basic human rights by litigating issues of community concern, defending the politically unpopular, monitoring governmental activities that affect the Black and minority communities, and challenging attempts to decrease the Black bar through lower law school admissions, discriminatory bar examinations, and judicial or bar sanctions.

In the early years of its existence, the National Conference of Black Lawyers recognized that the struggle in the United States was inextricably tied to the struggle for human rights being waged throughout the Third World. This broadened perspective caused NCBL to acquire the status of a non-governmental organization at the United Nations.

Petitioner, the **National Alliance Against Racist and Political Repression** (NAARPR), is a broad-based coalition of church, civic, community, student and professional groups formed in 1973 to fight against repression in its myriad forms. An integral part of NAARPR's work to secure justice for political prisoners in this country is the commitment to bring about an end to the brutal non-rehabilitative and oppressive racism of the prison system of the United States. NAARPR organizes mass support to repel the growing repression of leaders and activists involved in the movement for peace and justice and investigates and documents complaints and incidents brought to its attention by the American people.

Petitioner, the **United Church of Christ Commission for Racial Justice** (CRJ), was born as a result of crisis. In 1963, the assassination of the Black Mississippi civil rights leader *Medgar Evers*; the Birmingham, Alabama, church bombing which killed four Black children attending Sunday School; and other less spectacular crises spurred the United Church of Christ to become actively involved in the struggle for racial justice.

The Commission for Racial Justice was established by the Church to increase the United Church of Christ's participation in the continuing struggle for racial justice and to aid the Black and other minority communities to control the institutions and structures affecting their lives and to reshape them to answer their needs. For the Black community, the criminal justice system and penal reform must take the highest of priorities. Therefore, CRJ developed the National Black Investigation Task Force to utilize the skills of Black professionals, civil rights groups, and politicians to investigate incidents such as the Attica killings and the killing of the Soledad Brother, George Jackson.

The questionable imprisonment of many young Black leaders across North Carolina and the jailing of Rev. Ben Chavis, a CRJ staff member, led the Commission to focus heavily on that state as a place to develop a model for redressing the evils of the criminal justice system. Also, the Commission is endeavoring to keep before the United Church of Christ the plight not only of racially oppressed peoples in the U.S., but also those in South Africa.

The petitioners, National Conference of Black Lawyers, the National Alliance Against Racist and Political Repression, and the United Church of Christ's Commission for Racial Justice, by their history of work and advocacy in the United States, have established themselves as organizations that seek to uphold the principles and provisions embodied in the Universal Declaration of Human Rights and other applicable Covenants. It is within the letter and spirit of the Universal Declaration of Human Rights, the International Convention on the Elimination of All Forms of Racial

Discrimination, the International Covenant on Civil and Political Rights, and the International Covenant on Economic, Social and Cultural Rights, that Petitioners present the gross and consistent violations of basic human rights and fundamental freedoms as enumerated herein before the U.N. Commission on Human Rights and the Sub-Commission on Prevention of Discrimination and Protection of Minorities.

Endnotes

1 Interview in *Le Matin,* July 12, 1978.

2 In the early stages of the United Nations, when the number of Third World countries was very small, the United Nations voted on a request that India and the Union of South Africa report at the next session on treatment of Indians in South Africa, which had impaired relations between the two countries; the United States voted NO.

The United Nations proposed that negotiations take place between India, Pakistan and South Africa with respect to the treatment of Indian Peoples in South Africa. *The South African delegation voted NO, as was expected, and the U.S. voted NO with them.*

On the same day during the General Assembly plenary meeting, Resolution 616 (VII) A was passed to establish a United Nations Commission to study the government of South Africa and its system of apartheid. *The U.S. abstained from voting.*

Whatever America had advocated as being the assurance of human rights for all people, through its Declaration of Independence in 1776 and in the Bill of Rights of 1796, is certainly not evident in its voting practices concerning the disenfranchised people of the world, as set forth below:

Resolution 637VII, 16 December 1952

...The right to self-determination is a prerequisite among all people. *U.S. voted NO.*

...All means possible should be used to ensure self-determination among all people. *U.S. voted NO.*

...Native peoples should be used in the government of their territories. U.S. voted *NO.*

Draft Resolution a/4502, Session XV, 14 December 1960

...Calls for the elimination of Colonialism; that this act to eliminate colonialism will be entirely beneficial and to enter into negotiations with representatives of colonial territories. *U.S. voted NO.*

...Affirms importance of the universal realization of the right of all people to self-determination and of speedily granting independence to colonial countries and peoples for the effective guarantee and observance of human rights. *U.S. voted NO.*

...Notes with appreciation the report of the Committee on the Elimination of Racial Discrimination. *U.S. voted NO.*

...Reaffirms Apartheid is a crime against humanity. *U.S. abstained while 92 countries voted YES to pass the resolution.*

Resolution 3103XXVII, 12 December 1973
...Use of mercenaries by the colonial or racist regimes in these conflicts is considered a criminal act. *U.S. voted NO.*

Other resolutions condemning Portugal and declaring the legitimacy of the struggle of the peoples include:

1809XVIII, 14 December 1963, *U.S. voted NO*;
27107XX, 21 December 1965, *U.S. voted NO*;
2270XXII, 17 November 1967, *U.S. voted NO*;
2707XXV, 14 December 1970, *U.S. voted NO*;
2784XXVI, 6 December 1971, *U.S. abstained*;
3163XXVIII, 15 December 1973, *U.S. voted NO.*

Resolution 2918XXVII, 14 November 1972
...Reaffirms the inalienable rights of all indigenous peoples of Southern Africa; recognizes the national liberation movements as rightful. Condemns treatment of freedom fighters and asks racist governments to withdraw military forces immediately. *U.S. voted NO.*

[3] COINTELPRO is the shortened name of the Counter Intelligence Program of the FBI to discredit and destroy political activists, with a specific focus on Blacks involved in the civil rights struggle and other social protest movements. Also other activist Americans were placed by the government under illegal surveillance, mail interception, and wire-tapping and became the subject matter of informers and agent provocateurs. Such victims of COINTELPRO include Martin Luther King, Andrew Young, Angela Davis, and other civil rights activists prosecuted and jailed repeatedly for alleged violations of the criminal law. (See Chapter 3 for COINTELPRO documents.)

[4] See *Police Use of Deadly Force: Preliminary Report of the National Minority Advisory Council on Criminal Justice*, Dr. Gwynne W. Pierson, Senior Researcher, Law Enforcement Assistance Administration, U.S. Department of Justice. Also see Lennox S. Hinds, "The Police Use of Excessive and Deadly Force: Racial Implications," *Community Concern: Police Use of Deadly Force*, compiled by Robert N. Brenner and Majorie Kravitz. U.S. Department of Justice, January 1979.

Chapter Two
The Historical Basis for the Petition

The Petitioners contend that any serious examination of the effects and ramifications of the racist policies and practices related to basic human rights and fundamental freedoms within the United States of America must begin with an historical analysis of the unique relationships between the European colonizers and the Black, Brown, and Native American peoples from the country's inception. As Members of the Commission of Human Rights and the Sub-Commission for the Prevention of Discrimination and Protection of Minorities are aware, American society functions normally through an elaborate framework of law.

It was the law which transformed Black people into capital goods through the system of chattel slavery and denied them their humanity; and it was the law which divested the Native American tribes of their lands, their culture, and their future; and it was the law which guaranteed the continued exploitation of Spanish-speaking Americans as a cheap labor source.

This short, truncated history of American racism which follows seeks to provide the historical and factual foundation which undergirds these allegations and to establish that institutionalized racism permeates all aspects of American society and has done so since the founding of this country. Blacks, Puerto Ricans, Chicanos, Native Americans, and other minorities continue to suffer the results of racist and repressive policies and practices which every year become more firmly entrenched in the fabric of American society. While the U.S. government may attempt to minimize the objective realities of the economic, social, and political conditions of minorities in America by citing in their defense various types of legislation that have been adopted ostensibly to secure political and economic equality for minorities, such recent legislation has not altered the relationship of minorities to the material and social benefits of this society.

As but one instance of the unchanged status of minorities in the United States, Petitioners note that in 1951 a petition was filed by William L. Patterson with the General Assembly of the United Nations on behalf of

Black people in the United States documenting deliberate acts of violence and indifference to this violence by the government against Blacks and charging the United States with the crime of genocide. That petition was published under the title, *We Charge Genocide: The Crime of Government Against the Negro People.* In 1951, when this petition was filed with the United Nations, it was effectively ignored by the then-majority member states.

A. Oppression of Blacks in America

While the savage and brutal treatment to which Africans were subjected during the exploitative slave trade and inhumane system of slavery is well-documented, certain factors require special reconsideration for the purposes of this petition.

Twenty years after Columbus reached the New World, Africans, transported initially by the Spanish, Dutch, and Portuguese traders, were arriving in large numbers in the Caribbean Islands after being bound and sold into slavery. By 1600, there were more than half a million slaves in the Western Hemisphere, although several million Africans had been forcibly taken from their homeland. Hundreds of thousands of Africans died *en route* to the New World because of the barbaric conditions under which they were transported.

The first Africans landed in colonial America at Jamestown in August 1619. Within forty years, the Africans brought to America had become a group apart, separated from the rest of the population by custom and law. Classified as slaves for their lives, a status inherited by their children, forbidden to contract, learn, or intermarry with whites, deprived of their African traditions and dispersed among Southern plantations, Blacks in America lost tribal, regional, and family ties. Slavery, as it developed in the United States, is among the most odious and unspeakable examples of institutionalized and legally sanctioned oppressions in the history of humankind.

On July 4, 1776, the founders of the United States announced to the world:

> "We hold these truths to be self-evident: that all men are created equal; that they are endowed by their creator with certain inalienable rights; that among these rights are life, liberty, and the pursuit of happiness."

These words were loudly and widely proclaimed to the world by European landholders looking straight into the faces of 700,000 African slaves, one-fifth of the nation they declared to be free, while standing on land stolen from the Native American tribes.

The very Constitution of this new-found nation of "equally created men" rejected the humanity of the Africans brought to America in slavery by counting them as only *three-fifths* of a person for determining the number of elected representatives for which a state was eligible for the first national Congress.[1] That Blacks were viewed as something less than human was made explicit by the highest judicial tribunal within the United States. In 1857, Chief Justice Taney of the U.S. Supreme Court, in the infamous *Dred Scott Case (Dred Scott v. Sandford,* 60 U.S. (19 How.) 393 (1857)), defined the legal status of Blacks which was a reflection of the actual political, social, and economic practices embedded in American society. In pertinent part, the *Dred Scott* decision said:

> "In the opinion of the court, the legislation and histories of the times, and the language used in the Declaration of Independence, show, that neither the class of persons who had been imported as slaves, nor their descendants, whether they had become free or not, were then acknowledged as a part of the people, nor intended to be included in the general worth used in that memorable instrument.
>
> "It is difficult at this day to realize the state of public opinion in relation to that unfortunate race, which prevailed in the civilized and enlightened portions of the world at the time of the Declaration of Independence, and when the Constitution of the United States was framed and adopted. But the public history of every European nation displays it in a manner too plain to be mistaken.
>
> *"Blacks had for more than a century before been regarded as being of an inferior order, and altogether unfit to associate with the*

> *white race, either in social or political relations; and so far inferior, that they had no rights which the white man was bound to respect; and the negro might justly and lawfully be reduced to slavery for his benefit.* He was bought and sold, and treated as an ordinary article of merchandise and traffic, whenever a profit could be made by it. This opinion was at that time fixed and universal in the civilized portion of the white race. It was regarded as an axiom in morals as well as in politics, which no one thought of disputing, or supposed to be open to dispute; and men in every grade and position in society daily and habitually acted upon it in their private pursuits, as well as in matters of public concern, without doubting for a moment the correctness of this opinion." (Emphasis added.)

The Court's statement that Blacks "had no rights which the white man was bound to respect" is of particular relevance. The contemporary and continuing degradation faced by Blacks in the United States exemplifies this. One significant import of this statement is that people of color, whether slave or free, had no intrinsic right to be treated with and accorded the basic respect due to all human beings because of their color, not only because of their status as slaves.

The Emancipation Proclamation of 1863, which freed slaves from chattel property status, did not erase the badges of inferiority that had irrevocably been stamped upon Black men, women, and children in America. The Thirteenth Amendment to the U.S. Constitution abolished slavery; the Fourteenth Amendment granted citizenship to Blacks; and the Fifteenth Amendment guaranteed their right to vote. Nevertheless, Blacks still found themselves in a state of economic bondage and oppression because no provisions had been made for societally pervasive and effective enforcement of newly granted rights.[2]

More recently, legislation adopted in an effort to grant Blacks the same basic economic, political, educational, and social rights enjoyed by whites throughout the history of this country has been equally unsuccessful as remedies because any enforcement rests upon the aggrieved minorities' proofs in a court of law that they have been discriminated against.[3] Such remedies, therefore, rely upon access to lawyers, money for litigation, and the capacity to prove the racist intent of those whose conduct has caused the harm. Even when racist intent is proved in a court of law, as when a person is denied a job, a child denied an education, a family a home, a sick person medical treatment, many years pass between the discriminatory conduct and such limited relief as the court can order.

That Black people in America were never afforded status as equal persons under the law with white people is clear when one examines the *apartheid*-type of segregation that was codified in law and continued in fact and custom after the abolition of slavery. In 1896, the Supreme Court in *Plessy v. Ferguson*, (163 U.S. 537 (1896)) upheld the doctrine of "separate but equal" public facilities for Blacks and whites by holding that the Fourteenth Amendment was not designed "to abolish distinctions based upon color, or to enforce social, as distinguished from political, equality, or a commingling of the two races upon terms unsatisfactory to either." (p. 544) This decision established what Justice Harlan's dissenting opinion made clear when he observed that the "real meaning" of such legislation was "that colored citizens are so inferior and degraded that they cannot be allowed to sit in public coaches occupied by white citizens." (p.560)

After the *Plessy* decision made Black inferiority a matter of law, all the Southern states and many in the North expanded their "Jim Crow" segregation laws which had, until then, been limited primarily to public transportation and schools. The racist policy of segregation was extended to residential areas, parks, hospitals, theaters, waiting rooms, churches, and bathrooms. Some statutes and ordinances authorized separate phone booths for Blacks and whites as well as separate cemeteries. In the courthouse, Blacks and whites took the oath on separate Bibles.

The legacy of second-class citizenship remains the dominant fact of Black American life in the United States today. A survey of U.S. statistics indicates the ravages on Black people of continuing racist and oppressive governmental policies and practices:

- the life expectancy of a Black child is more than five years shorter than that of a white child;[4]
- the Black mother is over three times more likely to die of complications in childbirth;[5]

- the infant mortality rate for Blacks in approximately twice that for whites;[6]
- the median income of the Black family is only 60% that of the median income of a white family;[7]
- the percentage of Blacks who live in families with incomes below the poverty line is approximately four times greater than that of whites;[8]
- the unemployment rate for Black adults is at least twice that of whites and the unemployment rate is three times higher for Black teenagers;[9]
- a Black male who completes four years of college can only expect a median annual income of $110.00 more than a white male who has only a high school diploma.[10]

These shocking statistics barely reveal the degradation and despair of Black existence in the United States which grows from prevailing racist and oppressive governmental practices and government-sanctioned private policies. They do, however, permit a glimpse of the cycle of poverty and powerlessness which is the birthright of Black Americans.

B. Native Americans and Manifest Destiny: A Plan for Genocide

The arrival of the colonizers from Europe to the shores of America had a devastating impact on the very existence of Native Americans. As the new nation began to develop and expand across the North American continent during the early years of the nineteenth century, whites began to develop an image of Native Americans as savage, backward, uncivilized, and unworthy of holding their lands. The negative image of Native Americans was dramatized against the background of a stridently nationalistic and expansive white culture that was racist in nature—dependent as it was upon Black slavery.

Several historians have described that particular period as follows:

> "Beginning with the era of large scale expansion to the West following the War of 1812 and aided by developments in travel and communications, Americans began to feel that it was their ordained fate to inhabit the continent from east to west. By the mid-1840's, the

idea had a label—Manifest Destiny—and became an important part of American life and politics. Americans also possessed a sense of the inevitable progress of their civilization and its role in the world at large. There was little feeling for reds or blacks except as they presented obstacles to the idea of progress."[11]

The expansionist fever of white Americans brought them into direct conflict with Native Americans, since expansion of the former required the physical removal of the latter. Government sanctioned dispossession from their native lands of those whom Christopher Columbus dubbed "Indians" began with Thomas Jefferson, one of the founding fathers, when he negotiated the purchase of Louisiana from the French. While Presidents Jefferson and Madison were not willing to commit force to the project of relocation of the Native Americans, they sanctioned the use of force by the territorial governors who were often land speculators and who governed according to the needs of their white, land-hungry constituents. Because there were no governmental restraints, an increasing number of colonists resorted to murder and pillage of the tribes, who were forced to respond with violence of their own.

The end of the War of 1812 saw an intensification of the national pressure for the removal of the Native American. The U.S. government responded to this pressure by canceling treaties between the government and Native Americans which provided for government purchase of the Native lands, new territories in which they could settle, and assistance in moving. Through chicanery, intimidation, and bribery in land purchases, and inadequately funded removal procedures and provisions, and callous and brutal maltreatment, the treaties became null and void. As was the case with Blacks, the law was used as an oppressive instrument to facilitate the legal, social, political, and economic subjugation of Native American peoples.[12]

In 1830, the U.S. Congress passed the Indian Removal Act which formalized government policy and provided a firmer and broader framework for the relocation of Native American tribes. Consequently, the prevailing attitude that "according to the American way, the Indian has a right to be defrauded"[13] resulted in egregious thefts of their native lands under color of law. For example, in Kansas in the 1850's, Native Americans surrendered almost nine-tenths of their territory; in California, in 1851 alone, 119 tribes were deprived of half their lands by a series of extortionate treaties.

The migration of colonizing whites from the eastern part of the United States caused constant Indian uprooting and forced them to adapt inimical and alien life styles in unfamiliar environments, which, along with slaughter and starvation, had the effect of drastically diminishing the Native American population to about a third of its size in colonial times.

> "...Each new relocation brought the Indians to more isolated and less productive areas. The dwindling food supply and increased competition for it further eroded tribal independence. White diseases and liquor completed the cycle of destruction. By the time of the Civil War, not only had the territorial integrity of the Indian been threatened, but also his very survival. By the 1850s few tribes could get along without white technology, money, and amenities, so completely had their own cultures been transformed. Large numbers had been reduced to the status of indigent camp followers."[14]

Any ambiguities that may have existed as to the legal status of Native Americans within the United States prior to 1831 were settled by the U.S. Supreme Court in *Cherokee Nation vs. Georgia,* (30 U.S. (5Pet.) I (1831)). In *Cherokee*, Chief Justice Marshall characterized the precise nature of the relationship between the United States and the Native Americans: "[The Indians] are in a state of pupillage. Their relation to the United States resembles that of a ward to his guardian." (p. 17) This characterization concretely defined the legal status of Native Americans in United States to this day.

Native Americans, like Blacks and other minorities, find themselves victimized by the racist and oppressive government policies and practices that characterize majority rule in the United States. These remnants of Native Americans make up less than one percent of the population in the United States in 1978. Their economic standard of living is at least five times lower than the U.S. norm. Severe poverty results in some 75 percent of Native Americans suffering from malnutrition and their unemployment ranges between 75 to 80 percent. Native Americans have the highest suicide rate of any minority group in the society.

Those who have dared to break out of the cycle of oppression have met with racist and repressive force and brutality so that they and others can be kept in their "place". If Native Americans are able to survive the ravages of disease, malnutrition, social pathology, and racist attack, they will find themselves ensnared in the apparatus of the criminal justice system as a response to their resistance against oppression.

C. Mexican-Americans: Victims of American Racism

The end of the Mexican-American War brought significant results for the United States. First, there were new territories: the annexation of Texas and the area which now is New Mexico, Arizona, California, and Colorado. Second, there was a new racial minority group to provide a cheap labor force. The Treaty of Guadalupe Hidalgo, signed on February 2, 1848, codified the secession and annexation of the Southwest territories and at the same time guaranteed both the civil and property rights of the Mexicans who agreed to become American citizens. But, as with other "non-white" Americans, neither citizenship nor treaties would prove to be of any significance to ensure full citizenship rights.

The white American colonists who annexed its Southwest came with a heritage of racism and hostility and contempt for non-Anglo-Saxon cultures, which bred little appreciation for the economic, cultural, and political history of the Mexican-Americans (Chicanos). As had happened to Africans and Native Americans, the Chicanos fell victim to the brutality, economic oppression, and other bitter fruits of racism.[15]

This pattern of oppression and discrimination that has characterized Anglo-Hispano relations for more than a century emerged in the course of westward expansion, as white settlers took possession of the land. The pattern was easily reinforced when the demands of economic development created a need for cheap labor to sustain itself. In the ensuing competition for land and for control over other valuable resources, the guarantees of cultural autonomy and property rights of the Spanish-speaking inhabitants contained in the Treaty of Guadalupe Hidalgo were quickly forgotten by the government and the settler.

Discrimination against Chicanos is particularly obvious in the area of employment. Organized labor discriminates against Mexican-Americans by excluding them from established unions and by creating ethnic wage differentials.[16] While the salaries paid to Mexican-Americans are much lower than that paid to whites, the salaries are still high enough to induce Mexicans to journey from Mexico in search of a "better life." This has given rise to the notorious "border patrols" between the U.S. and Mexico which selectively enforce the U.S. government's racist immigration laws.

As Mexican-Americans continue to be victims of racist government policies and practices, their families earn a median income of only two-thirds that of white families in the Southwest. U.S. government statistics show that at least three million of the over seven million Mexican-Americans in that region are living at a meager subsistence level.[17] The long tradition of economic and social deprivation is found as well in the area of education. Mexican-Americans, like Blacks, are relegated to *de facto* segregated schools of deliberately inferior quality which contributes to the extremely high and chronic unemployment rate among Mexican-Americans. Statistics, which show that the unemployment rate for Mexican-Americans is twice that of whites, do not even include the chronically underemployed farm workers. In addition, in 1960 it was reported that 79 percent of Mexican-American workers held unskilled or semiskilled jobs.[18]

Economic and political attitudes toward Mexican-Americans of necessity infect their treatment in the criminal justice system. As recently as 1969, a California judge, while sentencing a Mexican-American youth who had confessed to incest, announced in open court, "You are lower than an animal....Mexican people, after 13 years of age, it's perfectly all right to go out and act like an animal....We ought to....send you back to Mexico.... You....haven't the right to live in organized society—just miserable, lousy, rotten people."[19]

D. Minorities in the Criminal Justice System

Blacks and other minority groups find themselves confronted and oppressed by a system of institutionalized, governmentally supported racism. This institutional racism in its most egregious and repressive form is graphically demonstrated in the processes of the criminal justice system and the selective enforcement of the laws against minorities.

An examination of government statistics reveals that Blacks, Hispanics, and Native Americans are arrested and incarcerated in disproportionate numbers when compared to their percentage of the total population, as can be seen in Tables I, II, and III (found on the following pages).[20] For example, in 1975 at least 8.4 percent of the total Black population was arrested, compared to 3.1 percent of the total white population. As Dr. W.E.B. DuBois pointed out, it "is not that we commit the most crimes, but that we are the most often arrested, convicted and sent to prison."

As a result of the constant and continuing state of racist oppression and subjugation which results in menial, poorly-paid work, wretched living conditions, substandard nutrition, and medical services, Petitioners allege that the victims are forced to exert resistance to the established mode of social control, and thereby become targets of the criminal law and its sanctions.

> "It is, of course, fundamental to the understanding of U.S. society, as in any capitalist society, that the system of law enforces the oppressive social and economic relationships. There are two different, but intimately related, ways in which this is accomplished:
>
> (1) "The laws that define what is and what is not "crime" are primarily defined by and for those who benefit most from the capitalist system; and
>
> (2) "Even within this inherently one-sided system of laws, the criminal law most especially has been used selectively, enforcing some of the laws against some kinds of people, while allowing other laws to fall into disuse or to be applied only against certain lawbreakers.
>
> "In the United States the main function of law enforcement and the criminal codes has been to protect the property and well-being of those who benefit most from an economy based on profit. The law is not intended to enforce the rights of those who rebel against this

TABLE ONE *(part 1)*

Table 4.7 Arrests, by offense charged, race, and age group, United States, 1975

NOTE: See NOTE, Table 4.1.

[7,993 agencies; 1975 estimated population 169,455,000]

Offense charged	Total arrests				
	Total	White	Negro	Indian	Chinese
Total	7 671,230	5,538,890	1,935,422	115,554	4,629
Criminal homicide:					
Murder and nonnegligent manslaughter	15,173	6,581	8,257	143	18
Manslaughter by negligence	2,971	2,316	555	21	2
Forcible rape	19,920	10,414	9,050	183	6
Robbery	110,411	43,598	64,867	808	65
Aggravated assault	180,668	105,226	71,360	2,145	139
Burglary	422,032	294,779	119,853	3,145	188
Larceny-theft	923,127	620,618	282,297	6,903	1,143
Motor vehicle theft	110,320	78,029	29,145	1,444	66
Violent crime [c]	326,172	165,819	153,534	3,279	228
Property crime [d]	1,455,479	993,426	431,295	11,492	1,397
Subtotal for above offenses	1 784 622	1,161,561	585,384	14,792	1 627
Other assaults	338,441	217 481	113,608	3,589	180
Arson	13,667	10,843	2,618	85	2
Forgery and counterfeiting	53 692	35,615	17,470	296	31
Fraud	141 866	99,972	40,476	850	59
Embezzlement	8,809	6,030	2,691	18	4
Stolen property; buying, receiving, possessing	93,148	60,111	31,462	165	60
Vandalism	165,846	138,107	25,149	1,247	64
Weapons; carrying, possessing, etc	123,114	69,843	51,028	826	79
Prostitution and commercialized vice	46,727	21,030	25,032	180	42
Sex offenses (except forcible rape and prostitution)	47,901	37,635	9,259	485	35
Narcotic drug laws	487,287	383,649	96,660	2,248	256
Gambling	47,798	11 960	34,424	30	73
Offenses against family and children	52,199	36,751	14,616	558	9
Driving under the influence	893,798	751,024	117,105	11,831	477
Liquor laws	263,051	233,061	21,337	6,716	121
Drunkenness	1,161,140	883,383	224,417	45,533	537
Disorderly conduct	578,630	390,194	174,517	10,218	217
Vagrancy	58,228	34,010	22,897	930	40
All other offenses (except traffic)	986,652	696 160	267,294	10 976	593
Suspicion	27,133	16,105	10,665	204	8
Curfew and loitering law violations	111 167	80 517	28,499	1,275	34
Runaways	186,314	163,515	18,814	2,172	72

TABLE ONE *(part 2)*

Table 4.7 *Arrests, by offense charged, race, and age group, United States, 1975*

NOTE: See NOTE, Table 4.1.

[7,993 agencies; 1975 estimated population 169,455,000]

Japanese	All others	Percent [a]						
		Total	White	Negro	Indian	Chinese	Japanese	All others
5,817	70,918	100.0	72.2	25.2	1.5	0.1	0.1	0.9
11	163	100.0	43.4	54.4	.9	0.1	0.1	1.1
3	74	100.0	78.0	18.7	.7	0.1	0.1	2.5
10	257	100.0	52.3	45.4	.9	([b])	0.1	1.3
78	995	100.0	39.5	58.8	.7	0.1	0.1	0.9
81	1,717	100.0	58.2	39.5	1.2	0.1	([b])	1.0
287	3,780	100.0	69.8	28.4	.7	([b])	0.1	0.9
1,088	11,078	100.0	67.2	30.6	.7	0.1	0.1	1.2
101	1,535	100.0	70.7	26.4	1.3	0.1	0.1	1.4
180	3,132	100.0	50.8	47.1	1.0	0.1	0.1	1.0
1,476	16,393	100.0	68.3	29.6	.8	0.1	0.1	1.1
1,659	19,599	100.0	65.1	32.8	.8	0.1	0.1	1.1
243	3,340	100.0	64.3	33.6	1.1	0.1	0.1	1.0
6	113	100.0	79.3	19.2	.6	([b])	([b])	0.8
14	266	100.0	66.3	32.5	.6	0.1	([b])	0.5
67	442	100.0	70.5	28.5	.6	([b])	([b])	0.3
4	32	100.0	68.5	30.5	.5	([b])	([b])	0.4
42	666	100.0	64.9	33.8	.5	0.1	([b])	0.7
73	1,206	100.0	83.3	15.2	.8	([b])	([b])	0.7
92	1,246	100.0	56.7	41.4	.7	0.1	0.1	1.0
63	380	100.0	45.0	53.6	.4	0.1	0.1	0.8
40	447	100.0	78.6	19.3	1.0	0.1	0.1	0.9
421	4,053	100.0	78.7	19.8	.5	0.1	0.1	0.8
310	1,001	100.0	25.0	72.0	.1	0.2	0.6	2.1
10	255	100.0	70.4	28.0	1.1	([b])	([b])	0.5
1,104	12,257	100.0	84.0	13.1	1.3	0.1	0.1	1.4
91	1,725	100.0	88.6	8.1	2.6	([b])	([b])	0.7
320	6,950	100.0	76.1	19.3	3.9	([b])	([b])	0.6
238	3,246	100.0	67.4	30.2	1.8	([b])	([b])	0.6
21	330	100.0	58.4	39.3	1.6	0.1	([b])	0.6
791	10,838	100.0	70.6	27.1	1.1	0.1	0.1	1.1
3	148	100.0	59.4	39.3	.8	([b])	([b])	0.5
75	767	100.0	72.4	25.6	1.1	([b])	0.1	0.7
130	1,611	100.0	87.8	10.1	1.2	([b])	0.1	0.9

TABLE TWO *(part 1)*

Table 6.18 ***Estimated number of inmates of State correctional facilities, by selected demographic characteristics, United State***
1974

NOTE: These data are estimates derived from a stratified probability sample of adult and youthful offenders held in the custody of State correctional authorities. The survey included n only those inmates detained in facilities directly administered by State correctional authorities, but also those in any public or private institution charged with the custody of perso under the jurisdiction of State correctional authorities. Examples of the latter arrangement are inmates committed to State mental hospitals and inmates housed in YMCA's while a signed to work-release programs. For discussion of the survey sampling procedures, standard error tables, and definitions, see Appendix 14. Juvenile offenders were excluded from t survey.

Characteristic	Number of inmates	Percent of inmates
Sex:		
Total [a]	191,400	100
Male	185,000	97
Female	6,300	3
Race:		
Total [a]	191,400	100
White	97,700	51
Black	89,700	47
Other	3,400	2
Not reported	600	([b])
Age:		
Total [a]	191,400	100
Under 18	1,800	1
18	5,500	3
19	7,900	4
20 to 24	57,100	30
25 to 29	44,900	23
30 to 34	27,300	14
35 to 39	16,300	9
40 to 49	19,600	10
50 and over	10,300	5
Not reported	600	([b])

Characteristic	Number of inmates	Percent of inmates
Armed forces service:		
Total [a,c]	187,500	100
Served	51,200	27
Never served	136,400	73
Personal income (year prior to arrest):		
Total [a,d]	168,300	100
No income	7,600	5
Less than $2,000	32,400	19
$2,000 to $3,999	30,700	18
$4,000 to $5,999	30,400	18
$6,000 to $9,999	29,900	18
$10,000 or more	23,000	14
Amount not known	12,600	8
Not reported	1,800	1
Length of time on last job:		
Total [a,d]	168,300	100
Less than 5 weeks	16,900	10
5 to 26 weeks	61,100	36
27 to 104 weeks	55,100	33
105 to 260 weeks	21,500	13
261 or more weeks	13,700	8

[a] Detail may not add to totals because of rounding. Percent distribution based on unrounded figures.
[b] Less than 0.5 percent.
[c] Includes sentenced inmates only.
[d] Includes only those inmates who had held a full-time job after December 1968 or who had been employed during most of the month prior to their arrest.

Source: U.S. Department of Justice, Law Enforcement Assistance Administration, ***Survey of Inmates of State Correctional Facilities 1974—Advance Repor*** **National Prisoner Statistics Special Report No. SD-NPS-SR-2 (Washington, D.C.: U.S. Government Printing Office, 1976), pp. 24, 25.**

TABLE TWO *(part 2)*

Table 6.18 ***Estimated number of inmates of State correctional facilities, by selected demographic characteristics, United States, 1974***

NOTE: These data are estimates derived from a stratified probability sample of adult and youthful offenders held in the custody of State correctional authorities. The survey included not only those inmates detained in facilities directly administered by State correctional authorities, but also those in any public or private institution charged with the custody of persons under the jurisdiction of State correctional authorities. Examples of the latter arrangement are inmates committed to State mental hospitals and inmates housed in YMCA's while assigned to work-release programs. For discussion of the survey sampling procedures, standard error tables, and definitions, see Appendix 14. Juvenile offenders were excluded from the survey.

Level of educational attainment:		
Total [a,c]	187,500	100
Eighth grade or less	49,000	26
1 to 3 years of high school	65,900	35
4 years of high school	52,200	28
1 to 3 years of college	14,300	8
4 years or more of college	1,500	1
Not reported	4,700	2
Employment status (month prior to arrest):		
Total [a]	191,400	100
Employed	131,000	68
Full-time	117,100	61
Part-time	13,800	7
Unemployed	59,000	31
Looking for work	23,800	12
Not looking for work	35,200	18
Wanting work	9,100	5
Not wanting work	26,100	14
Not reported	1,400	1
Marital status:		
Total [a,c]	187,500	100
Married	44,300	24
Widowed	5,800	3
Divorced	31,900	17
Separated	15,200	8
Never married	89,900	48
Not reported	300	([b])

Occupation at time of arrest:		
Total [a,d]	168,300	100
Professional and technical workers	4,900	3
Managers and administrators	9,500	6
Salesworkers	3,900	2
Clerical workers	7,000	4
Craftsmen and kindred workers	39,300	23
Carpenters	4,400	3
Auto mechanics	4,100	2
Painters	4,300	3
Other craftsmen	26,500	16
Operatives	48,100	29
Welders	3,700	2
Machine operators	3,800	2
Truck drivers	9,200	5
Other operatives	31,400	19
Nonfarm laborers	29,200	17
Construction laborers	8,200	5
Freight and material handlers	7,100	4
Other nonfarm laborers	13,800	8
Farmers and farm managers	400	([b])
Farm laborers and supervisors	4,000	2
Service workers	19,200	11
Others	500	([b])
Not reported	2,500	1

[a] Detail may not add to totals because of rounding. Percent distribution based on unrounded figures.
[b] Less than 0.5 percent.
[c] Includes sentenced inmates only.
[d] Includes only those inmates who had held a full-time job after December 1968 or who had been employed during most of the month prior to their arrest.

Source: U.S. Department of Justice, Law Enforcement Assistance Administration, *Survey of Inmates of State Correctional Facilities 1974—Advance Report*, National Prisoner Statistics Special Report No. SD-NPS-SR-2 (Washington, D.C.: U.S. Government Printing Office, 1976), pp. 24, 25.

TABLE THREE *(part 1)*

Table 6.61 ***Number of, and average sentence for, Federal prisoners confined in Federal institutions, by offense, type of commitment, race, and sex, on June 30, 1975***

NOTE: See NOTES, Tables 6.49 and 6.60. "Average sentence" is in months.

[Population 23,556. Data complete on 88.9 percent of the population.]

Offense	All prisoners			Prisoners under sentence		
				White		
	Total	Male	Female	Number	Average sentence	Male
Total	20,948	19,997	951	12,956	87.6	12,534
Total excluding immigration and violent crimes [a]	14,423	13,619	804	9,494	65.0	9,132
Assault	97	96	1	50	90.6	50
Bankruptcy	5	5	0	5	32.4	5
Burglary	203	201	2	112	81.1	112
Counterfeiting	395	380	15	323	70.8	312
Drug laws, total	5,569	5,285	284	3,786	73.3	3,613
Non-narcotics	1,117	1,055	62	1,042	50.1	989
Narcotics	3,979	3,790	189	2,404	86.2	2,306
Controlled substances	473	440	33	340	53.0	318
Embezzlement	159	142	17	109	43.9	97
Escape, flight or harboring a fugitive	132	127	5	106	40.2	104
Extortion	163	157	6	136	111.0	130
Firearms	1,022	1,007	15	642	54.5	633
Forgery	832	706	126	336	53.1	298
Fraud	368	350	18	283	50.3	275
Immigration	929	916	13	920	15.3	907
Income tax	111	110	1	83	36.1	82
Juvenile delinquency	337	319	18	208	39.0	199
Kidnaping	360	350	10	263	300.3	255
Larceny/theft, total	3,303	3,106	197	2,262	55.3	2,217
Motor vehicle, interstate	1,706	1,695	11	1,404	52.3	1,394
Postal	733	575	158	247	46.1	218
Theft, interstate	329	328	1	249	69.1	249
Other	535	508	27	362	63.5	356
Liquor laws	111	109	2	78	33.7	77
National security laws	7	6	1	6	298.0	5
Robbery	4,242	4,172	70	2,013	176.6	1,985
Selective Service Acts	7	5	2	6	36.0	4
Securities, transporting false or forged	582	540	42	390	70.5	371
White slave traffic	64	61	3	29	57.4	29
Other and unclassifiable	585	561	24	450	70.5	434
Government reservation, high seas, territorial, and District of Columbia	1,296	1,219	77	342	214.7	322
Assault	140	129	11	35	155.2	33
Auto theft	14	13	1	6	57.0	6
Burglary	115	113	2	22	83.0	22
Forgery	21	17	4	4	57.0	4
Homicide	385	357	28	118	386.8	111
Larceny/theft	119	111	8	45	67.4	42
Robbery	283	270	13	39	187.1	37
Rape	89	88	1	24	262.4	24
Sex offenses, except rape	17	17	0	5	175.2	5
Other and unclassifiable	113	104	9	44	55.4	38
Military court-martial cases	69	67	2	18	328.3	18

[a] This total line excludes the immigration law and violent crime offenses whose unusual sentence lengths distort the average sentence length statistic.

Source: U.S. Department of Justice, Federal Prison System, *Statistical Report, Fiscal Year 1975* (Washington, D.C.: Federal Prison System, *Statistical Report, Fiscal Year 1975* (Washington, D.C.: Federal Prison System, 1977), pp. 28, 29.

TABLE THREE *(part 2)*

Table 6.61 Number of, and average sentence for, Federal prisoners confined in Federal institutions, by offense, type of commitment, race, and sex, on June 30, 1975

NOTE: See NOTES, Tables 6.49 and 6.60. "Average sentence" is in months.

[Population 23,556. Data complete on 88.9 percent of the population.]

Prisoners under sentence					Prisoners not under sentence		Narcotic Addict Rehabilitation Act commitments included in total	
White	All other							
Female	Number	Average sentence	Male	Female	Male	Female	Under sentence	Not under sentence
422	7,732	109.0	7,217	515	246	14	316	55
362	4,743	69.3	4,312	431	175	11	281	49
0	43	106.9	42	1	4	0	0	0
0	0	X	0	0	0	0	0	0
0	89	73.7	87	2	2	0	1	1
11	70	51.9	66	4	2	0	5	0
173	1,739	89.9	1,630	109	42	2	152	19
53	67	65.7	59	8	7	1	14	3
98	1,542	92.2	1,452	90	32	1	133	15
22	130	74.3	119	11	3	0	5	1
12	46	41.2	41	5	4	0	1	0
2	25	74.7	22	3	1	0	1	0
6	21	69.1	21	0	6	0	0	0
9	363	48.0	357	6	17	0	3	1
38	486	52.1	400	86	8	2	18	3
8	78	38.0	68	10	7	0	1	0
13	9	23.3	9	0	0	0	0	0
1	28	51.1	28	0	0	0	0	0
9	123	42.2	115	8	5	1	0	0
8	90	321.3	88	2	7	0	0	0
45	1,003	47.6	856	147	33	5	44	8
10	284	54.0	283	1	18	0	6	0
29	474	42.2	348	126	9	3	29	4
0	78	49.7	77	1	2	0	2	1
6	167	51.1	148	19	4	2	7	3
1	33	24.6	32	1	0	0	0	0
1	1	240.0	1	0	0	0	0	0
28	2,180	161.2	2,139	41	48	1	30	4
2	1	18.0	1	0	0	0	0	0
19	186	58.4	163	23	6	0	10	0
0	35	72.5	32	3	0	0	0	0
16	117	86.5	109	8	18	0	4	0
20	915	162.4	861	54	36	3	46	19
2	102	91.9	94	8	2	1	1	1
0	7	64.9	6	1	1	0	0	0
0	81	83.9	79	2	12	0	15	10
0	14	83.1	10	4	3	0	4	3
7	261	274.1	241	20	5	1	0	0
3	69	70.9	64	5	5	0	7	3
2	239	150.2	228	11	5	0	4	1
0	65	187.7	64	1	0	0	0	0
0	11	89.5	11	0	1	0	0	0
6	66	79.8	64	2	2	1	15	1
0	51	254.5	49	2	0	0	0	0

* This total line excludes the immigration law and violent crime offenses whose unusual sentence lengths distort the average sentence length statistic.

Source: U.S. Department of Justice, Federal Prison System, *Statistical Report, Fiscal Year 1975* (Washington, D.C.: Federal Prison System, *Statistical Report, Fiscal Year 1975* (Washington, D.C.: Federal Prison System, 1977), pp. 28, 29.

TABLE FOUR *(part 1)*

Table 6.102 ***Prisoners executed under civil authority, by offense and race, United States, 1930–75***

[The years 1930-59 exclude Alaska and Hawaii except for three Federal executions in Alaska: 1939, 1948, 1950]

Year	All offenses				Murder				Rape				Other offenses[a]		
	Total	White	Black	Other	Total	White	Black	Other	Total	White	Black	Other	Total	White	Black
All years	3,859	1,751	2,066	42	3,334	1,664	1,630	40	455	48	405	2	70	39	31
Percent	100.0	45.4	53.5	1.1	100.0	49.9	48.9	1.2	100.0	10.6	89.0	0.4	100.0	55.7	44.3
1975	0	0	0	0	0	0	0	0	0	0	0	0	0	0	0
1974	0	0	0	0	0	0	0	0	0	0	0	0	0	0	0
1973	0	0	0	0	0	0	0	0	0	0	0	0	0	0	0
1972	0	0	0	0	0	0	0	0	0	0	0	0	0	0	0
1971	0	0	0	0	0	0	0	0	0	0	0	0	0	0	0
1970	0	0	0	0	0	0	0	0	0	0	0	0	0	0	0
1969	0	0	0	0	0	0	0	0	0	0	0	0	0	0	0
1968	0	0	0	0	0	0	0	0	0	0	0	0	0	0	0
1967	2	1	1	0	2	1	1	0	0	0	0	0	0	0	0
1966	1	1	0	0	1	1	0	0	0	0	0	0	0	0	0
1965	7	6	1	0	7	6	1	0	0	0	0	0	0	0	0
1964	15	8	7	0	9	5	4	0	6	3	3	0	0	0	0
1963	21	13	8	0	18	12	6	0	2	0	2	0	1	1	0
1962	47	28	19	0	41	26	15	0	4	2	2	0	2	0	2
1961	42	20	22	0	33	18	15	0	8	1	7	0	1	1	0
1960	56	21	35	0	44	18	26	0	8	0	8	0	4	3	1

TABLE FOUR *(part 2)*

Table 6.102 ***Prisoners executed under civil authority, by offense and race, United States, 1930–75***

[The years 1930-59 exclude Alaska and Hawaii except for three Federal executions in Alaska: 1939, 1948, 1950]

Year	All offenses				Murder				Rape				Other offenses[a]		
	Total	White	Black	Other	Total	White	Black	Other	Total	White	Black	Other	Total	White	Black
All years	3,859	1,751	2,066	42	3,334	1,664	1,630	40	455	48	405	2	70	39	31
Percent	100.0	45.4	53.5	1.1	100.0	49.9	48.9	1.2	100.0	10.6	89.0	0.4	100.0	55.7	44.3
1959	49	16	33	0	41	15	26	0	8	1	7	0	0	0	0
1958	49	20	28	1	41	20	20	1	7	0	7	0	1	0	1
1957	65	34	31	0	54	32	22	0	10	2	8	0	1	0	1
1956	65	21	43	1	52	20	31	1	12	0	12	0	1	1	0
1955	76	44	32	0	65	41	24	0	7	1	6	0	4	2	2
1954	81	38	42	1	71	37	33	1	9	1	8	0	1	0	1
1953	62	30	31	1	51	25	25	1	7	1	6	0	4	4	0
1952	83	36	47	0	71	35	36	0	12	1	11	0	0	0	0
1951	105	57	47	1	87	55	31	1	17	2	15	0	1	0	1
1950	82	40	42	0	68	36	32	0	13	4	9	0	1	0	1
1949	119	50	67	2	107	49	56	2	10	0	10	0	2	1	1
1948	119	35	82	2	95	32	61	2	22	1	21	0	2	2	0
1947	153	42	111	0	129	40	89	0	23	2	21	0	1	0	1
1946	131	46	84	1	107	45	61	1	22	0	22	0	2	1	1
1945	117	41	75	1	90	37	52	1	26	4	22	0	1	0	1
1944	120	47	70	3	96	45	48	3	24	2	22	0	0	0	0
1943	131	54	74	3	118	54	63	1	13	0	11	2	0	0	0
1942	147	67	80	0	115	57	58	0	25	4	21	0	7	6	1
1941	123	59	63	1	102	55	46	1	20	4	16	0	1	0	1
1940	124	49	75	0	105	44	61	0	15	2	13	0	4	3	1
1939	160	80	77	3	145	79	63	3	12	0	12	0	3	1	2
1938	190	96	92	2	154	89	63	2	25	1	24	0	11	6	5
1937	147	69	74	4	133	67	62	4	13	2	11	0	1	0	1
1936	195	92	101	2	181	86	93	2	10	2	8	0	4	4	0
1935	199	119	77	3	184	115	66	3	13	2	11	0	2	2	0
1934	168	65	102	1	154	64	89	[illegible]	14	1	13	0	0	0	0
1933	160	77	81	2	151	75	74	2	7	1	6	0	2	1	1
1932	140	62	75	3	128	62	63	3	10	0	10	0	2	0	2
1931	153	77	72	4	137	76	57	4	15	1	14	0	1	0	1
1930	155	90	65	0	147	90	57	[illegible]	6	0	6	0	2	0	2

[a] Includes 25 armed robbery, 20 kidnaping, 11 burglary, 6 sabotage, 6 aggravated assault, and 2 espionage.

Source: U.S. Department of Justice, Law Enforcement Assistance Administration, *Capital Punishment 1975*, National Prisoner Statistics Bulletin No. SD-NPS-CP-4 (Washington, D.C.: U.S. Government Printing Office, 1976), pp. 14, 15.

oppression; rather it is used to insure that they will continue to accept their place in the scheme of things.

"For example, in the nineteenth century the police did not shoot or beat the corporate executives of Carnegie Steel, the Pullman Company, or the Pennsylvania Railroad who subjected their workers to long hours, brutal working conditions, and low pay; instead they shot, beat, or arrested the workers who protested against those conditions.

"In the1960's the people who planned and directed U.S. aggression in Southeast Asia were not arrested or convicted of genocide, but those who protested against this aggression were arrested and convicted of crimes.

"When Black people in Harlem, Watts, and Newark rebelled against their joblessness and wretched living conditions, the police did not use teargas, weapons and criminal prosecutions against the landlords and merchants who victimized them, but against those who were victimized.

"Racism, sexism, and economic exploitation *are not defined as crimes.* It is not a criminal act to deny people jobs on the grounds of their sex or race; or to expose them to slow death and mutilations from violations of safety or anti-pollution regulations; or to exclude minority youth from educational opportunity; or to perform bio-medical experimentation on minority people.

"Even when the actions of the wealthy and powerful are defined as criminal and they are prosecuted, the penalties are relatively mild. Crimes against the State, as in Watergate, and offenses such as embezzlement, fraud, tax evasion, forgery and other serious property crimes result, in most cases, in fines and suspended sentences."[21]

A recent study by a committee of the U.S. Congress further indicates that there is a double standard of justice within this country based on race and class status. Someone Black and poor tried for stealing a few hundred dollars has a 90 percent likelihood of being convicted of robbery with a sentence averaging between 94 to 138 months. On the other hand, a white business executive who has "embezzled" hundreds of thousands of dollars has only a 20 percent likelihood of conviction with a sentence averaging about 20 to 48 months.[22]

The most potent evidence of the "stark racism" of the application of the penal law in the United States is an analysis of those sentenced to death or executed under process of law.[23] (See Table IV, found in the previous pages.) Between 1930 and 1968 (the period for which statistics have been maintained), 455 persons have been executed nationwide for rape, 405 of them Black. Of the 3,859 persons executed for all crimes in this same period, 2,066 (53.5%) were Black. Sixty percent (60%) were unemployed at the time of the alleged crime. Sixty-two percent (62%) were unskilled. Over fifty percent (50%) did not finish high school. Ninety percent were too poor to afford private counsel. Out of fifty states, eleven former slave-holding states were responsible for more than half of the state-perpetrated executions.

In July 1976, when the Supreme Court of the United States upheld the constitutionality of the death penalty, six hundred ten people were on Death Row nationally. North Carolina alone had one hundred and twenty-two people awaiting execution. Georgia, Florida, and Texas had a combined total of one hundred and sixty-six persons. Nationwide, over fifty percent were Black; ninety percent were poor. In the history of the United States, no white person has ever been executed for rape as a crime against a black woman.[24] The Supreme Court's 1976 decision validated the imposition of the death penalty and approved its use as a criminal sanction by upholding the statues of Florida, Georgia, and Texas. By 1978, 33 states had enacted statues conforming to the 1976 Supreme Court decision. It can be anticipated that these newly legislated death penalty statutes will be imposed in the same racially and economically biased fashion as the previous ones.

Petitioners will show that criminal law and imprisonment are used politically to control the poor and oppressed segments of the population routinely and are also used against those who consciously assert and advocate resistance to the established society and are therefore singled out for specially repressive and brutal treatment in violation of their human rights and fundamental freedoms.

Endnotes

[1] United States Constitution, Art. 1, Sec. 2, Clause 3.

[2] See John H. Franklin, *From Slavery to Freedom: A History of African Americans* (9th ed,, McGraw Hill Education, 2010)., 4th ed., (1974); C. V. Woodward, *The Strange Career of Jim Crow,* 3rd ed., Oxford University Press, NY (1974); and *Report of the National Advisory Commission on Civil Disorders* (1968).

[3] Legislation adopted in mid-twentieth century to grant civil rights to Blacks: Civil Rights Act of 1957 (17 Stat. 634); Civil Rights Act of 1960 (74 Stat. 86); Twenty-fourth Amendment to the U.S. Constitution (repealed poll tax requirement for purposes of voting); Civil Rights Act of 1964 (78 Stat. 241); Voting Rights Act of 1965 (79 Stat. 437); Civil Rights Act of 1968 (81 Stat. 73).

[4] U.S. Department of Commerce, Bureau of the Census, *Statistical Abstract of the United States 65* (1977); Table 94.

[5] *Ibid.*, p. 70; Table 102.

[6] *Ibid.*

[7] U.S. Department of Commerce, Bureau of the Census, *Current Population Reports, Series P-60*, No. 107, p. 7 (1977); Table 1.

[8] *Ibid.*, p. 20; Table 14.

[9] U.S. Department of Labor, Bureau of Labor Statistics, *Employment and Earnings,* January 1978, p. 170; Table 44.

[10] U.S. Department of Commerce, Bureau of the Census, *Current Population Reports, Series P-60,* No. 105, p. 19B (1977); Table 47.

[11] See P. Borden, "Found Cumbering the Soil: Manifest Destiny and the Indian in the Nineteenth Century," in *The Great Fear: Race in the Mind of America,* G. Nash and R. Weiss, eds. (1970).

[12] *Ibid.*

[13] *Ibid.*

[14] *Ibid.*

[15] See Derrick A. Bell, Jr., *Race, Racism and American Law,* (1973), Chapter 2.

[16] *Ibid.*

[17] *Ibid.*

[18] *Ibid.*

[19] *Ibid.*, quotation from 115 Congressional Record 32358 (1969).

[20] Also see U.S. Department of Commerce, Bureau of the Census as reported in *The Social and Economic Status of Negroes in the United States, 1970,* BLS Report No. 394, Current Population Reports, Series P-23, No. 38 Tables 1 and 6, pp. 7 and 12 respectively.

[21] Lennox S. Hinds, "Political Prisoners in the United States," *Africa* (No. 85, September 1978), pp. 92-93.

[22] *The Commercial Appeal,* Memphis, Tennessee, May 7, 1978.

[23] Former Attorney General of the United States Ramsey Clark in a speech at a Rally Against the Death Penalty, Atlanta, Georgia, April 1977.

[24] Death Penalty Project, NAACP Legal Defense Fund, Inc.

SECTION TWO OF THE PETITION
Political Abuse of the Law

Chapter Three
COINTELPRO and Other Government Misconduct

A. Introduction

There is merit in the argument that all victims of the political use of the law are, in fact, political prisoners, especially in light of the use of the law in the United States to maintain the *status quo* in the relationship of poor and minority people to the economic and social institutions of the society. However, for purposes of this Petition, the term "political prisoner" is used to describe those persons whose overt and expressed opposition and resistance to United States national and international practices place them in direct confrontation with the majority society; and who, by virtue of this opposition, become targets for criminal prosecution and illegal invasions of their rights in concerted governmental efforts to suppress and control their dissent.

Petitioners can show, as a matter of public record, that coincident with organized attempts of minority groups to redress their grievances through petitions, peaceful demonstrations and organizing, and passive and overt resistance to detrimental economic and political conditions, agencies of the U.S. Government have employed legally sanctioned and illegally executed methods to control, destroy, and harass social emergence of Black and other communities. Such covert and overt governmental misconduct have particularly focused on movements, associations, and organizations that are vocal and visible in those communities' struggle for fundamental social and economic equities and basic human rights. As part of the overall efforts to silence dissent and to control dissenters, government agencies, by their agents, have singled out particular minority organizations and individuals for unique treatment to prevent their further development and influence.

In an obvious example, when Blacks in the 1960's began to protest openly in major U.S. ghettos (Watts, California; Detroit, Michigan; Newark, New

Jersey) against the substandard housing, lack of meaningful employment, educational opportunity, and other fruits of racism which have dominated their social conditions since slavery by demanding equality with majority citizens in economic, political and educational opportunities, their agitation was met with brute force and repressive measures. Such measures were taken by police and military as if these minority citizens seeking change in their conditions were an invading foreign enemy that had to be controlled and broken by armed attack. These explosions within the cities were understood by impartial observers to be responses to legitimate grievances by minority citizens.[1] Yet, neither systematic and pervasive efforts nor national efforts were devised to reorder the priorities of the society so that it might remedy the admittedly inhumane and inequitable conditions of minority peoples' existence. Black communities were among the first national minorities in the United States to organize for social justice and against racial oppression in what has become known as the Civil Rights Movement.

The governmental response on local and national levels to protests and passive resistance to white supremacy was the development, implementation, and refinement of illegal, unconstitutional, and repressive counterintelligence tactics designed to discredit and destroy these domestic organizations and their leaders. Official documents released by the Federal Bureau of Investigation (F.B.I.) of the U.S. Justice Department indicate that, as early as 1967, the government initiated a program to

"...expose, disrupt, misdirect, discredit, or otherwise neutralize the activities of black nationalist, hate-type organizations and groupings, their leadership, spokesmen, membership, and supporters, and to counter their propensity for violence and civil disorder....Efforts of the various groups to consolidate their forces or to recruit new or youthful adherents must be frustrated."[2]

Moreover, the only criterion for a group to be considered as "black nationalist" was that its membership be primarily Black.[3]

Apart from the specific Black membership groups targeted for surveillance purposes, dossiers were maintained on over five thousand Blacks who were viewed as threats to national security. This list included such advocates of non-violence as *Roy Wilkins*, Executive Director of the

National Association for the Advancement of Colored People (NAACP); *Roy Innis*, head of the Congress for Racial Equality (CORE); *Rev. Jesse Jackson*, Director of Operation PUSH, a self-help group in Chicago; *Rev. Martin Luther King, Jr.* and *Andrew Young* (now Ambassador to the United Nations). The surveillance did not stop with Black political leaders, but included such Black artists as *Harry Belafonte*, *Eartha Kitt*, *James Baldwin*, and *Ossie Davis*, among others; athletes such as *Muhammed Ali* and *Joe Louis;* as well as ordinary citizens, students and workers.[4] Blacks who were singled out for surveillance, blackmail, eavesdropping, and often arrest and prosecution ranged from non-violent disciples of *Gandhi* to articulate opponents of the American system. Many were merely people who have complained about injustice and racism in their communities.

The illegal counterintelligence program COINTELPRO was the acronym for the FBI efforts to destroy American political movements of which the FBI disapproved. The Civil Rights Movement was a primary target of such misconduct. In an official memorandum dated March 1968, the following long-range goals of COINTELPRO against Blacks were outlined:

(1) to prevent the "coalition of militant black nationalist groups," which might be the first step toward a real "Mau Mau" in America;

(2) to prevent the rise of a "messiah" who could "unify and electrify" the movement, naming specifically Martin Luther King, Jr., Stokely Carmichael, and Elijah Muhammed;

(3) to prevent violence on the part of black nationalist groups, by pinpointing "potential trouble-makers" and neutralizing them "before they exercise their potential for violence;"

(4) to prevent groups and leaders from gaining "respectability" by discrediting them to the "responsible" Negro community, to the white community and the "liberals" (the distinction is the Bureau's), and to "Negro radicals;" and

(5) to prevent the long range growth of these organizations, especially among youth, by developing specific tactics to "prevent these groups from recruiting young people."[5]

B. Church Committee Report

As a direct result of COINTELPRO activities and other counterintelligence activities, thousands of Blacks were kept under surveillance via wiretapping, mail interception, and other illegality as targets of political repression. The remainder of this chapter presents photostatic copies of passages from the *Church Committee Report* and of official FBI memoranda which were contained in Appendices IV and V of the original Petition.

94TH CoNGRESS } 2d, Session .SENATE { REPORT No. 94-755

SUPPLEMENTARY DETAILED STAFF. REPORTS ON INTELLIGENCE ACTIVITIES AND THE RIGHTS OF AMERICANS

BOOK III

FINAL REPORT

OF THE

SELECT COMMITTEE
TO STUDY GOVERNMENTAL OPERATIONS

WITH RESPECT TO

INTELLIGENCE ACTIVITIES

UNITED STATES SENATE

APRIL 23 (under authority of the order of APRIL 14), 1976

U.S. GOVERNMENT PRINTING OFFICE

69-984 0 WASHINGTON : 1976

For sale by the Superintendent of Documents, U.S. Government Printing Office
Washington, D.C. 20402 - Price $7.65

CONTENTS

COINTELPRO: THE FBI'S COVERT ACTION PROGRAMS AGAINST AMERICAN CITIZENS

I. INTRODUCTION AND SUMMARY

COINTELPRO is the FBI acronym for a series of covert action programs directed against domestic groups. In these programs, the Bureau went beyond the collection of intelligence to secret action designed to "disrupt" and "neutralize" target groups and individuals. The techniques were adopted wholesale from wartime counterintelligence, and ranged from the trivial (mailing reprints of *Reader's Digest* articles to college administrators) to the degrading (sending anonymous poison-pen letters intended to break up marriages) and the dangerous (encouraging gang warfare and falsely labeling members of a violent group as police informers).

This report is based on a staff study of more than 20,000 pages of Bureau documents, depositions of many of the Bureau agents involved in the programs, and interviews of several COINTELPRO targets. The examples selected for discussion necessarily represent a small percentage of the more than 2,000 approved COINTELPRO actions. Nevertheless, the cases demonstrate the consequences of a Government agency's decision to take the law into its own hands for the "greater good" of the country.

COINTELPRO began in 1956, in part because of frustration with Supreme Court rulings limiting the Government's power to proceed overtly against dissident groups; it ended in 1971 with the threat of public exposure.[1] In the intervening 15 years, the Bureau conducted a sophisticated vigilante operation aimed squarely at preventing the exercise of First Amendment rights of speech and association, on the theory that preventing the growth of dangerous groups and the propagation of dangerous ideas would protect the national security and deter violence.[2]

Many of the techniques used would be intolerable in a democratic society even if all of the targets had been involved in violent activity, but COINTELPRO went far beyond that. The unexpressed major premise of the programs was that a law enforcement agency has the duty to do whatever is necessary to combat perceived threats to the existing social and political order.

---

[1] On March 8, 1971, the FBI resident agency in Media, Pennslyvania, was broken into. Documents stolen in the break-in were widely circulated and published by the press. Since some documents carried a "COINTELPRO" caption—a word unknown outside the Bureau—Carl Stern, a reporter for NBC, commenced a Freedom of Information Act lawsuit to compel the Bureau to produce other documents relating to the programs. The Bureau decided because of "security reasons" to terminate them on April 27, 1971. (Memorandum from C. D. Brennan to W. C. Sullivan, 4/27/71; Letter from FBI headquarters to all SAC's, 4/28/71.)

[2] The Bureau's direct attacks on speaking, teaching, writing, and meeting are discussed at pp. 28–33, attempts to prevent the growth of groups are set forth at pp. 34–40.

4

A. "*Counterintelligence Program*": *A Misnomer for Domestic Covert Action*

COINTELPRO is an acronym for "counterintelligence program." Counterintelligence is defined as those actions by an intelligence agency intended to protect its own security and to undermine hostile intelligence operations. Under COINTELPRO certain techniques the Bureau had used against hostile foreign agents were adopted for use against perceived domestic threats to the established political and social order. The formal programs which incorporated these techniques were, therefore, also called "counterintelligence." [2a]

"Covert action" is, however, a more accurate term for the Bureau's programs directed against American citizens. "Covert action" is the label applied to clandestine activities intended to influence political choices and social values.[3]

B. *Who Were the Targets?*

1. The Five Targeted Groups

The Bureau's covert action programs were aimed at five perceived threats to domestic tranquility: the "Communist Party, USA" program (1956–71); the "Socialist Workers Party" program (1961–69); the "White Hate Group" program (1964–71); the "Black Nationalist-Hate Group" program (1967–71); and the "New Left" program (1968–71).

2. Labels Without Meaning

The Bureau's titles for its programs should not be accepted uncritically. They imply a precision of definition and of targeting which did not exist.

Even the names of the later programs had no clear definition. The Black Nationalist program, according to its supervisor, included "a great number of organizations that you might not today characterize as black nationalist but which were in fact primarily black." [3a] Indeed, the nonviolent Southern Christian Leadership Conference was labeled as a Black Nationalist "Hate Group." [4] Nor could anyone at the Bureau even define "New Left," except as "more or less an attitude." [5]

Furthermore, the actual targets were chosen from a far broader group than the names of the programs would imply. The CPUSA program targeted not only Party members but also sponsors of the

---

[2a] For a discussion of U.S. intelligence activities against hostle foreign intelligence operations, see Report on Counterintelligence.

[3] See Senate Select Committee Report, "Alleged Assassination Plots Involving Foreign Leaders" and Staff Report: "Covert Action in Chile."

[3a] Black Nationalist Supervisor deposition, 10/17/75, p. 12.

[4] Memorandum from FBI Headquarters to all SAC's, 8/25/67, p. 2.

[5] New Left Supervisor's deposition, 10/28/75, p. 8. The closest any Bureau document comes to a definition is found in an investigative directive: "The term 'New Left' does not refer to a definite organization, but to a movement which is providing ideologies or platforms alternate to those of existing communist and other basic revolutionary organizations, the so-called 'Old Left.' The New Left movement is a loosely-bound, free-wheeling, college-oriented movement spearheaded by the Students for a Demorcatic Society and includes the more extreme and militant anti-Vietnam war and anti-draft protest organizations." (Memorandum from FBI Headquarters to all SAC's, 10/28/68; Hearings, Vol. 6, Exhibit 61, p. 669.) Although this characterization is longer than that of the New Left Supervisor, it does not appear to be substantively different.

National Committee to Abolish the House Un-American Activities Committee [6] and civil rights leaders allegedly under Communist influence or simply not "anti-Communist." [7] The Socialist Workers Party program included non-SWP sponsors of antiwar demonstrations which were cosponsored by the SWP or the Young Socialist Alliance, its youth group.[8] The Black Nationalist program targeted a range of organizations from the Panthers to SNCC to the peaceful Southern Christian Leadership Conference,[9] and included most black student groups.[10] New Left targets ranged from the SDS [11] to the Interuniversity Committee for Debate on Foreign Policy,[12] from all of Antioch College ("vanguard of the New Left") [13] to the New Mexico Free University [14] and other "alternate" schools,[15] and from underground newspapers [16] to students protesting university censorship of a student publication by carrying signs with four-letter words on them.[17]

C. What Were the Purposes of COINTELPRO?

The breadth of targeting and lack of substantive content in the descriptive titles of the programs reflect the range of motivations for COINTELPRO activity: protecting national security, preventing violence, and maintaining the existing social and political order by "disrupting" and "neutralizing" groups and individuals perceived as threats.

1. Protecting National Security

The first COINTELPRO, against the CPUSA, was instituted to counter what the Bureau believed to be a threat to the national security. As the chief of the COINTELPRO unit explained it:

> We were trying first to develop intelligence so we would know what they were doing [and] second, to contain the threat. . . . To stop the spread of communism, to stop the effectiveness of the Communist Party as a vehicle of Soviet intelligence, propaganda and agitation.[17a]

Had the Bureau stopped there, perhaps the term "counterintelligence" would have been an accurate label for the program. The ex-

---

[6] Memorandum from FBI Headquarters to Cleveland Field Office, 11/6/64.

[7] One civil rights leader, the subject of at least three separate counterintelligence actions under the CPUSA caption, was targeted because there was no "direct evidence" that he was a communist, "neither is there any substantial evidence that he is anti-communist." One of the actions utilized information gained from a wiretap; the other two involved dissemination of personal life information. (Memorandum from J.A. Sizoo to W.C. Sullivan, 2/4/64; Memorandum from New York Field Office to FBI Headquarters, 2/12/64; Memoranda from FBI Headquarters to New York Field Office, 3/26/64 and 4/10/64; Memorandum to New York Field Office from FBI Headquarters, 4/21/64; Memorandum from FBI Headquaters to Baltimore Field Office, 10/6/65.)

[8] Memorandum from FBI Headquarters to Cleveland Field Office, 11/29/68.

[9] FBI Headquarters memorandum, 8/25/67, p. 2.

[10] Memorandum from FBI Headquarters to Jackson Field Office, 2/8/71, pp. 1–2.

[11] Memorandum from FBI Headquarters to San Antonio Field Office, 10/31/68.

[12] Memorandum from FBI Headquarters to Detroit Field Office, 10/26/66.

[13] Memorandum from FBI Headquarters to Cincinnati Field Office, 6/18/68.

[14] Memorandum from FBI Headquarters to Albuquerque Field Office, 3/14/69.

[15] Memorandum from FBI Headquarters to San Antonio Field Office. 7/23/69.

[16] Memorandum from FBI Headquarters to Pittsburgh Field Office, 11/14/69.

[17] Memorandum from FBI Headquarters to Minneapolis Field Office, 11/4/68.

[17a] COINTELPRO Unit Chief deposition, 10/16/75, p. 14.

pansion of the CPUSA program to non-Communists, however, and the addition of subsequent programs, make it clear that other purposes were also at work.

2. Preventing Violence

One of these purposes was the prevention of violence. Every Bureau witness deposed stated that the purpose of the particular program or programs with which he was associated was to deter violent acts by the target groups, although the witnesses differed in their assessment of how successful the programs were in achieving that goal. The preventive function was not, however, intended to be a product of specific proposals directed at specific criminal acts. Rather, the programs were aimed at groups which the Bureau believed to be violent or to have the potential for violence.

The programs were to prevent violence by deterring membership in the target groups, even if neither the particular member nor the group was violent at the time. As the supervisor of the Black Nationalist COINTELPRO put it, "Obviously you are going to prevent violence or a greater amount of violence if you have smaller groups." (Black Nationalist supervisor deposition, 10/17/75, p. 24.) The COIN TELPRO unit chief agreed: "We also made an effort to deter or counteract the propaganda . . . and to deter recruitment where we could. This was done with the view that if we could curb the organization, we could curb the action or the violence within the organization."[17b] In short, the programs were to prevent violence indirectly, rather than directly, by preventing possibly violent citizens from joining or continuing to associate with possibly violent groups.[18]

The prevention of violence is clearly not, in itself, an improper purpose; preventing violence is the ultimate goal of most law enforcement. Prosecution and sentencing are intended to deter future criminal behavior, not only of the subject but also of others who might break the law. In that sense, law enforcement legitimately attempts the indirect prevention of possible violence and, if the methods used are proper, raises no constitutional issues. When the government goes beyond traditional law enforcement methods, however, and attacks group membership and advocacy, it treads on ground forbidden to it by the Constitution. In *Brandenberg* v. *Ohio*, 395 U.S. 444 (1969), the Supreme Court held that the government is not permitted to "forbid or proscribe advocacy of the use of force or law violation except where such advocacy is directed toward inciting or producing imminent lawless action and is likely to incite or produce such action." In the absence of such clear and present danger, the government cannot act against speech nor, presumably, against association.

3. Maintaining the Existing Social and Political Order

Protecting national security and preventing violence are the purposes advanced by the Bureau for COINTELPRO. There is another purpose for COINTELPRO which is not explicit but which offers

---

[17b] Unit Chief deposition, 10/16/75, p. 54.

[18] "Possibly violent" did not necessarily mean likely to be violent. Concededly non-violent groups were targeted because they might someday change; Martin Luther King, Jr. was targeted because (among other things) he might "abandon his supposed 'obedience' to 'white, liberal doctrines' (non-violence) and embrace black nationalism." (Memorandum from FBI Headquarters to all SAC's, 3/4/68, p. 3.)

> programs I have ever seen the Bureau handle as far as any group is concerned.[87]

5. *Black Nationalist-Hate Groups.*[88]—In marked contrast to prior COINTELPROs, which grew out of years of intensive intelligence investigation, the Black Nationalist COINTELPRO and the racial intelligence investigative section were set up at about the same time in 1967.

Prior to that time, the Division's investigation of "Negro matters" was limited to instances of alleged Communist infiltration of civil rights groups and to monitoring civil rights protest activity. However, the long, hot summer of 1967 led to intense pressure on the Bureau to do something to contain the problem, and once again, the Bureau heeded the call.

The originating letter was sent out to twenty-three field offices on August 25, 1967, describing the program's purpose as

> . . . to expose, disrupt, misdirect, discredit, or otherwise neutralize the activities of black nationalist, hate-type organizations and groupings, their leadership, spokesmen, membership, and supporters, and to counter their propensity for violence and civil disorder. . . . Efforts of the various groups to consolidate their forces or to recruit new or youthful adherents must be frustrated.[89]

Initial group targets for "intensified attention" were the Southern Christian Leadership Conference, the Student Nonviolent Coordinating Committee, Revolutionary Action Movement, Deacons for Defense and Justice, Congress of Racial Equality, and the Nation of Islam. Individuals named targets were Stokely Carmichael, H. "Rap" Brown, Elijah Muhammed, and Maxwell Stanford. The targets were chosen by conferring with Headquarters personnel supervising the racial cases; the list was not intended to exclude other groups known to the field.

According to the Black Nationalist supervisor, individuals and organizations were targeted because of their propensity for violence *or* their "radical or revolutionary rhetoric [and] actions":

> Revolutionary would be [defined as] advocacy of the overthrow of the Government. . . . Radical [is] a loose term that might cover, for example, the separatist view of the Nation of Islam, the influence of a group called U.S. Incorporated. . . . Generally, they wanted a separate black nation. . . . They [the NOI] advocated formation of a separate black nation on the territory of five Southern states.[90]

---

[87] Moore, 11/3/75, p. 31.

[88] Note that this characterization had no substantive meaning within the Bureau. See p. 4.

[89] Memorandum from FBI Headquarters to all SAC's, 8/25/67.

[90] Black Nationalist supervisor, 10/17/75, pp. 66–67. The supervisor stated that individual NOI members were involved with sporadic violence against police, but the organization was not itself involved in violence. (Black National supervisor, 10/17/75. p. 67.) Moore agreed that the NOI was not involved in organizational violence, adding that the Nation of Islam had been unjustly blamed for violence in the ghetto riots of 1967 and 1968: "We had a good informant coverage of the Nation of Islam. . . . We were able to take a very positive stand and tell the Department of Justice and tell everybody else who accused the Nation of

The letter went on to direct field offices to exploit conflicts within and between groups; to use news media contacts to disrupt, ridicule, or discredit groups; to preclude "violence-prone" or "rabble rouser" leaders of these groups from spreading their philosophy publicly; and to gather information on the "unsavory backgrounds"—immorality, subversive activity, and criminal activity—of group members.[91]

According to George C. Moore, the Southern Christian Leadership Conference was included because

> . . . at that time it was still under investigation because of the communist infiltration. As far as I know, there were not any violent propensities, except that I note . . . in the cover memo [expanding the program] or somewhere, that they mentioned that if Martin Luther King decided to go a certain way, he could cause some trouble. . . . I cannot explain it satisfactorily . . . this is something the section inherited.[92]

On March 4, 1968, the program was expanded from twenty-three to forty-one field offices.[93] The letter expanding the program lists five long-range goals for the program:

> (1) to prevent the "coalition of militant black nationalist groups," which might be the first step toward a real "Mau Mau" in America;
>
> (2) to prevent the rise of a "messiah" who could "unify, and electrify," the movement, naming specifically Martin Luther King, Stokely Carmichael, and Elijah Muhammed;
>
> (3) to prevent violence on the part of black nationalist groups, by pinpointing "potential troublemakers" and neutralizing them "before they exercise their potential for violence;"
>
> (4) to prevent groups and leaders from gaining "respectability" by discrediting them to the "responsible" Negro community, to the white community (both the responsible community and the "liberals"—the distinction is the Bureau's), and to Negro radicals; and

---

Islam . . . [that they] were not involved in any of the riots or disturbances. Elijah Muhammed kept them under control, and he did not have them on the streets at all during any of the riots." (Moore, 11/3/75, p. 36.)

When asked why, therefore, the NOI was included as a target, Mr. Moore answered: "Because of the potential, they did represent a potential . . . they were a paramilitary type. They had drills, the Fruit of Islam, they had the capability because they were a force to be reckoned with, with the snap of his finger Elijah Muhammed could bring them into any situation. So that there was a very definite potential, very definite potential." (Moore, 11/3/75, p. 37.)

[91] The unit chief, who wrote the letter on instructions from his superiors, concedes that the letter directed field offices to gather personal life information on targets, not for "scandalous reasons," but "to deter violence or neutralize the activities of violence-prone groups." (Unit chief, 10/16/75, p. 66.)

[92] Moore, 11/3/75, pp. 37, 39, 40.

[93] Primary targets listed in this second letter are the Southern Christian Leadership Conference, the Student Nonviolent Coordinating Committee, Revolutionary Action Movement, Nation of Islam, Stokely Carmichael, H. "Rap" Brown, Martin Luther King, Maxwell Stanford, and Elijah Muhammed. CORE was dropped for reasons no witness was able to reconstruct. The agent who prepared the second letter disagreed with the inclusion of the SCLC, but lost. (Black Nationalist supervisor, 10/17/75, p. 14.)

(5) to prevent the long range growth of these organizations, especially among youth, by developing specific tactics to "prevent these groups from recruiting young people." [94]

6. The Panther Directives.—The Black Panther Party ("BPP") was not included in the first two lists of primary targets (August 1967 and March 1968) because it had not attained national importance. By November 1968, apparently the BPP had become sufficiently active to be considered a primary target. A letter to certain field offices with BPP activity dated November 25, 1968, ordered recipient offices to submit "imaginative and hard-hitting counterintelligence measures aimed at crippling the BPP." Proposals were to be received every two weeks. Particular attention was to be given to capitalizing upon the differences between the BPP and US, Inc. (Ron Karenga's group), which had reached such proportions that "it is taking on the aura of gang warfare with attendant threats of murder and reprisals." [95]

On January 30, 1969, this program against the BPP was expanded to additional offices, noting that the BPP was attempting to create a better image. In line with this effort, Bobby Seale was conducting a "purge" [96] of the party, including expelling police informants. Recipient offices were instructed to take advantage of the opportunity to further plant the seeds of suspicion concerning disloyalty among ranking officials.[97]

Bureau witnesses are not certain whether the Black Nationalist program was effective. Mr. Moore stated:

> I know that the . . . overall results of the Klan [COINTELPRO] was much more effective from what I have been told than the Black Extremism [COINTELPRO] because of the number of informants in the Klan who could take action which would be more effective. In the Black Extremism Group . . . we got a late start because we did not have extremist activity [until] '67 and '68. Then we had to play catch-up. . . . It is not easy to measure effectiveness. . . . There were policemen killed in those days. There were bombs thrown. There were establishments burned with molotov cocktails. . . . We can measure that damage. You cannot measure over on the other side, what lives were saved because somebody did not leave the organization or suspicion was sown on his leadership and this organization gradually declined and [there was] suspicion within it, or this organization did not join with [that] organization as a result of a black power conference which was aimed towards consolidation efforts. All we know, either through their own ineptitude, maybe it emerged through counterintelligence, maybe, I think we like to think that that helped to do it, that there was not this development. . . . What part did counterintelligence [play?] We hope that it did play a part. Maybe we just gave it a nudge." [98]

---

[94] Memorandum from FBI headquarters to all SAC's, 3/4/68, pp. 3–4.

[95] Memorandum from FBI Headquarters to Baltimore Field Office, 11/25/68.

[96] Memorandum from FBI Headquarters to all SAC's. 1/30/69.

[97] This technique, the "snitch jacket," was used in all COINTELPRO programs.

[98] Moore, 11/3/75, pp. 34, 50–52.

23

7. New Left.—The Internal Security Section had undergone a slow transition from concentrating on the "Old Left"—the CPUSA and SWP—to focusing primarily on the activities of the "New Left"—a term which had no precise definition within the Bureau.[99] Some agents defined "New Left" functionally, by connection with protests. Others defined it by philosophy, particularly antiwar philosophy.

On October 28, 1968, the fifth and final COINTELPRO was started against this undefined group. The program was triggered in part by the Columbia campus disturbance. Once again, law enforcement methods had broken down, largely (in the Bureau's opinion) because college administrators refused to call the police on campus to deal with student demonstrations. The atmosphere at the time was described by the Headquarters agent who supervised the New Left COINTELPRO:

> During that particular time, there was considerable public, Administration—I mean governmental Administration—[and] news media interest in the protest movement to the extent that some groups, I don't recall any specifics, but some groups were calling for something to be done to blunt or reduce the protest movements that were disrupting campuses. I can't classify it as exactly an hysteria, but there was considerable interest [and concern]. That was the framework that we were working with. . . . It would be my impression that as a result of this hysteria, some governmental leaders were looking to the Bureau.[100]

And, once again, the combination of perceived threat, public outcry, and law enforcement frustration produced a COINTELPRO.

---

[99] As the New Left supervisor put it, "I cannot recall any document that was written defining New Left as such. It is my impression that the characterization of New Left groups rather than being defined at any specific time by document, it more or less grew. . . . Agreeing it was a very amorphous term, he added: "It has never been strictly defined, as far as I know. . . . It is more or less an attitude, I would think." (New Left supervisor, 10/28/75, pp. 7–8.)

[100] New Left supervisor, 10/28/75, pp. 21–22.

The attacks on speaking, teaching, writing, and meeting have been examined in some detail because they present, in their purist form, the consequences of acting outside the legal process. Perhaps the Bureau was correct in its assumption that words lead to deeds, and that larger group membership produces a greater risk of violence. Nevertheless, the law draws the line between criminal acts and constitutionally protected activity, and that line must be kept.[146] As Justice Brandeis declared in a different context fifty years ago:

> Our government is the potent, the omnipresent teacher. For good or for ill, it teaches the whole people, by its example. Crime is contagious. If the Government becomes a lawbreaker, it breeds contempt for law: it invites every man to become a law unto himself. To declare that in the administration of the criminal law the end justifies the means—to declare that the Government may commit crimes in order to secure the conviction of the private criminal—would bring terrible retribution. Against the pernicious doctrine this Court should resolutely set its face. *Olmstead* v. *U.S.*, 277 U.S. 439, 485 (1927)

IV. COINTELPRO TECHNIQUES

The techniques used in COINTELPRO were—and are—used against hostile foreign intelligence agents. Sullivan's testimony that the "rough, tough, dirty business"[147] of foreign counterintelligence was brought home against domestic enemies was corroborated by George Moore, whose Racial Intelligence Section supervised the White Hate and Black Nationalist COINTELPROs:

> You can trace [the origins] up and back to foreign intelligence, particularly penetration of the group by the individual informant. Before you can engage in counterintelligence you must have intelligence. . . . If you have good intelligence and

---

[143] Memorandum from FBI Headquarters to El Paso Field Office, 12/6/68.

[144] Memorandum from FBI Headquarters to New York Field Office, 3/19/65.

[145] Memorandum from FBI Headquarters to Cleveland and Boston Field Offices, 5/5/64.

[146] Mr. Huston learned that lesson as well:

"We went from this kind of sincere intention, honest intention, to develop a series of justifications and rationalizations based upon this . . . distorted view of inherent executive power and from that, whether it was direct . . . or was indirect or inevitable, as I tend to think it is, you went down the road to where you ended up, with these people going into the Watergate.

"And so that has convinced me that you have just got to draw the line at the top of the totem pole, and that we would then have to take the risk—it is not a risk-free choice, but it is one that, I am afraid, in my judgment, that we do not have any alternative but to take." (Huston, 9/23/75, p. 45.)

[147] Sullivan, 11/1/75, pp. 97–98.

> know what it's going to do, you can seed distrust, sow misinformation. The same technique is used in the foreign field. The same technique is used, misinformation, disruption, is used in the domestic groups, although in the domestic groups you are dealing in '67 and '68 with many, many more across the country . . . than you had ever dealt with as far as your foreign groups.[148]

The arsenal of techniques used in the Bureau's secret war against domestic enemies ranged from the trivial to the life-endangering. Slightly more than a quarter of all approved actions were intended to promote factionalization within groups and between groups; a roughly equal number of actions involved the creation and dissemination of propaganda.[149] Other techniques involved the use of federal, state, and local agencies in selective law enforcement, and other use (and abuse) of government processes; disseminating derogatory information to family, friends, and associates; contacting employers; exposing "communist infiltration" or support of target groups; and using organizations which were hostile to target groups to disrupt meetings or otherwise attack the targets.

A. Propaganda

The Bureau's COINTELPRO propaganda efforts stem from the same basic premise as the attacks on speaking, teaching, writing and meeting: propaganda works. Certain ideas are dangerous, and if their expression cannot be prevented, they should be countered with Bureau-approved views. Three basic techniques were used: (1) mailing reprints of newspaper and magazine articles to group members or potential supporters intended to convince them of the error of their ways; (2) writing articles for or furnishing information to "friendly" media sources to "expose" target groups;[150] and (3) writing, printing, and disseminating pamphlets and fliers without identifying the Bureau as the source.

1. Reprint Mailings

The documents contain case after case of articles and newspaper clippings being mailed (anonymously, of course) to group members. The Jewish members of the Communist Party appear to have been inundated with clippings dealing with Soviet mistreatment of Jews. Similarly, Jewish supporters of the Black Panther Party received articles from the BPP newspaper containing anti-Semitic statements. College administrators received reprints of a *Reader's Digest* article[151] and a *Barron's* article on campus disturbances intended to persuade them to "get tough."[152]

Perhaps only one example need be examined in detail, and that only because it clearly sets forth the purpose of propaganda reprint mailings. Fifty copies of an article entitled "Rabbi in Vietnam Says With-

[148] Moore, 11/3/75, pp. 32–33.

[149] The percentages used in this section are derived from a staff tabulation of the Petersen Committee summaries. The numbers are approximate because it was occasionally difficult to determine from the summary what the purpose of the technique was.

[150] The resulting articles could then be used in the reprint mailing program.

[151] Memorandum from FBI Headquarters to Minneapolis Field Office, 11/4/68.

[152] Memorandum from FBI Headquarters to Boston Field Office, 9/12/68.

drawal Not the Answer," described as "an excellent article in support of United States foreign policy in Vietnam," were mailed to certain unnamed professors and members of the Vietnam Day Committee "who have no other subversive organizational affiliations." The purpose of the mailing was "to convince [the recipients] of the correctness of the U.S. foreign policy in Vietnam." [153]

Reprint mailings would seem to fall under Attorney General Levi's characterization of much of COINTELPRO as "foolishness." [154] They violate no one's civil rights, but should the Bureau be in the anonymous propaganda business?

2. "Friendly" Media

Much of the Bureau's propaganda efforts involved giving information or articles to "friendly" media sources who could be relied upon not to reveal the Bureau's interests.[155] The Crime Records Division of the Bureau was responsible for public relations, including all headquarters contacts with the media. In the course of its work (most of which had nothing to do with COINTELPRO) the Division assembled a list of "friendly" news media sources—those who wrote pro-Bureau stories.[156] Field offices also had "confidential sources" (unpaid Bureau informants) in the media, and were able to ensure their cooperation.

The Bureau's use of the news media took two different forms: placing unfavorable articles and documentaries about targeted groups, and leaking derogatory information intended to discredit individuals.[157]

A typical example of media propaganda is the headquarters letter authorizing the Boston Field Office to furnish "derogatory information about the Nation of Islam (NOI) to established source [name excised]": [158]

---

[153] Memorandum from FBI Headquarters to San Francisco Field Office, 11/1/65.

[154] Levi 12/11/75, Hearings, Vol. 6, p. 318.

[155] "Name checks" were apparently run on all reporters proposed for use in the program, to make sure they were reliable. In one case, a check of Bureau files showed that a television reporter proposed as the recipient of information on the SDS had the same name as someone who had served in the Abraham Lincoln Brigade. The field office was asked to determine whether the "individuals" were "identical." The field office obtained the reporter's credit records, voting registration, and local police records, and determined that his credit rating was satisfactory, that he had no arrest record, that he "stated a preference for one of the two major political parties"—and that he was not, in fact, the man who fought in the Spanish Civil War. Accordingly, the information was furnished. (Memorandum from Pittsburgh Field Office to FBI Headquarters, 12/26/68; memorandum from FBI Headquarters to Pittsburgh Field Office, 1/23/69.)

[156] The Bureau also noted, for its files, those who criticized its work or its Director, and the Division maintained a "not-to-contact" list which included the names of some reporters and authors. One proposal to leak information to the *Boston Globe* was turned down because both the newspaper and one of its reporters "have made unfounded criticisms of the FBI in the past." The Boston Field Office was advised to resubmit the suggestion using another newspaper. (Memorandum from FBI Headquarters to Boston Field Office, 2/8/68.)

[157] Leaking derogatory information is discussed at p. 50.

[158] The Committee's agreement with the Bureau governing document production provided that the Bureau could excise the names of "confidential sources" when the documents were delivered to the Committee. Although the staff was permitted to see the excised names at Bureau headquarters, it was also agreed that the names not be used.

> Your suggestions concerning material to furnish [name] are good. Emphasize to him that the NOI predilection for violence,[159] preaching of race hatred, and hypocrisy, should be exposed. Material furnished [name] should be either public source or known to enough people as to protect your sources. Insure the Bureau's interest in this matter is completely protected by [name].[160]

In another case, information on the Junta of Militant Organizations ("JOMO", a Black Nationalist target) was furnished to a source at a Tampa television station.[161] Ironically, the station manager, who had no knowledge of the Bureau's involvement, invited the Special Agent in Charge, his assistant, and other agents to a preview of the half-hour film which resulted. The SAC complimented the station manager on his product, and suggested that it be made available to civic groups.[162]

A Miami television station made four separate documentaries (on the Klan, Black Nationalist groups, and the New Left) with materials secretly supplied by the Bureau. One of the documentaries, which had played to an estimated audience of 200,000, was the subject of an internal memorandum "to advise of highly successful results of counterintelligence exposing the black extremist Nation of Islam."

> [Excised] was elated at the response. The station received more favorable telephone calls from viewers than the switchboard could handle. Community leaders have commented favorably on the program, three civic organizations have asked to show the film to their members as a public service, and the Broward County Sheriff's Office plans to show the film to its officers and in connection with its community service program.
>
> This expose showed that NOI leaders are of questionable character and live in luxury through a large amount of money taken as contributions from their members. The extreme nature of NOI teachings was underscored. Miami sources advised the expose has caused considerable concern to local NOI leaders who have attempted to rebut the program at each open meeting of the NOI since the program was presented. Local NOI leaders plan a rebuttal in the NOI newspaper. Attendance by visitors at weekly NOI meetings has dropped 50%. This shows the value of carefully planned counterintelligence action.[163]

The Bureau also planted derogatory articles about the Poor People's Campaign, the Institute for Policy Studies, the Southern Students Organizing Committee, the National Mobilization Committee, and a host of other organizations it believed needed to be seen in their "true light."

---

[159] Note that Bureau witnesses testified that the NOI was not, in fact, involved in organization violence. See pp. 20–21.

[160] Memorandum from FBI Headquarters to Boston Field Office, 2/27/68.

[161] Memorandum from Tampa Field Office to FBI Headquarters, 8/5/68.

[162] Memorandum from Tampa Field Office to FBI Headquarters, 2/7/69.

[163] Memorandum from G. C. Moore to William C. Sullivan, 10/21/69.

37

3. Bureau-Authored Pamphlets and Fliers.

The Bureau occasionally drafted, printed, and distributed its own propaganda. These pieces were usually intended to ridicule their targets, rather than offer "straight" propaganda on the issue. Four of these fliers are reproduced in the following pages.

[**Note:** The four fliers have been omitted due to legibility issues]

40

B. Effects to Promote Enmity and Factionalism Within Groups or Between Groups

Approximately 28% of the Bureau's COINTELPRO efforts were designed to weaken groups by setting members against each other, or to separate groups which might otherwise be allies, and convert them into mutual enemies. The techniques used included anonymous mailings (reprints, Bureau-authored articles and letters) to group members criticizing a leader or an allied group; [164] using informants to raise controversial issues; forming a "notional"—a Bureau-run splinter group—to draw away membership from the target organization; encouraging hostility up to and including gang warfare, between rival groups; and the "snitch jacket."

1. Encouraging Violence Between Rival Groups

The Bureau's attempts to capitalize on active hostility between target groups carried with them the risk of serious physical injury to the targets. As the Black Nationalist supervisor put it:

> It is not easy [to judge the risks inherent in this technique]. You make the best judgment you can based on all the circumstances and you always have an element of doubt where you are dealing with individuals that I think most people would characterize as having a degree of instability.[165]

The Bureau took that risk. The Panther directive instructing recipient officers to encourage the differences between the Panthers and

[164] This technique was also used in disseminating propaganda. The distinction lies in the purpose for which the letter, article or flier was mailed.

[165] Black Nationalist supervisor, 10/17/75, p. 40.

U.S., Inc. which were "taking on the aura of gang warfare with attendant threats of murder and reprisals," [166] is just one example.

A separate report on disruptive efforts aimed at the Panthers will examine in detail the Bureau's attempts to foment violence. These efforts included anonymously distributing cartoons which pictured the U.S. organization gloating over the corpses of two murdered Panthers, and suggested that other BPP members would be next,[167] and sending a New Jersey Panther leader the following letter which purported to be from an SDS member: [168]

"To Former Comrade [name]

"As one of 'those little bourgeois, snooty nose'—'little schoolboys'—'little sissies' Dave Hilliard spoke of in the 'Guardian' of 8/16/69, I would like to say that you and the rest of you black racists can go to hell. I stood shoulder to shoulder with Carl Nichols last year in Military Park in Newark and got my a——whipped by a Newark pig all for the cause of the wineheads like you and the rest of the black pussycats that call themselves Panthers. Big deal; you have to have a three hour educational session just to teach those . . . (you all know what that means don't you! It's the first word your handkerchief head mamma teaches you) how to spell it.

"Who the hell set you and the Panthers up as the vanguard of the revolutionary and disciplinary group. You can tell all those wineheads you associate with that you'll kick no one's '. . . a—,' because you'd have to take a three year course in spelling to know what an a— is and three more years to be taught where it's located.

"Julius Lester called the BPP the vanguard (that's leader) organization so international whore Cleaver calls him racist, now when full allegiance is not given to the Panthers, again racist. What the hell do you want? Are you getting this? Are you lost? If you're not digging then you're really hopeless.

"Oh yes! We are not concerned about Hilliard's threats.

"Brains will win over brawn. The way the Panthers have retaliated against US is another indication. The score: US–6: Panthers–0.

"Why, I read an article in the Panther paper where a California Panther sat in his car and watched his friend get shot by Karenga's group and what did he do? He run back and write a full page story about how tough the Panthers are and what they're going to do. Ha Ha—B—— S——.

"Goodbye [name] baby—and watch out. Karenga's coming.

---

[166] Memorandum from FBI Headquarters to Baltimore Field Office, 11/25/68.

[167] Memorandum from San Diego Field Office to FBI Headquarters, 2/20/69; memorandum from San Diego Field Office to FBI Headquarters, 3/27/69; memorandum from FBI Headquarters to San Diego Field Office, 4/4/69.

[168] Memorandum from Newark Field Office to FBI Headquarters, 8/25/69. According to the proposal, the letter would not be typed by the field office stenographic pool because of the language. The field office also used asterisks in its communication with headquarters which "refer to that colloquial phrase . . . which implies an unnatural physical relationship with a material parent." Presumably the phrase was used in the letter when it was sent to the Panthers.

" 'Right On' as they say."

An anonymous letter was also sent to the leader of the Blackstone Rangers, a Chicago gang "to whom violent type activity, shooting, and the like, are second nature," advising him that "the brothers that run the Panthers blame you for blocking their thing and there's supposed to be a hit out for you." The letter was intended to "intensify the degree of animosity between the two groups" and cause "retaliatory action which could disrupt the BPP or lead to reprisals against its leadership." [169]

> EDITOR:
> What's with this bull—— SDS outfit? I'll tell you what they has finally showed there true color White. They are just like the commies and all the other white radical groups that suck up to the blacks and use us. We voted at our meeting in Oakland for community control over the pigs but SDS says no. Well we can do with out them mothers. We can do it by ourselfs.
>
> OFF THE PIGS   POWER TO THE PEOPLE
> Soul Brother Jake

In another case, the Bureau tried to promote violence, not between violent groups, but between a possibly violent person and another target. The field office was given permission to arrange a meeting between an SCLC officer and the leader of a small group described as "anti-Vietnam black nationalist [veterans'] organization." The leader of the veterans' group was known to be upset because he was not receiving funds from the SCLC. He was also known to be on leave from a mental hospital, and the Bureau had been advised that he would be recommitted if he were arrested on any charge. It was believed that "if the confrontation occurs at SCLC headquarters," the veterans' group leader "will lose his temper, start a fight," and the "police will be called in." The purpose was to "neutralize" the leader by causing his commitment to a mental hospital, and to gain "unfavorable publicity for the SCLC." [170]

At least four assaults—two of them on women—were reported as "results" of Bureau actions. The San Diego field office claimed credit for three of them. In one case, US members "broke into" a BPP meeting and "roughed up" a woman member.[171]

In the second instance, a critical newspaper article in the Black Panther paper was sent to the US leader. The field office noted that "the possibility exists that some sort of retaliatory actions will be taken against the BPP." [172] The prediction proved correct; the field office reported that as a result of this mailing, members of US assaulted a Panther newspaper vendor.[173] The third assault occurred after the

---

[169] Memorandum from Chicago Field Office to FBI Headquarters, 1/12/69; memorandum from FBI Headquarters to Chicago Field Office, 1/30/69.

[170] Memorandum from Philadelphia Field Office to FBI Headquarters, 11/25/68; memorandum from FBI Headquarters to Philadelphia Field Office, 12/9/68.

[171] Memorandum from San Diego Field Office to FBI Headquarters, 4/10/69, p. 4.

[172] Memorandum from San Diego Field Office to FBI Headquarters, 11/12/69.

[173] Memorandum from San Diego Field Office to FBI Headquarters, 11/12/69.

San Diego Police Department, acting on a tip from the Bureau that "sex orgies" were taking place at Panther headquarters, raided the premises. (The police department conducted a "research project," discovered two outstanding traffic warrants for a BPP member, and used the warrants to gain entry.) The field office reported that as a "direct result" of the raid, the woman who allowed the officers into the BPP headquarters had been "severely beaten up" by other members.[174]

In the fourth case, the New Haven field office reported that an informant had joined in a "heated conversation" between several group members and sided with one of the parties "in order to increase the tension." The argument ended with members hitting each other. The informant "departed the premises at this point, since he felt that he had been successful, causing a flammable situation to erupt into a fight."[175]

2. Anonymous Mailings

The Bureau's use of anonymous mailings to promote factionalism range from the relatively bland mailing of reprints or fliers criticizing a group's leaders for living ostentatiously or being ineffective speakers, to reporting a chapter's infractions to the group's headquarters intended to cause censure or disciplinary action.

Critical letters were also sent to one group purporting to be from another, or from a member of the group registering a protest over a proposed alliance.

For instance, the Bureau was particularly concerned with the alliance between the SDS and the Black Panther Party. A typical example of anonymous mailing intended to separate these groups is a letter sent to the Black Panther newspaper: [176]

In a similar vein, is a letter mailed to Black Panther and New Left leaders.[177]

> Dear Brothers and Sisters,
>
> Since when do us Blacks have to swallow the dictates of the honky SDS? Doing this only hinders the Party progress in gaining Black control over Black people. We've been ——— over by the white facists pigs and the Man's control over our destiny. We're sick and tired of being severly brutalized, denied our rights and treated like animals by the white pigs. We say to hell with the SDS and its honky intellectual approaches which only perpetuate control of Black people by the honkies.
>
> The Black Panther Party theory for community control is the only answer to our problems and that is to be followed and enforced by all means necessary to insure control by Blacks over all police departments regardless of whether they are run by honkies or uncle toms.
>
> The damn SDS is a paper organization with a severe case of diarhea of the mouth which has done nothing but feed us

[174] Memorandum from San Diego Field Office to FBI Headquarters, 12/3/69.

[175] Memorandum from New Haven Field Office to FBI Headquarters, 2/18/70.

[176] Memorandum from San Francisco Field Office to FBI Headquarters, 8/27/69; memorandum from FBI Headquarters to San Francisco Field Office, 9/5/69.

[177] Memorandum from Detroit Field Office to FBI Headquarters, 2/10/70; memorandum from FBI Headquarters to Detroit Field Office, 3/3/70.

lip service. Those few idiots calling themselves weathermen run around like kids on halloween. A good example is their "militant" activities at the Northland Shopping Center a couple of weeks ago. They call themselves revolutionaries but take a look at who they are. Most of them come from well heeled families even by honky standards. They think they're helping us Blacks but their futile, misguided and above all white efforts only muddy the revolutionary waters.

The time has come for an absolute break with any non-Black group and especially those ——— SDS and a return to our pursuit of a pure black revolution by Blacks for Blacks.

Power!

Off the Pigs!!!!

These examples are not, of course, exclusive, but they do give the flavor of the anonymous mailings effort.

3. Interviews

Interviewing group members or supporters was an overt "investigative" technique sometimes used for the covert purpose of disruption. For example, one field office noted that "other [BPP] weaknesses that have been capitalized on include interviews of members wherein jealousy among the members has been stimulated and at the same time has caused a number of persons to fall under suspicion and be purged from the Party." [178]

In another case, fourteen field offices were instructed to conduct simultaneous interviews of individuals known to have been contacted by members of the Revolutionary Union. The purpose of the coordinated interviews was "to make possible affiliates of the RU believe that the organization is infiltrated by informants on a high level.[179]

In a third instance, a "black nationalist" target attempted to organize a youth group in Mississippi. The field office used informants to determine "the identities of leaders of this group and in interviewing these leaders, expressed to them [the target's] background and his true intentions regarding organizing Negro youth groups." Agents also interviewed the target's landlords and "advised them of certain aspects of [his] past activities and his reputation in the Jackson vicinity as being a Negro extremist." Three of the landlords asked the target to move.[180] The same field office reported that it had interviewed members of the Tougaloo College Political Action Committee, an "SNCC affiliated" student group. The members were interviewed while they were home on summer vacation. "Sources report that these interviews had a very upsetting effect on the PAC organization and they felt they have been betrayed by someone at Tougaloo College. Many of the members have limited their participation in PAC affairs since their interview by Agents during the summer of 1968." [181]

4. Using Informants To Raise Controversial Issues

The Bureau's use of informants generally is the subject of a separate report. It is worth noting here, however, that the use of inform-

[178] Memorandum from Indianapolis Field Office to FBI Headquarters, 9/23/69.
[179] Memorandum from FBI Headquarters to all SACs, 10/28/70.
[180] Memorandum from Jackson Field Office to FBI Headquarters, 11/27/68.
[181] *Ibid.*

ants to take advantage of ideological splits in an organization dates back to the first COINTELPRO. The originating CUPSA document refers to the use of informants to capitalize on the discussion within the Party following Khrushchev's denunciation of Stalin.[182]

Informants were also used to widen rifts in other organizations. For instance, an informant was instructed to imply that the head of one faction of the SDS was using group funds for his drug habit, and that a second leader embezzled funds at another school. The field office reported that "as a result of actions taken by this informant, there have been fist fights and acts of name calling at several of the recent SDS meetings." In addition, members of one faction "have made early morning telephone calls" to other SDS members and "have threatened them and attempted to discourage them from attending SDS meetings." [183]

In another case, an informant was used to "raise the question" among his associates that an unmarried, 30-year old group leader "may be either a bisexual or a homosexual." The field office believed that the question would "rapidly become a rumor" and "could have serious results concerning the ability and effectiveness of [the target's] leadership." [184]

5. Fictitious Organizations

There are basically three kinds of "notional" or fictitious organizations. All three were used in COINTELPRO attempts to factionalize.

The first kind of "notional" was the organization whose members were all Bureau informants. Because of the Committee's agreement with the Bureau not to reveal the identities of informants, the only example which can be discussed publicly is a proposal which, although approved, was never implemented. That proposal involved setting up a chapter of the W.E.B. DuBois Club in a Southern city which would be composed entirely of Bureau informants and fictitious persons. The initial purpose of the chapter was to cause the CPUSA expense by sending organizers into the area, cause the Party to fund Bureau coverage of out-of-town CP meetings by paying the informants' expenses, and receive literature and instructions. Later, the chapter was to begin to engage in deviation from the Party line so that it would be expelled from the main organization "and then they could claim to be the victim of a Stalinist type purge." It was anticipated that the entire operation would take no more than 18 months.[185]

The second kind of "notional" was the fictitious organization with some unsuspecting (non-informant) members. For example, Bureau informants set up a Klan organization intended to attract membership away from the United Klans of America. The Bureau paid the informant's personal expenses in setting up the new organization, which had, at its height, 250 members.[186]

The third type of "notional" was the wholly fictitious organization, with no actual members, which was used as a pseudonym for mailing

---

[182] Memorandum from FBI Headquarters to New York Field Office, 9/6/56.

[183] Memorandum from Los Angeles Field Office to FBI Headquarters, 12/12/68, p. 2.

[184] Memorandum from San Diego Field Office to FBI Headquarters, 2/2/70.

[185] Memorandum from New York Field Office to FBI Headquarters, 7/9/64.

[186] Memorandum from C. D. Brennan to W. C. Sullivan, 8/28/67.

letters or pamphlets. For instance, the Bureau sent out newsletters from something called "The Committee for Expansion of Socialist Thought in America," which attacked the CPUSA from the "Marxist right" for at least two years.[187]

6. Labeling Targets As Informants

The "snitch jacket" technique—neutralizing a target by labeling him a "snitch" or informant, so that he would no longer be trusted—was used in all COINTELPROs. The methods utilized ranged from having an authentic informant start a rumor about the target member,[188] to anonymous letters or phone calls,[189] to faked informants' reports.[190]

When the technique was used against a member of a nonviolent group, the result was often alienation from the group. For example, a San Diego man was targeted because he was active in draft counseling at the city's Message Information Center. He had, coincidentally, been present at the arrest of a Selective Service violator, and had been at a "crash pad" just prior to the arrest of a second violator. The Bureau used a real informant to suggest at a Center meeting that it was "strange" that the two men had been arrested by federal agents shortly after the target became aware of their locations. The field office reported that the target had been "completely ostracized by members of the Message Information Center and all of the other individuals throughout the area . . . associated with this and/or related groups."[191]

In another case, a local police officer was used to "jacket" the head of the Student Mobilization Committee at the University of South Carolina. The police officer picked up two members of the Committee on the pretext of interviewing them concerning narcotics. By prearranged signal, he had his radio operator call him with the message, "[name of target] just called. Wants you to contact her. Said you have her number."[192] No results were reported.

The "snitch jacket" is a particularly nasty technique even when used in peaceful groups. It gains an added dimension of danger when it is used—as, indeed, it was—in groups known to have murdered informers.[193]

For instance, a Black Panther leader was arrested by the local police with four other members of the BPP. The others were released, but the leader remained in custody. Headquarters authorized the field office to circulate the rumor that the leader "is the last to be released" because "he is cooperating with and has made a deal with the Los Angeles Police Department to furnish them information concerning the BPP."

---

[187] Memorandum from F. J. Baumgardner to W. C. Sullivan, 1/5/65.

[188] Memorandum from FBI Headquarters to San Diego Field Office, 2/14/69.

[189] Memorandum from FBI Headquarters to Jackson Field Office. 11/15/68.

[190] Memorandum from FBI Headquaters to New York Field Office, 2/9/60.

[191] Memorandum from San Diego Field Office to FBI Headquarters, 2/17/69; memorandum from FBI Headquarters to San Diego Field Office, 3/6/69; memorandum from San Diego Field Office to FBI Headquarters 4/30/69.

[192] Memorandum from San Diego Field Office to FBI Headquarters, 1/31/69; memorandum from FBI Headquarters to San Diego Field Office, 2/14/69.

[193] One Bureau document stated that the Black Panther Party "has murdered two members it suspected of being police informants." (Memorandum from FBI Headquarters to Cincinnati Field Office, 2/18/71.)

The target of the first proposal then received an anonymous phone call stating that his own arrest was caused by a rival leader.[194]

In another case, the Bureau learned that the chairman of the New York BPP chapter was under suspicion as an informant because of the arrest of another member for weapons possession. In order to "cast further suspicion on him" the Bureau sent anonymous letters to BPP headquarters in the state, the wife of the arrested member, and a local member of CORE, saying "Danger-Beware-Black Brothers, [name of target] is the fink who told the pigs that [arrested members] were carrying guns." The letter also gave the target's address.[195]

In a third instance, the Bureau learned through electronic surveillance of the BPP the whereabouts of a fugitive. After his arrest, the Bureau sent a letter in a "purposely somewhat illiterate type scrawl" to the fugitive's half-brother:

> Brother:
> Jimmie was sold out by Sister [name—the BPP leader who made the phone call picked up by the tap] for some pig money to pay her rent. When she don't get it that way she takes Panther money. How come her kid sells the paper in his school and no one bothers him. How comes Tyler got busted up by the pigs and her kid didn't. How comes the FBI pig fascists knew where to bust Lonnie and Minnie way out where they were.
>
> —Think baby.[196]

In another example, the chairman of the Kansas City BPP chapter went to Washington in an attempt to testify before a Senate subcommittee about information he allegedly possessed about the transfer of firearms from the Kansas City Police Department to a retired Army General. The attempt did not succeed; the committee chairman adjourned the hearing and then asked the BPP member to present his information to an aide. The Bureau then authorized an anonymous phone call to BPP headquarters "to the effect that [the target] was paid by the committee to testify, that he has cooperated fully with this committee, and that he intends to return at a later date to furnish additional testimony which will include complete details of the BPP operation in Kansas City." [197]

In the fifth case, the Bureau had so successfully disrupted the San Diego BPP that it no longer existed. One of the former members, however, was "'politicking' for the position of local leader if the group is ever reorganized." Headquarters authorized the San Diego field office to send anonymous notes to "selected individuals within the black community of San Diego" to "initiate the rumor that [the target],

---

[194] Memorandum from San Diego Field Office to FBI Headquarters, 2/11/69; memorandum to San Diego Field Office from FBI Headquarters, 2/19/69.

[195] Memorandum from New York Field Office to FBI Headquarters, 2/14/69; memorandum from FBI Headquarters to New York Field Office, 3/10/69.

[196] Memorandum to FBI Headquarters from SAC, Newark, 7/3/69; memorandum to Newark Field Office from FBI Headquarters, 7/14/69.

[197] Memorandum from Kansas City Field Office to FBI Headquarters, 10/16/69; memorandum from FBI Headquarters to San Francisco Field Office, 11/3/69.

who has aspirations of becoming the local Black Panther Party Captain, is a police informant." [198]

In a sixth case, a letter alleging that a Washington, D.C., BPP leader was a police informant was sent "as part of our continuing effort to foment internal dissension within ranks of Black Panther Party:" [199]

> Brother:
> I recently read in the Black Panther newspaper about that low dog Gaines down in Texas who betrayed his people to the pigs and it reminded me of a recent incident that I should tell you about. Around the first part of Feb. I was locked up at the local pigpen when the pigs brought in this dude who told me he was a Panther. This dude who said his name was [deleted] said he was vamped on by six pigs and was brutalized by them. This dude talked real bad and said he had killed pigs and was going to get more when he got out, so I thought he probably was one of you. The morning after [name] was brought in a couple of other dudes in suits came to see him and called him out of the cell and he was gone a couple of hours. Later on these dudes came back again to see him. [Name] told me the dudes were his lawyers but they smelled like pig to me. It seems to me that you might want to look into this because I know you don't want anymore low-life dogs helping the pigs brutalize the people. You don't know me and I'm not a Panther but I want to help with the cause when I can.
>
> A lumpen brother

In a seventh case, the "most influential BPP activist in North Carolina" had been photographed outside a house where a "shoot out" with local police had taken place. The photograph, which appeared in the local newspaper, showed the target talking to a policeman. The photograph and an accompanying article were sent to BPP headquarters in Oakland, California, with a handwritten note, supposedly from a female BPP member known to be "disenchanted" with the target, saying, "I think this is two pigs oinking." [200]

Although Bureau witnesses stated that they did not authorize a "snitch jacket" when they had information that the group was *at that time* actually killing suspected informants,[201] they admitted that the risk was there whenever the technique was used.

---

[198] Memorandum to FBI Headquarters from San Diego Field Office, 3/6/70; memorandum from FBI Headquarters to San Diego Field Office, 3/6/70.

[199] Memorandum from Charlotte Field Office to FBI Headquarters, 3/23/71; memorandum from FBI Headquarters to Charlotte Field Office, 3/31/71.

[200] Memorandum from Charlotte Field Office to FBI Headquarters 3/23/71; memorandum FBI Headquarters to Charlotte Field Office, 3/31/71.

[201] In fact, some proposals were turned down for that reason. See, e.g., letter from FBI Headquarters to Cincinnati Field Office, 2/18/71, in which a proposal that an imprisoned BPP member be labeled a "pig informer" was rejected because it was possible it would result in the target's death. But note that just one month later, two similar proposals were approved. Letter from FBI Headquarters to Washington Field Office, 3/19/71, and letter from FBI Headquarters to Charlotte Field Office, 3/31/71.

> It would be fair to say there was an element of risk there which we tried to examine on a case by case basis.[202]

Moore added, "I am not aware of any time we ever labeled anybody as an informant, that anything [violent] ever happened as a result, and that is something that could be measured." When asked whether that was luck or lack of planning, he responded, "Oh, it just happened that way, I am sure." [203]

C. Using Hostile Third Parties Against Target Groups

The Bureau's factionalism efforts were intended to separate individuals or groups which might otherwise be allies. Another set of actions is a variant of that technique; organizations already opposed to the target groups were used to attack them.

The American Legion and the Veterans of Foreign Wars, for example, printed and distributed under their own names Bureau-authored pamphlets condemning the SDS and the DuBois Clubs.

In another case, a confidential source who headed an anti-Communist organization in Cleveland, and who published a "self-described conservative weekly newspaper," the *Cleveland Times*, was anonymously mailed information on the Unitarian Society of Cleveland's sponsorship of efforts to abolish the House Committee on Un-American Activities. The source had "embarrassed" the Unitarian minister with questions about the alleged Communist connections of other cosponsors "at public meetings." [204]

It was anticipated that the source would publish a critical article in her newspaper, which "may very well have the result of alerting the more responsible people in the community" to the nature of the movement and "stifle it before it gets started." [205]

The source newspaper did publish an article entitled "Locals to Aid Red Line," which named the Minister, among others, as a local sponsor of what it termed a "Communist-dominated plot" to abolish the House Committee.[206]

One group, described as a "militant anticommunist right wing organization, more of an activist group than is the more well known John Birch Society," was used on at least four separate occasions. The Bureau developed a long-range program to use the organization in "counterintelligence activity" by establishing a fictitious person named "Lester Johnson" who sent letters, made phone calls, offered financial support, and suggested action:

> In view of the activist nature of this organization, and their lack of experience and knowledge concerning the interior workings of the [local] CP, [the field office proposes] that efforts be made to take over their activities and use them in such a manner as would be best calculated by this office to

---

[202] Black Nationalist supervisor, 10/17/75, p. 39.

[203] Moore, 11/3/15, p. 64.

[204] The minister has given the Select Committee an affidavit which states that there was an organized attempt by the Bureau's source to disrupt the Church's meetings, including "fist fights." Affidavit of Rev. Dennis G. Kuby, 10/19/75.

[205] Memorandum from Cleveland Field Office to FBI Headquarters, 10/28/64; memorandum from FBI Headquarters to Cleveland Field Office, 11/6/64.

[206] Memorandum from FBI Headquarters to Cleveland Field Office, 11/6/64.

> completely disrupt and neutralize the [local] CP, all without [the organization] becoming aware of the Bureau's interest in its operation.[207]

"Lester Johnson" used the organization to distribute fliers and letters opposing the candidacy of a lawyer running for a judgeship [208] and to disrupt a dinner at which an alleged Communist was to speak.[209] "Johnson" also congratulated the organization on disrupting an anti-draft meeting at a Methodist Church, furnishing further information about a speaker at the meeting,[210] and suggested that members picket the home of a local "communist functionary." [211]

Another case is slightly different from the usual "hostile third party" actions, in that both organizations were Bureau targets. "Operation Hoodwink" was intended to be a long-range program to disrupt both La Cosa Nostra (which was not otherwise a COINTELPRO target) and the Communist Party by "having them expend their energies attacking each other." The initial project was to prepare and send a leaflet, which purported to be from a Communist Party leader to a member of a New York "family" attacking working conditions at a business owned by the family member.[212]

D. Disseminating Derogatory Information to Family, Friends, and Associates

Although this technique was used in relatively few cases it accounts for some of the most distressing of all COINTELPRO actions. Personal life information, some of which was gathered expressly to be used in the programs, was then disseminated, either directly to the target's family through an anonymous letter or telephone call, or indirectly, by giving the information to the media.

---

[207] Memorandum from Detroit Field Office to FBI Headquarters, 10/18/66, p. 2.

[208] Memorandum from Detroit Field Office to FBI Headquarters, 1/19/67. The lawyer was targeted, along with his law firm, because the firm "has a long history of providing services for individual communists and communist organizations," and because he belonged to the National Lawyers Guild.

[209] Memorandum from FBI Headquarters to Detroit Field Office, 1/16/67.

[210] Memorandum from FBI Headquarters to Detroit Field Office, 1/10/67.

[211] Memorandum from FBI Headquarters to Detroit Field Office, 11/3/66.

[212] Memorandum from F. J. Baumgardner to William C. Sullivan, 10/4/66; memorandum from FBI Headquarters to New York Field Office, 10/5/66.

A similar proposal attempted "to cause dissension between Negro numbers operators and the Italian hoodlum element" in Detroit. The Bureau had information that black "numbers men" were contributing money to the local "black power movement." An anonymous letter containing a black hand and the words "watch out" was sent a minister who was "the best known black militant in Detroit." The letter was intended to achieve two objectives. First, the minister was expected to assume that "the Italian hoodlum element was responsible for this letter, report this to the Negro numbers operators, and thereby cause them to further resent the Italian hoodlum element." Second, it is also possible that [the minister] may become extremely frightened upon receipt of this letter and sever his contact with the Negro numbers men in Detroit and might even restrict his black nationalist activity or leave Detroit. (Memorandum from the Detroit Field Office to FBI Headquarters, 6/14/68; Memorandum from FBI Headquarters to Detroit Field Office, 6/28/68.)

Several letters were sent to spouses; three examples follow.[213] The names have been deleted for privacy reasons.

The first letter was sent to the wife of a Grand Dragon of the United Klans of America ("Mrs. A"). It was to be "typed on plain paper in an amateurish fashion." [214]

"My Dear Mrs. (A),

"I write this letter to you only after a long period of praying to God. I must cleanse my soul of these thoughts. I certainly do not want to create problems inside a family but I owe a duty to the klans and its principles as well as to my own menfolk who have cast their divine lot with the klans.

"Your husband came to [deleted] about a year ago and my menfolk blindly followed his leadership, believing him to be the savior of this country. They never believed the "stories that he stole money from the klans in [deleted] or that he is now making over $25,000 a year. They never believed the stories that your house in [deleted] has a new refrigerator, washer, dryer and yet one year ago, was threadbare. They refuse to believe that your husband now owns three cars and a truck, including the new white car. But I believe all these things and I can forgive them for a man wants to do for his family in the best way he can.

"I don't have any of these things and I don't grudge you any of them neither. But your husband has been committing the greatest of the sins of our Lord for many years. He has taken the flesh of another unto himself.

"Yes, Mrs. A, he has been committing adultery. My menfolk say they don't believe this but I think they do. I feel like crying. I saw her with my own eyes. They call her Ruby. Her last name is something like [deleted] and she lives in the 700 block of [deleted] Street in [deleted.] I know this. I saw her strut around at a rally with her lustfilled eyes and smart aleck figure.

"I cannot stand for this. I will not let my husband and two brothers stand side by side with your husband and this woman in the glorious robes of the klan. I am typing this because I am going to send copys to Mr. Shelton and some of the klans leaders that I have faith in. I will not stop until your husband is driven from [deleted] and back into the flesh-pots from wherein he came.

---

[213] Letters were also sent to parents informing them that their children were in communes, or with a roommate of the opposite sex; information on an actress' pregnancy by a Black Panther was sent to a gossip columnist; and information about a partner's affair with another partner's wife was sent to the members of a law firm as well as the injured spouses.

Personal life information was not the only kind of derogatory information disseminated; information on the "subversive background" of a target (or family member) was also used, as were arrest records.

[214] Memorandum from Richmond Field Office to FBI Headquarters, 8/26/66.

"I am a loyal klanswoman and a good churchgoer. I feel this problem affects the future of our great country. I hope I do not cause you harm by this and if you believe in the Good Book as I do, you may soon receive your husband back into the fold. I pray for you and your beautiful little children and only wish I could tell you who I am. I will soon, but I am afraid my own men would be harmed if I do."

"A God-fearing klanswoman"

The second letter was sent to the husband ("Mr. B") of a woman who had the distinction of being both a New Left and Black Nationalist target; she was a leader in the local branch of the Women's International League for Peace and Freedom, "which group is active in draft resistance, antiwar rallies and New Left activities," and an officer in ACTION, a biracial group which broke off from the local chapter of the Congress of Racial Equality and which "engaged in numerous acts of civil disruption and disobedience." [215]

Two informants reported that Mr. B had been making suspicious inquiries about his wife's relationship with the Black males in ACTION. The local field office proposed an anonymous letter to the husband which would confirm his suspicions, although the informants did not know whether the allegations of misconduct were true. It was hoped that the "resulting marital tempest" would "result in ACTION losing their [officer] and the WILPF losing a valuable leader, thus striking a major blow against both organizations." [216]

Accordingly, the following letter,[216a] written in black ink, was sent to the husband:

---

[215] Memorandum from St. Louis Field Office to FBI Headquarters, 1/30/70.

[216] Memorandum from St. Louis Field Office to FBI Headquarters, 1/30/70. Note that there is no allegation that ACTION was engaged in violence. When the target was interviewed by the staff, she was asked whether ACTION ever took part in violent activities. She replied that someone once spat in a communion cup during a church sit-in and that members sometimes used four letter words, which was considered violent in her city. The staff member then asked about more conventionally violent acts, such as throwing bricks or burning buildings. Her response was a shocked, "Oh, no! I'm a pacifist—I wouldn't be involved in an organization like that." (Staff interview of a COINTELPRO target.)

[216a] Memorandum from St. Louis Field Office to FBI Headquarters, 1/30/70.

53

Dear Mr. B

Look man I guess your old lady doesn't get enough at home or she wouldn't be shucking and jiving with our Black Men in ACTION, you dig? Like all she wants to integrate is the bed room ~~and we~~ Black Sisters ain't gonna take no second best from our men. So lay it on her, man— or get her the hell off Newstead.

A Soul Sister

A letter from the field office to headquarters four months later reported as a "tangible result" of the letter that the target and her husband had recently separated, following a series of marital arguments:

> This matrimonial stress and strain should cause her to function much less effectively in ACTION. While the letter sent by the [field office] was probably not the sole cause of this separation, it certainly contributed very strongly.[217]

The third letter was sent to the wife of a leader of the Black Liberators ("Mrs. C"). She was living in their home town with their two daughters while he worked in the city. Bureau documents describe Mrs. C. as a "faithful, loving wife, who is apparently convinced that her husband is performing a vital service to the Black world. . . . She is to all indications an intelligent, respectable young mother, who is active in the AME Methodist Church." [218]

The letter was "prepared from a penmanship, spelling style to imitate that of the average Black Liberator member. It contains several accusations which should cause [X's] wife great concern." It was expressly intended to produce "ill feeling and possibly a lasting distrust" between X and his wife; it was hoped that the "concern over what to do about it" would "detract from his time spent in the plots and plans of his organization." [219]

The letter was addressed to "Sister C":

---

[217] Memorandum from St. Louis Field Office to FBI Headquarters, 6/17/70.

[218] Memorandum from St. Louis Field Office to FBI Headquarters, 2/14/69, p. 1.

[219] Memorandum from St. Louis Field Office to FBI Headquarters, 2/14/ 69, pp. 2–3.

55

Us Black Liberators are trained to respect Black Women and special are wifes and girls. Brother C keeps tellen the Brothers this but he dont treet you that way. I only been in the organisatoin 12 months but C been maken it here with Sister Marva Bass & Sister Tony and than he gives jive bout their better in bed then you and how he keeps you off his back by senden you a little dollah ever now an then. He says he gotta send you money the Draft board gonna chuck him in the army or somethen. This aint rite and were sayen that is treaten you wrong —

A Black Liberator

The Petersen Committee said that some COINTELPRO actions were "abhorrent in a free society." This technique surely falls within that condemnation.[220]

---

[220] House Judiciary Committee, Subcommittee on Civil and Constitutional Rights, Hearings, 11/20/74, p. 11.

E. Contacts with Employers

The Bureau often tried to get targets fired, with some success.[221] If the target was a teacher, the intent was usually to deprive him of a forum and to remove what the Bureau believed to be the added prestige given a political cause by educators. In other employer contacts, the purpose was either to eliminate a source of funds for the individual or (if the target was a donor) the group, or to have the employer apply pressure on the target to stop his activities.

For example, an Episcopal minister furnished "financial and other" assistance to the Black Panther Party in his city. The Bureau sent an anonymous letter to his bishop so that the church would exert pressure on the minister to "refrain from assistance to the Black Panther Party." [222] Similarly, a priest who allowed the Black Panther Party to use his church for its breakfast program was targeted; his bishop received both an anonymous letter and three anonymous phone calls. The priest was transferred shortly thereafter.[223]

In another case, a black county employee was targeted because he had attended a fund raiser for the Mississippi Summer Project and, on another occasion, a presentation of a Negro History Week program. Both functions had been supported by "clandestine CP members." The employee, according to the documents, had no record of subversive activities; "he and his wife appear to be genuinely interested in the welfare of Negroes and other minority groups and are being taken in by the communists." The Bureau chose a curiously indirect way to inform the target of his friends' Party membership; a local law enforcement official was used to contact the County Administrator in the expectation that the employee would be "called in and questioned about his left-wing associates." [224]

The Bureau made several attempts to stop outside sources from funding target operations.[225] For example, the Bureau learned that SNCC was trying to obtain funds from the Episcopal Church for a "liberation school." Two carefully spaced letters were sent to the Church which falsely alleged that SNCC was engaged in a "fraudulent scheme" involving the anticipated funds. The letters purported to be from local businessmen approached by SNCC to place fictitious orders for school supplies and divide the money when the Church paid the bills.[226] Similar letters were sent to the Interreligious Foundation for Community Organizing, from which SNCC had requested a grant for its "Agrarian Reform Plan." This time, the letters alleged kickback approaches in the sale of farm equipment and real estate.[227]

Other targets include an employee of the Urban League, who was fired because the Bureau contacted a confidential source in a foundation which funded the League; [228] a lawyer known for his representation

[221] There were 84 contacts with employers or 3 percent of the total.

[222] Memorandum from New Haven Field Office to FBI Headquarters, 11/12/69.

[223] Memorandum from FBI Headquarters to San Diego Field Office, 9/11/69.

[224] Memorandum from FBI Headquarters to San Francisco Field Office, 9/29/64.

[225] The FBI also used a "confidential source" in a foundation to gain funding for a "moderate" civil rights organization. (Memorandum from G. C. Moore to W. C. Sullivan, 10/23/68.)

[226] Memorandum from New York Field Office to FBI Headquarters, 6/18/70.

[227] Memorandum from New York Field Office to FBI Headquarters, 8/19/70.

[228] Memoranda from FBI Headquarters to Pittsburgh Field Office, 3/3/69 and 4/3/69.

of "subversives," whose nonmovement client received an anonymous letter advising it not to employ a "well-known Communist Party apologist";[229] and a television commentator who was transferred after his station and superiors received an anonymous protest letter. The commentator, who had a weekly religious program, had expressed admiration for a black nationalist leader and criticized the United States' defense policy.[230]

F. Use and Abuse of Government Processes

This category, which comprises 9 percent of all approved proposals includes selective law enforcement (using Federal, state, or local authorities to arrest, audit, raid, inspect, deport, etc.); interference with judicial proceedings, including targeting lawyers who represent "subversives"; interference with candidates or political appointees; and using politicians and investigating committees, sometimes without their knowledge, to take action against targets.

1. Selective Law Enforcement

Bureau documents often state that notifying law enforcement agencies of violations committed by COINTELPRO targets is not counterintelligence, but part of normal Bureau responsibility. Other documents, however, make it clear that "counterintelligence" was precisely the purpose. "Be alert to have them arrested," reads a New Left COINTELPRO directive to all participating field offices.[231] Further, there is clearly a difference between notifying other agencies of information that the Bureau happened across in an investigation—in plain view, so to speak—and instructing field offices to find evidence of violations—*any* violations—to "get" a target. As George Moore stated:

> Ordinarily, we would not be interested in health violations because it is not my jurisdiction, we would not waste our time. But under this program, we would tell our informants perhaps to be alert to any health violations or other licensing requirements or things of that nature, whether there were violations and we would see that they were reported.[232]

State and local agencies were frequently informed of alleged statutory violations which would come within their jurisdiction.[233] As noted above, this was not always normal Bureau procedure.

A typical example of the attempted use of local authorities to disrupt targeted activities is the Bureau's attempt to have a Democratic Party fund raiser raided by the state Alcoholic Beverage Control Commis-

---

[229] Memorandum from FBI Headquarters to New York Field Office, 7/2/64.

[230] Memorandum from FBI Headquarters to Cincinnati Field Office, 3/28/69.

[231] Memorandum from FBI Headquarters to all SAC's, 10/9/68.

[232] Moore, 11/3/75, p. 47.

[233] Federal agencies were also used. For instance, a foreign-born professor active in the New Left was deported by the Immigration and Naturalization Service at the Bureau's instigation. (Memorandum from FBI Headquarters to San Diego Field Office, 9/6/68.) The Bureau's use of the IRS in COINTELPRO is included in a separate report. Among other actions, the Bureau obtained an activist professor's tax returns and then used a source in a regional IRS office to arrange an audit. The audit was intended to be timed to interfere with the professor's meetings to plan protest demonstrations in the 1968 Democratic convention.

sion.[234] The function was to be held at a private house: the admission charge included "refreshments." It was anticipated that alcoholic beverages would be served. A confidential source in the ABC Commission agreed to send an agent to the fund raiser to determine if liquor was being served and then to conduct a raid.[235] (In fact, the raid was cancelled for reasons beyond the Bureau's control. A prior raid on the local fire department's fund raiser had given rise to considerable criticism and the District Attorney issued an advisory opinion that such affairs did not violate state law. The confidential source advised the field office that the ABC would not, after all, raid the Democrats because of "political ramifications.")[236]

In the second case, the target was a "key figure" Communist. He had a history of homosexuality and was known to frequent a local hotel. The Bureau requested that the local police have him arrested for homosexuality; it was then intended to publicize the arrest to "embarrass the Party." Interestingly, the Bureau withdrew its request when the target stopped working actively for the Party because it would no longer cause the intended disruption.[237] This would appear to rebut the Bureau's contention that turning over evidence of violations to local authorities was not really COINTELPRO at all, but just part of its job.

2. Interference With Judicial Process

The Bureau's attempts to interfere with judicial processes affecting targets are particularly disturbing because they violate a fundamental principle of our system of government. Justice is supposed to be blind. Nevertheless, when a target appeared before a judge, a jury, or a probation board, he sometimes carried an unknown burden; the Bureau had gotten there first.

Three examples should be sufficient. A university student who was a leader of the Afro American Action Committee had been arrested in a demonstration at the university. The Bureau sent an anonymous letter to the county prosecutor intended to discredit her by exposing her "subversive connections"; her adoptive father was described as a Communist Party member. The Bureau believed that the letter might aid the prosecutor in his case against the student. Another anonymous letter containing the same information was mailed to a local radio announcer who had an "open mike" program critical of

---

[234] The fund raiser was targeted because of two of the candidates who would be present. One, a state assemblyman running for reelection, was active in the Vietnam Day Committee; the other, the Democratic candidate for Congress, had been a sponsor of the National Committee to Abolish the House Committee on Un-American Activities and had led demonstrations opposing the manufacture of napalm bombs. (Memorandum from FBI Headquarters to San Francisco Field Office, 10/21/66.)

[235] Memorandum from FBI Headquarters to San Francisco Field Office, 11/14/66.

[236] *Ibid.*

[237] Memorandum from New York Field Office to FBI Headquarters, 2/23/60; memorandum from FBI Headquarters to New York Field Office, 3/11/60; memorandum from New York Field Office to FBI Headquarters, 11/10/60; memorandum from FBI Headquarters to New York Field Office, 11/17/60.

local "leftist" activity. The letter was intended to further publicize the "connection" between the student and the Communist Party.[239]

In the second example, a Klan leader who had been convicted on a weapons charge was out on bail pending appeal. He spoke at a Klan rally, and the Bureau arranged to have newsmen present. The resulting stories and photographs were then delivered to the appellate judges considering his case.[240]

The third instance involved a real estate speculator's bequest of over a million dollars to the three representatives of the Communist Party who were expected to turn it over to the Party. The Bureau interviewed the probate judge sitting on the case, who was "very cooperative" and promised to look the case over carefully. The judge asked the Bureau to determine whether the widow would be willing to "take any action designed to keep the Communist Party from getting the money." The Bureau's efforts to gain the widow's help in contesting the will proved unsuccessful.[241]

3. Candidates and Political Appointees

The Bureau apparently did not trust the American people to make the proper choices in the voting booth. Candidates who, in the Bureau's opinion, should not be elected were therefore targeted. The case of the Democratic fundraiser discussed earlier was just one example.

Socialist Workers Party candidates were routinely selected for counterintelligence, although they had never come close to winning an election. In one case, a SWP candidate for state office inadvertently protected herself from action by announcing at a news conference that she had no objections to premarital sex; a field office thereupon withdrew its previously approved proposal to publicize her common law marriage.[241a]

Other candidates were also targeted. A Midwest lawyer whose firm represented "subversives" (defendants in the Smith Act trials) ran for City Council. The lawyer had been active in the civil rights movement in the South, and the John Birch Society in his city had recently mailed a book called "It's Very Simple—The True Story of Civil Rights" to various ministers, priests, and rabbis. The Bureau received a copy of the mailing list from a source in the Birch Society and sent an anonymous follow-up letter to the book's recipients noting the pages on which the candidate had been mentioned and calling their attention to the "Communist background" of this "charlatan." [242] The

---

[239] Memorandum from FBI Headquarters to Minneapolis Field Office, 7/22/69; memorandum from FBI Headquarters to Minneapolis Field Office, 4/9/69. Charles Colson spent seven months in jail for violating the civil rights of a defendant in a criminal case through the deliberate creation of prejudicial pretrial publicity.

[240] Memorandum from FBI Headquarters to Miami Field Office, 6/23/66; memorandum from Miami Field Office to FBI Headquarters, 9/30/66.

[241] Memorandum from New York Field Office to FBI Headquarters, 4/5/67. The Bureau also obtained legal advice from a probate attorney on how the will could be attacked; contacted other relatives of the deceased; leaked information about the will to a city newspaper; and solicited the efforts of the IRS and state taxing authorities to deplete the estate as much as possible.

[241a] Memorandum from Atlanta Field Office to FBI Headquarters, 7/13/70.

[242] Memorandum from Detroit Field Office to FBI Headquarters, 9/15/65; memorandum from FBI Headquarters to Detroit Field Office, 9/22/65.

Bureau also sent a fictitious-name letter to a television station on which the candidate was to appear, enclosing a series of informative questions it believed should be asked.[243] The candidate was defeated. He subsequently ran (successfully, as it happened) for a judgeship.

Political appointees were also targeted. One target was a member of the board of the NAACP and the Democratic State Central Committee. His brother, according to the documents, was a communist, and the target had participated in some Party youth group activities fifteen years earlier. The target's appointment as secretary of a city transportation board elicited an anonymous letter to the Mayor, with carbons to two newspapers, protesting the use of "us taxpayers' money" in the appointment of a "known Communist" to a highly paid job; more anonymous letters to various politicians, the American Legion, and the county prosecutor in the same vein; and a pseudonymous letter to the members of the transportation board, stating that the Mayor had "saddled them with a Commie secretary because he thinks it will get him a few Negro votes.[244]

4. Investigating Committees

State and Federal legislative investigating committees were occasionally used to attack a target, since the committees' interests usually marched with the Bureau's.

Perhaps the most elaborate use of an investigating committee was the framing of a complicated "snitch jacket." In October 1959, a legislative committee held hearings in Philadelphia, "ostensibly" to show a resurgence of CP activity in the area.[245] The Bureau's target was subpoenaed to appear before the committee but was not actually called to testify. The field office proposed that local CP leaders be contacted to raise the question of "how it was possible for [the target] to escape testifying" before the committee; this "might place suspicion on him as being cooperative" with the investigators and "raise sufficient doubt in the minds of the leaders regarding [the target] to force him out of the CP or at least to isolate and neutralize him." Strangely enough, the target was not a bona fide CP member; he was an undercover infiltrator for a private anti-Communist group who had been a source of trouble for the FBI because he kept getting in their way.

A more typical example of the use of a legislative committee is a series of anonymous letters sent to the chairman of a state investigating committee that was designated to look into New Left activities on the state's college campuses. The target was an activist professor, and the letters detailed his "subversive background."

G. Exposing "Communist Infiltration" of Groups

This technique was used in approximately 4 percent of all approved proposals. The most common method involved anonymously notify-

[243] Memorandum from FBI Headquarters to Detroit Field Office, 10/1/65.

[244] Memorandum from Detroit Field Office to FBI Headquarters, 10/24/66; memorandum from FBI Headquarters to Detroit Field Office, 11/3/66.

[245] According to the documents, "operating under the direction of New York headquarters," a document was placed in the record by the Committee which according to the "presiding officer," indicated that the CP planned to hold its national convention in Philadelphia. The field office added, "This office is not aware of any such plan of the CP." Memorandum from, Philadelphia Field Office to FBI Headquarters, 11/3/59; memorandum from FBI Headquarters to Philadelphia Field Office, 11/12/59.

THE FBI'S COVERT ACTION PROGRAM TO DESTROY THE BLACK PANTHER PARTY

INTRODUCTION

In August 1967, the FBI initiated a covert action program—COINTELPRO—to disrupt and "neutralize" organizations which the Bureau characterized as "Black Nationalist Hate Groups." [1] The FBI memorandum expanding the program described its goals as:

> 1. Prevent a coalition of militant black nationalist groups. . . .
> 2. Prevent the rise of a messiah who could unify and electrify the militant nationalist movement . . . Martin Luther King, Stokely Carmichael and Elijah Muhammad all aspire to this position. . . .
> 3. Prevent violence on the part of black nationalist groups. . . .
> 4. Prevent militant black nationalist groups and leaders from gaining respectability by discrediting them. . . .
> 5. . . . prevent the long-range growth of militant black nationalist organizations, especially among youth." [2]

The targets of this nationwide program to disrupt "militant black nationalist organizations" included groups such as the Southern Christian Leadership Conference (SCLC), the Student Nonviolent Coordinating Committee (SNCC), the Revolutionary Action Movement (RAM), and the Nation of Islam (NOI). It was expressly directed against such leaders as Martin Luther King, Jr., Stokley Carmichael, H. Rap Brown, Maxwell Stanford, and Elijah Muhammad.

The Black Panther Party (BPP) was not among the original "Black Nationalist" targets. In September 1968, however, FBI Director J. Edgar Hoover described the Panthers as:

> "the greatest threat to the internal security of the country.
>
> "Schooled in the Marxist-Leninist ideology and the teaching of Chinese Communist leader Mao Tse-tung, its members have perpetrated numerous assaults on police officers and have engaged in violent confrontations with police throughout the country. Leaders and representatives of the Black Panther Party travel extensively all over the United States preaching their gospel of hate and violence not only to ghetto residents,

[1] For a description of the full range of COINTELPRO programs, see the staff report entitled "COINTELPRO: The FBI's Covert Action Programs Against American Citizens."

[2] Memorandum from G. C. Moore to W. C. Sullivan, 2/29/68, pp. 3–4.

> but to students in colleges, universities and high schools as well."[3]

By July 1969, the Black Panthers had become the primary focus of the program, and was ultimately the target of 233 of the total 295 authorized "Black Nationalist" COINTELPRO actions.[4]

Although the claimed purpose of the Bureau's COINTELPRO tactics was to prevent violence, some of the FBI's tactics against the BPP were clearly intended to foster violence, and many others could reasonably have been expected to cause violence. For example, the FBI's efforts to "intensify the degree of animosity" between the BPP and the Blackstone Rangers, a Chicago street gang, included sending an anonymous letter to the gang's leader falsely informing him that the Chicago Panthers had "a hit out" on him.[5] The stated intent of the letter was to induce the Ranger leader to "take reprisals against" the Panther leadership.[6]

Similarly, in Southern California, the FBI launched a covert effort to "create further dissension in the ranks of the BPP."[7] This effort included mailing anonymous letters and caricatures to BPP members ridiculing the local and national BPP leadership for the express purpose of exacerbating an existing "gang war" between the BPP and an organization called the United Slaves (US). This "gang war" resulted in the killing of four BPP members by members of US and in numerous beatings and shootings. Although individual incidents in this dispute cannot be directly traced to efforts by the FBI, FBI officials were clearly aware of the violent nature of the dispute, engaged in actions which they hoped would prolong and intensify the dispute, and proudly claimed credit for violent clashes between the rival factions which, in the words of one FBI official, resulted in "shootings, beatings, and a high degree of unrest . . . in the area of southeast San Diego."[8]

James Adams, Deputy Associate Director of the FBI's Intelligence Division, told the Committee:

> None of our programs have contemplated violence, and the instructions prohibit it, and the record of turndowns of recommended actions in some instances specifically say that we do not approve this action because if we take it it could result in harm to the individual.[9]

But the Committee's record suggests otherwise. For example, in May 1970, after US organization members had already killed four BPP members, the Special Agent in Charge of the Los Angeles FBI office wrote to FBI headquarters:

> Information received from local sources indicate that, in general, the membership of the Los Angeles BPP is physical-

---

[3] New York Times, 9/8/68.

[4] This figure is based on the Select Committee's staff study of Justice Department COINTELPRO "Black Nationalist" summaries prepared by the FBI during the Petersen Committee inquiry into COINTELPRO.

[5] Memorandum from Chicago Field Office to FBI Headquarters, 1/13/69.

[6] *Ibid.*

[7] Memorandum from FBI Headquarters to Baltimore Field Office (and 13 other offices), 11/25/68.

[8] Memorandum from San Diego Field Office to FBI Headquarters, 1/16/70.

[9] James Adams testimony, 11/19/75, Hearings, Vol. 6, p. 76.

> ly afraid of US members and take premeditated precautions to avoid confrontations.
>
> In view of their anxieties, it is not presently felt that the Los Angeles BPP can be prompted into what could result in an internecine struggle between the two organizations. . . .
>
> The Los Angeles Division is aware of the mutually hostile feelings harbored between the organizations and the first opportunity to capitalize on the situation will be maximized. It is intended that US Inc. will be appropriately and discreetly advised of the time and location of BPP activities *in order that the two organizations might be brought together and thus grant nature the opportunity to take her due course.* [Emphasis added.] [10]

This report focuses solely on the FBI's counterintelligence program to disrupt and "neutralize" the Black Panther Party. It does not examine the reasonableness of the basis for the FBI's investigation of the BPP or seek to justify either the politics, the rhetoric, or the actions of the BPP. This report does demonstrate, however, that the chief investigative branch of the Federal Government, which was charged by law with investigating crimes and preventing criminal conduct, itself engaged in lawless tactics and responded to deep-seated social problems by fomenting violence and unrest.

A. The Effort to Promote Violence Between the Black Panther Party and Other Well-Armed, Potentially Violent Organizations

The Select Committee's staff investigation has disclosed a number of instances in which the FBI sought to turn violence-prone organizations against the Panthers in an effort to aggravate "gang warfare." Because of the milieu of violence in which members of the Panthers often moved we have been unable to establish a direct link between any of the FBI's specific efforts to promote violence and particular acts of violence that occurred. We have been able to establish beyond doubt, however, that high officials of the FBI desired to promote violent confrontations between BPP members and members of other groups, and that those officials condoned tactics calculated to achieve that end. It is deplorable that officials of the United States Government should engage in the activities described below, however dangerous a threat they might have considered the Panthers; equally disturbing is the pride which those officials took in claiming credit for the bloodshed that occurred.

1. The Effort to Promote Violence Between the Black Panther Party and the United Slaves (US), Inc.

FBI memoranda indicate that the FBI leadership was aware of a violent power struggle between the Black Panther Party and the United Slaves (US) in late 1968. A memorandum to the head of the FBI's Domestic Intelligence Division, for example, stated:

> On 11/2/68, BPP received information indicating US members intended to assassinate Leroy Eldridge Cleaver . . .

---

[10] Memorandum from Los Angeles Field Office to FBI Headquarters, 5/26/70, pp. 1–2.

> at a rally scheduled at Los Angeles on 11/3/68. A Los Angeles racial informant advised on 11/8/68 that [a BPP member] had been identified as a US infiltrator and that BPP headquarters had instructed that [name deleted] should be killed.
>
> During BPP rally, US members including one [name deleted], were ordered to leave the rally site by LASS members (Los Angeles BPP Security Squad) and did so. US capitulation on this occasion prompted BPP members to decide to kill [name deleted] and then take over US organization. Members of LASS . . . were given orders to eliminate [name deleted] and [name deleted].[11]

This memorandum also suggested that the two US members should be told of the BPP's plans to "eliminate" them in order to convince them to become Bureau informants.[12]

In November 1968, the FBI took initial steps in its program to disrupt the Black Panther Party in San Diego, California by aggravating the existing hostility between the Panthers and US. A memorandum from FBI Director Hoover to 14 field offices noted a state of "gang warfare" existed, with "attendant threats of murder and reprisals," between the BPP and US in southern California and added:

> In order to fully capitalize upon BPP and US differences as well as to exploit all avenues of creating further dissention in the ranks of the BPP, recipient offices are instructed to submit imaginative and hard-hitting counterintelligence measures aimed at crippling the BPP.[13]

As the tempo of violence quickened, the FBI's field office in San Diego developed tactics calculated to heighten tension between the hostile factions. On January 17, 1969, two members of the Black Panther Party—Apprentice "Buchey" Carter and John Huggins—were killed by US members on the UCLA campus following a meeting involving the two organizations and university students.[14] One month later, the San Diego field office requested permission from headquarters to mail derogatory cartoons to local BPP offices and to the homes of prominent BPP leaders around the country.[15] The purpose was plainly stated:

> The purpose of the caricatures is to indicate to the BPP that the US organization feels that they are ineffectual, inadequate, and riddled with graft and corruption.[16]

In the first week of March, the first cartoon was mailed to five BPP members and two underground papers, all in the San Diego area.[17] According to an FBI memorandum, the consensus of opinion within

---

[11] Memorandum from G. C. Moore to W. C. Sullivan, 11/5/68.

[12] *Ibid.* An earlier FBI memorandum had informed headquarters that "sources have reported that the BPP has let a contract on Karenga [the leader of US] because they feel he has sold out to the establishment." (Memorandum from Los Angeles Field Office to FBI Headquarters, 9/25/68, p. 1.)

[13] Memorandum from FBI Headquarters to Baltimore Field Office (and 13 other field offices), 11/25/68.

[14] Memorandum from San Diego Field Office to FBI Headquarters, 1/20/69.

[15] Memorandum from San Diego Field Office to FBI Headquarters, 2/20/69.

[16] *Ibid.*

[17] See memorandum from San Diego Field Office to FBI Headquarters, 3/12/69.

the BPP was that US was responsible and that the mailing constituted an attack on the BPP by US.[18]

In mid-March 1969, the FBI learned that a BPP member had been critically wounded by US members at a rally in Los Angeles. The field office concluded that shots subsequently fired into the home of a US member were the results of a retaliatory raid by the BPP.[19] Tensions between the BPP and US in San Diego, however, appeared to lessen, and the FBI concluded that those chapters were trying "to talk out their differences." The San Diego field office reported:

> On 3/27/69 there was a meeting between the BPP and US organization. . . . Wallace [BPP leader in San Diego] . . . concluded by stating that the BPP in San Diego would not hold a grudge against the US members for the killing of the Panthers in Los Angeles (Huggins and Carter). He stated that he would leave any retaliation for this activity to the black community. . . .
>
> On 4/2/69, there was a friendly confrontation between US and the BPP with no weapons being exhibited by either side. US members met with BPP members and tried to talk out their differences.[20]

On March 27, 1969—the day that the San Diego field office learned that the local BPP leader had promised that his followers "would not hold a grudge" against local US members for the killings in Los Angeles—the San Diego office requested headquarters' approval for three more cartoons ridiculing the BPP and falsely attributed to US. One week later, shortly after the San Diego office learned that US and BPP members were again meeting and discussing their differences, the San Diego field office mailed the cartoons with headquarters' approval.[21]

On April 4, 1969 there was a confrontation between US and BPP members in Southcrest Park in San Diego at which, according to an FBI memorandum, the BPP members "ran the US members off."[22] On the same date, US members broke into a BPP political education meeting and roughed up a female BPP member.[23] The FBI's Special Agent in Charge in San Diego boasted that the cartoons had caused these incidents:

> The BPP members . . . strongly objected being made fun of by cartoons being distributed by the US organization (FBI cartoons in actuality) . . . [Informant] has advised on several occasions that the cartoons are "really shaking up the BPP." They have made the BPP feel that US is getting ready to move and this was the cause of the confrontation at Southcrest Park on 4/4/69.[24]

---

[18] Memorandum from San Diego Field Office to FBI Headquarters, 3/12/69, p. 4.
[19] Memorandum from Los Angeles Field Office to FBI Headquarters, 3/17/69.
[20] Memorandum from San Diego Field Office to FBI Headquarters, 4/10/69.
[21] Memorandum from San Diego Field Office to FBI Headquarters, 3/27/69.
[22] Memorandum from San Diego Field Office to FBI Headquarters, 4/10/69, p. 4.
[23] *Ibid.*
[24] *Ibid.*

192

The fragile truce had ended. On May 23, 1969, John Savage, a member of the BPP in Southern California, was shot and killed by US member Jerry Horne, aka Tambuzi. The killing was reported in an FBI memorandum which stated that confrontations between the groups were now "ranging from mere harrassment up to and including beating of various individuals." [25] In mid-June, the San Diego FBI office informed Washington headquarters that members of the US organization were holding firearms practice and purchasing large quantities of ammunition:

> Reliable information has been received . . . that members of the US organization have purchased ammunition at one of the local gun shops. On 6/5/69, an individual identified as [name deleted] purchased 150 rounds of 9 MM ammunition, 100 rounds of .32 automatic ammunition, and 100 rounds of .38 special ammunition at a local gun shop. [Name deleted] was tentatively identified as the individual who was responsible for the shooting of BPP member [name deleted] in Los Angeles on or about 3/14/69.[26]

Despite this atmosphere of violence, FBI headquarters authorized the San Diego field office to compose an inflammatory letter over the forged signature of a San Diego BPP member and to send it to BPP headquarters in Oakland, California.[27] The letter complained of the killing of Panthers in San Diego by US members, and the fact that a local BPP leader had a white girlfriend.[28]

According to a BPP bulletin, two Panthers were wounded by US gunman on August 14, 1969, and the next day another BPP member, Sylvester Bell, was killed in San Diego by US members.[29] On August 30, 1969, the San Diego office of US was bombed. The FBI believed the BPP was responsible for the bombing.[30]

The San Diego office of the FBI viewed this carnage as a positive development and informed headquarters: "Efforts are being made to determine how this situation can be capitalized upon for the benefit of the Counterintelligence Program. . . ." [31] The field office further noted:

> In view of the recent killing of BPP member Sylvester Bell, a new cartoon is being considered in the hopes that it will assist in the continuance of the rift between BPP and US.[32]

The San Diego FBI office pointed with pride to the continued violence between black groups:

> Shootings, beatings, and a high degree of unrest continues to prevail in the ghetto area of southeast San Diego. Although no specific counterintelligence action can be credited with contributing to this overall situation, *it is felt that a*

---

[25] Memorandum from San Diego Field Office to FBI Headquarters, 6/5/69, p. 3.
[26] Memorandum from San Diego Field Office to FBI Headquarters, 6/13/69.
[27] Memorandum from FBI Headquarters to San Diego Field Office, 6/17/69.
[28] Memorandum from San Diego Field Office to FBI Headquarters, 6/6/69.
[29] Memorandum from San Diego Field Office to FBI Headquarters, 8/20/69.
[30] Memorandum from San Diego Field Office to FBI Headquarters, 9/18/69.
[31] *Ibid*, p. 3.
[32] *Ibid.*, p. 1.

> *substantial amount of the unrest is directly attributable to this program.* [Emphasis added.] [33]

In early September 1969, the San Diego field office informed headquarters that Karenga, the Los Angeles US leader, feared assassination by the BPP.[34] It received permission from headquarters to exploit this situation by sending Karenga a letter, purporting to be from a US member in San Diego, alluding to an article in the BPP newspaper criticizing Karenga and suggesting that he order reprisals against the Panthers. The Bureau memorandum which originally proposed the letter explained:

> The article, which is an attack on Ron Karenga of the US organization, is self-explanatory. It is felt that if the following letter be sent to Karenga, pointing out that the contents of the article are objectionable to members of the US organization in San Diego, the possibility exists that some sort of retaliatory action will be taken against the BPP. . . .[35]

FBI files do not indicate whether the letter, which was sent to Karenga by the San Diego office, was responsible for any violence.

In January 1970, the San Diego office prepared a new series of counterintelligence cartoons attacking the BPP and forwarded them to FBI headquarters for approval.[36] The cartoons were composed to look like a product of the US organization.

> The purpose of the caricatures is to indicate to the BPP that the US Organization considers them to be ineffectual, inadequate, and [considers itself] vitally superior to the BPP.[37]

One of the caricatures was "designed to attack" the Los Angeles Panther leader as a bully toward women and children in the black community. Another accused the BPP of "actually instigating" a recent Los Angeles Police Department raid on US headquarters. A third cartoon depicted Karenga as an overpowering individual "who has the BPP completely at his mercy. . . ." [38]

On January 29, 1970, FBI headquarters approved distribution of these caricatures by FBI field offices in San Diego, Los Angeles, and San Francisco. The authorizing memorandum from headquarters stated:

> US Incorporated and the Black Panther Party are opposing black extremist organizations. Feuding between representatives of the two groups in the past had a tendency to limit the effectiveness of both. The leaders and incidents depicted in the caricatures are known to the general public, particularly among the Negroes living in the metropolitan areas of Los Angeles, San Diego and San Francisco.
>
> The leaders and members of both groups are distrusted by a large number of the citizen within the Negro commu-

---

[33] *Ibid.*, p. 2.
[34] Memorandum from San Diego Field Office to FBI Headquarters, 9/3/69.
[35] Memorandum from San Diego Field Office to FBI Headquarters, 11/12/69.
[36] Memorandum from San Diego Field Office to FBI Headquarters, 1/23/70.
[37] *Ibid.*, p. 1.
[38] *Ibid.*, p. 2.

194

> nities. Distribution of caricatures is expected to strengthen this distrust.[39]

Bureau documents provided to the Select Committee do not indicate whether violence between BPP and US members followed the mailing of this third series of cartoons.

In early May 1970, FBI Headquarters became aware of an article entitled "Karenga King of the Bloodsuckers" in the May 2, 1970, edition of the BPP newspaper which "vilifies and debases Karenga and the US organization."[40] Two field offices received the following request from headquarters:

> [s]ubmit recommendation to Bureau . . . for exploitation of same under captioned program. Consider from two aspects, one against US and Karenga from obvious subject matter; the second against BPP because inherent in article is admission by BPP that it has done nothing to retaliate against US for killing of Panther members attributed to US and Karenga, an admission that the BPP has been beaten at its own game of violence.[41]

In response to this request, the Special Agent in Charge in Los Angeles reported that the BPP newspaper article had already resulted in violence, but that it was difficult to induce BPP members to attack US members in Southern California because they feared US members.[42] The Los Angeles field office hoped, however, that "internecine struggle" might be triggered through a skillful use of informants within both groups:

> The Los Angeles Division is aware of the mutually hostile feelings harbored between the organizations and the first opportunity to capitalize on the situation will be maximized. It is intended that US Inc. will be appropriately and discretely advised of the time and location of BPP activities *in order that the two organizations might be brought together and thus grant nature the opportunity to take her due course.* [Emphasis added.] [43]

The release of Huey P. Newton, BPP Minister of Defense, from prison in August 1970 inspired yet another counterintelligence plan. An FBI agent learned from a prison official that Newton had told an inmate that a rival group had let a $3,000 contract on his life. The Los Angeles office presumed the group was US, and proposed that an anonymous letter be sent to David Hilliard, BPP Chief of Staff in Oakland, purporting to be from the person holding the contract on Newton's life. The proposed letter warned Hilliard not to be around when the "unscheduled appointment" to kill Newton was kept, and cautioned Hilliard not to "get in my way."[44]

---

[39] Memorandum from FBI Headquarters to San Diego Field Office, 1/29/70.

[40] Memorandum from FBI Headquarters to Los Angeles and San Francisco Field Offices, 5/15/70.

[41] *Ibid.*

[42] Memorandum from Los Angeles Field Office to FBI Headquarters, 5/26/70.

[43] *Ibid.*, pp. 1–2.

[44] Memorandum from Los Angeles Field Office to FBI Headquarters, 8/10/70.

FBI headquarters, however, denied authority to send the letter to Hilliard. Its concern was not that the letter might cause violence or that it was improper action by a law enforcement agency, but that the letter might violate a Federal statute:

> While Bureau appreciates obvious effort and interest exhibited concerning anonymous letter . . . studied analysis of same indicates implied threat therein may constitute extortion violation within investigative jurisdiction of Bureau or postal authorities and may subsequently be embarrassing to Bureau.[45]

The Bureau's stated concern with legality was ironic in light of the activities described above.

2. The Effort To Promote Violence Between the Blackstone Rangers and the Black Panther Party

In late 1968 and early 1969, the FBI endeavored to pit the Blackstone Rangers, a heavily armed, violence-prone organization, against the Black Panthers.[46] In December 1968, the FBI learned that the recognized leader of the Blackstone Rangers, Jeff Fort, was resisting Black Panther overtures to enlist "the support of the Blackstone Rangers." [47] In order to increase the friction between these groups, the Bureau's Chicago office proposed sending an anonymous letter to Fort, informing him that two prominent leaders of the Chicago BPP had been making disparaging remarks about his "lack of commitment to black people generally." The field office observed:

> Fort is reportedly aware that such remarks have been circulated, but is not aware of the identities of the individual responsible. He has stated that he would "take care of" individuals responsible for the verbal attacks directed against him.
>
> Chicago, consequently, recommends that Fort be made aware that [name deleted] and [name deleted] together with other BPP members locally, are responsible for the circulation of these remarks concerning him. It is felt that if Fort were to be aware that the BPP was responsible, it would lend impetus to his refusal to accept any BPP overtures to the Rangers and *additionally might result in Fort having*

[45] Memorandum from FBI Headquarters to Los Angeles Field Office, 9/30/70.

[46] There is no question that the Blackstone Rangers were well-armed and violent. The Chicago police had linked the Rangers and rival gangs in Chicago to approximately 290 killings from 1965–69. Report of Captain Edward Buckney, Chicago Police Dept., Gang Intelligence Unit, 2/23/70, p. 2. One Chicago police officer, familiar with the Rangers, told a Committee staff member that their governing body, the Main 21, was responsible for several ritualistic murders of black youths in areas the gang controlled. (Staff summary of interview with Renault Robinson, 9/25/75.)

[47] Memorandum from Chicago Field Office to FBI Headquarters, 12/16/68. Forte also had a well-earned reputation for violence. Between September 1964 and January 1971, he was charged with more than 14 felonies, including murder (twice), aggravated battery (seven times), robbery (twice), and contempt of Congress. (Select Committee staff interview of FBI criminal records.) A December 1968 FBI memorandum noted that a search of Forte's apartment had turned up a .22 caliber, four-shot derringer pistol. (Memorandum from Chicago Field Office to FBI Headquarters, 12/12/68, p. 2.)

active steps taken to exact some form of retribution toward the leadership of the BPP. [Emphasis added.] [48]

On about December 18, 1968, Jeff Fort and other Blackstone Rangers were involved in a serious confrontation with members of the Black Panther Party.

During that day twelve members of the BPP and five known members of the Blackstone Rangers were arrested on Chicago's South Side.[49] A report indicates that the Panthers and Rangers were arrested following the shooting of one of the Panthers by a Ranger.[49a]

That evening, according to an FBI informant, around 10:30 p.m., approximately thirty Panthers went to the Blackstone Rangers' headquarters at 6400 South Kimbark in Chicago. Upon their arrival Jeff Fort invited Fred Hampton, Bobby Rush and the other BPP members to come upstairs and meet with him and the Ranger leadership.[49b] The Bureau goes on to describe what transpired at this meeting:

> . . . everyone went upstairs into a room which appeared to be a gymnasium, where Fort told Hampton and Rush that he had heard about the Panthers being in Ranger territory during the day, attempting to show their "power" and he wanted the Panthers to recognize the Rangers "power." Source stated that Fort then gave orders, via walkie-talkie, whereupon two men marched through the door carrying pump shotguns. Another order and two men appeared carrying sawed off carbines then eight more, each carrying a .45 caliber machine gun, clip type, operated from the shoulder or hip, then others came with over and under type weapons. Source stated that after this procession Fort had all Rangers present, approximately 100, display their side arms and about one half had .45 caliber revolvers. Source advised that all the above weapons appeared to be new.
>
> Source advised they left the gym, went downstairs to another room where Rush and Hampton of the Panthers and Fort and two members of the Main 21 sat by a table and discussed the possibility of joining the two groups. Source related that Fort took off his jacket and was wearing a .45 caliber revolver shoulder holster with gun and had a small caliber weapon in his belt.
>
> Source advised that nothing was decided at the meeting about the two groups actually joining forces, however, a decision was made to meet again on Christmas Day. Source stated Fort did relate that the Rangers were behind the Panthers but were not to be considered members. Fort wanted the Panthers to join the Rangers and Hampton wanted the opposite, stating that if the Rangers joined the Panthers, then together they would be able to absorb all the other Chicago gangs. Source advised Hampton did state that they couldn't let the man keep the two groups apart. Source ad-

---

[48] Memorandum from Chicago Field Office to FBI Headquarters, 12/16/68, p. 2.
[49] Letter Head Memorandum, 12/20/68.
[49a] From confidential FBI interview with inmate at the House of Correction, 26th and California St. in Chicago, 11/12/69.
[49b] Letterhead Memorandum, 12/20/68.

> vised that Fort also gave Hampton and Rush one of the above .45 caliber machine guns to "try out."
>
> Source advised that based upon conversations during this meeting, Fort did not appear over anxious to join forces with the Panthers, however, neither did it appear that he wanted to terminate meeting for this purpose.[49c]

On December 26, 1968 Fort and Hampton met again to discuss the possibility of the Panthers and Rangers working together. This meeting was at a South Side Chicago bar and broke up after several Panthers and Rangers got into an argument.[49d] On December 27, Hampton received a phone call at BPP Headquarters from Fort telling him that the BPP had until December 28, 1968 to join the Blackstone Rangers. Hampton told Fort he had until the same time for the Rangers to join the BPP and they hung up.[49e]

In the wake of this incident, the Chicago office renewed its proposal to send a letter to Forte, informing FBI headquarters:

> As events have subsequently developed . . . the Rangers and the BPP have not only not been able to form any alliance, but enmity and distrust have arisen, to the point where each has been ordered to stay out of the other territory. The BPP has since decided to conduct no activity or attempt to do recruiting in Ranger territory.[50]

The proposed letter read:

> Brother Jeff:
>
> I've spent some time with some Panther friends on the west side lately and I know what's been going on. The brothers that run the Panthers blame you for blocking their thing and *there's supposed to be a hit out for you.* I'm not a Panther, or a Ranger, just black. From what I see these Panthers are out for themselves not black people. I think you ought to know what they're up to, I know what I'd do if I was you. You might hear from me again.
>
> (sgd.) A black brother you don't know.
> [Emphasis added.] [51]

The FBI's Chicago office explained the purpose of the letter as follows:

> It is believed the above may intensify the degree of animosity between the two groups and occasion Forte to take retaliatory action which could disrupt the BPP or lead to reprisals against its leadership.
>
> Consideration has been given to a similar letter to the BPP alleging a Ranger plot against the BPP leadership; however, it is not felt this would be productive principally because the BPP at present is not believed as violence prone as the Rangers to whom violent type activity—shooting and the like—is second nature.[52]

[49c] *Ibid.*, pp. 3–4.
[49d] FBI Special Agent Informant Report, 12/30/68.
[49e] *Ibid.*
[50] Memorandum from Chicago Field Office to FBI Headquarters, 1/10/69.
[51] Memorandum from Chicago Field Office to FBI Headquarters, 1/13/69, p. 1.
[52] *Ibid.*

On the evening of January 13, 1969, Fred Hampton and Bobby Rush appeared on a Chicago radio talk show called "Hot Line." During the course of the program Hampton stated that the BPP was in the "process of educating the Blackstone Rangers." [52a] Shortly after that statement Jeff Fort was on the phone to the radio program and stated that Hampton had his facts confused and that the Rangers were educating the BPP.[52b]

On January 16, Hampton, in a public meeting, stated that Jeff Fort had threatened to blow his head off if he came within Ranger territory.[52c]

On January 30, 1969, Director Hoover authorized sending the anonymous letter.[53] While the Committee staff could find no evidence linking this letter to subsequent clashes between the Panthers and the Rangers, the Bureau's intent was clear.[54]

B. The Effort To Disrupt the Black Panther Party by Promoting Internal Dissension

1. General Efforts to Disrupt the Black Panther Party Membership

In addition to setting rival groups against the Panthers, the FBI employed the full range of COINTELPRO techniques to create rifts and factions, within the Party itself which it was believed would "neutralize" the Party's effectiveness.[55]

Anonymous letters were commonly used to sow mistrust. For example, in March 1969 the Chicago FBI Field Office learned that a local BPP member feared that a faction of the Party, allegedly led by Fred Hampton and Bobby Rush, was "out to get" him.[56] Headquarters approved sending an anonymous letter to Hampton which was drafted to exploit dissension within the BPP as well as to play on mistrust between the Blackstone Rangers and the Chicago BPP leadership:

> Brother Hampton:
>
> Just a word of warning. A Stone friend tells me [name deleted] wants the Panthers and is looking for somebody to get you out of the way. Brother Jeff is supposed to be interested. I'm just a black man looking for blacks working together, not more of this gang banging.[57]

[52a] Memorandum from Special Agent to SAC, Chicago, 1/15/69.

[52b] *Ibid.*

[52c] Memorandum from Special Agent to SAC, Chicago, 1/28/69, reporting on informant report.

[53] Memorandum from FBI Headquarters to Chicago Field Office, 1/30/69.

[54] There are indications that a shooting incident between the Rangers and the Panthers on April 2, 1969, in a Chicago suburb may have been triggered by the FBI. According to Bobby Rush, coordinator of the Chicago BPP at the time, a group of armed BPP members had confronted the Rangers because Panther William O'Neal—who has since surfaced as an FBI informant—had told them that a Panther had been shot by Blackstone Rangers and had insisted that they retaliate. This account, however, has not been confirmed. (Staff summary of interview with Bobby Rush, 11/26/75.)

[55] The various COINTELPRO techniques are described in detail in the Staff Report on COINTELPRO.

[56] Memorandum from Chicago Field Office to FBI Headquarters, 3/24/69.

[57] Memorandum from FBI Headquarters to Chicago Field Office, 4/8/69.

Bureau documents indicate that during this time an informant within the BPP was also involved in maintaining the division between the Panthers and the Blackstone Rangers.[57a]

In December 1968, the Chicago FBI Field Office learned that a leader of a Chicago youth gang, the Mau Mau's, planned to complain to the national BPP headquarters about the local BPP leadership and questioned its loyalty.[58] FBI headquarters approved an anonymous letter to the Mau Mau leader, stating:

> Brother [deleted]:
>
> I'm from the south side and have some Panther friends that know you and tell me what's been going. I know those two [name deleted] and [name deleted] that run the Panthers for a long time and those mothers been with every black outfit going where it looked like they was something in it for them. The only black people they care about is themselves. *I heard too they're sweethearts* and that [name deleted] has worked for the man that's why he's not in Viet Nam. Maybe that's why they're just playing like real Panthers. I hear a lot of the brothers are with you and want those mothers out but don't know how. The Panthers need real black men for leaders not freaks. Don't give up brothers. [Emphasis added.] [59]
>
> A black friend.

The FBI also resorted to anonymous phone calls. The San Diego Field Office placed anonymous calls to local BPP leaders naming other BPP members as "police agents." According to a report from the field office, these calls, reinforced by rumors spread by FBI informants within the BPP, induced a group of Panthers to accuse three Party members of working for the police. The field office boasted that one of the accused members fled San Diego in fear for his life.[60]

The FBI conducted harassing interviews of Black Panther members to intimidate them and drive them from the Party. The Los Angeles Field Office conducted a stringent interview program

> in the hope that a state of distruct [sic] might remain among the members and add to the turmoil presently going on within the BPP.[61]

The Los Angeles office claimed that similar tactics had cut the membership of the United States (US) by 50 percent.[62]

57a Memorandum from Chicago Field Office to FBI Headquarters, 1/28/69.

58 Memorandum from Chicago Field Office to FBI Headquarters, 12/30/68.

59 Memorandum from FBI Headquarters to Chicago Field Office, 1/30/69.

60 Memorandum from San Diego Field Office to FBI Headquarters, 3/12/69. The FBI had success with this technique in other cases. For example, the FBI placed another anonymous call to Stokely Carmichael's residence in New York City. Carmichael's mother was informed falsely that several BPP members were out to kill her son, and that he should "hide out." The FBI memorandum reporting this incident said that Mrs. Carmichael sounded "shocked" on hearing the news and stated that she would tell Stokely when he came home. The memorandum observed that on the next day, Stokely Carmichael left New York for Africa. (Memorandum from New York Field Office to FBI Headquarters, 9/9/68, p. 2.)

61 Memorandum from Los Angeles Field Office to FBI Headquarters, 3/17/69, p. 1.

62 Memorandum from Los Angeles Field Office to FBI Headquarters, 2/3/69.

FBI agents attempted to convince landlords to force Black Panther members and offices from their buildings. The Indianapolis Field Office reported that a local landlord had yielded to its urgings and promised to tell his Black Panther tenants to relocate their offices.[63] The San Francisco office sent an article from the Black Panther newspaper to the landlord of a BPP member who had rented an apartment under an assumed name. The article, which had been written by that member and contained her picture and true name, was accompanied by an anonymous note stating, "(false name) is your tenant (true name)"[64] The San Francisco office secured the eviction of one Black Panther who lived in a public housing project by informing the Housing Authority officials that she was using his apartment for the BPP Free Breakfast Program.[65] When it was learned that the BPP was conducting a Free Breakfast Program "in the notorious Haight-Ashbury District of San Francisco," the Bureau mailed a letter to the owners of the building:

> Dear Mr. (excised):
>
> I would call and talk to you about this matter, but I am not sure how you feel, and I do not wish to become personally embroiled with neighbors. It seems that the property owners on (excised) Street have had enough trouble in the past without bringing in Black Panthers.
>
> Maybe you are not aware, but the Black Panthers have taken over (address deleted). Perhaps if you drive up the street, you can see what they are going to do to the property values. They have already plastered a nearby garage with big Black Panther posters.
>
> —A concerned property owner.[66]

The Bureau also attempted to undermine the morale of Panther members by attempting to break up their marriages. In one case, an anonymous letter was sent to the wife of a prominent Panther leader stating that her husband had been having affairs with several teenage girls and had taken some of those girls with him on trips.[67] Another Panther leader told a Committee staff member that an FBI agent had attempted to destroy his marriage by visiting his wife and showing photographs purporting to depict him with other women.[68]

2. FBI Role in the Newton-Cleaver Rift

In March 1970, the FBI initiated a concerted program to drive a permanent wedge between the followers of Eldridge Cleaver, who was then out of the country and the supporters of Huey P. Newton, who

---

[63] Memorandum from San Diego Field Office to FBI Headquarters, 9/8/69. The FBI discovered that the Indianapolis BPP would have difficulty in new quarters because of its financial plight, a fact which was discovered by monitoring its bank account. (Memorandum from Indianapolis Field Office to FBI Headquarters, 9/23/69.)

[64] Memorandum from San Francisco Field Office to FBI Headquarters, 9/15/69.

[65] Memorandum from San Francisco Field Office to FBI Headquarters, 10/21/70.

[66] Memorandum from San Francisco Field Office to FBI Headquarters, 10/22/70.

[67] Memorandum from San Francisco Field Office to FBI Headquarters, 11/26/68.

[68] The Bureau documents presented to the Committee do not record of this contact.

was then serving a prison sentence in California.[69] An anonymous letter was sent to Cleaver in Algeria stating that BPP leaders in California were seeking to undercut his influence. The Bureau subsequently learned that Cleaver had assumed the letter was from the then Panther representative in Scandanavia, Connie Matthews, and that the letter had led Cleaver to expel three BPP international representatives from the Party.[70]

Encouraged by the apparent success of this letter, FBI headquarters instructed its Paris Legal Attache to mail a follow-up letter, again written to appear as if Matthews was the author, to the Black Panther Chief-of-Staff, David Hilliard, in Oakland, California. The letter alleged that Cleaver "has tripped out. Perhaps he has been working too hard," and suggested that Hilliard "take some immediate action before this becomes more serious." The Paris Legal Attache was instructed to mail the letter:

> At a time when Matthews is in or has just passed through Paris immediately following one of her trips to Algiers. The enclosed letter should be held by you until such an occasion arises at which time you are authorized to immediately mail it in Paris in such a manner that it cannot be traced to the Bureau.[71]

In early May, Eldridge Cleaver called BPP national headquarters from Algeria and talked with Connie Matthews, Elbert Howard, and Roosevelt Hilliard. A Bureau report stated:

> Various items were discussed by these individuals with Hilliard. Connie Matthews discussed with Hilliard "those letters" appearing to relate to the counterintelligence letters, which have been submitted to Cleaver and Hilliard purportedly by Matthews. . . .
>
> It appears . . . that [Elbert Howard] had brought copies of the second counterintelligence letter to David Hilliard with him to Algiers which were then compared with the . . . letter previously sent to Cleaver in Algiers and that . . . discussed this situation. . . .[72]

The San Francisco Field Office reported that some BPP leaders suspected that the CIA or FBI had sent the letters, while others suspected the Black Panther members in Paris. A subsequent FBI memorandum indicated that suspicion had focused on the Panthers in Europe.[73]

On August 13, 1970—the day that Huey Newton was released from prison—the Philadelphia Field Office had an informant distribute a fictitious BPP directive to Philadelphia Panthers, questioning New-

---

[69] In September 1969, FBI Headquarters had encouraged the field offices to undertake projects aimed at splitting the BPP on a nationwide basis. (Memorandum from FBI Headquarters to Newark, New York, and San Francisco Field Offices, 9/18/69.)

[70] Memorandum from FBI Headquarters to Legat, Paris and San Francisco Field Office, 4/10/70.

[71] *Ibid.*, pp. 1–2.

[72] Memorandum from San Francisco Field Office to FBI Headquarters, 5/8/70.

[73] Memorandum from San Francisco Field Office to FBI Headquarters 5/28/70.

ton's leadership ability.[74] The Philadelphia office informed FBI Headquarters that the directive:

> stresses the leadership and strength of David Hilliard and Eldridge Cleaver while intimating Huey Newton is useful only as a drawing card.
>
> It is recommended this directive . . . be mailed personally to Huey Newton with a short anonymous note. The note would indicate the writer, a Community Worker in Philadelphia for the BPP, was incensed over the suggestion Huey was only being used by the Party after founding it, and wanted no part of this Chapter if it was slandering its leaders in private.[75]

Headquarters approved this plan on August 19, 1970.[76]

FBI officials seized on several incidents during the following months as opportunities to advance their program. In an August 1970 edition of the BPP newspaper, Huey Newton appealed to "oppressed groups," including homosexuals, to "unite with the BPP in revolutionary fashion."[77] FBI headquarters approved a plan to mail forged letters from BPP sympathizers and supporters in ghetto areas to David Hilliard, protesting Newton's statements about joining with homosexuals, hoping this would discredit Newton with other BPP leaders.[78]

In July and August 1970, Eldridge Cleaver led a United States delegation to North Korea and North Vietnam. *Ramparts* editor Robert Scheer, who had been a member of the delegation, held a press conference in New York and, according to the Bureau, glossed over the Panther's role in sponsoring the tour.[79] The New York office was authorized to send an anonymous letter to Newton complaining about Sheer's oversight to strain relations between the BPP and the "New Left."[80] On November 13, 1970, the Los Angeles field office was asked to prepare an anonymous letter to Cleaver criticizing Newton for not aggressively obtaining BPP press coverage of the BPP's sponsorship of the trip.[81]

In October 1970, the FBI learned that Timothy Leary, who had escaped from a California prison where he was serving a sentence for possessing marijuana, was seeking asylum with Eldridge Cleaver in Algiers. The San Francisco field office, noting that the Panthers were officially opposed to drugs, sent Newton an anonymous letter calling his attention to Cleaver "playing footsie" with Leary.[82] In January when Cleaver publicly condemned Leary, FBI headquarters approved sending Newton a bogus letter from a Berkeley, California commune condemning Cleaver for "divorcing the BPP from white revolutionaries."[83]

---

[74] Memorandum from Philadelphia Field Office to FBI Headquarters, 8/13/70.

[75] *Ibid.*, pp. 1–2.

[76] Memorandum from FBI Headquarters to Philadelphia and San Francisco Field Offices, 8/19/70.

[77] Memorandum from San Francisco Field Office to FBI Headquarters, 8/31/70.

[78] Memorandum from FBI Headquarters to San Francisco Field Office, 9/9/70.

[79] Memorandum from San Francisco Field Office to FBI Headquarters, 10/21/70.

[80] Memorandum from FBI Headquarters to San Francisco and New York Field Office, 10/29/70.

[81] Memorandum from FBI Headquarters to Los Angeles Field Office, 11/3/70.

[82] Memorandum from San Francisco Field Office to FBI Headquarters, 10/28/70.

[83] Memorandum from FBI Headquarters to San Francisco and New York Field Offices, 2/5/71.

In December 1970, the BPP attempted to hold a Revolutionary Peoples' Constitutional Convention (RPCC) in Washington, D.C. The Bureau considered the convention a failure and received reports that most delegates had left it dissatisfied.[84] The Los Angeles FBI field office suggested a letter to Cleaver designed to

> provoke Cleaver to openly question Newton's leadership . . . It is felt that distance and lack of personal contact between Newton and Cleaver do offer a counterintelligence opportunity that should be probed.
>
> In view of the BPP's unsuccessful attempt to convene a Revolutionary People's Constitutional Convention (RPCC), it is suggested that each division which had individuals attend the RPCC write numerous letters to Cleaver criticizing Newton for his lack of leadership. It is felt that, if Cleaver received a sufficient number of complaints regarding Newton it might . . . create dissension that later could be more fully exploited.[85]

FBI headquarters approved the Los Angeles letter to Cleaver and asked the Washington field office to supply a list of all organizations attending the RPCC.[86] A barrage of anonymous letters to Newton and Cleaver followed:

Two weeks later, the San Francisco office mailed Newton an anonymous letter, supposedly from a "white revolutionary," complaining about the incompetence of the Panthers who had planned the conference.[86a] The New York office mailed a complaint to the BPP national headquarters, purportedly from a black student at Columbia University who attended the RPCC as a member of the University's student Afro-American Society.[86b] The San Francisco office sent a letter containing an article from the *Berkeley Barb* to Cleaver, attacking Newton's leadership at the RPCC. Mailed with the article was a copy of a letter to Newton criticizing the RPCC and bearing the notation:

> Mr. Cleaver,
>
> Here is a letter I sent to Huey Newton. I'm sincere and hope you can do something to set him right and get him off his duff.[86c]

In January 1971, the Boston office sent a letter, purportedly from a "white revolutionary," to Cleaver, stating in part:

---

[84] Memorandum from FBI Headquarters to Los Angeles, San Francisco, and Washington Field Offices, 12/15/70.

[85] Memorandum from Los Angeles Field Office to FBI Headquarters, 12/3/70, p. 2.

[86] Memorandum from FBI Headquarters to Los Angeles, San Francisco, and Washington Field Offices, 12/15/70. A list of 10 organizations whose members attended the RPCC was forwarded to the FBI offices in Atlanta, Boston, Chicago, Detroit, New York, and San Francisco. (Memorandum from FBI Headquarters to Atlanta (and 5 other Field Offices), 12/31/70.) There is no indication concerning how the Bureau obtained this list.

[86a] Memorandum from FBI Headquarters to San Francisco Field Office, 12/16/70.

[86b] Memorandum from New York Field Office to FBI Headquarters, 12/14/70.

[86c] Memorandum from FBI Headquarters to San Francisco Field Office, 1/6/71.

204

Dear Revolutionary Comrade:

The people's revolution in America was greatly impeded and the stature of the Black Panther Party, both nationally and internationally, received a major setback as an outcome of the recent Revolutionary People's Constitutional Convention. . . .

The Revolutionary People's Constitutional Convention did little, if anything, to organize our forces to move against the evils of capitalism, imperialism and racism. Any unity or solidarity which existed between the Black Panther Party and the white revolutionary movement before the Convention has now gone down the tube. . . .

The responsibility of any undertaking as meaningful and important to the revolution . . . should not have been delegated to the haphazard ways of [name deleted] whose title of Convention Coordinator . . . places him in the . . . position of receiving the Party's wrath . . . Huey Newton himself (should) have assumed command. . . .

The Black Panther Party has failed miserably. No longer can the Party be looked upon as the "Vanguard of the Revolution."

Yours in Revolution,
Lawrence Thomas,
Students for a Democratic Society.

Memorandum from Boston Field Office to FBI Headquarters, 1/8/71. This letter was sent to Cleaver through Oakland BPP headquarters to determine whether the BPP in California would forward the letter to him. (*Ibid.*)

One letter to Cleaver, written to appear as if it had come from Connie Matthews, Newton's personal secretary read in part:

> Things around headquarters are dreadfully disorganized with the comrade commander not making proper decisions. The newspaper is in a shambles. No one knows who is in charge. The foreign department gets no support . . . I fear there is rebellion working just beneath the surface. . . .
>
> We must either get rid of the Supreme Commander [Newton] or get rid of the disloyal members.[87]

In a January 28, 1971, evaluation, FBI headquarters noted that Huey Newton had recently disciplined high BPP officials and that he prepared "to respond violently to any question of his actions or policies." The Bureau believed that Newton's reaction was in part a "result of our counterintelligence projects now in operation."

---

[87] Memorandum from San Francisco Field Office to FBI Headquarters, 1/18/70. FBI headquarters authorized this letter on January 21, 1971 stating that the Bureau must now seize the time and "immediately" send the letter. (Memorandum from FBI Headquarters to San Francisco Field Office, 1/21/71, p. 2.) Shortly afterward, a letter was sent to Cleaver from alleged Puerto Rican political allies of the BPP in Chicago, The Young Lords.

What do we get. A disorganized Convention, apologetic speakers and flunkys who push us around, no leadership, no ideas, no nothing. . . . [Y]our talk is nice, but your ideas and action is nothing. . . . You are gone, those you left behind have big titles but cannot lead, cannot organize, are afraid to even come out among the people. The oppressed of Amerikka cannot wait. We must move without you. . . . (Memorandum from Chicago Field Office to FBI Headquarters, 1/19/71; memorandum from FBI Headquarters to Chicago and San Francisco Field Offices, 1/27/71.)

> The present chaotic situation within the BPP must be exploited and recipients must maintain the present high level of counterintelligence activity. You should each give this matter priority attention and immediately furnish Bureau recommendations . . . designed to further aggravate the dissention within BPP leadership and to fan the apparent distrust by Newton of anyone who questions his wishes.[88]

The campaign was intensified. On February 2, 1971, FBI headquarters directed each of 29 field offices to submit within eight days a proposal to disrupt local BPP chapters and a proposal to cause dissention between local BPP chapters and BPP national headquarters. The directive noted that Huey Newton had recently expelled or disciplined several "dedicated Panthers" and

> This dissention coupled with financial difficulties offers an exceptional opportunity to further disrupt, aggravate and possibly neutralize this organization through counterintelligence. In light of above developments this program has been intensifield . . . and selected offices should . . . increase measurably the pressure on the BPP and its leaders.[89]

A barrage of anonymous letters flowed from FBI field offices in response to the urgings from FBI headquarters. A fictitious letter to Cleaver, signed by the "New York 21," criticized Newton's leadership and his expulsion of them from the BPP.[90] An imaginary New York City member of the Youth Against War and Facism added his voice to the Bureau's fictitious chorus of critics of Newton and the RPCC.[91] An anonymous letter was sent to Huey Newton's brother, Melvin Newton, warning that followers of Eldridge Cleaver and the New York BPP chapter were planning to have him killed.[92] The FBI learned that Melvin Newton told his brother he thought the letter had been written by someone "on the inside" of the BPP organization because of its specificity.[93] Huey Newton reportedly remarked that he was "definitely of the opinion there is an informer in the party right in the ministry."[93a]

On February 19, 1971, a false letter, allegedly from a BPP official in Oakland, was mailed to Don Cox, a BPP official close to Cleaver in Algeria. The letter intimated that the recent death of a BPP member in California was the result of BPP factionalism (which the Bureau knew was not the case.) The letter also warned Cleaver not to allow his wife, Kathleen, to travel to the United States because of the possibility of violence.[94]

A letter over the forged signature of "Big Man" Howard, editor of the BPP newspaper, told Cleaver:

---

[88] Memorandum from FBI Headquarters to Boston, Los Angeles, New York, and San Francisco Field Offices, 1/28/71.

[89] Memorandum from FBI Headquarters to 29 Field Offices, 2/2/71.

[90] Memorandum from FBI Headquarters to New York and San Francisco Field Offices, 2/3/71.

[91] Memorandum from FBI Headquarters to New York Field Office, 2/3/71.

[92] Memorandum from FBI Headquarters to San Francisco Field Office, 2/10/71.

[93] Memorandum from San Francisco Field Office to FBI Headquarters, 2/12 71.

[93a] The FBI was able to be specific because of its wiretaps on the phones of Huey Newton and the Black Panther headquarters.

[94] Memorandum from FBI Headquarters to San Francisco Field Office, 2/19/71.

> Eldridge:
> [Name deleted] told me Huey talked with you Friday and what he had to say. I'm disgusted with things here and the fact that you are being ignored.... It makes me mad to learn that Huey now has to lie to you. I'm referring to his fancy apartment which he refers to as the throne. . . .
> I can't risk a call as it would mean certain expulsion. You should think a great deal before sending Kathleen. If I could talk to you I could tell you why I don't think you should.[95]

The San Francisco office reported to headquarters that because of the various covert actions instituted against Cleaver and Newton since November 11, 1970:

> fortunes of the BPP are at a low ebb.... Newton is positive there is an informant in Headquarters. Cleaver feels isolated in Algeria and out of contact with Newton and the Supreme Commander's [Newton's] secretary (Connie Matthews) has disappeared and been denounced.[96]

On April 8, 1976 in Executive Testimony Kathleen Cleaver testified that many letters, written to appear as if they had come from BPP members living in California caused disruption and confusion in the relationship between the Algerian Section and the BPP leadership in Oakland. She stated:

> We did not know who to believe about what, so the general effect, not only of the letters but the whole situation in which the letters were part was creating uncertainty. It was a very bizarre feeling.[96a]

On February 26, 1971, Eldridge Cleaver, in a television interview, criticized the expulsion of BPP members and suggested that Panther Chief-of-Staff David Hilliard be removed from his post. As a result of Cleaver's statements, Newton expelled him and the "Intercommunal Section of the Party" in Algiers, Algeria.[97]

On March 25, 1971, the Bureau's San Francisco office sent to various BPP "Solidarity Committees" throughout Europe bogus letters on "fascsimiles of BPP letterhead" stating:

---

[95] Memorandum from FBI Headquarters to San Francisco Field Office, 2/24/71. The phone call from Cleaver to Newton mentioned in this letter had been intercepted by the FBI. An FBI memorandum commented that the call had been prompted by an earlier Bureau letter purporting to come from Connie Mathews: "The letter undoubtedly provoked a long distance call from Cleaver to Newton which resulted in our being able to place in proper perspective the relationship of Newton and Cleaver to obtain the details of the Geronimo [Elmer Pratt] Group and learn of the disaffections and the expulsion of the New York group." (Memorandum from San Francisco Field Office to FBI Headquarters, 2/25/71.)

[96] Memorandum from San Francisco Field Office to FBI Headquarters, 2/25/71.

[96a] Kathleen Cleaver testimony, 4/8/76, p. 34.

[97] Memorandum from San Francisco Field Office to FBI Headquarters, 3/2/71. FBI headquarters instructed the SAC, San Francisco to mail Cleaver a copy of the March 6 edition of the BPP newspaper which announced his expulsion from the BPP, along with an anonymous note saying, "This is what we think of punks and cowards." (Memorandum from FBI Headquarters to San Francisco Field Office, 3/10/71.)

207

To Black Panther Embassies,

You have received copies of February 13, 1971 issue of The Black Panther declaring [three BPP members] as enemies of the People.

The Supreme Servant of the People, Huey P. Newton, with concurrence of the Central Committee of the Black Panther Party, has ordered the expulsion of the entire Intercommunal Section of the Party at Algiers. You are advised that Eldridge Leroy Cleaver is a murderer and a punk without genitals. D.C. Cox is no better.

Leroy's running dogs in New York have been righteously dealt with. Anyone giving any aid or comfort to Cleaver and his jackanapes will be similarly dealt with no matter where they may be located.

[Three BPP international representatives, names deleted] were never members of the Black Panther Party and will never become such.

Immediately report to the Supreme Commander any attempts of these elements to contact you and be guided by the above instructions.

Power to the People
David Hilliard, Chief of Staff
For Huey P. Newton
Supreme Commander.[98]

On the same day, FBI headquarters formally declared its counterintelligence program aimed at "aggravating dissension" between Newton and Cleaver a success. A letter to the Chicago and San Francisco Field Offices stated:

Since the differences between Newton and Cleaver now appear to be irreconcilable, no further counterintelligence activity in this regard will be undertaken at this time and now new targets must be established.

David Hilliard and Elbert "Big Man" Howard of National Headquarters and Bob Rush of Chicago BPP Chapter are likely future targets. . . .

Hilliard's key position at National Headquarters makes him an outstanding target.

Howard and Rush are also key Panther functionaries; and since it was necessary for them to affirm their loyalty to Newton in "The Black Panther" newspaper of 3/20/71, they must be under a certain amount of suspicion already, making them prime targets.

San Francisco and Chicago furnish the Bureau their comments and recommendations concerning counterintelligence activity designed to cause Newton to expell Hilliard, Howard and Rush.[99]

---

[98] This letter was contained in a memorandum from San Francisco Field Office to FBI Headquarters, 3/16/71, pp. 1–2.

[99] Memorandum from FBI Headquarters to San Francisco and Chicago Field Offices, 3/25/71.

C. Covert Efforts To Undermine Support of the Black Panther Party and to Destroy the Party's Public Image

1. Efforts To Discourage and To Discredit Supporters of the Black Panthers

The Federal Bureau of Investigation's program to "neutralize" the Black Panther Party included attempts to deter individuals and groups from supporting the Panthers and, when that could not be accomplished, often extended to covert action targeted against those supporters.

The Bureau made a series of progressively more severe efforts to destroy the confidence between the Panthers and one of their major California supporters, Donald Freed, a writer who headed an organization of white BPP sympathizers called "Friends of the Panthers." In July 1969, the Los Angeles Field Office sent the local BPP office a memorandum bearing Freed's name and address to "Friends of the Panthers." Written in a condescending tone and including a list of six precautions whites should keep in mind when dealing with Panthers, the memorandum was calculated to cause a "rift between the Black Panther Party and their assisting organizations." [100] A few days later, the Bureau had leaflets placed in a park near a BPP-sponsored national conference in Oakland, California, alleging that Freed was a police informant.[101]

The FBI viewed with favor an intensive local investigation of Freed for "harboring" and "possession of illegal firearms."

> It is felt that any prosecution or exposure of either Freed or [name deleted] will severely hurt the BPP. Any exposure will not only deny the Panthers money, but additionally, would cause other white supporters of the BPP to withdraw their support. It is felt that the Los Angeles chapter of the BPP could not operate without the financial support of white sympathizers.[102]

The Bureau's Los Angeles Division also arranged for minutes of a BPP support group to be provided to the BPP when it was learned that statements of members of the support group were critical of Panther leaders.[103]

The FBI attempted to disaffect another BPP supporter, Ed Pearl of the Peace and Freedom Party, by sending him a cautionary letter bearing a fictitious signature. A Bureau memorandum describing the letter says:

> The writer states that although he is not a member of the BPP, he is a Mexican who is trusted by BPP members. The writer advises that he has learned from BPP members that certain whites in the PFP who get in the way of the Panthers will be dealt with in a violent manner. The object sought in this letter is to cause a breach between the PFP and the BPP. The former organization had been furnishing money and support to the latter.[104]

---

[100] Memorandum from FBI Headquarters to Los Angeles Field Office, 7/25/69.
[101] Memorandum from San Francisco Field Office to FBI Headquarters, 7/28/69.
[102] Memorandum from Los Angeles Field Office to FBI Headquarters, 9/24/69.
[103] Memorandum from Los Angeles Field Office to FBI Headquarters, 9/29/69, p. 1.
[104] Memorandum from G. C. Moore to W. C. Sullivan, 12/27/68.

Famous entertainment personalities who spoke in favor of Panther goals or associated with BPP members became the targets of FBI programs. When the FBI learned that one well-known Hollywood actress had become pregnant during an affair with a BPP member, it reported this information to a famous Hollywood gossip columnist in the form of an anonymous letter. The story was used by the Hollywood columnist.[105] In June 1970, FBI headquarters approved an anonymous letter informing Hollywood gossip columnist Army Archerd that actress Jane Fonda had appeared at a BPP fund-raising function, noting that "It can be expected that Fonda's involvement with the BPP cause could detract from her status with the general public if reported in a Hollywood 'gossip column.' "[106] The wife of a famous Hollywood actor was targeted by the FBI when it discovered that she was a financial contributor and supporter of the BPP in Los Angeles.[107] A caricature attacking her was prepared by the San Diego FBI office.[108]

A famous entertainer was also targeted after the Bureau concluded that he supported the Panthers. Two COINTELPRO actions against this individual were approved because FBI headquarters "believed" they:

> would be an effective means of combating BPP fund-raising activities among liberal and naive individuals.[109]

The Bureau also contacted the employers of BPP contributors. It sent a letter to the President and a Vice-President of Union Carbide in January 1970 after learning that a production manager in its San Diego division contributed to the BPP. The letter, which centered around a threat not to purchase Union Carbide stock, stated in part:

> Dear Mr. [name deleted]:
>
> I am writing to you in regards to an employee in your San Diego operation, [name deleted]. . . .
>
> I am not generally considered a flag-waving exhibitionist, but I do regard myself as being a loyal American citizen. I, therefore, consider it absolutely ludicrous to invest in any corporation whose ranking employees support, assist, and encourage any organization which openly advocates the violent overthrow of our free enterprise system.
>
> It is because of my firm belief in this self-same free enterprise, capitalistic system that I feel morally obligated to bring this situation to your attention.
>
> Sincerely yours,
>
> T. F. Ellis
> Post Office Box ——.
> San Diego, California [110]

---

[105] Memorandum from Los Angeles Field Office, to FBI Headquarters, 6/3/70.
[106] Memorandum from FBI Headquarters to Los Angeles Field Office, 6/25/70.
[107] Memorandum from San Diego Field Office to FBI Headquarters, 2/3/70.
[108] Memorandum from San Diego Field Office to FBI Headquarters, 3/2/70.
[109] Memorandum from FBI Headquarters to San Francisco Field Office, 3/5/70.
[110] Memorandum from San Diego Field Office to FBI Headquarters, 1/22/70. The name "T. F. Ellis" is completely fictitious and the Post Office Box could not have been traced to the FBI.

The response of Union Carbide's Vice President was reported in a San Diego Field Office memorandum:

> On 3/21/70, a letter was received from Mr. [name deleted], Vice President of the Union Carbide Corporation, concerning a previously Bureau-approved letter sent to the Union Carbide Corporation objecting to the financial and other support to the BPP of one of their employees, [name deleted]. The letter indicated that Union Carbide has always made it a policy not to become involved in personal matters of their employees unless such activity had an adverse affect upon that particular employee's performance.[111]

One of the Bureau's prime targets was the BPP's free "Breakfast for Children" program, which FBI headquarters feared might be a potentially successful effort by the BPP to teach children to hate police and to spread "anti-white propaganda." [112] In an admitted attempt "to impede their contributions to the BPP Breakfast Program," the FBI sent anonymous letters and copies of an inflammatory Black Panther Coloring Book for children to contributors, including Safeway Stores, Inc., Mayfair Markets, and the Jack-In-The-Box Corporation.[113]

On April 8, 1976 in Executive Testimony a former member of the BPP Central Steering Committee stated that when the coloring book came to the attention of the Panther's national leadership, Bobby Seale ordered it destroyed because the book "did not correctly reflect the ideology of the Black Panther Party . . ." [114]

Churches that permitted the Panthers to use their facilities in the free breakfast program were also targeted. When the FBI's San Diego office discovered that a Catholic Priest, Father Frank Curran, was permitting his church in San Diego to be used as a serving place for the BPP Breakfast Program, it sent an anonymous letter to the Bishop of the San Diego Diocese informing him of the priest's activities.[115] In August 1969, the San Diego Field Office requested permission from headquarters to place three telephone calls protesting Father Curran's support of the BPP program to the Auxiliary Bishop of the San Diego Diocese:

> All of the above calls will be made from "parishioners" objecting to the use of their church to assist a black militant cause. Two of the callers will urge that Father Curran be removed as Pastor of the church, and one will threaten suspension of financial support of the church if the activities of the Pastor are allowed to continue.
>
> Fictitious names will be utilized in the event a name is requested by the Bishop. It is felt that complaints, if they do not effect the removal of Father Curran . . . will at least result in Father Curran becoming aware that his Bishop is

---

[111] Memorandum from San Diego Field Office to FBI Headquarters, 6/1/70.

[112] Memorandum from FBI Headquarters to San Francisco Field Office, 7/30/69.

[113] *Ibid.;* Memorandum from San Francisco Field Office to FBI Headquarters, 11/30/70.

[114] K. Cleaver, 4/8/76, p. 16.

[115] Memorandum from San Diego Field Office to FBI Headquarters, 8/29/69; memorandum from FBI Headquarters to San Diego Field Office, 9/9/69.

> cognizant of his activities and will thus result in a curtailment of these activities.[116]

After receiving permission and placing the calls, the San Diego office reported: "the Bishop appeared to be . . . quite concerned over the fact that one of his Priests was deeply involved in utilization of church facilities for this purpose." [117]

A month later, the San Diego office reported that Father Curran had been transferred from the San Diego Diocese to "somewhere in the State of New Mexico for permanent assignment."

> In view of the above, it would appear that Father Curran has now been completely neutralized.
>
> The BPP Breakfast Program, without the prompting of Father Curran, has not been renewed in the San Diego area. It is not anticipated at this time that any efforts to re-establish the program will be made in the foreseeable future.[118]

In another case, the FBI sent a letter to the superior of a clergyman in Hartford, Connecticut who had expressed support for the Black Panthers, which stated in part:

> Dear BISHOP:
>
> It pains me to have to write this letter to call to your attention a matter which, if brought to public light, may cause the church a great deal of embarrassment. I wish to remain anonymous with regard to the information because in divulging it I may have violated a trust. I feel, however, that what I am writing is important enough that my conscience is clear.
>
> Specifically, I'm referring to the fact that Reverend and Mrs. [name deleted] are associating with leaders of the Black Panther Party. I recently heard through a close friend of Reverend [name deleted] that he is a revolutionist who advocates overthrowing the Government of the United States and that he has turned over a sizable sum of money to the Panthers. I can present no evidence of fact but is it possible Reverend [name deleted] is being influenced by Communists? Some statements he has made both in church and out have led me to believe he is either a Communist himself, or so left-wing that the only thing he lacks is a card.
>
> I beseech you to counsel with Reverend [name deleted] and relay our concern over his political philosophies which among other things involves association with a known revolutionist, [name deleted], head of the Black Panther Party in New Haven. I truly believe Reverend [name deleted] to be a good man, but his fellow men have caused him to go overboard and he now needs a guiding light which only you can provide.
>
> Sincerely,
>
> A Concerned Christian.[119]

---

[116] Memorandum from San Diego Field Office to FBI Headquarters, 8/29/69.

[117] Memorandum from San Diego Field Office to FBI Headquarters, 9/18/69.

[118] Memorandum from San Diego Field Office to FBI Headquarters, 10/6/69, p. 3.

[119] Memorandum from New Haven Field Office to FBI Headquarters, 11/12/69, p. 3.

Anonymous FBI mailings were also sent to public officials and persons whose help might sway public opinion against the BPP. In December 1969, the FBI mailed Bureau-reproduced copies of BPP "Seasons Greetings" cards to ten FBI field offices [120] with the following instructions:

> Enclosed for each office are 20 copies of reproductions of three types of Black Panther Party (BPP) "seasons greetings cards" which depict the violent propensities of this organization. You should anonymously mail these cards to those newspaper editors, public officials, responsible businessmen, and clergy in your territory who should be made aware of the vicious nature of the BPP.[121]

The San Francisco office mailed its cards to several prominent local persons and organizations.[122]

The Bureau also targeted attorneys representing Black Panther members. In July 1969, the Los Angeles Field Office suggested that a break between the BPP membership and Charles Garry, an attorney who frequently represented BPP members, might be accomplished by planting a rumor that Garry, Bobby Seale, and David Hilliard were conspiring to keep BPP leader Huey Newton in jail.[123] This proposal was rejected by FBI headquarters out of concern that the Bureau might be recognized as the source of the rumor.[124] Headquarters did suggest, however:

> Los Angeles should review the ideas set forth . . . especially as they pertain to Charles Garry, Bobby Seale, and David Hilliard, and prepare a specific counterintelligence proposal designed to create a breach between the BPP and Garry, Consider such things as anonymous communications and anonymous telephone calls as well as cartoons and other logical methods of transporting your idea.[125]

When the San Francisco Division learned that Garry intended to represent Bobby Seale at the Chicago 7 trial, it sent the Chicago office transcripts of hearings before the House Committee on Un-American Activities and the California State Senate's Report on Un-American Activities, which allegedly showed that Garry was connected with the Communist Party. It was intended to distribute this material "to cooperative news media in that city." [126]

---

[120] The offices were Baltimore, Boston, Chicago, Kansas City, Los Angeles, Newark, New Haven, New York, San Diego, and San Francisco.

[121] Memorandum from FBI Headquarters to Baltimore (and 9 other Field Offices), 12/24/69, p. 1.

[122] These included the Mayor; the Glide Foundation (church foundation); Catholic Archdiocese of San Francisco; Episcopal Diocese of California; Lutheran Church; Editor, *San Francisco Chronicle;* Editor, *San Francisco Examiner;* United Presbyterian Church, San Francisco Conference of Christians and Jews; San Francisco Chamber of Commerce; San Francisco Bar Association; and San Francisco Board of Supervisors. (Memorandum from San Francisco Field Office to FBI Headquarters, 1/12/70.)

[123] Memorandum from Los Angeles Field Office to FBI Headquarters, 7/1/69.

[124] Memorandum from FBI Headquarters to Los Angeles Field Office, 7/14/69.

[125] *Ibid.*

[126] Memorandum from San Francisco Field Office to FBI Headquartrs, 10/6/69.

Similarly, when two local BPP leaders filed suit against the San Diego Police Department charging harassment, illegal arrest, and illegal searches, the San Diego Field Office reviewed its files

> to determine if any public source information is available which describes [the attorney's] activities in behalf of CP (Communist Party) activities. If so, an appropriate request will be forwarded to the Bureau concerning a possible letter to the editor and/or an editorial.[127]

The FBI also sought to destroy community support for individual BPP members by spreading rumors that they were immoral. This idea was originally advanced in an August 1967 memorandum from FBI headquarters to all major field offices:

> Many individuals currently active in black nationalist organizations have backgrounds in immorality, subversive activity, and criminal records. Through your investigation of key agitators, you should endeavor to establish their unsavory backgrounds. Be alert to determine evidence of misappropriation of funds or other types of personal misconduct on the part of militant nationalist leaders so any practical or warranted counterintelligence may be instituted.[128]

An example of "successful" implementation of this program was a 1970 report from the San Diego Field Office that it had anonymously informed the parents of a teenage girl that she was pregnant by a local Panther leader:

> The parents showed extreme concern over a previously unknown situation and [name deleted] was forced to resign from the BPP and return home to live. It also became general knowledge throughout the Negro community that a BPP leader was responsible for the difficulty being experienced by [name deleted]. [129]

The field office also considered the operation successful because the mother of another girl questioned the activities of her own daughter after talking with the parent the agents had anonymously contacted. She learned that her daughter, a BPP member, was also pregnant, and had her committed to a reformatory as a wayward juvenile.[130]

2. Efforts To Promote Criticism of the Black Panthers in the Mass Media and To Prevent the Black Panther Party and Its Sympathizers from Expressing Their Views

The FBI's program to destroy the Black Panther Party included a concerted effort to muzzle Black Panther publications to prevent Panther members and persons sympathetic to their aims from expressing their views, and to encourage the mass media to report stories unfavorable to the Panthers.

---

[127] Memorandum from San Diego Field Office to FBI Headquarters, 1/2/70.

[128] Memorandum from FBI Headquarters to Albany (and 22 other Field Offices), 8/25/67, p. 2.

[129] Memorandum from San Diego Field Office to FBI Headquarters, 2/17/70, p. 3.

[130] *Ibid.*, p. 5.

In May 1970, FBI headquarters ordered the Chicago, Los Angeles, Miami, Newark, New Haven, New York, San Diego, and San Francisco field offices to advance proposals for crippling the BPP newspaper, *The Black Panther*. Immediate action was deemed necessary because:

> The Black Panther Party newspaper is one of the most effective propaganda operations of the BPP.
>
> Distribution of this newspaper is increasing at a regular rate thereby influencing a greater number of individuals in the United States along the black extremist lines.
>
> Each recipient submit by 6/5/70 proposed counterintelligence measures which will hinder the vicious propaganda being spread by the BPP.
>
> The BPP newspaper has a circulation in excess of 100,000 and has reached the height of 139,000. It is the voice of the BPP and if it could be effectively hindered it would result in helping to cripple the BPP. Deadline being set in view of the need to receive recommendations for the purpose of taking appropriate action expeditiously.[131]

The San Francisco Field Office submitted an analysis of the local *Black Panther* printing schedules and circulation. It discouraged disruption of nationwide distribution because the airline company which had contracted with the Panthers might lose business or face a law suit and recommended instead:

> a vigorous inquiry by the Internal Revenue Service to have "The Black Panther" report their income from the sale of over 100,000 papers each week. Perhaps the Bureau through liaison at SOG [seat of government] could suggest such a course of action. It is noted that Internal Revenue Service at San Francisco is receiving copies of Black Panther Party funds and letterhead memoranda.
>
> It is requested that the Bureau give consideration to discussion with Internal Revenue Service requesting financial records and income tax return for "The Black Panther."[132]

The San Diego Field Office, while noting that the BPP newspaper had the same legal immunity from tax laws and other state legislation as other newspapers, suggested three California statutes which might be used against *The Black Panther*. One was a State tax on printing equipment; the second a "rarely used transportation tax law"; and the third a law prohibiting business in a residential area.[133]

The San Diego Field Office had a more imaginative suggestion however; spray the newspaper printing room with a foul-smelling chemical:

> The Bureau may also wish to consider the utilization of "Skatol", which is a chemical agent in powdered form and when applied to a particular surface emits an extremely noxious odor rendering the premises surrounding the point of application uninhabitable. Utilization of such a chemical of

[131] Memorandum from FBI Headquarters to Chicago (and seven other Field Offices), 5/15/70.

[132] Memorandum from San Francisco Field Office to FBI Headquarters, 5/22/70.

[133] Memorandum from San Diego Field Office to FBI Headquarters, 5/20/70.

course, would be dependent upon whether an entry could be achieved into the area which is utilized for the production of "The Black Panther." [134]

The San Diego Division also thought that threats from another radical organization against the newspaper might convince the BPP to cease publication:

> Another possibility which the Bureau may wish to consider would be the composition and mailing of numerous letters to BPP Headquarters from various points throughout the country on stationary [sic] containing the national emblem of the Minutemen organization. These letters, in several different forms, would all have the common theme of warning the Black Panthers to cease publication or drastic measures would be taken by the Minutemen organization. . . .
>
> Utilization of the Minutemen organization through direction of informants within that group would also be a very effective measure for the disruption of the publication of this newspaper.[135]

On another occasion, however, FBI agents contacted United Airlines officials and inquired about the rates being charged for transporting the Black Panther magazine. A Bureau memorandum states that the BPP was being charged "the General Rate" for printed material, but that in the future it would be forced to pay the "full legal rate allowable for newspaper shipment." The memorandum continued:

> Officials advise this increase . . . means approximately a forty percent increase. Officials agree to determine consignor in San Francisco and from this determine consignees throughout the United States so that it can impose full legal tariff. They believe the airlines are due the differences in freight tariffs as noted above for past six to eight months, and are considering discussions with their legal staff concerning suit for recovery of deficit. . . . (T)hey estimate that in New York alone will exceed ten thousand dollars.[136]

In August 1970, the New York Field Office reported that it was considering plans:

> directed against (1) the production of the BPP newspaper; (2) the distribution of that newspaper and (3) the use of information contained in particular issues for topical counterintelligence proposals.
>
> The NYO [New York Office] realizes the financial benefits coming to the BPP through the sale of their newspaper. Continued efforts will be made to derive logical and practical plans to thwart this crucial BPP operation.[137]

A few months later, FBI headquarters directed 39 field offices to distribute copies of a column written by Victor Riesel, a labor columnist,

---

[134] Memorandum from San Diego Field Office to FBI Headquarters, 5/20/70, p. 2.

[135] *Ibid.*, p. 3.

[136] Memorandum from New York Field Office to FBI Headquarters and San Francisco Field Office, 10/11/69.

[137] Memorandum from New York Field Office to FBI Headquarters, 8/19/70.

216

calling for a nationwide union boycott against handling the BPP newspaper.

> Enclosed for each office are 50 reproductions of a column written by Victor Riesel regarding the Black Panther Party (BPP).
>
> Portions of the column deals with proposal that union members refuse to handle shipments of BPP newspapers. Obviously if such a boycott gains national support it will result in effectively cutting off BPP propaganda and finances, therefore, it is most desirable this proposal be brought to attention of members and officials of unions such as Teamsters and others involved in handling of shipments of BPP newspapers. These shipments are generally by air freight. The column also deals with repeated calls for murder of police that appear in BPP paper; therefore, it would also be desirable to bring boycott proposal to attention of members and officials of police associations who might be in a position to encourage boycott.
>
> Each office anonymously mail copies of enclosed to officials of appropriate unions, police organizations or other individuals within its territory who could encourage such a boycott....
>
> Handle promptly and advise Bureau of any positive results noted. Any publicity observed concerning proposed boycott should be brought to attention of Bureau.
>
> Be alert for any other opportunities to further exploit this proposal.[138]

Bureau documents submitted to the Select Committee staff do not indicate the outcome of this plan.

On one occasion the FBI's Racial Intelligence Section concocted a scheme to create friction between the Black Panthers and the Nation of Islam by reducing sales of the NOI paper, *Muhammed Speaks:*

> While both papers advocate white hate, a noticeable loss of revenue to NOI due to decreased sales of their paper caused by the BPP might well be the spark to ignite the fuel of conflict between the two organizations. Both are extremely money conscious.
>
> We feel that our network of racial informants, many of whom are directly involved in the sale of the NOI and BPP newspapers, are in a position to cause a material reduction in NOI newspaper sales. Our sources can bring the fact of revenue loss directly to NOI leader, Elijah Muhammad, who might well be influenced to take positive steps to counteract the sale of BPP papers in the Negro community. We feel that with careful planning and close supervision an open dispute can be developed between the two organizations.[139]

FBI headquarters promptly forwarded this suggestion to the field offices in Chicago, New York, and San Francisco with the express hope that Elijah Muhammed might be influenced "to take positive

[138] Memorandum from FBI Headquarters to SAC's in 39 cities, 11/10/70.
[139] Memorandum from G. C. Moore to W. C. Sullivan, 6/26/70.

steps to counteract the sale of BPP newspapers in the Negro community." [140] The following month, the Chicago Field Office advised against using informants for this project because animosity was already developing between the BPP and NOI, and any revelation of a Bureau attempt to encourage conflict might serve to bring the BPP and NOI closer together.[141]

Numerous attempts were made to prevent Black Panthers from airing their views in public. For example, in February 1969, the FBI joined with the Chicago police force to prevent the local BPP leader, Fred Hampton, from appearing on a television talk show. The FBI memorandum explaining this incident states:

> the [informant] also enabled Chicago to further harass the local BPP when he provided information the afternoon of 1/24/69 reflecting that Fred Hampton was to appear that evening at local TV studio for video tape interview. . . . The tape was to be aired the following day.
>
> Chicago was aware a warrant for mob action was outstanding for Hampton in his home town and the above information . . . was provided the Maywood Police Department with a suggestion that they request the Chicago Police Department to serve this arrest warrant. This was subsequently done with Hampton arrested at television studio in presence of 25 BPP members and studio personnel. This caused considerable embarrassment to the local BPP and disrupted the plans for Hampton's television appearance.[142]

Headquarters congratulated the Chicago Field Office on the timing of the arrest "under circumstances which proved highly embarrassing to the BPP." [143]

The Bureau's San Francisco office took credit for preventing Bobby Seale from keeping a number of speaking engagements in Oregon and Washington. In May 1969, while Seale was traveling from a speaking engagement at Yale University to begin his West Coast tour, a bombing took place in Eugene, Oregon which the FBI suspected involved the Black Panthers. The San Francisco Field Office subsequently reported:

> As this was on the eve of Seale's speech, this seemed to be very poor advance publicity for Seale. . . . It was . . . determined to telephone Mrs. Seale [Bobby Seale's mother] claiming to be a friend from Oregon, bearing the warning that it might be dangerous for Seale to come up. This was done.
>
> Shortly thereafter, Mrs. Seale reported this to BPP headquarters, claiming an unknown brother had sent a warning to Bobby from Oregon. Headquarters took this very seriously and when Bobby arrived shortly thereafter, he decided not to go north with "all the action going on up there." He subsequently cancelled a trip to Seattle. It is believed that the

---

[140] Memorandum from FBI Headquarters to Chicago, New York, and San Francisco Field Offices, 6/26/70.

[141] Memorandum from Chicago Field Office to FBI Headquarters, 7/15/70.

[142] Memorandum from Chicago Field Office to FBI Headquarters, 2/10/69.

[143] Memorandum from FBI Headquarters to Chicago Field Office, 2/20/69.

> above mentioned telephone call was a pivotal point in persuading Seale to stay home.[144]

The San Francisco office reported that not only had Seale been prevented from making his appearances, but that he had lost over $1,700 in "badly needed" fees and that relations between Seale and "New Left" leaders who had been scheduled to appear with him had become strained.

In December 1969, FBI headquarters stressed to the San Francisco Field Office the need to prevent Black Panther speaking engagements:

> Several recent communications received at the Bureau indicate the BPP is encouraging their branches to set up speaking engagements at schools and colleges and the showing of films in order to raise money. . . . San Francisco should instruct [local FBI] office covering to immediately submit to the Bureau for approval a counterintelligence proposal aimed at preventing the activities scheduled. . . .
>
> The BPP in an effort to bolster its weak financial position is now soliciting speaking engagements and information has been developed indicating they are reducing their monetary requirements for such speeches. We have been successful in the past through contacts with established sources in preventing such speeches in colleges or other institutions.[145]

In March 1970, a representative of a Jewish organization contacted the San Francisco FBI Field Office when it learned that one of its local lodges had invited David Hilliard, BPP Chief-of-Staff, and Attorney Charles Garry to speak. San Francisco subsequently reported to headquarters:

> Public source information relating to David Hilliard, Garry, and the BPP, including "The Black Panther" newspaper itself, was brought to [source's] attention. He subsequently notified the [FBI] office that the [name deleted] had altered their arrangements for this speech and that the invitation to Hilliard was withdrawn but that Charles Garry was permitted to speak but his speech was confined solely to the recent case of the Chicago 7.[146]

The FBI exhibited comparable fervor in disseminating information unfavorable to the Black Panthers to the press and television stations. A directive from FBI headquarters to nine field offices in January 1970 explained the program:

> To counteract any favorable support in publicity to the Black Panther Party (BPP) recipient offices are requested to submit their observations and recommendations regarding contacts with established and reliable sources in the television and/or radio field who might be interested in drawing up a program for local consumption depicting the true facts regarding the BPP.

---

[144] Memorandum from San Francisco Field Office to FBI Headquarters, 5/26/69.

[145] Memorandum from FBI Headquarters to San Francisco Field Office, 12/4/69.

[146] Memorandum from San Francisco Field Office to FBI Headquarters, 3/18/70.

> The suggested program would deal mainly with local BPP activities and data furnished would be of a public source nature. This data could be implemented by information on the BPP nationally if needed. . . .
> All offices should give this matter their prompt consideration and submit replies by letter.[147]

Soon afterward, the Los Angeles office identified two local news reporters whom it believed might be willing to help in the effort to discredit the BPP and received permission to

> discreetly contact [name deleted] for the purpose of ascertaining his amenability to the preparation of a program which would present the true facts about the Black Panther Party as part of a counterintelligence effort.[148]

Headquarters also suggested information and materials to give to a local newsman who expressed an interest in airing a series of programs against the Panthers.[149]

In July 1970, the FBI furnished information to a Los Angeles TV news commentator who agreed to air a series of shows against the BPP, "especially in the area of white liberals contributing to the BPP."[150] In October, the Los Angeles Division sent headquarters a copy of an FBI-assisted television editorial and reported that another newsman was preparing yet another editorial attack on the Panthers.[151]

In November 1970, the San Francisco Field Office notified the Director that Huey Newton had "recently rented a luxurious lakeshore apartment in Oakland, California." The San Francisco office saw "potential counterintelligence value" in this information since this apartment was far more elegant than "the ghetto-like BPP 'pads' and community centers utilized by the Party." It was decided not to "presently" leak "this information to cooperative news sources," because of a "pending special investigative technique."[152] The information was given to the *San Francisco Examiner*, however, in February 1971, and an article was published stating that Huey P. Newton, BPP Supreme Commander, had moved into a $650-a-month apartment

---

[147] Memorandum from FBI Headquarters to San Francisco Field Office (and 8 other offices), 1/23/70. The San Diego office had already made efforts along the lines proposed in this memorandum. In November 1969 it requested permission from headquarters to inform two newscasters "for use in editorials" that the sister and brother-in-law of a Communist Party member were believed to be members of the local Black Panthers. The office also proposed preparing "an editorial for publication in the Copley press." (Airtel from SAC, San Diego to Director, FBI, 11/12/69.) The San Francisco office had also leaked information to a *San Francisco Examiner* reporter, who wrote a front-page story complete with photographs concerning "the conversion by the BPP of an apartment into a fortress." (Memorandum from San Francisco Field Office to FBI Headquarters, 1/21/70.)

[148] Memorandum from Los Angeles Field Office to FBI Headquarters, 2/6/70; memorandum from FBI Headquarters to Los Angeles Field Office 3/5/70 (this memorandum bears Director Hoover's initials).

[149] Memorandum from FBI Headquarters to Los Angeles and San Francisco Field Offices, 5/27/70.

[150] Memorandum from Los Angeles Field Office to FBI Headquarters, 9/10/70, p. 2.

[151] Memorandum from Los Angeles Field Office to FBI Headquarters, 10/23/70.

[152] Memorandum from San Francisco Field Office to FBI Headquarters, 11/24/70.

overlooking Lake Merritt in Oakland, California, under the assumed name of Don Penn.[153] Headquarters approved anonymously mailing copies of the article to BPP branches and ordered copies of the article for "divisions with BPP activity for mailing to newspaper editors." [154]

The San Francisco office informed FBI headquarters later in February that

> BPP Headquarters was beseiged with inquiries after the printing of the San Francisco Examiner article and the people at headquarters refuse to answer the news media or other callers on this question. This source has further reported that a representative of the Richmond, Virginia BPP contacted headquarters on 2/18/71, stating they had received a xeroxed copy of . . . the article and believed it had been forwarded by the pigs but still wanted to know if it was true.[155]

D. Cooperation Between the Federal Bureau of Investigation and Local Police Departments in Disrupting the Black Panther Party

The FBI enlisted the cooperation of local police departments in several of its covert action programs to disrupt and "neutralize" the Black Panther Party. The FBI frequently worked with the San Diego Police Department, supplying it with informant reports to encourage raids on the homes of BPP members, often with little or no apparent evidence of violations of State or Federal law.[156]

Examples are numerous. In February 1969, the San Diego Field Office learned that members of the local BPP chapter were following each other to determine if police informants had infiltrated their organization. The field office passed this information to the San Diego police with the suggestion that BPP members engaged in these surveillances might be followed and arrested for violations of "local

---

[153] Memorandum from San Francisco Field Office to FBI Headquarters, 2/12/71.

[154] Memorandum from FBI Headquarters to San Francisco Field Office, 2/8/71.

[155] Memorandum from San Francisco Field Office to FBI Headquarters, 2/18/71. In a February 1971 report on recent COINTELPRO activity, the San Francisco Division described the *San Francisco Examiner* article as one of its "counterintelligence activities." This report said that because of the article, Newton had given an interview to another San Francisco daily to try to explain his seemingly expensive lifestyle. The report also states that copies of the article were sent to "all BPP and NCCF [National Committee to Combat Fascism] offices in the United States and to three BPP contacts in Europe." (Memorandum from San Francisco Field Office to FBI Headquarters, 2/25/71.)

[156] The suggestion of encouraging local police to raid and arrest members of so-called "Black Nationalist Hate Groups" was first put forward in a February 29, 1968 memorandum to field offices. This memorandum cited as an example of successful use of this technique: "The Revolutionary Action Movement (RAM). a pro-Chinese Communist group, was active in Philadelphia, Pa., in the summer of 1967. The Philadelphia office alerted local police who then put RAM leaders under close scrutiny. They were arrested on every possible charge until they could no longer make bail. As a result, RAM leaders spent most of the summer in jail and no violence traceable to RAM took place." (Memorandum from G. C. Moore to W. C. Sullivan, 2/29/68, p. 3.)

Motor Vehicle Code laws."[157] When the San Diego Field Office received reports that five BPP members were living in the local BPP headquarters and "having sex orgies on almost a nightly basis," it informed the local police with the hope that a legal basis for a raid could be found.[158] Two days later, the San Diego office reported to headquarters:

> As a result of the Bureau-approved information furnished to the San Diego Police Department regarding the "sex orgies" being held at BPP Headquarters in San Diego, which had not previously been known to the Police Department, a raid was conducted at BPP Headquarters on 11/20/69. [Name deleted], San Diego Police Department, Intelligence Unit, advised that, due to this information, he assigned two officers to a research project to determine if any solid basis could be found to conduct a raid. His officers discovered two outstanding traffic warrants for [name deleted], a member of the BPP, and his officers used these warrants to obtain entry into BPP Headquarters.
>
> As a result of this raid [6 persons] were all arrested. Seized at the time of the arrests were three shotguns, one of which was stolen, one rifle, four gas masks and one tear gas canister.
>
> Also as a result of this raid, the six remaining members of the BPP in San Diego were summoned to Los Angeles on 11/28/69. . . . Upon their arrival, they were informed that due to numerous problems with the BPP in San Diego, including the recent raid on BPP Headquarters, the BPP Branch in San Diego was being dissolved.
>
> Also, as a direct result of the above raid [informants] have reported that [name deleted] has been severely beaten up by other members of the BPP due to the fact that she allowed the officers to enter BPP Headquarters the night of the raid.[159]

A later memorandum states that confidential files belonging to the San Diego Panthers were also "obtained" during this raid.[160]

In March 1969, the San Diego Field Office informed Bureau headquarters:

> information was made available to the San Diego Police Department who have been arranging periodic raids in the

---

[157] The San Diego office reported to headquarters: "As of one week ago, the BPP in San Diego was so completely disrupted and so much suspicion, fear, and distrust has been interjected into the party that the members have taken to running surveillances on one another in an attempt to determine who the 'police agents' are. On 2/19/69, this information was furnished to the San Diego Police Department with the suggestion that possibly local Motor Vehicle Code laws were being violated during the course of these surveillances.'" (Memorandum from San Diego Field Office to FBI Headquarters 2/27/69.)

[158] Memorandum from San Diego Field Office to FBI Headquarters, 11/10/69. Headquarters told the San Diego office that if there was no legal basis for a raid, it should "give this matter further thought and submit other proposals to capitalize on this information in the counterintelligence field." (Memorandum from FBI Headquarters to San Diego Field Office, 11/18/69, p. 1.)

[159] Memorandum from San Diego Field Office to FBI Headquarters, 12/3/69, pp. 2–3.

[160] Memorandum from San Diego Field Office to FBI Headquarters, 2/17/70.

> hope of establishing a possession of marijuana and dangerous drug charge [against two BPP members]. . . .
> The BPP finally managed to rent the Rhodesian Club at 2907 Imperial Avenue, San Diego, which will be utilized for a meeting hall. A request will be forthcoming to have the San Diego Police Department and local health inspectors examine the club for health and safety defects which are undoubted by [*sic*] present.[161]

The San Diego office also conducted "racial briefing sessions" for the San Diego police. Headquarters was informed:

> It is also felt that the racial briefing sessions being given by the San Diego Division are affording tangible results for the Counterintelligence Program. Through these briefings, the command levels of virtually all of the police departments in the San Diego Division are being apprised of the identities of the leaders of the various militant groups. It is felt that, although specific instances cannot be attributed directly to the racial briefing program, police officers are much more alert for these black militant individuals and as such are contributing to the over-all Counterintelligence Program, directed against these groups.[162]

The Committee staff has seen documents indicating extensive cooperation between local police and the FBI in several other cities. For example, the FBI in Oakland prevented a reconciliation meeting between Huey Newton's brother and former Panthers by having the Oakland police inform one of the former Panthers that the meeting was a "set up." The San Francisco office concluded:

> It is believed that such quick dissemination of this type of information may have been instrumental in preventing the various dissidents from rejoining forces with the BPP.[163]

Another Bureau memorandum reflected similar cooperation in Los Angeles:

> The Los Angeles office is furnishing on a daily basis information to the Los Angeles County Sheriff's Office Intelligence Division and the Los Angeles Police Department Intelligence and Criminal Conspiracy Divisions concerning the activities of the black nationalist groups in the anticipation that such information might lead to the arrest of these militants.[164]

Information from Bureau files in Chicago on the Panthers was given to Chicago police upon request, and Chicago Police Department files were open to the Bureau.[165] A Special Agent who handled liaison between the FBI's Racial Matters Squad (responsible for monitoring BPP activity in Chicago) and the Panther Squad of the Gang Intelligence Unit (GIU) of the Chicago Police Department from 1967 through July 1969, testified that he visited GIU between three and

[161] Memorandum from San Diego Field Office to FBI Headquarters, 3/26/69.
[162] Memorandum from San Diego Field Office to FBI Headquarters, 12/15/69.
[163] Memorandum from San Francisco Field Office to FBI Headquarters, 4/21/69.
[164] Memorandum Los Angeles Field Office to FBI Headquarters, 12/1/69.
[165] Special Agent deposition, 2/26/75, p. p. 90.

C. Selected FBI Internal Memoranda on COINTELPRO Activities

In this section, we have selected 14 internal memoranda in which the Bureau's widespread lawlessness in its attempt to disrupt and destroy targeted individuals and organizations within the Black community is spelled out.

Note: Many of these memoranda began with the acronym "SAC." That acronym stands for "Special Agent in Charge."

SAC, Albany

August 25, 1967

PERSONAL ATTENTION TO ALL OFFICES

Director, FBI

1 - Mr. C.D. Brennan
1 -
1 -
1 -
1 -
1 -

COUNTERINTELLIGENCE PROGRAM
BLACK NATIONALIST - HATE GROUPS
INTERNAL SECURITY

Offices receiving copies of this letter are instructed to immediately establish a control file, captioned as above, and to assign responsibility for following and coordinating this new counterintelligence program to an experienced and imaginative Special Agent well versed in investigations relating to black nationalist, hate-type organizations. The field office control file used under this program may be maintained in a pending inactive status until such time as a specific operation or technique is placed under consideration for implementation.

The purpose of this new counterintelligence endeavor is to expose, disrupt, misdirect, discredit, or otherwise neutralize the activities of black nationalist, hate-type organizations and groupings, their leadership, spokesmen, membership, and supporters, and to counter their propensity for violence and civil disorder. The activities of all such groups of intelligence interest to this Bureau must be followed on a continuous basis so we will be in a position to promptly take advantage of all opportunities for counterintelligence and to inspire action in instances where circumstances warrant. The pernicious background of such groups, their duplicity, and devious maneuvers must be exposed to public scrutiny where such publicity will have a neutralizing effect. Efforts of the various groups

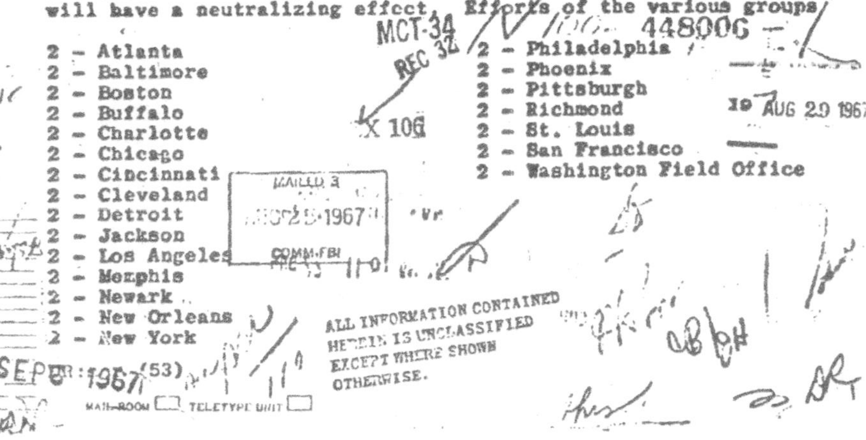
MCT-34 100-448006
REC 32

2 - Atlanta
2 - Baltimore
2 - Boston
2 - Buffalo
2 - Charlotte
2 - Chicago
2 - Cincinnati
2 - Cleveland
2 - Detroit
2 - Jackson
2 - Los Angeles
2 - Memphis
2 - Newark
2 - New Orleans
2 - New York
2 - Philadelphia
2 - Phoenix
2 - Pittsburgh
2 - Richmond
2 - St. Louis
2 - San Francisco
2 - Washington Field Office

19 AUG 29 1967

MAILED 3
AUG 25 1967
COMM-FBI

ALL INFORMATION CONTAINED HEREIN IS UNCLASSIFIED EXCEPT WHERE SHOWN OTHERWISE.

6 SEP 8 1967 (53)

MAIL ROOM ☐ TELETYPE UNIT ☐

Letter to SAC, Albany
RE: COUNTERINTELLIGENCE PROGRAM
BLACK NATIONALIST - HATE GROUPS

to consolidate their forces or to recruit new or youthful adherents must be frustrated. No opportunity should be missed to exploit through counterintelligence techniques the organizational and personal conflicts of the leaderships of the groups and where possible an effort should be made to capitalize upon existing conflicts between competing black nationalist organizations. When an opportunity is apparent to disrupt or neutralize black nationalist, hate-type organizations through the cooperation of established local news media contacts or through such contact with sources available to the Seat of Government, in every instance careful attention must be given to the proposal to insure the targeted group is disrupted, ridiculed, or discredited through the publicity and not merely publicized. Consideration should be given to techniques to preclude violence-prone or rabble-rouser leaders of hate groups from spreading their philosophy publicly or through various mass communication media.

Many individuals currently active in black nationalist organizations have backgrounds of immorality, subversive activity, and criminal records. Through your investigation of key agitators, you should endeavor to establish their unsavory backgrounds, Be alert to determine evidence of misappropriation of funds or other types of personal misconduct on the part of militant nationalist leaders so any practical or warranted counter-intelligence may be instituted.

Intensified attention under this program should be afforded to the activities of such groups as the Student Nonviolent Coordinating Committee, the Southern Christian Leadership Conference, Revolutionary Action Movement, the Deacons for Defense and Justice, Congress of Racial Equality, and the Nation of Islam. Particular emphasis should be given to extremists who direct the activities and policies of revolutionary or militant groups such as Stokely Carmichael, H. "Rap" Brown, Elijah Muhammad, and Maxwell Stanford.

At this time the Bureau is setting up no requirement for status letters to be periodically submitted under this program. It will be incumbent upon you to insure the program is being afforded necessary and continuing attention and that no opportunities will be overlooked for counterintelligence action.

This program should not be confused with the program entitled "Communist Party, USA, Counterintelligence Program, Internal Security - C," (Bufile 100-3-104), which is directed

-2-

Letter to SAC, Albany
RE: COUNTERINTELLIGENCE PROGRAM
BLACK NATIONALIST - HATE GROUPS

against the Communist Party and related organizations, or the program entitled "Counterintelligence Program, Internal Security, Disruption of Hate Groups," (Bufile 157-9), which is directed against Klan and hate-type groups primarily consisting of white memberships.

All Special Agent personnel responsible for the investigation of black nationalist, hate-type organizations and their memberships should be alerted to our counterintelligence interest and each investigative Agent has a responsibility to call to the attention of the counterintelligence coordinator suggestions and possibilities for implementing the program. You are also cautioned that the nature of this new endeavor is such that under no circumstances should the existence of the program be made known outside the Bureau and appropriate within-office security should be afforded to sensitive operations and techniques considered under the program.

No counterintelligence action under this program may be initiated by the field without specific prior Bureau authorization.

You are urged to take an enthusiastic and imaginative approach to this new counterintelligence endeavor and the Bureau will be pleased to entertain any suggestions or techniques you may recommend.

3/4/68

1 - Mr. C. D. DeLoach
1 - Mr. W. C. Sullivan
1 - Mr. G. C. Moore
1 -
1 -

AIRTEL

To: SAC, Albany PERSONAL ATTENTION

REC 18

From: Director, FBI (100-448006) — 17

COUNTERINTELLIGENCE PROGRAM
BLACK NATIONALIST-HATE GROUPS
RACIAL INTELLIGENCE

MAILED 12
MAR 5 1968
COMM-FBI

Title is changed to substitute Racial Intelligence for Internal Security for Bureau routing purposes.

PERSONAL ATTENTION FOR ALL THE FOLLOWING SACs

2 - Atlanta
2 - Baltimore
2 - Birmingham
2 - Boston
2 - Buffalo
2 - Charlotte
2 - Chicago
2 - Cincinnati
2 - Cleveland
2 - Denver
2 - Detroit
2 - Houston
2 - Indianapolis
2 - Jackson
2 - Jacksonville
2 - Kansas City
2 - Los Angeles
2 - Memphis
2 - Miami
2 - Milwaukee
2 - Minneapolis
2 - Mobile
2 - Newark
2 - New Haven
2 - New Orleans
2 - New York
2 - Omaha
2 - Philadelphia
2 - Phoenix
2 - Pittsburgh
2 - Portland
2 - Richmond
2 - Sacramento
2 - San Diego
2 - San Francisco
2 - Seattle
2 - Springfield
2 - St. Louis
2 - Tampa
2 - WFO

TJD:rmm (88)

ALL INFORMATION CONTAINED
HEREIN IS UNCLASSIFIED
EXCEPT WHERE SHOWN
OTHERWISE.

SEE NOTE PAGE SIX

54 MAR 18 1968

MAIL ROOM ☐ TELETYPE UNIT ☐

Airtel to SAC, Albany
RE: COUNTERINTELLIGENCE PROGRAM
BLACK NATIONALIST-HATE GROUPS

BACKGROUND

By letter dated 8/25/67 the following offices were advised of the beginning of a Counterintelligence Program against militant Black Nationalist-Hate Groups:

Albany	Memphis
Atlanta	Newark
Baltimore	New Orleans
Boston	New York
Buffalo	Philadelphia
Charlotte	Phoenix
Chicago	Pittsburgh
Cincinnati	Richmond
Cleveland	St. Louis
Detroit	San Francisco
Jackson	Washington Field
Los Angeles	

Each of the above offices was to designate a Special Agent to coordinate this program. Replies to this letter indicated an interest in counterintelligence against militant black nationalist groups that foment violence and several offices outlined procedures which had been effective in the past. For example, Washington Field Office had furnished information about a new Nation of Islam (NOI) grade school to appropriate authorities in the District of Columbia who investigated to determine if the school conformed to District regulations for private schools. In the process WFO obtained background information on the parents of each pupil.

The Revolutionary Action Movement (RAM), a pro-Chinese communist group, was active in Philadelphia, Pa., in the summer of 1967. The Philadelphia Office alerted local police, who then put RAM leaders under close scrutiny. They were arrested on every possible charge until they could no longer make bail. As a result, RAM leaders spent most of the summer in jail and no violence traceable to RAM took place.

The Counterintelligence Program is now being expanded to include 41 offices. Each of the offices added to this program should designate an Agent familiar with black

- 2 -

Airtel to SAC, Albany
RE: COUNTERINTELLIGENCE PROGRAM
BLACK NATIONALIST-HATE GROUPS

nationalist activity, and interested in counterintelligence, to coordinate this program. This Agent will be responsible for the periodic progress letters being requested, but each Agent working this type of case should participate in the formulation of counterintelligence operations.

GOALS

For maximum effectiveness of the Counterintelligence Program, and to prevent wasted effort, long-range goals are being set.

1. Prevent the coalition of militant black nationalist groups. In unity there is strength; a truism that is no less valid for all its triteness. An effective coalition of black nationalist groups might be the first step toward a real "Mau Mau" in America, the beginning of a true black revolution.

2. Prevent the rise of a "messiah" who could unify, and electrify, the militant black nationalist movement. Malcolm X might have been such a "messiah;" he is the martyr of the movement today. Martin Luther King, Stokely Carmichael and Elijah Muhammed all aspire to this position. Elijah Muhammed is less of a threat because of his age. King could be a very real contender for this position should he abandon his supposed "obedience" to "white, liberal doctrines" (nonviolence) and embrace black nationalism. Carmichael has the necessary charisma to be a real threat in this way.

3. Prevent violence on the part of black nationalist groups. This is of primary importance, and is, of course, a goal of our investigative activity; it should also be a goal of the Counterintelligence Program. Through counterintelligence it should be possible to pinpoint potential troublemakers and neutralize them before they exercise their potential for violence.

4. Prevent militant black nationalist groups and leaders from gaining respectability, by discrediting them to three separate segments of the community. The goal of discrediting black nationalists must be handled tactically in three ways. You must discredit these groups and individuals to, first, the responsible Negro community. Second, they must be discredited to the white community,

- 3 -

Airtel to SAC, Albany
RE: COUNTERINTELLIGENCE PROGRAM
BLACK NATIONALIST-HATE GROUPS

both the responsible community and to "liberals" who have vestiges of sympathy for militant black nationalist simply because they are Negroes. Third, these groups must be discredited in the eyes of Negro radicals, the followers of the movement. This last area requires entirely different tactics from the first two. Publicity about violent tendencies and radical statements merely enhances black nationalists to the last group; it adds "respectability" in a different way.

5. A final goal should be to prevent the long-range growth of militant black nationalist organizations, especially among youth. Specific tactics to prevent these groups from converting young people must be developed.

Besides these five goals counterintelligence is a valuable part of our regular investigative program as it often produces positive information.

TARGETS

Primary targets of the Counterintelligence Program, Black Nationalist-Hate Groups, should be the most violent and radical groups and their leaders. We should emphasize those leaders and organizations that are nationwide in scope and are most capable of disrupting this country. These targets should include the radical and violence-prone leaders, members, and followers of the:

Student Nonviolent Coordinating Committee (SNCC),
Southern Christian Leadership Conference (SCLC),
Revolutionary Action Movement (RAM)
Nation of Islam (NOI)

Offices handling these cases and those of Stokely Carmichael of SNCC, H. Rap Brown of SNCC, Martin Luther King of SCLC, Maxwell Stanford of RAM, and Elijah Muhammed of NOI, should be alert for counterintelligence suggestions.

INSTRUCTIONS

Within 30 days of the date of this letter each office should:

1. Advise the Bureau of the identity of the Special Agent assigned to coordinate this program.

Airtel to SAC, Albany
RE: COUNTERINTELLIGENCE PROGRAM
BLACK NATIONALIST-HATE GROUPS

2. Submit a very succinct summary of the black nationalist movement in the field office territory. Include name, number of members and degree of activity of each black nationalist group. Also state your estimate of each groups propensity for violence. This is for target evaluation only, not for record purposes. Second, list Rabble-Rouser Index subjects who are militant black nationalists and any other militant black nationalist leaders who might be future targets of counterintelligence action because of their propensity for violence. Include a minimum of background information on each person listed; a few descriptive sentences should suffice.

3. List those organizations and individuals you consider of such potential danger as to be considered for current counterintelligence action. Briefly justify each target.

4. Submit any suggestion you have for overall counterintelligence action or the administration of this program. Suggestions for action against any specific target should be submitted by separate letter.

5. Submit, by separate letter, suggestions for counterintelligence action against the targets previously listed as field-wide. These should not be general, such as "publicize Stokely Carmichael's travel to communist countries," but should be specific as to target, what is to be done, what contacts are to be used, and all other information needed for the Bureau to approve a counter-intelligence operation.

Thereafter, on a ninety-day-basis, each office is to submit a progress letter summarizing counterintelligence operations proposed during the period, operations effected, and tangible results. Any changes in the overall black nationalist movement should be summarized in this letter. This should include new organizations, new leaders, and any changes in data listed under number two above. Suggestions for counterintelligence operations should not be set out in this progress letter. Use the following captions:

1. Operations Under Consideration, 2. Operations Being Effected, 3. Tangible Results, and 4. Developments of Counterintelligence Interest. These 90-day progress letters are due at the Bureau the first day of March, June, September, and December, excepting March, 1968.

Airtel to SAC, Albany
RE: COUNTERINTELLIGENCE PROGRAM
BLACK NATIONALIST-HATE GROUPS

The effectiveness of counterintelligence depends on the quality and quantity of positive information available regarding the target and on the imagination and initiative of Agents working the program. The response of the field to the Counterintelligence Program against the Communist Party, USA, indicates that a superb job can be done by the field on counterintelligence.

Counterintelligence operations must be approved by the Bureau. Because of the nature of this program each operation must be designed to protect the Bureau's interest so that there is no possibility of embarrassment to the Bureau. Beyond this the Bureau will give every possible consideration to your proposals.

NOTE:

See memorandum G. C. Moore to Mr. W. C. Sullivan captioned as above dated 2/29/68, prepared by TJD:rmm.

Memorandum (1)

TO : Mr. W. C. Sullivan DATE: February 29, 1968

FROM : G. C. Moore

1 - Mr. C. D. DeLoach
1 - Mr. W. C. Sullivan
1 - Mr. G. C. Moore
1 -
1 -

SUBJECT: COUNTERINTELLIGENCE PROGRAM
BLACK NATIONALIST-HATE GROUPS
RACIAL INTELLIGENCE

PURPOSE:

To expand the Counterintelligence Program designed to neutralize militant black nationalist groups from 23 to 41 field divisions so as to cover the great majority of black nationalist activity in this country.

BACKGROUND:

By letter dated August 25, 1967, 23 field offices were advised of a new Counterintelligence Program designed to neutralize militant black nationalists and prevent violence on their part. Goals of this program are to prevent the coalit[ion] of militant black nationalist groups, prevent the rise of a leader who might unify and electrify these violence-prone elements, prevent these militants from gaining respectability and prevent the growth of these groups among America's youth.

CURRENT DEVELOPMENTS:

In view of the tremendous increase in black nationalis[t] activity, and the approach of summer, this program should be expanded and these goals should be reiterated to the field. Attached airtel also instructs the field to submit periodic progress letters to stimulate thinking in this area.

REC 18

Attached airtel also reminds the field that counterinte[l]ligence suggestions to expose these militants or neutralize them must be approved by the Bureau.

ACTION:

6 MAR 11 1968

That attached airtel expanding this program, defining goals and instructing periodic progress letters be submitted be sent Albany and the other listed field offices.

Enclosure 3/4-68

TJD:rmm (6)

ALL INFORMATION CONTAINED HEREIN IS UNCLASSIFIED EXCEPT WHERE SHOWN

TJD 5-TJD

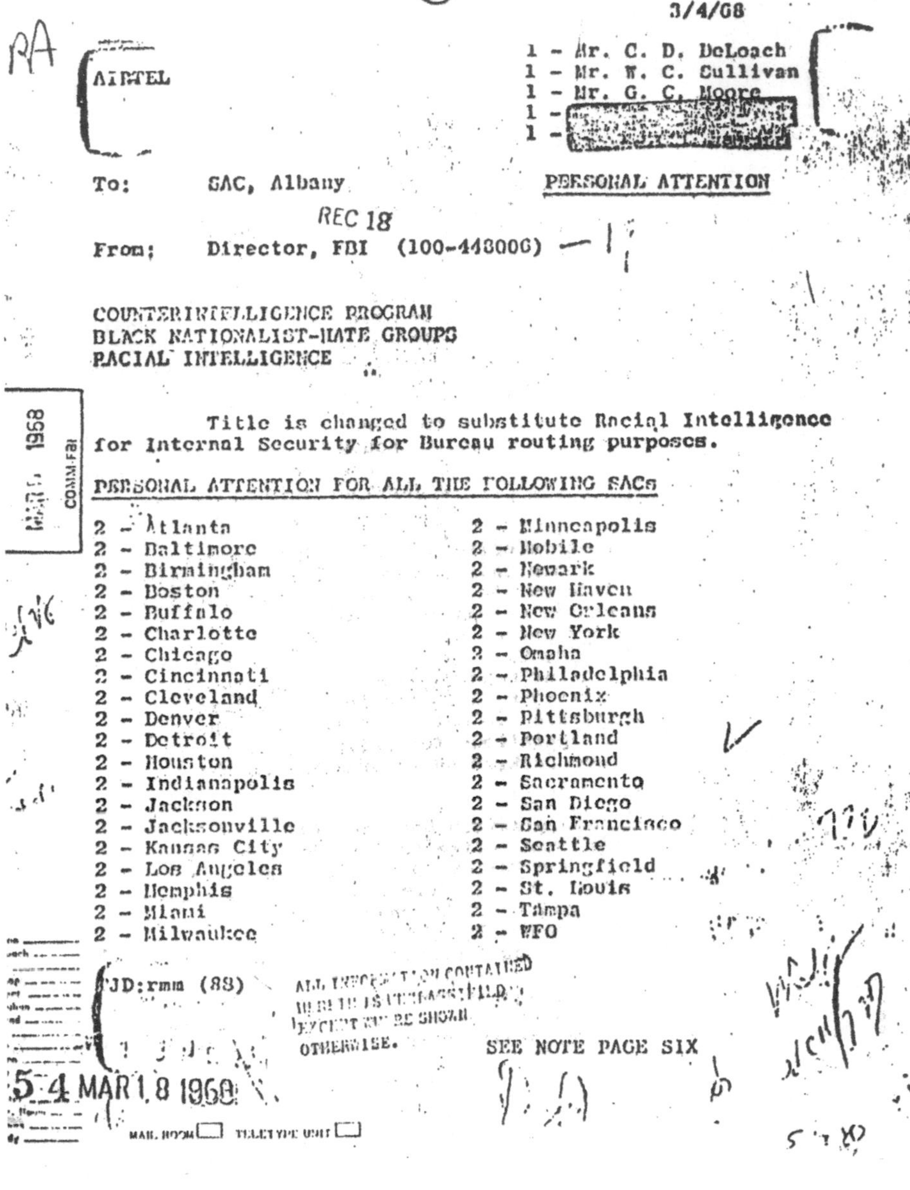

3/4/68

AIRTEL

1 - Mr. C. D. DeLoach
1 - Mr. W. C. Sullivan
1 - Mr. G. C. Moore
1 -
1 -

To: SAC, Albany

PERSONAL ATTENTION

REC 18

From: Director, FBI (100-448006)

COUNTERINTELLIGENCE PROGRAM
BLACK NATIONALIST-HATE GROUPS
RACIAL INTELLIGENCE

Title is changed to substitute Racial Intelligence for Internal Security for Bureau routing purposes.

PERSONAL ATTENTION FOR ALL THE FOLLOWING SACs

2 - Atlanta
2 - Baltimore
2 - Birmingham
2 - Boston
2 - Buffalo
2 - Charlotte
2 - Chicago
2 - Cincinnati
2 - Cleveland
2 - Denver
2 - Detroit
2 - Houston
2 - Indianapolis
2 - Jackson
2 - Jacksonville
2 - Kansas City
2 - Los Angeles
2 - Memphis
2 - Miami
2 - Milwaukee
2 - Minneapolis
2 - Mobile
2 - Newark
2 - New Haven
2 - New Orleans
2 - New York
2 - Omaha
2 - Philadelphia
2 - Phoenix
2 - Pittsburgh
2 - Portland
2 - Richmond
2 - Sacramento
2 - San Diego
2 - San Francisco
2 - Seattle
2 - Springfield
2 - St. Louis
2 - Tampa
2 - WFO

GCM:rmm (88)

ALL INFORMATION CONTAINED HEREIN IS UNCLASSIFIED EXCEPT WHERE SHOWN OTHERWISE.

SEE NOTE PAGE SIX

MAR 18 1968

MAIL ROOM ☐ TELETYPE UNIT ☐

(3)

Airtel to SAC, Albany
RE: COUNTERINTELLIGENCE PROGRAM
BLACK NATIONALIST-HATE GROUPS

BACKGROUND

By letter dated 8/25/67 the following offices were advised of the beginning of a Counterintelligence Program against militant Black Nationalist-Hate Groups:

Albany	Memphis
Atlanta	Newark
Baltimore	New Orleans
Boston	New York
Buffalo	Philadelphia
Charlotte	Phoenix
Chicago	Pittsburgh
Cincinnati	Richmond
Cleveland	St. Louis
Detroit	San Francisco
Jackson	Washington Field
Los Angeles	

Each of the above offices was to designate a Special Agent to coordinate this program. Replies to this letter indicated an interest in counterintelligence against militant black nationalist groups that foment violence and several offices outlined procedures which had been effective in the past. For example, Washington Field Office had furnished information about a new Nation of Islam (NOI) grade school to appropriate authorities in the District of Columbia who investigated to determine if the school conformed to District regulations for private schools. In the process WFO obtained background information on the parents of each pupil.

The Revolutionary Action Movement (RAM), a pro-Chinese communist group, was active in Philadelphia, Pa., in the summer of 1967. The Philadelphia Office alerted local police, who then put RAM leaders under close scrutiny. They were arrested on every possible charge until they could no longer make bail. As a result, RAM leaders spent most of the summer in jail and no violence traceable to RAM took place.

The Counterintelligence Program is now being expanded to include 41 offices. Each of the offices added to this program should designate an Agent familiar with black

Airtel to SAC, Albany
RE: COUNTERINTELLIGENCE PROG
BLACK NATIONALIST-HATE GROUPS

nationalist activity, and interested in counterintelligence, to coordinate this program. This Agent will be responsible for the periodic progress letters being requested, but each Agent working this type of case should participate in the formulation of counterintelligence operations.

GOALS

For maximum effectiveness of the Counterintelligence Program, and to prevent wasted effort, long-range goals are being set.

1. Prevent the coalition of militant black nationalist groups. In unity there is strength; a truism that is no less valid for all its triteness. An effective coalition of black nationalist groups might be the first step toward a real "Mau Mau" in America, the beginning of a true black revolution.

2. Prevent the rise of a "messiah" who could unify, and electrify, the militant black nationalist movement. Malcolm X might have been such a "messiah;" he is the martyr of the movement today. Martin Luther King, Stokely Carmichael and Elijah Muhammed all aspire to this position. Elijah Muhammed is less of a threat because of his age. King could be a very real contender for this position should he abandon his supposed "obedience" to "white, liberal doctrines" (nonviolence) and embrace black nationalism. Carmichael has the necessary charisma to be a real threat in this way.

3. Prevent violence on the part of black nationalist groups. This is of primary importance, and is, of course, a goal of our investigative activity; it should also be a goal of the Counterintelligence Program. Through counterintelligence it should be possible to pinpoint potential troublemakers and neutralize them before they exercise their potential for violence.

4. Prevent militant black nationalist groups and leaders from gaining respectability, by discrediting them to three separate segments of the community. The goal of discrediting black nationalists must be handled tactically in three ways. You must discredit these groups and individuals to, first, the responsible Negro community. Second, they must be discredited to the white community,

- 3 -

(5)

Airtel to SAC, Al
RE: COUNTERINTEL
BLACK NATIONALIST-HATE GROUPS

both the responsible community and to "liberals" who have vestiges of sympathy for militant black nationalist simply because they are Negroes. Third, these groups must be discredited in the eyes of Negro radicals, the followers of the movement. This last area requires entirely different tactics from the first two. Publicity about violent tendencies and radical statements merely enhances black nationalists to the last group; it adds "respectability" in a different way.

5. A final goal should be to prevent the long-range growth of militant black nationalist organizations, especially among youth. Specific tactics to prevent these groups from converting young people must be developed.

Besides these five goals counterintelligence is a valuable part of our regular investigative program as it often produces positive information.

TARGETS

Primary targets of the Counterintelligence Program, Black Nationalist-Hate Groups, should be the most violent and radical groups and their leaders. We should emphasize those leaders and organizations that are nationwide in scope and are most capable of disrupting this country. These targets should include the radical and violence-prone leaders, members, and followers of the:

Student Nonviolent Coordinating Committee (SNCC),
Southern Christian Leadership Conference (SCLC).
Revolutionary Action Movement (RAM).
Nation of Islam (NOI)

Offices handling these cases and those of Stokely Carmichael of SNCC, H. Rap Brown of SNCC, Martin Luther King of SCLC, Maxwell Stanford of RAM, and Elijah Muhammed of NOI, should be alert for counterintelligence suggestions.

INSTRUCTIONS

Within 30 days of the date of this letter each office should:

1. Advise the Bureau of the identity of the Special Agent assigned to coordinate this program.

(6)

Airtel to SAC, Albany
RE: COUNTERINTELLIGENCE PROGRAM
BLACK NATIONALIST-HATE GROUPS

2. Submit a very succinct summary of the black nationalist movement in the field office territory. Include name, number of members and degree of activity of each black nationalist group. Also state your estimate of each groups propensity for violence. This is for target evaluation only, not for record purposes. Second, list Rabble-Rouser Index subjects who are militant black nationalists and any other militant black nationalist leaders who might be future targets of counterintelligence action because of their propensity for violence. Include a minimum of background information on each person listed; a few descriptive sentences should suffice.

3. List those organizations and individuals you consider of such potential danger as to be considered for current counterintelligence action. Briefly justify each target.

4. Submit any suggestion you have for overall counterintelligence action or the administration of this program. Suggestions for action against any specific target should be submitted by separate letter.

5. Submit, by separate letter, suggestions for counterintelligence action against the targets previously listed as field-wide. These should not be general, such as "publicize Stokely Carmichael's travel to communist countries," but should be specific as to target, what is to be done, what contacts are to be used, and all other information needed for the Bureau to approve a counterintelligence operation.

Thereafter, on a ninety-day-basis, each office is to submit a progress letter summarizing counterintelligence operations proposed during the period, operations effected, and tangible results. Any changes in the overall black nationalist movement should be summarized in this letter. This should include new organizations, new leaders, and any changes in data listed under number two above. Suggestions for counterintelligence operations should not be set out in this progress letter. Use the following captions:

1. Operations Under Consideration, 2. Operations Being Effected, 3. Tangible Results, and 4. Developments of Counterintelligence Interest. These 90-day progress letters are due at the Bureau the first day of March, June, September, and December, excepting March, 1968.

(7)

Airtel to SAC, Albany
RE: COUNTERINTELLIGENCE PROGRAM
BLACK NATIONALIST-HATE GROUPS

The effectiveness of counterintelligence depends on the quality and quantity of positive information available regarding the target and on the imagination and initiative of Agents working the program. The response of the field to the Counterintelligence Program against the Communist Party, USA, indicates that a superb job can be done by the field on counterintelligence.

Counterintelligence operations must be approved by the Bureau. Because of the nature of this program each operation must be designed to protect the Bureau's interest so that there is no possibility of embarrassment to the Bureau. Beyond this the Bureau will give every possible consideration to your proposals.

NOTE:

See memorandum G. C. Moore to Mr. W. C. Sullivan captioned as above dated 2/29/68, prepared by TJD:rmm.

UNITED STATES GOVERNMENT
Memorandum

TO : DIRECTOR, FBI DATE: 2/28/68

FROM : SAC, NEW YORK (100-161140) (P)

SUBJECT: COUNTERINTELLIGENCE PROGRAM
BLACK NATIONALIST - HATE GROUPS
IS -

Re Bureau letter, 8/25/67.

Bureau authority is hereby requested to place the following counterintelligence technique into effect:

Anonymous and various other pretext telephone calls will be made to the below-listed subjects for the purpose of disruption, misdirection and to attempt to neutralize and frustrate the activities of these black nationalists.

These calls will be made to the subjects' residence or place of employment.

1. STOKELY CARMICHAEL
(New York File 100-153751)
Residence: 1810 Amethyst Street,
Bronx, New York
(phone 828-9179)
Employment: SNCC Headquarters
100 Fifth Avenue, New York City
(phone YU 9-1313)

REC-52

2 - Bureau (RM)
1 - New York

JJD:pm
(3)

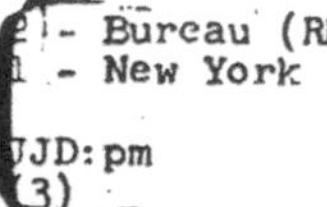

ALL INFORMATION CONTAINED
HEREIN IS UNCLASSIFIED
EXCEPT WHERE SHOWN
OTHERWISE.

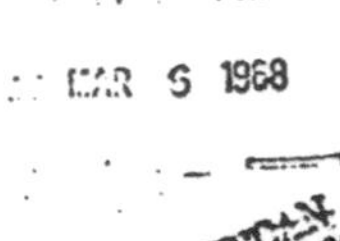

MAR 5 1968

LATIN-AMERICAN
RACIAL INT. SECT.

Buy U.S. Savings Bonds Regularly on the Payroll Savings Plan

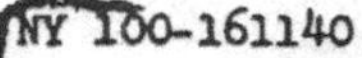
NY 100-161140

3. RAP BROWN
(New York File 100-160701)
Residing at 530 Manhattan Avenue,
New York City, with an individual
named WILLIAM HALL
(phone 865-5328)
Employment: National Leader, SNCC,
100 5th Avenue, New York City
(phone YU9-1313)

4.

5.

6.

-2-

SAC, New York (100-161140) 3/13/68

Director, FBI (100-448006) -11 1 -

REC-126
EX-105

COUNTERINTELLIGENCE PROGRAM
BLACK NATIONALIST - HATE GROUPS
RACIAL INTELLIGENCE

Reurlet 2/28/68.

Referenced letter requested authority to make anonymous and pretext telephone calls to 11 militant black nationalist leaders for the purpose of disruption, misdirection, and neutralization. In order to approve this recommendation, the Bureau needs to know what specific purpose these calls will have and how the calls will accomplish this purpose. For example, do you plan calls to the leader of one militant group telling him another group is trying to steal his followers?

The Bureau will be pleased to consider your recommendations in detail for disrupting these black nationalist leaders.

TJD:bjb
(4)
NOTE:

Relet merely requested authority to make these anonymous calls without specifying the nature of the calls or the objective sought.

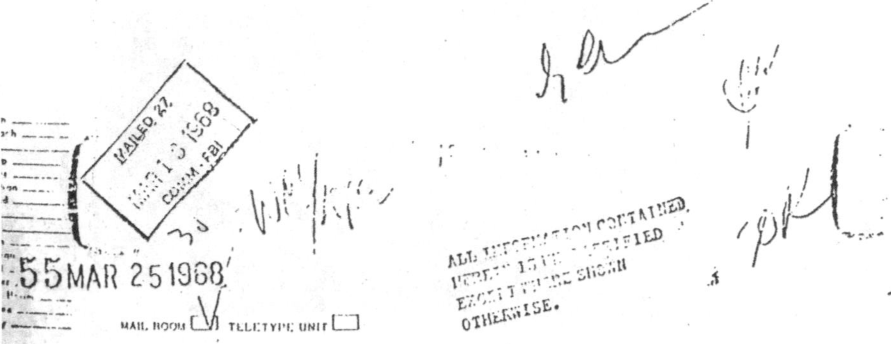

(1)

SAC, Los Angeles 4/25/68

Director, FBI (100-448006) 1 - [redacted]

COUNTERINTELLIGENCE PROGRAM
BLACK NATIONALIST - HATE GROUPS
RACIAL INTELLIGENCE
[redacted]

New York, in its overall counterintelligence letter 4/4/68, suggested ridicule of militant black nationalist leaders as a prime weapon to discredit these leaders, noting we should try to make militant black nationalism ludicrous to ghetto youth

[redacted]

Advise the Bureau in detail concerning initial contact and whether you

2 - Philadelphia
1 - New York

TJD:srs (7)

MAIL ROOM TELETYPE UNIT

REC 16

APR 25 1968

SAC, Los Angeles
RE: COUNTERINTELLIGENCE PROGRAM
100-448006

recommend further contact to develop this counterintelligence possibility.

Insure your initial pretext contact is sufficiently plausible to preclude any embarrassment to the Bureau. No contact should be made with [illegible] if there is any information in your files, or those of the Philadelphia Office, indicating such contact should not be made.

UNITED STATES GOVERNMENT

Memorandum

TO : DIRECTOR, FBI (100-448006) DATE: 7/2/68

FROM : SAC, CHICAGO (157-2209)

SUBJECT: COUNTERINTELLIGENCE PROGRAM
BLACK NATIONALIST - HATE GROUPS
RACIAL INTELLIGENCE

Re Bureau airtel, 3/4/68; Chicago airtels 4/22/68; Bureau letter 5/15/68 (re HERBERT C. MOHAMMED); Chicago airtel and Chicago letter, both 5/21/68.

Set forth below, under captions as instructed in re Bureau airtel, March 4, 1968, is a current progress letter regarding captioned matter.

1. Operations Under Consideration

In accordance with recent instructions from the Bureau (re Bulet, 5/15/68) Chicago has been directing consideration to DICK GREGORY as a counterintelligence target. As the Bureau is aware GREGORY is currently incarcerated in the State of Washington, serving a 90 day sentence based on his activities in behalf of Indian fishing rights.

The Chicago Office has organized a counterintelligence "team", made up of SA's experienced in RM and SM - C investigations including SA's with lengthy prior counterintelligence experience. This group, together with the RM supervisor, and the SA responsible for the coordination of this program, have devoted considerable effort to methods of inhibiting the effectiveness and credability of GREGORY. His file has been thoroughly and exhaustively reviewed to this end. The possibility has been noted that, in the final analysis, an individual such as GREGORY, so prone to erratic statements and actions, to such wild and obviously ridiculous charges, will in all probability destroy his own influence in this field and serve as a self-neutralizer.

REC-34 100-448006-

2 - Bureau (RM)
1 - Chicago

EX-105 25 JUL 5 1968

JCS:bab

5 JUL 12 1968

Buy U.S. Savings Bonds Regularly on the Payroll Savings Plan

CG 157-2209

however, subsequent investigation, as in Legat, London letter May 28, 1968, did not substantiate, or lend credence to GREGORY's use, or receipt of funds from abroad, primarily to have been utilized against the Democratic Convention, August, 1968, in Chicago.

Chicago is continuing to give the matter of discrediting GREGORY top priority, and Bureau authority will be promptly requested at the earliest opportunity in the event a specific counterintelligence device is formulated. It might also be noted, however, as in Chicago airtel of May 21, 1968, that GREGORY also faces a five month sentence, Cook County Jail, Chicago, as a result of the upholding of criminal charges against him, by the Illinois Appellate Court, of 1965 charges in connection with a local demonstration.

Chicago also has under consideration the review of federal income tax returns of HERBERT C. MOHAMMED, since he was pin-pointed as a counterintelligence target in Chicago airtel April 22, 1968, under the above caption, and that of the Nation of Islam (NOI).

These returns, referred to in Bureau letter May 15, 1968, have not as yet been received by Chicago, however, upon receipt, and subsequent review, a specific recommendation regarding counterintelligence action will be submitted.

In previous Chicago communications under above caption, Chicago has identified local Student Non-Violent Coordinating Committee (SNCC) official, as a possible target of counterintelligence action, with reference to his possible removal from an active role as a result of his refusal to cooperate with Selective Service officials over his imminent induction into the Armed Forces.

Although not a counterintelligence measure as such, Chicago has vigorously followed and pursued this situation, both with Selective Service and the Office of the United States Attorney. Recently refused to be inducted, his file is in the process of being forwarded by Selective Service to the United States Attorney (USA), who has advised case will be brought before the Federal Grand Jury at the earliest possible moment. The USA has advised that a warrant for the arrest of on above charges, will in all probability be

CG 157-2209

shortly forthcoming. Unquestionably this would serve to further inhibit local SNCC activities, and hopefully, would in some measure serve to neutralize [redacted] himself.

Chicago also feels that the Chicago Firearms Registration Ordinance, which went into effect May 15, 1968, has definite potential as a counterintelligence device, to be directed against local militants, as for example [redacted] In addition to the Chicago ordinance, a state law which requires registration of all persons possessing firearms will go into effect September 1, 1968. The penalty for violation of the local ordinance is a $500 fine, for violation of the state law, a $1,000 fine and a year incarceration.

Contact with the local office of gun registration has reflected that it will be approximately another 45-60 days before records are organized and alphabetized. [redacted] is identified as a possible target in this regard, however, there would appear to be a number of militants who may well be vulnerable.

As the Bureau has cautioned, Chicago assures that each specific future counterintelligence operation will be submitted for Bureau approval prior to taking any action.

2. Operations Being Effected

Chicago at present has no counterintelligence operation in progress, however, as noted will develop such, directed toward HERBERT MOHAMMED, upon receipt of his tax returns from the Bureau.

The impetus being provided to the efforts to expedite the handling of [redacted] Selective Service case is not a counterintelligence operation in the normal sense of the term, arising as it does from a substantive violation of federal law. However, the end result, that of reducing the effectiveness and hampering the activities of [redacted] is tantamount to that which might be achieved through any such operation with [redacted] as its target.

382

CG 157-2209

3. Tangible Results

With the possible exception of the imminent incarceration of [redacted] above, no tangible results have as yet been forthcoming since the inception of this program in the black nationalist field.

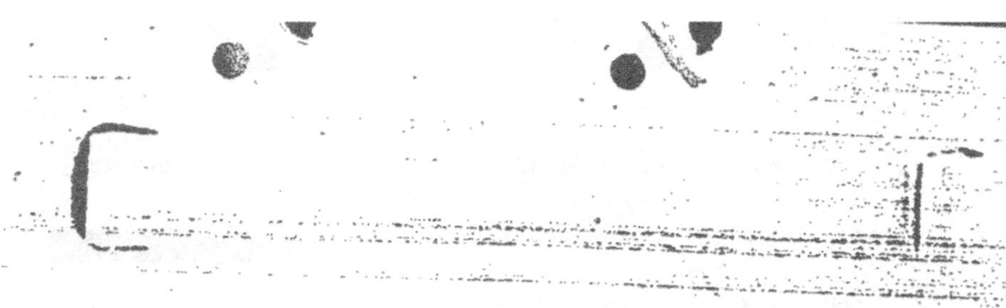

CG 157-2209

4. Developments of Counterintelligence Interest

There have been no significant developments in this field since my airtels of April 22, 1968, which would materially alter programs and approach previously suggested. Chicago appreciates, however, that changing times and developments in the general RM field can have an influence on any counterintelligence operation. Chicago will remain alert to any such development, and when any situation arises, relative to an individual or organization, which offers promise and potential as a counterintelligence operation, an appropriate communication will be promptly submitted.

It might also be noted that in general, the assessment of the local black nationalist movement, as set out in our airtel of April 22, 1968, under the above caption, remains as noted. It was pointed out that GREGORY had threatened to disrupt the Democratic National Convention, in August, 1968, however, as the Bureau is aware, he has cancelled his demonstration plans for before and during this convention, and is currently incarcerated.

Chicago assures the Bureau that full and continuing attention is devoted to this aspect of our operation, its potential value is well appreciated and this office will remain alert and receptive to any opportunity to accomplish and establish a productive counterintelligence operation.

284

SAC, New York (100-161140) 8-7-68

EX-103
Director, FBI (100-448006) — 213 1 - 

REC-126
COUNTERINTELLIGENCE PROGRAM
BLACK NATIONALIST - HATE GROUPS
RACIAL INTELLIGENCE
STUDENT NONVIOLENT COORDINATING COMMITTEE (SNCC)

Reurlet 7-25-68.

The Bureau appreciates your counterintelligence suggestion concerning the distribution of circulars indicating the Student Nonviolent Coordinating Committee (SNCC) and the Black Panthers organization are actually front groups established by police agencies.

As New York is aware, there is a dispute between these two groups in New York at present. If this counterintelligence operation was effected, there would be a possibility of uniting the two groups against a "common enemy," the intelligence agency that distributed this document.

Thus, New York should hold this suggestion in abeyance until the results of the dispute between SNCC and the Black Panthers are known.

(4)

MAILED 23
AUG 7 - 1968
COMM-FBI

Tolson
DeLoach
Mohr
Bishop
Casper
Callahan
Conrad
Felt
Gale
Rosen
Sullivan
Tavel
Trotter
Tele. Room
Holmes
Gandy

27·1
57 AUG 16 1968

MAIL ROOM ☐ TELETYPE UNIT ☐

OPTIONAL FORM NO. 10

UNITED STATES GOVERNMENT

Memorandum

TO : DIRECTOR, FBI (100-448006) DATE: 8/13/68

FROM : SAC, NEW YORK (100-161140) (P)

SUBJECT: COUNTERINTELLIGENCE PROGRAM
BLACK NATIONALIST - HATE GROUPS
RACIAL - INTELLIGENCE

ReBulet, 7/10/68; NY letters, 6/26/68, and 4/17/68.

The NYO desires to immediately place into effect counterintelligence device previously described in relets to Bureau in regard to [redacted] He will be pretexted late in the evening and told that various individuals in Harlem feel that he has been too disruptive and revolutionary and is causing repercussions by the power structure. He will also be told that [redacted] has been paid a sum of money to have [redacted] killed. The pretext will be conducted using a Negro dialect and by the use of ghetto language. [redacted] is still awaiting court action and it is felt that now is the time to place this pretext into effect against [redacted] and indirectly against [redacted]

In regard to the Black Panther organization in NY it is noted that [redacted] who is also known as [redacted] is reportedly the head man in the NY area. In order to exploit the break between SNCC and the Black Panthers and in order to put fear in the mind of Panther leader [redacted] the NYO desires to immediately place into effect the following counterintelligence device.

[redacted] will be telephonically contacted by pretext at which time he will be told that this individual had just attended a secret meeting of SNCC at which time [redacted] SNCC leader, let it be known that [redacted] will have to be eliminated. He will be told, in a Negro dialect, that [redacted] feels that [redacted] is becoming too powerful a figure so he will have to be "rubbed out". He will be cautioned to "keep looking over his

2 - Bureau (RM) REC 4
1 - New York

AUG 14 1968

54 SEP 3 - 1968

Buy U.S. Savings Bonds Regularly on the Payroll Savings Plan

NY 100-161140

shoulder" for sooner or later he will be taken care of. It is hoped that by use of such a pretext [redacted] might become disenchanted about future leadership in the Panther organization and "the word " might also get around to some of his friends causing them also to be disillusioned.

Bureau approval is requested to place above two techniques into operation.

-2-

SAC, New York October 12, 196

Director, FBI

SOCIALIST WORKERS PARTY
INTERNAL SECURITY - SWP
DISRUPTION PROGRAM

The Socialist Workers Party (SWP) has, over the past several years, been openly espousing its line on a local and national basis through running candidates for public office and strongly directing and/or supporting such causes as Castro's Cuba and integration problems arising in the South. The SWP has also been in frequent contact with international Trotskyite groups stopping short of open and direct contact with these groups. The youth group of the SWP has also been operating on this basis in connection with SWP policies.

Offices receiving copies of this letter are participating in the Bureau's Communist Party, USA, Counterintelligence Program. It is felt that a disruption program along similar lines could be initiated against the SWP on a very selective basis. One of the purposes of this program would be to alert the public to the fact that the SWP is not just another socialist group but follows the revolutionary principles of Marx, Lenin and Engels as interpreted by Leon Trotsky.

It is pointed out, however, that this program is not intended to be a "crash" program. Only carefully thought-out operations with the widest possible effect and benefit to the nation should be submitted. It may be desirable to expand the program after the effects have been evaluated

Each office is, therefore, requested to carefully evaluate such a program and submit their views to the Bureau regarding initiating a SWP disruption program on a limited basis.

MAY 1962 EDITION
GSA FPMR (41 CFR) 101-11.6
UNITED STATES GOVERNMENT
Memorandum

TO : DIRECTOR, FBI (100-448006) DATE: 10/16/68

FROM : SAC, DETROIT (100-34655)

SUBJECT: COUNTERINTELLIGENCE PROGRAM
BLACK NATIONALIST - HATE GROUPS
RACIAL INTELLIGENCE
(STOKELY CARMICHAEL)

Re Bureau letter to WFO, dated 7/1/68, captioned as above.

The Bureau in referenced letter indicated that it was desirous of spreading a rumor among black nationalists that CARMICHAEL is indeed a paid agent of a government intelligence or police agency. The Bureau further pointed out that due to CARMICHAEL's extensive travel overseas and black militants' distrust of the Central Intelligence Agency (CIA), it might be appropriate to tag CARMICHAEL with a "CIA label".

It is to be noted that CARMICHAEL is currently affiliated with the Black Panther Party (BPP), having recently severed his association with the Student Non-Violent Coordinating Committee (SNCC).

The Detroit Office proposes that when information is received that CARMICHAEL is to appear for a speech or any other activity in the Detroit area or in the territory of any other field office, that a throwaway be prepared and given widespread circulation in the black community of Detroit indicating in the throwaway information relative to the attempted purchase by CARMICHAEL in Washington, D.C. of a $70,000.00 home and further urging people not to attend the affair or give any financial support to CARMICHAEL

2 - Bureau (RM)
1 - WFO (157-1292) (Info) (RM)
2 - Detroit
DML/cmt
(5)

REC 46

OCT 18

RACIAL INT. SECT.

DE 100-34655

inasmuch as he is a traitor to the movement and it could further be implied in this throwaway that CARMICHAEL is a paid informant of a govenment intelligence agency, namely the CIA.

This throwaway would indicate that it was being distributed by such a fictitious organization as The Black Brotherhood to protect the brothers in Detroit.

In the event CARMICHAEL appears in the Detroit area, Detroit contemplates submitting the above proposed suggestion to the Bureau for Bureau approval.

UNITED STATES GOVERNMENT
Memorandum

2/25/70

TO : DIRECTOR, FBI (100-448006) DATE: 2/25/70

FROM : SAC, NEW YORK (100-161140) (P)

SUBJECT: COUNTERINTELLIGENCE PROGRAM
BLACK NATIONALIST - HATE GROUPS
RACIAL INTELLIGENCE

APPROPRIATE AGENCIES AND FIELD OFFICES ADVISED BY ROUTING SLIP(S) OF DATE

ReNYlet to Bureau, 11/28/69.

1. Operations Under Consideration

The NYO continues to give consideration to the disruption of BPP activities through the use of mailings directed to individuals or groups who do not have a complete understanding of BPP tactics or ideology.

These mailings would be prepared in such a way as to appear authentic in content and form as well as being topical. It is felt that they could be used as the vehicle to get inflamatory BPP literature and statements to those individuals who would not ordinarily have access to such material.

Handbills and throw-away type pamphlets would also be utilized in the above described consideration.

The study of the means and methods of distribution of the official BPP newspaper, "The Black Panther", in the NYC area continues but as yet the NYO has not derived a logical or practical plan to disrupt the circulation of this organization.

2. Operations Being Submitted

On 12/24/69, 20 reproductions of three types of BPP "Seasons Greetings Cards" were sent to various individuals in the NYC area, according to Bureau instructions given on 12/24/69.

REC-93

2- Bureau (RM)
1- New York (43)

FEB 27 1970

JLL:tf
(3)

5 MAR 6 1970

RACIAL INT. SECT.

Buy U.S. Savings Bonds Regularly on the Payroll Savings Plan

2/25/70

(2)

NY 100-161140

Source could furnish no positive information.

On 2/11/70, the NYO submitted an appropriate counter-intelligence proposal concerning a party given at the home of the well known [redacted] in NYC on 1/14/70, at which time money was raised for the aid and support of the BPP.

On 2/12/70, the NYO submitted observations and recommendations regarding contacts with established and reliable sources in the television and/or radio field, who might be interested in drawing up a program for local consumption, depicting the time facts regarding the BPP.

On 2/16/70, the NYO submitted a counterintelligence proposal for the Bureau's approval, which concerned the sending of a "BPP solicitation letter" to a "store owner" and the "store owner's reply letter" to the BPP.

On 2/17/70, two letters to the Editor of "Life" Magazine were prepared by the NYO from the point of view of a reader who would be a middle-class Black man. The letters concerned the writer's views on an article in February 6, 1970, edition of "Life" Magazine which could be construed favorable or at least sympathetic towards the BPP.

3. Tangible Results

Inasmuch as the majority of New York's counterintelligence activities since the submission of referenced quarterly letter have occured near the end of instant quarter it is not felt that the captioned category can be properly evaluated at this time.

It is felt that if utilized a favorable reaction from counterintelligence proposals as submitted by New York can be obtained in the future.

4. Developments of Counter-Intelligence Interests

NY 100-161140

The activities of those involved in the New York State trial of the "Panther 21" in New York City are closely monitored as reported by the local media so that appropriate counterintelligence proposals can be submitted.

Also the NYO is acutely aware of the significance of the actions of those who would closely associate themselves with the BPP, the Young Lords or the Young Patriots, as a source of timely counterintelligence proposals.

The activities of the RNA in the NYC area are minimal and therefore, no counterintelligence proposals concerning that organization can be made at this time.

The NYO will immeidately inform the Bureau of any situations or developments that occur where counterintelligence techniques may be utilized.

SAC, San Francisco 5/11/70

Director, FBI

COUNTERINTELLIGENCE AND SPECIAL OPERATIONS
(RESEARCH SECTION)

The Bureau would like to offer for your consideration a proposal for a disruptive-disinformation operation targeted against the national office of the Black Panther Party (BPP). This proposal is not intended to be all inclusive or binding in any of its various phases, but only is a guide for the suggested action. You are encouraged to submit recommendations relating to revisions or innovations of the proposal.

1. The operation would be effected through close coordination on a high level with the Oakland or San Francisco Police Department.

2. Xerox copies of true documents, documents subtly incorporating false information, and entirely fabricated documents would be periodically anonymously mailed to the residence of a key Panther leader. These documents would be on the stationery and in the form used by the police department or by the FBI in disseminating information to the police. FBI documents, when used, would contain police routing or date received notations, clearly indicating they had been pilfered from police files.

3. An attempt would be made to give the Panther recipient the impression the documents were stolen from police files by a disgruntled police employee sympathetic to the Panthers. After initial mailings, brief notes by the alleged disgruntled employee would be included with the mailed documents. These notes would indicate the motive and sympathy of the police employee, his bitterness against his department, and possibly a request for mone

4. Depending on developments, at a propitious time, consideration would be given to establishing a post office box or other suitable "drop" address for the use of the alleged disgruntled employee to receive responses, funds and/or specifications relating to the documents from the Panthers.

(2)

SAC, San Francisco 12/24/70

Director, FBI

ReSFairtel 12/7/70 captioned "Counterintelligence and Special Operations," and previous correspondence under the counterintelligence caption, outlining a proposed disruptive technique to be applied against leader / with the objective of neutralizing the

Recent information indicates has broken with the organization and is in the process of forming a new group. For this reason, and because of the expanding complexities of the proposed technique, no further action should be taken on this suggested disruptive technique.

Letter to SAC, San Francisco
RE: COUNTERINTELLIGENCE AND SPECIAL OPERATIONS

San Francisco is requested to submit comments and/or recommendations relating to the implementation of this proposal.

Copies of this letter have been designated for Los Angeles for background and information purposes. Any suggestion Los Angeles may have for strengthening or further implementing the technique will be appreciated.

Letter to SAC, San Francisco
RE: COUNTERINTELLIGENCE AND SPECIAL OPERATIONS

5. Although the operation may not require inclusion of a live source to represent the disgruntled employee, circumstances might warrant the use of such a source for face-to-fac meetings with the Panthers. During early stages of the operat an effort should be made to locate and brief a suitable police employee to play the role of the alleged disgruntled employee.

6. A wide variety of alleged authentic police or FBI material could be carefully selected or prepared for furnishing to the Panthers. Reports, blind memoranda, LHMs, and other alleged police or FBI documents could be prepared pinpointing Panthers as police or FBI informants; ridiculing or discrediting Panther leaders through their ineptness or personal escapades; espousing personal philosophies and promot factionalism among BPP members; indicating electronic coverage ~~where none exists; outlining fictitious plans for police raids~~ or other counteractions; revealing misuse or misappropriation of Panther funds; pointing out instances of political disorientation; etc. The nature of the disruptive material and disinformation "leaked" would only be limited by the collection ability of your sources and the need to insure the protection of their security.

Effective implementation of this proposal logically could not help but disrupt and confuse Panther activities. Even if they were to suspect FBI or police involvement, they would be unable to ignore factual material brought to their attention through this channel. The operation would afford us a continuing means to furnish the Panther leadership true information which is to our interest that they know and disinformation which, in their interest, they may not ignore.

Although this proposal is a relatively simple technique, it has been applied with exceptional results in another area of intelligence interest where the target was of far greater sophistication. The Bureau believes with careful planning this technique has excellent long-range potential to disrupt and curtail Panther activity.

1/29/71

UNITED STATES GOVERNMENT

Memorandum

1 - Mr. W. C. Sullivan
1 - Mr. J. P. Mohr

TO : Mr. C. D. Brennan

DATE: 1/29/71

1 - Mr. C. D. Brennan
1 - Mr. J. J. Casper
1 - Mr. G. C. Moore
1 - [redacted]

FROM : G. C. Moore

SUBJECT: COUNTERINTELLIGENCE PROGRAM
BLACK PANTHER PARTY (BPP) - DISSENSION
RACIAL MATTERS

1 - Mr. A. B. Fulton

To recommend that the attached airtel be sent to all offices conducting investigations of the BPP with instructions for intensifying our counterintelligence program against the BPP to fully exploit increasing dissension within that organization and among its leaders.

Current evidence indicates BPP is experiencing increasing amount of dissension causing serious morale problem and a strained relationship among members of its hierarchy. Primary cause of these internal problems is dictatorial and irrational attitude of BPP leader Huey P. Newton. His extreme sensitivity to any criticism and jealousness of other top Panthers have recently led to his capricious expulsion of dedicated Panthers. Based on the above we have intensified our counterintelligence activity in selected offices to further disrupt and aggravate this situation and our efforts are undoubtedly responsible for some of the Panthers' current problems.

In view of this widespread dissension coupled with financial problems currently being experienced by BPP it is imperative we strike now and fully exploit this development. We should further intensify on a large scale the implementation of imaginative counterintelligence proposals aimed at increasing overall Panther internal problems, widening strained relations between its leaders and neutralizing the growth and effectiveness of this cancerous organization. Accordingly, attached airtel is being sent to all pertinent offices requesting timely suggestions for disruptive counterintelligence proposals against the BPP on both local and national level. All proposals to be approved by Bureau before implementation.

Enclosure sent 2-1-71

REC- 65

EX-114

ABF:drl (8)

1971

D. Conclusion

It is within this climate of U.S. Government lawlessness that the situation of political prisoners in the United States must be examined. The cases that are set forth within this Petition are not exhaustive of the list of U.S. political prisoners.[6] Rather, these cases are intended to provide examples to the Commission on Human Rights and the Sub-Commission on Prevention of Discrimination and Protection of Minorities that are representative of the class of political prisoners and the various ways and patterns in which the gross and consistent violations of human rights and fundamental freedoms alleged by Petitioners are instituted and practiced by agents of the United States Government.

Endnotes

[1] *Report of the National Advisory Commission on Civil Disorders,* "The Basic Causes", Chap. 4 (1968).

[2] The United States Senate, *Final Report of the Select Committee to Study Governmental Operations with Respect to Intelligence Activities,* Book III (1976), p. 20. (Hereinafter referred to as the *Church Committee Report.*)

[3] *Ibid.*, p. 4.

[4] The list of 5,700 names constituting the FBI Black Nationalist Surveillance List was contained in the original Petition as Appendix VI. Additional documentation is contained in testimony by Ramsey Clark on June 26, 1972, and by Jack Anderson on June 27, 1972, before the Congressional Black Caucus' Governmental Lawlessness Hearings. Transcripts of the Clark and Anderson testimony were contained in Appendix V of the original Petition.

[5] *Church Committee Report,* Book III, pp. 21-22.

[6] One list of political prisoners is that of Amnesty International (AI). AI is a highly respected, London-based international organization that works for the release of prisoners of conscience throughout the world. It received The Nobel Peace Prize in 1977 for its work. In November 1977, AI announced that it had adopted and had under investigation for future adoption the cases of eighteen prisoners in the U.S. whom it believed may have been jailed for their beliefs, origins, or involvement with unpopular political groups. The AI list currently includes the Wilmington 10, the Charlotte 3, Obadele (of the Republic of New Africa 11), Rice and Poindexter, and Tyler.

Chapter Four
The Wilmington Ten

Petitioners contend that the case known internationally as the *Wilmington Ten* is a clear and shocking example of gross violations of human rights instituted to intimidate not only these ten people but all citizens in the South who might have considered articulating opposition to racist practices.

Nine young Black men and one white woman have become known collectively as the Wilmington, N.C., Ten:

Rev. Benjamin Chavis, Jr. is the Director of the Washington, D.C. Field Office of the United Church of Christ's Commission for Racial Justice. Rev. Chavis is a graduate of the University of North Carolina in Charlotte and was in his final year of graduate studies at the Howard University School of Religion at the time of his surrender. He was a field organizer for the North Carolina-Virginia Field Office of the Commission for Racial Justice during the time of the Wilmington disturbance. He was 29 years old at the time of his incarceration in February 1976.

Reginald Epps is the oldest of nine children, was born and reared in Wilmington where he attended the New Hanover and Hoggard High Schools. At the time of the Wilmington disturbance, Mr. Epps was a junior at Hoggard. When arrested in March 1972, he had only a few weeks until graduation. While out on bail, Mr. Epps enrolled at Shaw University, where he majored in public administration. At the time of his surrender, he was in his junior year at Shaw.

Jerry Jacobs was born and reared in Wilmington where he attended Hoggard High School. At the time of the Wilmington disturbance, he was a junior and was a state tennis champion. Since graduation from high school and while out on bail, Mr. Jacobs attended Cape Fear Technical Institute in Wilmington. During his release on appeal bond, Mr. Jacobs married a local school teacher. They have a daughter.

James McKoy is a musician who plays the bass guitar and the bass clarinet. He was born in Brooklyn, New York, but moved to Wilmington at an early age. At the time of the Wilmington disturbance, Mr. McKoy, a senior at Hoggard, was the head of his own band. Following his release on bond, he studied electronics at Cape Fear Technical Institute in Wilmington.

Wayne Moore is one of eight children. He was born in New York but moved to Wilmington while still a child. At the time of the Wilmington disturbance, he was a senior at Hoggard High School. Following his release on bail, Mr. Moore entered Shaw University as a political science major. He hopes to pursue a legal career when he is released.

Marvin Patrick, a native of Wilmington, has two brothers and a sister. After being expelled from Williston High School for protest activities, he enlisted in the Army, where he served in Vietnam. Upon returning from the Army, Mr. Patrick has worked at several jobs and plans to finish high school when released.

Connie Tyndall is a native of Wilmington who was a star high school football player and a member of the glee club. At the time of the Wilmington disturbance, he was a senior at Hoggard High School. During his release on bail, Mr. Tyndall worked as a longshoreman.

Willie Earl Vereen is a musician, was a member of the Hoggard High School band and a drummer in the James McKoy band. He is a native of Wilmington and was in the tenth grade at the time of the Wilmington disturbance. While out on appeal, Mr. Vereen completed his GED and took some courses at the City College of San Francisco. He plans to pursue a career in entertainment after his release from prison.

William (Joe) Wright, a native of Wilmington, was a student leader at Hoggard High School prior to the Wilmington uprising. His arrest interrupted his studies, but he obtained his high school diploma at night school. After being released on appeal bond, Mr. Wright enrolled in Talladega College where he majored in history and pre-law until his imprisonment. Mr. Wright aided prisoners with their legal problems during his incarceration and wants to become a lawyer.

Anne Sheppard-Turner is a native of Auburn, New York, who moved to Wilmington in 1970, where she worked in a federal poverty program. Long active in civil rights matters, Ms. Turner was active in organizing Black and poor people to improve their lives and status in Wilmington. After her release on bond, Ms. Turner moved to Raleigh where she worked in a telephone answering service before her incarceration. She has three daughters.

Rev. Benjamin Chavis sent the following communication on the case of The Wilmington Ten from his cell in McCain, North Carolina, to the Belgrade Conference of the Thirty-Five Signatories to the Helsinki Final Act of 1975, in October 1977. Petitioners herein reproduce both his transmittal letter and that presentation of the facts which he prepared for that Conference as the definitive and most clearly attested version of this case whose principals have been declared Prisoners of Conscience by Amnesty International.

A. Introduction

From a torturous prison cell in the state of North Carolina I make to the world community and to the assembled conference in Belgrade, Yugoslavia, an urgent public appeal for human rights. As one of many victims, I shall not keep silent. I am compelled to speak out concerning human rights violations of the 1975 Helsinki Final Act by the United States of America.

Please permit me to state emphatically that I wish in no manner to embarrass or criticize my country unduly. I love my country. It is because I love my country that I decry publicly the domestic exploitation, persecution and imprisonment of innocent citizens for political, economic and racist motives.

No doubt I will face reprisals and retaliatory punishment for daring to write and speak these truths which are self-evident but I take the risk, accepting what may come with courage.

In the United States, the present reality for millions of Black Americans, Native American Indians, Puerto Ricans, Chicanos, Asian Americans and other oppressed national minorities is that the violations of fundamental human rights and freedoms are commonplace. We constitute the so-called "underclass"—the exploited and oppressed class. We are the victims of racism and monopoly economic exploitation. And, yes, we are the victims of governmental repression. The victimization is evident in our national poverty, high unemployment and unjust imprisonment.

Notwithstanding the rhetorical eloquence of President Jimmy Carter's foreign policy and of his human rights campaign directed abroad, inside our country the oppressed national minorities are confronted with the contradiction of continued racial discrimination, injustice, and inequality before the law. Here, equal justice under the law is prescribed only for the corporate rich and powerful. There are literally thousands of people imprisoned solely because of their race and poverty.

Today in the United States, in violation of the Helsinki Final Act, there are, in fact, many political "prisoners of conscience."

Therefore, I make this public appeal for human rights, in general, on behalf of the millions of oppressed in America and, in particular, on behalf of the Wilmington Ten and all other political prisoners presently incarcerated in the United States.

I send to the Belgrade Conference the details of the Wilmington Ten Case, not to present single, isolated case of human persecution, but to present our particular case as a clear factual example of the existence and continued persecution of the many "prisoners of conscience" in the nation.

In addition, I have compiled a partial list of the names of those I know to be political prisoners and/or imprisoned victims of racial injustice.

Lastly, I am issuing a brief Statement of Appeal to all freedom-loving peoples of the world. I pray that our cry for liberation, justice, human rights and peace will not fall on deaf ears.

Thank you.

In Christ's name,
Reverend Benjamin F. Chavis, Jr.
McCain, N.C. Prison
October 1977

B. The Facts of the Case

Six months after the United States "solemnly adopted" and signed the Helsinki Final Act, the United States Supreme Court in Washington, D.C. refused to hear the legal appeal of the Wilmington Ten by denying a petition for *writ of certiorari*. Without issuing a written or oral explanation for refusing to hear the appeal, the United States Supreme Court on January 19, 1976, stated merely, "*certiorari* is denied."

Despite the years-long litigation by a team of highly competent attorneys, presenting to nearly every appellate court level in the United States substantial civil rights and constitutional grounds for appellate review and relief, most courts have simply refused to hear the appeal. It should be noted that a year before the United States Supreme Court refused to hear the justice-pleas and freedom-pleas of the Wilmington Ten, the North Carolina Supreme Court likewise refused to hear the pleas for appeal.

In June 1977 at a news conference on foreign and domestic matters, the President of the United States was called on, in light of the United States' human rights campaign abroad, to comment on the unjust imprisonment of the Wilmington Ten. President Carter responded, "Well, the only comment I am free to make under our own system of Government is that I hope that justice will prevail, that the ones who are accused of the crime will be given a fair trial....This has been a matter of longstanding controversy both on the domestic scene and internationally as well....And I trust the system in its entirety....If there ever is a mistake made at a lower level in our judicial system, there's always a right to appeal....And I believe the history of our judicial system is that ultimately they make the right decision."

I, Marvin Patric, Connie Tyndall, Willie Earl Vereen, Jerry Jacobs, Anne Shephard-Turner, Reginald Epps, James McKoy, Joe Wright, and Wayne Moore are the Wilmington Ten. We are ten innocent victims of a racist and politically motivated and executed frame-up. We are not guilty of the alleged crime yet we are presently imprisoned in the State of North Carolina, sentenced to a collective total of 282 years. We are now incarcerated solely because of our past civil and human rights nonviolent protests and activities on behalf of young Black American students seeking an equal nondiscriminatory quality education. We are being punished to intimidate further and to repress the civil and human rights movement in the United States. We are in the clearest sense of the term: political prisoners of conscience.

Not only does the Wilmington Ten Case expose lack of a sincere commitment on the part of the United States to respect, ensure and protect the civil and human rights of minority citizens, but also the Wilmington Ten Case exposes the inherent institutionalized racism in the judicial system which systematically prevents equality before the law for Black Americans, Native American Indians, Puerto Ricans, Asian Americans, Chicanos and other oppressed national minorities.

Therefore, in the field of human rights and fundamental freedoms, the United States has not acted in conformity with the purposes and principles of the Charter of the United Nations, with the Universal Declaration of Human Rights and has not acted in conformity with the recently signed international covenants on human rights (the International Covenant on Civil and Political Rights and the International Covenant on Economic, Social and Cultural Rights).

Inasmuch as the courts have failed to render equal justice under the law, I have written two separate letters to President Carter appealing for his intervention and executive action to free the Wilmington Ten and all political prisoners in the United States. To date, I have not received a direct response from the President….

To enhance a fuller understanding of the enormous matrix of human rights issues evolving from the Wilmington Ten Case, I offer, in support of the appeal, the following background and chronology of events.

From 1966-1971, during the height of the Nixon Administration's repression against civil rights workers and anti-Vietnam War peace activists, many school districts in the United States were resisting the integration of Black and white students. Such was the case in Wilmington, N.C. However, through a successful civil rights suit filed by the National Association for the Advancement of Colored People (NAACP), the schools in Wilmington were forced to desegregate. Racist reactionary forces, including the Ku Klux Klan (KKK), the Rights of White People (ROWP) and other supremacist paramilitary organizations violently reacted against the orderly desegregation of the schools.

After receiving requests for assistance from local community leaders, I went to Wilmington, N.C., in February 1971, in the capacity of a community and civil rights organizer for the United Church of Christ's Commission for Racial Justice. I organized and led two nonviolent marches and demonstrations in support of the Black students' requests for fair and equal treatment in the school system.

Due to the prevailing violent threats and the intimidation of the Black community by the ROWP, the KKK and others who opposed school integration, I called on city and state officials to impose an official curfew to stop the "night riders" from terrorizing Black residents. However, the city officials of Wilmington refused to impose a curfew to avoid the increasing racial violence, and refused to protect Black citizens in their homes and churches from the bloodthirsty vigilantes roaming through and shooting up the Black community.

Gregory Congregational United Church of Christ, the focal religious worship and meeting place of the local civil rights movement, came under intense armed attack by the racist vigilantes. In the vicinity of, and within, Gregory Church, Black people were only attempting to exercise basic human rights and fundamental freedoms—including freedom of speech, freedom of religion, and freedom of conscience.

One year later, in March 1972, I, eight young Black student leaders and a vocal white woman supporter of the local civil rights movement were arrested and charged with a long series of felony offenses that had allegedly occurred in February 1971. We became known as the Wilmington Ten. From the moment of our unjust arrest to the present date, we have repeatedly and steadfastly declared our complete innocence of the charges.

While we were being held inside the New Hanover County Jail in Wilmington under a bond totaling over half-million dollars, we were viciously sprayed without provocation with tear gas and chemical mace.

In June, 1972, we were first brought to trial in Burgaw, N.C. We all entered pleas of "not guilty" to the Superior Court of Pender County. During the jury selection process, we accepted a jury composed of ten Black jurors and two white jurors. However, the state prosecutor, James T. Stroud, prevented the trial from proceeding by demanding a mistrial on the grounds that he had (conveniently) become suddenly ill. It became obvious that the state prosecutor was determined to keep the Wilmington Ten from having a fair trial before a jury composed of a majority of Black jurors.

In spite of legal objections raised by our defense attorneys, the judge granted the mistrial and thus denied the Wilmington Ten (in violation of the Constitution of the United States) the right to a fair trial before an impartial jury composed of our peers.

On September 11, 1972, we were brought to trial for a second time in Burgaw, N.C. During the jury selection process, the local state prosecutor, assisted by the North Carolina Attorney General's office, used all but one of the forty "pre-emptory challenges" to prevent in sequence thirty-nine Black jurors from being selected to serve on the jury. The presiding judge refused to take white jurors off the jury for "cause" although some admitted being members of the Ku Klux Klan.

Consequently, the Wilmington Ten went on trial before a prejudiced and hostile judge and before a jury composed of ten white jurors and two elderly Black jurors (the composition exactly the opposite of the first jury accepted by the defense). The wanton power of racist forces, acting in concert with the state judicial apparatus and its agents of racist injustice and political repression, conspired and set the stage to ensure the unjust conviction of the Wilmington Ten.

Only three state witnesses gave incriminating testimony against the Wilmington Ten at the trial. The names are Allen Hall, Jerome Mitchell, and Eric Junious. At the time of the trial, all three of these young men had previously been victimized by the vicious cycle of growing up in the United States in absolute poverty, running into trouble with the law at an early age, only to "graduate" eventually to the adult prison system, and living the life of "street" and "ghetto" survival. Hall, Mitchell and Junious were each under the detention and supervision initially of the state juvenile and later of the adult prison systems prior to their trial testimony.

The state conspiracy to silence and persecute the Wilmington Ten was planned months before our arrest. For example, in February, 1972, Allen Hall was taken by law enforcement from Lumberton, N.C., where he was incarcerated, to the Cherry Mental Hospital in Goldsboro, N.C., to meet with Jerome Mitchell who was there undergoing psychiatric observation. Hall himself had been confined there for psychiatric examination and observation in the fall of 1971. Hall and Mitchell, together, met at Cherry Hospital for several hours with J. Stroud, state prosecutor in charge of the Wilmington Ten case, local law enforcement officers, and William Walden, an agent of the Alcohol, Tobacco and

Firearms Division of the United States Treasury Department. Hall and Mitchell have testified that, at other meetings between Hall, Mitchell and Stroud, along with the other law enforcement officers plotting the frame-up, numerous attempts were made to coerce Hall and Mitchell to agree to lie against the Wilmington Ten. At the Cherry Hospital meeting Hall and Mitchell were shown photographs of each of us so that they could identify us in court. Following the meeting, Treasury Agent Walden prepared separate typewritten statements incriminating the Wilmington Ten which were later signed by Hall and Mitchell.

Eric Junious has now also publicly admitted in sworn statements that he was shown marked photographs of the Wilmington Ten and was instructed by the state prosecutor how to identify us prior to Junious's testimony in court.

The actions of the prosecution in exhibiting marked photographs of the Wilmington Ten to the state witnesses Hall, Mitchell, and Junious in order to enable them to identify us at the trial constituted an illegal, coercive and impermissibly suggestive identification procedure, in violation of our rights secured by Article I, Section 19, of the North Carolina Constitution, the due process and equal protection clause of the Fourteenth Amendment to the Constitution of the United States and Article 10 of the Universal Declaration of Human Rights.

The prosecution knew before and during the trial that the testimonies of Hall, Mitchell, and Junious were completely false, fabricated to facilitate the racist and political persecution of ten innocent civil and human rights activists. The use by the state prosecutors of testimony they knew was false denied the Wilmington Ten the rights of fair trial, due process and equal protection of the law, confrontation, cross-examination and effective assistance of counsel, in violation of Article I, Sections 19 and 23 of the Constitution of the State of North Carolina, the Sixth and Fourteenth Amendments to the Constitution of the United States and in violation of Articles 2, 7, 10, and 11 of the Universal Declaration of Human Rights.

The anfractuous frame-up of the Wilmington Ten, resulting in the unjust conviction and imprisonment for a total of 282 years for allegedly "unlawful burning" and "conspiracy to assault emergency personnel," is a classic reminder of the cases of Sacco and Vanzetti, the Scottsboro Nine, Julius and Ethel Rosenberg and Angela Davis, all of whom were prosecuted to satisfy the racist, political and repressive motives of those who subjugate, exploit and oppress.

In August, 1976, exactly one year after the United States signed the Helsinki Final Act, the facts and truth about the Wilmington Ten frame-up became publicly known throughout the nation and world. The chief state prosecution witness, Allen Hall, signed a sworn notarized statement declaring that his testimony against the Wilmington Ten in 1972 was completely false, that he had testified because of false information given to him by the state prosecutor and police officers and because he had been promised that he would be out of jail within a period of six months after he testified. It is a fact that, although Hall had received a regular twelve-year sentence in January, 1972, that sentence was unlawfully amended in October, 1972 (after Hall had lied in court against the Wilmington Ten) to make if possible for him to be eligible for immediate release. The amendment of Hall's sentence was made by Judge Marvin Blount at the instance of the state prosecutor Stroud.

In March, 1977, Hall testified before a federal grand jury in Raleigh, N.C., and again acknowledged that his testimony was false and that he had been induced to give that false testimony by the state prosecutor and by investigating officers. Hall testified that he had in fact been coached in giving his false testimony. Jerome Mitchell also appeared at that grand jury and testified that his trial testimony was false also and that he had been coached by the same persons. He had also been promised by the state prosecutor that he would be out of jail in six months. Mitchell, in a letter received by the North Carolina Parole Commission on June 10, 1974, and already notified the Commission that his testimony was false. This letter was not revealed, however, to our defense counsel until its contents appeared in the news media in April, 1977.

In January, 1977, Eric Junious stated in a sworn, notarized statement that he had been promised a job and a mini-bike motorcycle for his trial testimony against the Wilmington Ten. In 1972, at the time of his trial testimony, Junious was only thirteen years old. In April, 1977, Junious swore that his testimony at the trial was false and that he had been led to give false testimony because he had been told he would receive the mini-bike motorcycle. It should be noted that the state prosecutor,

J. Stroud, did in fact give Junious the mini-bike a month after the Wilmington Ten trial in 1972.

In May, 1977, a post-conviction hearing for the Wilmington Ten was held in the Superior Court of Pender County in Burgaw, North Carolina. The hearing lasted for two weeks (the longest post-conviction hearing in the history of North Carolina). However, we were not allowed to be present at the hearing. We were kept locked in prison cells hundreds of miles from the Pender County Courthouse.

The denial of the fundamental human right to be present at our trial-hearing is another deliberate and flagrant violation of Basket 1, Part A, Article VII of the Helsinki Final Act, Articles 2, 7, 10, and 11 of the Universal Declaration of Human Rights, and Article 14, Sections 1 and 3 of the International Covenant on Civil and Political Rights.

At the post-conviction hearing in May, 1977, Allen Hall, Jerome Mitchell, and Eric Junious all testified under oath that their trial testimony against the Wilmington Ten had been false and that they had all received promises from the prosecutor which caused them to give the false testimony.

Mitchell testified, "They told me to cooperate or I could face life in prison….they reminded me I had a brother who had just been convicted and that he also faced life in prison." Mitchell also testified that the state prosecutor J. Stroud and other law enforcement officers had kept him and Hall, during and before the Wilmington Ten trial in 1972, at a Carolina beach cottage where they were visited by a local leader of the Knights of the Ku Klux Klan, Tex Gross. The close relationship between Klan members and law enforcement officials in the Wilmington, N.C., area confirms the racist intentions of the judicial and law enforcement system at its base. A fair trial for the Wilmington Ten was (and is now) impossible in eastern North Carolina because of the close ties between the police, the courts, and the Ku Klux Klan. White robes are worn during the night at "cross-burnings"; in day time black robes are worn at judicial-lynchings in the county courthouses.

Allen Hall testified at the hearing, "I agreed to lie against the Wilmington Ten because J. Stroud said that he could get me out of prison in six months." Hall stated that U.S. Treasury Agent Walden and Wilmington detectives Ken Hooks, McQueen, and Robinson assisted Stroud in encouraging him to testify against the Wilmington Ten.

Eric Junious testified at the hearing, "I lied because Mr. Stroud asked me what I wanted for Christmas and I said a mini-bike.... Detective Brown showed me pictures of Chavis and another and so on....I knew what they wanted me to say and I knew I'd get a mini-bike...that's how they got me."

On May 12, 1977, the Reverend Eugene Templeton and his wife, Donna, testified at the post-conviction hearing in the Pender County Superior Court that I, Marvin Patrick, Connie Tindall and James McKoy were actually inside their home in Wilmington at the time Mike's Grocery Store burned in February, 1971. (The prosecution had accused the Wilmington Ten of burning the store.)

In 1971, Rev. Templeton was the pastor of Gregory Congregational United Church of Christ. At the May, 1977, post-conviction hearing Rev. Templeton testified that he had asked United Church of Christ officials to send me to Wilmington to help organize the local civil rights movement, particularly in regard to the rights of Black students struggling against racism in the school system.

The Assistant North Carolina Attorney General, Al Cole, cross-examined Rev. Templeton by asking, "Why didn't you just tell them all to leave?" (Mr. Cole was referring to the people in the church during the violence: the students, their parents and church members.) Rev. Templeton replied, "The feeling in the Black community at that time was they would not be intimidated by radical conservative whites....it seemed at the time necessary to stay and defend the right to assemble."

Mrs. Donna Templeton testified, "After the church received bomb threats, whites in pickup trucks, members of the Klan, began riding by and shooting at the church and our home....I was shot at twice."

John and Stephanie Green both testified at the post-conviction hearing that Wayne Moore could not have been at Mike's Grocery Store the night it burned because Wayne was at their house at the time.

Mrs. Slayton testified that Joe Wright could not have been at Mike's Grocery Store at the time it burned because Joe was at her house at the time.

When our chief defense counsel, James Ferguson, attempted to question the chief state prosecutor, J. Stroud, about the illegal coercion of state's witnesses Hall, Mitchell, and Junious, Mr. Stroud repeatedly responded, at the post-conviction hearing, "I do not recall."

In the face of all the state's major witnesses having recanted their testimony and alibi witnesses having testified that members of the Wilmington Ten were not at the scene of the alleged crime, at the conclusion of the post-conviction hearing, Superior Court Judge George Fountain refused to grant the Wilmington Ten a new trial. On May 20, 1977, Judge Fountain ruled, "I find no violations of constitutional rights." Thus, the conspiracy to persecute, deny basic human rights, and to silence the Wilmington Ten continues unabated….

Although I have highlighted only some of the events concerning the Wilmington Ten, the preceding chronology should indicate adequately and exemplify how it is possible in the United States for political prisoners of conscience to languish in prison for many years.

Basket I, Part A, Article II of the Helsinki Final Act states, "In the field of human rights and fundamental freedoms, the participating States will…fulfill their obligations as set forth in the international declarations and agreements in this field, including inter alia the International Covenants on Human Rights, by which they may be bound."

One of the primary contentions of this appeal is that the United States has violated not only the human rights clauses of the Helsinki Final Act but is presently violating Articles 2, 7 and 10 of the International Covenant on Civil and Political Rights (which President Carter signed recently).

> *Article 2, Section 1 of the International Covenant on Civil and Political Rights* states:
>
> "Each State Party to the present Covenant undertakes to respect and to ensure to all individuals within its territory and subject to its jurisdiction the rights recognized in the present Covenant, without distinction of any kind, such as race, colour, sex, language, religion, political or other opinion, national or social origin, property, birth or other status."
>
> *Article 2, Section 3 of the International Covenant on Civil and Political Rights* states:
>
> "Each State Party to the present Covenant undertakes: (a) To ensure that any person whose rights or freedoms are herein recognized are violated shall have an effective remedy, notwithstanding that the violation has been committed by persons acting in an official capacity; (b) To ensure than any person

claiming such a remedy shall have his right thereto determined by competent judicial, administrative, or legislative authorities, or by any other competent authority provided for by the legal system of the State, and to develop the possibilities of judicial remedy; (c) To ensure that the competent authorities shall enforce such remedies when granted."

In violation of the preceding two Sections of Article 2 of the International Covenant on Civil and Political Rights, there is in the United States *no effective remedy or procedure* to rectify the denial of fundamental political, civil and human rights of political prisoners of conscience and of imprisoned victims of racial injustice and judicial abuse. While we do have, as President Carter has stated in reference to the Wilmington Ten, "the right to appeal," we do not enjoy the privilege or have "the right to be heard." Appealing a violation of rights to an appellate court that refuses "to hear" the appeal is an exercise in futility. Most appellate courts in the United States only "hear" appeals of cases selected at the court's discretion. (The Wilmington Ten case has been on appeal for the last five years to no avail.)

Article 7 of the International Covenant on Civil and Political Rights states:

"No one shall be subjected to torture or to cruel, inhuman or degrading treatment or punishment. In particular, no one shall be subjected without the free consent to medical or scientific experimentation."

Article 10, Section 1 of the International Covenant on Civil and Political Rights states:

"All persons deprived of their liberty shall be treated with humanity and with respect for the inherent dignity of the human person."

Article 10, Section 3 of the International Covenant on Civil and Political Rights states:

"The penitentiary system shall comprise treatment of prisoners, the essential aim of which shall be their reformation and social rehabilitation. Juvenile offenders shall be segregated from adults and be accorded treatment appropriate to their age and legal status."

In violation of Article 7 and the two preceding Sections of Article 10 of the International Covenant on Civil and Political Rights, in the

United States there is cruel, inhuman and degrading treatment of the hundreds of thousands of men, women, and children held inside state and federal prisons, jails, and detention facilities.

The American penitentiary system's essential aim is punishment, not "reformation" and "social rehabilitation." I personally have seen, inside the prisons, the physical brutality of many inmates by prison officers. I have seen prisoners who were forced to submit to electric-shock treatment on their brains. I have seen prisoners "watered down" in their cells with a two-hundred-pound pressure water hose by prison officers. And I have seen elderly prisoners made to slave in plantation fields until their limbs gave out (often resulting in amputation of their legs).

On March 18, 1976, at Caledonia State Prison, as punishment for reading the Bible to fellow prisoners and speaking to them about prisoners' human rights, I was put into leg irons and chains, lifted up and placed on the back of a prison truck and transferred two hundred miles to McCain State Prison. At McCain Prison, for three months prison officials refused to let me touch my children and family when the would come to visit.

In May, 1976, because of the cruel and inhuman treatment I went on a one hundred thirty-one day "fast" and hunger strike to protest the unjust treatment and imprisonment of the Wilmington Ten and to protest the feculent conditions of the prison system.

Today, even as I write to appeal for human rights, I am only allowed to wear grey-colored, "gun clothes" uniforms. According to prison officials, "gun clothes" signify that if I were to try to go over the barbed wire fence to gain my freedom, I would be shot to death by prison guards using double barrel 12-guage shotguns with number 4 buckshot.

In summary, the struggle to free the Wilmington Ten continues. Since we are political prisoners of conscience, our fate shall not be determined by courts but by the will of the people. It is my sincere hope and prayer that the United States will acknowledge the moral necessity, and the injunction of the Helsinki mandate, for launching an honest human rights campaign at home.

I must point out that the persecution of the Wilmington Ten is clearly symptomatic of the continuing struggle of all of the oppressed national minorities in the United States struggling for justice, human rights and liberation from American racism and monopoly exploitation….

We shall overcome.

In Christ's name,
Rev. Benjamin F. Chavis, Jr.
McCain N. C., Prison
October, 1977

A few weeks after Judge Fountain's adverse decision, James Ferguson, Ben Chavis' attorney, formally petitioned North Carolina Governor James Hunt for pardons of innocence for the Wilmington Ten. Attorney General Griffin Bell, at the request of sixty members of Congress, urged Hunt to seriously consider the pardon request.[1]

In spite of significant domestic and international pressure and support for the release of the Wilmington Ten, who were declared prisoners of conscience by Amnesty International, Governor Hunt refused to pardon them. Instead, in January 1978, Hunt reduced their prison terms from a total of 282 years to 224 years, as a sop to these widespread protests.

In June 1978, Reverend Chavis' life was jeopardized by the North Carolina prison authorities who refused to secure proper medical treatment for him when he complained about symptoms that proved to be an acute appendicitis. Prison officials, having rejected medical advice to hospitalize Rev. Chavis at a nearby civilian hospital, strapped him down in a van and drove him 75 miles to a prison hospital, where after much delay and physical suffering, he was operated upon. His recovery was extended and complicated because of the peritonitis which resulted from the prison system's treatment of him. The Wilmington Ten, with the exception of Rev. Ben Chavis, became eligible for parole in 1978. To date, nine members of the Wilmington Ten have been paroled, in an effort to lessen public pressure; but any remedy short of public repudiation of the convictions will continue to compound these egregious violations of their human and constitutional rights and fundamental freedoms.[2] Nothing can restore the years lost to them or compensate for their suffering.

The widely held belief in the injustice of the conviction and imprisonment of the Wilmington Ten and the broad base of support for their freedom is demonstrated by the thousands who signed an open letter to President Carter requesting his intervention. The letter to President Carter, dated September 6, 1978, and a selected list of the signators, which was in Appendix I of the original Petition, follows below. Also included here is the last of three letters that Rev. Chavis sent to President Carter; all three letters (March 4, 1977; May 28, 1977 and March 16, 1978) were contained in Appendix I of the original Petition.

LETTER TO PRESIDENT CARTER SHOWING WIDESPREAD SUPPORT FOR WILMINGTON TEN.

6 September 1978

Dear Mr. President:

We are writing to respectfully request an appointment with you to discuss a matter of the greatest urgency, the continued incarceration of the civil rights workers known as "the Wilmington 10."

As you know, on February 1, 1976, the Reverend Benjamin F. Chavis, Jr., and nine co-workers entered North Carolina prisons. They were sentenced for a combined 282 years on alleged arson and conspiracy charges, growing out of their efforts for equal education on behalf of the Black community of the town of Wilmington. (The facts of the case are by now well known to millions around the world and it would be presumptuous to restate them for you who, we are sure, are already familiar with them).

A year after the defendants' incarceration, you came into office, speaking of a new direction for our country, and a criminal justice system with the emphasis on "justice." We were therefore heartened with your pronouncements, upon assuming office, that support for human rights would be a hallmark of your Presidency. That was nearly a year and a half ago.

Since then, every prosecution witness against the Wilmington 10 has recanted the trial testimony, telling both the state courts and a federal grand jury that their testimony had been induced by threats and bribery by state and federal officials. In addition, other witnesses have come forward who were at time of trial intimidated by an atmosphere of terror, to say that the defendants were with them in their homes at the time of the alleged arson. These facts, together with defense allegations of some 2,600 trial errors constitute the basis of appeals which have been sitting in federal district court for 29 months without action. In addition, the Justice Department has told the public for 14 months that it is investigating the matter. Meanwhile, precious years of dedicated young lives are being lost, not to mention the terrible suffering endured by their devoted families.

The Governor of North Carolina has abdicated his responsibility in the matter, the federal district court has declined to act in the case for more than two years, the Justice Department appears to be bogged down in its investigation. To this day, we have heard nothing from your office in support of the human rights of Rev. Chavis and his co-defendants. It is well and good to speak to the human rights of those in other lands but attention must be paid at least equally to those who suffer deprivation of those same rights in our own country. We now appeal to you to bring the moral weight of your office to bear to secure justice in this most important case.

Scores of newspapers have editorialized for pardons or at least a new trial for the defendants. They have been joined in these appeals by virtually every major Protestant denomination, a number of important trade unions, more than a dozen city councils and the entire range of civil rights leadership in our country. Around the world, heads of state, members of parliaments, prestigious international human rights organizations and church bodies have demonstrated such concern for the Wilmington 10 that a spokesman for the State Department has described the case as "an embarrassment."

It is now past time to end that embarrassment. We ask you to speak out for the human rights of the Wilmington 10 as you have done for those you have felt were persecuted in other lands. To use these persuasive powers would not violate any principles of federalism. We call upon you to urge a speedy conclusion, with a firm deadline set, of the Justice Department investigation. We also ask that the Justice Department submit an *amicus curiae* brief in support of the defendants.

Finally, we eagerly await your response to our request that a representative delegation from our numbers be given an appointment in your busy schedule to discuss this most urgent matter with you.

Respectfully,

(The following pages, from Appendix 1 of the original Petition, list the signers to this letter to Pres. Carter.)

UNITED STATES HOUSE OF REPRESENTATIVES

Hon. Joseph Addabbo, NY
Hon. Les Aucoin, OR
Hon. Berkley Bedell, IA
Hon. Jonathan Bingham, NY
Hon. David Bonoir, MI
Hon. William Brodhead, MI
Hon. George Brown, Jr., CA
Hon. John Buchanan, AL
Hon. Yvonne Brathwaite Burke, CA
Hon. John Burton, CA
Hon. Phillip Burton, CA
Hon. Shirley Chisholm, NY
Hon. William Clay, MO
Hon. Cardiss Collins, IL
Hon. John Conyers, MI
Hon. William Cotter, CT
Hon. Ronald Dellums, CA
Hon. Charles Diggs, Jr., MI
Hon. Christopher Dodd, CT
Hon. Robert Drinan, MA
Hon. Don Edwards, CA
Hon. Robert Edgar, PA
Hon. Walter Fauntroy, DC
Hon. Millicent Fenwick, NJ
Hon. Harold Ford, TN
Hon. Donald Fraser, MN
Hon. Robert Garcia, NY
Hon. Michael Harrington, MA
Hon. Augustus Hawkins, CA
Hon. Henry Haxman, CA
Hon. Ted Heiss, NY
Hon. Elizabeth Holtzman, NY
Hon. James Howard, NJ
Hon. Andrew Jacobs, IN
Hon. Barbara Jordan, TX
Hon. Robert Kastenmeier, WI
Hon. Robert Leggett, CA
Hon. William Lehman, FL
Hon. Paul McCloskey, Jr., CA
Hon. Stewart McKinney, CT
Hon. Ralph Metcalfe, IL
Hon. George Miller, CA
Hon. Norman Minetta, CA
Hon. Parren Mitchell, MD
Hon. Robert Nix, PA
Hon. Richard Nolan, MN
Hon. Lester Nolff, NY
Hon. James Oberstar, MN
Hon. Richard Ottinger, NY
Hon. Jerry Patterson, CA
Hon. Charles Rangel, NyY
Hon. Henry Reuss, WI
Hon. Frederick Richmond, NY
Hon. Benjamin Rosenthal, NY
Hon. Edward Roybal, CA
Hon. Leo Ryan, CA
Hon. Patricia Schroeder, CO
Hon. John Seiberling, OH
Hon. Stephen Solarz, NY
Hon. Fortney Stark, CA
Hon. Gerry Studds, MA
Hon. Louis Stokes, OH
Hon. Frank Thompson, Jr., NJ
Hon. Paul Tsongas, MA
Hon. Lionel Van Deerlim, CA
Hon. Henry Waxman, CA
Hon. James Weaver, OR
Hon. Lester Wolff, NY
Hon. Ted Weiss, NY

TRADE UNIONISTS

William Andrews, President, United Steel Workers of America, Local 1010

Stanley A. Aslanian, President, Graphic Arts International Union, Local 1-P

Charles W. Barton, Amalgamated Meatcutters and Butcher Workman of North America, Local P500

Willie H. Bell, Vice President, District Council 1, United Electrical, Radio and Machinists Workers,

Moe Biller, President, New York Metro Area Postal Union

Boris H. Block, Secretary-Treasurer, United Electrical, Radio and Machinists Workers

Warren Bunn, Assistant Director, Oil, Chemical and Atomic Workers, District 8, AFL-CIO

Sydney Bykofsky, Co-Manager, Amalgamated Clothing and Textile Workers Union, Local 166

Alzada F. Clark, Second Vice President, Coalition of Black Trade Unionists, United Furniture Workers

Marion T. Calligaris, Co-Chair, Trade Unionists for Action and Democracy

John Chico, United Steel Workers of America, Local 65

Leroy Clark, United Furniture Workers of America

Richard A. Days, Vice President, United Auto Workers, Local 259

C.L. Dellums, International President, Brotherhood of Sleeping Car Porters

Steve D'inzillo, Business Agent, Motion Picture Machine Operators, IATSE, Local 306

Henry B. Epstein United Public Workers, American Federation of State, County and Municipal Employees, Local 646

Abe Feinglass, International Vice President, Amalgamated Meatcutters and Butcher Workmen of North America

Willie W. Felder, International Representative, United Auto Workers

Harold Fisher, American Federation of Teachers, AFL-CIO, Local 6

Charles B. Folks, President International Union of Electrical Workers, AFL-CIO, Local 431

Henry Foner, President, Fur, Leather and Machine Workers Joint Board

Moe Foner, Executive Secretary, National Union of Hospital and Health Care Employees

Patrick E. Gorman, Board Chairman, Amalgamated Meatcutters and Butcher Workmen of North America

Leon Hall, Amalgamated Clothing and Textile Workers Union

Hilton E. Hanna, Vice President Emeritus, Executive Assistant, Amalgamated Meatcutters and Butcher Workmen of North America

Charles Hayes, International Vice President, Amalgamated Meatcutters and Butcher Workmen of North America

Howard M. Horn, Business Agent, Provision Salesmen and Distributors Union, Local 627

Paul S. Kaczocha, President, United Steel Workers of America, Local 6787

Nathan Katz, President, Leather Goods, Plastics, Handbags and Novelty Workers Union

Roy Arnold Keith, Stearns Striker

Charles Klare, Brewery and Soft Drink Workers, BT

Eddie Lapa, Vice President, International Longshore Workers, Union, Local 142

Ellen Lavroff, Colorado Federation of Teachers

Peggy Lipschutz, Actors Equity

William Lucy, Secretary—Treasurer, American Federation of State, County and Municipal Employees

Julius Margolin, New York City Central Labor Council

Thomas Martinez, National Maritime Union

Thomas F. Miechur, President, United Cement, Lime and Gypsum Workers International Union

Phillip H. Nezart, Executive Council, Coalition of Black Trade Unionists, Teamsters Local 988

William H. Nuchow, Secretary-Treasurer, International Brotherhood of Teamsters, Local 840

Gilbert B. Podolner, United Auto Workers, Local 719

Jordan Pola, Secretary-Treasurer, Restaurant Employees Union

Jesse Prosten, Vice President, Amalgamated Meatcutters and Butcher Workmen of North America

Bruce Raynor, Education Director, Amalgamated Clothing and Textile Workers Union

Bettye W. Roberts, President, District Council 1707

Cleveland Robinson, Secretary-Treasurer, Distributive Workers of America

Max Roffman, Retirees Committee, United Public Workers American Federation of State, County and Municipal Employees, Local 646

Ray Rogers, Corporation Campaign Manager, Amalgamated Clothing and Textile Workers Union

Frank Rosen, President, United Electrical, Radio and Machine Workers, District Council 11

Max Roth, Secretary-Treasurer, Los Angeles Leather, Luggage, and Handbag Workers Union, Local 213

Norman C. Roth, Trade Unionists for Action and Democracy

Harold L. Shapiro, President, Furriers Joint Council of New York City
Horace Sheffield, President, Detroit Coalition of Black Trade Unionists
William H. Simons, Treasurer, Coalition of Black Trade Unionists
Robert Simpson, Corresponding Secretary, Coalition of Black Trade Unionists
Laurie Slavin, President, American Federation of Government Employees, AFL-CIO, Local 2667
Jacqueline E. Storey, Equal Opportunity Employment Committee, American Federation of Government Employees, AFL~CIO, Local 2667
Leon Sverdlove, President, International Jewelry Workers Union, AFL-CIO
Brian T. Tamamoto, Hawaii State Federation of Labor, AFL-CIO
Joseph Tarantola, President, International Jewelry Workers Union, Local 1
Eleanor Tilson, Vice President, United Storeworkers Union, AFL-CIO
Edward Todd, Amalgamated Clothing and Textile Workers Union
Doris Turner, Vice President, District 1199, National Union of Hospital and Health Care Employees
Barbara P. Van Blake, American Federation of Teachers
Larry Wahl, President, United Electrical, Radio and Machine Workers, Local 1111
Samuel Williams, President, Allied Service Workers, Local P80
Clifford Wilson, President, Coalition of Black Trade Unionists
Robert H. Wilson, Butchers, Food Handlers and Allied Workers of Greater NY and NJ, Local 174
Addie Wyatt, Human Rights Director Amalgamated Meatcutters and Butcher Workmen of North America

CLERGY

Nora Adelman, Third Unitarian Church
Samuel S. Ailey, Chairperson, North Carolina Council of Churches
James V. Albertini, Catholic Action of Hawaii
Bob Alpern, Unitarian-Universalist Association
Rev. David T. Anderson, Mediator Lutheran Church
B. Tartt Bell, American Friends Service Committee
Rev. Van S. Bird, Episcopal Diocese of Pennsylvania
Rev. Charles L. Briem, Association Conference Minister, Iowa Conference United Church of Christ
Rev. Charles Briody, Unitarian Church, Chile Legislative Center
Rev. Arie R. Brouwer, Reformed Church in America
Rev. John P. Brown, Executive Director, Northern California Ecumenical Council
Frank Chapman, Field Secretary, American Friends Service Committee

Dr. Charles Cobb, Executive Director, Commission for Racial Justice, United Church of Christ
Milton M. Cohen, Jewish Council on Urban Affairs
Dr. Jerome Cooper, National Caucus, Black Presbyterians United, U.S.A.
Sister Carol Coston, 0P, Network
Calvin C. Craig, General Baptist State Convention of North Carolina Churches
A.C. Cuppy, *Christian Church Commission
Robert L. Diwitt, Witness Magazine, Episcopal Church
Jim Eller, Unitarian-Universalist Association
Rev. Fred Eyster, National Farm Workers Ministry
Rev. Dewey Fagerburn, Greater Cleveland Interchurch Council
Rev. W.W. Finlator
Rev. Robert Froeschmer, St. John's United Church of Christ
Rev. David Garcia, St. Mark's Church-in-the-Bowery
Rev. John Gugel
Reginald Harris, Bibleway Evangelistic Church
Dr. Donald Jacobs, Greater Cleveland Interchurch Council
Rev. Arthur B. Jellis, Unitarian Society of Germantown
Stanley E. Kain, Executive Director, Hawaii Council of Churches
Rev. Onaje Kazana, Temple of the Black Messiah
Julian J. Keiser, Community Religious Conference of Southern California
Mrs. Donneter E. Lane, San Francisco Council of Churches
J. M. Lawson, Holman United Methodist Church
Ian Y. Lind, American Friends Service Committee
Rev. Robert C. Loveless, Oahu Association, United Church of Christ
C. Gresham Marmion, *Retired Bishop, Diocese of Kentucky
Rev. Paul Mayer, New York Theological Seminary Mobilization for Survival
Rev. Jonas Miller, Bethesda Mennonite Church
Rev. Onaje Mpandaji, Temple of the Black Messiah
Sister Annette Mulry, Office of Social Concerns, Maryknoll Sisters
Mr. George Outen, Board of Church and Society, United Methodist Church
Mary Jane Patterson, Washington Office, United Presbyterian Church
Frederick J. Perella, Jr., Office of Urban Affairs, Archdiocese of Hartford, Roman Catholic Church
Ruby Rhoades, Church of the Brethren
Rev. Del Rupiper, Catholic Church Mobilization for Survival
Rev. Al Sampson, Fernwood United Methodist Church.
Louis W. Schneider, American Friends Service Committee

Bebe Simon, Third Unitarian Church
Rev. William D. Stickney, St. Peter's Episcopal Church
James R. Stormes, Jesuit Social Ministries
Rev. Thomas W. Strieter, Grace Lutheran Church
Edward F. Snyder, Friends Committee on National Legislation
Rev. James Thcmas, Calvin Memorial Presbyterian Church
Dr. Wyatt Tee Walker, Canaan Baptist Church of Christ
Rev. Tony Watkins, Church of the Living God (CWFF)
Rev. Donald H. Wheat. Third Unitarian Church
Dr. F. B. Williams, Church of the Intercession

*For Identification Only

ARTISTS AND INDIVIDUALS

Edward Albee, Playwright
Dr. Herbert Aptheker, American Institute for Marxist Studies
Edward Asner, Actor
James Baldwin, Author
David Baltimore, Nobel Laureate
Harry Belafonte, Actor
St. Clair Bourne, The Chamba Organization
Kevin Brophy, MGM studios
Hon. Margaret Burnham, Boston Judge
Mary E. Charlson, M.D.
Noam Chomsky, Professor, Massachusetts Institute of Technology
Ramsey Clark, Attorney, Clark, Wulf & Levine
John Bolt Culbertson, Attorney
Sarah Cunningham, Actress
Ossie Davis, Author, actor
Ruby Dcc, Actress
Mike Farrell, Actor, 'MASH', 20th Century Fox
Bernard P. Gray, CA-FAM III, Miya Gallery
Prof. Ewart Guinier, Harvard University
R. David Hall, Washington, D.C. Street Academy
Carroll Hollister, Musician
Nat Hentoff, Writer, music critic
James Hillman, Unified Industries, Inc.
Vernon Jarrett, Reporter, Chicago Tribune

Lyman T. Johnson
Prof. Donald Kalish, University of California at Los Angeles
Thomas Kilgore, Jr., Chairman, Board of Trustees, Morehouse College
Betty Lee, Editor, Proud Magazine
Edward Lewis, Edward Lewis Productions
Dr. Richard A. Lobban, Jr., *Associate Professor of Anthropology and African Studies, RI College
Jamal Long, Black Theology Center
Sidney Lumet, Warner Brothers
Norman Mailer, Author
Arthur Miller, Author
Hon. Claudia Morcum, Detroit Judge
Toni Morrison, Author, editor
Leora Mosston, Center for Legal Education, City College of New York
Madeline W. Murphy, Columnist, Afro-American newspaper
Gil Noble, WABC-TV
William L. Patterson
Atty. Jerry Paul, Executive Board, National Alliance Against Racist and Political Repression
Brock Peters, Actor, Producer
Hamilton Pitt, Jr., Instructor, Political Science, Malcolm X. College
Tony Randall, Actor
John Randolph, Actor
Beatrice Rippy, Concert singer
Jerome Robbins, Director, choreographer
Dr. Calvin W. Rolark, Publisher, Black Media Inc.
Pete Seeger, Folk singer
Dr. Benjamin Spock, Physician, author
Chuck Stone Philadelphia Daily News
Charles E. Tate, Vice President, Booker T. Washington Foundation
Prof. Ronald Walter, African Heritage Studies Association
James D. Watson, Nobel Laureate, Cold Springs Harbour Laboratory
Melvin L. Wulf, Attorney, Clark. Wulf & Levine
Isaac Zafrani, President, Harbor Lumber Company, Inc.

*For Identification Only

POLITICAL ACTIVISTS

Walter Albertson, California Democratic Council
Bob Christian, Democratic Committeeman, Gravois Township
Angela Y. Davis, Communist Party U.S.A.
David Fontaine, Sacramento Area Black Caucus
Raymond Garrison, North Philadelphia Political Action Group
Ruth B. Harper, North Central Women's Political Caucus
David Randall Luce, 25th Assembly District Unit, Democratic Party of Wisconsin

WOMEN'S ORGANIZATIONS

Vinie Burrows, Actress, Women for Racial and Economic Equality
Frieda Cohen, President, Emma Lazarus Clubs
Merrie M. Felder, Women's International League for Peace and Freedom
Jean Harnish, Women's International League for Peace and Freedom
Joesetta Lawus, President, Women for Racial and Economic Equality
Pamela McAllister, Chair, Honolulu Branch, Women's International League for Peace and Freedom
Melve L. Mueller, Executive Director, Women's International League for Peace and Freedom
Sarah Shuldiner, Chair, Women's International League for Peace and Freedom
Eldora Spiegelberg, President, Women's International League for Peace and Freedom
Edith Villastrigo, Women Strike for Peace

REGIONAL AND NATIONAL ORGANIZATIONS

Wale Amusa, President, Nigerian Students Union, St. Louis, Mo. Branch
Vernon M. Bahlinger, Los Angeles Chapter, National Association of Social Workers
Black Student Association, Executive Board, Southern Illinois University
Mildred Cater Bradhorn, Zeta Phi Beta Sorority, Inc.
Adjoa Burrow, President, National Association of Black Social Workers
Tommy Chung, National Asian Pacific Substance Abuse Network
Charles E. Daye, President, North Carolina Black Lawyers Association
James M. Evans, Jr., National Association of Social Workers
Leroy S. Gaillano, National Association of Minority Contractors
Dr. Thomas Hart, Omega Psi Phi Fraternity
Lydia A. Hill, National Association of Minority, CPA Firms
Janice G. Kissner, Zeta Beta Sorority, Inc.
Rev. A.J. McKnight, President, Southern Cooperative Development Fund
Pluria W. Marshall, Chairman, National Black Media Coalition

Jeffrey W. Matthew, Esq., Barristers Association of Philadelphia
Earl A. Morris, Executive Secretary, Kappa Alpha Psi Fraternity
Vicki Otten, Americans for Democratic Action
Gregory N. Paneologos, President, Connecticut Chapter of National Association Of Social Workers
Kirkpatrick Sale, Vice President, PEN American Center
Stephen P. Thaman, Alameda County Public Defenders Association
Frank X. Viggiano, President, U.S. National Student Association
Cenie J. Williams, Jr., President, National Association of Black Social Workers

STATE LEGISLATORS

Hon. Paul Carpenter, California State Senate
Hon. Bill Green, 29th District, California State Senate
Hon. Teresa P. Hughes, California State Assembly
Hon. Herschel Rosenthal, California State Assembly
Hon. Alan Sieroty, California State Senate
Hon. Maxine Waters, California State Assembly
Hon. Chet Hray, California State Assembly
Hon. Henry E. Parker, Treasurer, State of Connecticut
Hon. Julian Bond, Georgia State Senate
Hon. Anson Chong, Hawaii State Senate
Hon. Jean King, Hawaii State Senate
Hon. Georgia M. Powers, Kentucky State Senate
Hon. Aubrey Williams, *Kentucky State Assembly,
Hon. Estella B. Diggs, New York State Assembly
Hon. Arthur O. Eve, Deputy Majority Leader, New York State Assembly
Hon. Thomas R. Fortune, New York State Assembly
Hon. Richard N. Gottfried, New York State Senate
Hon. Carl McCall, New York State Senate
Hon. Jerrold Nadler, New York State Assembly
Hon. Jose E. Serrano, South Bronx, New York State Assembly
Hon. Stanley Steingut, New York State Assembly
Hon. Albert Vann, New York State Assembly
Hon. John White, Jr., Pennsylvania State Assembly

*For Identification Only

MAYORS

Hon. Tom Bradley, Mayor, Los Angeles, CA

Hon. Charles Evers, Mayor, Fayette, MS

Hon. Richard Hatcher, Mayor, Gary, IN

Hon. Basil Patterson, Deputy Mayor, New York, NY

Hon. Paul Soglin, *Mayor, Madison, WI

Hon. Lionel J. Wilson, Mayor, Oakland; CA

*For Identification Only

HUMAN RIGHTS

Rev. Ralph David Abernathy, Southern Christian Leadership Conference

Bernida Amerson, Roots Activity Learning Center

Rev. James E. Barnett, People United for Justice

Henry B. Dotson. Jr., National Association for the Advancement of Colored People

Heeley Epstein, Freedom of Residence

John G. Gloster, Opportunity Funding Corporation

Dr. Carlton B. Goodlett, President, National Black United Fund

Lennox Hinds, Esq., Director, National Conference of Black Lawyers

Carl Holman, National Urban Coalition

Benjamin Hooks, Executive Director, National Association for the Advancement of Colored People

Wilhelm H. Joseph, North Mississippi Rural Legal Services

Charisse R. Lillie-Andrews, National Conference of Black Lawyers

Dr. Joseph E. Lowery, President, The Southern Christian Leadership Conference

Enola McMillan, Baltimore Branch of the National Association for the Advancement of Colored People

Charlene Mitchell, Executive Secretary, National Alliance Against Racist and Political Repression

Reinhard Muhr, Director, American Civil Liberties Union of Hawaii

Norma D. Murphy, Secrctary, Philadelphia Chapter, National Conference of Black Lawyers

Suzy Post, *National Board, American Civil Liberties Union

Yvonne Price, Leadership Conference on Civil Rights

Joseph L. Rauh, Jr., Council, Leadership Conference on Civil Rights, Americans for Democratic Action

William Schnapp, Esq., Chairman, Washington D.C. National Lawyers Guild

Rev. Bennett W. Smith, Sr., National Board, Operation PUSH

Lynn S. Spradley, Black American Law Students Association, Georgetown University Law Center

Doris E. Strieter, Chicago Committee to Save Lives in Chile

Laverne Tong, President, Hawaii Association of Asian and Pacific Peoples

George E. Williams, Save the Children

Kathy Wilsey, Citizens Commission on Human Rights

*For Identification Only

SOCIAL AND ECONOMIC JUSTICE

Asekia T. Bey, Neighbors United

Anne Braden, Co-chair, Southern Organizing Committee for Social and Economic Justice

Brad Castlebury, Coordinator, Kentucky Coalition Against the Death Penalty

Bobby Cheeks, Baltimore Welfare Rights Organization

Ron Clark, RAP, Inc.

David Cortright, Friends Committee on National Legislation

Ron Freund, Clergy and Laity Concerned

Jomarie Griesgraber, Executive Director, SANE

Morton Halperin, Campaign to Stop Government Spying

Robert J. Haberman, President, Metro Omaha Peace Association

Esther Herst, National Committee Against Repressive Legislation

Brenda Maisha Jefferson Jackson, Tenant Action Group

Kentucky Prisoners Support Committee

Michael Kroll, National Moratorium on Prison Construction

Sylvia Kushner, Chicago Peace Council

Sarah Luria, Gray Panthers of Philadelphia

Christine Marwick, Centre for National Security Studies

Maxine Maye, National Black Parents Organization

Audrey A. Myers, National Committee to Support the Marion Brothers

Rose Paull, South Jersey Coalition to Defend the Bill 047 Rights

Bill Pennington, Illinois Prisoners Organization

Mayant Phillip, St. Louis Moratorium Committee

Mary Alice Rankin, Illinois Coalition Against the Death Penalty

Rachel Rosen, Chicago Committee to Defend the Bill of Rights

John E. Schleh, Teen Haven

Phillip Shinnick, Sports for the People, Sports Studies, Rutgers University

Walter Simpson, Coordinator, Western New York Peace Center

John S. Smith, Des Moines Area Justice and Peace Center
Robert T. Yeager, Clinton County Legal Aid
Richard Ziegler, Micronesia Support Committee

President Jimmy Carter
The White House
Washington, D.C. 20500

Dear Mr. President:

I pray that you will take time to read thoroughly this letter because the issue of human rights violations here inside the United States of America should be of a priority to you in light of your recent statements concerning alleged violations of human rights abroad.

I write to you with the utmost respect and sincerity, and I trust you will receive this letter in the spirit of equal justice and freedom for all people.

It has been exactly one full year since my first letter to you about the national disgrace and injustice of the Wilmington Ten and other "political prisoners of conscience" imprisoned in the nation. And I might add that this is my third letter to you appealing for action from your good office to free the Wilmington Ten, the Charlotte Three, George Merritt, Imari Obadeli and all political prisoners who have been persecuted in the United States as a result of racial and political repression through the deliberate abuse of the judicial system.

Yes, Mr. President, I am aware it may be embarrassing to admit that there are in fact political prisoners in our country. But certainly, it has become extremely hypocritical for you to remain silent about the domestic violations of human rights while proceeding to proclaim a selective foreign policy based on human rights.

Should not the protection of human rights begin at home?

Is it not proper for me to appeal directly to you? Do you not have a sworn responsibility to "preserve, protect, and defend" the civil rights of all citizens?

In regard to the Wilmington Ten, do you, as President, intend to permit the State of North Carolina to continue to violate the Constitution of the United States, the Universal Declaration of Human Rights, the International Covenant on Civil and Political Rights and the Helsinki Final Act?

At 12:00 noon on March 18, 1978 thousands of freedom-loving people will be marching to the White House asking for our freedom. Millions of justice-seeking peoples throughout the world will be watching to see if you are for real about human rights.

In the name of Jesus of Nazareth, I ask you to immediately free all political prisoners in the United States.

Respectfully,

Rev. Benjamin F. Chavis, Jr.

Rev. Benjamin F. Chavis, Jr.
March 16, 1978

Endnotes

[1] See article in *Greensboro (N.C.) Daily News*, "How Due Process Died in Wilmington, North Carolina," Stan Swoffard, 1977. See also Michael Myerson, *Nothing Could Be Finer,* International Publishers (New York) 1978.

[2] As of October 1978, the following individuals have been released on parole: Anne Sheppard Turner, Willie Vereen, James McKoy, Jerry Jacobs, Joe Wright, Wayne Moore, Reginald Epps, Connie Tyndall, and Marvin Patrick. Rev. Chavis is not *eligible* for parole until January 1980.

CHAPTER FIVE
The Charlotte Three
(Listed by Amnesty International)

Although this case has not been as widely publicized as the Wilmington Ten, it evolved in the same racially tense atmosphere in North Carolina during the 1960's described above, involves some of the same state officials, and some of the same paid government informers. The Charlotte Three are all Black men. The attested and well-documented facts of the Charlotte Three case follow.

James Earl Grant, Jr., is a native of Hartford, Connecticut, with a doctorate in chemistry from Penn State University. He came to Charlotte, North Carolina, as a VISTA worker in 1968 and later worked for the Southern Christian Leadership Conference and the Southern Conference Education Fund, both civil rights groups.

Thomas James (T.J.) Reddy, a native of Savannah, Georgia, is a writer whose books of poetry have been published by Random House. He attended Johnson C. Smith University and later transferred to the University of North Carolina at Charlotte, where he helped organize a Black student union. He graduated from UNCC in 1972.

Charles Parker, of Osierfield, Georgia, attended Johnson C. Smith University and University of North Carolina at Charlotte, where he majored in business administration. He later worked for the Charlotte Urban Ministry and the Charlotte Mental Health Clinic.

In September 1967, T.J. Reddy and Charles Parker were students at colleges in Charlotte, North Carolina. Grant was finishing his Ph.D. at Pennsylvania State University and had not yet come to Charlotte. At that time, Reddy was dating a young white woman whom he later married. He and his white friend, along with two of her co-workers, both white, went to the Lazy B Stables to ride horses. They were refused service because Reddy is Black. They returned the following day with a larger group, which included both Blacks and whites, and were allowed to use the facilities and ride the horses. As far as Reddy was concerned, the matter was forgotten because the management apparently had a change of heart and was willing to allow Black and white people to ride the horses together.

A year later, on September 24, 1968, the stables burned and a number of horses died in the fire. The initial investigation by local police concluded that the fire was deliberately set with incendiary devices. (The local fire marshal had determined the fire was accidental.) No one was charged with the burning until more than three years later, when indictments were returned against Reddy, Grant, and Parker by a Mecklenburg County Grand Jury on January 6, 1972, despite the fact that the physical evidence had disappeared.

The indictments resulted from statements obtained in the summer of 1971 from Walter David Washington[1] and Theodore Alfred Hood[2] after they were placed in custody on a host of federal charges, including bail jumping and possession and manufacturing of explosives. Upon their arrest, Hood and Washington were initially placed under secured bonds of $165,000 and $100,00 each respectively. After they agreed to testify against Reddy, Grant, and Parker in this case and Grant and Benjamin Chavis in another case,[3] they were both released on their own recognizance.

A long period of negotiation proceeded Washington and Hood's agreement to testify. A memorandum dated June 28, 1971, prepared by Bill Walden, an agent of the Alcohol, Tobacco, and Firearms Unit of the U.S. Treasury Department, reveals that before Washington and Hood agreed to testify, Walden arranged for Hood to be transported from Charlotte to Raleigh, North Carolina, where Washington was incarcerated so that Washington could convince Hood to testify in accordance with Washington's version of events.

The negotiations with Hood and Washington were conducted by federal agents who were anxious to secure the convictions, either state or federal, of Grant and Chavis who were characterized in a United States Justice Department memo as "black militants". As soon as Hood and Washington agreed to give statements and testimony, the federal agents called in state authorities so that they could take full benefit of the bargaining for Hood and Washington's testimony.

An agreement was apparently reached between federal authorities and local authorities that the federal authorities would furnish local authorities copies of statements made by Washington and Hood. Local authorities therefore relied upon federal authorities for the statements and testimony of Washington and Hood.

The final agreement reached between federal and state law enforcement authorities provided that (1) Washington and Hood would be given complete immunity for anything they might say; (2) they would be provided housing, food, clothing, and subsistence money for themselves and their families by the federal government until they testified; (3) the local prosecutor, Thomas F. Moore, would have Washington's probation terminated after he testified in the state trial; and (4) each of them would be paid an unspecified amount of cash by the federal government after they had completed their testimony.

After the indictments were returned, the attorneys for Reddy, Grant, and Parker filed written motions in court requesting that they be apprised of any deals made with the witnesses to obtain their testimony. The Assistant District Attorney, William Austin, stated in open court:

"If any arrangements [with prosecuting witnesses] are made prior to the trial or during the trial, the state will immediately stipulate what they are in open court."

Thereafter, neither Mr. Austin nor Mr. Moore, nor anyone else associated with the prosecution of the case, including the federal agents, revealed the promise made to Washington concerning the termination of his probation or the promise of cash payments to both Washington and Hood.

The only evidence which linked Reddy, Grant, and Parker to the burning of the Lazy B Stables was the testimony of Washington and Hood. There was no other evidence whatsoever even remotely pointing to Reddy, Grant, and Parker, although a full investigation had been carried out by the local police. Nevertheless, they were convicted of the burning by the virtually all-white jury. Following their convictions, they were given active sentences as follows: Dr. Grant, 25 years; Mr. Reddy, 20 years; and Mr. Parker, 10 years.

Throughout the proceedings, each of these men insisted upon their innocence. Reddy testified in his own behalf that he did not participate in the burning, but, due to the lapse of time between the event and the indictment, was unable to state specifically where he was at the time of the burning four years earlier. Several witnesses testified as to their recollection that Grant was teaching a class at State College, Pennsylvania, at the time of the burning. Parker offered no testimony, but stood on his plea of not guilty.

Reddy, Grant, and Parker appealed their convictions unsuccessfully. The North Carolina Court of Appeals affirmed the convictions on September 9, 1973. The North Carolina Supreme Court declined review on November 1, 1973.

On March 24 and 25, 1974, the *Charlotte Observer,* the largest newspaper in the state, disclosed for the first time that Washington and Hood had been paid the cash sum of $4,000 each by federal authorities for their testimony against Reddy, Grant, and Parker, as well as for the testimony they had given against Dr. Grant and Rev. Benjamin Chavis in a federal trial in Raleigh. The Justice Department paid $3,000 to each witness. The Treasury Department paid each witness $1,000. The Treasury Department characterized the payment as a "reward" for information and testimony against Grant, Reddy and Parker.

On July 11, 1974, Reddy, Grant, and Parker filed a petition for post-conviction relief in Mecklenburg County Superior Court, alleging that their rights had been violated at trial by the failure of the prosecution to disclose to them, upon request, the secret agreement for money payments to the witnesses and the secret agreement by Tom Moore to terminate Washington's probation. An adverse ruling against the Charlotte Three was entered by Judge Sam Ervin, III, on September 24, 1975, following which review was sought and denied by the North Carolina Court of Appeals on March 11, 1976.

On April 5, 1976, the Charlotte Three filed a petition for a *writ of habeas corpus* in the federal district court for the Western District of North Carolina. The case initially came before Judge James B. McMillian who entered a preliminary order on June 22, 1976, admitting Reddy and Grant to bail. Parker, by this time, was already free on parole.

Before ruling on the merits, Judge McMillian, without stating reasons, disqualified himself from further consideration of the case. On December 29, 1976, Judge Woodrow Wilson Jones, without a hearing, without briefs, without oral argument, and without consideration of controlling cases favorable to the Charlotte Three, entered an adverse ruling denying them a new trial and ordering them taken into immediate custody. The men took an appeal and applied to the late Judge J. Braxton Craven for an order continuing them on bail.

Judge Craven entered an order staying Judge Jones' order and allowed them to remain free on bail pending resolution of Grant and Reddy's claims in the Fourth Circuit Court of Appeals, observing that this was the first time he had ever entered such an order and they had shown a strong likelihood of success on the merits.

On November 3, 1977, the Fourth Circuit Court of Appeals entered a *per curiam* order affirming on the basis of Judge Jones' opinion.

On November 14, 1977, the Charlotte Three filed a petition for rehearing, with a suggestion for rehearing *en banc*. The Court requested a response from the state which was filed on December 9, 1977. When the Court ruled against the Charlotte Three, an appeal was taken to the U.S. Supreme Court.

On October 1, 1978, the U.S. Supreme Court refused to hear the appeal of the Charlotte Three which charged prosecutorial misconduct and denial of fundamental rights. As a result of that ruling, Dr. Grant and Mr. Reddy have been ordered back to the North Carolina prison system where they continue serving their sentences. All state and federal remedies have been exhausted.

Additional details of the case were presented in a petition for pardon submitted to Governor Hunt in December 1977. Their petition for pardon and selected exhibits, which were in Appendix I of the original Petition to the United Nations follows.

STATE OF NORTH CAROLINA

OFFICE OF THE GOVERNOR

IN THE MATTER OF:

THOMAS JAMES REDDY, JAMES EARL GRANT, JR. and CHARLES PARKER

PETITION FOR PARDON

TO: THE HONORABLE JAMES B. HUNT, JR.
GOVERNOR
STATE OF NORTH CAROLINA

Thomas James Reddy, James Earl Grant, Jr. and Charles Parker, petitioners herein, by and through their undersigned counsel, pursuant to Article III, Section 5 of the Constitution of the State of North Carolina and North Carolina General Statutes, Section 147-21, hereby respectfully request a pardon of innocence for the crime of unlawful burning which they were convicted of on July 15, 1972. The grounds for granting a pardon of innocence are as set forth below:

PRELIMINARY STATEMENT

Petitioners are here seeking to invoke the special constitutional powers of your office to grant them a pardon because they have been wrongfully and unjustly convicted and vindictively sentenced for a crime of which they are innocent. They were convicted and sentenced because of their racial and political activities. So intent were state and federal authorities upon convicting petitioners that they secretly paid cash money, promised freedom from imprisonment and openly and unabashedly made other important concessions to known criminals in return for their testimony against them.

Reddy, Grant and Parker are three known black civil rights activists who have been adopted as political prisoners of conscience by Amnesty International, the London-based human rights organization which received the 1977 Nobel Peace Prize for its efforts in working to free political prisoners. The prosecution's ostensible theory was that Reddy, who was dating the white woman to whom he is now married, in the company of a racially integrated group, attempted to ride horses at the Lazy B Riding Stables in September or October, 1967, was refused service and returned to burn the stables down a year later in September, 1968. They were convicted at their 1972 trial by a jury of eleven whites and one black solely on the basis of the unsupported testimony of two witnesses, both with long criminal records and both facing potentially long sentences for their own admitted crimes, who were secretly paid $4,000 each by government authorities for their testimony. These witnesses were granted absolute immunity for their own admitted crimes and one of the witnesses was secretly promised by the prosecutor that he would not have to serve a 25 year probationary sentence for armed robbery, although the witness was in violation of the terms of probation. The promise of cash payments and the promise of probation termination were kept secret from the petitioners, the jury, the judge and their attorneys until long after trial when the secret arrangements were uncovered by an investigation conducted by reporters for the Charlotte Observer newspaper who publicly reported the details of the money payments.

After the public revelations of the secretly arranged payments of the witnesses and secret promise of probation termination, thousands of citizens of this state and this country and even in other countries were properly outraged and called upon the Governor's Office to intervene in the case to assure that justice was done. They viewed the case as an instance of governmental over-reaching to secure convictions of persons whose political beliefs and racial activities were unpopular at the time. It was in this context that Amnesty International investigated the case and concluded that these men were indeed prosecuted and convicted because of their political beliefs or ethnic background and added them to the list of political prisoners throughout the world. The nature of the case, the secret deals which were made and the irrational and inordinately long sentences which were imposed have all combined to bring our system of justice into serious disrepute locally, nationally and internationally because of the patently unfair and unjust manner in which it has dealt with these men. Many people

-3-

properly view this case as one where young black activists have been singled out for summary treatment in an effort to silence racial protest. The growing concern about the case has caused and is continuing to cause an unnecessary division between the races on a state level, thus having the potential to destroy the racial goodwill and progress which have been brought about over the years through the efforts of many of our citizens, black and white, and the Office of the Governor under this and previous administrations.

The incredible and unconscionable deals made between the two criminal witnesses for the prosecution, the known involvement of Reddy, Grant and Parker in racial and political protests, the unlawful and inordinately long sentences imposed upon them and the prevailing atmosphere of racial hysteria at the time demonstrate that the prosecution, conviction and sentencing of these men were the product of improper political and racial motivation.

Since July, 1974, Reddy, Grant and Parker have been engaged in an effort to have their convictions overturned though litigation in state and federal court. Although it is undisputed that the two witnesses were paid $4,000 each by the federal government and that one witness was promised probation termination and that these deals were not disclosed to the defense before or during the trial, the courts have refused to overturn these convictions. Most recently, a three-judge panel of the United States Fourth Circuit Court of Appeals, in a non-published *per curiam* opinion, refused to give any relief in the case. We have filed a petition for rehearing by the full panel with that court and are awaiting action on the petition.

Reddy and Grant have both served two and one-half years on their sentences, but have been free on bail since June of 1976, pending action on their petition for a writ of habeas corpus. Parker has been free on parole since December of 1975. Grant and Reddy are in immediate jeopardy of being re-incarcerated if the Fourth Circuit Court of Appeals rules adversely on their petition for rehearing. The order admitting them to bail is effective only until the Fourth Circuit acts on their petition for rehearing. Even though they can seek further review of their case from the United States Supreme Court, their chances of remaining free on bail pending action by the Supreme Court are slim.

The only realistic hope of meaningful relief in these cases is through gubernatorial action at this time. It is therefore not only appropriate, but necessary that the gubernatorial powers to grant a pardon of innocence be exercised on behalf of Reddy, Grant and Parker in order to correct an obvious injustice which the courts have proven unready, unwilling or unable to deal with.

FACTS

In September, 1967, T. J. Reddy and Charles Parker were students at local Charlotte colleges at the time. Grant was finishing his Ph.D at Pennsylvania State University and had not yet come to Charlotte. At that time, Reddy, himself black, was dating a young white woman whom he later married. He and his white girlfriend, along with two of her co-workers, both white, went to the Lazy B Stables to ride horses. They were refused service because Reddy was black. They returned the following day with a larger group which included both blacks and whites, at which time they were allowed to use the facilities and ride the horses. As far as Reddy was concerned, the matter was forgotten because the management apparently had a change of heart and was willing to allow black people, as well as white people, to ride the horses.

A year later, on September 24, 1968, the stables burned and a number of horses died in the fire. The initial investigation by local police concluded that the fire was deliberately set with incendiary devices. No one was charged with the burning until more than three years later, when indictments were returned against Reddy, Grant and Parker by a Mecklenburg County Grand Jury on January 6, 1972.

The indictments resulted from statements obtained in the summer of 1971 from Walter David Washington and Theodore Alfred Hood after they were placed in custody on a host of federal charges, including bail jumping and possession and manufacturing of dynamite. Upon their arrest, Hood and Washington were initially placed under secured bonds of $165,000 and $100,000 each, respectively. After they agreed to testify against Reddy, Grant and Parker in this case and Grant and Benjamin Chavis in a federal case, they

-5-

were both released on their own recognizance.

A long period of negotiation preceded Washington and Hood's agreement to testify. A memorandum dated June 28, 1971, prepared by Bill Walden, an agent of the Alcohol, Tobacco and Firearms Unit of the Treasury Department, reveals that before Washington and Hood agreed to testify, Walden arranged for Hood to be transported from Charlotte to Raleigh where Washington was incarcerated so that Washington could convince Hood to testify in accordance with Washington's version of events. This same memorandum contained statements from Washington which were materially inconsistent with his trial testimony and background information on Washington which could have been used for impeachment purposes at trial, had petitioners known of its existence. The existence of this memorandum was not revealed to petitioners until Walden was deposed during post-conviction proceedings. A copy of this memorandum is attached to this petition as Exhibit 1.

Washington initially demanded the sum of $25,000 for his testimony. Hood demanded $50,000. They both bargained for complete immunity from prosecution, state and federal, for any self-incriminating statements they might make and Washington further demanded that his probation, which was then in effect, be terminated in order that he could avoid having to serve a 25 year sentence. He was then in violation of probation and would likely have had his probation revoked, thus requiring him to serve the sentence.

The negotiations with Hood and Washington were conducted by federal agents who were primarily interested in securing convictions, either state or federal, of Grant and Chavis who were characterized in a United States Justice Department memo as "black militants". As soon as Hood and Washington agreed to give statements and testimony, the federal agents called in state authorities so that they could take full benefit of the bargaining for Hood and Washington's testimony. Tom Moore, local prosecutor of Mecklenburg County, sent Joe Europa of the intelligence unit of the Charlotte Police Department to Raleigh, North Carolina to participate in the taking of statements from Washington and Hood. An agreement was apparently reached between federal authorities and local authorities that the federal authorities would furnish local authorities copies of statements made by Washington and Hood. Local authorities therefore relied upon federal authorities for the statements and testimony of Washington and Hood.

The final agreement reached between Washington and law enforcement authorities provided that: (1) Washington and Hood would be given complete immunity for anything they might say; (2) They would be provided housing, food, clothing and subsistence money for themselves and their families by the federal government until they testified; (3) The local prosecutor, Thomas F. Moore, would have Washington's probation terminated after he testified in the state trial; and (4) Each of them would be paid an unspecified amount of cash by the federal government after they had completed their testimony.

After the indictments were returned, the attorneys for Reddy, Grant and Parker filed written motions in court requesting that they be apprised of any deals made with the witnesses to obtain their testimony. The Assistant District Attorney, William Austin, stated in open court:

> "If any arrangements [with prosecuting witnesses] are made prior to the trial or during the trial, the state will immediately stipulate what they are in open court."

Thereafter, neither Mr. Austin, nor Mr. Moore, nor anyone else associated with the prosecution of the case, including the federal agents, revealed the promise made to Washington concerning the termination of his probation or the promise of cash payments to both Washington and Hood. The attorneys for Reddy, Grant and Parker had earlier learned of the promises of immunity and that the federal government had provided living expenses and accommodations for the witnesses prior to trial. Not only did District Attorney Moore fail to reveal the full bargain that had been made with Washington and Hood, he told the jury twice in his closing argument that the only concession made to Washington and Hood was the grant of immunity from prosecution for the burning of the Lazy B Stables. The jury was therefore left with the impression that Hood and Washington were motivated solely by altruism in testifying against these three men.

The only evidence linking Reddy, Grant and Parker to the burning of the Lazy B Stables was the testimony of Washington and Hood. There was no other evidence whatsoever, even remotely pointing to Reddy, Grant and Parker, although a full investigation had been carried out by the local police. Nevertheless, they were convicted of the burning by the virtually all-white jury. Following their convictions, they were given active sentences as follows: Grant - 25 years; Reddy - 20 years; and Charles Parker - 10 years. Grant had no previous convictions, other than a federal conviction in April, 1972 of aiding and abetting Washington and Hood in jumping bail and conspiracy to have Washington and Hood flee the country.[1/] Grant had a Ph.D in chemistry which he earned from Pennsylvania State University, prior to coming to Charlotte to live. He had moved from his home in Hartford, Connecticut and relocated in Charlotte in 1968 as a VISTA volunteer to work in the community. Reddy had no previous convictions whatsoever and was a student at Johnson C. Smith University at the time. He has since completed his bachelor's degree and master's degree at the University of North Carolina at Charlotte, by attending classes and completing course requirements while in prison. Parker only had a conviction for possession of drugs at the time of conviction. He was then a student at a local college.

Throughout the proceedings, each of these men insisted upon their innocence. Reddy testified in his own behalf that he did not participate in the burning but, due to the lapse of time between the event and the indictment, was unable to state specifically where he was at the time of the burning four years earlier. Several witnesses testified as to their recollection that Grant was in State College, Pennsylvania at the time of the burning. Parker offered no testimony, but stood upon his plea of not guilty.

Reddy, Grant and Parker all appealed their convictions to no avail. The North Carolina Court of Appeals affirmed the convictions on September 9, 1973. The North Carolina Supreme Court declined review on November 1, 1973.

On March 24 and 25, 1974, the Charlotte Observer disclosed for the first time that Washington and Hood had been paid the cash sum of $4,000

1/ Ironically, Washington and Hood were granted immunity on the very same bail jumping charges for which Grant was convicted. Grant's conviction on these charges was based solely on Washington and Hood's statement that Grant had masterminded their leaving the country to avoid coming to trial on (Continued on page 8) each by federal authorities for their testimony against Reddy, Grant and Parker, as well as for testimony they had given against Grant and Benjamin Chavis in a federal trial in Raleigh. The Justice Department paid $3,000 to each witness. The Treasury Department paid each witness $1,000. The Treasury Department characterized the payments as a "reward" for information and testimony against Grant, Reddy and Parker. Copies of the relevant documents of the Treasury Department are attached hereto as Exhibits 2 through 10 and incorporated by reference, the same as if fully set forth herein. Records from the Justice Department and the Treasury Department show that the money was paid to these witnesses within three working days after the trial of Reddy, Grant and Parker. The federal trial against Grant and Chavis had been completed three months earlier in April, 1972. No attempt was made by anyone to secure cash money for the witnesses until after the state trial in Charlotte.

Although the portion of the money paid by the Justice Department was characterized as "relocation assistance" payments, neither Washington nor Hood ever actually relocated.[2/]

Shortly after learning of the secret deal for money payments, petitioners' counsel, through investigation, learned that in a probation revocation proceeding in April, 1973, Tom Moore, then Mecklenburg County District Attorney, had attempted to make good his promise that he would terminate Washington's probation on a 25 year armed robbery conviction so that Washington could avoid service of the 25 year sentence. Moore's position was contrary to that of the probation officer who, being fully familiar with Washington's record and background, sought to have the sentence put into

---

1/ (Continued from page 7)
charges of possessing and manufacturing of dynamite. Still more ironically, Grant was charged, but never tried, with possessing and manufacturing the very same dynamite which was found in a car occupied by Washington and Hood when they were arrested for curfew violation. Washington and Hood's testimony in connection with these federal charges against Grant and Benjamin Chavis resulted from the same bargain described above.

2/ Hood was known to have remained in Charlotte following the trial. He was charged with several offenses in Charlotte after July of 1972, including murder and felony possession of drugs. The murder charge and one drug possession charge were dismissed. Other drug possession charges are stil outstanding, even to the present day.

Washington was also charged with offenses in Charlotte after July, 1972 and was never brought to trial. He was also convicted of armed robbery in Chester, South Carolina.

effect. Much to Moore's chagrin, he learned at the probation revocation hearing that he did not have the power to terminate probation. Moore was successful, however, in persuading the judge not to effectuate the sentence, although the probation was not technically terminated.

On July 11, 1974, Reddy, Grant and Parker filed a petition for post-conviction relief in Mecklenburg County Superior Court, alleging that their rights had been violated at trial by the failure of the prosecution to disclose to them, upon request, the secret agreement for money payments to the witnesses and the secret agreement by Tom Moore to terminate Washington's probation.[3/] An adverse ruling against the petitioners was entered by Judge Sam Ervin, III, on September 24, 1975, following which review was sought and denied by the North Carolina Court of Appeals on March 11, 1976.

On April 5, 1976, petitioners filed a petition for a writ of habeas corpus in the federal district court for the Western District of North Carolina. The case initially came before Judge James B. McMillan who entered a preliminary order on June 22, 1976, admitting Reddy and Grant to bail. Parker, by this time, was already free on parole.

Before ruling on the merits, Judge McMillan, without stating reasons, disqualified himself from further consideration of the case. On December 29, 1976, Judge Woodrow Wilson Jones, without a hearing, without briefs, without oral argument and without consideration of controlling cases favorable to the petitioners, entered an adverse ruling denying petitioners a new trial and ordering them taken into immediate custody. The men took an appeal and applied to the late Judge J. Braxten Craven for an order continuing them on bail.

Judge Craven entered an order staying Judge Jones' order and allowing Reddy and Grant to remain free on bail pending resolution of their claims in the Fourth Circuit Court of Appeals, observing that this was the first time he had ever entered such an order and that petitioners had shown a strong likelihood of success on the merits.

On November 3, 1977, the Fourth Circuit Court of Appeals entered a *per curiam* order affirming.on the basis of Judge Jones' opinion.

3/ Petitioners later amended their petition to include the concealment of Walden's memorandum.

On November 14, 1977, petitioners filed a petition for rehearing, with a suggestion for rehearing en banc. The Court requested a response from the state which was filed on December 9, 1977. We are presently awaiting action by the court on the petition for rehearing.

If the Court rules adversely to the petitioners, they will be in jeopardy of immediate incarceration. Even if they seek further review from an adverse decision of the Fourth Circuit, they are likely to be incarcerated while seeking discretionary review in the United States Supreme Court, unless the possibility of further incarceration is removed by favorable action from your office.

REASONS FOR GRANTING THE PARDON

1. The conviction of the petitioners was unfairly procured by the use of bought testimony and other fulfilled promises from unsavory and unreliable witnesses. It is undisputed that without the testimony of Walter David Washington and Theodore Alfred Hood, there could have been no conviction. It is further uncontradicted that within three working days after the trial of the petitioners, Hood and Washington were paid $3,000 each by the Justice Department and on the following day were paid an additional $1,000 each by the United States Treasury Department. The Treasury Department documents describe and characterize the money payments to these witnesses as a "reward" for their testimony against the petitioners.

Washington had been medically discharged from the United States Marine Corps as a 100% mentally disabled person with homicidal schizophrenic tendencies. He had been convicted of armed robbery, breaking and entering, larceny, damage to property and assault with a deadly weapon. Although petitioners did not know it at the time of their trial, he was a suspect in 5 murders in Mecklenburg County, as shown by the document, Exhibit 1, in the possession of William Walden at the time of trial. Walden himself felt that because of Washington's background, his testimony, standing alone, would be of little or no value. However, Washington had told Walden that if he (Washington) could spend some time alone with Hood, he could get Hood to support his testimony. Walden then arranged for them to get together alone.

-11-

Hood had previously been convicted of assault with a deadly weapon with intent to kill, assault on a police officer, carrying a concealed weapon and auto theft. He provided no incriminating information against petitioners until after he was left alone with Washington. He began his negotiations with law enforcement authorities by demanding $50,000 for his testimony and stating that he would provide such testimony only if "certain conditions were met". Ultimately, the conditions were met: (1) an agreement to pay him and Washington an unspecified amount of money for their testimony; (2) an agreement to terminate Washington's probation; and (3) other inducements which were known to the petitioners, including complete immunity for any criminal implications of themselves and an agreement to provide living expenses and accommodations for themselves and their families up until their testimony was completed.

The procuring of testimony by a promise of financial reward, at worst, debases our system of criminal justice by encouraging, if not soliciting, perjury and, at best, is of dubious ethical propriety. Ethical consideration 7-28 of the ABA Code of Professional Responsibility provides as follows:

> "Witnesses should always testify truthfully and should be free from any financial inducements that might tempt them to do otherwise. A lawyer should not pay or agree to pay a non-expert witness an amount in excess of reimbursement for expenses and financial loss incident to being a witness; however, a lawyer may pay or agree to pay an expert witness a reasonable fee for his services as an expert. But in no event should a lawyer pay or agree to pay a contingent fee to any witness. A lawyer should exercise reasonable diligence to see that his client and lay associates conform to these standards."

Disciplinary Rule 7-190 (C) clarifies this important ethical standard:

> "A lawyer shall not pay, offer to pay, or acquiesce in the payment of compensation to a witness contigent upon the content of his testimony or the outcome of the case. But a lawyer may advance, guarantee, or acquiesce in the payment of:
> (1) Expenses reasonably incurred by a witness in attending or testifying.
> (2) Reasonable compensation to a witness for his loss of time in attending or testifying.
> (3) A reasonable fee for the professional services of an expert witness."

In support of this rule, the ABA Code notes that:

> "There certainly can be no greater incentive to perjury than to allow a party to make payments to its opponents witnesses under any guise or on any excuse, and at least attorneys who are officers of the court to aid it in the administration of justice, must keep themselves clear of any connection which in the slightest degree tends to induce witnesses to testify in favor of their clients." In re Robinson, 151 App. Div. 589, 600, 136 N.Y.S. 548, 556-57 (1912), aff'd, 209 N.Y. 354, 103 N.E. 160 (1913)." (Emphasis added).

Apart from the unfulfilled, constitutional duty the prosecutor had to disclose to petitioners and their counsel the full details of the deal negotiated for testimony of these witnesses, any conviction premised upon bought testimony should not be allowed to stand. That should be so in any case, but compellingly so in this case where the only incriminating evidence was the bought testimony.

The witnesses not only received financial rewards, they received other benefits as well. They were given absolute immunity from prosecution for their own admitted crimes. Again, such benefits encouraged perjury. It was easy for the witnesses to claim participation in a crime with petitioners, knowing that no matter what they said, they would not be prosecuted. Still further inducement to perjure themselves was provided by the agreement of the federal government to pay all the living expenses for them and their families for a period of approximately nine months under the guise of protective custody.[4/]

Courts, because of the peculiar context in which they operate, are not concerned with the moral or ethical dimensions of prosecutions unless a legally defined violation of due process is involved. Governors, on the other hand, in whom the power of pardon is wisely reposed, cannot ignore the moral and ethical implications of convictions that defy notions of basic fairness and essential justice. It is for this reason that we now seek a pardon of innocence to correct the egregious wrong heaped upon the petitioners

---

4/ The record in this case contains no showing of a need for protective custody for Washington and Hood, except they were negotiating for money and this was the only way it could be provided to them. Federal Agent Stanley Noel, a principal in the negotiations, testified that the only reason for providing "relocation assistance" was that the witnesses requested it, and once they were given the money they did not have to use it to relocate, but could use it for any purpose. (Deposition of Noel, pp. 46-47)

-13-

through the government's unabashed use of bought testimony, perjurious by its very nature.

2. The unfair use of bought testimony by the prosecutor was compounded by his concealment from the defense of the details of the full deal made with the witnesses. Not only did the government enter into an unconscionable bargain for perjurious testimony. The prosecutor refused to tell the defense about the deal, although his assistant had falsely promised in court to reveal to the court and the defense any deals which were made with prosecution witnesses. The failure of the prosecutor to disclose the deal is at odds with basic fairness and runs far afoul of his constitutional duty to reveal any inducements offered for the testimony of witnesses. Brady v. Maryland, 373 U.S. 83, 10 L.Ed 2d 215 (1963); Giglio v. United States, 405 U.S. 150, 31 L.Ed 2d 104 (1972); United States v. Agurs, __U.S.__, 49 L.Ed 2d 342 (1976); Boone v. Paderick, 541 F.2d 447 (4th Cir. 1976); United States v. Sutton, 542 F.2d 1239 (4th Cir. 1976).

The prosecutor's failure to disclose the deal was not an inadvertent oversight; it was deliberate and purposefully deceitful. The assistant prosecutor, after first strenuously objecting to the defense request for disclosure, stated in open court:

> "If any arrangements [with prosecuting witnesses] are made prior to trial or during trial, the State will immediately stipulate what they are in open court." (Trial Transcript, p. 128).

The prosecution then told the defense that they had only granted the witnesses immunity for their testimony in the Lazy B burning case. During the trial, the prosecutor told the jury twice during his final argument:

> "I told Washington and Hood that I wouldn't prosecute them about this case, this one case."

These statements by the prosecutor and assistant prosecutor establish beyond cavil that the revelation of any deal was of crucial importance in the case. Their concealment of the full deal was a calculated move, designed to bring about a conviction. And it did. Only those prosecutions premised on principle should be allowed to stand. Unprincipled prosecutions produced by improper political and racial motivations, as the one involved here, should be discouraged by corrective action by the Chief Executive of the State.

There is no need or reason for hesitancy on the part of the Governor in acting to correct abuses of the system which result in unfair convictions and vindictive, irrational sentences. It is precisely because the system sometimes produces unfair convictions which the courts either will not or cannot correct that the power of pardon is reposed in the Office of the Governor. The long course of post-conviction proceedings in this case is indicative of the inability or unwillingness of the courts to correct the clear abuse involved. It would be hard to imagine a case more appropriate for gubernatorial action than this one is.

3. The unduly and irrationally harsh sentences imposed upon the petitioners can be removed only by gubernatorial action. We have outlined above in the preliminary statement the general background of the petitioners. Parker, who received the lightest sentence, was the only one of the three who had a prior conviction unrelated to testimony obtained as a result of the unconscionable bargain with Washington and Hood. His sentence, like the others, was inordinately long, all things considered; however, the fact that he received the lightest sentence clearly demonstrates that the sentences were unrelated to the petitioners' background or other objective factors. The sentences merely reflected the biases and emotions of the sentencing Judge who, in the midst of the trial, had ordered the petitioners locked up over night for no reason.

In an editorial on July 18, 1972, the Charlotte Observer compared sentences of persons who had been convicted of burning offenses. This comparison, though limited to information in the files of the Charlotte Observer, illustrates the lack of objectivity in the sentencing of the petitioners. In no case had anyone received a sentence as heavy as petitioners for a single burning offense. Persons convicted of burning offenses where human life was placed in jeopardy or taken received substantially lighter sentences than did the petitioners.

The colossal and pointless waste of human life and human talent occasioned by the outrageously long sentences imposed upon these men, without regard to improper motivation, would be reason enough for gubernatorial action. Reddy is now married and has a wife and baby daughter who was born on

October 11, 1977. Since the conviction, he miraculously earned both his bachelor's degree and master's degree during the period of his incarceration. While behind bars, he wrote a book of poetry, Less Than A Score, But A Point, which has been published by Random House. While out on bail, he served as a counsellor in a local pretrial diversion program and counselled high school students in a government funded summer program. Both in and out of prison, he has been a prolific artist, producing over 300 works of art since his initial imprisonment. Grant served as a librarian and teacher for other inmates while incarcerated in federal prison. He received an official commendation from prison authorities for his outstanding work. Parker's activities have been less spectacular. He has maintained steady employment since his release on parole.

There is no explanation for the harshness of the sentences imposed upon the petitioners other than that the same improper emotional, political and racial motivation which produced the prosecution and convictions affected, if not determined, the sentences. Under our system, no procedure is available for review and correction of the improper sentencing, so long as a given sentence falls within the statutory maximum for the offense. Short of ordering a new trial, there is no action the courts can take affecting the sentences. Action by your office is the only direct means by which the unjust sentences in these cases can be corrected.

The sentences imposed in this case are so inextricably interwoven into the entire tainted process which produced the convictions, that the only meaningful way to effectively remove the resultant injustice would be to grant a pardon of innocence, thereby eradicating not only an unjust sentence, but an unjust conviction as well.

4. The manner in which the petitioners were convicted and the circumstances surrounding their prosecution and convictions have produced a justified and widespread belief that they were prosecuted, convicted and sentenced because of their racial protests and political beliefs, rather than for the commission of any crime. All of the petitioners have been adopted as prisoners of conscience by Amnesty International, the foremost non-governmental human rights organization in the world. The conscientious, responsible and

effective work that Amnesty International has done on behalf of political prisoners throughout the world was recognized by the Nobel Peace Prize Committee when it awarded Amnesty International the Prize for 1977. Amnesty concluded after an investigation of the case that these petitioners had been imprisoned for their ethnic origin and their political beliefs.

Others who have looked into the case have come to basically the same conclusion. The North Carolina Legal Foundation, Inc., the legal arm of the North Carolina Chapter of the American Civil Liberties Union, has filed an amicus brief in the Fourth Circuit Court of Appeals, urging that the convictions be overturned because of the blatant violations of petitioners' rights. Two members of the United States House of Representatives cited this case as an example of racial inequity in the operation of our system of criminal justice. Congressional Record, Volume 121, No. 98, June 20, 1975, No. 121, October 2, 1975. On December 16, 1977, twelve Congressmen corresponded with you, asking for a pardon of the petitioners, pointing out that civil rights and religious leaders throughout the country have appealed for their release. The two Senators from the State of Connecticut, petitioner Grant's home state, have already corresponded with you, asking you to review this case, one simply asking that you review the case, the other urging you to grant a pardon or parole to Dr. Grant. Other persons, titled and untitled. have expressed their concern over the obvious injustice involved in this case.

In July, 1976, the Office of the Mayor of Hartford, Connecticut, petitioner Grant's hometown, established a Committee to seek the unconditional release of petitioner Grant. On December 13, 1976, the Hartford City Council passed a resolution calling upon the Governor of North Carolina to release all of the petitioners.

The Governor of the State of Connecticut has already requested of you to grant a pardon in this case.

Many news commentators, both in the state and out of the state, have written about this case, calling for the correction of the injustice which the petitioners have suffered and continue to suffer. We are attaching hereto copies of some representative editorial comments from the Greensboro

-17-

Daily News, The New York Times, the Charlotte Observer, the Washington Post and Encore Magazine.

The unjust convictions and sentences of the petitioners have placed a blight on our system of criminal justice which has served and will continue to serve as a source of divisiveness between the races in our state because many who believe in racial justice and equal justice view the case as a glaring example of racial inequity emphasizing the disparity of treatment accorded black citizens by governmental institutions. This blight can be removed only by decisive favorable action by your Office, granting to these petitioners the pardon of innocence which they justly deserve.

CONCLUSION

We therefore urge you in the name of fairness, justice, human dignity, human rights and racial equality to immediately grant a pardon of innocence to each of the petitioners.

This 30th day of December, 1977.

Respectfully submitted,

James E. Ferguson II

JAMES E. FERGUSON, II
JAMES C. FULLER, JR.
Chambers, Stein, Ferguson & Becton, P.A.
951 S. Independence Boulevard
Charlotte, North Carolina 28202
(704) 375-8461

ADAM STEIN
Chambers, Stein, Fergu n & Becton, P.A.
Post Office Drawer 720
Chapel Hill, North Carc na 27514
(919) 967-7066

EXHIBIT 1

June 28, 1971

To: Chief Special Investigator
Charlotte, North Carolina

From: Special Investigator William S. Walden
Raleigh, North Caroline

NCLI 7103(T-II) Re: NCS 16,198 (T-II) (T-VII)

On May 14, 1970 at Oxford, North Carolina, during a civil disturbance which resulted in the destruction of over $1,000,000.00 worth of property, Joseph Preston Goines, Theodore Alfred Hood, and Walter David Washington were arrested for violation of Title II of the Gun Control Act (possession of three dynamite bombs and firearms) – see attached 1540.

All three defendants in this case made bond and this case was scheduled for the next term of Federal Court. The defendants Hood and Washington failed to show and warrants for their arrest were issued. Hood and Washington were later apprehended in this case which is now set for the September session of Federal Court. It was learned that Joseph Preston Goines was an alleged informer for the FBI, but during the time of this disturbance, his presence or whereabouts were unknown to them.

On March 15, 1971, Alfred Hood was interviewed at the Mecklenburg County Jail, Charlotte, North Carolina. At this time, he gave me a signed sworn statement which in essence said that after he and Washington were released from jail the first time, he was contacted by James Earl Grant and told that they were going to have to leave the country because he did not think it was wise for them to go to court in this case. Hood goes on to say in this statement that Grant made arrangements for them to go to Canada, giving them names and addresses of people to contact after they got there. Grant then furnished Hood a check for the amount of $150.00 drawn on the Black Peoples Society, Shelby, North Carolina, signed by Grant as Treasurer of this organization.

Grant then put Hood and Washington on a bus for Durham, North Carolina, instructed them to contact Ben Chavis in Oxford, North Carolina. Upon arriving in Oxford, Chavis cashed the above mentioned check and gave Hood and Washington additional money after which he transported them to the outskirts of Oxford, North Carolina, and giving them instructions that it would be better to thumb than catch the bus, that it would be no record that way.

Hood and Washington then made their way to Canada where they contacted the people as they had been instructed. Arrangements were then initiated to get both Hood and Washington either to Hanoi or Algeria. After about two weeks, Hood and Washington decided they were being used by Grant to protect Goines and both returned to Charlotte, North Carolina. Both were apprehended shortly thereafter. (See attached statement and background information on Grant.)

A preliminary investigation was run to see if possible Grant could be named as a conspirator in the above cited case. This investigation revealed that a check in the amount of $150.00 drawn on the Black Peoples Society and signed by Grant had cleared the Mechanics & Farmers Bank, Charlotte, North Carolina. This check was made out to Alfred Hood and cleared by a bank in Durham, North Carolina. At this time, no further evidence was obtained and this information along with Hood's statement was turned over to the FBI agent Koon, Charlotte, North Carolina, in the anticipation that they would proceed towards an indictment on this aiding and abetting on the bond default case already initiated by the FBI against Hood and Washington. It stands to become obvious that the FBI is not going to take any action in this case and that agent Koon is apparently more interested in making an informer out of Grant than prosecuting.

On June 23, 1970, the defendant Washington was interviewed at Releight, North Carolina, by this investigator in the presence of his attorney, John Cutter, Charlotte, North Carolina, Assistant U.S. Attorney David Long, and FBI Agent Jim Roach. At this time, Attorney Cutter indicated that his client, Washington, would be willing to become a witness if he could be granted immunity, his family afforded protection, and he be provided the financial means to leave this country after the government was through with him.

Assistant District Attorney Long indicated to Washington and his attorney that his office would be willing to go along with this proposal.

I then informed District Attorney Long, defendant Washington, and his attorney Cutter that I would be more than willing to entertain this idea going along with the immunity, protection of his family, but that as far as his leaving the country, this would be contingent on authorization of our department.

Washington was then questioned about this association with James Earl Grant and related as follows: Washington says that he first met James Earl Grant in September 1968, at which time Washington inquired about them and finally met him and asked him to attend a meeting over on East 10th Street, Charlotte, North Carolina. Washington attended this meeting along with T. J. Reddy, Charles Parker, and Stan Alexander and [sic] which time Jim Earl Grant was present. He said they rapped about things in general and that he had no further contact with James Earl Grant until sometime later 1968. Washington related the incidents involving the fire bombing of the Lazy Boy Stable at Charlotte, North Carolina (the exact information concerning this fire bombing will follow in another report after this information is obtained from the Charlotte POD). Prior to this incident, Washington said he was with T. J. Reddy, Charles Parker, Alfred Hood, Mary Smith, and Jim Grant. At this time, Grant put together a Molotov cocktail using various ingredients and transported this bomb along with T. J. Reddy, Charlie Parker, Al Hood, and David Washington to the Lazy Boy Stable. Washington states that he did not see who actually threw the bomb but that this fire bombing resulted from a group of negroes being refused service at this stable.

Washington then related the facts concerning the fire bombing of Norman's Market on Roberson Ferry Road, Charlotte, North Carolina. The exact date he did not know but figured it was later on in 1968. At this time, he stated that James Earl Grant put together a fire bomb in a quart 45 Colt beer bottle and that Charles Parker, Jim Earl Grant, T. J. Reddy, Alfred Hood, and himself went to Norman's Market at which time Charles [sic] Grant took the fire bomb from his vehicle and gave it to Charlie Parker with instructions as to where to throw it to do the most damage. (A complete report of this fire bombing will follow on receipt of this information from the Charlotte POD.)

Washington further related that on or about May 14, 1970, he went to the residence of James Earl Grant and that Grant was not home at this time, however, Grant had left a message with his roommate David

Belvins that he wanted Washington and Alfred Hood to come to Oxford, North Carolina. Washington and Hood then drove to Oxford, North Carolina, where they joined James Earl Grant and Ben Chavis at the Soul Kitchen, operated by Ben Chavis. At this time, Jim Grant and Ben Chavis told them that they would pay them $5,000.00 to kill Robert Gerald Teal and Robert Larry Teal accused of murdering Henry Marrow, negro male, in Oxford, North Carolina. (A report of this incident to follow.) At this time, Grant went behind Ben Chavis' house and returned carrying a 22 Magnum rifle and an air flight bag containing three dynamite bombs complete with caps and put them in the vehicle being driven by Grant and Hood.

Washington stated that he and Al Hood were joined by Joseph Preston Goines during this time and that they departed the Soul Kitchen and in the company of some girls and drove in to Oxford, North Carolina. Somewhere around 11:00 P.M. [then] departed the girls and decided to return to Soul Kitchen at which time they were apprehended at a road block set up by the State Highway Patrol and other officers. At this point Washington states that he and Al Hood had decided not to complete the contract on the Teals but it is this investigator's contention that they were returning to the Soul Kitchen to get further instructions.

Washington, at this time, stated that if he could have a few minutes with Alfred Hood that he believed that Alfred Hood would testify to the same facts. At this time, the DA office is preparing a rit to have Neal transferred from Mecklenburg County Jail where he is incarcerated to Raleigh, North Carolina, so that Washington and Hood can be allowed to discuss this matter.

At an earlier interview with this investigator, Alfred Hood indicated that he would testify as to his relationship and activity with James Earl Grant. He related to some of the same bombing incidents as Washington has but refused at this time to give enough evidence to implicate Grant until he was granted certain conditions.

Background of David Washington: David Washington has been discharged from the armed services under Section 8 and is currently under a 100% disability. He has been committed to various mental institutions since his discharge from the service and has been adjudicated a schizophrenic with homicidal tendencies. Sergeant Joseph Uropa of the Charlotte Police Department (Intelligence Division) said that he has information that leds [sic] him to believe that David Washington is a prime suspect in five murders in the Charlotte area, however, this is not supported by enough evidence for indictment. After his arrest on May 14, 1970 for violation of the Gun Control Act, Judge Larkin had David Washington committed for observation and at this time, the doctors in their medical reports state that Washington has schizophrenic tendencies but at this time is confident and rational. In my opinion, Washington's testimony in the case against James Earl Grant and Ben Chavis would be attacked most viciously and would probably be of little or no value except to use as corroboration in the event that Alfred Hood does and will testify.

Conclusion: It is my opinion that Alfred Hood will be willing to be a government witness in a case against James Earl Grant and Ben Chavis. This case can be written as a conspiracy under the Title II Section as relates to the three dynamite bombs and the guns arising out of the Oxford incident in Case No. NC E-16, 198(T-I) (T-VII). Other cases issuing out of their testimony would be a case of conspiracy to commit murder which would have to be prosecuted by the state (SSI) and possibly as aiding and abetting in the bomb default case on Washington and Hood.

Subject to a meeting of Washington and Hood the later part of this week and Hood's willingness to testify, a signed sworn statement will be taken from both of the men. In my opinion, their testimony can be corroborated resulting in a conspiracy case against both James Grant and Ben Chavis.

/s/ William F. Walden

On the following pages there are copies of ten editorials written about the Charlotte Three case. The first seven are from The Charlotte Observer, a North Carolina newspaper which followed the case closely.

The Charlotte Observer

TUESDAY, JULY 18, 1972

JAMES L. KNIGHT, *Publisher* C A MCKNIGHT, *Editor*

BEVERLY R. CARTER *General Manager* JAMES K. BATTEN *Executive Editor* REESE CLEGHORN *Editor of the Editorial Pages*

The Sentences In The Stable Fire

The prison sentences of 25, 20 and 10 years which Judge Frank Snepp imposed on three men Saturday for fire-bombing the Lazy B Stables and killing 15 horses four years ago seem to be out of line with sentences imposed in other unlawful burning cases in North Carolina in recent years. A search of Observer clippings for the past 10 years reveals only one case in which a stiffer sentence was imposed.

Judge Snepp gave James Earl Grant, a chemist, 25 years; writer-poet T. J. Redly, 20 years; and Charles Parker, 10 years. All are black militants.

Here are some samples of the trial courts' sentences:

—April, 1962 — Judge William K. McLean (known as a "tough" judge) sentenced a man who pleaded guilty to burning his own house to collect insurance to three to five years in prison.

—August, 1962 — A 15-year-old Gastonia boy pleaded guilty to setting fire to South Gastonia High School and was given 10 years.

—September, 1964 — Two white men in Wilson got 18 to 24 months and three to four years for setting fire to a black church that was being painted by an integrated organization.

—October, 1964 — A 15-year-old Kinston boy was given 8 to 15 years for burning a black church.

—January, 1965 — A Mt. Airy businessman who burned a store, killing an employe, was given five to eight years.

—June, 1966 — Four Wilkesboro people charged with burning a relative's residence pleaded guilty to a lesser offense and got two years, suspended.

—June, 1966 — A former state forestry employe in Whiteville pleaded guilty to setting eight fires in one day on timber land owned by the International Paper Co. and was given a four-month suspended sentence and fined $100.

—September, 1967 — A 17-year-old Monroe boy got a total of 15 years (five years per offense) for burning three occupied houses.

— September, 1968 — A Charlotte man got three to five years (with a recommendation for work-release) for fire-bombing a grocery store.

— October, 1968 — Five blacks got 12 years each for burning a Ku Klux Klan hut at Benson.

—December, 1969 — A student discharged from the N.C. Central University Law School got 10 years for a $1 million fire that burned the law library.

—March, 1970 — A Stanley 17-year-old got 10 years for fire-bombing a residence when the family was at home.

—April, 1970 — A Charlotte man got four to five years for burning the home occupied by his estranged wife.

—December, 1971 — A 25-year-old former volunteer fireman got 5 to 10 years at Hendersonville for burning three schools.

—February, 1972 — Judge Snepp sentenced the burglar who burned down the C'est Bon night club in Charlotte to seven years.

The only case that exceeded Judge Snepp's sentence in the Lazy B Stables fire was in April 1968, when a former Murfreesboro policeman was sentenced to 35 to 38 years for seven instances of arson.

The charge in the Lazy B Stables fire was not arson but unlawful burning. The maximum sentence allowable is 30 years in prison. Fifteen horses died in the fire, representing a considerable loss in property and a blow to horse-lovers' sentiment. But was the offense greater than the others cited here? Are those 15 horses worth 25, 20 and 10 years of three men's lives?

The Charlotte Observer
TUESDAY, MAY 8, 1973

JAMES L. KNIGHT, Publisher
C. A. McKNIGHT, Editor

BEVERLY R. CARTER
General Manager

JAMES K. BATTEN
Executive Editor

REESE CLEGHORN
Editor of the Editorial Pages

Tom Moore Bends A Court Order

Those who believe that the law should be applied with an even hand will not be encouraged by a recent proceeding in a Mecklenburg County courtroom. There was Solicitor Thomas F. Moore arguing that a convicted felon who had violated his probation be let off that probation entirely.

The man Mr. Moore argued for was Walter David Washington. In 1969, Mr. Washington pleaded guilty to armed robbery and was sentenced to 20 to 25 years. He was then put on probation. As two state probation officers testified at the recent hearing, he never complied with the terms. Subsequently, Mr. Washington became a government witness at a trial in Raleigh and the Lazy B burning trial in Charlotte that resulted in the conviction of several blacks. In exchange for his cooperation, other federal charges against him were dropped. Mr. Moore apparently promised him he would not prosecute him for probation violations and would seek the end of his probation.

It is a proper and frequent practice for prosecutors to grant immunity in return for testimony. But there is a serious question whether prosecutors in this case went too far. Since the federal government already had dropped charges of illegal possession of dynamite and firearms against Mr. Washington, why should it also seek to help him with probation violation? That would seem to be an action that might be held contempt of court.

The judge found that Mr. Washington did indeed violate the terms of probation by not paying a fine, not observing a curfew and not reporting to probation officers. But he said these violations were not "serious" and in continuing the probation period for 15 months said Mr. Washington need not observe them. Well, obviously the judge who put him on probation in the first place felt that Mr. Washington needed supervision. And a case can be made that the need for supervision still exists.

By his action bending a court order — the one establishing probation — Mr. Moore has acted in a way that lends credence to those who see a perversion of judicial processes to "get" certain black activists in North Carolina. Can he also wink at judicial orders in other cases? The court ought not to stand for that.

News Article - Charlotte Observer (published as The Charlotte Observer) - July 1, 1974 - page 24
July 1, 1974 | Charlotte Observer (published as The Charlotte Observer) | Charlotte, North Carolina | Volume 89 | Page 24

Holshouser And The Lazy B

It has been more than a month since state investigators submitted their final report on the Lazy B Stables fire to Gov. Jim Holshouser. If the governor does not intend to act on the request for clemency raised in that case, he should say so.

As state investigators found, the evidence that convicted three black men of illegal burning in that case raises many questions. They were convicted largely on the statements of two other men who were paid $4,000 and given immunity from prosecution on other charges for their testimony.

Once convicted, the three men were sentenced to unusually long terms for such a case. James Earl Grant, a chemist and black activist, was sentenced to 25 years. T. J. Reddy, a poet and sculptor, was sentenced to 20 years. And Charles Parker, an anti-poverty worker, was sentenced to 10 years.

Attorneys for the three appealed to Gov. Holshouser in January. The governor turned their appeal over to the Parole Board. By mid-April, investigators had filed their report to the Parole Board. By mid-May, the board's report had been submitted to the governor.

The Lazy B case has attracted national attention. The governor's office has received more than 10,000 letters supporting the request for clemency. Many people see the case as a miscarriage of justice and the three men as political prisoners. In our view the numerous questionable aspects of the case establish a strong argument for clemency.

The governor has had ample time to review the findings. We hope he will avoid the temptation to simply let the case lie because it is controversial.

The Charlotte Observer

C. A. McKNIGHT, Editor — ERWIN R. POTTS, General Manager

JAMES K. BATTEN, Executive Editor — REESE CLEGHORN, Editor of the Editorial Pages

WEDNESDAY, JANUARY 23, 1974

An Injustice?

Lazy B Case Needs Inquiry

In his first year as governor, Jim Holshouser proved to be reluctant to exercise his powers of executive clemency. He has granted fewer pardons and commuted fewer sentences than any governor since 1941. But he has a petition before him that begs for careful attention and study within the next week.

The three men convicted of burning the Lazy B Stables in Charlotte on September 24, 1968, have appealed to the governor to commute their sentences to the eight months they already have served in jail. Their case raises many questions.

The three — Dr. James Earl Grant, a chemist and writer; T. J. Reddy, a poet and sculptor; and Charles Parker, a poverty worker — were convicted under some unusual circumstances and given long sentences.

At their 1972 trial in Mecklenburg Superior Court, no physical evidence was presented to link them to the stable burning four years earlier. Officers who investigated the fire had misplaced the firebombs the three were accused of using to burn the Lazy B barns and 15 horses.

The three men were convicted almost entirely on the testimony of two others who were granted immunity from prosecution on a number of charges in exchange for their testimony in at least four trials of black activists in North Carolina.

The two witnesses, Walter David Washington and Theodore Alfred Hood, had been sought on a number of charges, including illegal possession of dynamite and firearms, armed robbery and illegal flight to avoid prosecution. Washington had been discharged from the Marines for mental instability.

Arrested in North Carolina after a flight to Canada, they agreed to give testimony in four cases in exchange for immunity from prosecution and protection by state and federal law-enforcement officers.

They claimed they helped Grant, Reddy and Parker burn the Lazy B Stables as retribution for the stables' discrimination against blacks.

Following conviction, the three defendants were given some of the longest sentences ever handed down in such a case, in which human lives were not endangered. Grant was sentenced to 25 years in prison; Reddy, who had not been convicted of a previous crime, was sentenced to 20 years; and Parker, the youngest of the three, was sentenced to 10.

The three petitioned Gov. Holshouser after exhausting appeals in the state courts. If the governor does not intercede before Jan. 29, their sentences begin. (Reddy and Parker are out of jail on bond. Grant is already serving time in federal prison in Atlanta, having been convicted on charges corroborated by testimony from Washington and Grant in another trial.)

The governor, legal aide Fred Morrison and the N. C. Parole Board should inquire carefully into the Lazy B convictions and the circumstances of the trial.

The Charlotte Observer

C. A. McKnight Editor Erwin R. Potts. General Manager

James K. Batten. Executive Editor Reese Cleghorn. Editor of the Editorial Pages

TUESDAY, MARCH 26, 1974

The Lazy B

New Facts Call For Review

The question of fair trial is the one that arises most prominently from new information about prosecution witnesses whose testimony sent three men to prison in the Lazy B stable-burning case.

The basic question of guilt or innocence is not answered by that information. Other questions, including one about the fairness of the sentences given to the three, are unchanged. But the new information clearly shows that jurors who found James Grant, T. J. Reddy and Charles Parker guilty of unlawful burning were denied important facts that have a bearing upon the credibility of the prosecution witnesses.

The new information was developed during an eight-week investigation by The Observer, which followed continuing reports of special treatment accorded to witnesses Walter David Washington and Theodore Alfred Hood in exchange for their testimony. A well-placed source in the U.S. Department of Justice has now confirmed that the government paid them at least $4,000 in reward and relocation money and granted them wide-ranging immunity from prosecution.

This fact was unknown to the jurors or to Superior Court Judge Frank Snepp, who presided at the trial. Nor was it known by the defense. All, in fact, heard Hood testify that he had not received "monetary gain" from the federal or state government except for living in protective custody at government expense, even though he apparently already had received $1,000 and a promise of $3,000 more after the trial.

The Juror's Information

Did Hood's testimony on that point, which went without contradiction, influence the jurors? Would they have been less likely to convict Grant, Reddy and Parker if they had known of the rewards which these two key prosecution witnesses were receiving from the government for their testimony? Were they entitled to know of this, and of the possible perjury Hood may have committed in denying that he had received payments?

Those questions, which go to the heart of the issue of whether this was a fair trial, should be heavily weighed now by the Mecklenburg County Superior Court and by Gov. Jim Holshouser, who had ordered an inquiry to determine whether he should commute the sentences of Grant (25 years), Reddy (20 years) and Parker (10 years).

Guilt or Innocence

We have no conclusion about whether they, in fact, did burn the stables in Charlotte on the night of Sept. 24, 1968. If they did, they should pay for that serious crime with prison sentences.

But ever since their trial in 1972, the case has been clouded by contradictions in the testimony of the two men who claimed to be eyewitnesses to the event, and by evidences [sic] that the government had overstepped the bounds of judicial propriety in order to "get" the defendants in this case because of a view that they were dangerous militants.

In using Hood and Washington as the key witnesses, two men called "criminals" even by Mecklenburg Solicitor Thomas F. Moore Jr., the government was not acting in an unusual manner. The criminal records of Hood and Washington would not in themselves disqualify them as witnesses. Nor is there evidence proving they did not tell the truth about the three

The Charlotte Observer

C. A. McKnight Editor
Erwin R. Potts, General Manager
James K. Batten, Executive Editor
Reese Cleghorn, Editor of the Editorial Pages

TUESDAY, MARCH 26, 1974

men convicted.

The Federal Payments

But more than a nicety of detail is involved in the fact that Hood and Washington were being paid substantial sums by the government and that the judge and jury were allowed to believe this was not so. If the jurors had known this, as they knew of the contradictions in the testimony by Hood and Washington about important facts in the case, the outcome might have been different.

That suggests to us that this was not a fair trial and that it must have the most serious scrutiny.

How may it be reexamined, not with the object of freeing the three convicted men but with the object of learning the truth?

Their convictions have been upheld at the appellate level. Since that is the case, the only recourse would seem to be through a new trial or through a communication of the sentences by Gov. Holshouser.

The Governor's Power

The commutation process exists because, in the state's view, there sometimes are cases in which a judicial outcome should be altered in the interest of justice. During the six administrations preceding that of Gov. Holshouser, 3,251 sentences were commuted: an average of 542 per administration. In more than a year in office, Gov. Holshouser has granted 20 commutations.

It is clear that Gov. Holshouser does not easily and readily move toward that kind of remedy, but he has been giving the Lazy B case careful study, with the help of the Board of Paroles. We believe he will not lightly dismiss the troublesome aspects of the case. Not only the fates of the three convicted men are at stake; the state's reputation for fairness also is involved.

But commutation would not settle the question of guilt or innocence. If that question is now open, it can be fully settled only by a new trial, one in which the judge, jury and defense are not denied important information that is properly relevant to the case.

A New Trial?

The best way to resolve the matter legally in our view, would be for a judge to formally deliberate whether the new information might establish "reasonable doubt" in the minds of a new jury about the guilt of the convicted men. We therefore believe there should be a motion for a new trial to bring the matter again before the courts.

In the absence of new judicial examination of the evidence, however, Gov. Holshouser should study the new information and set forth in detail not only his decision about commutation but also the reasoning that led to it.

The Charlotte Observer

C. A. McKnight, Editor — Erwin R. Potts, General Manager

James K. Batten, Executive Editor — Reese Cleghorn, Editor of the Editorial Pages

THURSDAY, JULY 4, 1974

Gov. Holshouser On The Lazy B

Gov. Jim Holshouser has responded to the Lazy B case in a careful, deliberative manner. That is the responsible way to approach any quasi-judicial decision such as the use of a governor's clemency powers.

The governor shared some of his thoughts about the matter with the press on Tuesday. It was almost as if he were thinking out loud. He had no decision to announce; but he wanted to let the public know he is wrestling with the case and may yet use his clemency powers.

He indicated that he will not grant full pardons to the three sentenced men, James Earl Grant Jr., T. J. Reddy and Charles Parker, who were convicted of burning the Lazy B stables in Charlotte in 1972. But, he said, he is "still struggling" with the question of whether he should shorten their sentences, which range from 25 to 10 years.

It seems to us highly significant that Gov. Holshouser, emphasizing that he was speaking as a lawyer rather than as governor, suggested that there is a case for a new trial for the three. He did not do so on the basis of any hasty look at the case or on the strength of emotion. His office has exhaustively examined the case. The governor first had a legal aide, Fred Morrison, look into it. He then called for an investigation of it by the Board of Paroles, which gave him a still-secret report six weeks ago. Since then he has examined the findings further.

On the basis of all that, the governor suggested that defense attorneys can make a good argument for a new trial. We do not believe he would have made that suggestion if he had not come to the conclusion that at least one aspect of the case — the $4,000 secretly paid by the government to each of the two key witnesses against those who were sentenced — was very questionable.

The Observer's investigation of the case, which led to discovery of the government payment to the witnesses, also turned up other aspects that make their convictions highly questionable, in our view. Further, we believe the sentences were clearly excessive. The fact that Gov. Holshouser has come to at least some of these same views of the matter, after extensive inquiry by the state investigators and legal advisers, should carry substantial weight.

We have said before that we believe defense attorneys should ask for a new trial. But the governor has a further responsibility whether they do or not. Governors are given the power of clemency not so that they frequently will second-guess judges and juries but so that, in occasional cases in which an injustice may have been done, they can grant remedy. To abandon the use of that power is to abandon a part of one's constitutional duty as governor.

The governor should shorten these excessive sentences, at the least, not waiting to see whether there will be a new trial, a development that would relieve him of some of the pressure for action.

His own duty is not related to whether there is a new trial. His duty requires a decision on clemency. If that decision were unpopular, Gov. Holshouser nevertheless would have earned respect for acting courageously in the discharge of official duties. We hope that, having shared his conscientious reflections with the public, he will now act upon them.

The Charlotte Observer

C. A. McKnight, Editor — Erwin R. Potts, General Manager

James K. Batten, Executive Editor — Reese Cleghorn, Editor of the Editorial Pages

MONDAY, SEPTEMBER 23, 1974

Case Dismissed

Lazy B Trial Was Similar

U.S. District Judge Fred Nichol cited government "misconduct" this week when he dismissed charges against two men who led a 71-day Indian takeover of Wounded Knee, S.D. last year. Some of that government conduct looks strikingly similar to what the government did in the 1972 trial of three men in Charlotte for the Lazy B stables fire.

In both trials, the inducements offered to key government witnesses—and the concealment of those inducements from the jury—raise grave doubts about the fairness of the trials.

The fact that the government did not reveal that it paid key witnesses to testify and offered them other rewards does not establish the guilt or innocence of the defendants, of course. But it could have affected the credibility that jurors attached to the testimony of those witnesses, and therefore the verdict.

In the Wounded Knee trial, government witness Louis Moves Camp, a Sioux, said he saw defendants Dennis Banks and Russell Means commit criminal acts during the Indian occupation of Wounded Knee. It was later proved that he lied.

Defense attorneys moved for dismissal partly on ground that the prosecutor had misled the court by implying that Mr. Moves Camp had received only the standard $36-a-day witness fee to testify. Instead, the judge said, the government had paid him more that $2,000; housed him in a plush Wisconsin resort; bought him liquor; and possibly quashed a rape charge against him.

Government treatment of two witnesses who said they helped burn the Lazy B stables here were also generous. The witnesses and their families lived in "protective custody" at government expense for nine months, including three months in a beach-front apartment in Atlantic Beach, N.C. The government granted them a wide-ranging immunity for prosecution—including one arrest for possession of three dynamite bombs and a large quantity of marijuana. The government also dropped federal bail-jumping charges and helped get a parole violation quashed that could have meant a 25-year prison sentence for one of the witnesses. After the trial, the government paid them $4,000 each for "relocation money."

Yet in the Lazy B case the government told neither Superior Court Judge Frank Snepp nor the jurors of the cash payments of the wide-ranging immunity from prosecution these two witnesses received for testifying. In fact, when a defense attorney asked one of the witnesses whether he had received any "monetary gain" for testifying, he said no.

Three men—James Earl Grant, T. J. Reddy and Charles Parker—were sentenced to prison, largely on the basis of these two witnesses' testimony.

There may be occasional need for granting witnesses immunity from prosecution, holding them in protective custody and giving them relocation money, though some of these practices raise grave questions. In any event, such benefits can be distressingly like payoffs in some cases.

Jurists and judges should be allowed to decide whether such benefits affect the credibility of government witnesses. Concealing the information can raise serious doubts about the fairness of a trial. In the case of the Lazy B defendants, we think a new trial is necessary to establish their guilt of innocence. As Judge Nichol said of the Wounded Knee trial, the function of the government is not to convict defendants but to seek justice.

The Washington Post

AN INDEPENDENT NEWSPAPER

March 5, 1974

Colman McCarthy

NORTH CAROLINA JUSTICE

In the annals of government lawlessness, not all the anguish suffered by citizens involves actual breakage of the law by officials. At times, the law can work against citizens in more subtle abuses. Thanks to the crudeness and arrogance that characterized John Mitchell's regime as Attorney General, the public has recently seen how the law can be used against citizens judged to be a threat to "law-and-order." The Harrisburg trial of Philip Berrigan and others was one of the more publicized of these prosecutions. Some would add to the list the trials of Daniel Ellsberg, the Gainesville 8 and the Camden 28. These cases reveal the immense discretionary power of the government to prosecute the citizens it chooses to pick on. Terror is in this power; none of the above defendants was ever convicted of the major "crimes" charged by their government, but their lives were disrupted severely, and large amounts of money were wasted on both sides—the public's money in prosecuting them and the persecuted's in defending themselves.

In North Carolina, a recent case involving three black men has many responsible people in the state and elsewhere convinced or suspicious that another repressive prosecution has occurred. Two differences in this case are that the citizens—called the Charlotte Thre—are already serving prison terms, and second, little national attention has been given the case. Within North Carolina, though, a state whose civic boosters like to identify it as leading the way of the "New South," the energies of The Charlotte Observer and a citizens group called the North Carolina Political Prisoners Committee, are determined not to abandon the prisoners by letting the case pass into obscurity. The national significance of the Charlotte Three is its suggestion that political repression at the state level can match or even pass what has been seen on the federal level.

The conviction of T. J. Reddy, Dr. James Grant and Charles Parker came in 1972 on a charge of burning the Lazy B stable in Charlotte and killing 15 horses. Reddy, a poet whose first volume of verse will be published by Random House this summer, had been in a small group that went to the Lazy B stable in 1967. They were denied riding privileges, apparently because of race. Eleven months later, the stable burned. Three years later, Reddy, along with Grant, a former VISTA and SCLC worker, and Parker, a youth counselor, were indicted.

In a January 1974 editorial entitled "An Injustice?" written one week before the appeals of the case ran out, The Charlotte Observer said the "case raises many questions," and added that at the trial "no physical evidence was presented to link (the defendants) to the stable burning four years earlier. Officers who investigated the fire had misplaced the firebombs the three were accused of using to burn the Lazy B barns and 15 horses." After noting the lack of evidence that sent Grant to prison for 25 years, Reddy for 20 years and Parker for 10, The Observer describes the "star" witnesses used by the state as two men "who were granted immunity from prosecution on a number of charges in exchange for their testimony in at least four trials of black activists in North Carolina." The Observer went on to say that the two witnesses, Walter David Washington and Theodore Alfred Hood, "had been sought on a number of charges, including illegal possession of dynamite and firearms, armed robbery and illegal flight to avoid prosecution. Washington had been discharged from the Marines for mental instability. Arrested in North Carolina after a flight to Canada,

The Washington Post

AN INDEPENDENT NEWSPAPER

March 5, 1974

North Carolina Justice (continued)

they agreed to give testimony in four cases in exchange for immunity from prosecution and protection by state and federal law enforcement officers."

Many in North Carolina were astonished at the severity of the sentences: 25, 20 and 10 years. The Observer checked its files of other unlawful burnings and found some disturbing facts. In 1965, a Mt. Airy, N.C. businessman burned a store, killing an employee and received only five to eight years. A Charlotte man got four to five years for burning the home occupied by his ex-wife. A Hendersonville man got five to 10 years for burning three schools. In 10 years, only one burning case exceeded the Charlotte Three's terms, and that was for seven instances of arson by the same person. Not only were the sentences astonishingly severe compared to other North Carolina burning convictions, but when compared to the 20 years Lt. William Calley (who now walks free) got for murdering 22 Vietnamese civilians, the severity is even more striking. Fifteen horses in Charlotte are apparently worth more than 22 human beings in Mylai.

The judge in the case was Frank Snepp. When asked in a phone interview last week about the case—about the severity of sentences, the reliability of the state's witnesses and the $50,000 bond imposed on Reddy even though he had no previous convictions—the judge said "the men had a fair trial. I thought they were dangerous to the community and I gave them the maximum sentence." As for the steady run of newspaper stories and editorials, Snepp charged that "the people who write them don't know the facts of the case."

In an ironic way, the judge may be right. The full facts may not be known, which is why reports from Charlotte say that The Observer, already editorially suspicious, has put two investigative reporters on the story. As the paper editorialized a year ago: "The conduct of the trial and various elements in it have so many troublesome aspects that the appeal may very well turn the conviction around." That didn't happen, but it did prompt Frye Gallard, an Observer reporter, to comment in a recent Progressive magazine article that "the same pattern—using criminals to testify against activists—has been applied to at least a half dozen other trials around the state."

Because Grant (a Ph.D. in chemistry) is a Hartford, Conn. native, the editorial page editor of the Hartford Times, Don O. Noel Jr., went to Charlotte. "It is remotely possible," he wrote, "that he is guilty of that charge (burning the stable), but I did not find, among several knowledgeable Charlotte newsmen I talked with, anyone who was persuaded of that, based on the evidence presented in court. Some clearly believe him the victim of a frame-up. Most, with the careful newsman's objectivity, concluded simply that his guilt was far from proven."

In America, and presumably North Carolina, court trials are meant to use the law as a means of settling doubts. But here, the opposite has happened—doubts have been raised. Those raising them are not the prison reformers who chant "free everybody" but parts of the rational and established community that have deep suspicions that these three men are victims of government oppression. Clearly, the governor of North Carolina has an obligation to act, either to remove all doubts about the case so that the guilt is factually based, or to drop the sentences so that justice in North Carolina is no longer mocked.

The Washington Post
AN INDEPENDENT NEWSPAPER
August 30, 1974

A Crucial Court Case in North Carolina

In Raleigh, N.C., yesterday, in the North Carolina Court of Appeals, the case of a group of citizens known as the Wilmington 10 was appealed. The group was convicted in October 1972 on firebombing and conspiracy charges. The alleged crime occurred in early 1971 in Wilmington, N.C., a time when that city was in turmoil with racial unrest. Following conviction of the group (eight were teenage students and none had criminal records), astonishingly severe sentences were imposed, with 1994 being the date before minimum imprisonment would be reached by most in the group. The case of the Wilmington 10 has received considerable attention in North Carolina. But many outside the state are also watching closely, and asking the same questions: Did the Wilmington 10 receive a fair trial? Or were they possible victims of tainted evidence and errors in proceedings and judicial rulings?

One of those interested is The Charlotte Observer. The newspaper has taken particular notice of the Rev. Ben Chavis, an ordained minister who went to Wilmington to help avoid violence by counseling the youth of the black community. The Observer examined the Rev. Chavis' treatment at the hands of North Carolina officials, going back through a series of criminal charges to 1968. The Observer called his treatment "harassment" and "persecution," noting that the Rev. Chavis is "beginning to look more and more like the target of political rather than criminal prosecutions." One group standing behind the Wilmington defendants is the Commission of Racial Justice of the United Church of Christ. The commission rallied the entire church to provide bail money of $400,000.

Although civic interests in North Carolina like to present the state as the epitome of the "New South," parts of its judicial system suggest that the methods of the "Old South" are still at work. There is also the case of the Charlotte 3 in which, according to The Observer, the government's star witnesses were secretly paid at least $4,000 each by the Justice Department. Another case involves James Grant, a Penn State Ph.D. in chemistry and former VISTA worker in Charlotte, who now does time in federal prison in Atlanta; many believe that questionable testimony was admitted in his trial also.

In sum, questions have been raised about the availability of justice for all of North Carolina's citizens. The appeal by the Wilmington group offers a clear opportunity for the state either to make its case conclusively—so that doubts are stilled—or else to recognize that there was never a case to be made in the first place.

The New York Times

Founded in 1851

ADOLPH S. OCHS, *Publisher 1896-1935*
ARTHUR HAYS SULZBERGER, *Publisher 1935-1961*
ORVIL E. DRYFOOS, *Publisher 1961-1963*

What Is Subversive?

Alongside the famous cases of the Chicago 7, the Gainesville 8 and the Camden 28, the overdrawn early campaign of the Nixon Administration against so-called domestic subversives continues to touch the lives of lesser known people in far-flung parts of the country.

Three young black activists in Charlotte, N.C. settled into prison this week on sentences of 10 to 25 years, convicted of arson in the mysterious destruction of a riding stable near Charlotte in 1968. One of the group, James Earl Grant, holds a Ph.D. in organic chemistry from the University of Chicago; another, T. J. Reddy, is publishing a volume of poetry later this year. All were active in anti-war and Black Action movements.

The evidence on which they were convicted last July seemed extraordinary from the start—the unsupported statements of two convicted felons whom the Government agreed to let off in return for their testimony. But the real controversy in North Carolina arose from the severity of the sentences, far in excess of the average prison terms for similar offenses.

Without attempting to untangle the political or racial motivations in their prosecution, a campaign is under way in North Carolina to persuade Gov. James Holshouser to commute their sentences. The Governor would enhance the stature of his fellow southern Republican moderates—to say nothing of furthering the cause of justice and defense of civil liberties—if he agreed to re-examine this strange case.

Endnotes

1 Walter David Washington was given a medical discharge by the U.S. Marines in 1967 and was diagnosed as a schizophrenic after he admitted trying to shoot his first sergeant in Vietnam. In 1969 he was convicted of the armed robbery of a 7-11 grocery store and was given a 20-25 year *suspended* sentence and placed on probation for five years.

2 Theodore Alfred Hood is also a Vietnam veteran. He has attended Central Piedmont Community College where he was active in the formation of a Black students union. In September, 1972, Hood was charged with second-degree murder in the death of a suspected heroin dealer. In November, 1972, he was charged with possession of marijuana. *Neither case has ever been tried.*

3 Chavis and Grant were accused by the federal government of helping Hood and Washington escape bond (bail) in a firearms case. Rev. Ben Chavis was acquitted, but Dr. James Grant was convicted and sentenced to two five-year terms in federal prison. He was freed on bail just before the stable-burning trial began in state court.

Chapter Six
Assata Shakur

The case of Assata Shakur, previously known as Joanne Chesimard, exemplifies U.S. governmental patterns and practices of racism, political repression, and sexism.

Assata Shakur, born in 1948 in New York City, is a student, poet, and mother, and was an active participant in the social and political activities of the Black community during the latter part of the 1960's. She became a member of the Black Panther Party, which was attracting young Blacks from urban centers faced with poverty, unemployment, police brutality, and conscription into the army during the Vietnam War. The Black Panthers had also won support from the segment of the majority population which had participated in the southern civil rights struggles, the anti-war movement, and the trauma from the epidemic of assassinations during the 1960s (Malcolm X, John Kennedy, Martin Luther King, Jr., and Robert Kennedy).

The Black Panther Party was uniquely singled out by then-director of the FBI, J. Edgar Hoover, as "the greatest threat to the internal security of the country.[1]" To ensure the destruction of the Black Panther Party, the FBI, through COINTELPRO, mounted an intensive repressive campaign against the Party. Activities in that campaign included charging persons with crimes and arresting them without regard to the factual basis of such charges; detaining persons in prisons for long periods of time on the basis of unfounded serious charges of which they were innocent; instigating various illegal acts and thereafter charging targeted Panther members with those crimes; creating and distorting disputes between persons and groupings within the Black Panther Party and with others outside the Party; utilizing the disputes to provoke and cause serious physical conflicts between such persons and groups; utilizing these disputes as a cover for shooting and otherwise seriously harming targeted persons; increasing the infiltration of the Party with paid informers and provocateurs and subjecting it to extensive electronic surveillance, burglaries, and other illegalities.[2]

By 1970, Assata Shakur had been targeted by the government as one of the "Black Nationalist" activists to be subjected to these strategies. The result was that she was charged with one serious crime after another—murder, bank robbery, kidnapping—and was also accused of conspiracy in a host of other crimes. The FBI circulated charges and accusations against her to its offices and to state and local law enforcement agencies throughout the country. The New York Police Department (NYPD) identified her both publicly and to other law enforcement agencies as the perpetrator of or co-conspirator in many major crimes.

The FBI and NYPD further charged her as being a leader of the Black Liberation Army (BLA), which they described as an organization engaged in the shooting of police officers. This description of the Black Liberation Army and the accusation of Assata Shakur's alleged relationship to it was widely circulated by government agents among police agencies and units.

As a result of this governmental misconduct, Ms. Shakur became a hunted person. Posters in police precincts and banks described her as a bank robber. She was highlighted on the FBI's most-wanted list and became a "shoot-to-kill" target throughout the country.

Various government agencies on the federal and state level brought six separate criminal indictments on federal and state charges within New York City against Assata Shakur, charging her with twenty different felonies. These indictments were accompanied by extensive publicity and embodied some, but not all, of the charges against her that the government had circulated to police units throughout the country.

All of these charges resulted in either dismissal or acquittal. These acquittals and dismissals were obtained notwithstanding the attempts to fabricate evidence against her, including the use of an FBI informer as the alleged victim of an alleged kidnapping and FBI procurement of identifications through improper use of an FBI "Black Nationalist" Photograph Album.

None of the other false and unfounded charges against Assata Shakur which had been publicly announced or circulated to police units became the subject of any criminal indictment or trial. Nevertheless, these charges, emanating from New York, along with the criminal indictments, made her a target to be hunted down and caused her to be in constant fear for her life.

In an effort to avoid the most intensive area of the hunt for her, Ms. Shakur was a passenger in an automobile on the New Jersey turnpike on May 2, 1973, when the vehicle was stopped by New Jersey state police. A shoot-out followed in which she was seriously injured and a companion in the vehicle and a state trooper were killed. Assata Shakur was thereafter charged with murder, assault, and related offenses for the events involving the shoot-out. Since May 2, 1973, the baseless New York charges against her of committing more than a score of felonies and the description of Assata Shakur as the "leader," "soul," and "queen" of the "cop-hating" Black Liberation Army have continued to be widely circulated. In May 1977, she was tried for murder arising out of the shoot-out and was convicted by an all-white jury in New Jersey. On March 29, 1978, she was sentenced to life imprisonment. That conviction is presently on appeal.

During her pre-trial detention and since her conviction, Assata Shakur has been subjected by New Jersey authorities to conditions of incarceration unprecedented in American penal history. During pre-trial detention, she was held in solitary confinement for one year in the basement of the Middlesex County Jail—an all-male facility where, in the words of the American Foundation, Inc., Institute of Corrections, her "dormitory was hidden from view from the rest of the basement....The basement area was musty, ventilation extremely poor, and natural light practically non-existent." Ten days after her conviction, Assata Shakur was placed in solitary confinement at the Yardville Youth Reception and Correctional Institution where she was the sole female inmate.

Notwithstanding the facts that Assata Shakur has never been accused of participating or conspiring in any prison escape or attempted escape and despite concessions by prison officers that she has presented no disciplinary problems throughout her incarceration, she has been subjected to extraordinary segregation by being the only woman in this century to be confined in an all-male correctional facility. The reasons given for this treatment rely upon the wrongful and groundless charges of numerous felonies and the FBI portrayal of her as the leader of a "cop-hating" group. The impact of this misconduct has been to create a myth of a person who is such a danger and risk that she must be uniquely confined in isolation.

Ms. Shakur's confinement as a pre-trial detainee and at Yardville as described above were unsuccessfully challenged in the United States District Court for the District of New Jersey. She was subsequently transferred to New York to stand trial on one of the false charges pending against her. Prior to her return to New Jersey, the State Department of Corrections advised the United States Court of Appeals for the Third Circuit that the New Jersey correctional system did not provide a women's institution with the degree of maximum security that New Jersey believed was required for Assata Shakur, and that it was the intention of the Department of Corrections to transfer her immediately to federal custody at Alderson Correctional Facility for Women in West Virginia upon her return to New Jersey.

Although the basis of the decision to transfer Assata Shakur to West Virginia was the false perception created by the illegal government activity, the Court agreed with the New Jersey Department of Corrections' decision and ordered that Ms. Shakur be transferred to federal custody. The transfer of Assata Shakur to the Alderson facility in West Virginia has resulted in depriving her of the right to participate effectively in her appeal, as well as denying her contact with her family and young child.[3]

Endnotes

[1] *Church Committee Report*, Book III, p. 187 (reprinted above in Chapter Three).

[2] Ibid., pp. 187-223 (reprinted above in Chapter Three).

[3] Since the filing of this Petition, the many federal suits challenging the conditions of Ms. Shakur's confinement bore some fruit. In the spring of 1979, she was transferred back to New Jersey and confined at the Clinton Reformatory for Women, albeit still in close confinement under maximum security conditions. Copies of the legal papers filed on her behalf in state and federal courts were included in the original Petition as Appendix VIII.

Chapter Seven
The Republic of New Afrika Eleven
(Obadele listed by Amnesty International)

One of the political responses by Black people in the turbulent 1960's to the racist and oppressive governmental policies and practices was the formation of organizations that advocated the establishment of a separate Black nation within the United States. One such group was the Republic of New Afrika (RNA), whose mission was to secure sovereignty by means of a peaceful plebiscite over the Black majority counties and parishes of Mississippi, Louisiana, and Arkansas, and establish a country to be known as Kush. The RNA, like so many other Black organizations, immediately became a target of the repressive COINTELPRO activities.

In August 1971, a force of heavily armed police and FBI agents, without prior warning or provocation, conducted a dawn raid on the official residence of the Provisional Government of the Republic of New Afrika in Jackson, Mississippi, under the guise of serving warrants on a fugitive alleged to be in the house. Five men and two women who were asleep in the house were given 75 seconds to come out after a bullhorn announcement calling for their surrender. Since no one was able to comply with the order, the police immediately opened fire. The seven people in the house fortunately escaped injury but a policeman lost his life in the attack, and an FBI agent and policeman were wounded.

A smaller but similar force simultaneously raided the office of the Republic of New Afrika several blocks away, where the President of the Provisional Government, Imari Abubakari Obadele I, two men, Aisha Salim (a female and the national Minister of Information) had spent the night. No shooting occurred here, but all four persons, together with the seven at the Residence, were arrested, and were charged with murder and with waging war against the state of Mississippi. They became known as the RNA Eleven.

The backgrounds of the RNA Eleven suggest the kinds of activism the United States government is anxious to suppress.

Imari Abubakari Obadele I was born Richard Bullock Henry on May 2, 1930, in Philadelphia. The Henry family, the Urban League's 1966 "Family of the Year," includes Dr. Walter Lester Henry, Jr., chairman of Howard University's Department of Medicine; Attorney Milton R. Henry, former City Councilman of Pontiac, Michigan; and Rev. Lawrence George Henry, pastor of the Union Baptist Church of Philadelphia. Obadele attended college at the University of Ottawa, Temple University, and Wayne State University. He is married, has four children, and six grandchildren. He became RNA President in March, 1970.

Hekima Ana was born Thomas Edward Norman on August 21, 1944, in Charlotte, North Carolina. During his first year at North Carolina College in Durham, his mother became a member of the Nation of Islam, an event which Ana said, "would be a force that would overshadow the influence of my college education." He later attended graduate school at the University of Wisconsin and became a citizen of the Republic of New Afrika in 1968. In 1970 he was elected RNA Vice President of the Midwest Region.

Aisha Salim was born Brenda Blount in Philadelphia. She attended Lincoln University and Harvard, majoring in political science. She was one of the first Black women to be hired as a stewardess by an American international airline, and has traveled extensively. She speaks and has taught French and Swahili. Also she worked as a reporter for a Philadelphia newspaper and for an African-affairs periodical. She is Minister of Information for RNA.

Offagga Quadduss was born Wayne James in Mt. Holly, New Jersey. After attending public schools in Camden, he enlisted in the Air Force when he was 17 and was honorably discharged four years later. In the service he was a fighter for civil rights and was instrumental in the decision to allow Black GIs to wear Afro hairstyles. He studied psychology and journalism at Rutgers University; also a musician, he studied under Black composer and artist Sun Ra. He is Delta Interior Minister for the RNA.

Addis Ababa was born Dennis Paul Shillingford in River Rouge, Michigan, and was raised in a middle class Black neighborhood in Detroit. After graduating from high school, he enrolled in Port Huron Community College in Port Huron, Michigan, and Washtenaw Community College in

Ypsilanti, where he majored in business administration. While in college, Ababa was active in the Black Students Union and also with the Malcolm X Center in Inkster, Michigan. He became a citizen of the RNA shortly before coming to Mississippi.

Chumaimari Fela Askadi was born Robert Charles Allen Stalling on October 23, 1951, in Duluth, Minnesota. He attended Lincoln Junior and Senior High School on the East Side of Milwaukee, Wisconsin. He dropped out after eleventh grade. He says, "The reason I left school is because I had somewhat of an idea that schools were teaching youth what to think instead of how to think." Later, as an RNA citizen, he attended nation-building classes. "That's when I really began to be interested in gaining complete freedom and building my own nation."

Tamu Sana was born Anne Lockhart. She is from Milwaukee, where she attended the University of Wisconsin at Milwaukee School of Education. She had worked as a teacher's aide in the Milwaukee Head Start Program. Tamu Sana was married to Hekima Ana in a ceremony conducted by the New Afrikan nation.

Spade de Mau Mau, born S. W. Alexander, attended public school in New Orleans, Louisiana. He is a Marine Corps veteran and saw combat service in Vietnam. He attended Tougaloo College outside of Jackson, Mississippi, where his family now lives. His mother is Margaret Walker, author of *Jubilee*.

Tawwab Nkrumah was born George L. Mathews in Birmingham, Alabama. He served for four years in the U.S. Marine Corps and saw extensive service in the Pacific. A lecturer at Boston's Black Topographical Research Center during 1970, he brought his skills to Mississippi in the Republic of New Afrika's Information Ministry.

Njeri Quadduss was born Toni Renee Austin. She was raised in Camden, New Jersey. After graduating from high school in Camden, she attended Rutgers University, where she met Offagga Quadduss. Their marriage ceremony was conducted by the nation in Mississippi on July 18, 1971. She was pregnant at the time of the raid, and her son, Antar Objereka

Offie Quadduss, was born on January 19, 1972, while pretrial hearings were being held.

Karim Hekima Omar Wadu Njabafudi is from New Orleans. He was born Larry Jackson in Bogalusa, Louisiana. He was president of a club called the Black Somalis which had about 100 members. When the Republic of New Afrika came to New Orleans, one of the club members told him about the new nation. He attended nation-building classes and became a citizen of the RNA. Njabafudi is the youngest of the RNA Eleven.

In September 1973, Imari Obadele and six others were tried in federal court in Biloxi, Mississippi, and found guilty of conspiracy to assault federal officers, assault, and the use of firearms to commit a felony. President Obadele was sentenced to twelve years, despite his motion to dismiss on the grounds that these attacks were part of an illegal conspiracy by the FBI and state officials to destroy the Black Liberation movement. In March 1976, the Fifth Circuit Court of Appeals confirmed all by one conviction. The conviction of Tamu Sana was reversed because at the time of the alleged conspiracy she was in Africa.

The U.S. Supreme Court denied *certiorari* in October 1976. Imari Obadele, free on bond, surrendered and was sent to the U.S. Penitentiary at Terre Haute, Indiana. He is presently serving his sentence at the U.S. Penitentiary in Atlanta, Georgia. Three other members of the RNA are serving life sentences in the state penitentiary of Mississippi. They have exhausted all legal remedies.

Long after their conviction, documents were released from the FBI COINTELPRO files which outlined the plot against the Republic of New Afrika and Imari Obadele. A petition for a *writ of habeas corpus* seeking the release of Obadele and others was filed in the Federal District Court for the Middle District of Pennsylvania. An FBI memorandum from the Jackson, Mississippi, field office to the Washington headquarters, written less than a month after the 1971 shoot-out and only recently released to attorneys for the RNA, makes clear the intensity of the FBI's involvement in the case. The memorandum dated September 8, 1971, reads in pertinent part as follows:

"If Obadele can be kept off the streets, it may prevent further problems involving the RNA, inasmuch as he completely dominates this organization and all members act under his instructions. It is the contention of the Jackson office that Obdale (sic) should be included with at least the aiding and abetting charges, particularly in regards to firearms violations, inasmuch, by this own admission, he controls all actions of the RNA.

"It should be noted: there are no federal charges pending against Obadele and the other three arrested at 1320 Lynch Street (the other house). Although these four are charged with local violations of murder and treason, the state feels they have a weak case in regard to these four men and may not be able to sustain successful prosecution."

An FBI memo from Jackson to Washington two years later, as the trial was about to begin, complained that the Justice Department was asking for a continuance, "as certain aspects of the case are being reevaluated at the highest levels of the Justice Department." The July 12, 1973, memo continued that unnamed officials felt there might not be sufficient evidence to prosecute, an attitude Jackson agents found "completely intolerable and unjustifiable." No legal remedies remain for the RNA Eleven.

Copies of three of Imari Obadele's challenges to his conviction were annexed to the original Petition as Appendix IX. We call your particular attention to them because he authored them himself.

Chapter Eight
The Puerto Rican Nationalists

The extended imprisonment and isolation of the five Puerto Rican Nationalists, Lolita Lebron, Rafael Cancel Miranda, Andres Figueroa Cordero, Irving Flores, and Oscar Collazo, jailed since 1954, must be examined within the context of the historic and continuing struggle for the independence of Puerto Rico. The United States took possession of Puerto Rico, then a Spanish possession, after a military invasion in 1898 called the Spanish-American War. The Treaty of Paris ceded the island to the U.S. after the defeat of Spain. All semblance of self-government was eliminated, and American economic penetration and exploitation of Puerto Rico was substituted for the Spanish.

Over the years, U.S. control and domination over the economic and political life of Puerto Rico has been most destructive. A 1976 U.S. Congressional Committee Report found that unemployment in the island approached nearly forty percent, and that over seventy percent of the island's population were eligible by their poverty for federal food stamps and nutritional assistance.

The Puerto Rican Nationalists, who have been in prison longer than any other U.S. political prisoners, are a particularly vivid example of the American government's remorselessness towards national minorities who oppose and resist oppressive governmental policies and practices. The backgrounds of these four men and a woman are outlined below.

Lolita Lebron was born in the mountainous agricultural region of Lares, Puerto Rico, where her family worked on a hacienda. In 1940, at the age of 21, she sailed for New York, where she worked as a seamstress. Active in the New York City branch of the Nationalist Party during the late '40's and '50's, she was named Delegate of the Nationalist Party in the U.S. in 1954. She is incarcerated in the federal prison for women at Alderson, West Virginia, where she continues to write poetry and practice Roman Catholicism.

Rafael Cancel Miranda is a native of Mayaguez, Puerto Rico, grew up in a prominent Nationalist family, and has been active in the Nationalist Party since childhood. At the age of 17, he was imprisoned for two years in Tallahassee Federal prison for refusing to register for military service in the U.S. Army during the Korean War. Since his imprisonment in 1954, he has struggled for prisoners' rights and has spent more than seventeen months in solitary confinement over the last five years of imprisonment. He is currently incarcerated at the federal prison in Marion, Illinois.

Andres Figueros Cordero was born in Aguada, Puerto Rico. He worked in the fields with his father until the age of 12, and slept on the floor "as a child and as an adult." In Aguada, he joined the Nationalist Party. In prison in the United States, he suffered cancer without diagnosis for over fourteen months, after which he endured three major operations. After his release on October 6, 1977, he returned to Puerto Rico where he was welcomed as a beloved patriot. He is currently receiving medical treatment in San Juan, but even this was made difficult by prison officials' delay in sending his medical records to Puerto Rico.

Irving Flores was born in Cabo Rojo and joined the Nationalist Party at a young age. After traveling to New York to look for work, he found a job as a tailor and became active in organizing for better working conditions. He is currently incarcerated at the federal prison in Springfield, Illinois.

Oscar Collazo was born the youngest of fourteen children in Manati, a coffee-growing area of Puerto Rico. With the expansion of the U.S. sugar corporations, his family became increasingly impoverished. He moved to New York to find a job. He worked as a dishwasher, cook, and hat-maker. He became active in the Nationalist Party in 1931, was later elected as president of the New York City branch, and then alternate delegate to the United Nations. He is currently incarcerated at the federal prison in Leavenworth, Kansas.

The acts for which the Puerto Rican Nationalists were prosecuted can best be understood in the context of the United States' colonization of Puerto Rico. In 1950, the U.S. Congress passed *Public Law 600,* which permitted Puerto Rico to draft its own Constitution as long as it did not repeal the colonial laws already governing the island. To suppress the growing opposition to American rule of the Puerto Rican people, the U.S. National Guard, assisted by the colonial police, mounted unrestrained attacks against the leaders and members of the Nationalist Party of Puerto Rico, which is dedicated to an independent Puerto Rico.

Meanwhile, in the United States in 1950, the government had begun to conduct an unreasoned and ruthless witch-hunt, prosecuting and discrediting Communists, labor leaders, teachers, and liberals from all walks of life and occupations. It was in this year and climate that Ethel and Julius Rosenberg were convicted and sentenced to death.

On October 30, 1950, threatened with the elimination of their political party by the police and National Guard, the Puerto Rican Nationalists encouraged island-wide resistance. It was rapidly suppressed; hundreds were wounded, many killed and thousands jailed on the flimsiest pretexts.

On November 1, 1950, as part of the revolution against American domination, Oscar Collazo and Griselio Torresola, both members of the Nationalist Party, carried out an armed attack against Blair House, the temporary residence of President Truman. Torresola and one presidential guard were killed, and Collazo was wounded. He was tried and given the death penalty. But in response to international pressure, the sentence was commuted to life imprisonment.

In the wake of the severe repression on the island, the U.S. government held a referendum on the new Constitution of Puerto Rico. Although 48 percent of the voting population boycotted the referendum, it passed and provided the basis for the U.S. government's claim that Puerto Ricans had freely chosen commonwealth status by an overwhelming majority. In December 1953, the United Nations removed Puerto Rico from its list of non-self-governing territories.

A similar decision was expected at the Tenth Pan-American Conference, opening in Caracas, Venezuela, under the auspices of the Organization of American States on March 1, 1954. On that same day, Lolita Lebron, Rafael Cancel Miranda, Andres Figueroa Cordero and Irving Flores fired guns from the visitors' gallery into the U.S. Congress, unfurling the Puerto Rican flag, and crying, "Viva Puerto Rico Libre!" Five Congressmen were wounded, none seriously. All four Puerto Ricans were tried and convicted of five counts of assault with a deadly weapon. Ms. Lebron was given 40 months to 10 years on each count, and the men 5 to 15 years, all sentences to be served consecutively, adding up to a total of 16 to 50 years for Lolita Lebron and 25 to 75 years for the other three Nationalists.

Lolita Lebron, Cancel Miranda, Figueroa Cordero and Irving Flores hoped to make their trial a public forum for explaining the issues surrounding Puerto Rico, but such evidence was not permitted by the court at the trial which was conducted in the atmosphere of the politically repressive fifties.

During their incarceration, the five Puerto Rican Nationalists have been subjected to a conscious program and policy by the U.S. Government to isolate them from communication with friends, family, and supporters from the outside. They have been harassed by arbitrary rules, and their mail and visiting rights have been severely limited. They are not allowed to correspond among themselves. Visitors coming from Puerto Rico have been allowed to visit for only an hour, or in some cases, not at all. Publications which contain news about the Puerto Rican struggle for independence are denied them. The have been placed in solitary confinement for peaceful protests against inhuman prison conditions.

The cruelest punishment of all was meted out to Andres Figueroa Cordero who was placed in the "hole"—solitary confinement—in Leavenworth Penitentiary when he was persistent in his complaints about bleeding from the rectum. For six months, he was kept there before it finally became obvious to the prison doctors that he was suffering from more than hemorrhoids. He was shipped to Springfield Medical Center, where it was discovered he has cancer of the lower colon, and a colostomy was immediately performed. Two more operations later, when it was apparent he didn't have long to live, a successful application for his release on medical parole was made, but the Chief Medical Officer refused to acknowledge his condition was terminal. Finally, in September, 1977, prison doctors admitted Cordero had only four to eight weeks to live and recommended a medical parole. Cordero refused release under those conditions and President Carter finally granted him executive clemency.

Today, twenty-five years later, four of the Puerto Rican Nationalists are still imprisoned although international attention and United Nations' inquiries are examining and questioning the continued neo-colonial rule of Puerto Rico by the United States. No legal remedies are available to them.

Chapter Nine
American Indian Movement Defendants: Wounded Knee and Its Aftermath

In the mid-1960's, Native American struggles for self-determination and economic and social dignity intensified as representatives of various tribes organized in activist groupings. The American Indian Movement (AIM) has been most successful in mobilizing groups who had traditionally been kept divided by language, geography, and custom. Much Native American discontent was focused on the dependent and quasi-feudal character of Indian life on the U.S. government-controlled reservations.

The 1973 siege at the Pine Ridge Reservation in Wounded Knee, South Dakota, precipitated the most recent series of governmental prosecutorial and armed ferocity against the Indian Nations and flowed directly from the land thefts, under guise of treaty, conducted by the U.S. government and its Bureau of Indian Affairs. Pine Ridge Reservation came into being after the treaty of Fort Laramie, signed in 1868 between the chiefs of the Sioux and the U.S. government. The treaty recognized the Sioux nation as a sovereign nation. It guaranteed to the Sioux Nation fifty million acres of land in their traditional homeland (now in the states of Nebraska, North and South Dakota, Montana, and Wyoming). When the area's natural resources such as gold, timber, oil, gas, coal, uranium, and grazing land were appraised, the government and private corporations took back the land in violation of this treaty—as has happened with so many other treaties with the Indian Nations.

Despite the provisions of the U.S. Constitution which make treaties between the United States and other sovereign nations the supreme law of the land, at least four hundred treaties with the Native American peoples have been ignored. In 1934, in order to destroy the tribes' causes of legal action against the United States, the sovereign state concept of the tribes and their traditional forms of self-rule were abolished. A "Tribal Council System" under the control of the U.S. Bureau of Indian Affairs (BIA) was unilaterally substituted and imposed upon the Native Americans without their consent, even though a treaty provision required that all such changes of political control could only be implemented with the consent of seventy-five percent of adult males.

The Pine Ridge Reservation in southwestern South Dakota was one of the parcels of land allocated to the Sioux, to which they were forcibly relocated after the violation of the treaty provisions. The reservation extends 4,500 square miles without any public transportation. Its one library and bank are located in the white settlement areas. Less than one percent of the land is cultivated by Native Americans, while more than half of the total acreage is used by whites for grazing and other purposes, at minimal rents.

Economic and social inequities press upon the Oglala Sioux people, as upon other Native American peoples, because of the quasi-indentured status. By 1973, about 70 percent of those at Pine Ridge were unemployed and dependent upon BIA largesse for survival; the life expectancy was 44 years, 30 years less than that of white persons. Reservations are managed by the Bureau of Indian Affairs' bureaucracy under policies designed to maintain Indian dependency. While the BIA and other federal agencies billed the American tax payers over $8,000 a year per Oglala Sioux family at Pine Ridge, the median family income there remained at less than $2,000.

After the unpunished murders of two Oglala by whites in 1972, the Native American community in Pine Ridge established the Oglala Sioux Civil Rights Organization (OSCRO) to press for justice on the reservation and to resist encroachments on Indian autonomy by the BIA. Their demands included a U.S. congressional investigation of the BIA; construction of Indian-owned and run cooperatives on the reservation, as opposed to white owned businesses "leased" out by the BIA; and the eviction from office by Richard Wilson, the chairman of the tribal council set up by the BIA, who maintained control of Pine Ridge through hired vigilantes and business corruption.

Six of the reservations' eight districts held meetings and voted to demand Wilson's impeachment. Wilson and the BIA called in federal marshals in February 1973, to repel the movement for civil rights, with violence if necessary. Tribal council meetings were banned so that no district resolutions could be acted upon. OSCRO continued to meet in spite of the ban. On February 27, supported by the American Indian Movement (AIM), the organization called a meeting at Wounded Knee, the historic site of the 1890 massacre of more than 300 Native American men, women, and children by a U.S. cavalry expeditionary force. More than 300 Native Americans, representing 75 different nations, met at Wounded Knee and developed new demands of government authorities: the dissolution of Wilson's tribal council and a reorganization after new elections; replacement of two senior BIA officials on the reservation; and an investigation by the Senate Foreign Relations Committee of violations of 400 treaties by the United States.

The government's reaction to the situation was swift and remorseless. About 90 police officers sealed off all the roads leading into Wounded Knee. The BIA police and an additional 250 U.S. marshals and FBI agents, armed with M-16 rifles, cordoned off the village. Fifteen armored personnel carriers with mounted .50 caliber machine guns surrounded the area. Twenty tanks were brought in and the 82nd Airborne was bivouacked nearby. The one-day meeting was converted into a seventy-one-day armed siege.

Despite government control and distortion of information reported from Wounded Knee, there was massive public support for the Native Americans. During the government's continued assault of Wounded Knee, two Native Americans were killed and scores wounded. To avoid an armed invasion, the Native Americans relinquished control of Wounded Knee after an agreement that there would be no reprisals. Despite the agreement, over 400 persons were arrested and many charged with conspiracy and other serious crimes.

Of the three hundred and twenty individuals selectively indicted and prosecuted for events at Wounded Knee, not one of the indictees was a federal marshal or BIA official. The majority of these charges have subsequently been thrown out of court because of government misconduct or contradictory, unsubstantiated evidence. The prosecutions since 1973 of some of the Native Americans' leaders at the Wounded Knee incursion is illustrative of the disparate ways in which Indian activists have been treated.

Russell Means is one of the organizers and founders of AIM. Since the 1973 events of Wounded Knee, Means has been subjected to twelve different criminal trials by both federal and state authorities. Most charges have been dismissed upon proof of governmental misconduct; he has been acquitted on others.

In a last attempt by the government to prosecute Means, he was tried and convicted in 1975 under a South Dakota law which has since been repealed. Sentenced to four years for "rioting to obstruct justice," he filed an unsuccessful appeal. In July 1978, he was ordered to prison. Numerous threats against his safety in prison have been reported, and within six months he had been stabbed.

Dennis Banks is another organizer and founder of AIM. After being convicted in Custer, South Dakota, in 1975 on riot and assault charges along with Russell Means, Banks fled to California in fear of his life. There he was arrested in January 1977, by the FBI on federal fugitive charges. As a result of public outcry, the governor of California refused to extradite Banks to South Dakota, but because the government is still determined to press charges, Dennis Banks remains a prisoner in federal custody.

Since the 1973 occupation of Wounded Knee, the people of the Pine Ridge Reservation have become increasingly determined to exercise their sovereignty and to force the U.S. government to uphold treaty agreements with the Sioux Nation. The success of the Oglala people in this pursuit would have implications for all Native American nations in the United States.

On June 26 and 27, 1975, BIA-imposed Council President Dick Wilson, after secret tribal council meetings, authorized transfer of land known as the Gunnery Range to the U.S. Department of Parks for incorporation in the Badlands National Monument without the knowledge of the tribal members. The area transferred included some 133,000 acres of Indian lands. The opposition to the contemplated land transfer precipitated another invasion of the reservation by governmental troops and agents.

FBI and BIA police presence increased steadily during that period, including helicopter surveillance of the reservation and patrols with para-military weapons. A number of supporters of the American Indian Movement were beaten, shot at, maced, or had their homes firebombed. Other residents of the reservation were detained for long periods for questioning.

On June 26, two heavily armed FBI agents, Jack Coler and Ronald Williams, entered the reservation, allegedly with arrest warrants for two men not known to frequent the area. Gunfire was heard shortly after they left the first house at which they stopped. At some time after their arrival on the reservation, the two agents were killed.

Additional agents, BIA police, and state and county officers surrounded the reservation. The FBI called for reinforcements from other local offices in Minneapolis and Denver. The 82nd Airborne Division was alerted. U.S. Army equipment, including two Armored Personnel Carriers, was requisitioned. Agents' arms included AR-15s and M-16s. A van of ammunition was driven into Oglala. A special team of chemical warfare men were on hand, as well as a sniper team. Equipment was sent from as far away as Quantico, Virginia, Marine Base. This rapid delivery of arms and material supplies suggests that the raid was pre-planned.

The South Dakota Attorney General announced his intention to go to Pine Ridge, though without jurisdiction on Indian reservations under Federal trust responsibility. He gave authorization for the use of state police units and special State Tactical Squads. Reports were circulated by state officials that the two FBI agents had been "executed", "ambushed", and their bodies "riddled" with twenty or more bullets each. The FBI reported finding Joseph Stuntz, a Native Oglala, dead in a jacket belonging to one of the dead FBI agents. The FBI issued warrants for four people from the list of "undesirable Wounded Knee militants" and charged them with the murder of the agents.

Leonard Peltier, Bob Robideau, Dino Butler and Jimmy Eagle were the four chosen. Robideau and Butler were acquitted by a jury. Charges against Eagle were dropped before his case went to trial, but after he was held in jail for a year and a half. Despite the lack of evidence, the government continued to prosecute Leonard Peltier, a 32-year-old Chippewa-Sioux from Grand Forks, North Dakota, who as a teenager had demonstrated against the destitute condition of the people on his home reservation, had initiated Native American self-help cooperative projects, and who had become an American Indian Movement activist known to FBI and state governmental agents.

Under threat of his life, Peltier fled to Canada, where he was arrested in February 1976. Despite international demonstrations of support, he was extradited to the United States in December 1976, to stand trial. The charges against him were based on two affidavits signed by Myrtle Poor Bear. They stated that she had been present and had watched Peltier shoot the agents. In contradiction to these affidavits indicating that Poor Bear had seen the shooting, the FBI also possessed a conflicting affidavit in which she stated that she had left the area the day before the shooting.

When defense attorneys interviewed Poor Bear, she maintained that she had never been anywhere near Oglala during that time, but had signed the conflicting affidavits because the FBI had threatened her by accusing her of the shooting and had threatened to put her in jail for life if she did not cooperate.

Poor Bear testified to all of this at a hearing at Peltier's trial in Fargo, North Dakota. The judge refused to permit her to give testimony before the jury. In this way, the government, which had obtained Peltier's extradition from Canada on the basis of Poor Bear's testimony, kept the jury from hearing her story at the trial.

Other instances of biased judicial rulings during the Peltier trial included a refusal to allow the defense to introduce an FBI agent's report into evidence while cross-examining the agent witness. The court also denied testimony which tended to establish that the reservation was so violent that the people of Oglala were acting in self-defense by returning fire that day, even though such testimony was an important part of the defense in the acquittal of Dino Butler and Bob Robideau.

In the spring of 1977, Leonard Peltier was sentenced to two consecutive life terms in prison. Although the U.S. attorney admitted the falsity of the Poor Bear affidavits on appeal to the Eighth Circuit Court of Appeals, the court refused to reverse the conviction. No meaningful legal remedies remain for Leonard Peltier.[1]

Appendix X of the original Petition included selected portions of a report, "Violations of American Indian Human Rights by the United States," which was prepared by the International Indian Treaty Council, 777 United Nations Plaza, Suite 10F, New York, NY 10017. Most of the report that appear in the Appendix of the original Petition follows.

INTERNATIONAL INDIAN TREATY COUNCIL
International Indian Treaty Council Report

VIOLATIONS OF AMERICAN INDIAN HUMAN RIGHTS BY THE UNITED STATES

Case History – Wounded Knee 1973

Indian peoples have tried to function through the colonial system imposed by the Indian Reorganization Act of 1934. They have seen their land taken away and their hopes destroyed. The liberation of Wounded Knee was an effort to regain power over their land and lives.

The Sioux Nation, like every Indian nation in the U.S., has ceded land to the U.S. government. In return, the government was to provide goods and services. At Wounded Knee, the Sioux demanded that the government honor its treaties. Hundreds of Indians representing more than 75 different nations supported this demand.

The Wounded Knee siege itself, the text of the agreement between the U.S. federal government and the Sioux people, the breaking of the agreement by the U.S. government, the harassment which followed, and the summary of legal cases were compiled by the Wounded Knee Legal Defense/Offense Committee set up by Indian and non-Indian people after it became clear that a massive defense effort would be necessary in order to keep the U.S. government from putting a large number of American Indian Movement members in jail.

A summary of the Wounded Knee siege and the events that ensued follows. It is followed by a description of FBI activities at Pine Ridge. Further information and documentation, including depositions and eyewitness accounts, can be found in Supplements IV A 1, B 1, C 1.

On February 26, 1973, the Civil Rights Organization on the Pine Ridge Reservation met openly to discuss their grievances concerning the tribal government and the BIA. Since similar meetings had produced no results, the people decided to ask for some assistance from the American Indian Movement.

After another open meeting on February 27, a caravan of some 300 people drove to Wounded Knee Village, site of the 1890 massacre and a prime example of the treatment of Indians since the European invasion. Ironically, the number of Indians in 1973 was approximately the same as the number massacred less than 100 years ago.

On arrival, the people continued the meetings that brought them to Wounded Knee. Within hours, police had set up roadblocks, cordoned off the area and began arresting people leaving the town. The people prepared to defend themselves against the government's aggression.

The federal government brought in armored personnel carriers and an arsenal of weapons, including AR-15's, M-16's, 30, 50 and 60 caliber machine guns, as well as grenade launchers, flares, CS gas and helicopters. BIA police, FBI and local vigilantes ringed the area. Hundreds of thousands of rounds of ammunition were fired into Wounded Knee; flares were shot off, burning up the countryside; and gas was released to rout the defenders.

On April 5, after holding off the government for 37 days, the residents of the Pine Ridge Reservation and leaders of AIM signed a 6 point agreement with White House representatives. Russell Means called the agreement "a small victory, a preliminary victory in the war with the United States over our treaty rights." The agreement provided for a meeting between traditional Indian leaders and White house representatives to re-examine U.S. obligations under the 1868 Treaty, investigation of the functioning of the BIA and tribal governments on the Reservation and inquiring into possible violations of civil rights and criminal laws. Promise of a preliminary meeting immediately after the signing of the agreement was instantly broken when the government demanded the Indians first surrender their arms and submit to arrest – a direct contradiction to the disarmament understanding reached during negotiations. The Indian people did not surrender. It was a month before a new agreement was signed and the people of Wounded Knee at last left the Village.

The government siege claimed its first life when Frank Clearwater was shot in the head while lying in a church on April 17. He died April 25. Then, on April 27, another defender was murdered. Buddy Lamont was killed while attempting to retrieve desperately needed food being airdropped.

The government tried starving out the defenders. Only food and medical supplies that were smuggled in by night reached the people. The goon squad roadblock set up by Dick Wilson and tacitly supported by the government was in direct violation of a Federal Court order won by the Wounded Knee Legal Defense/Offense Committee. Communications were cut for over a month and the press was prevented from getting first-hand information. Freedom of the press was obstructed throughout the liberation. Communications with attorneys and negotiations with government officials were continually hampered.

On April 28, negotiations began for the first time since the abortive April 5 "peace" settlement. On May 5 an agreement was reached for disarmament and on May 8 the siege ended and the Village was evacuated. After 71 days an agreement had been reached.

The primary issues in the accord were a re-examination of the 1868 Fort Laramie Treaty and a democratized tribal government. As with the 1868 Treaty, the government still has not implemented its latest agreement with the Sioux people. Instead, 317 people were charged with conspiracy, larceny and numerous other charges.

Lawyers for the Wounded Knee Legal Defense/Offense Committee personally witnessed the disregard of the May 5 Agreement – done in the spirit of a recent statement by South Dakota Senator George McGovern: "I think the treaties were abrogated by an act of Congress over 100 years ago and that it is ridiculous to talk about the Treaty of 1868 being carried out."

--Almost simultaneously with the signing of the Agreement, government personnel shot flares and tracers into the village, lighting the grass and sending smoke fumes into the tipi.

--The agreement that the attorneys would be present and supervise the stand-down was ignored until one of the defendants refused to leave the area without an attorney, precipitating a near crisis.

--The agreement that those arrested would be taken to Rapid City was initially violated by taking one group to the Pine Ridge jail, precipitating another crisis.

--The U.S. attorney has repeatedly violated the promise not to make bond recommendations, and instead has recommended and fought for outrageously high bonds.

--The agreement provided that permanent residents would be "escorted to their homes by government officials", and that a "search...monitored by attorneys" would be conducted "with minimum inconvenience to the occupants". This agreement was broken immediately and totally by the government. The residents were not permitted to return to their homes. escorted or otherwise. The search was conducted without the presence of attorneys, who demanded and were refused the right to be present, and without the presence of the residents. Far from being at a "minimum of inconvenience", the search actually was an excuse for massive destruction of personal property and homes by government officials. Repeated vociferous objections to these government procedures were ignored.

--The agreement that government roadblocks be eliminated was ignored for days, as was the promise that lawful access would be resumed.

--Despite the promise that lawful political activity would not be interfered with, no political activity has been permitted on the reservation unless approved by the tribal government.

--The promise to prevent civil rights violations by government authorities has been ignored; in fact terrorism on the reservation has increased since the stand-down.

--None of the promised civil suits to protect the personal property and civil, legal and political rights of Pine Ridge residents has been instituted by the federal government.

--The promised actions against unlawful tribal council actions, resolutions or ordinances have not been taken.

--None of the promised actions against tribal counts of BIA police has been taken.

In total disregard for the May 5 Agreement, BIA police, unattended by impartial observers, swept through the village, breaking into every automobile, prying open every trunk, smashing down even unlocked doors, ripping apart and confiscating the personal belongings of Wounded Knee families and Indian holy men.

Several supporters of the liberation were fired from their jobs, including the director of the Community Health Representative program and five employees of the Public Health Service hospital. Although their dismissal was overturned by the unemployment compensation board, the Wound Knee Legal Defense/Offense Committee filed a suite, Janis et al. v. Wilson et al. on their behalf.

On most occasions, the harassment far exceeded loss of jobs, withholding of welfare checks or arrests without cause. Beatings by BIA police and goons have become a fact of life for residents of the reservation. Homes have been firebombed and shot at, including those of Frank Fool's Crow, a traditional Sioux chief; Eddie White Dress, a former policeman who stayed inside Wounded Knee during the liberation; and Severt Young Bear, a vocal AIM supporter and district councilman for Porcupine. One such incident resulted in nine-year-old Mary Ann Little Bear losing sight in one eye as the car she was riding in with her family was shot at by goon squad leaders John Hussman, Francis Randall and Woody Richards. Law enforcement officials were notified, but when FBI agents arrived—hours later—they made a cursory survey of the area and left, taking no statements and no action. Meanwhile, members of the Wounded Knee Legal Defense/ Offense Committee investigations team had taken 20 signed statements by witnesses.

That such violence could go uninvestigated and unchecked made almost inevitable the murders of Clarence Cross and Pedro Bissonette. Clarence Cross, his brother Vernal, and their friend, William Spotted Eagle, were asleep in a car, en route to their home in Kyle, South Dakota. They were awakened and shot by two members of the BIA police force, who took Billy into the squad car. Clarence, mortally wounded, was left lying in the road. He died several weeks later as a result of these injuries and this neglect. Vernal was shot twice, then maced as he lay seriously wounded in his car. Vernal continues to be the subject of violence, his home shot at on many occasions, his car pursued as far as Rapid City, over 100 miles away, and his life threatened.

Pedro Bissonette was murdered on October 17 by members of the BIA police. Much evidence has come to light that federal and tribal authorities conspired to cover up facts and alter hospital records. It appears that the official account of Pedro's death—the murder weapon, the time of death, the distance and angle of the shots, and Pedro's alleged possession of a gun—is a fabrication. A founder and officer of the Oglala Sioux Civil Rights Organization and a leading figure during the 71-day liberation, Pedro was perhaps the most important defense witness for the upcoming trials. He had personal and extensive knowledge of the way that BIA police, Wilson's "goon squad", and the FBI, the Justice Department and the courts had acted in concert against Indians working for self-determination and recognition of their civil rights. Neither the BIA police nor the FBI has done anything more than question its own agents and harass the more than 2000 people who came to pay their respects and express their grief and outrage at the three-day wake and funeral.

Summary of Legal Cases

As a result of Wounded Knee, there were over 400 arrests resulting in 317 cases covering civil, criminal and tribal charges.

The first trial, that of Russell Means and Dennis Banks, began on January 8, 1974 before Chief Judge Fred J. Nichol of South Dakota who moved the case to St. Paul for trial.

On March 13, 1973, a Federal Grand Jury returned indictments including separate nine count indictments against Russell Means, Dennis Banks, Clyde Bellecourt, Carter Camp and Pedro Bissonette. These indictments were each mimeographed copies of each other with only the names changed. Approximately 40 other persons were indicted at the same time.

Subsequently, each of the five persons was named in identical two count indictments, and at the same time Stanley Holder and Leonard Crow Dog were named in 11 count indictments. The result was that each faced the same 11 charges. These charges were Count I (burglary), Count II (larceny), Count III (assault on a federal officer), Counts IV and V (impeding federal officers in the course of a civil disorder), Count VI (arson of a motor vehicle), Count VII (possession of unauthorized firearms), Count VIII (theft of a motor vehicle) and Count IX (conspiracy to commit each of the other acts). Counts I and II of the additional indictments, often referred to as Counts X and XI are the additional assault on federal office charges.

Count VI (arson of a motor vehicle) has been dismissed by the Court as improper.

All cases were originally set before Federal Judge ANDREW BOGUE of Rapid City, S.D. A massive series of affidavits were served showing Judge Bogue's prejudice against all the defendants. Judge Bogue removed himself from the Russell Means and Dennis Banks cases but refused to remove himself from the others. A writ of mandamus was filed in the Court of Appeals (8th Circuit) which transferred the Bellecourt, Camp, Bissonette and Holder and Crow Dog cases to Judge Fred J. Nichol, who then had the Means and Banks cases, but refused to remove Judge Bogue from the other cases.

From the beginning the defendants wanted to be tried together. The government opposed all efforts to obtain joint trials. Judge Nichol ruled that only the Banks and Means cases would be tried together at the first trial. The Court of Appeals refused to order Judge Nichol to consolidate the cases.

An in-depth study was made of the jury wheel for the Western Division from which the Grand Jury was selected. This study was conducted by the leading geographers and social scientists in the Midwest. It demonstrated that Indians were grossly unrepresented in the jury wheel. The court denied all motions based on this discrimination.

The defendants placed before the court overwhelming evidence that it would be impossible to obtain a fair trial in South Dakota. This involved a statewide survey of attitudes, a compilation of newspaper articles, and evidence of the government's press activities. The court found that: "... there exists in the District of South Dakota so great a prejudice against defendants that they cannot obtain a fair and impartial trial at any place fixed by law for holding trial in South Dakota." (See Supp. IV.E. 3)

The over-riding constitutional questions are those involving treaty rights. The defendants challenged the Major Crimes Act which makes acts on a reservation which violate state law federal crimes. Counts I, II, VI (dismissed) and VIII are based on this Act. The defendants also challenged the constitutionality of the Civil Disobedience Act of 1968 which forms the basis of the charge of obstructing federal officers in the course of a civil disorder (Counts IV and V) and the particular provisions of the Firearms Control Act dealing with registering Molotov cocktails (Count VII).

There were also serious constitutional questions in the indictments themselves. It is virtually unprecedented in modern American jurisprudence to charge individuals not only with conspiracy but also with responsibility for the allegedly criminal acts of hundreds or thousands of others. The Bill of Particulars by the government increases the problem for it discloses that the government does not claim to know who did many of the acts for which the defendants were being charged.

The defendants also argued that the indictments themselves were brought for the purpose of preventing Indian people from uniting and struggling against the oppressive conditions of their lives and further to destroy the American Indian Movements.

In summary of the original 317 indicted cases, only 138 were pursued by the U.S. government. Many of these cases were eventually dropped, since they had been brought on insufficient evidence or evidence which was illegally introduced into the courts of U.S. law. Charges against 70 persons were dropped as a result of information concerning the participation at Wounded Knee of the U.S. Army and Air Force, which is illegal in a civil disorder except by special declaration by the U.S. President or Congress. Some charges were based on testimony from Indian people who had participated in the liberation of the village and who had been threatened and/or bribed by federal agents. Most of these people refused to testify, and more cases were dropped. In the end, the U.S. government had only a 7% conviction rate—an unusually low rate which attests to the allegation that the government wanted above all to tie American Indian Movement members up in court cases and jail terms. The U.S. agencies and individual employees were never investigated or called to account for their actions in Wounded Knee. This is a clear example of selective prosecution.

Update

The present situation on the Pine Ridge Reservation is the same or worse than prior to the takeover. The unemployment, poverty, FBI harassment and other genocidal activities continue unabated. A specific example is the recent death of Jerry Williams, a veteran of Wounded Knee, under suspicious circumstances while in police custody in Oklahoma.

The following is a list of AIM members and supporters murdered on the Pine Ridge Reservation in the past four years.

Victim	Date	Solved by Police	Legal Status
Raymond Yellow Thunder	1-72	Yes	Acquitted
Wesley Bad Heart Bull	1-73	Yes	Acquitted
Edward Burns Prairie	2-1-73	No	No investigation
*Frank Clearwater	4-25-73	No	No investigation
*Buddy Lamont	4-27-73	No	No investigation
Julius Bad Heart Bull	7-30-73	Yes	1 man convicted
*Clarence Cross	6-73	No	No investigation
Donald He Crow	8-27-73	No	No investigation
Aloysius Long Soldier	10-5-73	No	No investigation
*Pedro Bisonette	10-17-73	No	No investigation
Philip Little Crow	11-14-73	No	No investigation
Allison Little Spotted Horse	11-23-73	No	Under investigation
Melvin Spider	9-22-73	No	No investigation
Verlyn Dale Bad Heart Bull	2-18-74	No	No investigation
Edward Standing Soldier	2-18-74	No	No investigation
Charlene Lame	Missing since 1960	No	No investigation
Dennis LeCompte	9-7-74	Yes	Not Guilty
Jesse Trueblood	11-17-74	No	No investigation
Elaine Wagner	11-30-74	No	No investigation
Robert Reddy	9-16-74	No	Under investigation
William J. Steele	3-9-75	Yes	1 man convicted
Stacey Kotier	3-20-75	Yes	1 man convicted
Edith Eagle Hawk	3-21-75	No	No investigation
Linda Eagle Hawk	3-21-75	No	No investigation
Earl W. Janis, Jr.	3-21-75	No	No investigation
Jeannette M. Bisonette	3-25-75	No	No investigation
Rosewood Buffalo	3-75	No	No investigation
*Joseph Stuntz Kills Right	6-26-75	No	No investigation
Homer Blue Bird	9-9-75	Yes	1 man convicted
James Little	9-10-75	Yes	3 men convicted
Janice Black Bear	10-26-75	Yes	1 man convicted
Lydia Cut Grass	1-5-76	Yes	No conviction
Byron L. DeSersa	1-31-76	Yes	Pending court action
Lena R. Slow Bear	2-6-76	No	No conviction
Cleveland Reddest	3-26-76	No	No conviction
Anna Mae Aquash	2-76	No	No investigation
Martin Two Two	5-6-76	No	Under investigation
Sam Afraid of Bear	5-24-76	No	No investigation
Julia Pretty Hips	5-9-76	No	Under investigation
Lyle Dean Richards	7-31-73	No	No investigation
Sandra Wounded Foot	Unknown	No	No investigation

**Victims known to have been murdered either by BIA police or the FBI.*

This list was taken from the government's reservation police file. We believe that more than 300 people have been murdered on the Pine Ridge Reservation since 1973.

The FBI, in conjunction with the reservation police and the Justice Department, intends to destroy the American Indian Movement by whatever means necessary. One of its own agents (Douglas Durham) who had infiltrated the A.I.M. is implicated in the murder of a taxi driver in California. Russell Means, a leader of the movement, has been shot three times since 1973, and has faced nine trials.

Case Histories of Military and FBI Misconduct at Wounded Knee

FBI misconduct with native peoples has become so blatant that on May 10, 1976, Arthur S. Fleming, chairman of the United States Commission on Civil Rights, wrote the U.S. Attorney General to demand an investigation of improper and illegal activities by the FBI at Pine Ridge.

OPLAN GARDEN PLOT became the Army's program for implementing the Interdepartmental (Army, FBI, BIA) Action Plan. An analysis of the government's response to the 1973 events at Wounded Knee, South Dakota, demonstrates the tangible practice of GARDEN PLOT, and how SWAT type units fit into an overall plan for domestic counter-insurgency.

The BIA contacted the Justice Department, which ordered a detachment of the U.S. Marshals Service Special Operations Group (SOG) to the reservation on Feb. 12, 1973. SOG was created in 1971 by Wayne Colburn, the Director of the Marshals Service, and had been used to protect federal buildings and property during the 1971 "May Day" anti-war demonstrations. SOG had also seen action in evicting members of the American Indian Movement from Alcatraz Island and the Twin Cities Naval Air Station.

When SOG arrived, they turned the BIA Building on Pine Ridge into an armed fort; sand bags were placed on the roof to form gun emplacements; 24-hour a day patrols of the reservation were begun; and SOG began to train BIA police in the use of carbines and shotguns. It was after two weeks of the SOG operations on Pine Ridge that the Oglala Sioux Civil Rights Organization (OSCRO) held a series of meetings and voted to ask AIM to come to Pine Ridge.

On March 1, Attorney General Richard Kliendienst requested that the Department of the Army send a representative to Wounded Knee to help coordinate and evaluate the situation. After conference between Gen. Alexander Haig, who was to have the final approval on all Army activities at Wounded Knee, and Gen. Hay, the commander of the XVIII Airborne Corps, Col. Volney Warner was designated the PLOCSA for Wounded Knee.

At 3:30 a.m. on March 3, 1973, Col. Warner arrived at Ellsworth AFB and was met by Marshal Colburn and FBI Special Agent in Charge Joseph Trimbach. The law enforcement officers wanted an immediate commitment from Warner that 2000 members of the 82nd Airborne would be committed to Wounded Knee.

Rather than bring in military troops that would create an unfavorable public impression, Warner asked the Marshals and FBI to increase their contingents and utilize support provided by the military to conduct a cordon operation against the Indians. The entire Special Operations Group was called to Wounded Knee, and the FBI brought in additional men. Even the riot squad from the Border Patrol was brought in to make a consolidated federal force of over 340. Col. Warner immediately began his work as a military advisor. In the first days of his stay, he helped the Justice Department establish an emergency operations center, complete with a tactical intelligence component; he procured over 100 M-16 rifles and ammunition, 17 Armored Personnel Carriers (APCs), and other logistical items needed by an Army conducting a siege, from "C" rations to field jackets. Most important of all, Col. Warner devised an attack plan to take Wounded Knee by force, which was never put into operation.

Several incidents were provoked on March 11th. First, four armed postal inspectors were sent into Wounded Knee, allegedly to investigate the conditions at the post office located inside the Trading Post. Seen as a pretext for securing intelligence on the strength and deployment of the Indian people, the postal inspectors were stopped at the Indian roadblock, arrested, disarmed and detained for several hours. At about the same time FBI agents pulled alongside a van of Indian people returning from a nearby community. A witness described: "…a sedan pulled alongside and all of a sudden he hit the siren. I was going to pull over but he put an M-16 out the window and fired."

The roadblocks then went back up to stay. But the military's attack plan for March 12 was cancelled in favor of a siege to starve out the occupants. After five unsuccessful weeks of siege, on April 27, preparations were made again with a modified plan devised after Warner made a trip to the Pentagon. The attack date was set. If negotiations failed to reach a settlement by May 9, an attack would take place on the morning of May 10. Army officers from Fort Carson were brought in to assist with the attack. The state was set, and the countdown was below 96 hours when a settlement was reached. A virtual repeat of the 1890 massacre of over 300 Oglalas was narrowly averted.

Throughout it all, the 82nd Airborne and the 4th Infantry were placed on and off alert. Even though the troops were never brought in, a domestic form of Vietnamization occurred. From all appearances, the Army actually controlled much of the operations.

Massive amounts of military equipment went through the pipelines to Wounded Knee, including back-pack radios, mine detectors, 17 APCs, 200 flakvests, 177 M-16 and sniper rifles, 9,100 "star" parachute flares, and 123,000 rounds of ball and tracer ammunition. All of this, of course, was in addition to the supplies brought in from Justice Department resources.

Wounded Knee was a practical application of the interdepartmental Action Plan, GARDEN PLOT, and the lessons of GRAM METRIC and CABLE SPLICER operations. The entire law enforcement community looked to Wounded Knee as a test of the theory and tactics that had been promoted at SEADOC and the California Specialized Training Institute (CSTI). CSTI sent an observer to Wounded Knee to make recommendations on how the Institute could best prepare for any similar operations. That observer was Major Victor Jackson, an instructor in the Civil Disturbance Course offered by CSTI.

For his role at Wounded Knee, Col. Volney Warner was promoted to Brigadier General and made the Assistant Division Commander of the 82nd Airborne. For their role in the Siege of Wounded Knee, over 200 Oglalas and AIM members and supporters were indicted on a variety of charges.

After the June 26, 1975, deaths, the FBI conducted a paramilitary operation, claiming to be seeking anyone connected with the shootings. Homes and autos were surrounded by the fatigue-clothed counter-insurgency units of the FBI SWAT squads. Helicopters hovered overhead while sometimes as many as a score of agents threatened old people and children by brandishing automatic weaponry of AR-15 and M-16 types. No Indian family or home was secure from illegal entry and search, often with no concern for private property. Many objects were confiscated and have not been seen since. Even cars were towed away and totally dismantled. Legal workers who sought to assure Indian residents of their legal rights frequently entered a home to find a father and his children literally cowering with fear in a corner of their own living room.

The combinations of arrests, court actions and harassments point more and more to a state-federal-local conspiracy to deal expediently, efficiently and thoroughly with native activists.

In early winter, 1974, Richard LaCourse of the American Indian Press Association outlined the cooperative effort then developing between the Bureau of Indian Affairs and the FBI. The information came directly from documents released by Attorney General William Saxbe and other material brought to light during the Wounded Knee trials.

James Cooper, according to this information, is coordinator for Special Operations Service (SOS) and collects basic intelligence from the U.S. Marshals, the FBI, the Secret Service, local BIA police units, and state law enforcement agencies.

From the FBI documents, LaCourse listed eight goals of the FBI's program against what it terms Indian "militants". One of those goals is to "have local police put leaders under close scrutiny and arrest leaders on every possible charge until they can no longer make bail."

Wanda Siers was forced to leave her six-month-old baby, sick with measles, to head for Rapid City voluntarily or face arrest by the FBI for failure to appear. Lou and Billy Bean were ordered by agents to head for Rapid City, even though their six children would come home from school unaware of their parent's absence.

In Rapid City, 11-year-old Jimmy Zimmerman was picked up by FBI agents and taken before the grnad jury. He was asked where he was June 26, but he said he would not testify without an attorney. He stood on his rights, and finally was released when even R.D. Hurd could not bring himself to charge an 11-year-old with contempt of court. Zimmerman had already gotten his political education during the siege on the Jumping Bull house near where the FBI agents had died. He had come out of the house with his hands held high, shouting at the hundreds of policemen to stop shooting. However, police continued firing on him, and he was forced to take cover in an outhouse.

Also taken before the grand jury was Jean Bordeaux. She was not subpoenaed, but instead was placed under arrest as a "material witness". She was placed in the lock-up despite a doctor's appointment for much needed medical attention. Judge Andrew Bogue said he had ordered her arrest to ensure that she would appear, although she had never been subpoenaed previously.

Although Hurd had threatened to re-subpoena some 30 to 40 persons from the reservation, he called only two more, brought in from the Pennington County Jail. They were Angie and Avis Long Visitor, who had been jailed since September 16 for refusing to testify before earlier grand jury sessions.

The Long Visitors had stood on their treaty rights, insisting that the grand jury had no business on the reservation. They had appealed their case, but their application for bail during the waiting period was denied. They took the matter as far as the U.S. Supreme Court, which declined to grant bail. That made it clear the Long Visitors would have to testify—they have three children under four years of age, and the conditions in the Rapid City jail are intolerable. The couple were not allowed to visit each other, even on visiting days.

Actually, the FBI had already implicated all persons now arrested for the slayings even before the grand jury was convened. Prosecutors had asked for high bonds on two persons arrested in other incidents on the grounds that they were involved in the June 26 FBI deaths.

The re-convening of the grand jury was carefully concealed from lawyers from the Wounded Knee Legal Defense/Offense Committee (WKLDOC), who had been representing the Long Visitors. US Attorneys had told WKLDOC lawyers it would take a week or two to get the grand jury together, but the U.S. would not object to releasing the Long Visitors if they would promise to reappear. When they appeared in Judge Bogue's court to give that pledge, Bogue said the grand jury would be ready to hear their testimony in a half-hour. Government officials knew that lawyers who had represented the Long Visitors previously would be out of town at that time.

Joanna LaDeaux had been returning to Oglala from Rapid City on the morning of June 26 when she was stopped by FBI agent David Price, who commandeered the car to be driven to the area of the shooting. He had blown up his own car engine in his haste to return there after delivering a prisoner to Hot Springs, South Dakota.

They arrived to find police shooting at the homes where Joanna knew women and children and old people lived. The FBI say they ordered firing to cease while Joanna, a legal worker, entered the area. The firing continued, however. After leaving the area, she returned to bearing a signed authorization from the White Clay District Tribal Council for her to mediate in the shooting, to seek a cease fire on their behalf.

Although federal law prohibits mediators and arbitrators from divulging information relative to the situation they enter, Judge Bogue says that this requirement does not hold in the case of an alleged murder, although the law itself does not seem to make this distinction.

Because of her stance, she had been singled out for more than the usual harassment. The home where she had been staying was on more than one occasion encircled by heavily armed FBI agents. Finally, the FBI obtained a warrant for her arrest as a material witness, a term which implies that exact knowledge of a specific crime is known—which is not true in her case. The warrant was issued on July 12, but she was not arrested until late August at her parent's home, although her exact whereabouts were known to the FBI constantly.

Joanna LeDeaux is separated from her Danish-national husband, Poul Johannesen. He had come to the U.S. to visit their two children who had been staying with their grandparents in Sioux Falls ever since the Oglala shootings. Poul headed east from Sioux Falls by airplane on Sunday morning August 24, at 7 a.m., and by 8:30 a.m., six FBI agents in the company of a Sioux Falls uniformed patrolman pushed their way past Joanna's 12-year-old son, and entered the home to arrest her. She was sleeping at the time, but agents refused her demand that she be allowed to dress. When asked to show an arrest or search warrant, they replied, "We don't need one."

Joanna was taken to jail, and later before U.S. Magistrate David Vroman. The U.S. wanted to hold her on $50,000 bail until September 2, when the grand jury was scheduled to meet.

In Chicago, Poul Johannesen changed planes. He was met by FBI agents from the Chicago office, and two FBI flown from Pine Ridge—David Price and Dean Hughes—the SWAT leaders from the June 26 assault on the Oglala houses. Poul says the FBI threatened to have "the shit beat out of him". They told him he would not be allowed back in the U.S. to visit his children and that he had been harboring a fugitive, even though Joanna had committed no crime. Most seriously, they threatened Poul with having the children taken into "protective custody", suggesting that if the children returned to Pine Ridge with Joanna, both children would be killed.

Joanna was eventually released on Monday, August 24, on $50,000 personal recognizance bond by Federal Judge Fred Nichol.

On the Rosebud Reservation, FBI agents, BIA police, and U.S. Marshals carried off a dawn raid on Crow Dog's Paradise and Leonard Crow Dog's brother-in-law's home adjoining his land. They arrested seven persons at that time, and later in Los Angeles they arrested an eighth.

In Kansas, seven persons, including two juveniles and a one-year-old child, were arrested. The car they were said to have been riding in exploded and burned.

At Oglala, former tribal councilman Jim Little was beaten to death by four men close to the present tribal administration. During his wake, three persons were arrested for allegedly having firearms.

Many members of the Lakota Treaty Council have themselves been victimized by the violence. Within a week of Frank Starr's being appointed to the White Clay Law and Order Committee in June to deal with the increased harassment by the FBI after June 26, his brother was beaten almost to death.

Respected chief Frank Fools Crow's home was firebombed in March, and in July the FBI refused to allow a truck to deliver cinderblocks for reconstruction, saying he might build bunkers with them.

Fools Crow's interpreter, Matthew King, had his home shot up.

Marvin Ghost Bear, an elected tribal council member from Batesland, was held hostage in the Pine Ridge jail when he came to Pine Ridge tribal court on February 26. His life has been threatened many times, and at one time, his home was shot at so often he was forced to move off the reservation for awhile.

Last March, Eugene White Hawk's niece and her two children died when goons ran their car off the road.

Kenny Loud Hawk was threatened with an indictment if he didn't answer FBI questions, and his father, also a delegate, was fired from the job he had held for ten years, and for which he was under contract for a full year more.

It is impossible to get an accurate count of Pine Ridge Reservation residents out on bond awaiting trial in Federal Court. Certainly it is close to a dozen or more, most of them "traditionals" or AIM members. However, two cases which related indirectly to the June 26 FBI deaths are indicative of the U.S. assault on native people, reprisals on uncooperative Indians.

Donny Hudson, age 13, is charged with stealing an automatic weapon from a white rancher, Orville Schwaring. No one else is charged, and Hudson was in Deadwood riding in a rodeo when the robbery was alleged to take place. Hudson was charged after he refused to testify at a July 14 grand jury investigating the FBI agents' deaths, and his family was warned by the FBI that they "would get it" if they didn't answer questions.

Jerry Bear Shield is accused of murder of his close friend, Stacy Cottier. On March 20, snipers shot at Bear Shield, Cottier, and Norman Bear Shirt as they walked along the road. Bear Shield was shot in the throat, and Cottier was killed. Tribal police tried to charge Bear Shield with murder, and then let him go, but in early September, a federal grand jury indicted him after he refused an FBI offer of $800 to testify before the grand jury about the murder on March 9 of Josh Steele, alleged to have been a member of the goon squad.

Bear Shield was indicted for murder March 21 for Steele's death, the same day goons killed an eye-witness to Steele's murder who could have cleared Bear Shield. The youth is an AIM member, a Wounded Knee defendant for whom charges were dropped, and a traditional Oglala who speaks little English. He has been a constant victim of FBI harassment, especially since June 26.

A Letter Written by William F. Muldrow, Rocky Mountain Regional Office, U.S. Commission on Civil Rights

Subj: Monitoring of Events Related to the Shooting of Two FBI Agents on the Pine Ridge Reservation.

Date: July 9, 1975

At about 1:00 p.m., on June 26, two FBI agents were shot to death on the Pine Ridge Reservation near the town of Oglala, South Dakota. The FBI immediately launched a large-scale search for the suspected slayers, which has involved 100 to 200 combat-clad FBI agents, BIA policemen, SWAT teams, armored cars, helicopters, fixed-wing aircraft, and tracking dogs. An increasing volume of requests for information regarding the incident and numerous reports and complaints of threats, harassment, and search procedures conducted without due process of law by the FBI, prompted my visit to the reservation to gather firsthand information. NSRO was involved at Pine Ridge during the investigation of the tribal election held there in 1973. This office also was called upon to do a preliminary investigation of an incident involving the shooting of AIM leader Russell Means on the Standing Rock Sioux Reservation in North Dakota last month.

I was on the reservation from July 1-3, and during that time had the opportunity to talk with the Acting BIA Superintendent (Kendall Cuming), the President of the Tribal Council (Dick Wilson), FBI agents, BIA police officials, numerous residents of the reservation including several who lived in the vicinity of the scene of the shooting, and media correspondents from NBC, CBS, and National Public Radio. FBI officials were too busy to see me when I visited their headquarters to arrange for an appointment. Part of the time I traveled in the company of Mario Gonzales, an attorney and enrolled member of the tribe, who has been designated chairman for the South Dakota Advisory Committee.

This particular incident of violence must be seen in the context of tension, frustration, and crime which has increasingly pervaded life on the reservation during the last three years. Unemployment approaches 70 percent and the crime rate is four times that of Chicago. There have been eighteen killings on the reservation so far this year and uncounted beatings, fights, and shootings. Many of these incidents have never been explained or, in the minds of many residents, even satisfactorily investigated.

Tensions are exacerbated by irresponsible statements by State Officials.

Many of the facts surrounding the shooting are either unknown by officials or have not been made public. Media representatives felt that the FBI was unnecessarily restrictive in the kind and amount of information it provided. It is patently clear that many of the statements that have been released regarding the incident are either false, unsubstantiated, or directly misleading. Some of these statements are highly inflammatory, alleging that the agents were "led into a trap" and "executed". As a result, feelings have run high.

The FBI had arrest warrants for four Native Americans who had allegedly assaulted, kidnapped, and robbed a white man and a boy. Residents of the reservation and an attorney from the Wounded Knee Legal Defense/Offense Committee with whom I talked felt that the warrants were issued merely on the word of the white people without adequate investigation. Such a thing, they point out, would never have happened had the Indians been the accusers and typifies unequal treatment often given to Indian people.

The two agents killed in the shooting had been to several houses on the reservation looking for the wanted men. The occupants of some of these houses claimed that the agents had been abusive and threatening. Some of the Native Americans that I talked with, who had been involved in the Wounded Knee incident, have a genuine fear that the FBI is "out to get" them. When the two agents were killed they had no warrants in their possession.

The bodies of the agents were found down in the valley several hundred yards from the houses where the shooting supposedly occurred. "Bunkers" described in newspaper accounts turned out to be aged root cellars. "Trench fortifications" were non-existent. Persons in the houses were in the process of preparing a meal when the shooting occurred. One of the houses, owned by Mr. and Mrs. Harry Jumping Bull, contained children and several women, one of whom was pregnant. The Jumping

Bulls had just celebrated their 50th wedding anniversary. As a result of the incident Mrs. Jumping Bull had a nervous breakdown and is now in a Chadron, Nebraska, hospital.

The body of Joseph Stuntz, the young Native American killed in one of the houses during the shooting, was seen shortly after the shooting lying in a mud hole as though it had been dumped there on purpose. He was later given a traditional hero's burial attended by hundreds of people from the reservation.

Sixteen men were reportedly involved in the shooting, though no one knows how this figure was determined. The FBI has never given any clear indication that it knows the identity of these men. Incredibly, all of them, though surrounded by State and BIA police and FBI agents, managed to escape in broad daylight during the middle of the afternoon.

In the days immediately following the incident there were numerous accounts of persons being arrested without cause for questioning, and of houses being searched without warrants. One of these was the house of Wallace Little, Jr., next door neighbor to the Jumping Bulls. His house and farm were surrounded by 80-90 armed men. He protested and asked them to stay off his property. Eliot Daum, an attorney with the WKLD/OC who had been staying in the house with Little's family, informed the agents that they had no right to search without a warrant. They restrained him and prevented him from talking further with Little while two agents searched the house.

Daum was also present when David Sky, his client, was arrested in Pine Ridge as a material witness to the shooting. Sky was refused permission to talk with Daum before he was taken to a Rapid City jail, a two hour drive.

Several questions and concerns arise as a result of these observations. The FBI is conducting a full-scale military operation on the reservation. Their presence there has created deep resentment on the part of many of the reservation residents who do not feel that such a procedure would be tolerated in any non-Indian community in the United States. They point out that little has been done to solve the numerous murders on the reservation, but when two white men are killed, "troops" are brought in from all over the country at a cost of hundreds of thousands of dollars.

No FBI agents actually live on the reservation and none of them are Native Americans. They are a completely outside group with remarkably little understanding of Indian society. Questions are raised as to the basis for FBI jurisdiction on the reservation, the seeming conflict and overlap with the jurisdiction of the BIA police, and the propriety of the FBI, which furnished adversary witnesses for the Wounded Knee trials, acting as an investigatory body on the Pine Ridge Reservation. Many Native Americans feel that the present large-scale search operation is an overreaction which takes on aspects of a vendetta.

The jurisdictional problem, like the present shooting incident, cannot be divorced from the other pressing concerns of Pine Ridge Reservation residents which relate to their basic rights as human beings and citizens of the United States. The climate of frustration, anger, and fear on the reservation, which results from poverty, ill health, injustice, and tyranny, would indicate that the latest incident of violence will not be the last.

/S/ William F. Muldrow
Equal Opportunity Specialist

Endnotes

[1] Peltier was acquitted in January, 1978, of an attempted-murder charge upon a police officer in Milwaukee. The charge is viewed as another example of repeated prosecutions of minority political activists intended to persecute and harass them.

Chapter Ten
David Rice and Edward Poindexter
(Listed by Amnesty International)

David Rice and Ed Poindexter are serving life sentences in the penal complex in Lincoln, Nebraska. They were convicted of first-degree murder of a policeman. The convictions were based on the testimony of a frightened teenager, who admitted to the crime, and on explosives allegedly found in Rice's house. The search of his house was declared illegal by the Federal District Court of Nebraska and the U.S. Eighth Circuit Court of appeals. They reversed Rice's conviction because it was based in large part on an illegal search of his home. The Eighth Circuit Court went on to say that the conduct of the Omaha police represented, "…a negligent disregard…for the rights of not only the petitioner (Rice) but possibly for other citizens as well."

On July 6, 1976, however, the United States Supreme Court agreed that the search of Rice's house violated his Constitutional rights but ruled that the two federal courts should not have reviewed the case, and that henceforth the only appeal route in such cases would be directly from the State Supreme Court to the U.S. Supreme Court. A direct appeal to the U.S. Supreme Court by attorneys on behalf of Rice was then refused hearing by the Court.

This U.S. Supreme Court decision, which eroded the Fourth Amendment protection of citizens' right to be free from unreasonable searches and seizures and expanded police powers, has generated much concern throughout the United States. On July 12, 1976, one newspaper editorial, in the *Boston Globe,* criticized the decision thus:

> "In the session that ended last week, the U.S. Supreme Court took a number of steps along the road toward expanded police powers—expanded powers that may add to the confusion in the administration of justice rather than improve control of crime…
>
> "The Supreme Court did not repeal the Fourth Amendment, of course. But it did throw virtually the entire burden of enforcing its provisions onto the state courts. Some states will do that job well….

"The danger is that there will now be 50 different interpretations of the Fourth Amendment—not tomorrow, but over time. Judges are human. State judges don't like their rulings to be overturned by federal courts. As long as their Fourth Amendment rulings were subjected to federal review, state judges could be expected to try to be consistent with federal precedents. Now, no longer subject to that review, individual state judges may well take a less rigorous stance on the meaning of the Fourth Amendment.

"There are a number of important ingredients to justice. One of them is uniformity of application. Whatever the court's motives, it has clearly moved away from that principle.

"Justice, with time, will suffer accordingly."

That the Rice/Poindexter case should have expanded the powers of the police is uniquely ironic, since as past members of the Black Panther Party in the 1960's, they were targeted by the Omaha, Nebraska, FBI Field Office as part of the COINTELPRO counter-intelligence program. According to FBI files made public by the *Omaha World Herald,* December 6, 1977, under the headline, "FBI Targeted Area Panthers," the Omaha Police Department, under the supervision of the FBI in the 1960's, instituted a harassment campaign against Black Panther Party members by stopping vehicles registered to them at every opportunity. Attorney General inquiries into fiscal management of the Omaha Panther Children's Breakfast Program resulted in its disruption without any proof that any money or food had been extorted.

David Rice and Ed Poindexter were leaders of the Nebraska Black Panther Party and its successor, the National Committee to Combat Fascism (NCCF).

Their case must be examined in the context of an intense period of conflict between the police and the Black community in Omaha. The shooting of 14-year-old Vivian Strong by a policeman in June 1969, was one such event. The girl was running from a vacant apartment where a group of young people had been playing records and dancing. A neighbor called the police because the young people were not supposed to be in the vacant apartment. When the police arrived, the children began running and Patrolman Loder shot them. The bullet struck Vivian Strong in the back of the head and killed her.

Days of protest in the Black community followed the child's death. Patrolman Loder was fired and charged with manslaughter. An all-white jury acquitted him in March 1970. The City Personnel Board then reinstated him on the police force and awarded him back pay for the entire period he was off the force. Between July 1966, and July, 1969, police killed four Blacks and two whites (Omaha's Black population is slightly over 10% of the total population). Racial harassment had become more widespread after Gov. George C. Wallace of Alabama spoke at a rally in Omaha in March 1968. Racist elements in the community were inspired to action against Black and white demonstrators who were protesting Wallace's speech. A Black youth was killed by police a few hours after Wallace's rally. From then on, there were frequent arrests of Black people on the slightest excuse. Some were beaten and some were shot.

This police violence spilled over into the white community. On August 24, 1969, the *Omaha World Herald* printed an article entitled, "Incidents Blur Image of Police." This article documented the following incidents which occurred within a few months: Vivian Strong's death resulting from police shooting; hospitalization of an assistant city attorney's son who claimed he was beaten by four policemen; handcuffing and arrest of two lawyers (one was the son of a former Nebraska governor, the other was the son of a retired city assistant prosecutor) following an argument over an illegally parked car; roughing-up by police of a leading trial lawyer; police shooting of two apparently drug-crazed men, one of whom died and the other was critically wounded.

Among the most vocal critics of such police abuse of power were members of the local chapter of the Black Panther Party and its successor, the National Committee to Combat Fascism (NCCF). Critics of police abuses were themselves harassed extensively. For example, Eddie Bolden, a Black Panther leader, was arrested 15 times in two years between 1968 and 1970 on a variety of charges, most of which were eventually dropped. Among leaders of the NCCF who were frequently arrested were Ed Poindexter and David Rice. Ed Poindexter was Chairman of the NCCF and Rice was the Minister of Information.

In August 1970, Patrolman Larry Minard was killed by a bomb. A 15-year-old youth, Duane Peak, admitted planting the bomb and calling the police to the site of the bomb. Peak had been the victim of police beatings on at least two occasions. Shortly after the killing of Minard, Peak told his sister that he had acted alone. After his arrest, he made a number of sworn statements to the police which did not mention Rice or Poindexter. According to later testimony by Peak, he was threatened by the police with death in the electric chair. A deal was made between Peak's attorney and the county attorney in which Peak would be permitted to plead guilty to "lesser charges" in exchange for implicating Rice and Poindexter. Thereafter, Peak changed his story and Rice and Poindexter were charged with murder.

At a preliminary hearing, the prosecuting attorney asked Peak whether Rice and Poindexter had had anything to do with the killing. The youth said they had not. The prosecutor then asked for and obtained a recess. When the hearing resumed a few hours later, Peak changed his story. He said Rice and Poindexter were involved.

Later at the trial of Rice and Poindexter in the spring of 1971, Peak not only implicated Rice and Poindexter, but four others as well. None of the others was ever charged in the case. Art O'Leary, a prosecuting attorney, made a statement that they were only interested in Rice and Poindexter. In exchange for this testimony, Duane Peak was allowed to plead guilty to juvenile delinquency while Rice and Poindexter were sentenced to life imprisonment. Peak was moved out of the state under the Federal Witness Relocation Program, and his whereabouts are unknown at this time.

The main evidence to support Peak's story was dynamite that police allegedly found in Rice's home days after the incident. Officers entered the home with an arrest warrant for Rice and an invalid search warrant. They said they found dynamite and other materials and tools that could be used to make bombs. David Rice was out of the city at the time this search was conducted. He later said that police or someone must have planted the dynamite, tools, or box in which they said the dynamite had been stored.

Poindexter had been arrested a few hours before Rice's house was searched. He was held for three days. On the third day, his clothing was taken from him. He was released later that day with no charges filed against him. He was arrested again after a government laboratory said that certain chemical elements that are in dynamite had been found in his shirt pockets. After learning that an arrest warrant had been issued for him, Rice, knowing his innocence, gave himself up to the police.

Officials claimed that dynamite particles were found in the pocket of the pants Rice wore when he gave himself up and in the pocket of the shirt Poindexter was wearing when he was first arrested. The forensic chemist from the government laboratory admitted that

1. the particles found were not oily, though particles from a stick of dynamite would normally be oily;
2. there were no traces of paraffin as would normally be expected if the particles had come from dynamite sticks;
3. there were no traces of the alleged dynamite particles anywhere else on any of the clothing of either man, as would normally be expected and as had been found on the clothing of others not brought to trial;
4. hand swabs to test for dynamite particles on the hands of Rice and Poindexter showed no traces of dynamite particles, though similar swabs on at least one other person not charged had shown traces of such particles.

Furthermore, the chemist had not tested for percentages of elements in the composition of the particles; this was especially important since, as indicated in a chemical report obtained by the defense, the same elements described as present are also found in kitchen matches, phosphorus detergents, gunpowder, ammonia fertilizer, and other common substances. Peak's clothing was never tested for traces of such particles.

The trial judge overruled motions by the defense to suppress evidence which police claimed to have found in the search of Rice's home and in the clothes of the two men. A jury convicted Rice and Poindexter of first degree murder and sentenced them to life imprisonment.

The Nebraska Supreme Court upheld the conviction of both men, but Rice's conviction was later overturned by the Federal District Court and the U.S. Circuit Court of Appeals. Both federal courts held that the search warrant for Rice's house was illegal, and that the search of his house and clothing violated his rights under the Fourth Amendment of the U.S. Constitution.

After denial of federal protection of their Constitutional rights and after having exhausted their state and federal remedies, Rice and Poindexter remain in prison. Their attorneys hope that delivery of their FBI files to Rice and Poindexter may open the possibility of new trials for either or both men because of evidence of government misconduct.

Chapter Eleven
Gary Tyler
(Listed by Amnesty International)

Gary Tyler is another young Black man whose conviction for murder coincided with white majority opposition to changes in the economic, political and social status of minority people in his community. Until his arrest for murder on October 7, 1974, Gary was a student at Destrehan High School in St. Charles Parish, Louisiana, an area which is one-third Black and the scene of long and bitter strikes against the major local petro-chemical industries.

White resistance to school desegregation had often turned to violence after a federal court had ordered change in 1968. On October 7, 1974, a brick and bottle-throwing mob of white youths and adults surrounded the Black students' school bus as it left the schoolyard. Gary Tyler was on that bus. Black students saw a white man in the mob with a shotgun. They ducked under the bus seats for cover. A shot rang out; 13-year-old Timothy Weber, a white student standing near the bus, fell dead.

Police searched the bus and its occupants twice, for three hours, without finding any guns. They forced the Black students to lie on the ground while being searched. During a second search at the police station, female students were forced to strip; several male students were beaten. No one from the white mob was arrested or searched.

Gary Tyler protested police harassment of his cousin. For this, he was arrested for disturbing the peace. Police severely beat Gary, trying to force him to say he had seen who fired the shot. One of the deputies who beat him was V. J. St. Pierre, a cousin of the dead youth. Gary was later charged and convicted at the age of seventeen of first degree murder.

Only one witness said she saw Gary Tyler fire a gun: Natalie Blanks, who was then 14 years old. She was one of the 65 students on the bus. She later admitted that she had lied under coercion by the prosecution.

The .45 which police claim killed Timothy Weber had disappeared from a firing range used by the police. Bus driver, Earnest Cojoe, a 25-

year veteran of the U.S. Marines, testified that no one could have fired a .45 from within the bus, that the sound would have burst eardrums. Inside the bus, all witnesses agreed the shot sounded like a fire-cracker.

No fingerprints were found on the gun. The all-white jury deliberated only two hours before finding Gary Tyler guilty of first degree murder. Judge Marino handed down the mandatory death sentence and sent Gary Tyler to Death Row.

The Louisiana death penalty was subsequently declared unconstitutional by the United States Supreme Court, and the Louisiana Supreme Court re-sentenced Gary Tyler to life imprisonment, without possibility of parole for twenty years, even though Gary was a juvenile at the time of conviction. The Court denied his appeal from the conviction and ignored the law governing prosecution of juveniles, which did not provide for life imprisonment. The U.S. Supreme Court refused to hear Gary's petition for a new trial. Gary Tyler's new attorney has filed a *writ of habeas corpus* challenging the legality of the trial, citing the recantation of the main prosecution witness, fourteen-year-old Natalie Blanks, who testified that she had not seen anyone fire a gun. She had been told by police that she and another witness would be charged as accessories to the murder unless she testified against Gary. The racially tense environment, including Ku Klux Klan (KKK) demonstrations during the trial and jury deliberation, is also an element of the *habeas corpus* petition.

Meanwhile, since the trial, the Tyler family and other supporters of Gary have been harassed by police and others.

(1) On March 27, 1976, white nightriders shot and killed Richard Dunn, a young Black man who was returning from a fund-raising dance for Gary Tyler at Southern University in New Orleans.

(2) Racists dressed in KKK robes have driven through the Tylers' community and followed the Tyler family.

(3) Gary's brother, Terry, 16, and a key defense witness, Donald Files, were both arrested on charges of simple burglary. The supposed burglary occurred while Terry was in Detroit speaking on his brother's behalf at a public rally on May 16, 1976. The same judge who tried Gary set bond at $5,000 for each.

(4) In June 1976, the judge held yet another brother, Steven, on

$2,700 bond for a charge of disturbing the peace. On January 5, 1977, the police invaded Mrs. Tyler's home at gunpoint, searching it for several hours. They then arrested her son in connection with a robbery, but released him without charging him.

Despite mass popular and international support, Gary Tyler remains in prison. At the hearing for a new trial, 400 people came to the courthouse to show their support for Gary. Mrs. Tyler and Terry Tyler have spoken about Gary in many cities to thousands of people. Support had come from many prominent civic, political, and religious leaders. Thousands have signed petitions to free him. The American Federation of Teachers passed a resolution in support of Gary at their 1976 National Convention. Amnesty International in West Germany has adopted Gary's case. Gary's classmates at Destrehan High School have organized the Gary Tyler Freedom Fighters to mobilize community support for Gary.

On July 24, 1976, more than 1,000 people from around the nation marched and rallied demanding Gary's freedom. No legal redress seems possible.

SECTION THREE OF THE PETITION
Racist Application of the Criminal Law

A. Introduction

This section provides evidence of the patterns and practices of the criminal justice system which demonstrate its abusive and racially unjust application to minorities. Characteristically, the prisoners discussed in this section will have attempted to extricate themselves from the consequences of the patently oppressive circumstances of their arrests, prosecution, and incarcerations by repeated appeal to the legal process.

Ostensibly neutral, the implementation of the legal process by which relief is sought is as tainted by racism and abusive discretion as the initial proceedings being challenged. These legal remedies are, therefore, a totally ineffective method of obtaining relief, but create an illusory and temporary expectation of individual vindication.

The conditions of penal confinement of named prisoners, and the hundred of thousands similarly situated persons also described in this section, reflect the politically determined priorities and decisions of those in power that aggrieved poor and minority people can be controlled by brutality and that it is desirable for this society to do so.

This combination of the racist application of the law, the disparate racial and economic imposition of the processes and procedures, and the inhumane and cynically callous disregard for the human and legal rights of imprisoned people produces the second and third categories of political prisoners in the United States:

Persons imprisoned initially for conviction of crimes who receive additional and extended sentences and are subjected to harsh and brutal treatment as a result of their political activities within the prison to bring about changes in specific dehumanizing conditions and the treatment of prisoners in general;

and

Prisoners whose race, ethnic identity, and poverty have exposed them to the politically selective application of the law and have made them victims of abusive criminal justice processes. The treatment of such prisoners during arrest, trial, sentencing, and incarceration reflects the callous disregard for their human and legal rights which characterizes their conditions in all other phases of American society and is intended to ensure political control of this segment of the population.

Those persons discussed and conditions described specifically in this section are a small, but representative, sample of the situation of many thousands in the United States.

Chapter Twelve
George Merritt

Newark, New Jersey, exploded during the racially tense summer of 1967. Three days later, Plainfield, New Jersey, Policeman John V. Gleason, Jr., notorious in the Black ghetto for his abuse of the legal and human rights of Black citizens, was on traffic patrol in the bordering white business district. He left his post to enter the Black community to pursue a Black youth. His chase caused a crowd of hundreds of people to gather. A rock was thrown at Gleason and he responded with gunfire, pumping three bullets into the unarmed Black youth, Bobby Lee Williams, critically wounding him. Several outraged onlookers came from the crowd and attacked Gleason, who was beaten to death.

Two months later, police broke down doors and invaded the homes of a number of Black persons in Plainfield. Dozens were charged with the murder of Gleason. George Merritt, along with eleven others, was subsequently indicted and held for trial. Of the twelve, only George Merritt and Gail Madden, a mother of two, were convicted and sentenced to life imprisonment after being forced into a group trial, in denial of their right to be tried individually. This was George Merritt's first criminal charge.

After three years in prison, the Appellate Division of the Superior Court of New Jersey unanimously reversed their convictions. In reversing their convictions, the Appellate Division held that the "pressure to convict someone" was inherent in a mass trial. The unanimous court also held that the only "eye-witness" who testified against George Merritt was "unreliable" and his testimony "flimsy and questionable."

To date, the Appellate Division of the New Jersey Supreme Court has twice unanimously reversed George Merritt's conviction. The second reversal was based on error at the trial court level, charging violations of the rules of evidence. A third trial, conducted in front of an all-white jury, resulted in a life sentence for George Merritt. At this trial, the same evidence that was found to be prejudicial in the previous trials was allowed to be introduced.

Merritt's ten-year ordeal reveals that he cannot expect justice in the courts of New Jersey. He has taken the only recourse left to him (other than further appeal), a request to the governor to exercise his executive prerogative to free the innocent Merritt. This request was made almost one year ago, and as of this date, no action has been taken.

In September 1978, the Appellate Court in New Jersey granted George Merritt bail, pending appeal. Less than 24 hours later, the prosecutor and the State Attorney General moved to block Merritt's release by appealing to the New Jersey Supreme Court, which ruled in their favor. George Merritt remains in prison.

Chapter Thirteen
J. B. Johnson

J. B. Johnson was arrested in Missouri in January 1970, as he was getting into a cab, and was later charged as an accomplice in a jewelry store robbery which had resulted in the death of a St. Louis County policeman. Johnson denied from the very beginning any involvement in the crime, but he was tried, convicted, and sentenced to 99 years and a day for his supposed participation in the robbery and murder that had occurred.

An examination of the J. B. Johnson case is illuminating on the racist application of the law while seeming to provide "due process" safeguards. J. B. Johnson was tried by an all-white, middle-aged jury. The sole eyewitness to the crime was unable to identify J. B. Johnson in the police line-up. He had, in fact, identified another man, saying, "All coloreds look alike." The prosecutor, during his summation to the jury, justified this wrong identification by saying, "Let's face it, to many of us, they do all look alike." Other evidence used to convict Johnson were footprints in the snow leading in the opposite direction from the escape route he was accused of taking.

Robert Lee Walker, who had already been convicted of the murder, stated in a sworn affidavit that he did not know Johnson until after the crime. The police testified that several days after Johnson's arrest, they had found two rings from the jewelry store in his shoe. These rings supposedly matched two rings photographed in the evidence bag on the day of the crime, but were later reported missing.

While on bail prior to his first trial, Johnson was subjected to constant harassment from the police. He was arrested seven consecutive times and was told by the county police that whenever they saw him on the street, he would be arrested and held for twenty-four hours.

Because the prosecution withheld exculpatory evidence, Johnson's conviction was reversed. He was subsequently retried and convicted by another all-white jury in the same jurisdiction. All defense motions were denied in spite of the overwhelming evidence that J. B. Johnson could not get a fair trial in that community because of the continuous and inflammatory pretrial publicity.

The second conviction is presently on appeal on further grounds of prosecutorial misconduct. During that trial, the prosecutor made the following remark in the closing arguments, "J. B. Johnson must be guilty since the jury in the first trial found him guilty."

J. B. Johnson has been incarcerated for seven years and there are no realistic prospects for him obtaining a fair hearing or release.

Chapter Fourteen
Delbert Tibbs

On December 14, 1974, Delbert Tibbs, a 36-year-old Black man, a writer and student of theology from Chicago, Illinois, was convicted by an all-white jury of raping a 16-year-old white woman and of killing her male companion in Fort Myers, Florida.

In Lee County, Florida, where Mr. Tibbs was prosecuted, prospective jurors are supposedly drawn at random from the 74,200 registered voters. However, despite a 16 percent Black population in the court district, only one Black was called to jury duty and immediately dismissed by the challenge of the state, resulting in the all-white jury.

There is ample evidence that at the time of the crimes, Tibbs was in Daytona Beach, 200 miles away. The State could never place Tibbs closer than 213 miles to the scene of the crime, and could not produce anyone who ever saw Tibbs in the Ft. Myers area. Evidence was produced to this effect.

The suspect was described as being a big "Black nigger with woolly hair." Delbert is of medium build and is light-brown-skinned. The prosecution suggested that he had "lightened up" many shades while in prison. A Florida State Trooper had questioned Delbert Tibbs three days after the crime in response to a state bulletin in search of the rapist-killer. He had been released because he did not match the physical description and because he could prove that he was nowhere near the vicinity of the crime.

One of the most controversial aspects of this rape-murder case is whether there was, in fact, a rape. A dead male body was found; the dead male was a companion of the alleged rape victim, Cynthia Nadeau. Ms. Nadeau was then a 16-year-old and a frequent drug user who had a long history of being a runaway and of living with various men. The examining physician testified under oath that semen was found in the vagina, indicating sexual activity, but that rape was not indicated by the physical evidence. Ms. Nadeau claimed later that she was pregnant because of the "rape", and was carrying Tibbs' child as a result. The child was born with obvious Caucasian features. She then said that she was mistaken and the child's father was the man she had been living with up to the night prior to the crime, when she had run away with Terry Milroy, the man who was killed. She also admitted that she had been under the influence of drugs at the time of the crime, which could distort her concept of time, place and person.

Ms. Nadeau identified Tibbs from a single photograph, even though it did not match her initial description of the murderer.

The testimony of Sylvester Gibbs was given at trial, in which he testified that Tibbs had confessed to him while they were fellow prisoners in Lee County Jail, after Gibbs had known him for two or three days. However, Tibbs had arrived at the jail only one day before he is alleged to have confessed to Gibbs, who had been convicted of rape and admitted having read of the crimes in the newspapers.

Delbert Tibbs was sentenced to execution on December 15, 1975, for the February 3, 1974, crime, becoming one of thirty-three Black men then on the death row of Florida.

In 1977, the Florida Supreme Court ruled that Tibbs should be released or retried. The lower court has chosen to retry him but, because of a recent U.S. Supreme Court ruling on double-jeopardy, there is a possibility that the State of Florida may be barred from retrying him. As of the writing of this petition, the court has not yet ruled on the State's motion to be allowed to retry the case, while Delbert Tibbs remains out of prison on bail.[1]

Endnotes

[1] Since the filing of the U.N. Petition, the Supreme Court of Florida ruled that Delbert Tibbs could not be retried.

Chapter Fifteen
Imani (Johnny Harris)

Imani was convicted by a Baldwin County, Alabama, jury of capital murder under an old Civil War era law requiring the death penalty for an inmate under life sentence who commits murder. He was serving five life sentences on convictions for rape and robbery when he was accused of killing a guard at Holman Prison during prisoner protests held at both Holman and the Atmore Prison Farm. These demonstrations objected to brutal and negligent treatment of prisoners.

Imani's current defense attorneys contend that Imani's original convictions, which caused him to be incarcerated in the first place, were the result of the typically negligent legal representation provided for poor and minority people charged with crimes. These attorneys point to the invalid circumstances of his arrest, the denial of counsel, guilty pleas extracted from him coercively, the unconstitutional line-up, and illegal sentencing procedures as indicative of the inadequacy of his legal representation and the callous disregard of the legal rights of poor people in the courts.

After Imani's conviction and confinement at Holman Prison, he became a much-respected leader and advocate for other prisoners. He articulated their grievances in regard to the racist application of the criminal law and processes to them and the oppressive and brutal conditions in which they were confined.

It is generally believed that Imani was selected for prosecution for the killing of the guard during the prison demonstration because of opposition to the leadership role he played during the prisoners' protests. The state was unable to establish any proof against Imani, other than that he had participated in the prison protest.

Imani's trial for killing the prison guard was conducted in rural Baldwin county, near Atmore Prison Farm, before an all-male, all-white jury, and is illuminating not only of Imani's situation but also of the ways racism permeates the patterns and practices of the criminal justice system despite constitutional guarantees of due process to the accused.

According to the U.S. Constitution, a person is entitled to a jury of his or her peers. This has been interpreted by the American courts to mean that juries must be drawn from a group of names, a jury pool, which is supposed to be randomly chosen from a cross-section of the community, using such sources as voter registration lists, phone books, and city directories. Jury commissioners in charge of placing names in the pool are required to include everyone other than those they personally know to be ineligible. The pool must be entirely replaced every few years. The evidence presented at Imani's hearing raises the question of whether there was any possibility of him being tried by a jury of his peers.

In Baldwin County, where he was tried, there are 5,023 Black people and 33, 707 white people over the age of 21. Blacks make up 15.2% of the population. They make up only 7.7% of the names in the jury pool. This means that they are underrepresented by 49.3% or that just about half of the Black people in Baldwin County are excluded from jury duty. Black women are 8.2% of the population, but make up only 2.9% of the names in the jury pool.

In Escambia County, where Imani and the other activist Atmore/Holman prisoners were indicted, the percentage of under representation is perhaps even greater. According to another survey, Blacks constitute 13.9% of the jury pool and are therefore excluded by about 50%. Women in Escambia are underrepresented by 21.3%, while the figure in Baldwin County is 34.1%.

That this exclusion is systematic and not inadvertent is shown by the testimony of the jury commissioners. They stated that they only include people whom they "know" in the book, and admitted that they know few Blacks other than their own and their white friends' housemaids and employees. They also testified that they never entirely renew the jury pool.

Throughout the hearing, lawyers for the state implied that most Black people in both counties are either convicted felons or habitual drunkards or both and are therefore ineligible for jury duty. They also suggested that census data for numbers of Blacks in the counties were inflated by the seasonal presence of migrant farmworkers. This implication was supported by Baldwin Probate Judge D'Olive, who stated that most of the farmworkers were from Texas and Mexico, and that he considered them Black despite the fact that they are Chicanos.

Another issue significant to the racist application of the criminal justice system raised during the hearing of Imani's case is that of discriminatory application of the death penalty. William Bowers, a noted scholar from Northeastern University in Boston, testified on the history of the use of the death penalty in Alabama. Eighty-two percent of executions in Alabama between 1927 and 1965 were of Black people. Blacks executed were younger than whites, and few Blacks had appeals taken.

Bowers also testified about race-of-victim studies he is currently conducting. In 1976, 94% of 400 homicide arrests in Alabama were of people of the same race as the victim. Twenty percent of the arrests were of whites accused of killing Blacks; 4% were of Blacks whose alleged victims were white. Although they were only 4% of the arrestees, Blacks convicted of homicide against whites constitute 47% of the Alabama's death row population. Forty-six percent on death row are whites convicted of killing whites. Seven percent are for Black-on-Black homicides. No white person on death row is there for the killing of a Black person.

The practices in Florida, Georgia and Texas, where Bowers has also conducted studies, produce similar results. The 4% arrested for alleged Black-on-white homicide leads to 36% of those arrested sentenced to death in those states. Bowers' study reveals a subtle form of discrimination practiced in the application of the death penalty. Both Black and white poor people are sentenced to the death penalty, so long as their alleged victims are white, but not if they are Black. Imani is but one such Black prisoner, victimized by the institutionalized racism of the criminal justice system. He awaits death absent outside intervention.

Chapter Sixteen
The Death Penalty in the United States: *A Consistent Pattern of Gross Violations*

(This chapter has been added in 2019; it was not in the original Petition to the UN.)

Perhaps no other single event to occur in the bicentennial year (1976—the year the U.S. Supreme Court reinstated the death penalty) more aptly symbolizes the ways in which legal argument can be used to mask and justify the perpetuation of the two parallel systems of justice which have marked this country's history since its inception. From our arrival as slaves in Jamestown in 1619 until 1865, the law justified our condition as chattel slaves and the brutal quelling of our rebellions; after 1865, the law was used to suppress our disconcerting struggles to achieve the rights of citizens and to create and maintain our second-class status on constitutional grounds.

Throughout this country's history, lynching, bombing, burning, rape, and murder against Black, Brown, and Red people, have been disregarded by federal law enforcement agencies as "outside their jurisdiction," while they have initiated and encouraged illegal surveillance of our struggles as rebellious minorities, controlled by constitutionally acceptable armed force. Racist application of state criminal law enforcement continues to select Black and poor people for arrest, prosecution, conviction, imprisonment, and death, no differently in 1976 than in 1876.[1]

Introduction

The legal tolerance of the imposition of the death penalty, the ultimate criminal sanction, has always been, in the United States, intimately related to majority attitudes to the acceptability of manifestations of overt racism and callous disregard for the rights of poor people. As will be discussed in this article and elsewhere in this volume, the open and violent racism that characterized the 1980's in communities throughout the society[2] has been mirrored in legal opinions that reversed the hard won, albeit limited, civil rights gains in the economic sector and in the criminal justice system. This article will discuss the history of court-sanctioned capital punishment in the United States its relationship to the history of African-Americans and other oppressed segments of society, in the context of international norms.

Some recent cases particularly germane to this discussion that will be considered are *McCleskey v. Kemp,*[3] *Thompson v. Oklahoma,*[4], *Atkins v. Virginia,*[5] *Domingues v. U.S.,*[6] and *Roper v. Simmons.*[7] Each has drawn international attention to the unique role the death penalty plays in the United States as compared to almost every other society in violation of norms of international law.

A. Applicable Norms of Domestic Statutory Law Affecting the Imposition of the Death Penalty

The United States federal system permits each of the fifty states and the federal government to establish its own law regarding capital punishment and, in most cases, the minimum age at which it can be imposed, resulting in "a hodge-podge of legislation" in the words of the Inter-American Commission on Human Rights[8] leading to arbitrary, inconsistent, and discriminatory sentencing based more on the race and economic status of the accused and where the crime took place[9] than the nature of the crime.

Federal Statutory Law

In 1994, a wide sweeping crime bill expanded the federal death penalty to over 60 different offenses, the majority of which are variations of felony murder. Under current federal law, the death penalty may also be imposed for the following:

- trafficking in large quantities of drugs (18 U.S.C. 3591(b)),
- civil rights offenses resulting in death (18 U.S.C. 241, 242, 245, 247),
- genocide (18 U.S.C. 1091),

and, in this post-9/11 era:

- destruction of aircraft, motor vehicles, or related facilities, resulting in death (18 U.S.C. 32-34),
- death resulting from offenses involving transportation of explosives, destruction of government property, or destruction of property related to foreign or interstate commerce (18 U.S.C. 844(d), (f) (i),
- willful wrecking of a train resulting in death (18 U.S.C. 1992),
- terrorist murder of a U.S. national in another country (18 U.S.C. 2332),
- murder by the use of a weapon of mass destruction (18 U.S.C. 2332a),
- murder involving torture (18 U.S.C. 2340),
- death resulting from aircraft hijacking (49 U.S.C. 1472-1473),

- espionage (18 U.S.C. 794), and
- treason. (18 U.S.C. 2381).

These statutes currently apply to adults.[10]

Statutory State Law

Each state determines its own laws regarding the imposition of the death penalty, presumptively within the parameters of the U.S. Constitution. Currently 37 states have death penalty statutes.[11] A total of 16 have ruled the death penalty as unconstitutional. Fifteen states specify a minimum age of 18, five states set the threshold at 17, and the remaining fifteen remain steadfast with a minimum imposable age of 16.[12]

The methods of execution authorized by state law include lethal injection (37 states); electrocution (10 states); lethal gas (5 states); hanging (2 states); firing squad (2 states). Thirteen states authorize more than one method (lethal injection and an alternative method) based on the election of the condemned or the date of sentencing. The method of execution for federal offenders is that of the state in which the execution takes place.[13] If the state has no death penalty, the judge may choose the method of another state. For offenses under the 1988 Drug Kingpin Law, the method of execution is lethal injection, pursuant to 28 CFR, part 26.

Domestic Case Law

Prior to the Supreme Court's decision in *Thompson v. Oklahoma,* discussed below, the Supreme Court had never ruled on the constitutionality of the death penalty for juveniles.

In 1976, the United States Supreme Court in *Gregg v. Georgia* ruled that the death penalty was not an unconstitutionally "cruel and unusual"[14] punishment, ending a decade of controversy—and hope— that the Bill of Rights adopted in 1791 by the U.S. would be interpreted as condemning the death penalty for any and all crimes.[15] Since *Gregg*, very few constitutional challenges to the death penalty have been successful.[16]

As will be discussed below, the apparent random pattern and idiosyncratic imposition of the death penalty in the United States is coherent and establishes an extremely consistent pattern when the race and economic status of those selected for execution are examined.

McCleskey v. Kemp

On October 12, 1978, the State of Georgia found Warren McCleskey, a Black man, guilty of murdering a white police officer during the course of a robbery. After a legally mandated sentencing hearing, the jury imposed the death penalty on him. After a number of appeals, McCleskey challenged his death sentence before the federal courts on the ground that the system that imposed it was racially discriminatory and violated his rights under the Eighth and Fourteenth Amendments[17] to the U.S. Constitution.

In support of this theory, McCleskey offered analyzed data compiled from over 2,000 murder cases that occurred in Georgia in the 1970's from a statistical research project directed by Dr. David C. Baldus *et al.*[18] (Hereinafter this data report will be referred to as the Baldus Study.) This evidence of race discrimination in the application of Georgia's death penalty was overwhelming. The data showed that, when a white person was the victim, the probability that the accused murderer would be sentenced to death was more than four times greater than when a Black person was murdered.[19] The Baldus Study which has been described as "... the most complete and thorough analysis of sentencing that has ever been done," revealed that Georgia's administration of the death penalty is marked by persistent racial disparities in capital sentencing—disparities by the race of the victim and by race of the defendant—that are highly significant and cannot be explained by any other sentencing factors.[20] The study also showed that, among all persons indicted for the murder of whites, Black defendants are sentenced to death nearly three times as often as white defendants, 22% to 8%.[21]

"Notwithstanding the unrebutted proofs of systematic and substantial disparities...imposed upon homicide defendants in Georgia based on the race of the...victim...and that the factors of race of the victim and defendant were at work in Fulton County,"[22] the Eleventh Circuit Court of Appeal denied McCleskey's Eighth and Fourteenth Amendment claims on the grounds that the statistics were "insufficient to demonstrate discriminatory intent . . . (and) insufficient to show irrationality, arbitrariness, and capriciousness under any kind of Eighth amendment analysis . . . "[23]

The Supreme Court of the United States granted *certiorari*, but held that McCleskey's Eighth Amendment rights were not violated because the results of the study did not demonstrate a constitutionally significant risk of racial bias affecting Georgia's capital sentencing process.[24] Furthermore, the Court held that McCleskey's Fourteenth Amendment rights were not violated because the Baldus Study failed to prove that any of the decision makers involved in his specific case acted with a discriminatory intent specific to Mr. McCleskey.[25]

Thompson v. Oklahoma

The Thompson case involves a brutal murder committed by three adult men accompanied by William Wayne Thompson, a fifteen-year-old boy. The victim was the ex-husband of Thompson's sister who according to testimony, was very abusive to Thompson and his sister. Apparently in retaliation for this abuse, Thompson participated with the men in the murder and was convicted and sentenced to death.[26] In addition to the Eighth and Fourteenth Amendment constitutional issues raised on his behalf The International Human Rights Law Group and Amnesty International filed *amicus curiae* briefs arguing that international legal principles applied to the analysis under federal common law and that an Eighth Amendment prohibition against cruel and unusual punishment should be informed by international law principles.[27]

The views of the international community and the norms of the European community discussed below were apparently ignored by the Supreme Court in its decision in *Thompson* which falls very short of bringing the United States into accord with international law and the practices of most other nation states.[28] The Court's narrow ruling in this case concludes that only state statutes that failed to set any minimum age for the imposition of the death penalty on offenders are unconstitutional, because there is no evidence that the legislatures in those states have considered the law's impact on those under sixteen. Therefore, the Court held the death penalty cannot be imposed on youths under the age of sixteen at the time they committed the crime, only if the death penalty statute in the state where the crime was committed fails to set a minimum age.[29] It should be noted that the children that have been selected for the death penalty throughout the history of the United States are disproportionately people of color. Nearly two-thirds of all child offenders currently sitting on death row are ethnic or racial minorities,[30] with 75% of youthful offenders executed since 1990 being African American.[31] Moreover, since 1900, over 200 minors have been executed in the United States; the large majority have been Black, including the execution of at least 40 Black juveniles for rape of white women. In 1944, a fourteen-year-old Black child named George Stinney was electrocuted in South Carolina for the murder of two white girls. In

May 1984, the last execution of a juvenile before the 1985 prohibition of the death penalty for juveniles, the death penalty was imposed in Texas on James Andrew Echols, a Black youth convicted of raping a white woman when he was seventeen. Between the years 1990 and 2002, eighteen juvenile offenders were executed in the United States; eleven (61%) were Black, the majority of whom committed murder against white victims and were sentenced to death by all white juries.[32] The only two 10-year-olds to have been legally executed in the United States were a Black child in 1855 and a Cherokee (Native American) who was hanged in 1885.[33]

B. The Historic Background to the Racist Imposition of Capital Punishment in the United States

While Justices of the Supreme Court have generally chosen to ignore racial issues in their opinions, it is only through such an analysis that the enduring impact on U.S. society of the death penalty can be understood.[34] Since slavery, Blacks who committed crimes against whites have been selected for the death sentence more than any other group.[35] Justice Thurgood Marshall was unequivocal on the disproportionate race and class assumptions inherent in the application of the death penalty in *Furman v. Georgia* when he wrote,

> "It ... is evident that the burden of capital punishment falls upon the poor, the ignorant, and the underprivileged members of society. It is the poor and the members of minority groups who are least able to voice their complaints against Capital Punishment. Their impotence leaves them victims of a sanction that the wealthier, better-represented, just-as-guilty person can escape. So long as the capital sanction is used only against the forlorn, easily forgotten members of society, legislators are content to maintain the status quo because change would draw attention to the problem and concern might develop."

Commenting on recent research establishing that, over a period of several years in South Carolina, the death penalty was requested by the prosecution in 49% of the cases in which a Black defendant was accused of murdering a white, but in only 11% of cases in which there is both a Black victim and a Black accused, former Justice of the Supreme Court Arthur J. Goldberg[36] also observed that this disparity is racial. "There is no other explanation."[37] He concluded ". . . the death penalty is uniformly imposed only on the poor, and the poor, unfortunately, are largely Black and Hispanic. Rich or establishment people also commit murder, but to my knowledge no such people wait in death cells. This disparity makes a mockery of the concept of Equal Justice For All, emblazoned on the edifice of the Supreme Court of the United States . . . ." [38]

The discriminatory use of the death penalty has deep and hardy roots in the first contacts with the criminal justice system of Africans brought on the slave ships to labor in the colonies in the seventeenth century.[39] The Slave Codes, enacted in a majority of the colonies between 1680 and the late 1800's, made conduct by African slaves criminal that was legal for whites.[40] These race specific laws provided the substantive foundation for the development of the U.S. criminal justice system.[41] As slavery expanded and became more important to the national economy, Southern Slave Codes became more complex and pervasive. Discriminatory regulations were adopted, not only to control African slaves' conduct, but to relegate all Black people to a permanent subordination devoid of equality or the expectation of the rights and privileges of citizens of the new country.

The stark racist intent of the white propertied legislators was nowhere more clear than in the area of criminal sanctions. The laws of the Southern states prescribed race specific punishments.[42] For example, in the states of Virginia, Louisiana, Tennessee, and Alabama, slaves and free Blacks were subject to the death penalty for burglary, arson, destruction of any house, building or other property, including grain, corn, and any other goods or chattel produced by whites. Whites convicted of these crimes had to pay the value of the property destroyed or to serve a two-to-five year prison term.[43]

Southern statutes provided that any Black man convicted of raping a white woman should be castrated, or receive the death penalty. White men did not face these automatic penalties. The law did not even recognize the rape of Black women as crimes.[44]

While the law failed to recognize Black women as victims of rape, white men raped Black women with impunity. Black men who engaged in consensual sex with white women committed capital offenses.[45] The race of the accused *and* the victim consistently distinguished capital crimes from non-capital crimes.

Every Southern state defined a substantial number of felonies carrying a capital punishment for slaves and lesser punishments for whites. In addition to murder of any degree, slaves received the death penalty for attempted murder, manslaughter, rape and attempted rape upon a white woman, rebellion and attempted rebellion, poisoning, robbery, and arson.[46] For the most part, whites were not affected by capital punishment for first degree murder. The death penalty could be imposed on whites for aiding or encouraging insurrection, whether or not the insurrection actually occurred.[47] North Carolina made "concealing a slave with the intent and for the purpose of enabling such a slave to escape" punishable by death.[48]

The permanent domination of Africans and their relegation to subordinate positions in society was clearly the intention of these race-specific criminal laws. Louisiana law gave jurors the discretion to sentence slaves to death for "grievously wounding a white person, merely shedding the blood of the master, a member of his family, or the overseer, and for the third offense of striking a white.'"[49] In Alabama, a Black perpetrator or accessory could receive the death penalty for insurrection or rebellion against whites, murder, attempted murder, rape, attempted rape of white women, burglary, or arson. Murder of a slave by a slave or freeman, however, was not punishable by death, but rather by the branding of the hand or one hundred lashes.[50] In Virginia, the discrepancy between punishments for slaves and whites was even greater. Virginia laws contained over 70 potential capital crimes for slaves and only three for whites.[51]

In addition to the racially disparate substantive criminal law, rules of criminal procedure restricted the rights of Black defendants. Even free Blacks, in all but two Southern states, were prohibited from testifying against whites in court[52], thereby preventing them from seeking redress for crimes against them.[53] Slaves could testify against other Blacks but could never testify against whites in any court.[54] No slave states allowed Blacks to serve on juries, whatever the race of the accused.[55]

This dual system of justice did not end in 1865 with the Civil War. Following emancipation and the passage of the Thirteenth Amendment, former slave states enacted the Black Codes as a substitute for the Slave Codes.[56] The Fourteenth Amendment was an effort to inhibit the South's continued repression of its newly made Black citizens. But judicial interpretation by the Supreme Court ensured the perpetuation of racially disparate justice and eliminated equal protection under the law for Black people.[57] When legal means were unavailable to enforce the subjugation of African-Americans, extra-legal methods were developed.[58]

During the Reconstruction period, when whites claimed that Blacks were an uncontrollable danger to white society, lynching arose as a means of terrorizing Blacks.[59] In both the South and the North, lynching became a second method of capital punishment aimed chiefly at Black citizens accused of crimes or minor indignities against white citizens. Prominent white citizens and elected officials continued to defend lynching as a "necessary" replacement for the Black Codes, long after whites had recaptured complete control of the Southern legal system.[60]

In fact, lynch mobs, although nominally outside the law, often worked with its cooperation.[61] The presence of lynch mobs often encouraged or forced the authorities to conduct hasty trials and exacerbated the prejudice of the entirely white judiciary and jury pool against the defendant. After a court of law pronounced a defendant guilty, it was not uncommon for a mob to administer his death sentence by hanging, or some more brutal means such as burning, mutilation, or shooting. Lynchers, on the other hand, were rarely punished.[62]

The South also used legal means to maintain social control over Blacks.[63] After the Black Codes were outlawed, Southern states adopted criminal systems with facially neutral statutes that allowed prosecutors, judges, and jurors broad discretion to mete out widely varying punishments.[64] In addition, some statutes, which expressly discriminated on the basis of race, remained.[65] Despite the end of slavery and the adoption of the Fourteenth Amendment, Southern states continued to subjugate their Black population through criminal law.

Southern states expanded their capital statutes to include many of the crimes previously contained in the Black Codes. For example, the crimes of burglary in the night, arson to an occupied building, and horse stealing, considered "typical of freemen",[66] were made punishable by death, imprisonment or fines at the discretion of the prosecution, the court, or jury. Rape and insurrection also continued to be punishable by death. Courts regularly applied the facially neutral sentencing statutes in a racially disproportionate fashion.[67] The legal system did not treat similar crimes in a similar manner. Whether Black defendants suffered at the hands of a mob or the law, they were treated more severely than similarly situated white defendants.

Meanwhile, lynching or the threat of racially motivated violence resulted in the control of African-Americans almost as effectively as race-specific criminal and civil codes and slavery itself. Discriminatory application of criminal punishment avoided the constitutional requirements of the criminal law.[68]

The passage of the Civil Rights Act of 1875 was an effort to redress some of the inequities of criminal justice systems run by and for white citizens only. Although the Act prohibited states from excluding qualified persons from a jury on the basis of their race[69], unequal justice thrived. However, in *Strauder v. West Virginia*[70], the Supreme Court struck down a state statute which barred Blacks from jury service, on the ground that the statute violated the equal protection clause.[71] The Court found that denying Blacks the right to serve on juries and participate in the criminal and civil process encouraged prejudice and the belief that Blacks were inferior.[72] One year later, in *Neal v. Delaware*,[73] the Court held that the racially discriminatory application of facially neutral jury selection laws also violated the equal protection clause. Both rulings, however, involved evidence of discriminatory intent, *Strauder* on the face of a statute, *Neal* in the actions and record of a state court. While the Court's rulings ostensibly vindicated Black rights, they had little affect on the racial composition of juries. In subsequent cases, the Court either found no evidence of intent or shut its eyes to such evidence, and Blacks continued to be excluded from jury service.[74]

In a survey done in the early twentieth century, questionnaires were sent to every county in the South in which Blacks represented more than half of the population. The results of the survey showed that Blacks had rarely been permitted to sit on juries in Southern state courts in the past, and were unlikely to be allowed to serve in the future. Respondents indicated that, in those instances in which Black names were accidentally selected from the jury roster, the Blacks were subsequently excluded. The respondents asserted that Blacks were poor jurors because of their ignorance. Blacks were frequently described as having failed the suffrage test, and therefore were unable to qualify for jury service under the law.[75]

The exclusion of Blacks from jury selection continued in the South for the next fifty years, in part because Blacks were not permitted to register to vote. Jurors were drawn from voter registration lists. Consequently, disenfranchised Black citizens did not appear on the jury roster. Hence Black defendants faced an entirely white courtroom: the judge, prosecutor, and jury were all white. Of equal importance, exclusion meant that Blacks in the community at large were denied their right to participate in the community's legal process.[76]

C. Discriminatory Imposition of the Death Penalty in the Modern Era (1954-2004)

After the Second World War, African-Americans joined by other people of color and white supporters began organizing systematic attacks on official *de jure* and *de facto* segregation.

By the middle of the 1950's and continuing into the 1960's, federal legislation was passed to remedy some forms of discrimination in the areas of public education,[77] public accommodations and transportation,[78] voting,[79] housing,[80] and employment.[81]

However, as earlier, the area of criminal justice remained a fertile ground for the retention and growth of the problems flowing from racially disparate standards and discretion tainted with racial animus. African-American adults and children accused of capital crimes anywhere in the nation were more likely to be sentenced to death. By 1974, more than half of the people who had been executed or condemned to die were Black.[82] Long before Professor Baldus provided statistical support for Mr. McCleskey's contentions before the Supreme Court that there was a pervasive and discernable pattern of racism in capital sentencing in Georgia, there was a wealth of research support for the hypothesis that the application of the death penalty and the criminal justice system in the United States was riddled with racial discrimination.[83] All the studies support the widespread belief in the African-American community that injustice flowing from the racism, which has characterized the imposition of the death penalty for 300 years, continues to define the value of Black lives.

Black defendants are sentenced to death more frequently than whites who are convicted of the same or more heinous crimes.

Crimes against white victims are more likely to result in death sentences than identical crimes against Black victims. As of October 2002, the ACLU reported that 12 people have been executed where the defendant was white and the murder victim Black, compared with 178 Black defendants executed for murders of white victims.[84]

Since African-Americans constitute a minority in most communities, and because prosecutors often use peremptory challenges to strike Black jurors,[85] the vast majority of jurors in death penalty cases continue to be white or death penalty advocates.[86]

A clear example of this consistent pattern of the racist application of the pre-emptory challenges resulting in the systematic exclusion of Blacks from prospective juries to the detriment of Black death penalty defendants is illustrated in the most recent U.S. Supreme Court decision in *Flowers v. Mississippi*. (*Flowers v. Mississippi.* US ___ 2019; argued March 28, 2019; decided June 21, 2019.) Notwithstanding the prior Supreme Court decision in *Batson v. Kentucky* in 1986, prohibiting prosecutors from using the pre-emptory challenges to remove Blacks from juries, the trial courts in *Flowers* turned a blind eye to obvious racism in the jury selection process. This resulted in Flowers being tried six times for capital murder. In the first five trials, the prosecution removed 41 of 42 prospective Black jurors. While this most recent Supreme Court decision reversed Flowers' conviction of murder, it illustrates the persistent and systemic pattern of the illegal removal of Blacks from prospective juries resulting in Black death penalty defendants being convicted by white juries.

Disparate treatment and impact toward Blacks has even been acknowledged as a problem by the federal government. A study was conducted by the U.S. Justice Department at the request of President Bill Clinton and released on September 12, 2000. The study entitled, "The Federal Death Penalty System: A Statistical Survey (1988-2000)," was aimed at unraveling the decision-making process behind prosecutors' decisions to seek the death penalty, as well as to provide statistical information relating to race, ethnicity, and demographic qualities of defendants and their victims. When all was said and done, the survey found numerous racial and geographic disparities, revealing that

- 80% of the cases submitted by federal prosecutors for capital punishment review between the years 1995 and 2000 have involved racial minorities as defendants;
- in more than half of those cases, the defendant was African American;
- even after review by the Attorney General, 72% of the cases approved for death penalty prosecution involved minority defendants;
- according to an analysis of 146 cases prosecuted under the federal death penalty statute since 1988, 60% of white defendants avoided a death sentence through plea bargaining, whereas only 41% of Black defendants had the same outcome.
- Forty-percent of the 682 cases sent to the Justice Department for approval to seek capital punishment were filed by only five jurisdictions.[87]

In the face of the unequivocal and unchallenged body of evidence demonstrating racial discrimination in the imposition of the death penalty and the Supreme Court's most recent callous indifference to the proofs of obvious systematic racism in the criminal justice system, after 300 years of unchecked *de facto* and *de jure* imposition of the death penalty, the inability to find redress in domestic law for these continuing violations of human rights of people of color in the United States suggests review of the available remedies under international law.

D. The Death Penalty As Applied in the United States Violates International Human Rights Law

(See Appendix II for International Standards Relevant to the Death Penalty)

In their report,[88] Amnesty International finds that, "No means of limiting the death penalty can prevent its being imposed arbitrarily or unfairly. This is borne out by the experience in the USA, where the introduction of elaborate judicial safeguards has failed to ensure that the death penalty is fairly and consistently applied."[89] The report calls upon the federal and state governments "to abolish the death penalty for all offenses in law. All measures to abolish the death penalty or restrict its use should be applied retroactively to prisoners under sentence of death, in accordance with international standards."[90]

Outside of the legislatures of the United States, there is growing international consensus that the death penalty is incompatible with the Universal Declaration of Human Rights and other international human rights instruments in which the right to life and the right not to be subjected to cruel, inhuman, or degrading treatment or punishment are incorporated.[91]

Other international and regional agreements restricting the imposition of the death penalty and supporting its abolition can be found in Article 4(2) of the American Convention on Human Rights (ACHR) stating that the "application of [capital punishment] shall not be extended to crimes to which it does not presently apply." Article 4(3) states: "The death penalty shall not be re-established in states that have abolished it." Article 6 of the International Covenant on Civil and Political Rights (ICCPR) imposes restrictions on the use of the death penalty "in countries which have not abolished it" and states, "Nothing in this article shall be invoked to delay or to prevent the abolition of capital punishment by any State Party to the present Covenant."

The United States has signed but not ratified the above treaties. However, as a signatory nation, it has an obligation under the Vienna Convention on the Laws of Treaties to do nothing to "defeat the object and purpose" of signed treaties.[92]

During its 63rd session, in 1984, the Inter-American Commission on Human Rights decided, in accordance with the spirit of Article 4 of the ACHR and the universal trend to eliminate the death penalty, to call on all countries in the Americas to abolish the death penalty. On 15 December 1980, the United Nations General Assembly adopted Resolution 35/172 urging all member states to "respect as a minimum standard the content of the provisions of articles 6, 14 and 15 of the International Covenant on Civil and Political Rights."[93]

Before 2005, U.S. laws allowing the execution of juveniles were in direct conflict with minimum recognized safeguards and standards of fairness (such as those contained in ECOSOC Resolution 1984/50, to be discussed later in this article) applying to those countries which retain the death penalty. This recently changed, however, with the Supreme Court's finding that the death penalty, in fact, violates the U.S. Constitution. The Court's holding in *Roper v. Simmons* asserts the Eighth and Fourteenth Amendments forbid the imposition of the death penalty on offenders who were under the age of 18 when their crimes were committed.[94] The above treaties and the 1949 Geneva Convention concerning the protection of civilians in time of war provide for the exclusion from the death penalty in all circumstances of people under 18 at the time of the crime. The wide adherence to this standard in practice, including the reversal of the U.S. on its age-old policy allowing for a structured system of juvenile capital punishment, together with the relevant treaties and guidelines, suggests that this provision is also *jus cogens,* part of customary international law. This peremptory norm had been previously argued by the Inter-American Commission in the case of *Domingues v. U.S.,*[95] with the United States issuing a strong opposition to the Commission's accusations of U.S. violations of customary international law.

The U.S. Government issued a statement asserting, among other things, that (as summarized by the Commission) "neither the state practice identified by, nor the legal standards cited in the Commission's report, are sufficient to establish either a customary or *jus cogens* prohibition of the execution of juvenile offenders" and that "in focusing on the domestic practice of states, the Commission's report ignored *opinio juris* as a necessary element of customary international law," as it had failed "to establish that states have discontinued the process of executing juvenile offenders out of a sense of legal obligation rather than, for example, out of courtesy, fairness, or morality."

After considering these arguments, the Commission stated that "Where an instrument [such as a human rights treaty] is widely ratified or endorsed by members of the international community and speaks to the legality of certain actions, the provisions of that instrument might themselves properly be considered as evidence of *opinio juris,*" and that "state measures in eradicating the juvenile death penalty may properly be considered to have been undertaken out of a sense of legal obligation to respect fundamental human rights." In its report on the case, adopted in October 2002, the Commission concluded that the U.S. "has acted contrary to an international norm of *jus cogens* as reflected in Article I of the American Declaration [on the Rights and Duties of Man] by sentencing Michael Domingues to the death penalty for crimes that he committed when he was 16 years of age" and that "should the State [the U.S.] execute Mr. Domingues pursuant to this sentence, it will be responsible for a grave and irreparable violation of Mr. Domingues' right to life under Article I of the American Declaration."[96] Domingues was spared three years later as a result of *Roper*, which not only forced all U.S. states retaining the juvenile death penalty to conform to the new national minimum threshold age of 18, but also affirmed the Inter-American Commission's argument opposing the U.S. violating *jus cogens* international norms forbidding juvenile capital punishment of those under the age of 18.

As noted above, prior to the *Roper* decision, US juvenile death penalty laws were in direct conflict with prohibition of the execution of minors contained in standards of fairness and safeguards guaranteeing protection of the rights of those facing the death penalty, such as those adopted by the United Nations Economic and Social Council in May 1984 (ECOSOC Resolution 1984/50). Some state practices not discussed here would appear to be in conflict with some other safeguards which include guidelines on prisoners who have become insane and on the provision of legal assistance for condemned prisoners at all stages of the proceedings.

The pre-*Roper* era ECOSOC safeguards were endorsed by the Seventh United Nations Congress on the Prevention of Crime and the Treatment of Offenders (Milan, 26 August-6 September 1985) in a resolution in which it invited "all States retaining the death penalty and whose present standards fall short of the safeguards" to adopt them and to take the necessary steps to implement them by, among other things

"(a) Incorporating or making provision for the safeguards in national legislation and regulations;

"(b) Ensuring that judges, lawyers, police officers, prison officials and other persons, including military personnel, who may be concerned with the administration of criminal justice, are familiar with the safeguards, and any corresponding provisions in national legislation and regulations, by including them in courses of instruction and by disseminating and publicizing them and by other appropriate means."

ECOSOC, in a resolution adopted at its spring session on 21 May 1986, urged, "Member States that have not abolished the death penalty to adopt the safeguards . . . and the measures for the implementation of the safeguards approved by the Seventh United Nations Congress on the Prevention of Crime and the Treatment of Offenders . . . "[97]

Amnesty International believes that the involvement of doctors and other health professionals in executions is contrary to the *Principles of Medical Ethics Relevant to the Role of Health Professionals, Particularly Physicians, in the Protection of Prisoners and Detainees against Torture or Other Cruel, Inhuman or Degrading Treatment or Punishment*, adopted by the United Nations General Assembly in December 1982.

The involvement of physicians in some U.S. executions (especially by lethal injection) has appeared contrary to the ethical principles laid down by the World Medical Association in 1981.[98]

The inability to obtain redress in the courts of the United States for "the consistent pattern of gross, well documented and attested violations of human rights and freedoms"[99] reflected in the imposition of the death penalty in the United States upon African-Americans and other people of color, upon the poor, upon children, and the mentally retarded[100], suggests the careful consideration of these international forums for remedies for those unremitting violations of human rights discussed here.[101]

The appeal of the execution of James Terry Roach[102], taken to the Inter-American Commission on Human Rights, may be instructive in the possibilities and limitations of such initiatives.

The "hodge-podge of legislation" [103] discussed above leading to arbitrary, inconsistent sentencing based on the race of the accused, the race of the victims, and where the crime took place led the Inter-American Commission on Human Rights, the advisory body on Human Rights within the Organization of American States (OAS), [104] in March 1987 to find the United States in violation of its international obligations for executing

James Terry Roach who was seventeen at the time he committed a capital crime.[105] The Commission held that the United States was in violation of a norm of *jus cogens*[106] prohibiting the state execution of children in the OAS system[107], which has been accepted by all Inter-American states including the United States.[108]

The decision by the IACHR, for the first time in its twenty-seven year history, finding the United States in violation of international human rights law, did not materially affect the Supreme Court's decision in *Thompson v. Oklahoma* discussed above. The Inter-American Commission findings in response to the arguments of the petitioners provided a useful framework for the applicability of international law to the application of the death penalty in the United States while revealing "the consistent pattern of gross and reliably attested violations of the human rights and fundamental freedoms"[109] of African-Americans, other people of color, and juveniles.

Although surprisingly the Inter-American decision did not find that the execution of Roach violated a customary norm of law binding the state as *jus cogens* prohibiting "the state execution of children,"[110] it did ultimately hold that the United States had, in fact, violated the American Declaration, not because the U.S. had failed to prevent the execution of Roach, or even because the American Declaration forbids the execution of children under 18, but because of the variety of individual state practices within the United States respecting the death penalty.[111] In the words of the Inter-American Commission,

> "The Commission finds that the diversity of state practice in the United States . . . results in very different sentences for commission of the same crime . . . Under the present system of laws in the United States, a hypothetical sixteen-year-old who commits a capital offense in Virginia may potentially be subject to the death penalty, whereas if the same individual commits the same offense on the other side of the Memorial Bridge, in Washington, D.C., where the death penalty has been abolished for adults as well as for juveniles, the sentence will not be death."[112]

The Commission then stated its holding:

> "The failure of the federal government to preempt the states as regards this most fundamental right—the right to life—results in a

pattern of legislative arbitrariness throughout the United States which results in the arbitrary deprivation of life and inequality before the law, contrary to Articles I and II of the American Declaration of the Rights and Duties of Man, respectively."[113]

Although the Inter-American decision has been sharply criticized because it found that the U.S. had violated the American Declaration on an article that petitioners never suggested had been violated, on an issue that neither the petitioners nor the U.S. had been given the opportunity to argue, it reaffirms the binding character of the American Declaration on OAS member states[114], including the United States.[115]

The substantive holding of the Commission appears to be that the United States, by allowing individual states to adopt varying legislation with respect to the death penalty, denied Roach equality before the law. Article II of the American Declaration states: "All persons are equal before the law and have the rights and duties established in this declaration, without distinction as to race, sex, language, creed or any other factor."[116] The decision of the Commission, finding a violation of Article II, seems to imply that the United States federal system of criminal justice violates international law.[117]

E. The Impact of International Standards on U.S. Law

International standards can be considered in the interpretation of the U.S. Constitution through Article VI of the Constitution.[118] International standards are already an established aspect of the Eighth Amendment analysis regarding limits on the use of executions as a penalty. In *Edmund v. Florida,*[119] the United States Supreme Court used the "climate of international opinion"[120] as one basis for finding that imposition of the death penalty on a defendant who had not intended to kill was cruel and unusual punishment. In *Coker v. Georgia*[121], the Court found a Georgia death penalty for rape to be cruel and unusual punishment, noting that only three major nations still applied the death penalty for rape.[122] In *Trop v. Dullest*[123], the Court took cognizance of other nations' practices in determining that denaturalization as a punishment for desertion violates the Eighth Amendment. *Atkins v. Virginia*[124] dealt with whether the Eighth and Fourteenth Amendments prohibited executing mentally disabled individuals as dictated by current standards of human decency. The court in *Atkins* took particular note of an *amicus curiae* brief filed by the European Union[125] supporting such a ban and recognized that "within the world community, the imposition of the death penalty for crimes committed by mentally retarded offenders is overwhelmingly disapproved."[126] The Court's goal in making specific reference to the brief was to make known that international opinion played a large role in determining the standards of decency as they evolved in a maturing society. The body of 18 states barring such executions fell short of a majority of the death penalty states, yet the Court found evidence of a consensus when these states were supported by numerous peripheral factors, including world opinion. More recently, the Supreme Court's bearing on considering international legal norms further resonated in its landmark decision in *Roper.* Justice Kennedy's majority opinion notes,

> "Respondent and his *amici* have submitted, and petitioner does not contest, that only seven countries other than the United States have executed juvenile offenders since 1990: Iran, Pakistan, Saudi Arabia, Yemen, Nigeria, the Democratic Republic of Congo, and China. Since then, each of these countries has either abolished capital punishment for juveniles or made public disavowal of the practice. (Brief for Respondent 49-50.) In sum, it is fair to say that the United States now stands alone in a world that has turned its face against the juvenile death penalty…It does not lessen our fidelity to the Constitution or our pride in its origins to acknowledge that the express affirmation of certain fundamental rights by other nations and peoples simply underscores the centrality of those same rights within our own heritage of freedom."[127]

In addition to using international law to interpret provisions of the Constitution, the Supreme Court has also recognized that international law is part of United States law. Treaties to which the United States is a party become binding on the states through the supremacy clause of the Constitution.[128] The Inter-American decision questioned the legality, under the American Declaration, of the death penalty administered under the U.S. federal system of criminal justice[129] and declared the U.S. system as denying equality before the law.

The invocation of a customary norm of international law in a domestic court might have prevented Thompson's execution[130] as it later would for petitioner in *Roper.* In addition to the custom and practice of nations,[131] the Supreme Court can look at the decisions of international tribunals to determine international law in the absence of a treaty.[132] The Commission unfortunately ignored its opportunity to assist either the Supreme Court or Thompson by basing its decision in *Roach* on the lack of a federal legislative or judicial prohibition of juvenile executions.[133]

Notwithstanding the defects in law and logic in the Inter-American decision on *Roach,* [134] this decision is extremely important because it places the United States on notice that, like any other nation in the world community, it can be found in violation of international human rights law, and that it is bound, as are all other OAS member states[135], to the American Declaration of the Rights and Duties of Men.[136]

Since 1948, the inter-American human rights system has evolved into the most ambitious institutional framework in the world for promoting and protecting human rights.[137]

The Inter-American system has two legal sources, one of which is the OAS Charter.[138] The other source is the American Convention on Human Rights.[139] The basic legal documents of the system within the context of the Organization of American States (OAS) recognize civil, political, social, and cultural rights.[140] The enabling documents of the OAS also established the Inter-American Commission on Human Rights[141] and the Inter-American Court of Human Rights.[142] These legal instruments grant the Commission the authority to review complaints from individuals and groups or to initiate its own proceedings into human rights violations by an OAS member state.

Among the very important features which distinguish this human rights forum from other international bodies which have the discretion to consider human rights complaints are

- the automatic right of an individual or non-state party to petition[143];
- the Commission has the power to undertake country-wide studies of human rights practices, including on-site investigations;[144]
- the Commission has the right to take urgent, interim measures where

necessary to avoid irreparable harm;[145]

- it has the authority to make recommendations to States regarding the promotion and protection of human rights;[146]
- where appropriate, the Court may award compensation to victims of human rights violations;[147]
- the Court has the most extensive advisory jurisdiction of any international judicial body.[148]

The extent of the enumerated human rights and the extensive enforcement powers of these inter-American bodies create the potential for an extremely effective human rights system for the western hemisphere which has been largely ignored by groups complaining of continuing gross and widespread violations of their human rights by the United States, although its provisions have successfully been invoked by persons in other countries in the region, leading to increased international concern, and in some cases, political change.[149]

As discussed above, an international system to defend human rights requires specific provisions to make it an effective remedy. They include the capacity to respond quickly; the resources and powers to obtain credible evidence; the ability to draft well-reasoned authoritative legal opinions; and the will and methodology to disseminatc results widely.[150]

Both the inter-American Commission and the inter-American Court, which only has jurisdiction over contentious cases involving states parties to the Convention, are able to take immediate steps with extraordinary speed compared to other human rights institutions.[151] For example, the Executive Secretary of the Inter-American Commission arrived in Santiago, Chile, less than a month after the *coup d'etat* in 1973.[152] The United Nations official on-site visit occurred in 1978.[153]

As in the case of challenges to the death penalty, speed is particularly important. During the challenge of the execution of the youth discussed above before the Commission, the United States refused requests from the Commission to stay the execution pending decisions on their petition. The Commission concluded that, in carrying out the execution, the United States government violated Article I (right to life) and Article II (equality of treatment and equality before the law) of the American Declaration of the Rights and Duties of Man,[154] causing serious embarrassment to the nation. The Commission's Country Reports are the most effective of all other human rights institutions. [155]

Amendments to the rules of procedure have eliminated some problems like the appearance of conflicts of interest in the study team.[156] The regulations also provide access to persons and documents during fact-finding.[157] However, standards for the collection of the evidence would strengthen the procedures.[158]

The Commission serves as fact-finder and decision-maker. As a decision-maker, some human rights legal experts consider the Commission to be at its weakest.[159] The recent opinion on the execution of juvenile offenders has been criticized for failing to apply controlling procedural rules and for ignoring international canons of interpretation.[160] This opinion, which has been read by some as finding the federal system of criminal justice in violation of international human rights law, has been interpreted to mean that varying punishments are also in violation of human rights laws when the punishment affects a fundamental right such as the right to life.

It has also been suggested that the Commission should refer difficult interpretative legal questions to the Court when asked for an advisory opinion.[161]

> "It has the ability to shape the interpretation and application of the Convention, Declaration, and other human rights instruments through its opinions and decisions. Advisory opinions in particular are well suited to the enunciation of general legal principles, which may contribute to the development of human rights law in the Western Hemisphere."[162]

Since the mobilization of public opinion remains a major vehicle for improving the behavior of nation states in respect to human rights issues, the poor delivery of information about the Inter-American system can present difficulties.[163]

The current publications policy also is unclear. Under the Convention, if a case is not referred to the Court or settled, the Commission may, by majority vote, issue an opinion and conclusions concerning the issue.[164] If the Commission adopts a report, the report must include recommendations and a prescribed period within which the state must take remedial measures. After the expiration of the specific time period, another Commission vote decides whether the state has taken adequate measures and whether to publish the report.[165]

For non-states parties to the Convention, the Regulations provide that the Commission may publish the final decision on a petition after issuing it to the state with any recommendations and a deadline for their implementation.[166] Only when the state does not adopt the recommendations of the Commission within the deadline, should the Commission publish failures to respond or to adopt Commission recommendations; if that interpretation is correct, the Commission has not followed this policy.[167] Commission policy requires clarification, if necessary, by an amendment to the Regulations specifying a general policy in favor of publication. As the policy is currently implemented, no one reading the Regulations and reports of the Commission can be certain what the Commission will publish and what it will not.

F. Conclusion

The Inter-American system is an ambitious initiative providing procedures for the promotion and protection of human rights under international law. It provides extraordinary opportunities for human rights activists in the Americas to obtain support and evidence to be presented in domestic cases where the human rights violations of a specific country are being challenged, as in *Filartiga v. Pena-Irala*[168] and in the *Haitian Refugee Cases*.[169] It also can provide an extremely potent and expedited (as compared to United Nations procedures) process by which racist application of the death penalty in the United States can be scrutinized and provide recourse in the international courts of law and opinion for victims of the persistent abuse of their human rights in the criminal justice processes of the United States.

Endnotes

[1] Hinds, Lennox S., "The Death Penalty: Continuing Threat to America's Poor," in *Freedomways*, First Quarter, 1976 at 39.

[2] See, *inter alia, The State of Black America 1990*, National Urban League, Inc., New York, January, 1990.

[3] 481 US 279 (1987), permitting execution even if statistics prove racial disparity in the imposition of the sentence.

[4] 107 S. Ct. 1284 (1987) vacated, 56 US Law 4892, Jun. 29, 1988, permitting the execution of a child who was 15 at the time the crime for which he was convicted was committed.

[5] See *Atkins v. Virginia*. 536 US 304 (2002) 260 Va. 375, 534 S.E. 2d 312, reversed and remanded, hereinafter, *Atkins*.

[6] See *Domingues* v. U.S. Case 12.285 (2002), hereinafter, *Domingues*.

[7] See *Roper v. Simmons*. 543 US 551 (2005), hereinafter, *Roper*.

[8] Resolution No. 3/87 case No. 9647 (United States), Inter-American Commission on Human Rights, OEA/see L/V/11.69, Doc 17,27 March 1987 (hereinafter *Inter-American Decision*).

[9] Inter-American Decision § 58,62 and Amnesty International, United States of America; The Death Penalty (1987) hereinafter *USA Death Penalty*.

[10] The current Federal death penalty law as decided in *Roper v. Simmons* 543 US 551 (2005) specifies a minimum age of 18.

[11] CAPITAL OFFENSES, BY STATE, 2005

Alabama. Intentional murder with 18 aggravating factors (Ala. Stat. Ann. 13A-5-40(a)(1)-(18)). **Arizona***. First-degree murder accompanied by at least 1 of 10 aggravating factors (A.R.S. § 13-703(F)). Arkansas*. Capital murder (Ark. Code Ann. 5-10-101) with a finding of at least 1 of 10 aggravating circumstances; treason. **California***. First-degree murder with special circumstances; train wrecking; treason; perjury causing execution. **Colorado***. First-degree murder with at least 1 of 17 aggravating factors; treason. **Connecticut***. Capital felony with 8 forms of aggravated homicide (C.G.S. 53a-54b). **Delaware***. First-degree murder with aggravating circumstances. **Florida***. First-degree murder; felony murder; capital drug trafficking; capital sexual battery. **Georgia***. Murder; kidnapping with bodily injury or ransom when the victim dies; aircraft hijacking; treason. **Idaho***. First-degree murder with aggravating factors; aggravated kidnapping; perjury resulting in death. **Illinois***. First-degree murder with 1 of 21 aggravating circumstances. **Indiana***. Murder with 16 aggravating circumstances (IC 35-50-2-9). **Kansas***. Capital murder with 8 aggravating circumstances (KSA 21-3439). **Kentucky***. Murder with aggravating factors; kidnapping with aggravating factors (KRS 532.025). **Louisiana***. First-degree murder; aggravated rape of victim under age 12; treason (La. R.S. 14:30, 14:42, and 14:113). **Maryland***. First-degree murder, either premeditated or during the commission of a felony, provided that certain death eligibility requirements are satisfied. **Mississippi**. Capital murder (97-3-19(2) MCA); aircraft piracy (97-25-55(1) MCA). **Missouri***. First-degree murder (565.020 RSMO 2000). **Montana**. Capital murder with 1 of 9 aggravating circumstances (46-18-303 MCA); capital sexual assault (45-5-503 MCA). **Nebraska***. First-degree murder with a finding of at least 1 statutorily-defined aggravating circumstance. Nevada*. First-degree murder with at least 1of 15 aggravating circumstances (NRS 200.030, 200.033, 200.035). **New Hampshire**. Six categories of capital murder (RSA 630:1, RSA 630:5). **New Jersey**. Murder by one's own conduct, by solicitation, committed in furtherance of a narcotics conspiracy, or during commission of a crime of terrorism (NJSA 2C:11-3c). **New Mexico***. First-degree murder with at least 1 of 7 statutorily-defined aggravating circumstances (Section 30-2-1 A, NMSA). **New York****. First-degree murder with 1 of 13 aggravating factors (NY Penal Law §125.27). **North Carolina***. First-degree murder (NCGS §14-17). **Ohio**. Aggravated murder with at least 1 of 10 aggravating circumstances (O.R.C. §§. 2903.01, 2929.02, and 2929.04). **Oklahoma**. First-degree murder in conjunction with a finding of at least 1 of 8 statutorily defined aggravating circumstances. **Oregon**. Aggravated murder (ORS 163.095). **Pennsylvania**. First-degree murder with 18 aggravating circumstances. **South Carolina***. Murder with 1 of 11 aggravating circumstances (§ 16-3-20(C)(a)). **South Dakota***. First-degree murder with 1 of 10 aggravating circumstances; aggravated kidnapping. **Tennessee***. First-degree murder with 1 of 15 aggravating circumstances (Tenn. Code Ann. § 39-13-204). **Texas**. Criminal homicide with 1 of 8 aggravating circumstances (TX Penal Code 19.03). **Utah***. Aggravated murder (76-5-202, Utah Code Annotated). **Virginia***. First-degree murder with 1 of 13 aggravating circumstances (VA Code § 18.2-31). **Washington***. Aggravated first-degree murder. **Wyoming**. First-degree murder.

*As of December 31, 2004, 26 States excluded mentally retarded persons from capital sentencing:
Arizona, Arkansas, California, Colorado, Connecticut, Delaware, Florida, Georgia, Idaho, Illinois, Indiana, Kansas, Kentucky, Louisiana, Maryland, Missouri, Nebraska, Nevada, New Mexico, New York, North Carolina, South Dakota, Tennessee, Utah, Virginia, and Washington. Mental retardation is a mitigating factor in South Carolina.
**As of June 24, 2004, the New York death penalty statute was ruled unconstitutional.

Bureau of Justice Statistics *Bulletin Capital Punishment 2004*, hereinafter *Bulletin.*

12 **MINIMUM AGE AUTHORIZED FOR CAPITAL PUNISHMENT BY STATE, YEAR END 2005**

Age 18	***Age 17***	***Age 16***	***Unconstitutional***
California	Florida	Alabama	Alaska
Colorado	Georgia	Arizona	Hawaii
Connecticut	New Hampshire	Arkansas	Iowa
Illinois	North Carolina	Delaware	Kansas
Indiana	Texas	Idaho	Maine
Maryland		Kentucky	Massachusetts
Montana		Louisiana	Michigan
Nebraska		Mississippi	Minnesota
New Jersey		Missouri	New York
New Mexico		Nevada	North Dakota
Ohio		Oklahoma	Rhode Island
Oregon		Pennsylvania	South Dakota
Tennessee		South Carolina	Vermont
Washington		Utah	Washington DC
		Virginia	West Virginia
			Wisconsin
			Wyoming

13 *Id, Bulletin.*

14 *Gregg v. Georgia* 428 U.S. 153 (1976)

15 Bedau, Hugo, "The Death Penalty and State Constitutional Rights in the United States of America" in "*United Nations Crime Prevention and Criminal Justice Newsletter*" Numbers 12

and 13, November 1986; hereinafter Bedau.

[16] *Woodson v. North Carolina*, 428 US. 280 (1976) Statute failed to permit individualized sentencing creating separate sentencing hearing requirement after determination of guilt; *Coker v. Georgia*, 433 U.S. 584, 1977, "disproportionate" in the case of rape; *Eberheart v. Georgia*, 433 U.S. 917 (1977) disproportionate for kidnapping.

[17] The Eighth Amendment provides: "excessive bail shall not be required, nor excessive fines imposed, nor cruel and unusual punishments inflicted." U.S. Const, Amend. VIII. The Fourteenth Amendment provides: "No state shall . . . deny to any person within its jurisdiction the equal protection of the laws." U.S. Const, Amend XIV, Art. 1.

[18] Baldus, David C., Charles Pulaski and George Woodworth, "Comparative Review of Death Sentences: An Empirical Study of the Georgia Experience," *Journal of Criminal Law and Criminology*, 74 (3), Chicago, IL: Northwestern Univ. School of Law (1983), pp. 661-753. The "McCleskey Theory" was developed by the NAACP Legal Defense and Educational Fund, Inc. (LDF).

[19] *McCleskey*, 481 US at 321 (Brennan J. dissenting).

[20] Testimony at *McCleskey* hearing of Dr. Richard Beck, a renowned social scientist in the field of sentencing research.

[21] *McCleskey* petition for *writ of certiorari*.

[22] *McCleskey v. Kemp*, 753 Fd2d 877, 895 (llth Cir. 1985) - Appellate decision before Supreme Court appeal, *supra*.

[23] *Id.* at 891

[24] *McCleskey*, 107 S. Ct. at 1777-78.

[25] *Id.* at 1756.

[26] Brief for the Petitioner. *Thompson v. Oklahoma*, 724 p. 2d 780 (Okla. Crim. App. 1986) Cert, granted 107 S Ct. 1284 (1987)

[27] "Death at an Early Age: International Law Arguments Against the Death Penalty for Juveniles", *Crim. Law Review* Vol. 57, 245. (1988). Although most state laws permit the execution of minors (see note 10) significant sectors of the public oppose it. The ABA which has not taken an official position on the death penalty otherwise adopted a resolution in August 1983 opposing" . . . the imposition of capital punishment upon any person for an offense committed while under the age of 18" stating "Retribution or legal vengeance seems difficult enough for a government to justify when adult offenders are involved and vengeance against children seems quite beyond justification."

[28] The imposition of death sentences on minors is in contradiction of international human rights standards. Article 6(5) of the International Covenant on Civil and Political Rights (ICCPR): "Sentence to death shall not be imposed for crimes committed by persons below eighteen years of age and shall not be carried out on pregnant women." Article 4(5) of the American Convention on Human Rights (see document below) "Capital Punishment shall not be imposed upon persons who, at the time the crime was committed, were under 18 years of age or over 70 years of age; nor shall it be applied to pregnant women; the United States executed these treaties (1977) but has not ratified them. Also see ECOSOC Resolutions 1984/50 25 May 1984 and by analogy the Geneva Covenant holding that "... the death penalty may not be pronounced on a protected person who was under eighteen years of age at the time of the offense."

[29] *Thompson, supra* at 107 S Ct. 1307.

[30] Amnesty International, *Facts and Figures on the Death Penalty 2005.*

[31] *Youth Advocate Program International* (Online) Evidence of Bias – Juvenile Death Penalty.

32 Amnesty International, *Children and the Death Penalty: Executions Worldwide Since 1990* (2002).
33 Streib, "Capital Punishment of Children in Ohio", 18 Akron Law Rev. 51,52 (1984). Also see *Death Penalty USA, supra.*
34 See generally *Harvard Civil Rights-Civil Liberties Law Review* (Vol. 24, 1989) and *Harvard Law Review* Volume 101 (May 1988). In 1985 48% of prisoners awaiting execution nationally were Black, Latino or Native American. But in some states the proportion of Blacks on death row is much higher. In Alabama 67% are Black (55 out of 82); over 50% of prisoners on death row in Georgia, Illinois, Mississippi, North Carolina, South Carolina and Pennsylvania are Black. In California and Texas a relatively high proportion are Latinos; NAACP Legal Defense and Educational Fund, Inc. statistics.
35 Between 1930-1969 when Blacks were approximately one-eleventh of the population, 3,859 persons were executed, of these, 2,066 (54%) were Black; 3,334 were executed for murder; 49% (1,630) were Black. For rape, a total of 455 were executed, 405 or 90% were Black.
36 1962-1965. Justice Goldberg resigned the court to accept a Presidential appointment as ambassador of the United States at the United Nations.
37 "The Death Penalty Revisited", *Hastings Constitutional Law Quarterly* 16:1. (Fall 1988) at 2.
38 *Idem.*
39 See, Higginbotham, Leon, *In the Matter of Color: Race and the American Legal Process: The Colonial Period* (1978).
40 Slave Codes in Virginia, enacted in 1680, barred Blacks from carrying arms, leaving their owner's plantation without a pass, or from "lifting up their hands against any Christian —regardless of provocation." *Id.* The Boston Black Codes, enacted in the eighteenth century, prohibited Blacks from engaging in street gambling, carrying weapons, or gathering in groups. The Codes also imposed curfews on Blacks. See *id.* at 76-80. See generally, Stampp, Kenneth, "Chattels Personal," in *Slavery in America* (1976) (reading and writing by Black slaves criminalized); see also Goodell, William, *The American Slave Code in Theory and Practice* 319-20 (1969) (South Carolina Act of 1740, prohibiting slaves from writing; South Carolina Another Act in 1800, and Virginia Revised Code of 1819, both prohibiting slaves from assembling for the purpose of learning to read or write).

Like the slave Codes in the North, southern Slave Codes made it criminal for slaves to be "at large" (off their master's property without a valid pass) or for more than a few slaves to gather together at any place. K. Stampp, *supra* at 94-95. Most cities forbade Blacks from making loud noises, smoking, or walking with canes in public. Blacks were prohibited from drinking, subjected to strict curfew laws, and generally required to be respectful of whites. See Flanigan, Daniel, *The Criminal Law of Slavery and Freedom, 1800-1868*, at 31-36 (1987).
41 Stampp, *idem* at 90-95.
42 See, Flanigan, *idem* at 24-27. That legacy continues since the abolition of slavery prior to 1972 half of all executions occurred in the southern states; since 1977 three states account for more than two-thirds of all executions carried out—Florida, Texas and Georgia. A fourth, California has the third largest number of prisoners under sentence of death, but no executions have been carried out under the post 1972 statute. 63% of those currently under sentence of death are held by southern states. *Bulletin Capital Punishment* 1988.
43 *Idem.*
44 Genovese, E., *Roll Jordan Roll: The World the Slaves Made* (1972). Also see Hooks, Bell, *Ain't I a Woman: Black Women and Feminism,* (1981) describing the frequency of rape of Black

women by both white men and Black men during slavery.

45 Spear, C., *Essays on the Punishment of Death* 220-31 (Appendix 1) (1845) citing laws on punishment of slaves and Alabama 1, 1843.

46 Stampp, *The Peculiar Institution: Slavery in the Ante-Bellum South*, 210 (1956).

47 Stampp, *supra* at 97.

48 *Idem.*

49 Flanigan, *supra* at 26.

50 *Idem* at 25.

51 Capital Punishment in Virginia 58 Va. L. Rev. 97, 103 (1972).

52 Genovese, *supra* at 38-39.

53 *Idem* at 407.

54 Flanigan, *supra* at 109-110, 116.

55 *Idem* at 379-80.

56 *Idem.*

57 See, e.g., *The Civil Rights Cases*, 109 US. 3 (1883); *s*ee also, "Developments in the Law-Race and the Criminal Process", 101 Harv. L. Rev. 1472, 1483-86 (1988) (explaining how the Equal Protection Clause failed to serve as a mechanism for upholding the rights of Blacks both within the criminal justice system and society at large because of the Supreme Court's failure to uphold Section 5 of the Fourteenth Amendment).

58 See, Cutler, J. E., "*Capital Punishment and Lynching"*, 29 Annals Am. Acad. Pol. & Soc. Sci. 622-23 (1907).

59 Lynching was used to "intimidate, degrade and control Black people throughout the southern and border states, from Reconstruction to the mid-twentieth century." R. Zangranado, The NAACP Crusade Against Lynching 1919-1950, at 3 (1980). Between 1882 and 1968 approximately 4743 lynchings were recorded in the United States. Of those lynchings, 3446 of those lynched, or 72.6% were Black. While the excuses for lynching Blacks varied from accusations of rape or murder to vague accusations of disrespectful behavior towards a white person, the justification for a particular lynching was not necessarily important to the mob. *Id.* at 4-8. "Mob violence transcended the victim's behavior and reminded all Black people of white America's determination to impose its will and authority in a bi-racial society." *Id.* at 8; see also Chadbourn, James, "Lynching and the Law" 4-6 (1933). Also see Belknap, Michael, *Federal Law and Southern Order; Racial Violence and Constitutional Conflict in the Post-Brown South* 8-9 (1987). Belknap explains that lynch mobs had "little to fear from those who administered the southern legal system."

60 The attitude of the Columbus, Texas prosecutor who in 1935 dismissed a lynching as "an expression of the will of the people", was typical. South Carolina's Governor Cole Blease, that state's chief executive from 1911 to 1915, was even more tolerant of mob violence, proclaiming himself willing to participate personally in the lynching of any Black man who attacked a white woman. Like Blease, local sheriffs generally shared the attitudes of their constituents. In any event, they needed the votes of mob members and their friends to stay in office. Id. at 8-9.

61 Chadbourn, *supra* at 3-12. See also White, Walter, *Rope and Faggot: A Biography of Judge Lynch*, 19-39 (1969).

62 *Idem*, Chadbourn, *supra* at 13-24.

63 After Emancipation, Blacks continued to be excluded from participation in the legal system. Poll taxes, literacy tests and grandfather clauses disenfranchised millions of Black voters, keeping them out of jury pools in the South. See Smead, Howard, *Blood Justice: The Lynching of Mack Charles Parker* 32 (1986). After Reconstruction, fear of mob retaliation kept other Blacks from voting, being elected to office, or bringing their claims to court. See

generally, Belknap, *supra* at 1-16 (describing lynching as a means of social control, which worked to prevent Blacks from exercising their right to participate in the political process).

64 South Carolina and Alabama, for example, continued to make rape a capital offense only for Black defendants. D. Flanigan, *supra* at 274.

65 See generally Wilson, Theodore, *The Black Codes of the South* (1965) (describing the revised criminal laws of the South: Georgia (burglary in the night, arson in occupied building), Tennessee (horse stealing, burglary, burning of houses or bridges and felonious robbery), North Carolina (assault with an attempt to commit rape upon the body of a white female) and Virginia (rape, burglary, armed robbery). See also Flanigan, *supra*, at 275-76.

66 See generally Flanigan, *supra*, at 271-76.

67 *Id.*

68 *See* Bowers, William, *Executions in America* 68 (1974).

69 Civil Rights Act of 1875, ch. 114, §4,18 Stat. 336 (codified at 18 U.S.C. §243 (1982).

70 100 US. 303 (1879).

71 *Id.* at 308.

72 See Johnson, Sheri, "Black Innocence and the White Jury", 83 Mich. L. Rev. 1611, 1652; see also *Strauder*, 100 U.S. at 308; *ExParte Virginia*, 100 US. 339 (1879) (nondiscrimination rules regarding jury selection apply to grand juries).

73 103 US. 370 (1881).

74 See, e.g., *Virginia v. Rives*, 100 U.S. 313 (1879) (conviction of Black defendants by all white jury, coupled with assertion that no Blacks had ever been allowed to serve as jurors in trials with Black defendants within the county, did not establish denial of equal protection of the laws); *Williams v. Mississippi*, 170 U.S. 213 (1898) (literacy test as prerequisite for voting and for jury service which produces total absence of Blacks from jury pool, though passed with discriminatory purpose, does not violate defendant's right to equal protection of the laws); *Franklin v. South Carolina*, 218 U.S. 161 (1910) (poll tax and literacy test do not violate defendant's equal protection rights absent specific proof that they operated to exclude qualified Black jurors).

75 Stephenson, Gilbert, "Actual Jury Service by Negroes in the South," in *Race Distinctions and American Law* 247 (1910).

76 *Idem.*

77 See, e.g., *Brown v. Board of Educ.*, 347 U.S. 483 (1954) (holding racial segregation in public education unconstitutional).

78 Civil Rights Act of 1964, 42 U.S.C. §§2000b-3 (1982).

79 Voting Rights Act of 1965, 42 U.S.C. §§1971 to 173aa-3 (1982 & supp. IV 1986).

80 Civil Rights Act of 1968, 42 U.S.C. §§3601-3631 (1982).

81 Civil Rights Act of 1964, 42 U.S.C. §§200e-17 (1982).

82 Available statistics suggest that Blacks and other people of color have never represented more than 15% of the U.S. population

83 An accumulation of systematic scientific research on racial discrimination in the application of the death penalty in America was begun in the 1940's. *See* W. Bowers *supra*, at 18 (citing Magnum, Charles, *The Legal Status of the Negro* (1940) (among those sentenced to death in nine southern and border states, Blacks were more likely than whites to have their death sentences carried out in every state); Johnson, Guy, "The Negro and Crime," 271 The Annals 93 (1941) (in murder cases in selected jurisdictions in Virginia, North Carolina and Georgia the death sentence was disproportionately imposed upon Black defendants convicted of murdering white victims). For executions between 1930 and 1950, the tabulated number of executions by type of offense and race of the defendant indicated that "black men had

been the principal victims of the death penalty in America." Bowers, *supra*, at 18-19 (citing *National Prisoner Statistics* (1950). In 800 North Carolina homicide trials occurring from 1930 to 1940,43% of Blacks that killed whites received the death penalty (29% of homicide indictments), whereas only 15% of whites that killed whites received the death penalty (7% of indictments). Only 5% of Blacks that killed Blacks received the death penalty (3% of indictments). Garfinkel, Research Note on Inter- and Intra-racial Homicides, 27 Soc. Forces 369, 374 (1949), cited in Gross & Mauro, "Patterns of Death: An Analysis of Disparities in Capital Sentencing and Homicide Victimization", 37 Stan. L. Rev. 27,39(1984). Garfinkel's research showed that in general, defendants who killed whites were more likely to receive the death penalty than defendants who killed Blacks. Further, when Garfinkel controlled for the race of the homicide victim, Black defendants were more likely to receive the death penalty than whites. See also Bureau of Statistics, *National Prison Statistics*, US. Dept. of Justice, Capital Punishment, 1979, at 18 (1980). While these figures alone do not prove that capital punishment had been applied in a discriminatory manner, they did inspire further inquiry into discriminatory application of the death penalty in the United States. This inquiry produced an extensive body of evidence on discriminatory treatment of white and Black life by the death penalty system. Subsequent studies have confirmed the conclusion that courts applied the death penalty disproportionately to Blacks. In a study of every execution that occurred in the United States from 1864 to 1967, Bowers found that Blacks sentenced to death were more likely to be executed without an appeal than whites. Bowers, William, *Legal Homicide: Death as Punishment in America 1864-1982*, at 81 (1984). Bowers concluded that Blacks, as of 1967, continued to have significantly less access to the protections of the legal system than whites. Also see note 29.

84 American Civil Liberties Union, *Race and the Death Penalty* (Online) 02/26/2003.

85 *Batson v. Kennedy* 476 U.S. 79, 103 (1986).

86 In most states, opponents of the death penalty are systematically excluded from serving as jurors in capital trials. In *Lockhart v. McCree* (1986) the Court held (6-3) that the Constitution did not prohibit the exclusion of committed opponents of the death penalty from serving as jurors at both the trial of guilt and innocence and the sentencing phase.

87 U.S. DOJ, "The Federal Death Penalty System: A Statistical Survey (1988-2000)", hereinafter, *DOJ Survey.*

88 USA The Death Penalty, *supra.*

89 *Idem*, at 189.

90 *Idem.*

91 Article 3 of the Universal Declaration of Human Rights. In December 1971 the United Nations General Assembly adopted Resolution 2857 (XXVI), in which it affirmed that: "... in order fully to guarantee the right to life, as provided for in article 3 of the Universal Declaration of Human Rights, the main objective to be pursued is that of progressively restricting the number of offenses for which capital punishment may be imposed, with a view to the desirability of abolishing the punishment in all countries." This decision was reaffirmed by the General Assembly in Resolution 32/61 of 8 December 1977.

92 Article 18, Vienna Convention.

93 UN. Doc.A/35/48.

94 *Roper, supra.*

95 *Domingues, supra.*

96 Amnesty International, *The Exclusion of Child Offenders From the Death Penalty Under General International Law* (Online) 2003.

[97] Resolution 1986/102/May.
[98] See Appendix II for excerpts of other Treaties and Standards.
[99] ECOSOC Resolution 1503 (VXLII) of 27 May 1970 Sub-Commission for Prevention of Discrimination and Protection of Minorities.
[100] *USA The Death Penalty*, "Execution of the Mentally Ill" at 76-87.
[101] See for example, "The Domestic Effects of International Norms restricting the Application of the Death Penalty" in the *University of Cincinnati Law Review*, Vol. 52,1983.
[102] Executed in South Carolina, 10 January 1986 by means of electric chair.
[103] Resolution No. 3/87, Case No. 9647 (United States), Inter-American Commission on Human Rights, OEA/Ser. L/V/II.69, Doc. 17,27 March 1987, §58,62 (hereinafter Inter-American decision).
[104] The OAS is an organization open to all American nations "to achieve an order of peace and justice, to promote their solidarity, to defend their sovereignty, their territorial integrity and their independence. Within the United Nations, the Organization of American States is a regional agency." *Handbook of Existing Rules Pertaining To Human Rights in The Inter-American System*, OEA/Ser.L/V/11.60 Doc. 28, July 26, 1983, at 3. The Inter- American Commission on Human Rights is a consultative organ of the OAS whose principle function is to "promote the observance and protection of human rights." *Id.* at 5.
[105] Inter-American Decision §58 discussing the execution of Jay Pinkerton and James Terry Roach.
[106] *Jus cogens* is a peremptory norm or general international law that cannot be superseded by any treaty or customary rule of law. Vienna Convention on the Law of Treaties, at art. 53,64. UN. Doc. A.CONF. 39/27 (1969) entered into force Jan. 27,1970 (transmitted to the Senate for advice and consent on Nov. 21, 1971, but not yet ratified).
[107] *Id.*
[108] The more than 40 other countries that retain the death penalty do not execute juveniles.
[109] U.N. Economic and Social Council Resolution 1503 (XLVIII) (1970), (see Appendix 1) was drafted to provide a mechanism for consideration of systematic, massive violations of human rights involving all the UN. human rights organs; the General Assembly, ECOSOC, the Commission on Human Rights, and the Sub-Commission on Prevention of Discrimination and Protection of Minorities. It is intended to identify and correct, if possible "situations which appear to reveal a consistent pattern of gross violations of human rights."
[110] Inter-American Decision §56.
[111] *See* discussions in "Death at an Early Age: International Law Arguments Against the Death Penalty for Juveniles" comments, 57 Crim. Law Rev. 245 (1988).
[112] Inter-American Decision §62
[113] *Idem.*
[114] See esp. "Execution of Juveniles" 3 AM UJ. Int'l L. & Pol'y 339 (1988).
[115] Inter-American Decision §46-48.
[116] *Idem.*
[117] "Execution of Juveniles" at 359-360.
[118] US. Const. Art. VI, C1.2.
[119] 458 US. 782, (1982).
[120] *Edmund*, 458 US 782, *supra* at 796 n.22.
[121] 433 US. 584 (1977)
[122] *Idem*, at 596.
[123] 356 U.S. 86 (1958).
[124] *Atkins, supra.*

[125] Brief for the European Union as *Amicus Curiae in McCarver v. North Carolina*, O.T. 2001, No. 00-8727, p. 4.
[126] *Atkins, supra* at 317, n. 21.
[127] *Roper, supra* (Online Findlaw.com version, under Section IV).
[128] See *The Paquete Habana*, 175 U.S. 677, (1900) (asserting that internal law is part of United States law); *The Nereide*, US. (9 Cranch.) 388, (1815) (declaring that the Court is legally bound by the law of nations).
[129] Each state determines individually the existence and practices of capital punishment. Of the twenty OAS member states that retain the death penalty, only Argentina, Brazil and Mexico are federal states. *See* Amnesty International, *supra* (listing the three countries as retentionist as of April 1987). The laws of these countries provide for the death penalty only for exceptional crimes such as in wartime.
[130] See *Restatement (Revised) of the Foreign Relations Law of the United States* §131(1) (Tent. Draft. No.6, 1985) (asserting that international law is supreme over the law of several states of the United States). (Hereinafter *Restatement.*)
[131] See *The Paquete Habana, supra* at 700 (1900) (holding that international law is part of United States law and that when there is no treaty, executive or legislative act, or judicial decision to guide the Court, the Court looks to international law and custom).
[132] *Restatement, supra* at §131(2) (stating that "[(International law is determined and interpreted in the United States by reference to the sources of international law cited in §102, and the evidence of international law indicated in §103, *with particular attention to the decisions of international tribunals. Also see, Filartiga v. Pena-Irala*, 630 F.2d 876, 882-84 (2d Cir. 1980) relying in part on the resolutions of public international bodies to find a norm prohibiting torture).
[133] In fact, the finding of the Commission that no customary norm exists establishing 18 as the minimum age at which the death penalty may be imposed may well have damaged Thompson in his appeal. Both the International Human Rights Law Group and Amnesty International filed briefs *amicus curiae* arguing separately that Thompson's execution would violate international law; arguing that there is an internationally recognized legal standard and customary norm prohibiting the executions of juvenile offenders, disagreeing with the Inter-American decision.
[134] *Cf* "Execution of Juveniles", *supra.*
[135] 32 States of the western hemisphere are members of the OAS and are subject to its human rights program.
[136] American Declaration of the Rights and Duties of Man, adopted May 2, 1948, by the Ninth International Conference of American States, Bogota, Colombia, reprinted in *Handbook of Existing Rules Pertaining to Human Rights in the Inter-American System*, OEA/Ser L7v. II.65 Doc. 6 (1985) at 17-25 [hereinafter American Declaration]; the Statute of the Inter-American Commission on Human Rights, reprinted in *Handbook, supra*, at 103-13 [hereinafter Commission Statute]; Regulations of the Inter-American Commission on Human Rights, reprinted in *Handbook, supra*, at 115-42 [hereinafter Commission.]
[137] Shelton, Dinah, "Improving Human Rights Protections: Recommendations for Enhancing the Effectiveness of the Inter-American Commission and Inter-American Court of Human Rights," in 3 AM UJ. Int'l L.& Pol'y 323 (1988).
[138] Charter of the Organization of American States, April 30,1948,2 U.S.T. 2416, T.I.A.S. No. 2361,119 U.N.T.S. 3, protocol of Amend. Feb. 23,1967,21 U.S.T. 607, T.I.A.S. No. 6847 [hereinafter *OAS Charter*].
[139] American Convention on Human Rights, Nov. 22, 1969, O.A.S.T. No. 36, at 1, OEA/ser.

L/V/H.23, doc. 2 rev. 6,1, O.A.S.O.R. OEA/ser. K./XVI/I.l, doc. 65 rev. corr. 2 (1970), reprinted in 91.L.M. 673 (1970) [hereinafter American Convention]; the nineteen states that have ratified the Convention include: Argentina, Barbados, Bolivia, Colombia, Costa Rica, Dominican Republic, Ecuador, El Salvador, Grenada, Guatemala, Haiti, Honduras, Jamaica, Mexico, Nicaragua, Panama, Peru, Uruguay, and Venezuela. The non-ratifying OAS member states are Antigua and Barbuda, Bahamas, Brazil, Chile, Cuba, Dominica, Paraguay, Saint Kitts and Nevis, Saint Lucia, Saint Vincent and the Grenadines, Surinam, Trinidad and Tobago, and the United States

140 American Declaration, *supra.* The Declaration protects basic rights, including life, liberty, personal security, equality before the law, religious freedom, freedom of expression and opinion, privacy and family life, residence and movement, health and well-being, education, work, social security, civil rights, fair trial, nationality, vote, assembly, association, property, petition, due process, and asylum. The Convention contains 22 broad categories of guaranteed rights. A broad non-discrimination clause and an obligation on the part of all states to respect and ensure the rights and freedoms reinforce these provisions, art. I. *See Inter-Am. C.H.R., 1985-86 Annual Report* 22, OEA/ser. L/V/II.68, doc. 8 rev. 1 (1986) [hereinafter *IACHR Annual Report*] (inviting member states to present specific proposals for the draft of the Additional Protocol to the American Convention).

141 The imposition of death sentences on minors is in contradiction of international human rights standards. Article 6(5) of the International Covenant on Civil and Political Rights (ICCPR): "Sentence to death shall not be imposed for crimes committed by persons below eighteen years of age and shall not be carried out on pregnant women." Article 4(5) of the American Convention on Human Rights (see document below) "Capital Punishment shall not be imposed upon persons who, at the time the crime was committed, were under 18 years of age or over 70 years of age; nor shall it be applied to pregnant women; the United States executed these treaties (1977) but has not ratified them. Also see ECOSOC Resolutions 1984/50 25 May 1984 and by analogy the Geneva Covenant holding that "... the death penalty may not be pronounced on a protected person who was under eighteen years of age at the time of the offense."

142 American Convention, *supra*, art. 33. The Court consists of seven judges nominated from among nationals of the member states of the OAS, Id. art. 52. Judges are elected to the Court in an individual capacity by a vote of the state parties to the Convention. *Id.* art. 52 The Judges of the Court are to be of the highest moral authority, of recognized competence in the field of human rights, and must possess the qualifications required for the exercise of the highest judicial functions in the state of nationality or of the state, which nominates them. *Id.* The judges are elected for a term of six years and may be reelected only once. *Id.* art. 54. *See* Court Statute, arts, 18-20 (describing the duties and responsibilities of Inter-American Court judges).

143 Commission Statute arts. 18-20.

144 Commission Statute art. 18(c), (g).

145 *Idem*, art. 19(3).

146 *Idem*, arts. 18(b), 20(b).

147 American Convention art. 62.

148 Shelton, "Implementation Procedures of the American Convention on Human Rights", 26 GERM. Y.B. INT'L L. 238,251-61 (1983). See Convention, *supra* art 64 (defining the advisory power of the Inter-American Court); Buergenthal, "The Advisory Practice of the Inter-American Human Rights Court" 79 AM. J. INTL L. 1,2-5 (1985) (describing the advisory and jurisdictional capacity of the Inter-American Court).

149 INTER-AM. C.H.R., "Report on the Situation of Human Rights in Panama" 50-51, OEA/

ser. L/V/II.44, doc. 38 rev. 1 (1978) In Panama, government decree No. 342, affecting the right of fair trial, was repealed during the visit of the Commission; 17th Mtg. of Consultation of Ministers of Foreign Affairs (Washington, D.C.), OEA ser. F/II.17, doc. 40, rev. 2 (1979). The 1979 resolution on Nicaragua found that the inhumane conduct of the dictatorial regime governing the country, as evidenced by the report of the Inter-American Commission on Human Rights, was the fundamental cause of the situation facing the Nicaraguan people. The resolution declared that the solution to problems of Nicaragua should be based upon immediate and definitive replacement of the Somoza regime; Inter-Aa. C.H.R., "Report on the Situation of Human Rights in Nicaragua," 2, OEA/sr. L./V/II.53, doc. 25 (1981) at 2.

[150] Buergenthal, "Implementation in the Inter-American Human Rights System," in *International Enforcement of Human Rights* 75 (R. Berghardt & J. Jolowisz, eds. 1987).

[151] American Convention art. 61. But the Court's advisory jurisdiction however extends to all OAS member states and all OAS organs. Id. art. 64.

[152] Shelton, "Utilization of Fact-Finding Missions to Promote and Protect Human Rights; The Chile Case," 2 Hum. Rts. L.J. 1, (1981).

[153] UN GAOR, Protection of Human Rights in Chile: Report of the Economic and Social Council, Annex VII, UN. Doc A/33/331 (1978).

[154] Case 9647, Inter-Am. C.H.R. 147, OEA/ser. L./V/II. 69, doc. 17 rev. 3 (1987).

[155] Shelton at n. 108.

[156] Commission regulations art. 56 provides that a Commission member who is a national of or who resides in the State in which the on-site observation is to be carried out shall be disqualified from participating in the on-site observation.

[157] *Id.* art. 59.

[158] See International Law Association "Draft Minimal Rules of Procedure for International Human Rights Fact-Finding Missions," Belgrade Conference (1980), reprinted in *Protecting Human Rights, supra*, at 163-64.

[159] See Shelton *supra* at 332.

[160] Case 9647 *supra.*

[161] See Shelton, *Id.* a 332-335 for a complete analysis of the perceived technical errors in the juvenile execution decision.

[162] *Id.*

[163] *Id.*

[164] American Convention *supra* art. 51.

[165] *Id.*

[166] Commission regulation *supra* art. 53.

[167] See, e.g., Case 2141, Inter-Am. C.H.R. 25, 43, OEA/ser. L./V/II.54, doc. 9 rev. (1981) where the Commission found the United States not in violation of human rights, but published the decision in its 1979-80 Annual Report.

[168] 630 F2d 876 (2d Cir. 1980).

[169] Haitian Refugee Center K Civilette 503 F supp. 442. (S.D. Fla 1980).

Chapter Seventeen

Abuse of Power: Offenses and Offenders beyond the Reach of Law. Police Crimes in the United States

(This chapter has been added in 2019; most of this was presented at the Sixth UN Convention on Prevention of Crime and Treatment of Offenders in 1980 in Caracas, Venezuela. Some more recent data has been added in the Offenses and Victims section of this chapter.)

"To some Negroes. police have come to symbolize white power, white racism and white oppression. And the fact is that many police do reflect and express these white attitudes. The atmosphere of hostility and cynicism is reinforced by a widespread belief among Negroes in the existence of police brutality and in a double standard of justice and protection-- one for Negroes and one for whites."

-- *The National Advisory Commission on Civil Disorders, 1968, p.11*

"After the staccato of machine gun fire had died down and firemen in riot-ravaged Miami quenched the last embers of blazes that had reduced scores of business buildings to charred shells, as street crews hosed off the blood of 14 people beaten or shot to death, and 3,800 National Guardsmen withdrew from patrolling a 40-block by 60-block area of the shaken city, the nation had been jolted anew into a realization that Black outrage at a 'double standard of justice' still remains near flash point in many U.S. cities. While high unemployment, the ruinous impact of inflation, resentment at all the public help given the still rising tide of refugees inundating southern Florida from Cuba--all fed the fury of the Miami area's 233,000 Blacks. *Yet perhaps more clearly than in any other recent race conflict, the rage in Miami focused on police, prosecutors and the courts." (Emphasis added.)*

--*Time. June 2, 1980, p.10*

A. Introduction

The world is aware of the recent uprising of the Black citizens in Miami protesting the failure of an all-white jury to convict the police who brutally and unjustifiably murdered Arthur McDuffey. The world is not aware of the fact that McDuffey's murder is not an isolated incident. In fact, hundreds of Blacks and other minorities are killed by the police every year and their killers know that they can continue to maim, cripple, and kill minorities without any expectation of judicial reprimand or punishment because they operate behind the protective shield of racism. McDuffey's murder differed from the thousands of unreported cases of police misconduct because enraged citizens took to the streets in open rebellion against police lawlessness. They relentlessly exposed the facts of the case and managed to shatter the police efforts at a cover-up with the usual nomenclature of "justifiable homicide."

This paper is an attempt to bring the racist and pervasive nature of police misconduct in the United States to the attention of the international community.

The problem reaches every corner of America. And yet the American public, like the international community, is aware only of the most egregious and brutal abuses that garner the attention of the media. Seldom do local newspapers or national television provide information about its scope. If and when isolated incidents of gross abuses are reported, the primary source of information is the police department. Because police departments are considered more credible than the victims of abuse, the press and public media become unwitting tools to distort the truth and effectuate cover-ups by lawbreakers. Thus, what the majority culture views as an isolated incident which can be blamed on one or more "bad apples," the minority communities perceive as the reality of daily repression at the hands of the agents of an oppressive economic and political system designed to keep them at the bottom of the social and economic ladder. Put another way, the white majority of America views the role of the police as protective while racial minorities view that role as dominating, repressive, and violent.

B. Defining the Problem

The police have unique power. They are the only representatives of governmental authority who in the ordinary course of events are legally permitted to arrest citizens and use physical force against them. Other agencies of state power rely upon request, persuasion, public opinion, custody, and legal and judicial processes to gain compliance with rules and laws. Only the police can use firearms to compel the citizen to obey. The police are also in a special category in that they are sworn to enforce the law at all times, on or off duty in most jurisdictions, so that their power to arrest citizens and their access to firearms is constant and legal.[1]

The most frequent targets of police abuse of power are the powerless in society: Blacks, Browns, Native Americans and other racial minorities, the poor, the young, and people who challenge the economic or political order.[2] Various forms of police misconduct are widespread in the United States, ranging from extortions of false testimony and filing false charges against the victims to brutal beatings and the use of deadly force. Only when particularly atrocious incidents outrage an otherwise apathetic public is any official effort made to acknowledge the existence of a problem. And even in these few cases, the tragedy is that admission of a problem is substituted for a solution.

A survey in the *Sourcebook of Criminal Justice Statistics*, 1978, reports that in 1975 Third World peoples in the United States viewed the police more negatively than whites. Non-whites rated police performance "good" only half as often as whites; they used the rating "poor" twice as often.[3] Given the functional role the police serve in relation to the total society, these findings are not surprising.

> "In 1964, a *New York Times* study of Harlem showed that 43 percent of those questioned believed in the existence of police brutality. In 1965, a nationwide Gallup poll found that 35 percent of Negro men believed there was police brutality in their areas; 7 percent of white men thought so. In 1966, a survey conducted for the Senate Subcommittee on Executive Reorganization found that 60 percent of Watts Negroes aged 15 to 19 believed there was some police brutality. Half said they had witnessed such conduct. A University of California at Los Angeles study of the Watts area found that....74 percent (of Negro males) believed police use unnecessary force in making arrests. In 1967, an Urban League study of the Detroit riot area found that 82 percent believed there was some form of police brutality."[4]

The cases selected for presentation in this report are illustrative of the deep and extensive nature of the problem. They reflect the outrage felt by the minority communities at the failure and unwillingness of governmental entities to remedy the situation.

The tensions and hostilities between police and minorities are further exacerbated by the system of economic exploitation in the United States, which relegates minorities to the bottom of the barrel and relies on the police to keep them in their place. Minorities of all ages suffer greater unemployment than whites, but the 30-50% unemployment rate among inner-city youth which has existed for years creates a special problem that neither the local nor national government has made a serious effort to address. Indeed, current government policy is designed to stimulate unemployment in order to slow inflation. And today's youth, who are better educated and thus enter the job market believing they have a right to a job, may "foreshadow a more assertive and rebellious generation of workers."[5] Thus increased unemployment brings with it increased community struggles confronting the inequities of the existing economic order, and increased community struggles are met with increased repression by police. It is a debilitating spiral downward that all too often leads to open rebellion, injury, and death to those confronting the system that cripples their lives.

Whenever power is invested in persons, there exists the possibility of abuse. When the abusers of power comprise an entity, such as the law enforcement establishment in the United States, and when, time and again, these abuses are not met with effective remedies, a social problem of massive proportions develops. Under these conditions, it is inevitable that one segment of society--the powerless victims of pervasive police abuse--will view that abuse as lawlessness sanctioned by the ruling majority. Society is thus faced with offenses and offenders beyond the reach of the law.

C. Offenses and Victims

Police have used and continue to use unwarranted force which includes physical and/or psychological abuse shocking to the consciences of citizens living in a democratic society. All too often the targets of these acts are the powerless within the society and are members of racial minorities and poor communities.

Examples of such practices include, but are not limited to
(1) Physically abusing people who have committed no crime;
(2) Physically abusing arrestees and prisoners who are awaiting trial;
(3) Physically or psychologically intimidating arrestees and prisoners to extract confessions;
(4) Verbally abusing and detaining people without proper cause;
(5) Conducting illegal searches and seizures;
(6) Killing people who have committed no crime;
(7) Killing people who are not threatening the lives of others (including those who are fleeing from apprehension);
(8) Killing unarmed people of color;
(9) Engaging in practices to deliberately cover-up their own abuses of power and that of fellow officers.

The widespread nature of the problem is documented by the fact that upwards of 10,000 complaints involving denial of a citizen's rights by a law enforcement agent were submitted to the Civil Rights Division of the United States Department of Justice in 1977.[6] And the problem is increasing. In the six months between October 1979 and March 1980, the Department of Justice received 142% more complaints of police abuse of force than it had in the same time period a year before.[7]

Even these figures are misleading because many incidents of police brutality are never reported, since victims fear additional harassment or reprisal or even lawsuits by the police themselves. Some police unions file counter lawsuits anytime charges are brought against them.[8]

Not only is the enormity of police abuse overwhelming, but the racist nature of it is undeniable. There are currently no nationwide data kept on all forms of police abuse. Data on police-caused deaths are somewhat more adequate than on other types of misconduct and thus we shall use this data to demonstrate here the disproportionate impact of these practices on minority communities.

In the seven-year period, 1970-76, 2,392 civilians were killed by legal intervention, averaging 343 deaths per year.[9] During that same 7-year-period, 851 law enforcement officers were killed, averaging 122 deaths per year. From these figures, we can see that about 3 citizens are killed for each officer killed. A recent study by Lawrence Sherman and Robert Langworthy reveals the figures for citizen deaths are being under-reported by at least 50%.[10] Thus the ratio of citizens to officers killed is more like 6:1.

Fifty percent of the civilians killed from 1970 to 1976 were Black males. Black males make up only 6% of the United States population.[11] It should be noted that Hispanics are included in the figures for whites which are derived from Public Health Service data. If one adjusts the figures for whites by excluding Hispanics, the statistics indicate that Blacks have been killed at a rate 13 times higher than whites.[12]

Some people have tried to discredit this obvious discrepancy by arguing that Blacks have a higher arrest rate than whites.[13] This is done by comparing the percentage of Blacks killed by police to the percentage of Blacks arrested for *violent* crimes. To compare these two sets of statistics is totally inappropriate because victims of police use of deadly force cannot be equated with perpetrators of *violent* crimes. Kobler reports that, "...30% of the victims were either involved in no criminal activity or in a misdemeanor....An additional 27% were engaged in property crimes including auto theft."[14] In a Philadelphia study covering a 9-year span, it was found that nearly 50% of the victims were not engaged in any forcible felony or threatening serious bodily harm to the officer or others.[15]

"Data collected by *The Washington Post*...on the use of lethal force by police officers since 2015 indicate that, relative to the portion of the population, Blacks are over-represented among all those killed by police under all circumstances. As is evident in Figure 1 at the bottom of pg. 340, (looking at the top bar) according to the U.S. Census estimates, Blacks made up 13% of the population. However in 2015 they accounted for 26% of all those killed by police. In other words, Blacks were the victims of the lethal use of force by police at nearly twice their rate in the general population."[16] The racist nature of the killings cannot be denied.

1. Physical abuse of people who have committed no crime

Police engage in practices of inflicting severe physical injuries upon citizens who have committed no crimes whatsoever. These instances are provoked by the reckless abuse of power by the police. Their conduct and lack of regard for the rights of citizens is shocking, but seldom is it reprimanded and thus it continues. The following examples[17] illustrate this inexcusable practice; while the examples illustrate this category of offense, some also illustrate other offenses, such as filing charges in an attempt to blame the victim for the abuses perpetrated by the police.

--Wasco, CA, October, 1977: A verbal exchange resulted in the arrest of five youths, who were beaten and handcuffed tightly causing wrist bruises. Mr. Ramirez, a Hispanic friend of one of the youth's father, attempted to investigate the processing of the youths, which was carried out in secrecy. A couple of days later, officers Emerson and Snead arrived at Ramirez' home without warrants, entered the property, and began to beat Ramirez with clubs. When Mrs. Ramirez attempted to hold her husband, officers began to beat Mrs. Ramirez. They also tossed the children into some rosebushes when the children attempted to aid their parents. Ramirez was never charged with anything and it was never specified why the officers had gone to his house.

--Washington, D.C., 1977: Officers were stopping cars to check drivers' licenses. When one Black man was stopped, he and the

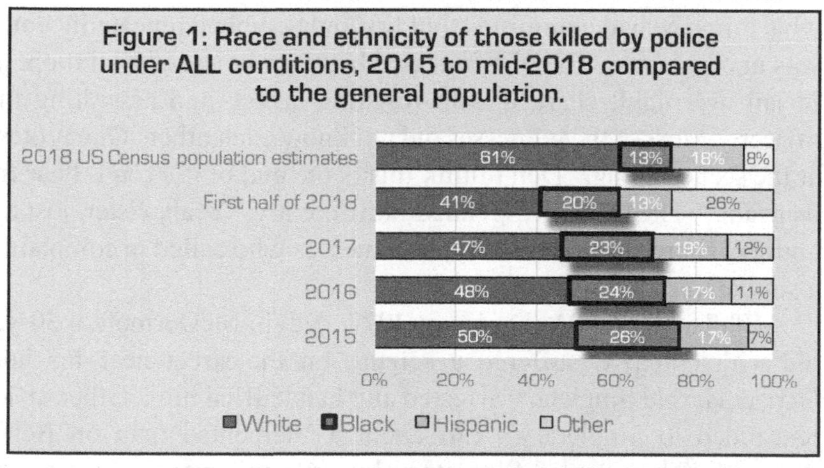

Figure 1: Race and ethnicity of those killed by police under ALL conditions, 2015 to mid-2018 compared to the general population.

officers became embroiled in a verbal confrontation. The man was then knocked down by officers, kneed in the face, restrained, and taken to the police station. There the officers began calling the man names and he became angry and hit at one. He was put in a cell and subjected to further beating. The incidents at the police station were witnessed by a Black policeman who was willing to testify on the man's behalf. Charges of assaulting a police officer were dropped to prevent a public hearing at which one policeman would testify against another.

--Brownsville, TX, October, 1977: Mr. Beltran, a Hispanic, was an eyewitness to the police shooting of Ventura Flores. Two officers handcuffed Flores and threw him to the ground. When he heard the shot that wounded Flores, he raised his head to get up, and Officer Hess kicked him in the face, causing abrasions.

--Bronx, NY, August, 1972: Two plainclothes policemen kidnapped a 20-year-old Golden Gloves boxer who was walking home. The officers roughed him up and forced him into a cab, drove him to a deserted area, beat him, and then as he fled, shot at him 11 times. The young man was a neighborhood hero and there were witnesses to the abduction. The District Attorney said the young man had done nothing wrong.

--Philadelphia, PA, 1977: A young Black man was beaten by 5 officers in view of 8 white witnesses. The young man begged to be told what crime he had committed, but was only clubbed repeatedly until he was unconscious. The victim was subsequently issued a citation, held in jail overnight, charged with resisting arrest, and assaulting three officers. Most of the witnesses did not know each other. One protested at the scene saying, "Don't think this is the end of it. You'll hear from us again." The officer responded indifferently, "Yeah, sister, just try it and see where it gets you." Other witnesses who called to complain got a similar verbal brush-off.

--Philadelphia, PA, February, 1977: Kevin McDermott, a 30-year-old with epilepsy, suffered a seizure on the street near his home. Officer Harold Singletary arrested and handcuffed him. Other officers responded to Singletary's call about a "demented man on Belfield Avenue." They denied Singletary his anti-epilepsy medication, beat him with batons, and jumped on him. After hospital treatment and lengthy detention, he was charged with aggravated assault and resisting arrest. The charges were dismissed. McDermott has filed a class action suit, still in its early stages, for relief against the police for failure to train and supervise officers to recognize symptoms of epilepsy and deal appropriately with epileptics.

--Philadelphia, PA, June 1976: A 25-year-old Hispanic, Louis Parrilla, was riding home with a friend after buying beer. Officers stopped the car, found the beer, and broke the bottle Parrilla was holding. When Parrilla protested, the officer grabbed him and punched him in the neck. When Parrilla's father and Anglo wife came to the police station, the police officer was apparently enraged at their presence; he then punched Parrilla in the right eye and beat him more. Parrilla was arrested for aggravated assault, resisting arrest, terrorist threats, and disorderly conduct. This was his first arrest. About 2 months later, the charges were dropped through a pretrial diversion program.

--Philadelphia, PA 1975: 40% of the citizens who filed complaints of police abuse with citizens' groups had no criminal charges lodged against them. But the examples show that, even when the citizens are not committing criminal acts, charges are often filed against them to cover for police abuse. Between January 1968 and July 1970, only 22% of those charged with assault and battery on police officers or resisting arrest were found or pled guilty.[18] These figures give additional proof of the extensive nature of the totally unnecessary and arbitrary use of power by law enforcement agents—and to their efforts to cover-up their misdeeds.

2. Physical abuse of arrestees and prisoners who are awaiting trial

Police officers engage in the use of excessive and unnecessary force before, during, and after the process of arresting citizens. This unwarranted use of force is illustrated by the following cases:

--Louisville, KY, June 1979: Fred Harris, a 23-year old Black man, was stopped by police who searched his car trunk. They handcuffed Harris without telling him that he was under arrest and hit him in the stomach with their flashlights. When he raised his leg to stop the blows, the flashlight broke on his knee. He was then hit in the face with the broken flashlight. This last blow made it necessary for doctors to remove Harris' eye. His bowels were paralyzed by the blows to his stomach. Harris was charged with theft of parts off an abandoned car which had been marked "junked vehicle" by the city.

--Boston, MA, December 1979: Bellana Borde, a 21-year-old Black woman, decided to wait for the bus in the entry foyer of an apartment building because it was such a cold, wintry day. A security guard saw her and called the police. When the police arrived, she tried to leave, but instead was handcuffed, knocked to the ground, and kneed in her stomach and breast by the officer who arrested her for trespassing. In the car on the way to the police station, the officer pinched her legs. At the station, when Ms. Borde refused to give her name, saying that she had done nothing wrong, the officer stood on her feet. She was then placed in a holding cell and the officer came in and sprayed mace in her face and slammed her against the wall. At that point Ms. Borde bit the officer's finger to get him to stop torturing her. The charges against Ms. Borde were dropped by Judge Harry Elam who said, "With all the crime in this state, I am appalled that I am here today because a police officer of 29 years [experience] doesn't have the judgment to say to a security guard with no experience and no training that this woman is just waiting for the bus."[19]

--Albuquerque, NM, July 1977: After being arrested, Mr. Maya, a Hispanic man, ran into his house. Police kicked the door in. Officer Babich went over to Mr. Maya who had made no movement (according to Babich's own testimony) and struck him over the head with a flashlight. After being dragged outside and beaten repeatedly with the flashlight, officers reported that Mr. Maya grabbed for the officer's gun. Officer Torbett choked Mr. Maya until he passed out. Mr. Maya was convicted and sentenced; no action was taken against either officer. Before Mr. Maya was sentenced, Officer Babich killed Andrew Ramirez in a similar flashlight beating.

--Gordon, NE, September 1976: Mrs. JoAnn Yellow Bird, a Native American woman who was 8-months pregnant, was kicked in the abdomen when she attempted to intervene in a fight between an officer and her brother. Her baby was later born dead. The officer stated in a deposition that the "higher class people" in Gordon receive preferential treatment from law enforcement agents. "'Higher class' people meant 'white people,'" the officer stated.[20]

--Detroit, MI, February 1980: Fred Warren was found dead in his cell a few hours after he was arrested for burglary. Two prisoners in the cell block charge that Warren was struck with a blackjack after he spit on an officer. When citizens began raising questions about Warren's death, it was discovered that electric cattle prods had been used on numerous occasions on prisoners in the Second Precinct. This precinct is made up primarily of Mexican-Americans and Appalachian whites.

--Philadelphia, PA, May 1977: Edward Duck, a 23-year-old Black man who works as a potter, was driving on Chestnut Street when he was stopped for a traffic violation. He was with a white woman. The two officers who stopped him fractured his nose and handcuffed him so tightly that he suffered-nerve damage to his right hand. Duck was charged with disorderly conduct but acquitted.

--Philadelphia, PA, January 1977: Richard Canady was arrested and taken to the Police Administration Building. Canady was placed in a cell and later handcuffed to a chair. While handcuffed, Canady was punched and beaten by Detective Chitwood and Detective Strohm.

--Philadelphia, PA: Kevin Carter, a 17-year-old Black male, reported that he was taken from the House of Corrections to the 35th District for a hearing. After the hearing, when he was put back in the cell, the officers came to unlock the cells and transport him back to the House of Corrections. Officer Seddon grabbed him by the shoulders and threw him against the bars saying, "Put your hands up." He then began patting down his legs. Carter told Seddon that he had stitches in his leg. The officer then said, "Shut the fuck up. This is my turf." He grabbed the area on the left leg where the stitches were. Carter complained again that he had stitches in the leg. Then Officer Wolk grabbed him by the front of the shirt and choked him. When Wolk let go, Seddon grabbed him again and hit him repeatedly in the left leg. Cuffs were then put on Carter and he was taken out of the cellblock. Seddon then pushed Carter into the door-way as they were leaving the building and said, "Oops, better watch where you are walking." Carter was then taken to the wagon. The other prisoners in the wagon were handcuffed together but Carter was handcuffed alone with his hands behind him. He was pushed by Officer Wolk as he climbed into the wagon and fell all the way to the front. Carter then sat on a bench at the back of the wagon and Seddon came up and said, "You're a wise ass, aren't you?" Then Seddon poked him in the face with a finger. Carter told the officer to leave him alone. Seddon then said, "Come here, smart ass, we're going to teach you a lesson."

Carter was then pulled from the wagon by his arms and taken back into the police station to the empty courtroom. Seddon threw him into the chair and he fell down. Seddon jumped on top of him with his knees in his chest, hands around his neck, choking him saying, "Don't you know I'll kill you, nigger?" Seddon kept shaking him. Officer Wolk was walking around, kicking him in the back and sides and told Seddon to take the handcuffs off Carter. Wolk then pulled Carter up off the floor saying, "Put your hands up, punk, put your hands up." Carter said, "No, man, I told you, I'm not going to fight."

A sergeant walked in. Carter asked him to tell the officers to stop; the sergeant left. Wolk then put the handcuffs back on Carter very tight and Seddon, as they were leaving the building, said, "I thought we had a hard guy. He's a pussy. You know where we stand, right." Carter was then put back in the wagon and all prisoners were driven to the detention center. The other inmates were taken out of the wagon at the detention center, but Officer Wolk closed the door on Carter, saying, "Hold on, chump, you're going for a ride." Then the officer got into the wagon, stepped on the gas, slammed on the brakes, and Carter flew all the way to the front of the wagon. This happened twice. Then Carter was taken into the House of Corrections.

The examples cited above, horrible as they are, represent only a minute number of the thousands of victims of such abuse. The results of a study in one American city, which we believe can be replicated across the country, are included below to demonstrate the pervasive nature of this problem. This data, in addition to the examples above, clearly provide evidence of the heavy impact of police brutality upon members of oppressed minorities.[21]

Citizens Who Have Suffered Physical Abuse at the Hands of Philadelphia Police Officers While Being Arrested or Held for Trial

Name	Date	Race
Edward David	7/14/74	Black
Joseph Lee O 'Neill	1/8/75	Black
Gregory Gallman	12/27/74	Black
Louis Africa	1/23/75	Black
Alberta Africa	1/12/75	Black
John J. Gush, aka John E. Gush	8/17/75	White

Name	Date	Race
Carmine DeNardis	3/9/75	White
Garfield Hedgman	4/17/75	Black
SunduSu Mohammad Loroma	6/18/75	Black
Edward Patrick Fields	7/11/75	White
Edward John Douglas	7/11/75	White
Kenneth Eugene Shostak	7/11/75	White
Paul Joseph Tannello	9/18/75	White
Veloso Jackson	9/24/75	Black
William Rot Hoskins	11/5/75	Black
John Joseph Naulty	11/16/75	White
James Warren Wyatt	11/20/75	Black
Leon Harasmowicz	6/27/76	White
William Robert Hanna, Sr.	12/15/76	White
William Robert Hanna, Jr.	12/15/76	White
Earl Franklin	9/28/76	Black
Robert Jackson	1/3/79	Black
William L. Cradle	4/29/77	Black
Richard James Rozanski	12/29/77	Black
Joseph James Kedra	12/22/75	White
Michael John Kedra	12/22/75	White
Patricia Kedra	12/22/75	White
Kenneth Kedra	12/22/75	White
John Andrew Clifton	4/22/77	Black
Bernard Cyril Meaton	6/12/76	White
Alvestuse Goode	4/26/77	Black
John J. Copelella	5/24/77	White
Robert Crenshaw	8/23/76	White
Joseph Bross	8/23/76	White
George Cassidy	8/23/76	White
John Moore	1/15/77	Black
Ronald E . Anderson	4/25/77	White
Charles Edward Thomas	3/5/77	White
Sheik Bishara Bey	6/15/77	Moorish/American
Theodore Pendergrass	11/22/76	Black
Clemon Jo Perry	12/21/76	Black
Everett J. Day	3/1/77	Black
William H . Williams	6/15/77	White
Edgardo Ralph Ortiz	6/18/77	White
Phillip Shepard Young	10/6/76	Black
Robert Rodriguez	1/12/76	Puerto Rican
Perry Joseph King	Easter 1976	Black

Name	Date	Race
Michael Wilber	3/24/77	White
Maryane Hornberger	6/30/77	White
Mark Kenny	5/13/77	White
Louis Roach	3/16/72	White
Joseph Ronald Bilhardt	9/19/76	White
Jon Davis Kennedy	11/1/75	Black
John Wardlow	6/9/73	Black
William Henderson Meekins	7/3/77	Black
Charles A . Murray	8/28/76	White
Delores Terry	8/2/75	Black
Clarence Terry, Sr.	8/2/75	Black
Clarence Terry, Jr.	8/2/75	Black
Andre Terry	8/2/75	Black
Tyrone Terry	8/2/75	Black
John-States McKinney	6/5/66	White
Samuel D. Jackson	8/18/77	Black
Robert Thomas	6/21/77	Black
Gee Robinson	6/22/77	Black
Joseph J, Berthesi	8/27/77	Black
Kevin Zienkewica	8/13/77	White
Howard Seiss	8/20/77	White
Leroy Davis	8/31/77	Black
Melvin S. Stacks	8/11/77	Black
Annette Bush	9/1/77	Black
Lindell Swinson	9/20/77	Black
Raymond S . Pratt	9/8/77	Black
Steven Borek	9/26/77	Black
Leroy Smith	12/16/75	Black
Lawrence Joseph O'Neill	10/1/77	White
Peter Frycyk	11/3/77	White
John Joseph Quinn	11/3/77	White
Augustine Acevedo	11/3/77	White
Royal Oscar Chambers, Jr.	11/19/77	Black
Joseph James Ebbinger	9/28/76	White
Margaret Dolores Ebbinger	9/28/76	White
Arthur M. Smith	12/3/78	Black
John. Bans Lima, Sr.	10/16/77	Black
William Thomas Kane	10/5/77	White
Joseph Lee Grace	2/2/78	Black
Joseph Rouse, Jr.	12/9/75	Black
Norman Wojciechowski	9/5/77	White

Name	Date	Race
Arthur Reid	4/2/78	Black
Lesley Charles Beasley	3/29/78	Black
Steven P. Newman	5/15/78	
Robert Lawhorn	5/13/78	Black
Mark Lamar Golden	11/20-21/71	Black
Franco Philip Montenegro	5/29/78	
William Paul Macchianerna	7/30/78	White
Harry Joseph Charlesworth	8/6/78	White
Delbert Orr Africa	8/10/78	Black
Cornell Warren (Deceased)	9/23/78	Black
Harry Joseph Burt	12/12/78	
Frank Clarence Leans	1/24/79	White
Will M. Claxton , Sr .	8/28/78	Black
Victoria Dawn Heffernan	2/25/79	White
Barry Young	6/15/77	Black
Jon Lelyn Douglas	2/28/77	Black
Monserate Colon	5/6/77	Hispanic
Thomas J. O'Connor	6/76	
Randolph Pitts	7/2/76	
Angel Sanchez	5/7/76	
William Simmans	10/2/76	
Stephen Barkley	5/30/76	

(3) Physical or psychological intimidation of arrestees and prisoners to extract confessions

The *Philadelphia Inquirer*:

"...documented that between 1974 and 1977, at least 80 criminal cases (of the 433 that the newspaper examined) were thrown out of court because of the tactics police used during interrogations to extract statements and confessions from suspects. Many of their grillings had gone on for as long as nine hours. And some of these 'illegally interrogated' suspects ended up in hospitals. Spencer Coxe of the American Civil Liberties Union in Philadelphia is convinced that: 'abuse is practiced... the policy of the department.... Torture has been practiced.... Judges know it.'"[22]

Case examples of physical intimidation to extract confessions are

--Philadelphia, PA: Norman Legg, a 24-year-old Black male, complained that his left arm was handcuffed to a chair while he was interrogated; that he was kicked in both legs, burned with a cigarette on the back of his left hand and forearm, hit in the back with a chair, and choked until he blanked out. These measures were taken by Detective Robert Murphy in a 12-hour attempt to get Legg to make a statement and sign it.

--Philadelphia, PA, December 1975: Joseph Rouse was punched in the jaw after he refused to sign a statement admitting a theft.

--Philadelphia, PA, 1976 or early 1977: Joseph Bilhardt said detectives punched him in the ribs, chest, and lower back while his right arm was stretched out and his left arm was handcuffed to a chair. This beating occurred for a couple of hours because he refused to answer questions until a lawyer was contacted on his behalf. His head was pounded with a book until he gave a statement.

--In South Dakota, FBI agents utilized a form of psychological intimidation to obtain testimony from a Native American woman. She was shown the autopsy pictures of a murdered woman and told that she and her children would suffer a similar fate if she didn't give false testimony at a trial.

(4) Verbal abuse and detention of people without proper cause

Stopping and holding people without cause and calling them names does not rank with maiming and killing. But, precisely because it is of a less violent nature, it is frequently used, becoming the daily fare of millions of Blacks, Browns, Native Americans, and other minorities and poor people. Several examples related to this category have already been given above under other categories. Some additional examples are:

--Washington, DC, July, 1980: A young Black mother with a child was standing on a curb. A white police officer who was backing up his cruiser told her to move. She indicated she was on the sidewalk and didn't need to move, to which he replied, "Fuck you, bitch."

--Omaha, NE, May 1980: Helen Hiatt, a Native American woman, was stopped by officers looking for a Spanish-speaking suspect. Ms.

Hiatt was taken to the police station and questioned at length, with officers insisting that she was able to speak Spanish.

--Los Angeles, CA: Gilbert Castillo, a light-skinned Chicano, came out of a movie and was asked for identification by an officer. When the officer read his name, he asked derogatorily, "You Mexican?" The officer threw Castillo's identification on the ground and ordered him to pick it up and leave.

The following example from Philadelphia files "plainly grew out of improper police persistence in a confrontation, and erroneous police views that 'boisterous' expression of resentment and peaceable departure when the police desire to continue questioning amount to offenses for which they may and should arrest."[23]

"Police stop to question two black men pushing an automobile on a lot. They are told that the automobile has just been purchased by the father and brother of one of them, the purchasers having just gone off to a notary to conclude the formalities. The father and brother return with the seller, a white man, who confirms that there is no occasion for police concern. The police nevertheless insist on 'identification.' According to the police account itself, the brother became indignant, loud, and disrespectful, but not profane or physically aggressive. The police then made the critical decision to 'take the whole job [that is, all four men] into the district where we can settle this quietly.' The brother then walked away towards his own car and drove off. He was followed by police cars, stopped, and severely beaten in the course of arrest. The arresting police and, later, the police investigator in his report, indicated that the arrest was proper on the ground that the complainant walked away from the police when they had indicated they proposed to take him into the district 'for investigation.'"[24]

(5) Illegal searches and seizures

In 1978-79, the rampant misuse of illegal strip search procedures by the Chicago Police Department was exposed. The victims were women, many of whom had not even been arrested. It is interesting to note that this practice had gone unchecked for many years. Only because the police unknowingly selected as one of their victims the wife of a white judge did the matter get brought to the attention of the public.

The judge's wife had been arguing with a taxi driver about a cab fare. Police called to the scene took her to the station where she was subjected to a strip search. Even the judge's wife felt so humiliated by the incident that she, at first, was frightened into silence. Fortunately she protested and, once she did, large numbers of victims of this same police crime emerged out of their fearful silence.

The Illinois chapter of the American Civil Liberties Union received some 200 calls. "Women in their sixties reported being strip-searched. Disabled women were strip-searched. One woman was arrested because she was with a known crime figure. He was patted down. She was strip-searched."[25]

This particular example of abuse of power by law enforcement agents points again to the fact that the victims selected are members of the powerless groups in the United States. Only because one of the victims happened to belong to the powerful segment of society did this matter become a concern needing correction. The Chicago Police Department adopted a new set of guidelines on strip-searches and state legislation was introduced to curb these offenses.

Notwithstanding the availability of constitutional protections against illegal searches and seizures,[26] the stark reality of daily existence in the ghettos and barrios throughout the United States evidences a constant and flagrant disregard of those protections for minorities. In fact, the police often break into homes of minority citizens with no search warrants and questionable justification.[27] Moreover, while the "exclusionary rule" has never served as an effective deterrent to these abuses, the United States Supreme Court in recent cases has limited the access to the courts by such victims,[28] resulting in a further insulation of the police from judicial review.

(6) Killing people who have committed no crime

Killing of citizens by police is, of course, the most serious offense for there is no way a person's life can be restored. To kill a person who has committed no crime is doubly inexcusable.

Figures collected by the Public Interest Law Center of Philadelphia (PILCOP) reveal that between 1970 and 1978, "...50% of Philadelphia police shootings were contrary to state law....the Philadelphia Police Department, on the average of once every two weeks, shoots a citizen who is charged with non-forcible felonies or misdemeanors."[29] In Philadelphia, 2 out of 3 victims of police killings are Black or Hispanic; the same is true in Los Angeles. Again we see incontrovertible evidence that police crimes impact most severely on members of the oppressed minority communities.

--Los Angeles, July 1980: Larry Morris, a 28-year-old Black man, was choked to death in the bathroom of his own apartment by police who had illegally entered his apartment. There had been no illegal activity in progress nor could any be inferred from the conduct of the individuals in front of the apartment. The police had heard firecrackers and had asked Morris' brother, who was on a second-floor balcony, "Hey, boy, where are the firecrackers?" When the brother replied that he wasn't a "boy," the officers charged into the apartment building and forced their way into the Morris apartment. A witness described the scene: "The cops came in....and we went into the bathroom. The next thing I saw was the police who had Larry's head hanging over the toilet bowl, with clubs on his neck and in his stomach....We didn't hear any arguing, no shouting. He had never been in trouble. He wasn't that kind. He didn't fight back, he didn't have the chance."[30]

--Boston, MA, July 1980: Levi Hart, a 14-year-old Black youth, was shot and killed while being arrested for alleged car theft. Levi Hart was a slow learner student, a "little thin guy," whom police say tried to grab the policeman's gun. People who knew Levi Hart do not believe the police story.

--Philadelphia, PA, 1980: Breaking into a home to investigate a gas leak, police killed a 94-year-old man armed with a starting pistol.

--Omaha, NE, August 1979: On orders to stop a car with Iowa license plates with three whites in it, police stopped a car with Nebraska plates driven by an unarmed 27-year-old Black man and killed him.

--Laredo, TX, July 1978: A 32-year-old Mexican citizen was killed at the border by an off-duty policeman. The officer held a shotgun to the victim's head while searching his companions, and the gun "went off."

--Seattle, WA, June 1978: A 21-year-old Black man was shot in the back and killed by a police officer. There was not even a claim that the man was armed or dangerous.

(7) Killing people who are not threatening the lives of others, including those fleeing from apprehension, where failure to apprehend poses no serious threat to the lives of others

Police officers engage in irresponsible and unjustified use of deadly force when people are not threatening the lives of others or are not fleeing from arrest. Even in cases when people are fleeing from arrest, if flight prevents immediate apprehension but does not pose any serious threat to the lives of others, the use of deadly force is unnecessary. It is true that some states have laws permitting police to shoot anyone who flees from arrest, but stolen or damaged property should not be seen as more valuable than a person's life. Thus we submit that deadly force should only be used when there is an immediate threat to the life of others.

--Birmingham, AL, August 1979: A 20-year-old Black woman, unarmed, was murdered by police investigating a disturbance at a grocery store in a Black community.

--Los Angeles, December 1979: A 16-year-old Black youth was shot in the head and killed by police after climbing on a fence near the home of person who was under police protection.

--New York City, August 1979: A 26-year-old Hispanic man was shot 21 times by five police officers. He had allegedly threatened them with a pair of scissors.

--Los Angeles, CA, January 1979: A Black woman hit a representative of the utilities company with a shovel when he came to turn off her gas. The police were summoned. When the police arrived, the woman brandished a knife. Two officers each fired six rounds at her.

--Flint, MI, July 1980: A 15-year-old Black youth was shot in the back of the head by a policeman who said the youth did not halt while allegedly leaving the scene of a burglary.

(8) Killing unarmed people of color 1999 – 2015 (This category has been added to the original paper.)

To illustrate the fact that police abuse of power continues to be an egregious violation of human rights in the United States, the descriptions below of killings of unarmed people of color are only sample cases from the period 1999 – 2015. Most of the data in this section has been obtained from two websites: gawker.com and mappingpoliceviolence.com. The **Key Findings** in the next paragraph *summarizes only the 104 cases from 2015*, the most recent year for which detailed data is available from the website, mappingpoliceviolence.org, the source of most of the data in this section.

Key Findings

• Police killed at least 104 unarmed black people in 2015, nearly 2 each week.

• Nearly 1 in 3 Black people killed by police in 2015 were identified as unarmed, though the actual number is likely higher due to underreporting.

• 36% of unarmed people killed by police were Black in 2015, despite Black people being only 13% of the U.S. population

• Unarmed Black people were killed at 5 times the rate of unarmed whites in 2015.

• Only 13 of the 104 cases in 2015 where an unarmed black person was killed by police resulted in officer(s) being charged with a crime. Four of these cases have ended in a mistrial or charges against the officer(s) being dropped and 4 cases are still awaiting trial or have a trial underway. Only 4 cases (Matthew Ajibade, Eric Harris, Paterson Brown Jr., and William Chapman) have resulted in convictions of officers involved, with a fifth case (Walter Scott) resulting in the officer pleading guilty.

• Of the 4 cases where the officer(s) involved have been convicted and sentenced, none were sentenced to serve more than 4 years in prison. Only 1 of 2 officers convicted for their involvement in Matthew Ajibade's death received jail time. He was sentenced to 1 year in jail and allowed to serve this time exclusively on weekends. The officer who killed Paterson Brown was sentenced to only 3 months in jail. Deputy Bates, who killed Eric Harris, was sentenced to 4 years in prison and Officer Cobb, who killed William Chapman, was sentenced to 2.5 years in prison. Officer Slager, who killed Walter Scott and pled guilty, was sentenced to 20 years in federal prison.

Sample Cases

Feb. 4, 1999, Amadou Diallo, Bronx, NY

Four plainclothes officers fired a total of 41 shots at Diallo outside of his apartment in the Bronx. Nineteen hit him. He was armed with a wallet, which an officer mistook for a gun when he pulled it out of his pocket. Officers initially approached him because he supposedly matched the description of a serial rapist. **The officers were acquitted of all charges. Diallo's mother and stepfather filed a $61 million ($20m plus $1m for each shot fired) wrongful death suit against the officers and New York city. They settled for $3 million.**

March 1, 2000, Malcolm Ferguson, New York, NY

Drug officers "noticed some movement" in the hallway of a public housing building and investigated. Ferguson, who was unarmed, ran up the stairs. "At some point, on the second-floor landing, there was a struggle," Chief John Scanlon said. "...[Officer Louis Rivera's] firearm discharged." **Rivera was cleared of wrongdoing. Ferguson's mom, Juanita Young, was awarded $10.5 million as a result of her wrongful death suit against the NYPD and the city.**

March 16, 2000, Patrick Dorismond, New York, NY

An undercover cop approached Dorismond and his friend, Kevin Kaiser, when they were standing outside of a lounge. The cop asked where he could buy marijuana. A scuffle ensued and another undercover cop, Anthony Vasquez, stepped in to help his partner. Vasquez claimed Dorismond grabbed his gun and caused it to discharge into his own chest. Vasquez said the first cop was in their face, and that he attempted to pull Dorismond out of the confrontation to no avail. **Vasquez was not indicted. New York paid the Dorismond family $2.25 million as a settlement in a wrongful death suit.**

June 12, 2000, Ronald Beasley and Earl Murray, St. Louis, MO

Beasley and Murray, described by family and friends as small-time drug dealers, were shot and killed during an attempted drug bust in a restaurant parking lot. One cop called the killings "unintended, but not a mistake." **The officers were cleared of wrongdoing after a yearlong investigation.**

Sept. 1, 2000, Prince Jones, Fairfax County, VA

An undercover narcotics agent followed the unarmed Jones, firing 16 shots at him while Jones was in his Jeep. Eight landed. Officials later confirmed that Officer Carlton Jones (no relation) mistook Prince Jones for someone else. **The Fairfax commonwealth's attorney and the Justice Department declined to file charges against the officer, Carlton Jones. The case was not put before a grand jury. Five years after the killing, Prince Jones's parents and daughter were awarded $3.7 million in a wrongful death lawsuit.**

April 7, 2001, Timothy Thomas, Cincinnati, OH

Nine officers pursued Thomas, who was wanted on 14 misdemeanor counts. Twelve of them were traffic violations. A chase ensued. Thomas ran into an alley and was shot by Patrolman Stephen Roach, who joined the group of nine officers during the pursuit. Roach said he believed Thomas was going for a gun, but an investigation later revealed that Thomas was attempting to pull up his pants. **Roach was acquitted on a charge of negligent homicide. An investigation later revealed that Roach lied on his incident report and broke protocol.**

February 28, 2003, Orlando Barlow, Las Vegas, NV

Barlow was hired to babysit seven children. After a supposed argument, his employer (the children's mother) called the police, saying that Barlow was holding her children hostage with a sawed-off shotgun. Police responded to the call. Barlow was shot while surrendering. He was unarmed. **A coroner's inquest labeled the shooting "excusable." The FBI looked into it. "The shooting was unanimously ruled justifiable, but Hartman and two other officers were fired after they printed T-shirts with the initials 'BDRT' — 'Baby's Daddy Removal Team,'" reported the Las Vegas Review-Journal.**

May 16, 2003, Alberta Spruill, New York, NY

Police knocked down Spruill's door, apparently acting on bad information that there were drugs and guns inside her apartment. They threw a concussion grenade into her home. She died of a heart attack. **The city paid Spruill's family $1.6 million as a settlement for the wrongful death lawsuit they filed.**

May 22, 2003, Ousmane Zongo, New York, NY

Zongo was shot four times (twice in the back) by officer Bryan Conroy during a police raid in a storage facility where Zongo worked. Zongo was unarmed and his business (art and musical instrument restoration) had nothing to do with what the police were investigating (CD and DVD piracy). **Conroy was convicted of criminally negligent homicide. He received five years probation and lost his job. Zongo's family received $3 million in a wrongful death suit.**

January 24, 2004, Timothy Stansbury, New York, NY

Officer Richard S. Neri Jr., testified that he shot the unarmed Stansbury by accident when Stansbury pushed open the rooftop door of a building Neri was patrolling. **Neri was not indicted. He was suspended for 30 days without pay and stripped of his gun permanently. The NYPD settled the wrongful death lawsuit of Stansbury's family for $2 million.**

Sept. 4, 2005, Ronald Madison and James Brisettem, New Orleans, LA

Police received a call claiming gunfire on the Danziger Bridge. Police opened fire upon arriving in a Budget Rental Truck. They hit Brisette. Madison, who was developmentally disabled, fled. Two cops chased him down. One, Robert Faulcon, shot him. The other, **Sgt. Kenneth Bowen, was convicted of stomping Madison on the back before he died. That conviction was later overturned. Police attempted a cover-up. Eventually five officers involved in the shooting were found guilty of various charges. Faulcon was sentenced to 65 years' imprisonment, Bowen and Robert Gisevius received 40 years, Anthony Villavaso got 38 years, and Arthur "Archie" Kaufman, who was the investigator placed on the case and eventually found guilty of conspiring to conceal evidence, received 6 years. A month later, the same judge who convicted them, Kurt Engelhardt, vacated their convictions and ordered a new trial as a result of the defendants' appeal and "highly unusual, extensive and truly bizarre actions" by prosecutors.**

September 2, 2005, Henry Glover, New Orleans, LA

Glover was shot in the chest by NOPD officer David Warren at a strip mall in the days following Hurricane Katrina. Glover, with the help of a friend, attempted to get aid, and ended up handcuffed. He died. NOPD Officer Greg McRae set fire to Glover's body in Glover's friend's car. **David Warren was sentenced to 25 years and 9 months on a manslaughter conviction. Greg MacRae got 17 years and 3 months for obstruction of justice. About a year and a half later, the Fifth Circuit Court of Appeals vacated Warren's convictions and two of MacRae's, ordering new trials. Warren was acquitted in the retrial.**

November 25, 2006, Sean Bell, New York, NY

On the night before Bell's wedding, Bell and his friends attempted to flee the scene of escalating tension with the police. The police fired about 50 shots into Bell's car, killing him in the process. **All three officers were acquitted on all charges. They and their commanding officer were fired/forced to resign. New York City agreed to pay Bell's family $3.25 million to settle their wrongful death suit.**

July 22, 2007, DeAunta Terrel Farrow, West Memphis, AR

Farrow was out walking with his 14-year-old cousin when gunned down by a police officer, Erik Sammis. Sammis claims that only after he shot Farrow did he realize that the gun Farrow was carrying was a toy. **Sammis wasn't indicted. He resigned from the force via a letter that contained the sentence, "Then there are others who are not rational and breed hate and racism in this community." Sammis and Jimmy Evans, who was also on duty with him July 22, 2007, were found not liable in Farrow's family's $250 million civil suit.**

January 4, 2008, Tarika Wilson, Lima, OH

A SWAT team arrived at Wilson's home with the intention of arresting her companion for dealing drugs. When they opened fire, they shot and killed Wilson. **Sgt. Joe Chavalia, who shot Wilson, was acquitted of two misdemeanors: negligent homicide and negligent assault. Wilson's family received a $2.5 million wrongful death settlement.**

January 1, 2009, Oscar Grant, Oakland, CA

After reports of a fight at the BART train station, police detained Grant and some of his friends. While Grant was lying face down, resisting arrest, a police officer named Johannes Mehserle shot him. The officer claimed he meant to taser Grant. **Mehserle was found guilty of involuntary manslaughter and not guilty of second-degree murder and voluntary manslaughter. He was sentenced to two years in prison. BART paid Grant's mother and daughter $2.8 million to settle the civil suit they filed. Grant's father lost a civil case against Mehserle.**

July 11, 2009, Shem Walker, New York, NY

Walker was shot when trying to eject an undercover officer from his stoop. Walker was unarmed. **No indictment for the officer. New York City paid $2.25 million to settle with Walker's family.**

October 3, 2009, Victor Steen, Pensacola, FL

Sheen rode his bike as a cop chased him. Steen refused to stop, and so the cop, Jerald Ard, tasered him. Steen fell from his bike and Ard ran him over, killing him. Ard also may have planted a gun on Steen after his death. **Ard was suspended from the force without pay for two weeks. The city of Pensacola paid Steen's mother a $500,000 settlement.**

October 9, 2009, Kiwane Carrington, Champaign, IL

Police investigating a suspected break-in at a house encountered the unarmed Carrington. A scuffle ensued and Officer Daniel Norbits's gun "went off," killing Carrington. **No indictment for Norbits, but he did receive a total of $423,697 in disability and worker's compensation payments. Carrington's family received $470,000 from Champaign in a settlement of their wrongful death lawsuit.**

January 29, 2010, Aaron Campbell, Portland, OR

Campbell was shot in front of his apartment after being reported to the police as suicidal and possessing a gun. Campbell was unarmed. Campbell was walked backward with his hands behind his head. Officer Frashour told Campbell to put his hands straight in the air. When Campbell did not comply, Frashour shot him. **No indictment for Frashour. He was fired for not following protocol, but then reinstated. Portland agreed to pay Campbell's family $1.2 million to settle their civil suit against the city.**

March 20, 2010, Steven Eugene Washington, Los Angeles, CA
Police officers spotted Washington on a Los Angeles street. He reportedly approached them, appearing to be removing something from his waistband. He was shot and killed. No weapon was found on him. Later, Washington's family revealed that he was autistic. **Police Chief Charlie Beck recommended that Officers Allan Corrales and George Diego be cleared of charges, but the civilian commission that oversees the LAPD disagreed. Washington's mother received $950,000 in a settlement with Los Angeles.**

May 16, 2010, Aiyana Jones, Detroit, MI
Seven-year-old Jones was shot when a Special Response Team raided the duplex she lived in. Officers threw a grenade into Jones' apartment. Officer Joseph Weekley claimed Jones's grandmother grabbed his gun, causing Jones to be shot. **Weekley was charged with involuntary manslaughter. His first trial ended in a mistrial. So did his second.**

October 17, 2010, Danroy Henry, Thornwood, NY
Officer Aaron Hess shot Henry through the windshield of Henry's car as Henry drove away from a chaotic altercation. **No indictment for Hess. Henry's family filed a wrongful death suit.**

November 8, 2010, Derrick Jones, Oakland, CA
Jones' neighbor accused him of assault. Police arrived and Jones fled. According to Officers Perez-Angeles and Daza-Quiroz, when they caught up with Jones, they thought that he was reaching for a gun, so they fired at him. Six of their nine shots hit Jones, who was unarmed. **No indictment. Oakland settled with Jones' parents and daughter for $225,000. His widow lost a $10 million civil suit.**

January 14, 2011, Reginald Doucet, Los Angeles, CA
Police responded to a "disturbing the peace" call, where Doucet was arguing with a taxi driver. Doucet had stripped down. Doucet reportedly resisted arrest, and a chase ensued. During a violent confrontation, the unarmed Doucet was fatally shot. **The Los Angeles Police Commission ruled that officer Aaron Goff was justified in shooting Doucet. A judge dismissed the wrongful death lawsuit filed by Doucet's family.**

January 22, 2011, Raheim Brown, Oakland, CA

During a struggle with the police, Brown was shot five times, including twice in the head. Police reports alleged that Brown was attempting to stab an officer with a screwdriver. **No indictment for Officer Barhin Bhatt. The Oakland Unified School District settled with Brown's parents for $995,000.**

July 16, 2011, Kenneth Harding, San Francisco, CA

Harding fled a routine Muni fare inspection. The police said that a shootout ensued, witnesses said that Harding did not have a weapon. **According to police Cmdr. Mike Biel, the caliber of the bullet that killed Harding did not match the caliber used by police. "We believe that the fatal wound on Mr. Harding's body was self-inflicted," Biel said. Harding's mother filed federal wrongful death and civil rights lawsuits against San Francisco.**

July 18, 2011, Alonzo Ashley, Denver, CO

Police were called by Denver Zoo security who were alarmed over Ashley's behavior. Ashley was confronted and tasered. He started convulsing and then stopped breathing. **Ashley's death was ruled a homicide by the coroner, but no officers were charged. The City of Denver paid Ashley's family $259,000.**

November 19, 2011, Kenneth Chamberlain, White Plains, NY

Chamberlain's Life Aid alert necklace was triggered by mistake, causing the police to respond. He refused to answer his door, saying he did not need help. Officer Steven Hart called Chamberlain a "nigger." The police broke down his door. They alleged that Chamberlain attempted to charge them with a butcher knife. They tasered him, and shot him dead. **No indictment for Officer Anthony Carelli, who shot Chamberlain twice. A jury rejected the $21 million wrongful death suit filed by Chamberlain's family.**

February 2, 2012, Ramarley Graham, Bronx, NY

Graham was shot and killed by police in the Bronx, who chased him into his home without a warrant. He was unarmed. **The officer, Richard Haste, was initially indicted in 2012, but the case was later overturned. A second grand jury decided not to indict Haste. The**

Graham family sought compensation for emotional damages, in addition to mistreatment by the NYPD. After Graham was killed, his grandmother, Patricia Hartley, was detained at the local precinct for seven hours and forced to give a statement against her will. Haste also allegedly threatened to shoot her. Hartley received $450,000; Graham's brother, who was also home during the shooting, received $500,000; Graham's mother received $40,000 and Graham's estate was awarded $2.95 million.

February 7, 2012, Sgt. Manuel Loggins, Jr., Orange County, CA

On a religious fast and off medication for ADHD, Loggins allegedly crashed into a gate at Orange County high school with his car carrying his two daughters. After walking to and returning from the school's athletic field with a Bible, he was approached by a police officer, who shot Loggins three times through his car window. He was unarmed. **Orange County paid $4.4 million to Loggins' family in a settlement last year.**

February 26, 2012, Trayvon Martin, Sandford, Florida

Martin, an unarmed 17-year-old, was walking back from a convenience store after purchasing candy and iced tea when George Zimmerman, a neighborhood watch volunteer, shot and killed him based on the deepest, ugliest stereotype still embodied in the American psyche—namely, that all Blacks are criminals. Despite the strides made by the Civil Rights Movement, eradicating Jim Crow Laws, teaching tolerance and electing an African-American president, **Zimmerman was acquitted of charges of second-degree manslaughter.** His acquittal ignited outrage throughout the African-American community nationwide. This outrage was later intensified and further inflamed by the chokehold death of Eric Garner in Staten Island and the shooting death of Michael Brown in Ferguson, Missouri (see below on July 17, 2014 and August 9, 2014) as well as other cases less well-known. This outrage culminated in the formation of the **Black Lives Matters Movement.**

February 27, 2012, Raymond Allen, Galveston, TX

Police responded to a complaint from a hotel that Allen was repeatedly jumping from the second story. Two officers tasered him. He stopped breathing, and died in the hospital. **His wife filed a lawsuit against Galveston, the county, and taser's manufacturer.**

March 1, 2012, Dante Price, Dayton, OH

Security guards ordered Price out of an apartment complex. They told him to leave his car, but instead he decided to drive away, so they fired 17 shots at him. **Justin Wissinger and Christopher Tarbert pled guilty to involuntary manslaughter and abduction. They were sentenced 3 to 11 years in prison.**

March 5, 2012, Nehemiah Dillard, Spring Hill, FL

Dillard was admitted to Meridian Behavioral Healthcare after "displaying strange behavior" in a stranger's yard. He allegedly struck a member of the hospital's staff, who called police. Officers shot him twice with tasers after he allegedly attacked them. After being handcuffed, the *Tampa Bay Times* reports, "a staffer at the facility injected him with drugs" and Dillard died soon after from cardiac arrest.

March 7, 2012, Wendell Allen, New Orleans, LA

Allen, unarmed, dressed only in jeans and sneakers, was shot and killed by New Orleans police officer Joshua Colclough executing a search warrant of Allen's home for marijuana. **Colclough pleaded guilty to manslaughter and was sentenced to four years in prison last year.**

March 15, 2012, Shereese Francis, New York, NY

Francis, a schizophrenic who at the time was not taking her medication, became "increasingly emotionally distraught" after an argument with her mother. Her sister called 311, hoping for an ambulance—four police officers arrived instead, who chased Francis through the home. All four allegedly pinned her down as they handcuffed her and she stopped breathing soon after. She was pronounced dead at the hospital. The coroner's report concluded Francis died of "compression of trunk during agitated violent behavior." **Her family filed a lawsuit after police dragged their feet on releasing records under the Freedom of Information Act.**

March 21, 2012, Rekia Boyd, Chicago, IL

Off-duty officer Dante Servin fired an unregistered firearm into an alleyway where four people were standing after he allegedly saw a man brandish a gun. One of the bullets hit Boyd in the back of the head. She died the next day. **The city of Chicago paid Boyd's family $4.5 million in a wrongful death suit. The officer was charged with last November**

with involuntary manslaughter, reckless discharge of a firearm, and reckless conduct.

March 24, 2012, Kendrec McDade, Los Angeles County, CA

McDade was chased and shot by two police officers after a 911 caller falsely reported he had been robbed at gunpoint by two Black men. Both were unarmed. McDade was shot seven times. **The police department and Los Angeles County District Attorney's Office cleared the officers of wrongdoing. Investigations by the FBI and Office of Independent Review are pending.**

March 24, 2012, Ervin Jefferson, Decatur, GA

Security guards shot Jefferson, 18, to death during a "bizarre chain of events" outside of an apartment complex. **Security guards Curtis Scott and Gary Jackson were arrested and charged with impersonating police.**

April 18, 2012, Tamon Robinson, Brooklyn, NY

Police responded to a call from Canarsie, Brooklyn that Robinson was stealing paving stones. When confronted by police, Robinson, unarmed, ran toward the building where his mother lived; officers chased him by car, hitting him. **Robinson's family reached a $2 million settlement in a wrongful death suit against the city.**

April 21, 2012, Sharmel Edwards, Las Vegas, NV

Edwards was suspected of stealing a vehicle. A police chase ensued. Cops said that when they were finally able to get her to leave her car, she pointed a gun at them and they opened fire. At least three witnesses disputed that claim, with two saying she wasn't carrying a weapon at all. **The Clark County DA office ruled that the five officers who killed Edwards acted "reasonably and lawfully."**

June 14, 2012, Shantel Davis, Brooklyn, NY

Police chased Davis in a stolen car through East Flatbush until it crashed. In the ensuing struggle at the vehicle, one officer fired one shot, killing Davis. She was unarmed. It's "not clear" if the plainclothes officers chasing knew the car was stolen. David was due in court the week she died for helping hold a man hostage as the group robbed his home. **The officers involved were placed on administrative duty.**

July 29, 2012, Chavis Carter, Jonesboro, AK

Police say Carter killed himself while handcuffed in the back of a police car. His mother pointed out that he was left-handed (he would have had to shoot himself with his right hand), detained for marijuana while his concealed weapon supposedly went undetected, and not suicidal. **The officers involved were placed on administrative leave and the FBI stepped in to "monitor and assess " the situation. His mother filed a wrongful death suit.**

September 7, 2012, Reynaldo Cuevas, Bronx, NY

Cuevas was shot and killed by police as he was fleeing armed men attempting to rob the bodega he worked at. **The Bronx District Attorney did not find the officer at fault and declined to move the case forward to a grand jury. His mother filed a $25 million wrongful death claim against the city last year.**

November 29, 2012, Malissa Williams and Timothy Russell, Cleveland, OH

Russell led 62 police cars on a chase that ended with 137 shots being fired at his car, killing him and Williams. Police believed someone in Russell's car had fired at them first. Cornered at a middle school, Cleveland Patrolman Michael Brelo jumped on top of Russell's car from behind, climbed to the hood, and fired 15 more shots. **A judge approved a settlement between the city and their two families—$1.5 million each. Brelo was tried for voluntary manslaughter and found not guilty.**

December 10, 2012, Johnnie Kamahi Warren, Houston, TX

A Houston County Sheriff's deputy spotted Warren struggling with three other men outside a bar. Upon approaching Warren, he used a taser at least twice. Soon after additional officers arrived and arrested him, he lost consciousness and died at the hospital. **An Alabama Bureau of Investigation probe was ordered; the sheriff's deputy was placed on paid leave.**

March 9, 2013, Kimani Gray, New York, NY

Police said Gray pointed a revolver at them as they attempted to question him. Friends and family say Gray had never had a gun, and a witness says he never pointed one at police. The cops shot a total of 11 rounds, striking Gray several times. **No indictments for the cops responsible for shooting Gray.**

May 5, 2013, Deion Fludd, New York, NY

Police say that a train clipped Fludd as they chased him for dodging subway fare. According to his mother, Fludd denied this before succumbing to his injuries. **Fludd's mother sued the officers involved, the NYPD, and the MTA.**

July 26, 2013, Larry Eugene Jackson, Austin, TX

Jackson was fatally shot during a scuffle resulting from a chase that took place when detective Charles Kleinert apprehended Jackson for trying to "defraud" a bank. **Kleinert was indicted on a manslaughter charge, but the indictment was dismissed.**

August 15, 2013, Carlos Alcis, New York, NY

Alcis died of a heart attack after the police mistakenly raided his home in search of a cell phone thief. **Alcis's family filed a wrongful death suit against the city and the NYPD for $10 million.**

September 14, 2013, Jonathan Ferrell, Charlotte, NC

Ferrell crashed his car and knocked on the door of a nearby house. The woman inside called the police. Police said that when Ferrell was apprehended, they shot him. Ten times. **Officer Randall Kerrick was indicted on a charge of voluntary manslaughter. It took two grand juries to get there.**

October 3, 2013, Miriam Carey, Washington, DC

While attempting to make a U-turn at a White House checkpoint, Carey allegedly hit a barricade and a Secret Service officer in front of the White House. After a high-speed chase, police surrounded her, weapons drawn. She was shot five times in the chase and died at the scene. She was unarmed. Her daughter was in the car with her and was unharmed. **The U.S. Attorney's Office declined to press charges.**

October 22, 2013, Andy Lopez, Santa Rosa, CA

Lopez was carrying a pellet gun that resembled an AK-47 assault rifle. After officers reportedly told Lopez to drop the gun, he turned toward them and they shot him. **No indictment.**

January 16, 2014, Jordan Baker, Houston, TX

An off-duty police officer thought Baker, 26, fit the description of robbery suspects—both they and he were wearing black hooded sweatshirts. A scuffle and foot chase ensued. Baker, who was unarmed, was fatally shot. Officer J. Castro, who killed Baker, was placed on administrative leave pending an investigation.

January 28, 2014, McKenzie Cochran, Southfield, MI

Cochran died of "position compression asphyxia" during struggle with mall security. Cochran told them, " I can't breathe." His death was ruled an accident by medical examiner. **No indictments for the security guards.**

February 16, 2014, Yvette Smith, Bastrop County, TX

Officers responding to a domestic disturbance call shot after Yvette Smith, 47, opened her front door to them. Initially, police claimed that Smith had a firearm, but the sheriff's office retracted this the next day. **Deputy Daniel Willis, who shot Smith, was indicted on a murder charge. Her family asked for $5 million in a wrongful death suit.**

March 22, 2014, Victor White III, Iberia Parish, LA

The coroner says he shot himself while handcuffed in the back of a police cruiser. The autopsy report claims, White's injuries "are possible to be self-inflicted even with the hands handcuffed behind the back." "Short of him being Houdini or David Copperfield, it's not possible," said White's family's attorney. **District Attorney Phil Haney of the 16th Judicial Circuit said he will let a federal investigation run its course before making a decision.**

July 17, 2014, Eric Garner, Staten Island, NY

Police alleged they saw Garner, 43, selling illegal untaxed cigarettes, but witnesses at the scene said he was stopped because he broke up a fight. After an argument, Officer Daniel Pantaleo placed Garner in a chokehold. Garner died of neck compression from the chokehold along with "the compression of his chest and prone positioning during physical restraint by police." **The New York City medical examiner ruled Garner's death a homicide. Pantaleo was not indicted. In May 2019 an administrative disciplinary hearing was held to consider evidence against Officer Daniel Pantaleo.** The case is now under consideration by a judge who will determine if the evidence equates to charges of first-degree strangulation and third-degree reckless assault. **The City also paid the family $5.9 million to settle a wrongful death claim.**

August 5, 2014, John Crawford III, Beavercreek, OH

Crawford, 22, was fatally shot while carrying a pellet gun in a Wal-Mart. The gun was unsold merchandise and out of its package. A man named Ronald Ritchie told 911 that he looked like he was pointing it at people, but a month later he admitted that Crawford was not pointing the gun at people. **No indictment.**

August 9, 2014, Michael Brown, Ferguson, MO

Shot by Officer Darren Wilson after an altercation that happened inside Wilson's car. Wilson reported that Brown "looked like a demon." Brown was 18 years old. **Wilson was not indicted by a grand jury. He resigned from the Ferguson police force. The U.S. Justice Department performed a probe and found a deeply entrenched and blatant racist bias in the Ferguson police Department. Subsequently the number of Black police officers has been increased and a Black police chief now heads the Police Department.**

August 12, 2014, Dante Parker, Victorville, CA

Police responded to a call about an attempted break-in. The suspect fled on a bicycle. Police found Parker, 36, nearby riding his bike. He was unarmed. He resisted arrest and a struggle ensued. Police tasered him and he died. **Pending. The NAACP has called for a federal investigation.**

August 12, 2014, Ezell Ford, Los Angeles, CA

Ford, 25, was shot by police who were conducting "an investigative stop." " A struggle ensued," read the LAPD's news release. Ford's family members say he was lying down when shot. **The LAPD, which hasn't closed the investigation into Ford's death, put an indefinite**

"investigative hold" on the coroner's autopsy report to prevent witness testimony from being tainted.

August 19, 2014, Kajieme Powell, St. Louis, MO

Powell was shot by police who responded to a 911 call accusing him of stealing some energy drinks and pastries. Cops claimed that he approached them holding a knife "in an overhand grip"; video footage of the incident shows that Powell did not come as close to the police as they reported and that his hands were by his side. Police shot him within 15 seconds of arriving at the scene. **Powell's family has filed a wrongful death suit against the St. Louis police chief and arresting officers.**

Nov. 20, 2014, Akai Gurley, New York, NY

Gurley, 28, was shot in a dark stairwell of an East New York housing project building by Officer Peter Liang. Gurley was unarmed. Police Commissioner William Bratton called Gurley "a total innocent." "The cop who was standing behind Officer Liang doesn't know what happened; the girlfriend doesn't know what happened," a senior police official told the New York Times. "There is a distinct possibility that Officer Liang doesn't quite understand what happened." **District Attorney Ken Thompson announced that he is investigating.**

Nov. 22, 2014, Tamir Rice, Cleveland, OH

Officer Tim Loehmann shot and killed Rice, 12, who was holding a BB gun, seconds after spotting him at a park. **Cleveland agreed to pay $6 million to the family of Tamir Rice.**

Dec. 2, 2014, Rumain Brisbon, Phoenix, AZ

Brisbon, 34, an unarmed Black father of four, was shot to death in when a police officer apparently mistook his bottle of pills for a gun. **Pending.**

January 1, 2015, Matthew Ajibade, Savannah, GA

Ajibade's girlfriend called 911 to ask police to take him to the hospital because he was having a manic episode (he had bipolar disorder). Instead, they arrested him and took him to the Chatham County Detention Center. The Sheriff's Office claims that he fought officers, so they put him in a restraining chair. He died in the restraining chair. **Deputy Kenny was convicted of cruelty to an inmate and Deputy Evans was convicted of**

public records fraud and three counts of perjury for killing Matthew. Deputy Kenny was sentenced to 1 year in jail - to be served only on weekends - and 3 years probation while Deputy Evans was sentenced to 6 years probation.

January 6, 2015, Leslie Sapp, Pittsburgh, PA

Marshals went to serve a warrant on Leslie. They shot and killed Leslie, claiming he pointed a toy gun at them. **No officers have been charged with a crime.**

January 6, 2015, Brian Pickett, Willowbrook, CA

Pickett's mother called police to report he was under the influence and had threatened her. When police arrived, Pickett allegedly charged at them and was tasered by a deputy. He stopped breathing when the paramedics arrived and was pronounced dead at an area hospital. **No officers have been charged with a crime.**

January 7, 2015, Andre Larone Murphy Sr., Norfolk, NE

An officer responding to a disturbance call at a Super 8 Motel struggled with Murphy, using a taser against him. Murphy died soon after at Faith Regional Health Services in Norfolk, NE. **No officers have been charged with a crime.**

January 22, 2015, Tiano Meton, El Paso, TX

Meton drove through a West Texas checkpoint without stopping and drove 30 more miles before he stopped. "Four agents approached the vehicle and one of them yelled 'gun,'" the AP reported. Two of the agents fired their weapons at the vehicle. A toy gun was found in Meton's vehicle. **No officers have been charged with a crime.**

February 8, 2015, Natasha, McKenna, Fairfax, VA

Police used a stun gun on McKenna, who had schizophrenia, claiming she "refused to comply" with deputies' commands and "physically resisted" them as they prepared her for transport to Alexandria to face charges there, the sheriff's office said. **No officers have been charged with a crime.**

February 20, 2015, Terry Price, Osage County, OK

Deputies responded to a call from casino security saying the subject who was banned from the premises was there and needed to be removed.

The subject fled the scene and then returned. He ran into the woods where police tasered him. The subject collapsed and died. **No officers have been charged with a crime.**

February 22, 2015, Calvon Reid, Coconut Bay, FL

Police said they found Reid injured and in an "agitated, combative state" in a gated retirement community. He was tasered at least three times and went into cardiac arrest, according to lawyers. **Authorities did not disclose the death until witness accounts were published by the media. Coconut Bay's police chief promptly retired. Medical examiners ruled the death a homicide by electrocution. No officers have been charged with a crime.**

February 28, 2015, Thomas Allen Jr., Wellston, MO

Allen and his young daughter were passengers in a car that was pulled over. The driver got out to talk to the officer. Allen climbed into the driver's seat and started to drive away. The officer fatally shot Allen, who died in the hospital the next day. **No officers have been charged with a crime.**

March 1, 2015, Deontre Dorsey, Waldorf, MD

Deontre Dorsey lost control of his car, coming to rest against a tree in a median. Witnesses called 911 saying Dorsey was "flopping like a fish." After Dorsey, who was having a seizure, rolled on his stomach and reached for a firefighter's leg, police ordered him to put his hands behind his back. When Dorsey failed to comply and tried to stand up, police tasered him in the back several times. Dorsey was later handcuffed and placed in leg shackles at the scene and stopped moving or breathing. He was a father of four. **No officers have been charged with a crime.**

March 1, 2015, Darrell Gatewood, Oklahoma City, OK

Police responded to a disturbance call about a man breaking things and "fighting with the air." When they arrived at the scene, Darrell started fighting with them. Deputies tasered Darrell an unknown number of times and he went into cardiac arrest and was pronounced dead at the hospital. **No officers have been charged with a crime.**

March 6, 2015, Tony Robinson

Police claim unarmed Tony Robinson attacked an officer who responded to calls for help from friends and nearby residents over his "erratic and aggressive behavior". The officer shot him seven times. Robinson's family filed a federal civil rights lawsuit against the officer and the city on August 12. **No officers have been charged with a crime.**

March 22, 2015, Denzel Brown, Bayshore, NY

Denzel Brown, 21, was suspected of shoplifting from a Best Buy. Police responded and found him hiding in the parking lot. Denzel attempted to open car doors in the lot. Police claim he tried to steal a car from a couple with children in back seat. Officers shot and killed him. **No officers were charged with a crime.**

April 2, 2015, Donald "Dontay" Ivy, Albany, NY

Officers questioned Ivy, a paranoid schizophrenic with a heart condition. He fled down Second Street. Officers chased Ivy, shooting him with a Taser at least once. The Taser failed to subdue Ivy, whom they chased and handcuffed. When he stopped breathing, officers attempted CPR and called for help. Ivy died at Albany Medical Center. **No officers have been charged with a crime.**

April 4, 2015, Walter Scott, North Charleston, SC

Scott was pulled over by North Charleston police officer Michael Slager for a minor traffic violation. Scott fled but Slager caught up with him and attempted to deploy his Taser. The Taser was not effective and as Scott ran away, Slager opened fire. The final altercation was caught on video. **Officer Slager pled guilty to 2nd degree murder and was sentenced to 20 years in federal prison.**

April 19, 2015, Freddie Gray, Baltimore, MD

Freddie Gray died from injuries sustained during a prolonged ride on the floor of a police van while handcuffed and shackled. He was arrested after catching the eye of a police officer and running away. **Six officers were charged with crimes including murder for killing Freddie. One officer's trial ended in a mistrial, three officers were found not guilty, all other charges were dropped.**

April 21, 2015, Samuel Harrell, Beacon, NY

Samuel Harrell, 30, was involved in a confrontation with corrections officers at the Fishkill Correctional Facility, during which up to 20 officers repeatedly punched and kicked him while he was handcuffed on the ground, according to a New York Times report. The Orange County medical examiner ruled Harrell's cause of death as homicide 'following physical altercation with corrections officers'. **No officers have been charged with a crime.**

May 6, 2015, Brandon Glenn, Los Angeles, CA

Glenn was allegedly panhandling outside a bar in Venice when a customer complained that he was harassing customers. He wound up in a scuffle with a bouncer and two officers, one of whom shot and killed him. After viewing unreleased tape of the incident, LAPD Police Chief Charlie Beck said: "Any time an unarmed person is shot by a Los Angeles police officer, it takes extraordinary circumstances to justify that. I have not seen those extraordinary circumstances." **No officers have been charged with a crime.**

June 15, 2015, Kris Jackson, Lake Tahoe, CA

An officer responding to a domestic disturbance fatally shot Jackson, claiming to see the 22-year-old man climb through a back window at a Lake Tahoe motel. Jackson's family questions whether the officer followed proper protocol. Jackson's girlfriend, who was at the scene, did not hear a command to stop from the officer. She also questions whether Jackson was a threat. "He was shot while climbing out a window," Laskin wrote. "Does that sound like he posed a threat?" **No officers have been charged.**

June 25, 2015, Spencer McCain, Baltimore, MD

Police responding to a domestic call entered a condominium after hearing arguing inside and fatally shot McCain, claiming they believed he had a gun. McCain was later revealed to be unarmed and died at a nearby hospital. **No officers have been charged with a crime.**

July 2, 2015, Victo Larosa III, Jacksonville, FL

Victo Larosa was shot after tripping and falling to the ground while fleeing officers following an undercover sting operation against drug deals, according to the sheriff's office. The officer alleged that he opened fire because Larosa reached into his waistband. No weapon was recovered from the scene. **No officers have been charged with a crime.**

July 17, 2015, Albert Davis, Orlando, FL

Albert Davis, 23, was shot and killed by an Orlando police officer who had been called after reports of a fight in the area involving five men. The officer deployed his taser and then fired his gun, after an alleged 'struggle' with Davis. Despite police saying Davis was "very, very violent" towards the officer, the officer did not sustain any injuries. **No officers have been charged.**

July 17, 2015, Darrius Stewart, Memphis, TN

Stewart was stopped by police for a broken headlight. Authorities said he was placed in the back of a patrol car, unhand-cuffed, while officers ran his name. When the officers returned to handcuff Stewart and take him into custody for outstanding warrants, police said he became "combative" and struck an officer with the handcuffs. The officer then drew his gun and fired. Stewart's mother told local news that her son had never been arrested and that the warrants were for someone else with the same name. **No officers have been charged.**

July 19, 2015, Samuel Dubose, Cincinnati, OH

Police initially said that an officer pulled DuBose over for a routine traffic stop which escalated into some type of altercation, and that DuBose dragged an officer with his vehicle for a distance before the officer fired. That account was later disproven by body camera footage released by Cincinnati prosecutor Joseph Deters. **University of Cincinnati Officer Ray Tensing has been charged with murder for killing DuBose.**

August 7, 2015, Christian Taylor, Arlington, VA

Taylor, 19, entered a car dealership after hours and can be seen in security surveillance footage jumping on cars and smashing the windows of several vehicles. Six Arlington police arrived and Brad Miller, a rookie cop, fatally shot unarmed Christian. He has since been fired from his station. **No officers have been charged.**

August 28, 2015, Felix Kumi, New York, NY

Kumi, 61, was an innocent bystander during a sting operation. He was shot by an undercover NYPD officer while allegedly standing near a suspect. **No officers have been charged.**

Sept. 7, 2015, Wayne Wheeler, Detroit, MI

A Lathrop police officer was grilling in his backyard when Wheeler, his 44-year-old neighbor, allegedly jumped the fence. The officer fought Wheeler and struck him in the head, knocking him down. Wheeler was pronounced dead at the scene by a medic. **No officers have been charged.**

Sept. 23, 2015, Keith McLeod, Baltimore, MD

An employee at a pharmacy called police to report that McLeod had tried to use a fake prescription. The responding officer spotted McLeod in a parking lot near the pharmacy and fatally shot him after claiming he reached "around to the small of his back and abruptly [whipped] his hand around and [pointed] it toward the officer, as if with a weapon," according to police. He was19-years-old and unarmed. **No officers have been charged.**

Sept. 28, 2015, Junior Prosper, Miami, FL

Junior Prosper crashed the car he was driving, a cab, on the highway and allegedly began to run away. An officer chased Prosper, claiming Prosper bit his finger before the officer shot and killed him. Prosper's mother, Marie, said the police were not telling the truth about him. "He's very nice, he's a person who respects all types of people. He's not aggressive. Whoever said that is lying." He leaves behind three children, and his wife is expecting a fourth. **No officers have been charged.**

Oct. 27, 2015, Anthony Ashford, San Diego, CA

A San Diego Harbor officer claimed he confronted Ashford, 29, after seeing him "looking into cars" near Nimitz Boulevard. After being tasered, police claim Ashford reached for the officer's gun before being shot and killed. **No officers have been charged.**

Nov. 1, 2015, Alonzo Smith, Washington, DC

Alonzo Smith, 27, died while handcuffed in the custody of DC special police officers. Special police officers are armed security guards licensed by the city. **No officers have been charged.**

Nov. 11, 2015, Michael Lee Marshall, Denver, CO

Marshall, a 50-year-old mentally ill man, apparently posed no physical threat when three sheriff's deputies restrained him into unconsciousness at the Denver jail. He died after nine days on life support. **No officers have been charged.**

Nov. 15, 2015, Richard Perkins, Oakland, CA

Oakland police were towing vehicles near 90th Ave. and Bancroft Ave. when they claim Perkins, 39, approached them and "pointed a firearm in their direction." They shot Perkins multiple times. Police later revealed Perkins' "firearm" was actually a toy gun. **No officers have been charged.**

Nov. 17, 2015, Chandra Weaver, Kansas City, MO

Chandra, 48, was killed by Kansas City, MO police, who crashed their patrol car into the driver's side of her Pontiac Grand Am. **No officers have been charged with a crime.**

Dec. 8, 2015, Miguel Espinal, Bronx, NY

Miguel Espinal, 36, was shot and killed by NYPD officers in an incident that started with a traffic stop in the Bronx. Espinal fled the stop, prompting a police chase that ended in a wrong-way crash. After the crash, Espinal left the vehicle and ran to the surrounding Tibbetts Brook Park, where police killed him. Espinal's family said he ran from officers because he doesn't have a license. "Whether he ran from the cops or not, it doesn't justify that he got shot. It doesn't justify that," Justin Juble, Espinal's brother, said. **No officers have been charged.**

Dec. 20, 2015, Leroy Browning, Palmdale, CA

Deputies say Browning, 30, fled when they were attempting to arrest him for a DUI. They claim he put deputies in a "bear hug" and reached for a firearm before being shot by deputies. **No officers have been charged.**

(9) Engaging in practices to deliberately cover-up their own abuses of power and that of fellow officers

Illustrations of extensive use of cover-charges by police have been included in previous categories above. An additional example is found in the next section. A few officers are beginning to break the "code of silence" and speak out about misconduct by their fellow officers. If an officer protests only within his department, administrators often ignore such protests. Furthermore, the officer who is courageous enough to speak out is usually subjected to harassment by his colleagues.[31]

One tactic used by police to cover-up killings is known as the "throw-away gun." This involves police planting on the victim a gun which will not be easily traced to the officers. One such case occurred in Houston, Texas in February 1977. A 17-year-old was shot by one officer as the youth was held on the ground by another officer. To make it appear that the victim had been armed so the officers could claim self-defense, a 22-caliber pistol was planted on the body. Eventually the gun was traced to the police property room; it was one of a number of weapons supposedly destroyed in 1968.

Cover-charging, failure to speak out or actually giving false accounts of events in order to protect fellow officers, and creation of false evidence are some of the crimes police engage in to hide their own misdeeds.

D. Mythical Remedies under the Law

Throughout the history of the Unites States, law has been the politically motivated instrument of racism. It has been used both overtly and covertly to enforce and legitimize enslavement, segregation, murder, and theft of land as well as for systematic political, social, and economic oppression of minorities. As a Black lawyer, teacher and student of history, this author could no longer participate without comment in the illusions of justice, in that endless and intricate labyrinth of legal process which holds tantalizing promises of relief, but which in practice merely validate the results of the proceedings tainted with racism and political expediency.

A. Criminal Sanctions

Because of the interrelated roles of the police and the District Attorney's Office, that Office has not been and cannot be an effective instrument for controlling police violence.[32]

In theory, police misconduct can be deterred by the possibility that an officer may be prosecuted under state criminal statutes for complaints ranging from murder in the first degree to simple assault and battery. Also, federal statutes provide for the imposition of criminal sanctions under 18 U.S.C. Section 241-242.[33] But police agencies in the United States make the arrests and gather the evidence upon which government prosecutors rely. Consequently, under these circumstances, District Attorneys and

U. S. Attorneys are reluctant to prosecute officers upon whom they must depend for the successful completion of other prosecutions they initiate. Thus an atmosphere of protection from external investigation settles in, and the police, unlike other citizens, are freed from the fear of punishment. Prosecutors exercise their discretion by not filing charges against officers whose actions make them liable for criminal prosecution.

Illustrative of the degree of hesitancy of prosecutors to file charges against police officers is the fact that there were no indictments against police officers in Los Angeles from 1950 to 1967. When this lack of prosecution is coupled with the fact that a majority of the victims were non-white, it is apparent why minorities view the courts and law enforcement establishment in the United States as being indistinguishable.

Prosecutors also collaborate with police in filing "cover charges"—i.e., charges against the victims of police abuse rather than charges against those who perpetrated the brutality. A vivid example of cover-charging is the case of Wallace Davis, a 25-year-old Black man living in Chicago. Davis had surprised two men in the act of robbing the restaurant he owned and called the police for assistance. The police did not respond promptly to the call and the robbers managed to flee. Finally Davis left his business, only to have the police arrive and assume he was one of the culprits. He tried to explain that he was the owner of the restaurant, but complied with the officers' orders. After the officer searched Davis, he was kicked to the ground and shot in the back. As Davis pled with the officer not to shoot or kick him again, the officer put his gun between Davis' eyes and said, "Die, Nigger, die or else I'll kill you." Subsequently, charges were filed against him for attempted murder. No criminal charges have been placed against the officer involved in the shooting.[34]

Even if the intrinsic conflicts of interest arising from the inter-related roles of prosecutors and police officers in prosecutions of police crimes were abated, *the federal criminal statutes, 18 U.S.C. Section 241-242 were never designed adequately to curb the widespread, arbitrary and unreasonable physical abuse described in the preceding section of this paper.* U.S. Federal District Judge Jon O. Newman has pointed out the limitation of those statutes which makes it difficult to successfully prosecute a criminal case against law enforcement agents under these statutes: the statute "requires not only evidence that a constitutional right was denied, but proof beyond a reasonable doubt that the wrongdoer acted with specific intent to deny such a right. That requirement, never easily met, coupled with the understandable reluctance of jurors to brand as criminals those who, however misguidedly, are seeking to enforce the law, assures that, even when prosecutions are brought, convictions will be rare."[35]

The process of insulating police from external investigation and imposition of sanctions is further entrenched by the investigative processes used in the few cases where charges are filed. Police departments and the officers within these departments have initiated, approved, enforced and pursued internal investigative practices and procedures which are calculated to and do result in the acquiescence to and approval of denials of citizens' rights by police officers.[36]

One researcher[37] discusses the following investigative procedures which constitute additional protections for police against successful prosecution by the District Attorney's Office:

(1) An unusually heavy initiative and burden of proof is placed on the complainant. It is customary that, when a complaint of criminal conduct is made against anyone other than a police officer, a positive effort is made to follow-up, find supporting witnesses, and so forth. In the case of complaints against the police, the bulk of the file is made up of statements by police witnesses.

(2) Witnesses against the police are generally examined in a hostile atmosphere and their testimony unfairly deprecated.

(3) Police never take lie detector tests and always insist that the complainant take one. Refusal by officers to take lie detector tests, even those administered by the police department itself, is understandable in light of the refusal of the Fraternal Order of Police to supply free counsel to an accused police officer if he submits to such a test.[38] When a complainant agrees to take a test, it is administered by a police lieutenant under circumstances not disclosed in the files. The lieutenant's report of the complainant's performance is entirely summary: "Complainant appears to be lying."

(4) While the police investigators are free to interview anyone during the course of the investigation, officers involved in an incident

of police brutality are under orders not to talk with anyone outside the police department while the investigation is pending. This restraint prevents the complainant from acquiring a freshly recalled account of what happened, even though the police can obtain such an account. By the time anyone else is allowed to interview the accused officer(s), the insulation has solidified, contradictions have been ironed out, and informal pressures have been brought to bear on fellow officers to keep them from saying anything which would prejudice the hearing against the officer.

Notwithstanding the availability of the criminal statutes which provide relief from violations of law at the hands of law enforcement agents, very few officers are convicted, and, if convicted, the sentences imposed are so inappropriate the victims and the community interpret them as a miscarriage of justice.[39]

It is a myth that remedies under the law currently exist to prevent abuse of power by law enforcement officers in the United States. It is a myth because

(1) The interrelated roles of police and prosecutors constitute a built-in conflict of interest preventing the impartial initiation of prosecution against law enforcement officers who perpetrate physical and psychological abuse on citizens.

(2) The federal criminal statutes require a nearly impossible defense to be presented by the complainant.

(3) Investigation procedures carried out by the police department which also hires the accused officer are designed to give maximum protection to the officer and little, if any, aid to the complainant.

B . Civil Remedies—Suing the Lawbreakers

When victims of police abuse seek relief in court for police misconduct, they find that the burden of proof required to establish a case against the defending police officer is almost insurmountable. The high burden of proof placed upon the complainant, the jury's racial bias, the ignorance and poverty of the victim, and the prevailing nationwide clamour for law and order all operate to foreclose the courts as an effective forum for relief.[40] Furthermore, the availability and application of civil damages in federal courts have been severely restricted[41] and similarly, but to a lesser extent, civil damages do not serve a compensatory or deterrent function in the federal or state court context.[42]

As a practical matter, the principal federal statute authorizing a damage suit for deprivation of constitutional rights is [42] U.S.C. Section 1983.[43] The use of damage action became a virtual necessity after the U.S. Supreme Court in a series of cases slammed the court doors shut in the faces of victims of police crimes by severely restricting the power of the federal courts to intervene through injunctive actions into patently gross illegal patterns of police crimes.[44]

Newman[45] argues that, whenever it appears that the Constitution or laws of the United States have been violated, the United States itself should be permitted to sue to redress the wrong. That proposition has been dealt a very serious setback by the incredible decision of the United States District Court for the Eastern District of Pennsylvania in its decision in *United States v. City of Philadelphia.*[46] In dismissing this law suit, the Court held that the Attorney General of the United States lacked the constitutional authority to bring such a lawsuit[47] and further accused the Justice Department of "abuse of power."[48]

Since the efficacy of a civil action depends upon adjudication before an impartial jury, the impact of intrinsic race and class biases affect the ultimate decisions of the fact-finders. A group of researchers reporting on their findings on racial prejudice in jury determinations in Connecticut noted that white plaintiffs won approximately 43% of their cases while Black plaintiffs won only 19% of their cases.[49]

Racism unquestionably impacts the difference in damage awards between successful white and Black plaintiffs. This conclusion is supported by the results of the Connecticut study which revealed that, although the total number of verdicts in favor of plaintiffs in general was small, the award differential was unmistakable; for example, the average award for the three successful whites was over $7600; the average award for the three successful Blacks was $1400.[50]

It is important to examine this pattern of damage awards against the backdrop of an inherent racial bias in the jury selection process in the United States. In many court districts, juries are selected from a pool of names drawn from voter registration lists from that area. Blacks do not register to vote in the same proportions as do whites, and thus fewer are included on the juror lists. Since jurors, when interviewed, explain their inability to reach a verdict as a function of racial attitudes, different lifestyles, backgrounds, and dealings with the police, and because defense attorneys concede they prefer all-white, middle-class juries, it is clear that a jury selection process that regularly includes few Blacks systematically discriminates against members of oppressed minorities, whom we have already seen are disproportionately the victims of police misconduct. Thus entrenchment of racism which characterizes police abuse of power is given additional support through court responses to the victims ' attempts to gain relief.

If one of the objectives in civil suits against the police is to compensate individuals for violations of their constitutional rights, then major impediments operate to nullify that objective. It has been argued that a more significant objective, albeit more theoretical than actually obtainable, is to deter police misconduct.[51] However, to the extent that the deterrent effect depends chiefly upon holding those responsible for police crimes financially accountable, the facts demonstrate that the realization of this objective is also unattainable. In most jurisdictions, police officers are provided free legal counsel and are indemnified for any settlement or judgment by the municipality or its insurance carrier. Some municipalities are self-insured; others purchase insurance from a carrier for the benefit of their employees. Under these circumstances, the general procedure followed once a complaint is filed against an officer requires that the insurance company be notified, and it retains an attorney to represent the police officer. If the municipality is self-insured, its corporation counsel handles the police officer's defense.

In summary, when looking at civil remedies available to victims of police abuse, it is again clear that, while the remedies may exist in theory, in actuality they are myths. This is true for three reasons:

(1) Victims must overcome substantial impediments to present an adequate defense;

(2) Financial awards do not adequately compensate victims for the violations of their constitutional rights;

(3) Both individual police officers and police departments are insulated from the financial burden consequent to a civil law suit.

The inescapable fact facing the victim of police crimes, therefore, is that efforts to sue the lawbreaker in court have almost no impact on controlling or alleviating patterns and practices of police abuse.

Obviously, minorities and the poor who become victims of police crimes in the United States realize that the biased legal process is manipulated to subvert national standards of decency and democracy and to encourage an increasing national tolerance of domestic indifference to brutality and injustice which places the wrongdoer beyond the reach of the law.

Endnotes

[1] Kobler, Arthur L., "Police Homicide in a Democracy," *Journal of Social Sciences,* Vol. 31, No. 1, Winter 1975, p. 163.

[2] Minority community witnesses told the National Minority Advisory Council on Criminal Justice that police often use excessive and deadly force against them to quell their political activities which are devoted to improving their status in American society; to evict people who are behind in their rent or mortgages; to arrest people who complain to or argue with a storekeeper who sells rotten foods at high prices. Minorities have watched police stand by or even aid in allowing right-wing groups to beat, maim or kill minority peoples.

[3] *Sourcebook of Criminal Justice Statistics,* 1978, United States Department of Justice (Washington, DC), "Table 2.35 -- Ratings of Local Police-by Demographic Characteristics, 13 Selected American Cities (Aggregate), 1975." p. 301.

[4] *Report of the National Advisory Commission on Civil Disorders,* Government Printing Office (Washington, DC) 1968, p. 158.

[5] Takagi, Paul, from his statement made to the consultation on "Police Practices and the Preservation of Civil Rights" sponsored by the United States Commission on Civil Rights, Washington, DC, December 12-13, 1978, p. 34.

[6] From a statement by Drew Days, Assistant Attorney General, Civil Rights' Division, United States Department of Justice, at a consultation on "Police Practices and the Preservation of Civil Rights" sponsored by the United States Commission on Civil Rights, Washington, DC, December 12-13, 1978, p. 139.

[7] Hudson, Brian, "Police Abuse and National Unrest," *The Guardian,* June 25, 1980, p. 6.

[8] Rollins, Thomas M., "Mean Beats: Police Brutality in America," *Politics Today,* p. 50.

[9] Figures for the number of civilians killed by police have to be obtained from U.S. Public Health Service data. One indicator that killings and beatings of civilians by police are tacitly considered outside the framework of the justice system is that there are no statistics on these subjects in the U. S. Justice Department's *Sourcebook of Criminal Justice Statistics.* In contrast, the Justice Department each year publishes two detailed sets of statistics about law enforcement agents who have been killed by citizens: one set in the *Sourcebook* and one set in a monograph entitled *Law Enforcement Officers Killed.*

[10] Sherman, Lawrence W. and Robert H. Langworthy, "Measuring Homicide by Police Officers," *The Journal of Criminal Law and Criminology,* Vol. 70, No. 4, December 1979, p. 546-560.

[11] Blacks make up 12% of the U.S. population. We have estimated Black males are about half of that number to arrive at the 6% figure for Black male population.

[12] Takagi, Paul, "Death by 'Police Intervention,'" *A Community Concern: Police Use of Deadly Force,* National Institute of Law Enforcement and Criminal Justice, Washington, DC, p. 33.

[13] Black, Donald J. and Albert J, Reiss, "Patterns of Behavior in Police and Citizen Transactions," in Reasons, Charles E. and Jack L. Kuykendall (eds.), *Race, Crime, and Society* (Pacific Palisades, CA: Goodyear, 1972) p. 203; and Piliavin, Irvin and Scott Briar, "Police Encounters with Juveniles," in Cressey, Donald and David Ward (eds.), *Delinquency, Crime, and Social Process* (New York: Harper and Row, 1969), p. 159.

[14] Kobler, Arthur, "Figures (and Perhaps Some Facts on Police Killings of Civilians in the United States, 1965-1969," from synopsis in *A Community Concern: Police Use of Deadly Force,* National Institute of Law Enforcement and Criminal Justice, Washington, DC, p. 74.

[15] Statement of Anthony E. Jackson, Esq., Director, Police Project, Public Interest Law Center

of Philadelphia, April 19, 1979; p. 1.

[16] Beer, Todd, "Police Killing of Blacks: Data for 2015, 2016, 2017, and First Half of 2018," *TheSocietyPages.org: Sociology Toolbox*, March, 2018, https://thesocietypages.org/toolbox/police-killing-of-blacks/, (May 9, 2019).

[17] For further information on any of the cases in this section, contact the author: Lennox Hinds, (Professor Emeritus, Rutgers University, Department of Administration of Justice), 126 Spring Meadow Dr., Bluffton, SC 29910.

[18] Figures from answers to interrogations in the case *United States v. City of Philadelphia et al.,* Civil Action No. 79-2937, Eastern District Court of Pennsylvania.

[19] "Up Against the Law," *Equal Times: Boston's Newspaper for Working Women,* Vol. 5, No. 80, February 3, 1980, p. 9.

[20] "Gordon Police Told Not to Stop Couple, Ex-officer Testifies," *North Platte Telegraph,* North Platte, Nebraska, July 2, 1979.

[21] The data is taken from answers to interrogatories in the case, *United States of America v. City of Philadelphia* (note 18 supra). Data of this sort is available for each of the categories of offenses discussed in this paper. We are only including this one set just to convey the enormity of the problem of law enforcement officers who abuse their power.

[22] Rollins, *supra*, p. 49. Rollins points out that six detectives convicted of criminal charges for excessive use of force during interrogations are still working for the Philadelphia police.

[23] Schwartz, Louis B., "Complaints against the Police: Experience of the Community Rights Division of the Philadelphia District Attorney's Office," *University of Pennsylvania Law Review,* v.118:1023, 1970, p. 1033.

[24] Schwartz, p. 1032-1033.

[25] "Chicago Police Methods Exposed," *Ms. Magazine,* June 1979, p. 23.

[26] The U.S. Supreme Court in the landmark decision in *Mapp v. Ohio,* 367 U. S. 643 (1961) read the exclusionary rule into the Fourth Amendment, as incorporated against the states: "The exclusionary rule is an essential part of both the Fourth and Fourteenth Amendments…."

[27] See examples of Mr. Ramirez in category (1) and Mr. Morris in category (6).

[28] See *Stone v. Powell,* 428 U. S. 465 (1976).

[29] Jackson, note 15 *supra*, p. 3.

[30] "L.A. Cops Use of Deadly Force Rises," *The Guardian,* July 23, 1980, p. 7.

[31] Sherman, Lawrence, "The Breakdown of the Police Code of Silence," *Criminal Law Bulletin,* Mar./Apr. 1978.

[32] Schwartz, note 23 supra, p. 1024.

[33] The legislative history of 18 U.S.C. Section 241-242 demonstrates that, although these provisions were designed to provide protection to all inhabitants of the United States without regard to race, the level of violence visited upon Black citizens in the southern states continued to rise. Congress finally passed the Ku Klux Klan Act, 17 Stat. 13 (1871) in a further attempt to address the problem. Notwithstanding these provisions, Black citizens continued to suffer severe deprivations of their constitutional rights under the color of law—and they still suffer today.

[34] Payne, Ethel L., "The Judge Said 'No,'" *The Chicago Defender,* Oct. 14, 1977.

[35] Newman, Jon O., "Suing the Lawbreakers: Proposals to Strengthen the Section 1983 Damage Remedy for Law Enforcers' Misconduct," *Yale Law Journal,* Vol. 87, No. 3, January 1978, p. 449-450.

[36] Police investigations of police are not and cannot be neutral. They tend to be defensive of the police and slanted against complainants. Assuming that investigating officers are attempting to do a good job in most cases, the conflict of interest which frustrates a fair and

credible disposition of citizens' complaints by the District Attorney's office operates even more strongly when the police department investigates itself on complaints filed by persons whom the police department has already identified as violent criminals, some with long records. The investigating officers or the commanding officers who report on the incident are often superiors who have previously given favorable performance ratings to the subject policeman and who are likely to continue in a daily working relationship with him.

[37] Schwartz, note 23 *supra*, p. 1028-1031.

[38] Schwartz, note 23 *supra*, p. 1029.

[39] The most recent, widely known example of such a miscarriage of justice was the acquittal of the officers involved in the flashlight bludgeoning of Arthur McDuffey in Miami.

Another widely publicized case was that of Jose Campos Torres. Torres was arrested for drunkedness, handcuffed and beaten severely by three Houston police. One of them then pushed Torres, still hand-cuffed, into a bayou, saying, "Let's see if this wetback can swim."

The three officers received no punishment from the state court that tried them. They were then tried in federal court for violating Torres' civil rights and sentenced to one year. "I thought the federal government was going to take care of everything," said the victim's mother. "It's just a slap in the face."

In stark contrast to the despair of Ms. Torres was the jubilation of a fellow Houston police officer, "That ain't bad at all. They won't be there [in prison] but six months." (These responses of Ms. Torres and the police officer were reported in *The Washington Post,* March 29, 1978.)

One study by Arthur Kobler found that, out of 1500 police-caused deaths, only 3 resulted in a criminal conviction of a police officer for homicide. (Kobler, *Journal of Social Issues,* v. 31, n. 1, 1975, p. 177.) This is a conviction rate of 0.2%. In contrast, between 1965 and 1974, of 1,337 civilians identified in killing law enforcement officers, 827 were convicted of murder or a charge related to murder or committed to a mental hospital; this is a 62% conviction rate. In addition to this remarkable conviction rate, an additional 175 people (13%) were killed on the spot and another 44 either committed suicide or died in custody. Thus 78% of people identified were either killed on the spot, died, or were convicted. (Based on figures found in Table 3.103, "Persons Identified in the Killing of Law Enforcement Officers, by Type of Disposition, U.S., 1965-1974 (Aggregate)," *Sourcebook of Criminal Justice Statistics,* 1978, p. 464.)

[40] *U.S. Commission on Civil Rights Report,* Vol. 5, p. 25, note 63 (1961). (Hereinafter cited as 1961 *Civil Rights Report.*) Figures given by Drew Days (note 6 *supra*) reveal that of 10,000 complaints filed in 1977, 26 officers were convicted; this is a 0.2% conviction rate.

[41] See 1961 *Civil Rights Report, supra,* p. 25 at note 70-71.

[42] *1961 Civil Rights Report, supra* note 25 at 80. The President's Commission on Law Enforcement and Administration o f Justice Task Force Report: The Police 199 (1967).

43 Section 1983 provides: "Every person who under color of any statute, ordinance, regulation, custom, or usage, of any State or Territory, subjects, or causes to be subjected, any citizen of the United States or other person within the jurisdiction thereof to the deprivation of any rights, privileges, or immunities secured by the Constitution and laws, shall be liable to the party injured in an action at law, suit in equity, or other proper proceeding for redress." 42 U.S.C. Section1983 (1970).

[44] See, for example, *Rizzo v. Goode,* 423 U.S. 362 (1976). In the *Goode* case, the plaintiffs contended that certain police officers were biased against Blacks and other minority groups and habitually violated their legal and constitutional rights; that the proclivities of these officers were well known to their superiors in the department; and that the persons in control of the supervision of police conduct, by failing to take appropriate disciplinary action, condoned these illegal and unconstitutional activities as a matter of policy. Plaintiffs in *Goode* offered

a mass of evidence, including expert testimony, to show that the existing complaint procedure was inadequate and that departmental resistance to the creation or implementation of adequate complaint procedures justified the conclusion that it was the policy of the department to condone racially discriminatory actions by the police.

45 Newman, *supra*, p. 453.

46 In this far-reaching lawsuit, the United States, through its Attorney General, attempted to secure broad declaratory and equitable relief against an allegedly pervasive pattern of police abuse in Philadelphia, the effect of which was to deny basic federal constitutional rights to persons of all races, colors and national origins. This abuse was said to consist of such practices as, for example, using deadly force where it is unnecessary, physically abusing arrestees and prisoners, extracting information and concessions by means of physical brutality, stopping persons without probable cause and conducting illegal searches and seizures.

47 In his decision, Judge Ditter, at page 36 of his opinion in *United States v. City of Philadelphia et al.,* Civil Action No. 79-2937, says the following:

> "While pondering all this, it is important to remember that the Attorney General and his subordinates are not elected officials. They are not subject to the sobering influence of the ballot box, and they never need to worry about the whim or desire of any electorate. Yet they stand before this court today and claim the power to decide what will serve the nation's interest and the people's 'welfare.' I am persuaded that such a power was never intended to lie in the hands of an executive appointee. Rather, I hold that these decisions are best made by Congress alone….
>
> "It is clear to me, therefore, that the authority to bring a lawsuit of this kind should never be vested in the Attorney General. This conclusion is fully in accord with the decisions of the Courts of Appeals for the Fourth and Ninth Circuits in *Mattson* and *Solomon, supra.*"

48 See Judge Ditter's opinion *supra* at p. 39.

49 See "Project: Suing the Police in Federal Court," *Yale Law Journal,* Vol. 88, No. 4, March 1979, note 62 at p. 794.

50 *Ibid.*

51 Takagi argues with some persuasion that "to pay money to the victim or someone else representing him is distributive justice and not social justice. Distributive justice means simply 'what's good for the goose is good for the gander.' Social justice, on the other hand, means that the rights of liberty, equality, and security are not elements to be exchanged for money or for property rights; nor should they be expressed in relative terms, that is, greater or less than property rights. One person's life and liberty is the same as the next person's. But in a society that equates the right of private property with human rights, they become inevitably reduced to standards and consequences that value some lives less than others. The system of coercion and punishment is intimately connected with the unequal distribution of wealth, and provides the legitimization under the perverted notion that 'ours is a government of laws' even to kill in order to maintain social priorities based upon property rights." Note 12 *supra*, p. 37.

Chapter Eighteen
Prison Conditions

No more striking or persuasive argument in support of petitioners' contention that the criminal justice system of the United States is a façade for gross and shocking violations of the legal and human rights of minorities and poor citizens can be made than an examination of the prisons of the society. The Thirteenth Amendment to the United States Constitution provides:

"Neither slavery nor involuntary servitude, except as a *punishment for crime* whereof the party shall have been duly convicted, shall exist within the United States, or any place subject to its jurisdiction." (Emphasis added.)

Although the Thirteenth Amendment abolished one class of the oppressed, it provides legal sanction for the creation and maintenance of another. The prisons and jails in the United States have become bulging warehouses for the poor Black minority, and for the uneducated and unemployed. They provide a legally sanctioned instrumental for social, political and economic control. Prisoners lose, as a matter of law, their civil and constitutional rights and are subjected to treatment designed to divest them of personal and cultural identity. Upon entrance into prison, one is stripped naked, forced to undergo a rectal and other body cavity searches, denied personal clothing and effects, and given an institutional number in place of a name. One prisoner has described this process as follows:

> "They put you thru (sic) a status degradation ceremony, stripping you—deliberately and with relish in some cases—of all self-esteem, self-respect, human sensibility, and sense of responsibility. This is designed to punish you, humble you, humiliate you, and shame you. I've seen guys in here that have been literally destroyed, broken, turned into a mass of jelly, into vegetables."[1]

One result of the harshness of prison life is a suicide rate among prisoners that is disproportionate to that of society as a whole. For example, in New York City jails, during the eight week period between August and October,

197, six persons in New York State correctional facilities committed suicide; in 1973, the rate was one death for every 1,000 prisoners, six times the rate for the general population.[2]

Prisoners do not have a right to education, vocational training, meaningful work, or other rehabilitative opportunities while incarcerated. These opportunities are "privileges" which may be granted or denied at the discretion of local authorities, contrary to the spirit and letter of Sections 65 and 66 of the United Nations Standard Minimum Rules for the Treatment of Prisoners and Related Recommendations (hereinafter referred to as the U.N. Minimum Rules) which state respectively in pertinent part that:

> "65. The treatment of persons sentenced to imprisonment or a similar measure shall have as its purpose, so far as the length of the sentence permits, to establish in them the will to lead law-abiding and self-supporting lives after their release and to fit them to do so. The treatment shall be such as will encourage their self-respect and develop their sense of responsibility.
>
> 66. (1) To these ends, all appropriate means shall be used, including religious care in the countries where this is possible, education, vocational guidance and training, social casework, employment counseling, physical development and strengthening of moral character, in accordance with the individual needs of each prisoner, taking account of his social and criminal history, his physical and mental capacities and aptitudes, his personal temperament, the length of his sentence and his prospects after release."

Typically the norm in prisons or jail of the United States is enforced idleness in physically degrading conditions, often accompanied by physical and emotional brutality. Prisoners leave prison less able to lead a productive, law-abiding life; typically angrier; less able to find employment; and more likely to commit future criminal offenses. In these ways the prison system in the United States is a significant factor in the perpetuation of crime rather than its alleviation.

Many prisoners spend the majority of their time locked in small, dark, dirty cells, without being provided meaningful physical or mental activity. Many of the prisoners most articulate on the inhumanity and brutality of the penal system are kept in solitary confinement, forced to spend as much as twenty-three hours a day in their cells, allowed out only for short periods of recreation and infrequent showers. All other activities occur within the parameters of the cramped cell under perpetual artificial light.

Although most prisoners who enter the system are uneducated and unemployed, only about 5 percent of the prison budget throughout the 50 states goes for services labeled as rehabilitation.[3]

When prisoners are given the opportunity to work, it is to provide physical maintenance of the institution and not to train or provide experience that will prepare them for meaningful work in the community upon release. A 1972 survey of vocational training in prisons showed that of a total population of 130,800 prisoners only 12,868, or less than 10%, were enrolled in programs designed to provide work skills and trades. More than half of the institutions evaluated offered only five or fewer vocational programs and, in all, only 855 vocational programs were in existence.[4] An analysis by a member of the Federal Bureau of Prisons staff of such programs underscores their cursory and serious character. She concedes that much of the training whether in institutional maintenance or prison industries, or in vocational training shops and related classroom instruction, uses obsolete equipment and production standards that are much lower than those in private industry. As a result, she concludes that most prison occupational training programs have been useless in preparing prisoners for post-release employment.[5]

The resources allocated to such vocational programs confirm the view widely held in the minority community of the United States that the role of prisons is to provide warehouses for poor people and not to eliminate crime. The maintenance of an under-skilled menial labor force who will continue to be underemployed and unemployed after release is the true objective of the prison system.

The following conclusion is a reasonable inference from the facts:

> "One who visits prisons commonly sees prisoners lying on their beds, milling about courtyards, lifting barbells and passing the time with other forms of indolence. Prisoners who are not assigned to prison industries are put to work keeping the institution clean. Thus most employment in prison is simple housekeeping: the maintenance

> of the institution overcomes the purposes of its existence. When we visited the federal penitentiary in Atlanta, we discovered that half the prisoners worked in a textile mill making mail bags; the other half devoted their working hours to maintaining the institution. According to a letter we received from one inmate, 'The institution is now in the ludicrous position of offering valuable training to arm convicts for jobs in a highly competitive society: plunging johns, mopping floors, mowing grass. The truth is most time is wasted.'
>
> "To cite a few illustrative examples, the San Quentin Prison in California operates a cotton mill that, according to former prison employees, is the only one in the state—and thus hardly good preparation for future jobs. The irrelevance of prison labor to the world of work is not restricted to California. Recently a New York judge, on questioning a fugitive about his failure to rehabilitate himself during his imprisonment in New York's Green Haven Prison, asked whether he had been taught a trade. The defendant replied, 'I was learning textile weaving, but there isn't a textile mill in the state of New York, Your Honor.'"[6]

It is instructive to note that 58% of the prisoners thus employed as domestic help and producers of "State Use" items and services (institutional laundry, license plates, mail bags, road building, farming, *et al.*) are paid less that twenty cents per hour, and twenty-nine percent of those are not paid at all, despite the economic value of their productivity.[7]

In the words of the judge in *Ruffin v. Commonwealth,* (62 Va. 790, (1871), p. 796), prisoners are "slaves of the state." As such, the prisoners do not have the right to choose to work or choose not to work. It may be required or it may be forbidden, and, if ordered, may not be refused, even though the work assigned is inconsistent with a prisoner's health, physical constitution, or level of skills. As a worker, a prisoner in the United States is subject to the arbitrary and often capricious discretion of his keepers. In light of the segregation of disproportionate number of minorities and poor people in prisons, the conditions of work and other aspects of the conditions of incarceration reflect the patterns and practices of racism.

In no particular do American prisons comport with United Nations Standard Minimum Rules for the Treatment of Prisoners. Most particularly, petitioners urge this body to review these charges in light of the mandate of the following U.N. standards:

> "60.(1) The regime of the institution should seek to minimize any differences between prison life and life at liberty which tend to lessen the responsibility of the prisoner or the respect due to their dignity as human beings.
>
> "60.(2) Before the completion of the sentence, it is desirable that the necessary steps be taken to ensure for the prisoner a gradual return to life in society. This aim may be achieved, depending on the case, by a pre-release regime organized in the same institution or another appropriate institution, or by release on trial under some kind of supervision which must not be entrusted to the police but should be combined with effective social aid.
>
> "61. The treatment of prisoners should emphasize not their exclusion from the community, but their continuing part in it. Community agencies should, therefore, be enlisted wherever possible to assist the staff of the institution in the task of social rehabilitation of the prisoners. There should be in connextion (sic) with every institution social workers charged with the duty of maintaining and improving all desirable relations of a prisoner with his family and with valuable social agencies. Steps should be taken to safeguard, to the maximum extent compatible with the law and the sentence, the rights relating to civil interests, social security rights and other social benefits of prisoners."

Prisons in the United States serve to isolate from, rather than integrate the offender into, society. Most prisons are located in rural areas, often hundreds of miles from urban centers where most offenders have lived. Isolation and segregation of inmates are the hallmarks of the American prison system.

> "Historically the correctional institution was based on the concept of separation, punishment, and isolation. Prisons, both rural and urban, were built to keep the prisoner in and the community out. It simply was not considered necessary to make provisions for visiting, family relations, community involvement, or work releases; and there was no effort to secure staffs that were professional and of racial balance to match the racial makeup of the inmates. The old corrections succeeded

in isolation and control functions but was (sic) markedly unsuccessful in preparing offenders for life in the real world."[8]

New correctional institutions have perpetuated prisons' isolation:

"This hope and the reality that we found were two different things. With the exceptions of jails which were usually located in the county seats and small special purpose facilities such as halfway houses, all of the new correctional institutions which we visited were rurally located. They were far removed from universities, unable to be reached by public transportation, and seemingly designed to discourage citizen and community involvement. In addition, they were usually staffed by rural person unsympathetic, even antipathetic, to the aspirations, life styles, and ethnic values of the prisoners who were mostly Black, Brown, Red and urban."[9]

Physical isolation of prisons serves to destroy a prisoner's social ties and communications with families and society. Isolation geographically creates circumstances for the most heinous violations of the human rights of prisoners, since they are subject to the almost unbridled discretion of prison administrators, hidden from the scrutiny of the outside world.

"Screened from public visibility and immune from effective accountability to other branches of the government, the predictable abuses took place and continue occur. There is almost nothing the prison cannot do, and does not do, to inmates, including keeping them beyond the expiration dates of their sentences (via procedures declaring them dangerous or mentally ill). It can and does transfer them far from their families; limit and restrict their visitors; censor what they read, what they may write; decide whom they may associate with inside, what medicine, what education they may or may not have, whether the will be totally locked up, for weeks, months, occasionally even years, or enjoy limited physical freedom. Inmates' personal property may be misplaced and destroyed, incoming and outgoing letters sometimes not delivered, and, in the extreme, prisoners may be starved, brutalized and killed.

"Administrative decisions within the prison including punitive measures such as transfer and solitary confinement are not subject to due process procedures and are ordinarily immune from review....

"Prison administrators understand the vulnerability and powerlessness of inmates, parolees, and their families. Indeed, reprisals can be so severe against prisoners who attempt to obtain redress in any way but the most supplicant manner that many used to prefer (and some still do) to suffer in silence, rather than risk years in solitary or a denial of parole. Administrators act with total, arbitrary authority to avoid any action—whether legislative or judicial, or from the community or from attorneys—which asserts an inmate's rights or desires as against the desires of the prison system. The taxpayer's money is spent to pay the Attorney General to oppose any attempts in court to change these conditions, whether it be to get access to prisoners' files, or have inmates represented at the parole hearing, or to permit the public to see the strip cells or hear the prisoners testify in open court as to these conditions."[10]

As in all other aspects of the criminal justice system of the United States, racism permeates all aspects of the prison system, as Blacks and minority prisoners are placed in a position of powerlessness under domination by white guards and prison administrators. Although minorities are at least seventy-five percent of a state's prison population, only two states in the U.S. employ more than thirty percent minority correction officers. For example, in New York State where minority prisoners comprise seventy-five percent of the population, only eighteen percent of corrections staff are minority people.[11]

"None of the maximum security facilities are in or even very near the state's large cities, and thus they are staffed by rural whites who entered government employment for pretty much the same reasons a million other employees of state and local government in New York did: their fathers or mothers had worked for the state, job opportunities were scarce, pay, advancement opportunities and fringe benefits were relatively favorable.

"Thus, the 29 facilities, from Ossining on the lower Hudson to Clinton on the Canadian border and Attica an hour from Lake Erie are, not by design but by happenstance, racial hotbeds. They bring urban minority inmates into a pointed relationship with the power and authority of government, and the upstate guards into daily confrontation with the products of crumbling social order. It is an unnatural situation for both groups, and one that cannot avoid breeding hostility.

"Racial antagonism is certainly a major factor, if not the exclusive cause, in prisoners' protests against the system that confines them. The discovery last year of an active Ku Klux Klan membership among guards at the Eastern Correctional Facility at Napanoch illustrates the kind of racial hostility that can be spread in prison staffs.

"Thus incidents with racial overtones are common in the prisons, though with some reform and luck the Department has avoided a repetition of the major revolt at Attica in 1971."[12]

Petitioners presentation herein of necessity is neither exhaustive nor complete on the subject of the brutalization of prisoners in the United States which results from racist and political oppression and which arises to a consistent pattern of human rights violations.

We can but mention for this body's consideration the following nationwide patterns and practices of well-documented abuse for which the class of persons Petitioners represent have no legal or equitable domestic remedies.

(1) The sexual abuse of prisoners, male and female, by guards personally and by their indifference to attacks on young prisoners by the more experienced.[13]

The well-known case of Joan Little who was acquitted of the murder of her jailer who forced her into sexual relations with him is unique only because of her acquittal, which is attributed in large measure to the international and national scrutiny of the trial. She was in many ways prototypical of imprisoned women in the United States and their experiences.

Joan Little is the oldest of nine children. Her educational career was prematurely ended when she left school in the twelfth grade for medical and economic reasons. After that, Joan held jobs as waitress, garment factory worker, and sheet-rock finisher.

In June 1974 she was convicted of breaking, entering, and larceny and given a seven-to-ten year sentence. Instead of being sent to North Carolina Correction Center for Women in Raleigh, North Carolina, after her conviction and while awaiting her appeal, Joan was confined in the women's cellblock of Beaufort County Jail for approximately three months.

During the majority of the three months, Joan was the only woman confined in the cellblock. All the jailers in the Beaufort County Jail are white males.

On August 27, 1974, a jailer, Clarence Alligood, was found dead in the cell assigned to Joan. He was apparently stabbed a number of times with an icepick. The icepick belonged to the jailers and was kept in their desk drawer.

The autopsy report which the prosecution attempted to conceal showed that:

> "His (Alligood's) shoes were in the corridor, socks on feet but otherwise naked from the waist down with open yellow plaid shirt and undershirt on. The left arm was under the body and clutching his pants...extending from his penis to his thigh was a stream of what appeared to be seminal fluid...the urethral fluid was loaded with spermatozoa."

Miss Little fled from the jail and hid from Beaufort County authorities for a week. Although she wanted to turn herself in, she was afraid to do so. On September 3, 1974, Joan surrendered to the State Bureau of Investigation in Raleigh, North Carolina. "The only thing I have to say is the reason I ran is self-defense...if I had stayed in Beaufort County, the authorities there, if they had gotten to me, I know I wouldn't have been able to be here to tell what really happened."

Joan Little remains a symbol of racial injustice and resides in New York State.

(2) The use of chemical weapons on prisoners trapped in confined spaces.

Chemical weapons are in widespread use in American prisons. The chemicals employed include chloroacetophenone, commonly found in tear gas, mace and CN gas, and ortho-chlorobenzylidenemalononitrile, commonly referred to as irritant gas or CS gas. Several instruments are employed to administer the gases: hand-held applicators, various types of grenades, and fog-generating machines. Originally developed for riot control purposes and used in open spaces, they are generally believed to have no adverse effects.

In fact, these gases, in sufficient concentrations, produce serious toxic effects: first and second degree burns to the skin, dermatitis, permanent eye injuries, damage to the respiratory tract including pulmonary eczema and chemically induced pneumonia, and neurological damage including cerebral anoxic necrosis. These toxic effects are particularly indicated when the gases are administered in closed spaces and the victim is mentally disturbed, thus rendering their use in prisons particularly dangerous, since most prison rooms are small and poorly ventilated and prisons contain a high percentage of mentally unstable individuals.

In several documented cases, the use of gas in prison has resulted in death. One such case, in 1975, concerned a 48-year-old Black inmate of the Queens (New York) House of Detention. This individual had been diagnosed as psychotic and was awaiting transfer to a mental hospital when, early one morning, he was found to be agitated and acting erratically, cursing, spitting, and eating soap. A nurse tried to administer a tranquilizing drug to the inmate through the bars of his cell, but was unsuccessful because of his resistance. It was decided to use gas in order to put an end this resistance. Gas was administered twice, followed by the tranquilizer. Approximately one hour after the gas was administered, he was removed from the cell and taken to a psychiatric hospital. The following day, he developed a fever of 107 and succumbed to "massive hemorrhagic bronchial pneumonia" caused by exposure to the gas.

In other cases prisoners have died of extreme mental and physical exhaustion. When gases are used against extremely agitated or psychotic persons, rather than having a sedative effect, they sometimes cause these persons to enter an extremely hyperactive state in which they struggle until all strength is gone and they literally die of exhaustion.

As the example indicates, these weapons are used not only when there is a rebellious group of prisoners who pose a threat to prison security or when a prisoner is armed and dangerous, but also routinely to control disruptive or disorderly individuals. They are commonly used, for example, on the prisoner who refuses to leave his cell when ordered to, or the prisoner who shouts loudly or argues loudly with a guardian, or who perhaps begins to throw items within his cell. In the majority of these cases, the individual is locked securely in a cell and presents no threat of riot, escape, or physical injury.

The use of chemical weapons in such circumstances is clearly unwarranted. Moreover, the use of such potentially dangerous weapons appears to violate internationally established standards for the protection of prisoners. Article 10 of the International Covenant on Civil and Political Rights requires that prisoners be treated "with humanity." Advocates of prison reform have long been attacking this abhorrent method of disciplining inmates. Some successes have been realized, notably the 1976 court decision of *Spain v. Procunier* (US District Court, Northern District of California) and the 1971 decision *Landman v. Royster* (US District Court, Eastern District of Virginia), both of which held gassing of inmates already confined to their cells to be unconstitutional. Also regulations effective 1 March 1978 pertaining to local facilities in New York no longer allow gas to be used "to effect the movement of recalcitrant and belligerent inmates," but require that the use of gas "is necessary to protect any person from serious physical injury."

While such developments are important, they have only local effect. Experts in this area believe that not only is the practice widespread throughout the country, but that in most areas the courts do not give relief to prisoners who complain of this practice unless exceptional circumstances exist, such as permanent injury to the victim. Such judicial reluctance to grant relief does not help curb the practice. The limited success of domestic efforts to remedy this problem after years of indicate that a demonstration of concern by the international community might be timely and appropriate.[14]

(3) The use of prisoners for medical experiments by private drug companies, who have infected prisoners with virulent diseases to test new drugs.[15]

This practice has been suspended by the federal government and some states because of widespread protest and litigation. Informed written consent from experimental subjects is required by the Nuremburg Code. Petitioners question whether any captive person can voluntarily agree to such experimentation when prisoners are offered small comforts, money, and parole considerations as inducements. Internationally agreed-upon standards of human decency must be concerned about the discretion which can and has been used for drug and surgical experimentation. At least one American experimenter thinks that "Criminals in our penitentiaries are fine experimental material—and much cheaper than chimpanzees."[16]

(4) The excessive and medically-contraindicated use of tranquilizing drugs to control the conduct of prisoners without medical supervision.[17]

(5) Psycho-surgical operations on prisoners without consent and for the purpose of behaviour control.[18]

Petitioners suggest that the well-attested and continuing abuse of prisoners by knowing physical and psychological torture, by neglect, and by design constitute patterns and practices of abuse and gross violation of human and legal rights of these Americans because of their race, ethnic identity and political beliefs, for which they have no redress in the United States.

Endnotes

[1] H. Jack Griswold, et al., *An Eye for an Eye.* P. 225.

[2] *Instead of Prisons,* Prison Research Education Action Project, Syracuse, New York, 1976.

[3] Mitford, Jessica, *Kind and Usual Punishment: The Prison Business,* 1973, p. 106.

[4] U.S. Department of Justice, *Job Training and Placement for Offenders and Ex-Offenders,* 1975, p. 8.

[5] Ibid., p. 9.

[6] Singer and Goldfarb, *After Conviction,* 1973.

[7] Sources of this information were provided in Appendix XI in the Original Petition.

[8] Nagle, William, *The New Red Barn,* pp. 47-48.

[9] *Ibid.*

[10] Greenberg, David F. and Fay Stender, "The Prison as a Lawless Agency," *Buffalo Law Review,* (1972) p. 807 and 809.

[11] *Sourcebook of Criminal Justice Statistics,* Table 1.122. Provided in the original Petition in Appendix XI.

[12] Buck, Rinker, "Corrections: Prisoner of Inertia," Empire State Report, May 1978, pp. 143-144.

[13] In addition to the specific case example of Joan Little, documentation of sexual abuse in prison can be found in material such as *Sexual Assault and Forced Homosexual Relationships: Cruel and Unusual Punishment,* 36 Albany L.R. 428 (1972); Weiss and Friar, Terror in Prisons, Bobbs-Merrill, 1974.

[14] The findings of the International Commission of Jurists, published as "United States: The Use of Chemical Weapons in Prison," Review (June, 1978). See also "The Death of John Wesley Thompson," *New York City Board of Corrections Report,* January 29, 1976, which reports on the death of Mr. Thompson while incarcerated in the Queens (New York) House of Detention from the lethal application of tear gas to him by correction guards. It also documents the death of a number of other prisoners as a result of gas.

[15] See, for example, Irvin Gilchrist, "Medical Experimentation on Prisoners Must Stop," Urban Information Interpreters, Inc., College Park, MD, 1974.

[16] Quoted in M.H. Pappworth, MD, *Human Guinea Pigs,* (1967). Petitioners request this forum to investigate widespread rumors that these practices are still being continued in a number of states in the United States today.

[17] See, for example, Mitford, Jessica, *Kind and Usual Punishment, supra.*

[18] See, for example, Breggin, "Psycho Surgery for the Control of Violence," 118 Cong. Rec. E 3380, March 30, 19; Frank Ervin, "Biological Intervention Technologies and Social Control, *American Behavioral Scientist,* Vol. 18, No. 5, May/June 1975, p. 633; Hearings before the Subcommittee on Health of the Committee on Labor and Public Welfare, US Senate, 93rd Cong. *Quality of Healthcare—Human Experimentation,* Part 3, March 7 and 8, 1973, pp. 1029-1060 (hereinafter cited as "Hearings Report"); Hearings before the Subcommittee on Courts, Civil Liberties and the Administration of Justice of the House Committee on the Judiciary, 93rd Cong., *Behavior Modification Programs: Federal Bureau of Prisons,* February 27, 1974, p. 30; Martin Groder, MD, "Psychological, Behavioral and/or Social Research Involving Prisoners as Voluntary Subjects," *Research Involving Prisoners,* The National Commission

for the Protection of Human Subjects of Biomedical and Behavioral Research, 1976; David Rothman, "Behavioral Modification in Total Institutions," *Hastings Center Report,* 5 (February 1975), p. 17.

Chapter Nineteen
Attica Prison Uprising: Mirror of American Prisons

On September 9, 1971, the prisoners at Attica Prison in New York State rebelled against their maltreatment, isolation from loved ones, idleness, over-crowding, physical and mental abuse from corrections guards (who were almost exclusively rural, white males and were unrestrained by supervision), inadequate and nonexistent medical treatment, arbitrary lockup in solitary confinement, and meaningless educational and vocational programs. At the time of the 1971 rebellion, Black and Spanish-speaking prisoners made up seventy percent of the prison population and were from New York City, many hundreds of miles away. Fifty percent of the prison population received twenty-five cents a day for their labors. Prisoners were fed on a daily budget of sixty-five cents each in an atmosphere of daily degradation and humiliation charged with racism.[1]

One of the prisoners proclaimed as he offered their collective grievances, "We don't want to be treated as statistics, as numbers….We want to be treated as human beings."[2]

The prisoners of Attica had exhausted every possible avenue for redress of their grievances which had been festering for many years before they rebelled and seized hostages and major parts of the prison. During the takeover of the prison, several guards were injured when prisoners, overcome with rage over years of maltreatment, struck them with clubs. The most seriously injured was William Quinn, who was hit by at least 25 inmates armed with clubs, sticks, and bats after a prison yard gate was broken. The more seriously injured guards, including Quinn, were released by the prisoners that afternoon after a leadership structure was established in D Yard.

While the inmates were protecting the hostages and attempting to negotiate a peaceful end to years of oppression, the State was gathering a vast force of troopers and correction officers from all over the state to recapture the prison through the use of deadly weapons, even though they were aware that the prisoners were not armed. At the same time no real provisions were being made to provide medical treatment to the hundreds who would inevitably be injured by this kind of force.

Many prisoners were subsequently murdered and one-quarter of the inmates in D Yard were injured in the massacre which took place. Thousands of rounds of ammunition were fired on unarmed men. After the assault was over, the inmates were tortured by state troopers, sheriff's departments, and guards in what the United States Court of Appeals for the 2nd Circuit terms "an orgy of brutality." *Inmates of Attica v. Rockefeller,* 453 F. 2d 12 (2nd Cir., 1971). At the same time, state officials of New York State were lying to the people and press about the true facts of the Attica Massacre.

From the first lie told by Assistant Commissioners Houlihan and Dunbar to the press, the State of New York, from the Governor down to the state police, then spent its resources in covering up the true facts of Attica. The officials, including but not limited to, Rockefeller, Lefkowitz, Oswald, Fischer, and Simonette, were setting up the structure to blame the inmates for the State's inhumanity.[3] At the same time, the state police were "cleaning up" the yard, destroying the evidence, moving the positions of the bodies, not marking who had what weapons, and failing to follow every police tactic dictated by law.

In a sworn affidavit[4] filed by Malcolm H. Bell, former Special Assistant Attorney General of the State of New York, he testifies to the systematic slaughter and abuse of prisoners by state police and guards after the retaking of the prison, when they killed thirty-nine people, including ten hostages, almost ten times as many people as the prisoners were accused of killing—four. Mr. Bell's graphic account of the vicious and brutal lawlessness of these law enforcement officers is instructive on the atmosphere and conditions of United States prisons. Conditions at Attica Prison before and since the rebellion still reflect the most blatant and debasing racism and inhumanity.[5]

Evidence existed that following the shootings on September 13, 1971, state police and correction officers committed numerous assaults and other crimes of brutality against inmates who had surrendered. According to the evidence, law officers beat inmates with clubs and gun butts, smashed wristwatches, eye glasses, and false teeth, permitted cigarettes to burn out upon the flesh of naked inmates and smashed them, attempted to jam a Phillips head screwdriver up the anus of an inmate, forced inmates to run barefoot over broken glass, smashed a guitar over the head of an inmate, dumped injured inmates off stretchers onto the ground, attempted to insert night sticks into the wounds of inmates, broke bones and committed other assaults. Those post-shooting assaults and other crimes should have been comparatively easy to prosecute. Whereas the shooters wore gas masks, fired mostly untraceable weapons and would have escaped identification almost entirely were it not for their BCI statements, the ravagers had taken off their masks by then and were easily recognizable. Many photographs indicated who stood where during the brutality. The brutality happened without the smoke and noise of the armed assault and occurred over a long period of time. It should have been comparatively easy, under the Investigation mandate to prosecute all crimes at Attica, to arm investigators with current photographs of all the officers who went inside the prison that day, interview all the witnesses promptly before they forgot a face, and ask simple questions about who saw what. Moreover, there were a host of disinterested witnesses, including National Guard litter bearers, local medical personnel and others. On information and belief, this failure of the Investigation to prosecute crimes of brutality by law officers stands in stark contrast to the systematic effort which the Investigation made to prosecute crimes of brutality by inmates.[6]

Dacajeweiah (John Hill)

On December 18, 1972, the State of New York handed down thirty-seven indictments, plus five more in August 1973, with a total of sixty-two prisoners being prosecuted as an outcome of the forty-two indictments. Only one state law enforcement officer was ever indicted as a result of the Attica slaughter: Trooper Gregory Wildridge for "reckless endangerment," a minor charge, in October 1975.

After an expenditure by the State of New York of $12,000,000 for the prosecution of these cases, thirty-four of the forty-two indictments were dismissed. Six cases were tried before juries, and four of the Attica prisoners were exonerated. Only two Attica prisoners were convicted: two young Native Americans, Charley Joe Pernasilece and Dacajeweiah (John Hill), for the alleged murder of correction officer William B. Quinn.

On December 30, 1976, New York Governor Hugh Carey announced that, after reading reports he had commissioned, he wanted to "close the book" on the Attica rebellion.[7] He decreed that no disciplinary or legal action would be taken against the state officers and employees inculpated by his commission reports; he pardoned seven Attica indictees and commuted the sentence of Dacajeweiah so that he could be eligible for immediate parole.

Dacajeweiah was denied parole by a board which included a former Attica prosecutor involved in the cover-up of law enforcement officers' misconduct, a cousin to the victim, William Quinn, a former secretary of Governor Rockefeller, and a parole officer.

As Malcolm H. Bell states in his affidavit: "I am aware of no circumstances which make the lack of fairness and evenhandedness of the Attica prosecution any less applicable to John Hill (Dacajeweiah) than it was to (any other) inmates charged with serious felonies."[8]

The fundamental difference was that the Corrections Guards Union has publicly repeated since 1971 that "someone will pay for Billy Quinn's death." That someone is Dacajeweiah. No one will pay for the dead and brutalized prisoners and state employees killed by the wanton ferocity of state law enforcement officers.

Dacajeweiah has been denied parole and a new trial. Despite massive public protests and petitions, he remains confined in Sing-Sing Prison.[9]

The Malcolm H. Bell Affidavit

On the following pages is the complete text of the Malcolm Bell affidavit and the memorandum which was attached as Exhibit A to that affidavit.

ADDITIONAL SPECIAL AND TRIAL TERM
OF THE SUPREME COURT OF THE STATE
OF NEW YORK: COUNTY OF ERIE

--x

PEOPLE OF THE STATE OF NEW YORK

AFFIDAVIT

v.

IND. NO. 1/72

JOHN HILL,
Defendant.

--x

STATE OF NEW YORK)
ss.:
COUNTY OF NEW YORK)

MALCOLM H. BELL, being duly sworn, deposes and says:

1. I am a member of the bar of the State of New York, and a former Special Assistant Attorney General of the State of New York assigned to the Attica Investigation, in which capacity I was charged with prosecuting crimes and possible crimes committed by the State Police, Correction Officers and other State employees at and after the riot at the Attica Correctional Facility (hereinafter "Attica") in September, 1971. I make this affidavit at the request of counsel for John Hill.

2. My background is as follows: I received an A.B. degree cum laude from Harvard College in 1953, served two years in the United States Army, and received an LL.B. degree from Harvard Law School in 1958. I was employed by Dewey, Ballentine, Bushby, Palmer & Wood, 140 Broadway, New York, New York, from October 1958 through February 1968; by Mermelstein, Burns & Lesser (now Burns & Jacoby), 445 Park Avenue, New York, New York, from March 1968 through November 1970, and by the Law Firm of Malcolm A. Hoffman, 12 East 41st Street, New York, New York, from December 1970 until September 1973, all primarily in litigation. Besides the

New York Bar, I am a member of the bars of the United States District Courts for the Southern and Eastern District of New York, the United States Court of Appeals for the Second Circuit and the Supreme Court of the United States. I am also a member of the National Panel of Arbitrators, American Arbitration Association.

3. In the summer of 1973, I answered a "blind" ad for prosecutors in the New York Law Journal, and was employed by the Attica Investigation on September 20, 1973. In January 1974, I became the Chief Assistant to the Attica Investigation, under Assistant Attorney General Anthony G. Simonetti (hereinafter "Simonetti), who had recently risen from Chief Assistant to being In Charge of the Attica Investigation, succeeding Robert E. Fischer. By Executive Order of October 1971, the Attica Investigation superseded the District Attorney of Wyoming County where Attica is located and was charged with the investigation and prosecution of all crimes committed in connection with the riot and retaking of Attica on September 9-13, 1971. In May 1974 a Supplemental Grand Jury was convened in Wyoming County specifically to investigate and prosecute crimes and possible crimes committed by the State Police, Correction Officers and other State employees at and after riot, such crimes and possible crimes not having been fully and systematically investigated and prosecuted prior to that date. On December 11, 1974, I resigned from the Attica Investigation, when my belief became a certainty that the investigation and prosecution of such crimes and possible crimes by State employees lacked integrity and was being intentionally aborted. Thereafter, I have engaged in the private practice of law as a sole practitioner.

4. On information and belief based upon my examination of the Attica Investigation (hereinafter "Investigation") files and conversations with Simonetti and other Investigation employees, the prosecution of crimes and possible crimes committed by State employees was programmed for failure from the start. Whereas it was apparent in September 1971 that the State Police and guards had killed 39 people, including ten hostages, almost ten times as many people as the inmates had killed (4), the meager forces of the Investigation were deployed in inverse proportion to the magnitude of the

problems facing them. Thus, my notes of a Simonetti memorandum dated December 18, 1971, show that eight Investigation and State Police Investigators were looking into homicides and other crimes committed by inmates; seven were looking into a possible conspiracy among inmates to start the riot; and only two were looking into the thirty-nine homicides and the other crimes and possible crimes committed by law officers. This was the deployment of investigators notwithstanding the fact that by then it was established that over one hundred State Police and guards had admitted firing their weapons during the assault; that they had shot approximately one hundred twenty-eight people, and the accounts of criminal assaults by officers upon inmates after the shooting stopped were common knowledge. The decision to investigate the riot before the retaking, and inmate crimes before law officer crimes, was crucial to the failures of the Investigation to accord equal justice at Attica.

5. The initial programming of the Investigation for failure was reinforced by three additional factors:
   (a) During the crucial first year following September 1971, the Investigation had approximately the full time services of two lawyers and eight investigators, plus several State Police investigators. That number fell woefully shy of the number that the task required. The crimes and possible crimes at Attica involved hundreds of possible perpetrators, thousands of potential witnesses, hundreds of photographs, thousands of weapons and other forms of tangible evidence, and thousands of pages of documents. Whereas the McKay Commission, which Governor Rockefeller established to investigate and report to the public upon the riot, had a far smaller job than the Investigation, which had not only to learn what happened at the riot but also to develop proof of a host of individual crimes and the identities of numerous perpetrators thereof beyond a reasonable doubt, the staff of the McKay Commission was several times larger than the staff of the Investigation.
   (b) Whereas it is the duty of the police to cooperate with the prosecution and whereas the law and the State Police Manual provides that every trooper may be answerable in a Grand

Jury for shots he fires, the State Police who participated in the assault would only consent to be interviewed by the Investigation in the presence of a State Police detective. Moreover, the State Police repeatedly refused to turn over evidence to the Investigation, or turned it over only gradually, or in response to repeated demands, or after they had indicated that they had already turned over everything.

(c) Whereas the Investigation was charged with investigating all crimes and possible crimes committed by the State Police, and whereas it appears that scores or even hundreds of such crimes may have been committed, the Investigation worked with and relied upon State Police detectives. Thus, on information and belief, Captain Henry Williams, Chief of the State Police Bureau of Criminal Investigation (hereinafter "BCI") for Troop A, in whose jurisdiction Attica is located, worked in the office and had access to the files of the Investigation until January 1972; other BCI detectives worked in the Investigation office until June 1972. It is my best recollection that in the Fall of 1974, BCI investigators were still working with the Investigation on inmates prosecutions, and specifically on the prosecution of John Hill. The reliance of the Investigation upon State Police BCI detectives to prosecute inmates created an obvious conflict of interest, in that the Investigation could not vigorously prosecute crimes committed by the State Police without incurring a palpable risk of alienating the State Police upon whom the investigation was relying to prosecute inmates. This conflict of interest was obvious from the start; Simonetti acknowledged to me that it existed; but so long as I remained with the Investigation, it was never remedied.

6. During the first two years that the Investigation was presenting evidence to the (first) Attica Grand Jury, which was convened, I believe, in November 1971, no systematic effort was made to prosecute crimes committed by State Police, guards and other State employees at and after the riot and retaking. While a few isolated cases were prepared, the Investigation remained content for the most part to accept the self-serving and self-justifying statements which

were given by the State Police and guards who fired their weapons during the assault, in spite of the fact that most of these statements did not accord with the photographic, eye-witness and other evidence and many of these statements were absurd or improbable on their face. The McKay Commission reported publicly in September 1972 that there was "much unnecessary shooting" during the assault, and much brutality by law officers after the shooting – "unnecessary shooting" in the context of Attica being presumptively criminal. During this two year period after the riot, sixty-two inmates were indicted by the Attica Grand Jury for crimes ranging from homicide to commandeering an electric cart. No State personnel were indicted.

7. The Investigation's staff, which had been far too small for its task, grew only gradually during the two years following the riot, in spite of written requests from Simonetti, which I saw in the file, for a larger staff. Then in the Summer and Fall of 1973, when the trials of the indicted inmates began to appear imminent, State officials amazingly permitted the staff to expand approximately double, to, I believe, fourteen lawyers and thirty investigators.

8. At the end of 1973, Robert E. Fischer resigned from his position In Charge of the Investigation, having been elected to the Supreme Court of the State of New York in the November 1973 election. Simonetti succeeded Fischer In Charge of the Investigation. Prior to joining the Investigation under Fischer in September 1971, Simonetti had been employed by the State Organized Crime Task Force under Fischer. Simonetti also spoke of returning to the Organized Crime Task Force after the Investigation concluded. To the best of my information and belief, the Organized Crime Task Force has little or no investigative staff of its own, but relies upon the investigative work of State Police detectives who are assigned to it. Insofar as Simonetti had a future with the Organized Crime Task Force, it obviously depended importantly upon his not alienating the State Police investigators whom he would have to rely upon later, by prosecuting the State Police who committed crimes at Attica with the vigor which he showed in prosecuting inmates.
9. Notwithstanding this apparent conflict of interest, Simonetti conducted in the first three months of 1974 the first systematic

analysis of all evidence which the Investigation possessed of all shots fired by the approximately one hundred and eleven troopers and guards who admitted firing their weapons at inmates during the retaking of Attica. I attribute this analysis of evidence by Simonetti to three factors:

(a) Such an analysis was required by the Executive Order of October 1971 which established the Investigation, by Simonetti's plain duty as a prosecutor, and, in light of the prosecutions of inmates for crimes committed at Attica, by the principles of due process, equal protection and equal justice which are embodied in the Constitution and inherent in our system of justice.

(b) Such an analysis had not been done during the first two and one-quarter years of the Investigation.

(c) Due to the fact that shotgun pellets are not ballistically traceable to the weapons which fired them, and to the astounding fact that the State Police failed to perform their elementary duty to record which trooper was assigned which rifle at Attica, the highest crime for which most of the admitted shooters could be prosecuted was reckless endangerment in the first degree, a class D felony. As of December 1973, two brief memoranda of law existed in the Investigation files, one by Simonetti and one by another Assistant Attorney General, both concluding in effect that reckless endangerment could not be applied to the shooters at Attica. With Simonetti's approval, I researched the subject as carefully as I could and wrote a memorandum of approximately thirty-eight pages which concluded that reckless endangerment in the first degree did indeed fit the Attica situation, and that many of the shooters at Attica were subject to prosecution under it. Upon reading my memorandum, Simonetti agreed with that conclusion, as did Maxwell B. Spoont, who succeeded Fischer as head of the Organized Crime Task Force and whom the Investigation frequently consulted at that time on questions of law.

10. The systematic analysis conducted by Simonetti during the Winter of 1974 consisted of matching each shot admitted by each trooper

and guard in each of his several written statements against the photographic evidence, such ballistic evidence as existed, the autopsy reports on the dead, and such eye-witness evidence as existed, to see if the justification for the shots which almost invariably appeared in the shooters' statements was corroborated or contradicted by the other evidence. For example, a trooper's statement might say that he fired his shotgun at an inmate who was about to throw a Molotov cocktail at him as he advanced down A Catwalk, whereas none of the assault photos shows such an inmate, no non-shooter eye-witness saw any such inmate and all the evidence showed that before any trooper went out onto A Catwalk all the inmates went down and stayed down except for three who tried to flee. Or a trooper's statement might say that as he advanced down C Catwalk he fired his shotgun at an inmate who was standing on top of a barricade midway down the catwalk brandishing a sword, whereas all the photos fail to show that inmate, none of the non-shooter eye-witnesses saw him, no sword was found near the barricade, and there was no way that an inmate could have lived to mount the barricade under the dozen or so rifles and shotguns firing from C Block above it. Upon this systematic analysis, Simontetti and I concluded that at least sixty-five or seventy shooters were subject to possible indictment for murder, attempted murder, reckless endangerment and other felonies.

11. It is important to note that this evidence of unjustified shots fired by officers at inmates and hostages existed in 1974, and presumably it still exists today, in spite of certain official statements to the effect that time has eroded the evidence. The core of this evidence is the written, signed statements in which approximately one hundred eleven State Police and guards admit firing weapons at other human beings in the crowded conditions within Attica. These shooters gave such statements to BCI detectives within two days of the shooting, followed by other written statements in the Fall of 1971. Nor has time eroded the State Police assault photos and videotape of the assault, such as they are. Moreover, whereas an eye-witness may have forgotten an individual face in the intervening years (most of the shooters wore gas masks, and are identified by the admissions in their written statements rather than by eye-witness), many eye-witnesses to the assault appear capable of still recalling whether any inmate

was attacking any trooper or anyone else at any time after the initial barrage in the first few seconds of the assault.

12. It appeared to Simonetti and me that it would not be appropriate to present the shooter cases to the sitting Attica Grand Jury for several reasons. They had sat for over two years. It was increasingly difficult to convene a quorum. Several were farmers, and Spring planting would occur during the time we wanted to start. After two years of hearing mainly about inmate crimes, such objectivity as they may have started with was likely gone. They had not been selected for maximum objectivity to start with. For example, their foreman ran a school bus company in the town of Attica which employed a number of Attica prison guards as drivers. We applied to the Honorable Carman F. Ball, Supreme Court, Wyoming County, to convene a new Grand Jury. He, in turn applied to the Appellate Division, Fourth Department. A Supplemental Grand Jury for Attica was convened on approximately May 2, 1974. Although I had never presented evidence to a Grand Jury, Simonetti placed me in charge of presenting the evidence to the Supplemental Grand Jury. As I understood its purpose, it was to be primarily concerned with the shooting, post-shooting brutality, hindering prosecution (i.e., obstruction of justice) and other crimes and possible crimes committed by State employees at and after the Attica riot.

13. From May 8 through August 1, 1974, the Supplemental Grand Jury, sitting about three days a week, received evidence of the shooter crimes during the retaking, presented mainly by me. They attended well, asked perceptive questions, and appeared to be doing a conscientious job. Although I had little staff support, Simonetti read the Grand Jury transcripts and made suggestions which appeared helpful to the prosecution. The nature of the evidence of the retaking lent itself to presenting most of the cases to the jury to vote upon indictments at the end of the shooter case presentation rather than voting them one at a time as we went along. Moreover, the Investigation had failed to question an amazing number of eye-witnesses to the assault in detail as to what they saw, a job which easily could have been done far better than it had been during the more than two and one-half years since the riot, even with the

Investigation's small staff; so that we could not be certain of the extent to which the eye-witnesses would corroborate, or conceivably repudiate, our substantial evidence of virtually no inmate resistance after the tear gas and first barrage of gunfire went down. Nonetheless, Simonetti (on the basis of his statements to me) and I considered it appropriate to present several cases for votes by the jury as we went along. Among other things, both Simonetti and I were dismayed at the extent to which trooper eye-witnesses who had not fired their weapons appeared to be lying and "forgetting" what they witnessed during the retaking, in their sworn testimony to the jury. I understood Simonetti to agree with me that a perjury indictment might well have a salutary effect of reducing this lying and obstructionism. Simonetti also was actively considering criminal contempt remedies against some of these trooper witnesses. Accordingly, I prepared two reckless endangerment cases and a perjury case for presentation and vote by the Supplemental Grand Jury on August 1, 1974, the last day the jury was to sit before a three week mid-summer recess. One reckless endangerment case involved a correctional officer who admitted firing a Thompson submachine gun at several inmates who were in A Yard, when it contained no hostages or officers and very few other inmates, the inmates he fired at were posing an imminent threat to no one, and any substantial overfire would have endangered the lives of the crowd of people in D Yard on the other side of the D Tunnel from A Yard. The other reckless endangerment case I prepared involved Trooper Gregory Wildridge, the one "token" trooper who was over indicted for all the shooting at Attica (in October 1975) approximately ten months after I first charged that the prosecution of law officers was being aborted. The perjury case involved a commissioned officer of the State Police who admitted watching the retaking from an elevated part of C Block but maintained under oath that he had seen no shooting whatsoever, in spite of the cannonading which is audible on the videotape of the assault and the troopers who admitted firing scores of shots from shotguns and pistols within plain sight of him, and the numerous inmates on the catwalk beneath his gaze whose bodies absorbed much of that gunfire. I prepared two packages of the evidence (mainly xeroxed copies of prior testimony to the jury) which I intended to rely upon for each of these cases, leaving one with Simonetti in New York City and taking the other to the Supplemental

Grand Jury in Warsaw in order to make the presentation to them of the three cases. Simonetti never criticized the contents of these cases, but he refused to permit me to present them to the Supplemental Grand Jury for votes.

14. Though I did not know it at the time, the August 1974 jury recess effectively marked the end of the presentation of shooter cases to the Supplemental Grand Jury so long as I remained with the Investigation, although that presentation was very far from complete. It was Simonetti's stated intention as of the Fall of 1974 to discharge the Supplemental Grand Jury without ever giving them the substantial additional evidence necessary for that presentation. On information and belief, while the Supplemental Grand Jury continued to sit through 1975 and further evidence was presented to them on shooter cases, such presentation basically constituted a "going through the motions" and only a bare handful of the sixty-five to seventy murder, attempted murder, assault and reckless endangerment cases which Simonetti and I contemplated when the Supplemental Grand Jury was convened were ever presented to them for a vote. By way of example only, and upon the basis of the evidence possessed by the Investigation, those felony cases not presented include the following:
    (a) Trooper A* fired his pistol numerous times into inmate Kenneth Malloy in the C Yard corner of Upper Times Square in the center of the prison, apparently when Malloy was surrounded by troopers and was not posing a threat to anyone's life. Four .357 magnum bullets taken from the body of Malloy were ballistically traced to Trooper A's pistol. On information and belief, neither a murder case nor any other case against Trooper A was ever presented to an Attica Grand Jury for a vote.
    (b) Trooper B also shot Malloy. Certain cases against him were presented to the first Attica Grand Jury and a no bill was voted. Simonetti stated that the circumstances of those votes, and also of the evidence as it existed at the time of those votes, warranted an application to the Court to resubmit Trooper B to the Supplemental Grand Jury for votes of murder, attempted murder and/or other crimes. On information and belief, such a

* I am not certain whether I am permitted to identify these officers by name. The Attorney General's office should be readily able to identify them. If they have any difficulty, I am prepared to help.

resubmission as to Trooper B was never made or even sought.

(c) As James Robinson lay mortally wounded, threatening no one, with a .270 bullet in his chest on the B Yard side of Upper Times Square, Trooper C fired a shotgun round through the neck of inmate Robinson at a range of from two to five feet, breaking Robinson's neck and killing him instantly. On information and belief, the case of Trooper C was never presented to an Attica Grand Jury for a vote.

(d) Inmate Ramon Rivera was shot to death and another inmate was shot in the foot by 00 buckshot while they were cowering in a hole that was dug under the sidewalk that runs beside B Tunnel in D Yard, where they were threatening no one. As of the time I left the Investigation, Trooper A was also the leading suspect in that case. Simonetti was refusing to permit that case to be developed properly, in particular, refusing to permit me to question witnesses who may have seen that shooting, and refusing to permit me to question a State Police Senior Investigator who appeared to have material information concerning knowledge of the shotgun used in that shooting. On information and belief, no case against Trooper A or any other officer was presented to any Attica Grand Jury in connection with the homicide of inmate Ramon Rivera or the assault upon the other inmate.

(e) A number of troopers admitted firing their shotguns into holes which had been dug in D Yard without looking first to see if anyone was inside, despite the probability that inmates would be hiding there to escape the volume of gunfire which came down on D Yard from the cellblocks and catwalks above them. (With uncanny similarity, these troopers later changed their statements to allege that they fired their shotguns into the ground in front of these foxholes.) Amazingly, no one other than Rivera appears to have been shot to death in any of these holes. On information and belief, no reckless endangerment or any other case was ever presented to an Attica Grand Jury against any of these troopers.

(f) One or more Correctional Officers fired submachine guns into holes and tents in D Yard (in violation of the order that Correction Officers were not to participate in the assault), endangering the lives of troopers and probably hostages as well as inmates in D Yard. On information and belief, no reckless endangerment or any other case was ever presented to an Attica Grand Jury against any such Correction Officer.

(g) Correctional Officer D fired his personal .44 Ruger magnum carbine, killing a hostage. Correctional Officer D may have been subject to charges for certain other acts. On information and belief, based on conversations with Simonetti and my own knowledge of the case, charges against Correctional Officer D were not properly presented to an Attica Grand Jury. Correctional Officer D's attorney, moreover, agreed with me to let him testify to the Supplemental Grand Jury under a waiver of immunity, but Simonetti would not permit me to call him.

(h) In C Tunnel, where a teargas projectile may or may not have come down the tunnel at the troopers from Lower Times Square, troopers admitted firing approximately fifty to one hundred rounds of 00 buckshot at inmates down the tunnel. There was evidence that as the first rank would empty their shotguns, they would fall back to reload and others would come up and fire. One State Police Commissioned Officer in C Tunnel saw no reason for the shooting; another State Police Commissioned Officer in the tunnel admitted firing his shotgun eight times. Several inmates were apparently wounded in Times Square and others were saved only by lying behind a metal apron at the bottom of the Times Square gate, as hundreds of deadly pellets came at them in what was grimly known at the Investigation as the State Police "Happy Hour". Numerous patched bullet holes were evident in the concrete rafters of C Tunnel when I was there in 1973 and 1974. On information and belief, no reckless endangerment or any other case was ever presented to an Attica Grand Jury in connection with all this shooting.

(i) Several troopers admitted firing their shotguns from A Catwalk down into A Yard, where there were no hostages or troopers, at an inmate who allegedly threw an object, which is not claimed to have struck anyone, up onto the catwalk approximately fifteen feet above. Inmate William Allen was the indicated deceased. On information and belief, no Attica Grand Jury was given the opportunity to vote whether or not to indict any of these troopers.

(j) A similar event occurred in D Yard under D Catwalk, the

indicated deceased being inmate Willy West. On information and belief, no case was ever presented to any Attica Grand Jury against any perpetrator of this homicide.

(k) Trooper E admitted shooting an inmate indicated as Lorenzo McNeil, in the back of the head with his shotgun from D Catwalk as McNeil was allegedly getting off the ground to throw a hatchet at Trooper F down in D Yard. To the best of my information and belief, it was not established that Trooper F was in D Yard at that time; and I was aware of no evidence which corroborated that alleged justification. No hatchet was recovered and none is shown in the photos of McNeil's body. On information and belief, no case was ever presented to an Attica Grand Jury against Trooper F.

(l) State Police Noncommissioned Officer G admitted firing his shotgun from D Catwalk at one or more inmates down in D Yard. In his statements to BCI and Investigation investigators, he gave five different versions of what the inmates he fired at were doing when he fired, ranging from an inmate diving into a trench (clearly not justified) to inmates running at troopers (maybe justified, but not established that such troopers were in D Yard at such time). On information and belief, no reckless endangerment, false official statement, or any other case was ever presented to an Attica Grand Jury concerning this officer.

(m) The shooting to death of eight hostages in the circle where inmates held them in D Yard during the riot is "officially" attributed to shotgun fire from B Catwalk which was allegedly necessary to save Police Lieutenant Joseph Christian from an attacking inmate as Christian rushed across D Yard towards the hostage circle. (There is substantial evidence, however, that Christian was saved by brother officers who struck the attacking inmate with their shotgun butts.) The "official" version persists despite the fact that three of the eight hostages were apparently killed by rifle fire which was not related to the Christian incident. Be that as it may, Trooper H admitted firing his shotgun from the B Catwalk four times at an alleged group of armed blacks who were apparently rushing the hostage circle after the Christian incident occurred. All other evidence that I am aware of, however, including the statements of troopers who were with Christian, and of the hostages, indicates that no such rush by armed blacks occurred. Trooper H's four shots (36-48 lethal pellets which, at the range of the hostage circle, went out in approximately four foot patterns) likely killed and/or injured a number of hostages and inmates. It only took one stray pellet, for example, to kill Correction Officer Sergeant Cunningham. Since pellets cannot be traced ballistically, Trooper H was subject only to charges of reckless endangerment and perhaps attempted murder, if the evidence was fully developed and remained consistent with what it was at the time I left the Investigation. On information and belief, no charge against Trooper H was ever presented to an Attica Grand Jury.

(n) Trooper I admitted firing his shotgun at an inmate who was coming up the nearly perpendicular iron stairs from Lower Times Square to Upper Times Square and allegedly attacking Trooper I with a knife. Trooper I admitted that the inmate's head had not even reached the level of the floor in which Trooper I was standing when he fired, and to the best of my information, no such knife was ever recovered. Trooper I's statement was consistent with the shotgun pattern in the side of the deceased inmate Edward Menefee, and two witnesses had told me that a body they saw lying at the foot of the Times Square stairs looked to them like Menefee, though they stopped short of making a positive identification. Simonetti prevented me from following several leads to get a positive identification of that body. When I was questioning a witness concerning Trooper A, for example, the witness pulled from his pocket a piece of paper, (never previously collected by our Investigation) on which he had written Trooper A's name on September 13, 1971; on the back of that piece of paper was a list of several Correctional Officers who had been in C Tunnel and may have been near the body in Lower Times Square that morning. Simonetti, however, never permitted me an opportunity to question those Correctional Officers about that body or show them Menefee's picture. On information and belief, no murder or any other case was ever presented against Trooper I to any Attica Grand Jury.

(o) Prior to May 1974, I was told a number of times by Simonetti and others at the Investigation that Correctional Officer Michael Smith, a hostage who was being held on A Catwalk at the time the retaking commenced, was injured by fragments of a single bullet which had disintegrated upon striking the catwalk or a railing. In approximately May 1974, I inspected Mr. Smith myself and observed four full round bullet holes in a vertical line in his abdomen resulting in horrible exit wounds (such observations being supplemented and confirmed by Dr. Michael Baden). On the evidence, it appears that Smith had been shot four separate times (and nearly killed) by a correctional officer firing an automatic weapon from A Block (probably an AR-15, not a Thompson submachine gun); several AR-15s were checked out of the Attica arsenal that day, and evidence existed that at least one was in A Block. Simonetti did not permit the case against Smith's assailant to be properly pursued. On information and belief, no perpetrator was ever identified to or voted upon by an Attica Grand Jury.

(p) Correction Officer O admitted firing approximately 16 rounds from A Block during the retaking. It is my best recollection that few if any of Correction Officer O's shots were justified, even under his own admissions. On information and belief, no case against Trooper O was ever presented to any Attica Grand Jury.

(q) Trooper P admitted firing at inmates who were running down B Catwalk away from any hostages or troopers. Simonetti spoke of this as a clear case of reckless endangerment. It was also possibly attempted murder. On information and belief, the case of Trooper P was never presented to any Attica Grand Jury.

15. On information and belief, the Supplemental Grand Jury was prepared to vote numerous indictments of State Police and Guards who fired their weapons without justification during the retaking of Attica on September 13, 1971, if such cases had been properly and timely presented to them. On information and belief, a significant number of Supplemental Grand Jurors considered that the prosecution of law officers was grossly mismanaged and/or intentionally mismanaged. On information and belief, neither the Meyer Commission nor Special Deputy Attorney General Alfred Scotti nor anyone else assigned to investigate the conduct of the Attica

Investigation ever questioned the Supplemental Grand Jurors on these subjects.

16. During the aforementioned analysis of shooter cases in early 1974 before the Supplemental Grand Jury was convened, Simonetti, several other Assistant Attorneys General and I prepared written analyses of most of the written statements of troopers and guards who admitted firing their weapons, together with such evidence as we then had which tended to corroborate or contradict the justification which they alleged for their shots fired. These analyses totaled several hundred pages, a set of them being in my possession and additional sets presumably being in the possession of the Attorney General. In my opinion, these analyses clearly tend to establish that John Hill was subject to selective prosecution. They show the basis upon which dozens of felony cases against law officers (perhaps even more than the sixty-five to seventy cases which Simonetti and I were projecting in the spring of 1974) should have been pursued and presented to the Supplemental Grand Jury but apparently never were; whereas cases against sixty-two inmates were prosecuted past indictment, and, in John hill's case, to the point of conviction for murder. These analyses describe in substantially greater detail the cases I have summarized under Paragraph 14, above, in addition to many other cases. Since these analyses contain the names of suspects and witnesses, however, I am not certain whether I am permitted to turn them over to counsel for John Hill even though I understand it to be his opinion that he is entitled to them under the doctrine of Brady v. Maryland, 373 U.S. 83 (1968). I am prepared to turn these over to counsel for John Hill if I am directed to do so by the Court; and I am, of course, prepared to submit them to the Court if so requested by the Court.

17. When the Supplemental Grand Jury three week recess commencing on August 2, 1974, began, I fully expected on the basis of conversations with Simonetti and the incompleteness of the shooter cases so far, that the prosecution of the shooter cases would resume when the jury reconvened on August 27. I left instructions in my usual manner with the Investigation to notify a number of non-shooter State Police eye-witnesses to the assault to be at the Jury to testify on August 27, 28 and 29, and left on vacation, planning, with

Simonetti's approval, to return to the Investigation on August 26. Of possible major significance, during the three week Jury recess in August 1974, President Nixon resigned, Vice President Ford became President, and former Governor Nelson A. Rockefeller was nominated for Vice President. When I returned to the Investigation on August 22 at Simonetti's urgent request, I found that he had suddenly and without warning made a radical change in the order of presentation of evidence to the Supplemental Grand Jury. He was halting the presentation of the shooter case evidence though that presentation was far from completed; and he was commencing the presentation of a major hindering prosecution (i.e., obstruction of justice) case against the State Police, although that case was far from ready for presentation, and although this sudden shift would obviously cause great confusion to the jurors. Simonetti had directed my attention to the existence of a possible hindering prosecution case against the State Police as early as the Fall of 1973; but our previous discussions had been in terms of presenting it after the shooter cases had been voted by the Jury, not in the middle of presenting them and so as to delay those votes for many months at least. On returning to the office on August 22, 1974, I found that the witnesses I had left word to be notified for the jury for the next week had not been notified, and that in their place Simonetti was calling a whole new slate of witnesses, some of whom I had never even heard of. Simonetti and I had worked closely and harmoniously heretofore. On this "August Switch" as I came to call it, Simonetti and I had our first major policy disagreement. He took the position that "breaking" the hindering prosecution case would probably cause the State Police trooper witnesses to stop lying to the Supplemental Grand Jury. I took the position that indicting a relatively small handful of higher-ups, which is what we projected for the hindering prosecution case, was unlikely to cause the average trooper suddenly to remember seeing his buddy shoot someone; and that a far better way to do this, to the extent that is could be done at all, was to vote the indictment of the State Police Commissioned Officer I wanted to present for a vote on August 1, and perhaps of a few others, for perjury. I argued further that, as just stated, the shooter cases were far from finished and the hindering prosecution case was far from ready. I estimated at the time that at least one month more of solid presentation to the Supplemental Grand

Jury was necessary to complete the shooter cases; in retrospect, it would have had to be at least another three months. I argued further that the sudden switch was likely to cause great and unnecessary confusion to the Supplemental Grand Jury; on information and belief, the jurors in fact found the switch extremely confusing. Again, of possible significance, a few days after the Attica riot in 1971, then Governor Rockefeller announced publically that the State Police had done a "superb job" at Attica; the effect upon his pending nomination for Vice President in 1974, if his pronouncement was officially repudiated by the indictment of several dozen State Troopers for shooting felonies at Attica, does not appear difficult to infer. The "August Switch" had the effect of assuring that such indictments would not occur during the pendency of Rockefeller's nomination for Vice President. Whether or not it was intended to have such effect, I have no direct knowledge beyond the legal principle that the people in charge of the Investigation are presumed to have intended the natural and probable results of their acts. Be that as it may, Simonetti, being In Charge of the Investigation under the Attorney General, prevailed, and the "August Switch" in fact occurred. I, and now other assistants as well, commenced presenting evidence of hindering prosecution by the State Police to the Supplemental Grand Jury.

18. In or about early September, 1974, Simonetti was called upon by the Federal Bureau of Investigation to provide such information as he could about Nelson A. Rockefeller, as part of the F.B.I. investigation of Rockefeller upon his nomination for Vice President. Simonetti, together with Investigator Michael McCarron and me acting under Simonetti's close supervision, questioned several members of Rockefeller's Executive Chamber and top State Police officials about Rockefeller's involvement at Attica. In my opinion, such investigation by Simonetti was superficial and designed to avoid probing the full facts. As I so often observed at the Investigation, Simonetti went through the motions of doing the right thing without actually doing it. I concluded at the time that Simonetti failed and refused to ask questions of Michael Whiteman, Robert Douglass and Howard Shapiro of the Executive Chamber that should have been asked in order to accomplish his stated purpose. Simonetti admonished me for sounding "too much like a prosecutor" after I

attempted to supplement his inadequate questioning of Douglass. On the morning of September 5, 1974, Simonetti kept me literally up in the air, flying from New York City to Buffalo on the 9:00 a.m. flight and from Buffalo to New York City on the 11:25 a.m. flight, so that I was unable to participate in questioning either Howard Shapiro or Wyoming County District Attorney Louis James (whom Rockefeller had superseded with Robert E. Fischer to head the Attica Investigation and who was on Simonetti's list to question for the F.B.I. Investigation), in Buffalo, both of whom were questioned very inadequately that morning. Though Simonetti had included me in his important conferences all year, he excluded me without explanation when the F.B.I. agent came to the office to receive the report he gave them of his inadequate investigation of Mr. Rockefeller.

19. The Supplemental Grand Jury had wanted Nelson A. Rockefeller questioned in the jury from the start. Approximately in late August or early September 1974, after Rockefeller's nomination for Vice President, their requests for him became intense. Simonetti asked them to wait, claiming that calling Rockefeller then would disrupt the orderly presentation of evidence to them (Simonetti told them this shortly after he had completely abandoned orderly presentation by halting the shooter cases that were far from finished and commencing the hindering prosecution case when it was far from ready), that there was no "foundation" for calling Rockefeller (this was neither true nor relevant), and that the jury lacked the power to subpoena Rockefeller (that is believed not to be true, and it diverted the jury away from their option of simply asking Rockefeller to appear before them). In my opinion, this advice to the jury by Simonetti violated the duty of the prosecutor to serve as legal advisor to the Grand Jury. As a result, Rockefeller was not called before the Supplemental Grand Jury until approximately one year later, in late August 1975 long after his confirmation as Vice President, and at a time when, I am informed, the Investigation was simply "going through the motions" of making an adequate presentation to the jury (with the sole exception of the Wildridge indictment, which came as a pleasant surprise to a number of jurors). In October and November 1974, it had been Simonetti's plan to dissolve the Supplemental Grand Jury without ever calling Rockefeller. In my opinion, Rockefeller was a potentially

important witness in the State Police hindering prosecution case and possibly in cases against others, though he was not a target of any investigation upon the basis of evidence known to me at the time I left the Investigation in December 1974. On information and belief, the Investigation never similarly frustrated the desire of any Attica Grand Jury to call before it any potentially important witness against inmates.

20. The Investigation possessed substantial evidence of hindering prosecution by the State Police. Elements of the State Police's pervasive effort to prevent and obstruct the prosecution of officers for their crimes at Attica included the following elements (what Simonetti referred to as "The Mosaic"):

(a) Weapon serial numbers were not recorded, making it often impossible to determine what trooper fired what weapon during the assault, and there was no ammunition accountability. The dereliction, especially as to serial numbers, was a flagrant and inexcusable violation of basic State Police procedure. Ballistics shows, for example, that one .270 rifle (serial number 468-488) killed three people, and that another .270 rifle (serial number 768-064) killed two people and injured one. The failure to record serial numbers meant that the Investigation did not know who fired those shots.

(b) Shotgun serial numbers, too, should have been recorded; while shotgun ammunition usually cannot be traced ballistically (a rifled deer slug can sometimes be traced if the front sight of the shotgun projects down the barrel), the empty shell casings can be so traced by the hammer mark on them, and a trooper can be located as having ejected a spent round at the location at which the casing is found.

(c) The empty shell casings were not picked up and tagged by location as they should have been, though they lay in some places about Attica for days after the riot.

(d) The standard State Police Discharge of Fire Arms form, which requires the listing of the serial number of the weapon fired, was not used at Attica. State Police procedure indicated that it should have been used and several officers actually inquired about using it. The form also requires the shooter to identify at whom or what the shot or shots were fired and state the circumstances of shooting. (State Police officials later contended that the form was used only for shots fired at animals, in spite of the "at whom" language on it; and Simonetti refused to let me subpoena such completed forms from the State Police to check whether their story about using it only for animals was true.)

(e) The videotape of the assault made from the roof of A Block by State Police shows no shooting, though the sounds of hundreds of shots can be counted on the videotape, and the troopers admitted to firing hundreds of shots. There was evidence that the State Police shortened the tape from approximately six minutes of assault to approximately four minutes of assault before turning it over to the Investigation, although Simonetti never permitted me properly to pursue that lead.

(f) State Police Investigator Jerome O'Grady took a number of 35mm color slides from C Roof during the assault. The film as numbered by Kodak shows two gaps in the sequence of photographs taken by O'Grady. The first shows a gap of one or two pictures occurring at about the time that Trooper C was firing his shotgun through the neck of inmate James Robinson in the vicinity Times Square. The second gap consisting of approximately four photographs, occurred at about the time Trooper A, Trooper B, and possibly some other officer were firing their pistols into inmate Kenneth Malloy in the vicinity of Times Square.

(g) State Police Sergeant Frank Strasser, who began the assault in A Block and followed the assault troopers down A Catwalk gave evidence tending to show that a number of his 35mm assault photographs are also missing.

(h) There was also an amazing series of claimed malfunctions by State Police personnel assigned to photograph the assault in operating their cameras or in having the photographs properly developed, resulting in an absence of photographs corroborating crimes and possible crimes by officers.

(i) State Police photographers undertook to make the autopsy photographs while Doctors Edlund and Abbott were performing the autopsy on most of the gunshot-killed hostages and inmates. I am informed, however, that the State Police neglected to perform the very basic operation of identifying which photograph went with which body, so that their autopsy photographs were rendered substantially useless. So far as I know, this information, the alleged failure of autopsy photos by the State Police, was never developed by the Investigation or presented to any Attica Grand Jury, although Edlund was obviously a person who should have been questioned. I first learned of it in the Summer of 1976 by talking to Edlund myself. Autopsy photos are, of course, vital to any investigation of gunshot homicides. It was only the good fortune that Dr. Baden was able to take additional photographs when he was called from New York City to review Dr. Edlund's work, which permitted the Investigation to have autopsy photos of the gunshot deceased. I personally found these photographs invaluable in the investigation of the homicides. (See, for example, Para. 14(c) and 14(n) above.)

(j) The State Police withheld from the Investigation a photograph depicting a big black inmate lying on his back in A Yard balancing a football on his chest and two white inmates balancing shotgun shells on their knees, the accompanying story being that if these objects fell, officers would blow the inmates' heads off. (The Investigation only obtained such photograph when it applied directly to the Monroe County Deputy Sheriff who took it.)

(k) There are two instances in which early photographs on the morning of September 13 of inmates (one dead, one unconscious) do not show weapons lying beside them, whereas photographs taken later do show weapons lying beside them which were apparently added well after the assault. A trooper admitted to me that he had added one of those weapons.

(l) Death scenes which should have been preserved were destroyed, contrary to basic State Police procedure; and bodies were moved away before they were even pronounced dead, contrary to State law.

(m) A State Police photographer took death scene photos in

D Yard and says he later saw them; but they were never produced for the Investigation.

(n) The locations of bodies were never properly measured before the bodies were moved.

(o) Inmate weapons were never properly collected and tagged by location.

(p) The State Police statements from all troopers on or before September 15, 1971, appear calculated to protect the State Police who committed crimes rather than to ascertain what actually happened. For instance, the main focus of the statements concerning the shooting appear to be what the inmates were saying and doing by way of provocation before the assault began. The troopers were almost always not asked their weapon serial numbers. In most cases the troopers were asked whether they saw members of other departments fire weapons but they were not asked whether they saw other troopers fire weapons, the troopers, of course, having done most of the firing. An early statement by one trooper described how the troopers fired their shotguns in waves in C Tunnel (see Par. 14(h), above); the final version of that statement (the only one originally submitted to the Investigation, I believe) omitted that. No matter how ridiculous or absurd a trooper's statement about why he fired his weapon, follow-up questions were seldom if ever asked by the BCI detective doing the interviewing (or, for that matter, by the Investigation investigators who later interviewed these troopers).

(q) A number of Trooper BCI statements failed to include justification for their shots fired. In most or all of these instances State Police officers such as Captain Malovich and Captain Parmeter obtained from the shooters (apparently on instructions from State Police headquarters in Albany) supplemental statements which added justification after the fact.

(r) State Police and Investigation interviews of inmate witnesses to the riot, in an extraordinary number of instances, asked the inmates what occurred during the first days of the riot, but failed to question them on what they saw, heard and did during the assault.

(s) Trooper A, who as indicated above, was implicated in perhaps two homicides and admitted having nightmares about seeing brains (inmate Malloy was shot in the head as well as other places), was permitted to resign from the State Police and was sent away from the Investigation and the prison in September 1971, and the Investigation, with its minuscule staff then, did not follow him. I am aware of no similar instances in which the State Police dropped an investigation of any inmate implicated in homicide.

(t) Having been removed from the death scenes before being pronounced dead, the bodies of the deceased were sent to a wholly inadequate local funeral home in the town of Attica for autopsies, before a State Police Investigator blew the whistle by telling the State Police command post that it was inadequate for the necessary autopsies, having no x-ray (vital in these multiple gun shot cases), sewage, etc. The bodies were then returned to the prison and eventually sent to Dr. Edlund in Rochester and a few other places for competent autopsies. If this had not been done, it is problematical whether the official (false) story that the hostages had died from having inmates slash their throats would ever have been exposed for the falsehood that it was.

(u) When news of Dr. Edlund's findings that the hostages had been shot to death reached the prison, a witness I consider reliable reported that a member of Governor Rockefeller's Executive Chamber from Albany stated "Who is this guy Edlund? We've got to get something on him." Simonetti never permitted me to give this evidence to the Supplemental Grand Jury, or otherwise to pursue effectively the possibility that the Executive Chamber was implicated in a possible hindering prosecution.

(v) After Edlund's findings were announced, State Police visited local undertakers at night and persuaded them to give statements to the effect that there was no evidence of gunshot wounds on the dead hostages they had seen.

(w) The State Police radio log of State Police Radio at the prison command post was composed by the State Police back at the Troop A barracks in Batavia several days after the riot, instead of contemporaneously at the radio, contrary to the usual State Police procedure. It was made from notes which were then apparently destroyed. (The usual State Police practice is to keep notes prior to the disposition of a case.) An account of what went on over the State Police radio during the assault which appeared in the New York Times on September 14, 1971 is more complete than the official State Police Radio Log turned over to the Investigation.

(x) After the shooting stopped, D Yard was filled with tents, tables, benches and other objects containing numerous bullet holes. Instead of analyzing these objects to ascertain trajectories, volumes of fire and so forth, the State Police, on information and belief, dug a big hole in back of the prison and buried it.

(y) State Police, including a high-ranking official, observed shotgun shells lying on the ground at the entrance of the hole in which inmate Ramon Rivera was shotgunned to death; yet they failed to collect those shells or analyze the hammer marks to see whether they matched a shotgun which Trooper A turned in to the command post or any other traceable shotgun.

(z) On information and belief, neither the State Police nor the Investigation were guilty of any such systematic or effective effort to fail to collect or to destroy evidence of crimes committed by inmates.

21. Four Commissioned Officers of the State Police were the chief suspects, or the prime targets, of the hindering prosecution presentation to the Supplemental Grand Jury. In October 1974, Simonetti, astoundingly, granted immunity from prosecution to two of these four chief suspects, allegedly to gain information about the case against the other two, but without reason or benefit to the Investigation, without adequate preparation, and without questioning of at least seventy-three witnesses and categories of witnesses concerning possible criminal acts by these two suspects and about evidence which such witnesses might have provided with

the "need" to question these two suspects. I protested strenuously against these decisions; a copy of the memorandum which I gave to Simonetti (with the letter designations substituted for the names which appeared in the original memorandum) after he immunized the first such suspect is attached hereto and made a part hereof as Exhibit A. Having granted them immunity, Simonetti then failed to question them fully or adequately and declined to permit me to question the first suspect adequately and the second suspect at all, concerning such information as they possessed about the hindering prosecution case. Without consulting the Supplemental Grand Jury, Simonetti thus deprived them of the opportunity to determine whether or not to indict these two prime suspects. On information and belief, certain Grand Jurors were incensed at this usurpation of their function by Simonetti. I know of no inmate prime suspect who was ever granted immunity from prosecution under these circumstances or any other circumstances.

22. During the period from late August through early November 1974, Simonetti repeatedly refused to permit me to call witnesses to the Grand Jury who needed calling, to ask questions which needed asking of those who were called, and to follow leads which needed following, in order to give the jury the evidence it needed to fairly pass upon the hindering prosecution case which Simonetti allegedly intended to develop. Prior to the "August Switch" I had not encountered these difficulties with Simonetti. On information and belief, prosecutors were not similarly prevented from presenting evidence against inmates to any Attica Grand Jury.

23. Evidence existed that following the shootings on September 13, 1971, State Police and Correctional Officers committed numerous assaults and other crimes of brutality against inmates who had surrendered. According to the evidence, law officers beat inmates with clubs and gun butts, smashed wristwatches, eyeglasses and false teeth, permitted cigarettes to burn out upon the flesh of naked inmates, ripped bottles of plasma from the arms of injured inmates and smashed them, attempted to jam a Phillips head screwdriver up the anus of an inmate, forced inmates to run barefoot over broken glass, smashed a guitar over the head of an inmate, dumped injured

inmates off stretchers onto the ground, attempted to insert night sticks into the wounds of inmates, broke bones and committed other assaults. These post-shooting assaults and other crimes should have been comparatively easy to prosecute. Whereas the shooters wore gas masks, fired mostly untraceable weapons and would have escaped identification almost entirely were it not for their BCI statements, the savagers had taken off their masks by then and were easily recognizable. Many photographs indicated who stood where during the brutality. The brutality happened without the smoke and noise of the armed assault and occurred over a long period of time. It should have been comparatively easy under the Investigation's mandate to prosecute all crimes at Attica, to arm investigators with current photographs of all the officers who went inside the prison that day, interview all the witnesses promptly before they forgot a face, and ask simple questions about who saw what. Moreover, there were a host of disinterested witnesses, including National Guard litter bearers, local medical personnel and others. On information and belief, this failure of the Investigation to prosecute crimes of brutality by law officers stands in stark contrast to the systematic effort which the Investigation made to prosecute crimes of brutality by inmates.

24. In late October, Simonetti informed the Supplemental Grand Jury that the presentation of evidence to them had been thorough, although that was palpably untrue. He recessed them in early November for a period of appraising the evidence. Before that recess began, Special Assistant Attorney General Edward Perry, who had by then succeeded me as Simonetti's Chief Assistant, informed the Supplemental Grand Jury that they would only sit for two more weeks at most after the recess before the Grand Jury would be dissolved. In other words, at this point Simonetti planned, and told me he planned, to have the Supplemental Grand Jury reconvene only to consider such cases as then existed on the record and perhaps to hear a few additional witnesses to fill in any gaps in any such cases. I understood him to have no intention whatsoever: (a) to finish presenting the three or more months of shooter case witnesses who were necessary in order to complete those cases, (ii) to permit the jury to hear the remaining evidence on the hindering prosecution case although that presentation, too, was far from complete at that point, (iii) to commence any of

the cases concerning post-shooting brutality crimes by law officers, or (iv) to consider the possibility that any officials from Albany bore responsibility for hindering prosecution of the crimes committed by law officers at Attica. On information and belief, the Investigation never similarly sought to close off prematurely the presentation of evidence of serious crimes by inmates to any Attica Grand Jury.

25. Commencing the Fall of 1973, Simonetti had planned to write and seek publication of a report or reports to the public on what occurred at Attica. When the Supplemental Grand Jury was convened, it became his stated intention to have them produce the report on the shooting, post-shooting brutality and hindering prosecution aspect of the events at and after Attica. If he could not secure its publication as a Grand Jury Report with leave of the Court, he proposed to make it public as a Report to the Attorney General. On information and belief (and putting to one side the rather general description of events in the McKay Report), whereas publication of the inmates' deeds were made de facto through the prosecution of inmates, no similar report as to the acts of law officers at Attica was ever made.

26. In late October 1974, Simonetti assigned me the task of determining what additional investigations were necessary in connection with the prosecution of crimes and possible crimes committed by law officers. The derelictions by the Investigation which I determined in this regard were appalling. For example, it appeared that many of the inmates who had a grandstand view of the retaking from their cells in C Block had never been properly questioned about what they saw of the retaking. National Guard litter bearers who were in the prison during many of the brutality crimes which followed the retaking were never questioned by the Investigation about what they saw. Many of the inmates who were wounded by gunfire had never been examined about the circumstances of their being wounded. I continued to bring such matters to Simonetti's attention until I received a written memorandum from Perry (then Simonetti's Chief Assitant) directing me to stop writing memoranda. On information and belief, the investigation of crimes by inmates was not similarly cut off.

27. On December 6, 1974, I received information from a confidential informant to the effect that certain tape recordings of telephone conversations between State Police at Attica and Albany made during the riot and retaking, which the Investigation had been informed had been routinely destroyed, in fact existed. The informant gave me this information, and the identity of an individual he believed to have custody of the tapes and of other individuals he believed to have knowledge of the tapes, upon my promise that I would not disclose such informant's identity even to Simonetti. This information obviously warranted prompt and decision action to ascertain whether it was accurate and to retrieve such State Police tapes if it was. I promptly reported this information to Simonetti, but consistent with my promise to the informant, declined to disclose his identity. Simonetti thereupon suspended me "pending investigation", but on information and belief did not promptly or precisely follow up the lead. Having concluded that at this point I had done all that I could as a State employee towards a fair and honest Investigation and towards making the Grand Jury system work as it is supposed to work in the context of Attica, I submitted my resignation, by a letter dated December 11, 1974, to Attorney General Louis Lefkowitz, advising him of my reluctantly reached conclusion that the Investigation of crimes by officers lacked integrity and was being aborted. On December 17, 1974, I spent an hour in the office of the Attorney General advising him orally in the presence of Simonetti, Perry and a Samuel Hershowitz (who was introduced as an assistant to the Attorney General), of the basis for my conclusions. Attorney General Lefkowitz told me that these were "very serious charges" and left me with the understanding that he and Mr. Hershowitz would be back to me if they had further questions. Instead of questions, I received from the Attorney General on December 27, 1974, a letter which stated merely that he accepted my resignation and wished me success in my future ventures. On information and belief, there was no similar lack of interest and integrity in prosecuting crimes by inmates.

28. From the Attorney General's letter and the fact that I received no other communication from him upon my complicated and serious charges, I concluded that he intended to take no serious steps to

investigate the charges or rectify what I considered a grave and continuing injustice. Therefore, I typed an eighty-nine page report, appending to it seventy-one pages of supporting documents, and mailed it on about January 30, 1975, to the new Governor, Hugh Carey, with a copy to Judge Carman Ball so that he would know what I believed to be happening with his Grand Juries. (I had previously telephoned my concerns to Judge Ball on the evening of December 10, 1974, since I had considerable fear that Simonetti would try to get him to dissolve the Attica Grand Juries prematurely.) Little of significance happened as a result of my report to the Governor, until April 1975 when my charges became public through The New York Times. Thereupon, Governor Carey and Attorney General Lefkowitz appointed Bernard Meyer as Special Deputy Attorney General to investigate my charges and the overall conduct of the Investigation. Meyer was given thirty days to report, an unreasonably and unrealistically short time in my judgment. On information and belief, he took six months and produced a 570 page report which concluded, in effect, that the Investigation had been very one-sided in favor of law officers and against inmates but that nobody intended it that way; rather, that one-sidedness resulted, in his opinion, merely from mis-ordered priorities, bad judgment and the like. It is incomprehensible to me how Mr. Meyer could objectively have concluded that Messrs. Lefkowitz, Fischer, Cimonetti and possibly those above them could have chosen day by day throughout a four year period, excepting only the first seven months of 1974, to bias the Attica prosecutions strongly in favor of State employees and against inmates, without intending to do that. As a result of Meyer's conclusions, Simonetti was replaced by Special Deputy Attorney General Alfred Scotti who made more forceful admissions of selective prosecution than Meyer had made but, nevertheless, continued the Investigation's one-sided failure to prosecute law officers and other employees for their provable crimes.

29. The only indictment of inmates which I became familiar with was Indictment Number 10, which named ten inmate defendants in connection with assaults upon correction officers in the C Block office on the morning of September 9, 1971. In my opinion, the evidence against several of the inmates who were indicted in that case was substantially weaker than the evidence that existed against

dozens of State Police and Correction Officers whose cases were never presented for a vote by any Attica Grand Jury.

30. On information and belief, the Supplemental Grand Jury with which I worked for six months would have indicted numerous officers for felonies if given a fair opportunity to do so. First, the evidence of many such cases existed in the Investigation. Second, the Supplemental Grand Jury did indict Trooper Gregory Wildridge for the felony of reckless endangerment in the first degree, in October 1975, i.e., even after the attrition of time and of what I am informed was a merely pro forma presentation of evidence during 1975 had reduced the morale and the numbers of the jury. Third, apparently my superiors at the Investigation and/or in the Attorney General's office agreed that the Supplemental Grand Jury would likely indict numerous officers if given a fair opportunity to do so, or else they would not have found it necessary to stop me from giving the jury large amounts of the evidence the jury needed in order to do that job. Fourth, on information and belief, numerous Supplemental Grand Jurors were disappointed and incensed that they were not given far more officer indictments to vote upon, that they were not given such cases as they did receive far sooner, that they were never given a systematic presentation of the post-shooting brutality cases, that numerous trooper witnesses lied to them under oath without perjury cases being prepared by the Investigation and presented to them for votes as a result of such lies, and that such cases against officers as were presented to them were not presented in an orderly, systematic and professional manner.

31. It has been said often, though apparently without evidentiary foundation, that there was too much confusion at Attica on September 13, 1971, for the prosecution to be able to identify and indict specific perpetrators for specific crimes. I have studied the evidence in great detail. In my opinion, such a conclusion about the confusion on September 13 is wholly unwarranted as to scores of officers who committed felonies. On information and belief, there was far greater confusion when the riot erupted on September 9, 1971, when (as was not true on September 13) there was general bedlam and numerous fires, no photographers present, no trained law enforcement

observers watching from safe areas, no opportunity to inspect the scenes immediately after the crimes, no signed admissions by inmates such as the approximately 111 signed shooter statements, and no disinterested observers mingling with the perpetrators such as the National Guard litter bearers mingling with the officers who were physically assaulting inmates after the shooting stopped. Failures to obtain or preserve evidence doubtless resulted in many crimes committed on both September 9 and September 13 remaining unsolved. Nevertheless, confusion did not prevent the Investigation from indicting dozens of inmates for crimes committed on September 9, 1971. There is no reason that confusion should have prevented the Investigation from indicting several score law officers for crimes committed on September 13, 1971.

32. Supplemental Grand Jurors wanted to hear Russell Oswald testify. He had been Commissioner of Corrections and Governor Rockefeller's "Man-In-Charge" at Attica at the time of the riot. I believed Russell Oswald might well have been able to shed much valuable light on the State Police hindering prosecution case and also on the possibility that officials from Albany were implicated in an overall cover-up of crimes committed by officers at Attica. When the time came to examine Oswald before the Supplemental Grand Jury in November 1974, Simonetti suddenly reassigned me to work on Indictment No. 10, where by then I was useless, and assigned Special Assistant Attorney General Frank Cryan to examine Oswald, even though Cryan was not familiar with the hindering prosecution case or with the thousands of pages of testimony that had already come into the jury on it, and even though Cryan had never yet appeared before the Supplemental Grand Jury. At Simonetti's request I prepared and had delivered to Cryan an outline of questions to explore in the jury with Oswald. (Simonetti then took the position that the outline was prepared too late to reach Cryan, but Special Assistant Attorney General Perry informed me that he (Perry) had in fact personally handed it to Cryan in time.) Cryan, however, did not question Oswald from the outline or explore areas useful to the hindering prosecution case with Oswald. Instead, Cryan gave the Supplemental Grand Jury, in effect, an irrelevant and meaningless show of Oswald. On information and belief, this failure properly to elicit evidence from

Oswald was never corrected. Oswald, on the other hand, was questioned fully in the first Attica Grand Jury about the period prior to September 13, 1971, relating to crimes and possible crimes by inmates.

33. In September and October, 1974, Simonetti repeatedly refused to let me ask important questions of witnesses in the Supplemental Grand Jury, to let me call necessary witnesses and to follow potentially important leads. It became a struggle for me even to be allowed to ask witnesses to the retaking if they saw anyone shoot anyone. Of the seventy-three witnesses and categories of witnesses I listed to be called before Simonetti gave immunity from prosecution to the first of the chief suspects in the State Police hindering prosecution case, Simonetti brushed many aside, refusing to let them be called at all, or questioned adequately if called, before he recessed the Supplemental Grand Jury in November 1974 prior to his proposed dissolution of the Grand Jury. As of the time I left the Investigation in December 1974, the Investigation had somchow never gotten around to having most of the ballistics evidence taken from the bodies of hostages and inmates who were killed and wounded by State Police analyzed by anyone but State Police.

One day I was about to put a correctional officer before the jury to introduce a tape recording he had made on September 13, 1971, in which he described his observations from A Block of how the inmates "were mowed down like wheat" by the State Police "fire power that came out," and of how the correctional officer standing next to him in A Block was firing into bodies on the catwalk. Simonetti, who was at the jury that day too, sent the witness home before I could call him. I was never permitted to recall him to the jury. Numerous other leads which the Investigation failed to follow adequately or at all as of the time I left the Investigation are listed in my Preliminary Report on the Attica Investigation dated January 29, 1975. On information and belief, leads were generally diligently followed and appropriate questions asked of Grand Jury witnesses in the prosecution of crimes by inmates, in stark contrast to the prolonged and flagrant dereliction of the Investigation in these respects when it came to prosecuting crimes by law officers and other State employees.

34. On information and belief, seven potential murder cases against members of the State Police were never adequately investigated or prosecuted, and were never investigated with the diligence used to investigate murders committed by inmates.

35. The figure of 65-70 felony cases against State Police and Correctional Officers for shooting crimes is a minimal figure, since many shooting crimes were not fully analyzed or investigated as of the time I left the Investigation. Moreover, many of the 65-70 troopers and guards involved in such cases and potential cases fired multiple unjustified shots, so that the minimal number of separate felony counts which should have been given to the Supplemental Grand Jury to vote upon (but were not) numbered in the hundreds. This stands in stark contrast to what I am informed are the more than 1,000 crimes charged against inmates by the Attica prosecution and Grand Juries.

36. On information and belief, in late February 1976, a number of Attica inmate defendants were coming to trial on charges of kidnapping in the first degree and other serious felonies. Superseding Special Prosecutor Alfred J. Scotti applied to the Court to dismiss these indictments on the grounds that the Attica prosecution had been grossly one-sided and lacked fairness and evenhandedness. The Court granted the application and dismissed the serious charges against these inmates. I am aware of no circumstances which make the lack of fairness and evenhandedness of the Attica prosecution any less applicable to John Hill than it was to these inmates charged with serious felonies.

____

MALCOLM BELL

Sworn to before me, this
28th day of June, 1978.

____

JUDITH E. POWELL
Notary Public, State of New York
No. 31-4519525
Qualified in New York County
Term Expires March 30, 1980

EXHIBIT A

STATE OF NEW YORK
ATTICA INVESTIGATION
MEMORANDUM

TO: A. G. Simonetti
OFFICE: New York City
FROM: M. H. Bell
DATE: October 17, 1974
SUBJECT: Supplemental Grand Jury

This is to record my respectful but deep dissent from your decision to grant immunity from prosecution to J at this time, as expressed in our conversations of yesterday and today prior to the time you questioned him in the Grand Jury, thus immunizing him; my request made to you as a matter of my conscience that I at least not be required to participate in immunizing J at this time; and your direction to me to participate nevertheless. A summary of my stated reasons for not immunizing J now were:

1. The record contains substantial evidence that members of the Division of State Police withheld evidence, destroyed evidence, fabricated evidence, and failed to collect evidence in violation of their duty.
2. J was .... at Attica, located physically and by authority at or near the center of events there.
3. Evidence exists which tends to establish that it was J's decision not to obtain rifle and shotgun serial numbers from individuals who shot circa 100 people, and that at one point he shared with K the questioning of Tpr. A.
4. At your request I gave you, prior to your immunizing J, a list of 74 witnesses and categories of witnesses all or many of whom, I suggested, should be questioned before J, both as to the facts he might supply and the facts they might supply about him. (The list was prepared in haste and is not complete.)
5. Since last August several thousand pages of testimony have been taken in the jury on the current SP investigation but not digested or appraised by our office. Some of this evidence concerns J. Besides

not knowing the future evidence, we do not yet understand the past evidence concerning him.

6. The appraisal of evidence which you contemplate shortly should be time enough to decide whom to immunize at or near the center of the case.

My respect for your judgment and my own view of the J situation were such that I complied with your direction. Once J was immunized, I questioned him myself as aptly as I could at one point, and I hope to complete his questioning as thoroughly as possible when he is recalled. Nevertheless, occasions are conceivable in which you or I or anyone else would be required not to follow the direction of a superior, no matter how sincere the superior's motive. Only last week, for example, it was your decision not to immunize Capt. L on account of his prior testimony (given under a waiver of immunity) to the effect that he had followed directions of his superiors which may have contravened his duty as an officer.

Endnotes

[1] See *Attica: The Official Report of the New York Commission on Attica* (New York) Bantam, 1972.

[2] *Ibid.*

[3] See "Three Secret Meetings", *Attica: My Story,* Russell G. Oswald.

[4] This affidavit, included at the end of this chapter in its entirety, was Appendix XIII in the original petition. It provides a complete and verified statement on the gross and shocking details of the Attica Massacre and cover-up by state officials, including the Governor and State Chief Prosecutor. The suppression by the State of New York of Mr. Bell's well-attested and convincing evidence and report to the Governor on the criminal conduct of state troopers, Attica guards, and other state officials was the basis of his resignation as a Special Prosecutor.

[5] See, for example, "Attica Is Termed as Bad as before 1971 Rebellion", *New York Times,* July 21, 1976; Tom Wicker, *A Time to Die,* (New York) Ballantine, 1975.

[6] *Affidavit, People of the State of New York v. John Hill,* Malcolm H. Bell, at 32.

[7] "Attica lurks as a dark shadow over our system of justice. The time has come to firmly and finally close the book on this unhappy chapter of our history...." New York Governor Hugh Carey, December 30, 1976, press release.

[8] Bell affidavit found in its entirety at the end of this chapter.

[9] After the filing of the Petition, Dacajeweiah was released in the spring of 1979.

Chapter Twenty
Behavior Control in Prisons: Marion, Illinois

Petitioners respectfully draw the United Nation's attention to the use by state and federal authorities of long-term "Behavior Control" units to suppress activist prisoners. The model for such oppression was created by the federal government at the United States Penitentiary at Marion, Illinois, the replacement for Alcatraz in San Francisco harbor.

Marion is the U.S. prison which houses prisoners from all the federal prisons, many state prisons, and U.S. protectorates such as the Virgin Islands and Puerto Rico.

Throughout the United States, correctional departments are holding in solitary confinement units the prisoners who articulate the grievances of institutional populations. These units are variously called Management Control Units, Protective Custody Units, Readjustment Units, or merely Control Units.

Whatever they are called, they share certain characteristics in common. Isolation of prisoners in such units is done under the guise of classification, i.e., decisions are allegedly made not for purposes of punishment but in the best interests of the security of the institution. Prisoners placed in this "classification" are expected to cause problems and such placement is done in *anticipation and expectation of wrongdoing.* The conditions in such units are even more brutal than is usual and include twenty-three-hour or more lock-up in isolation from other prisoners in very small cells; extremes of temperature; extremely limited visitation rights; limits on the reading and writing materials that may be kept in cells; repeated rectal and other degrading body searches on any pretext; minimal nutrition; and minimal access to medical personnel. Such units are always under the supervision of guards with the most notorious reputations for physical assaults on prisoners and verbal abuse.

This increasingly sophisticated method of suppressing political prisoners is consistent with the continuing search by federal and state authorities for effective ways to break the will of prisoners who maintain their individuality and humanity.[1] State and federal legal remedies and citizens' petitions have not been able to impede this development. As this Petition is being written, thousands are incarcerated in interminable isolation without hope or domestic remedy to change their conditions.

These experiments in behavior modification began at Marion in 1972 when prison officials put over 100 prisoners in solitary confinement to break a work stoppage. The officials claimed the men were being put in solitary to undergo a "treatment program" officially labeled the Long-Term Control Unit Treatment Program. Despite the official sounding title and detailed description of the "treatment program," the control unit offered solitary confinement in 6'x9' cells, 23.5 hours-a-day for an indefinite term. Visiting rights were severely restricted and correspondence closely watched. Some of the cells, known as sensory-deprivation boxcar cells, were specially equipped with closed-font doors. Their purpose was to completely isolate a prisoner by eliminating sound and sunlight from his environment. A 60-watt light bulb burned constantly in these cells.

The prisoners who were put in this unit immediately brought a class action suit, *Adams v. Carlson* (352 F. Supp. 882 (E.D. Ill., 1973)), charging that the unit was a punishment unit, not a treatment unit. After being denied relief in federal district court, their claims were upheld in federal appeals court. As a result, many prisoners were released from the unit.

Soon after, however, the control unit was filled again (this time with seventy-two men). The Bureau of Prisons dropped its "treatment" claims and said that the unit was, in fact, a punishment unit. Again the prisoners, now known as the Marion Brothers, filed another class action suit, *Bono v. Saxbe* (74-81E (E.D. Ill., 1978)), charging, among other things, that indefinite solitary confinement in the control unit was cruel and unusual punishment and that the unit was being used specifically to punish activist prisoners, jail-house lawyers, and other prison critics.

Bono v. Saxbe was tried in July 1975, in the same federal district court as the *Adams v. Carlson* case. Numerous prisoners testified at the trial. They pointed out that five prisoners had committed suicide as a result of long confinement in the control unit and that more suicides would occur if the unit remained in operation. Revealing testimony about the purpose of the unit also came from Bureau of Prison officials. "The purpose of the long-term control unit," testified former Marion warden Ralph Aron, "is to control revolutionary attitudes in the prison system and in the society at large."

It was three years before Federal Judge James Foreman ruled on the case. During that time, three more prisoners committed suicide and a fourth, Hiller "Red" Hayes, died of a heart attack after being held in the control unit for nearly six years. Finally, in April 1978, Judge Foreman ruled. Under the pressure of a *writ of mandamus* filed by attorneys, he described the unit as a modern unit of medieval torture and ordered it to be modified. But he allowed the control unit to remain in operation and upheld the policy of indefinite solitary confinement.

Judge Foreman's ruling contained many inconsistencies. On the one hand, he admitted that the control unit had been used "to silence prison critics. It has been used to silence religious leaders and economic and philosophical dissidents." On the other hand, he justified the use of indefinite solitary confinement in the unit on the basis of the "preventive detention" doctrine.

Preventive detention is the by-word of the control unit today. According to a "Revised Control Unit Program," released in July 1978, by the Bureau of Prisons, prisoners may be put in the control unit for a variety of non-criminal reasons: insolence to an officer, unauthorized contacts with the public, participating in or encouraging a group demonstration, unauthorized meetings or gatherings, refusing to work or participate in a prison program, or encouraging a work stoppage. Even more crucial is the last statement in the program, "Attempting to commit any of the above offenses, or planning to commit any of the above offenses, shall be considered the same as a commission of the offense itself."

The high suicide rate in the control unit is the highest per-capita in the federal system according to the Bureau's own statistics. There are numerous documented cases in which activist prisoners, jail-house lawyers, Muslims, and Marxists from other federal and state prisons have been put in the control unit to stop opposition to prison conditions in other prisons.

Petitioners urge the commissioners to note most especially that political prisoners, such as Rafael Miranda (of the Four Puerto Rican Nationalist Prisoners) and Leonard Peltier (the American Indian Movement activist), are being kept at Marion in isolation from family, friends, and supporters.

The Marion prisoners' lawyers have announced they will appeal Judge Foreman's decision in the Bono v. Saxbe case. The National Committee to Support the Marion Brothers is planning a series of public protests over the next six months. They are seeking support in Congress.

Whatever the final outcome, it will be a key to future U.S. prison policies. Already the Bureau of Prisons is helping to plan a regional prison for the Rocky Mountain states to be modeled after Marion. In addition the Department of Justice is helping to plan a control unit for 500 prisoners in the Missouri State Penitentiary in Jefferson City, Missouri.

Endnotes

1 "We are the ones who, because of racial or cultural backgrounds, political or religious beliefs, feel compelled to speak out against the inhumanities of the prison system. Because of this, we are subjected to these psychogenocide programs." Alberto Mares, released from the control Unit as a result of a federal court order, December 6, 1973. He was placed there with others for participating in a peaceful work stoppage to protest the brutal beating of a Chicano by prison officials. Statement on file with Prison Research Education Project, Syracuse, New York.

Chapter Twenty-One
The "Olympic Prison"

In 1980, Lake Placid, New York, will host the Winter Olympic Games from February 13-24. The Olympic construction program will bring an estimated seventy million dollars in state and federal money to the economically depressed Lake Placid Region. The federal government is currently constructing an athletic housing facility for the games. The present plan is to turn this facility into a five hundred bed federal youth prison, most of whose inmates will be incarcerated for non-violent offenses.

This Olympic Prison will violate the Federal Bureau of Prison's own policy of locating new prisons only *in or near* the prisoners' community, as Lake Placid is more than three hundred miles from *any* major city. Since it can be reasonably anticipated that the prisoners confined in that prison will be urban, poor, minority youth, this location will ensure these young prisoners' isolation from friends and family who will neither have the means nor time to spend a weekend in travel to this remote northern rural community.

Petitioners urge this international forum to consider the travesty of the Olympic spirit this decision to build a prison on the site of an Olympic Village represents. Can nation states participate in the 1980 Winter Games in the spirit of humanity, community, and celebration on the site of what will become cages for Black and Puerto Rican youth, confined under brutal and destructive conditions?[1] Petitioners seek international support to help prevent the conversion of an international festival into a further instrument for domestic oppression and the violation of the human rights of poor and minority persons in the United States.

Endnotes

1 In the last five years, the number of Black people in federal prisons has increased at a rate five times that of whites (111% as opposed to 22% for whites). Our present federal prison population is 40% Black, up from 27% Black in 1968. Statistics were provided in the original Petition in Appendix XI.

SECTION FOUR OF THE PETITION
Appeal to the United Nations

Chapter Twenty-Two
Violations of International Covenants

Petitioners contend that the evidence and documentation presented herein clearly define consistent patterns and practices of gross and reliably attested violations of human rights and fundamental freedoms in the United States, contrary to the tenets of international law and universally accepted standards of humanitarianism. Petitioners further contend that the facts herein set forth the situations of some prisoners punished for their political beliefs and others selected for punishment by virtue of their race, ethnic origins, and poverty, and demonstrate that such abridgment of the legal and human rights and fundamental freedoms by federal, state, and local governments of the United States is particularly focused on Blacks, Puerto Ricans, Native Americans, Mexican-Americans, and other national minorities who rights have been violated historically by the majority population and whose continuing oppression is based upon their race, color, descent, or national or ethnic origin and political beliefs.

The ongoing racially selective and repressive government policies and practices have resulted in gross violations of *The United Nations Charter, The Universal Declaration of Human Rights, The International Convention on the Elimination of All Forms of Racial Discrimination, The International Covenant on Civil and Political Rights,* and *The International Covenant on Economic, Social, and Cultural Rights.*

As a member of the United Nations, the United States is legally and expressly bound by the provisions of *The United Nations Charter* and *The Universal Declaration of Human Rights.* Despite the United States Senate's refusal to ratify *The International Convention on the Elimination of All Forms of Racial Discrimination, The International Covenant on Civil and Political Rights,* and *The International Covenant on Economic, Social, and Cultural Rights,* which seek the transformation of the principles of human rights into binding legal obligations, the United States government is constructively and morally bound by their enumerated principles as a member of the international body and because of their espousal by United States' delegates to the United Nations.

Petitioners further allege that the United States government, by its domestic conduct herein documented, violates the spirit and letter of its legal and moral obligations as a member of the United Nations and the international community of humankind. In this context, Petitioners allege that the knowing, conscious, and deliberate racist and repressive policies and practices of the government towards prisoners herein discussed and the class of persons they represent violate the following provisions of international law, most specifically and in pertinent part:

The Charter of the United Nations

ARTICLE 55

With a view to the creation of conditions of stability and well-being which are necessary for peaceful and friendly relations among nations based on respect for the principle of equal rights and self-determination of peoples, the United Nations shall promote:

(a) higher standards of living, full employment, and conditions of economic and social progress and developments;...

(c) universal respect for, and observance of, human rights and fundamental freedoms for all without distinction as to race, sex, language, or religion.

ARTICLE 56

All members pledge themselves to take joint and separate action in co-operation with the Organization for the achievement of the purposes set forth in Article 55.

The Universal Declaration of Human Rights

ARTICLE 1

All human beings are born free and equal in dignity and rights. They are endowed with reason and conscience and should act towards one another in a spirit of brotherhood.

RTICLE 2

Everyone is entitled to all the rights and freedoms set forth in this Declaration, without distinction of any kind, such as race, color, sex, language, religion, political or other opinion, national or social origin, property, birth or other status.

Furthermore, no distinction shall be made on the basis of the political, jurisdictional or international status of the country or territory to which a person belongs, whether it be independent, trust, or non-self-governing or under any other limitation of sovereignty.

ARTICLE 3

Everyone has the right to life, liberty and security of person.

ARTICLE 4

No one shall be held in slavery or servitude; slavery and the slave trade shall be prohibited *in all their forms*. (Emphasis added.)

ARTICLE 5

No one shall be subjected to torture or to cruel, inhuman or degrading treatment or punishment.

ARTICLE 6

Everyone has the right to recognition everywhere as a person before the law.

ARTICLE 7

All are equal before the law and are entitled without any discrimination to equal protection of the law. All are entitled to equal protection against any discrimination in violation of this Declaration and against any incitement to such discrimination.

ARTICLE 8

Everyone has the right to an effective remedy by the competent national tribunals for acts violating the fundamental rights granted him by the constitution or by law.

ARTICLE 9

No one shall be subjected to arbitrary arrest, detention or exile.

ARTICLE 10

Everyone is entitled in full equality to a fair and public hearing by an independent and impartial tribunal, in the determination of his rights and obligations and of any criminal charge against him.

ARTICLE 11

1. Everyone charged with a penal offense has the right to be presumed innocent until proved guilty according to law in a public trial at which he has had all the guarantees necessary for his defense….

ARTICLE 12

No one shall be subjected to arbitrary interference with his privacy, family, home or correspondence, nor to attacks upon his honour and reputation. Everyone has the right to the protection of the law against such interference or attacks….

ARTICLE 18

Everyone has the right to freedom of thought, conscience and religion; this right includes freedom to change his religion or belief, and freedom, either alone or in community with others and in public or private, to manifest his religion or belief in teaching, practice, worship and observance.

ARTICLE 19

Everyone has the right to freedom of opinion and expression; this right includes freedom to hold opinions without interference and to seek, receive and impart information and ideas through any media regardless of frontiers….

ARTICLE 22

Everyone, as a member of society, has the right to social security and is entitled to realization, through national effort and international co-operation and in accordance with the organization and resources of each State, of the economic, social and cultural rights indispensable for his dignity and the free development of his personality.

ARTICLE 23

1. Everyone has the right to work, to free choice of employment, to just and favorable conditions of work and to protection against unemployment.

2. Everyone, without any discrimination, has the right to equal pay for equal work.

3. Everyone who works has the right to just and favorable remuneration ensuring for himself and his family an existence worthy of human dignity, and supplemented, if necessary, by other means of social protection.

4. Everyone has the right to form and to join trade unions for the protection of his interests....

ARTICLE 25

1. Everyone has the right to a standard of living adequate for the health and well-being of himself and of his family, including food, clothing, housing and medical care and necessary social services, and the right to security in the event of unemployment, sickness, disability, widowhood, old age or other lack of livelihood in circumstances beyond his control....

ARTICLE 26

1. Everyone has the right to education. Education shall be free, at least in the elementary and fundamental stages. Elementary education shall be compulsory. Technical and professional education shall be made generally available and higher education shall be equally accessible to all on the basis of merit.

2. Education shall be directed to the full development of the human personality and to the strengthening of respect for human rights and fundamental freedoms. It shall promote understanding, tolerance and friendship among all nations, racial or religious groups, and shall further the activities of the United Nations for the maintenance of peace....

ARTICLE 28

Everyone is entitled to a social and international order in which the rights and freedoms set forth in this Declaration can be fully realized....

The International Convention on the Elimination of All Forms of Racial Discrimination

ARTICLE 1

1. In the convention the term "racial discrimination" shall mean any distinction, exclusion, restriction or preference based on race, color, descent,

or national or ethnic origin which has the purpose or effect of nullifying or impairing the recognition, enjoyment or exercise, on an equal footing, or human rights and fundamental freedoms in the political, economic, social, cultural or any other field of public life….

4. Special measures taken for the sole purpose of securing adequate advancement of certain racial or ethnic groups or individuals requiring such protection as may be necessary in order to ensure to such groups or individuals equal enjoyment or exercise of human rights and fundamental freedoms shall not be deemed racial discrimination, provided, however, that such measures do not, as a consequence, lead to the maintenance of separate rights for difference racial groups and that they shall not be continued after the objectives for which they were taken have been achieved.

ARTICLE 2

1. States Parties condemn racial discrimination and undertake to pursue by all appropriate means and without delay a policy of eliminating racial discrimination in all its forms, and promoting understanding among all races, and to this end:

(a) Each State Party undertakes to engage in no act or practice of racial discrimination against persons, groups of persons or institutions and *to ensure that all public authorities and public institutions, national and local, shall act in conformity with this obligation*; (Emphasis added)

(b) Each State Party undertakes not to sponsor, defend or support racial discrimination by any persons or organizations;

(c) Each State Party shall take effective measures to review governmental, national and local policies, and to amend, rescind or nullify any laws and regulations which have the effect of creating or perpetuating racial discrimination wherever it exists;

(d) Each State Party shall prohibit and bring to an end, by all appropriate means, including legislation as required by circumstances, racial discrimination by any persons, group or organizations;

(e) Each State Party undertakes to encourage, where appropriate, integrationist multi-racial organizations and movements and other means of eliminating barriers between races, and to discourage anything which tends to strengthen racial division.

2. States Parties shall, when the circumstances so warrant, take, in the social, economic, cultural and other fields, special and concrete measures

to ensure the adequate development and protection of certain racial groups or individuals belonging to them for the enjoyment of human rights and fundamental freedoms. These measures shall in no case entail as a consequence the maintenance of unequal or separate rights for different racial groups after the objectives for which they were taken have been achieved.

ARTICLE 3

States Parties particularly condemn racial segregation and apartheid and undertake to prevent, prohibit and eradicate, in territories under their jurisdiction all practices of this nature.

ARTICLE 4

States Parties condemn all propaganda and all organizations which are based on ideas or theories of superiority of one race or group of persons of one color or ethnic origin, or which attempt to justify or promote racial hatred and discrimination in any form, and undertake to adopt immediate and positive measures designed to eradicate all incitement to, or act of, such discrimination and to this end, with due regard to the principles embodied in *The Universal Declaration of Human Rights* and the rights expressly set forth in Article 5 of this Convention, *inter alia*:

(a) Shall declare an offense punishable by law all dissemination of ideas based on racial superiority or hatred, incitement to racial discrimination, as well as all acts of violence or incitement to such acts against any race or group of persons of another color or ethnic origin, and also the provision of any assistance to racist activities, including the financing thereof;

(b) Shall declare illegal and prohibit organizations, and also organized and all other propaganda activities, which promote and incite racial discrimination, and shall recognize participation in such organizations or activities as an offense punishable by law;

(c) *Shall not permit public authorities or public institutions, national, or local, to promote or incite racial discrimination.* (Emphasis added)

ARTICLE 5

In compliance with the fundamental obligations laid down in Article 2, States Parties undertake to prohibit and to eliminate racial discrimination in all its forms and to guarantee the right of everyone, without distinction as to race, color, or national or ethnic origin, to equality before the law, notably in the enjoyment of the following rights:

(a) The right to equal treatment before the tribunals and all other organs administering justice;

(b) The right to security of person and protection by the State against violence or bodily harm, whether inflicted by government officials or by any individual, group or institution;

(c) Political rights, in particular the rights to participate in elections, to vote and to stand for election—on the basis of universal and equal suffrage, to take part in the government, as well as in the conduct of public affairs at any level and to have equal access to public service;

(d) Other civil rights, in particular:….

(vii) the right to freedom of thought, conscience, and religion;

(viii) the right to freedom of opinion and expression;….

(e) Economic, social and cultural rights, in particular:

(i) the rights to work, free choice of employment, just and favorable conditions of work, protection against unemployment, equal pay for equal work, just and favorable remuneration;….

(iv) the right to public health, medical care social security and social services;

(v) the right to education and training;

(vi) the right to equal participation in cultural activities;….

ARTICLE 6

States Parties shall assure to everyone within their jurisdiction effective protection and remedies through the competent national tribunals and other State institutions against any act of racial discrimination which violate his human rights and fundamental freedoms contrary to this Convention, as well as the right to seek from such tribunals just and adequate reparation or satisfaction for any damage suffered as a result of such discrimination….

The International Covenant on Civil and Political Rights
(Adopted 16 December 1966)

....PART I
ARTICLE I

1. All peoples have the right of self-determination. By virtue of this right they freely determine their political status and freely pursue their economic, social and cultural development....

PART II
ARTICLE 2

....3. Each State Party to the present Covenant undertakes:

(a) To ensure that any person whose rights or freedoms as herein recognized are violated shall have an effective remedy notwithstanding that the violation has been committed by persons acting in an official capacity;

(b) To ensure that any person claiming such a remedy shall have his right thereto determined by competent judicial, administrative or legislative authorities, or by any other competent authority provided for by the legal system of the State, and to develop the possibilities of judicial remedy;

(c) To ensure that the competent authorities shall enforce such remedies when granted.

ARTICLE 3

The States Parties to the present Covenant undertake to ensure the equal right of men and women to the enjoyment of all civil and political rights set forth in the present Covenant....

ARTICLE 5

....2.There shall be no restriction upon or derogation from any of the fundamental human rights recognized or existing in any State Party to the present Covenant pursuant to law, conventions, regulations or customs on the pretext that the present Covenant does not recognize such rights or that it recognizes them to a lesser extent.

PART III
ARTICLE 6

1. Every human being has the inherent right to life. This right shall be protected by law. No one shall be arbitrarily deprived of his life.

2. In countries which have not abolished the death penalty, sentence of death may be imposed only for the most serious crimes in accordance with law in force at the time of the commission of the crime and not contrary to the provisions of the present Covenant and to *The Conventions on the Prevention and Punishment of the Crime of Genocide.* This penalty can only be carried out pursuant to a final judgment rendered by a competent court....

ARTICLE 7

No one shall be subjected to torture or to cruel, inhuman or degrading treatment or punishment. In particular, no one shall be subjected without his free consent to medical or scientific experimentation.

ARTICLE 8

1. No one shall be held in slavery; slavery and the slave-trade in all their forms shall be prohibited.

2. No one shall be held in servitude.

3.(a) No one shall be required to perform forced or compulsory labor;....

ARTICLE 9

1. Everyone has the right to liberty and security of person. No one shall be deprived of his liberty except on such grounds and in accordance with such procedure as are established by law.

2. Anyone who is arrested shall be informed, at the time of arrest, of the reasons for his arrest and shall be promptly informed of any charges against him.

3. Anyone arrested or detained on a criminal charge shall be brought promptly before a judge or other officer authorized by law to exercise judicial power and shall be entitled to trial within a reasonable time or to release. It shall not be the general rule that persons awaiting trial shall be detained in custody, but release may be subject to guarantees to appear for trial, at any other stage of the judicial proceedings, and, should occasion arise, for execution of the judgment.

4. Anyone who is deprived of his liberty by arrest or detention shall be entitled to take proceedings before a court, in order that such court may decide without delay on the lawfulness of his detention and order his release if the detention is not lawful.

5. Anyone who has been the victim of unlawful arrest or detention shall have an enforceable right to compensation.

ARTICLE 10

1. All persons deprived of their liberty shall be treated with humanity and with respect for the inherent dignity of the human person.

2. (a) Accused persons shall, save in exceptional circumstances, be segregated from convicted persons and shall be subject to separate treatment appropriate to their status as unconvicted persons;

(b) Accused juvenile persons shall be separated from adults and brought up as speedily as possible for adjudication.

3. The penitentiary system shall comprise treatment of prisoners the essential aim of which shall be their reformation and social rehabilitation. Juvenile offenders shall be segregated from adults and be accorded treatment appropriate to the age and legal status….

ARTICLE 14

1. All persons shall be equal before the courts and tribunals. In the determination of any criminal charge against him, or of his rights and obligations in a suit at law, everyone shall be entitled to a fair and public hearing by a competent, independent and impartial tribunal established by law….

2. Everyone charged with a criminal offense shall have the right to be presumed innocent until proved guilty according to law.

3. In the determination of any criminal charge against him, everyone shall be entitled to the following minimum guarantees, in full equality:

(a) To be informed promptly and in detail in a language which he understands of the nature and cause of the charge against him;

(b) To have adequate time and facilities for the preparation of his defense and to communicate with counsel of his own choosing;

(c) To be tried without undue delay;

(d) To be tried in his presence, and to defend himself in person or through legal assistance of his own choosing; to be informed, if he does not have legal assistance, of this right; and to have legal assistance assigned to him, in any case where the interests of justice so require, and without payment by him in any such case if he does not have sufficient means to pay for it;

(e) To examine, or have examined, the witnesses against him and to obtain the attendance and examination of witnesses on his behalf under the same conditions as witnesses against him;

(f) To have the free assistance of an interpreter if he cannot understand or speak the language used in Court;

(g) Not to be compelled to testify against himself; or to confess guilt....

6. When a person has by a final decision been convicted of a criminal offense and when subsequently his conviction has been reversed or he has been pardoned on the ground that a new or newly discovered fact shows conclusively that there has been a miscarriage of justice, the person who has suffered punishment as a result of such conviction shall be compensated according to law, unless it is proved that the non-disclosure of the unknown fact in time is wholly or partly attributable to him....

ARTICLE 16

Everyone shall have the right to recognition everywhere as a person before the law.

ARTICLE 17

1. No one shall be subjected to arbitrary or unlawful interference with his privacy, family, home or correspondence, nor to unlawful attacks on his honor and reputation.

2. Everyone has the right to the protection of the law against such interference or attacks.

ARTICLE 18

1. Everyone shall have the right to freedom of thought, conscience and religion. This right shall include freedom to have or to adopt a religion or belief of his choice, and freedom, either individually or in community with others and in public or private, to manifest his religion or belief in worship, observance, practice and teaching.

2. No one shall be subject to coercion which would impair his freedom to have or to adopt a religion or belief of his choice....

ARTICLE 19

1. Everyone shall have the right to hold opinions without interference.

2. Everyone shall have the right of freedom of expression; this right shall include freedom to seek, receive and impart information and ideas of all kinds, regardless of frontiers, either orally, in writing or in print, in the form of art, or through any other media of his choice….

ARTICLE 26

All persons are equal before the law and are entitled without any discrimination to equal protection of the law. In this respect the law shall prohibit any discrimination and guarantee to all persons equal and effective protection against discrimination on any ground such as race, color, sex, language, religion, political or other opinion, national or social origin, property, birth or other status.

ARTICLE 27

In those States in which ethnic, religious or linguistic minorities exist, persons belonging to such minorities shall not be denied the right, in community with the other members of their group, to enjoy their own culture, to profess and practice their own religion, or to use their own language….

The International Covenant on Economic, Social and Cultural Rights

(Adopted 16 December 1966)

….PART I

ARTICLE I

1. All peoples have the right of self-determination. By virtue of this right they freely determine their political status and freely pursue their economic, social and cultural development….

PART II

ARTICLE 2

1. Each State Party to the present Covenant undertakes to take steps, individually and through international assistance and co-operation especially economic and technical, to the maximum of its available

resources, with a view to achieving progressively the full realization of the rights recognized in the present Covenant by all appropriate means, including particularly the adoption of legislative measures.

2. The States Parties to the present Covenant undertake to guarantee that the rights enunciated in the present Covenant will be exercised without any discrimination of any kind as to race, color, sex, language, religion, political or other opinion, national or social origin, property, birth or other status.

PART III

ARTICLE 6

1. The States Parties to the present Covenant recognize the right to work, which includes the right of everyone to the opportunity to gain his living by work which he freely chooses or accepts, and will take appropriate steps to safeguard this right.

2. The steps to be taken by a State Party to the present Covenant to achieve the full realization of this right shall include technical and vocational guidance and training programs, policies and techniques to achieve steady economic, social and cultural development and full and productive employment under conditions safeguarding fundamental political and economic freedoms to the individual.

ARTICLE 7

The States Parties to the present Covenant recognize the right of everyone to the enjoyment of just and favorable conditions of work, which ensure, in particular:

(a) Remuneration which provides all workers as a minimum with:

(i) Fair wages and equal remuneration for work of equal value without distinction of any kind, in particular women being guaranteed conditions of work not inferior to those enjoyed by men, with equal pay for equal work; and

(ii) A decent living for themselves and their families in accordance with the provisions of the present Covenant….

ARTICLE 11

1. The States Parties to the present Covenant recognize the right of everyone to an adequate standard of living for himself and his family, including adequate food, clothing, and housing, and to the continuous improvement of living conditions. The States Parties will take appropriate

steps to ensure the realization of this right, recognizing to this effect the essential importance of international co-operation based on free consent....

ARTICLE 12

1. The States Parties to the present Covenant recognize the right of everyone to the enjoyment of the highest attainable standard of physical and mental health.

2. The steps to be taken by the States Parties to the present Covenant to achieve the full realization of this right shall include those necessary for:

....(d) The creation of conditions which would assure to all medical services and medical attention in the event of sickness.

ARTICLE 13

1. The States Parties to the present Covenant recognize the right of everyone to education. They agree that education shall be directed to the full development of the human personality and the sense of its dignity, and shall strengthen the respect for human rights and fundamental freedoms. They further agree that education shall enable all persons to participate effectively in a free society, promote understanding, tolerance and friendship among all nations, and all racial, ethnic or religious groups, and further the activities of the United Nations for the maintenance of peace....

Finally, Petitioners allege that the continuing torment, torture and imprisonment of prisoners herein enumerated and the class they represent is a clear and patent violation of the *1975 Helsinki Final Act*[1] to which the United States was a signator[2] at the Conference on Security and Cooperation in Europe, concluded on August 1, 1975:

1975 Helsinki Final Act

...Motivated by the political will, in the interest of peoples, to improve and intensify their relations and to contribute in Europe to peace, security, justice and cooperation as well as to rapprochement among themselves and with the other States of the world.

Determined, in consequence, to give full effect to the results of the Conference and to assure, among their states and throughout Europe, the benefits deriving from those results and thus to broaden, deepen and make continuing and lasting the process of détente.

The High Representatives of the Participating States have solemnly adopted the following:

...1.(a)Declaration of Principles Guiding Relations between Participating States

The Participating States,...

Expressing their common adherence to the principles which are set forth below and are in conformity with *The Charter of the United Nations,* as well as their common will to act, in the application of these principles, in conformity with the purposes and principles of *The Charter of the United Nations*;

Declare their determination to respect and put into practice, each of them in its relations with all other participating States, irrespective of their political, economic or social systems as well as of their size, geographical location or level of economic development, the following principles, which all are of primary significance, guiding their mutual relations;

VII. Respect for human rights and fundamental freedoms, including the freedom of thought, conscience, religion or belief

The participating States will respect human rights and fundamental freedoms, including the freedom of thought, conscience, religion or belief, for all without distinction as to race, sex, language or religion.

They will promote and encourage the effective exercise of civil, political, economic, social, cultural and other rights and freedoms all of which derive from the inherent dignity of the human person and are essential for his free and full development.

Within this framework the participating States will recognize and respect the freedom of the individual to profess and practice, alone or in community with others, religion or belief acting in accordance with the dictates of his own conscience.

The participating States on whose territory national minorities exist will respect the right of person belonging to such minorities to equality before the law, will afford them the full opportunity for the actual enjoyment of human rights and fundamental freedoms and will, in this manner, protect their legitimate interests in this sphere.

The participating States recognize the universal significance of human rights and fundamental freedoms, respect for which is an essential factor for the peace, justice and well-being necessary to ensure the development of friendly relations and cooperation among themselves as among all States.

They will constantly respect these rights and freedoms in their mutual relations and will endeavor jointly and separately, including in cooperation with the United Nations, to promote universal and effective respect for them.

They confirm the right of the individual to know and act upon his rights and duties in this field.

In the field of human rights and fundamental freedoms, the participating States will act in conformity with the purposes and principles of *The Charter of the United Nations* and with *The Universal Declaration of Human Rights*. They will also fulfill their obligations as set forth in the international declarations and agreements in this field, including *inter alia The International Covenants on Human Rights*, by which they may be bound.

Endnotes

1 Published in the United States by the Department of State Publication 8826, General Foreign Policy Series 298, Washington, DC (August1975).

2 The United States joined the High Representative of Austria, Belgium, Bulgaria, Canada, Cyprus, Czechoslovakia, Denmark, Finland, France, the German Democratic Republic, the Federal Republic of Germany, Greece, the Holy See, Hungary, Iceland, Ireland, Italy, Liechtenstein, Luxembourg, Malta, Monaco, the Netherlands, Norway, Poland, Portugal, Romania, San Marino, Spain, Sweden, Switzerland, Turkey, The Union of Soviet Socialist Republics, the United Kingdom and Yugoslavia in signing this Act.

Chapter Twenty-Three
Petition Summary and Prayer for Relief

From the arrival of the European colonizers to North America in the Fifteenth Century and continuing to date, Blacks, Native Americans, Puerto Ricans, Mexican-Americans and other national minorities within the United States have been the victims of racist and repressive government policies and practices, perpetrated in blatant and shocking disregard for Petitioners' human and legal rights and fundamental freedoms as defined by international law.

Petitioners have enumerated to this forum some cases representative of the class within the Petition. Other individual petitioners have addressed their grievances to the United Nations at other times and on behalf of other members of the class.[1] We respectfully urge this body to be mindful that the class of persons on whose behalf we petition number many thousands.

Verifiable and well-attested historical events and the record provided by this Petition establish the unique oppression inflicted under the pretense and color of domestic law, upon Black and Native American peoples and other national minorities in plain and unmistakable derogation of their human rights and fundamental freedoms solely on the basis of their history of servitude, race, color, descent, or national or ethnic origin and political beliefs.

Because of these long-standing policies and practices which have permeated and tainted the fabric of the United States' institutions of legality and the conduct of law enforcement and governmental officials, as well, Petitioners, on behalf of those whom they represent, have no adequate or effective national or state remedies for the amelioration of their grievances, and must seek redress before this international forum. No illusory existent domestic remedies can or will be invoked to compensate these victims of governmentally condoned and sanctioned illegality or prevent the continuous abuse and maltreatment of the members of the class whom they represent.

THEREFORE PURSUANT to *Resolution I (XXIV) of the Sub-Commission on Prevention of Discrimination and Protection of Minorities*, which provides, in part, the jurisdictional basis for the submission of this Petition, and which provides that the exhaustion of domestic remedies is not necessary when "it appears that such remedies would be ineffective or unreasonably prolonged." We submit this Petition to be considered by this international forum, because of the inefficacy and futility of relief from the United States governmental entities complained of herein. This international forum should also be mindful of legal precedent established in the United States to seek alternate forums for obtaining relief and redress of grievances.

The decision enunciated by the United States Supreme Court, the highest judicial tribunal, in *Monroe v. Pape,* (365 U.S. 176, 81 S.Ct. 473, 5 L.Ed.2d 492 (1961)), *McNeese v. Board of Education,* (373 U.S. 668, 83 S.Ct. 1433, 10 L.Ed.2d 622 (1963)), and their progeny[2] explicitly set forth the principle that the availability of state remedies, in theory though not in practice, need not serve as a bar to seeking necessary relief in an alternative forum.

The history and facts attested to on the conduct of the United States in regard to its minority citizens leave Petitioners no adequate remedy at domestic law as they seek justice in law and equity to redress these fundamental violations of their basic human rights and fundamental freedoms. It is Petitioners' firm and reasoned belief that investigations of these complains by the United Nations Commission on Human Rights and the Sub-Commission on Prevention of Discrimination and Protection of Minorities is their only hope of physical, cultural, economic, and political survival.

WHEREFORE, PETITIONERS RESPECTFULLY PRAY FOR THE FOLLOWING RELIEF:

1. That the Sub-Commission on Prevention of Discrimination and Protection of Minorities refer this Petition in its entirety to the Commission on Human Rights for consideration and investigations of the allegations of the consistent pattern of gross violations of human rights and fundamental freedoms, inflicted upon enumerated persons and the class they represent; and

2. That an *ad hoc* committee be immediately appointed by the Commission on Human Rights to conduct the necessary investigation of human rights violations in the United States; and

3. That the *ad hoc* committee of the Commission on Human Rights undertake an exacting investigation of the human rights violations alleged herein, including the preparation of a written report on the fruits of such investigation and study of the evidence, and that appropriate recommendations be made to the Economic and Social Council pursuant to Resolution 1503 (XLVIII); and

4. That based on its independent investigation as well as documentation presented by Petitioners, the Commission and other appropriate United Nations bodies should condemn the racist and repressive policies and practices of the U.S. Government that deny Blacks, Native Americans, and other national minorities their human rights and fundamental freedoms; and

5. That because of the egregious nature of the human rights violations presented by Petitioners, the Commission should make public the contents of this Petition by circulation throughout the United Nations community with a view towards increasing world-wide support for the plight of political prisoners and victims of racist represssion in the United States; and

6. That the Commission grant such other and further relief as may be deemed appropriate.

RESPECTFULLY SUBMITTED,

LENNOX S. HINDS
Attorney for Petitioners:

The National Conference of Black Lawyers
126 West 119th Street
New York, New York 10026
(212)866-3501
The National Alliance Against Racist and Political Repression
150 Fifth Avenue, Room 804
New York, New York 10011
(212)243-8555

United Church of Christ Commission for Racial Justice
297 Park Avenue South, Room 23
New York, New York 10010
(212)475-2121

DECEMBER 1978

Endnotes

1 See, for example, the petition presented to the United Nations in 1951 under the *Convention on the Prevention and Punishment of the Crime of Genocide* (ratified by the United Nations 16 June 1948; not ratified by the United States), sometimes referred to as the Patterson Petition. See also one example of an attempt by a state-wide community group (Georgia) to be heard by the United Nations on the endemic and oppressive racism of their state's legal, economic, and political institutions.

Petitioners respectfully submit that many such documents and pleas for assistance from the class represented by Petitioners are already in the possession of the Secretary General and other United Nations' offices.

2 *Damico v. California,* 389 U.S. 416, 88 S.Ct. 526, 19 L.Ed.2d 647; *King v. Smith,* 392 U.S. 309, 88 S.Ct. 2128, 20 L.Ed.2d 1118; *Houghton v. Shafer,* 392 U.S. 639, 88 S.Ct. 2119, 20 L.Ed.2d 1319; *Wilwerding v. Swanson,* 404 U.S. 249, 92 S.Ct. 407, 30 L.Ed.2d 418; *District of Columbia v. Carter,* 409 U.S. 418, 93 S.Ct. 602, 34 L.Ed.2d 613; *Prieser v. Rodriguez,* 411 U.S. 475, 93S.Ct. 1827, 36 L.Ed.2d 439; *Gibson v. Berryhill,* 411 U.S. 564, 93 S.Ct. 1689, 36 L.Ed.2d 488; *Allec v. Medrano,* 416 U.S. 802, 94 S.Ct. 2191, 40 L.Ed.2d 566; *Ellis v. Dyson,* 421 U.S. 426, 95 S.Ct. 1691, 44L.Ed.2d 274.

Appendix 1

REPORT OF INTERNATIONAL JURISTS VISIT WITH HUMAN RIGHTS PETITIONERS IN THE UNITED STATES AUGUST 3 — 20, 1979

REPORT AND FINDINGS

PETITION FILED WITH
U.N. COMMISSION ON
HUMAN RIGHTS
SUB-COMMISSION ON
PREVENTION OF DISCRIMINATION AND
PROTECTION OF MINORITIES
PURSUANT TO ECOSOC
RESOLUTION 1503 ON
DECEMBER 11, 1978

By: LENNOX S. HINDS
ATTORNEY FOR PETITIONERS

THE NATIONAL CONFERENCE OF
BLACK LAWYERS

THE NATIONAL ALLIANCE AGAINST
RACIST AND POLITICAL REPRESSION

UNITED CHURCH FOR CHRIST—
COMMISSION FOR RACIAL JUSTICE

INTERNATIONAL JURIST OBSERVERS:

MR. JUSTICE HARISH CHANDRA:
INDIA

CHIEF JUDGE PER EKLUND:
SWEDEN

RICHARD HARVEY:
GREAT BRITAIN

IFEANYI IFEBIGH:
NIGERIA

SERGIO INSUNZA BARRIOS:
CHILE (In Exile)

THE HON. SIR ARTHUR HUGH MCSHINE, T.C.,
TRINIDAD-TOBAGO

BABACAR NIANG:
SENEGAL

Introduction

On December 11, 19778, a Petition was filed with the United Nations Commission on Human Rights Sub-Commission on prevention of Discrimination and Protection of Minorities pursuant to ECOSOC Resolution 1503(XLVIII) *Procedure for Dealing with Communications Relating to Violations of Human Rights and Fundamental Freedoms* and Resolution 1(XXIV) of the Sub-Commission on Prevention of Discrimination and Protection of Minorities by Attorney Lennox S. Hinds on behalf of three petitioning organizations: The National Conference of Black Lawyers, The National Alliance Against Racist and Political Repression and The Commission for Racial Justice of the United Church of Christ. The petition alleged a consistent pattern of gross and reliably attested violations of human rights and fundamental freedoms of certain classes of prisoners in the United States because of their race, economic status and political beliefs.

This submission of a petition to Secretary General Kurt Waldheim of the United Nations defined its purposes and detailed the rights violated in one hundred and twenty-eight (128) pages and included a voluminous appendix containing extensive documentation of the allegations of the petitions. The date of submission coincided with the thirtieth anniversary of the signing of the United Nations Declaration of Human Rights. It is assumed that the Sub-Commission will consider the allegations of the petition at its regularly scheduled meeting in Geneva in August 1979.

The filing of the petition caused deep interest and support in the United States among domestic organizations and individual citizens who sought to assist the petitioning organizations in encouraging United Nations inquiry on the allegations of the petition.

It was determined to invite a representative delegation of jurists and lawyers to the United States despite the meager economic resources of the petitioning organizations. The purpose of the delegation was to review the allegations of the petition, and the documentation of those allegations, and the relevancy of the united Nations resolutions by arranging personal interviews with named prisoners and by making observations of conditions complained of so that these independent observers could determine if there were "reasonable grounds to believe that...(the conditions of prisoners in the United States named in the petition) reveal a consistent pattern of gross and reliably attested violations of human rights and fundamental freedoms, including policies of racial discrimination..." as enunciated in Sub-Commission Resolution 1(XXIV)1(b) requiring referral by the Sub-Commission to the Commission of Human Rights for thorough study as provided in Resolution 1503(XLVIII). To that end, eight (8) jurists were invited to the United States during August 3-20, 1979. They attended seminars, visited with prisoners, human rights activists and lawyers, elected officials and officials of the United States Departments of State and Justice to make an independent determination of the reliability of the allegations of the petition in accordance with recognized principles of human rights and in accordance with the criteria established by ECOSOC Resolution 1503(XLVIII) 27th of May, 1970 and Resolution 1(XXIV) 13th of August, 1971.

The Identities of the International Jurists

The eight (8) invited jurists were selected for professional standing in the international community, their demonstrated commitment to the fundamental principles of international human rights, prior experiences as legal advocates for human rights in their own societies and, to the extent possible in so small a group, geographical diversity.

The invited jurists, their nation-states of origin, and a short biographical sketch of each are as follows:

Professor A. K. Asmal: South Africa (in political exile); Law Professor, Trinity College, Dublin, Ireland. International Law Specialist. Professor Asmal was unable to attend.

Mr. Justice Harish Chandra: India; Judge of the High Court of Delhi; First Standing Counsel of the Government of India (1975); Secretary General of the Indian Association of Lawyers; Member of the Secretariat of the International Association of Democratic Lawyers.

Chief Judge Per Eklund: Sweden; Division Head of the Court of Appeal, Gothenberg (until retirement 1979); Chairman, Swedish Association of Democratic Lawyers, Specialist in Political and Trade Union Freedom.

Richard Harvey: Great Britain; Barrister; Member, executive Committee, British Section of the International Association of Democratic Lawyers (IADL), Specialist in Prisons and Southern Africa Affairs; Member, IADL Mission to Front Line States.

Ifeanyi Ifebigh: Nigeria; Legal Practitioner before the Supreme Court of Nigeria; former Cabinet Minister, Anambra and Imo States in charge of Education and Schools; International and Corporate Law Specialist.

Sergio Insunza Barrios: Chile (in political exile); Minister of Justice under President Salvador Allende; past Editor *Revista de Derecho y Jurisprudencia*, official publication of the Chilean Tribunals of Justice and the Lawyers Bar Association of Chile; Member, Secretariat of the International Association of Democratic Lawyers. Active before international tribunals (UN Committion on Human Rights, General Assembly, ILO *inter alia*); President, Chile Anti-Fasciata Office in Berlin.

The Honorable Sir Arthur Hugh McShine: T.C. Trinidad-Tobago; Chief Justice of the Court of Appeal (1968 until retirement in 1971); Judge of the Court of Appeal (1962); Acting Chief Justice, Supreme Court (1961-62); Judge of the Supreme Court (1953); Acting Governor-General of Trinidad and Tobago (1970 *inter alia*); Member of Boards of Directors; Member of Government Committees: Legal Services and professional status of appointee to Government Service.

Babacar Niang: Senegal; Practitioner; Member Senegal Bar Association, Senegal Association of Democratic Lawyers; Editor of political journal, *TAXAW*; Human Rights advocate.

Purpose of the Jurists' Inquiries in the United States

The jurists, based upon their observations and relevant information, will determine whether the petitioners have made a *prima-facie* case that the situations described reveal a consistent pattern of gross and reliably attested violations of Human Rights sufficient to recommend to the Sub-Commission that the Commission on Human Rights be requested to undertake a thorough study and report recommendations on the allegations of the petition.

A *prima-facie-case* in American jurisprudence and common law is: Such as will suffice until contradicted and overcome by other evidence. *Pacific Telephone & Telegraph Co. v. Wallace*, 158 Or. 210, 75 P. 2d 942, 947. A case which has proceeded upon sufficient proof to that stage where it will support finding if evidence to contrary is disregarded. *In re Hoagland's Estate*, 126 Neb. 377, 253 N.W. 416.

A litigating party is said to have a *prima-facie* case when the evidence in his favor is sufficiently strong for his opponent to be called on to answer it. A *prima-facie* case, then, is one which is established by sufficient evidence, and can be overthrown only by rebutting evidence adduced on the other side. In some cases the only question to be considered is whether there is a *prima-facie* case or no. Thus a grand jury are bound to find a true bill of indictment, if the evidence before them creates a *prima-facie* case against the accused; and for this purpose, therefore, it is not necessary for them to hear the evidence for the defense. Mosely & Whitley. And see *State v. Hardelein*, 169 Mo. 579, 70 S.W. 130; *State v. Lawlor*, 28 Minn. 216, 9 N.W. 698. See *Black's Law Dictionary* (rev. 4th ed. 1968) at 1353.

Sponsors of the International Jurists' Tour in the United States

The Petitioning Organizations
Commission for Racial Justice, United Church of Christ
National Alliance Against Racist and Political Repression
National Conference of Black Lawyers

Co-Sponsors
African National Congress of South Africa
American Baptist Church: National Ministries
Anderson, Jim* - Southwest Joint Regional Board
Amalgamated Clothing and Textile Workers Union
Black American Law Students Association of New York
Black Students Association, Webster College, Missouri

Church of the Brethren, Washington Office
Congressman William Clay, United States Congress
Elmwood Park Tenants Association (Missouri)
Female Offenders Resource Center
W. H. and Carol Ferry
Henry Foner* - Fur, Leather and Machine Workers Union Joint Board
Fund for Open Information and Accountability, Inc., New York
Paul E. Moore, Esq.* - Harlem Assertion of Rights
Kentucky Prisoners' Support Committee of the Southern Coalition on Jails & Prisons
Lutheran Church—Missouri Synod: Board of Social Ministry and World Relief
National Committee to Free J. B. Johnson
National Committee to Support the Marion Brothers
National Interreligious Task Force on Criminal Justice
National Lawyers Guild, Louisville, Kentucky Chapter
National Lawyers Guild, New York City Chapter
National Moratorium on Prison Construction
Southern Christian Leadership Conference
Southern Christian Leadership Conference
St. Stephens Episcopal Church, St. Louis, Missouri
Team Defense, Atlanta, Georgia
United Methodist Church: Office of Urban Ministries, National Division
Board of Global Mission

Section of Christian Social Relations,
Women's Division
United Presbyterian Church in the U.S.A.
United States Peace Council
Women for Racial and Economic Equality
World Peace Council

International Jurists' Orientation Seminar
Sponsor: Max E. & Filomen M. Greenberg Center for Legal Education & Urban Policy
City College, New York
August 4, 1979

PROGRAM

Presentation of Jurists
--Professor Haywood Burns, Director, Center for Legal Education

Greetings from Petitioning Organizations
--Rev. Leon White, Commission for Racial Justice, United Church of Christ
--Victor Goode, National Director, National Conference of Black Lawyers
--Prof. Angela Davis, Co-Chair, National Alliance Against Racist and Political Repression

History and Status of Petition to UN Alleging Human Rights Violations In the US
--Lennox S. Hinds, Esq., Attorney for the Petitioners

The United Nations as an International Court of Opinion
--Michael Posner, Executive Director, Lawyers' Committee for International Human Rights

The Repression of National Minorities in the United States
--Councilman Gilberto Gerena-Valentin, Eleventh District, New York City
--Prof. Angela Davis, Co-Chair, National Alliance Against Racist and Political Repression
--Antonio Bustamente, Esq., La Raza Legal Committee
--Bill Means, International Indian Treaty Council

Conditions in Prisons
--Dan Pachoda, Esq., American Corrections Associaltion
--Dacajewiah and Akil Ajundi, Attica Brothers
--Michael Kroll, Coordinator, National Moratorium on Prison Construction

Governmental Misconduct: The FBI; Victims of COINTELPRO; Police Misconduct; Repressive Legislation
--Esther Herst, Washington Coordinator, National Committee Against Repressive Legislation

--Marshall Perlin, Esq., Fund for Open Information and Accountability, Inc.
--Jose Antonio Lugo, Esq., Center for Constitutional Rights

The Next Steps
--Lennox S. Hinds, Esq., Attorney for Petitioners

International Jurists' Itinerary in the United States

The jurists were divided into the following four groups for the itinerary below:

Group A
Babacar Niang
Richard Harvey
Marlene Archer, Escort

Group B
Harish Chandra
Per Eklund
Philip John, Escort

Group C
Sir Arthur McShine, T.C.
John Garland, Escort

Group D
Sergio Insunza
Ifeanyi Ifebigh
Deborah Reyes, Escort

AUGUST	GROUP A	GROUP B	GROUP C	GROUP D
Fri - 3	Arrive in New York City			
Sat - 4	Orientation Seminar			
Sun - 5	Free			
Mon - 6	New Jersey	Chicago	Atlanta	Lake Placid
Tue - 7	"	Minneapolis	"	Louisville
Wed - 8	"	Pine Ridge	"	"
Thu - 9	Nanpanoch	"	Montgomery	"
Fri - 10	Alderson	Sioux Falls	"	Los Angeles
Sat - 11	Charlotte	Lincoln	Baton Rouge	"
Sun - 12	"	St. Louis	"	San Francisco
Mon - 13	Raleigh	Marion	Jackson	Kansas City
Tue - 14	"	"	"	"
Wed - 15 Thu - 16 Fri - 17	Washington DC			
Sat - 18	Philadelphia: Nat'l Conference of Black Lawyers Conference			
Sun - 19	Return to New York City			
Mon - 20	Depart			

Itinerary Stop	Prison or Prisoners
Atlanta, Georgia	Reidsville Brothers
Baton Rouge, Louisiana	Gary Tyler
Alderson, West Virginia	Lolita Lebron
Charlotte, North Carolina	The Charlotte Three
Chicago, Illinois	Statesville Penitentiary
	The Pontiac Seventeen
	(Cook County Jail)
Jackson, Mississippi	Republic of New Africa Defendants
	(Parchman Prisons)
Kansas City, Missouri	Oscar Collazo
	Irvin Flores Rodriguez
Lake Placid, New York	Site of Olympic Prison
Lincoln, Nebraska	David Rice
	John Rust
Louisville, Kentucky	Eddyville Penitentiary
Marion, Illinois	Fred Bustillo
	Rafael Cancel Miranda
	Imari Obadele
Minneapolis, Minnesota	Ed Poindexter
Montgomery, Alabama	Johnny Harris (Imani)
	Oscar Johnson (Gamba)
	Tommy Lee Hines
Napanoch, New York	Napanoch Defendants
	(Sing-Sing Prison)
New Jersey	Sundiata Acoli
	Gail Madden
	George Merritt
	Assata Shakur
Pine Ridge Reservation	Site of Wounded Knee Siege
Raleigh, North Carolina	The Wilmington Ten
St. Louis, Missouri	J. B. Johnson
San Francisco, California	Eugene Allen
	Ernest Graham
	Elmer "Geronimo" Pratt
Sioux Falls, South Dakota	Russell Means
	Ted Means
	Richard Marshall

International Jurists Findings on Allegations of Human Rights Violations in the United States

Criteria for Inquiring into Allegations of the Petition

Our purpose has been to assist the Sub-Commission in following its procedures for dealing with the question of admissibility in accordance with the standards and criteria adopted by virtue of ECOSOC Resolution (XLVIII), 27th of May 1970, and Resolution 1 (XXIV), of the 13th of August 1971. We have, therefore, been concerned throughout our inquiry to observe the highest standard of objectivity and impartiality and to apply the basic principles of International Law to all issues of fact which we have had to consider.

In particular, we have been guided by the definitions of fundamental human rights and freedoms delineated in the Universal Declaration of Human Rights the International Convention on the Elimination of all forms of Racial Discrimination, the International Covenant on Civil and Political Rights, the International Covenant on Economic, Social, and Cultural Rights, and the United Nations Standard Minimum Rules on the Treatment of Prisoners.

Methods of Inquiry

To accomplish the purpose in the time available, after initial joint examination of the Petition and ancillary documentation, we divided into four teams. Each team was accompanied in its travels by an escort from the National Conference of Black Lawyers. We visited prisons and conducted exhaustive interviews with the majority of those whose cases are set forth in the Petition.

In addition, we took evidence from several other alleged victims of human rights violations similar to those complained of in the Petition. We were frequently assisted by the individual's attorney in matters of United States federal and state law and procedure. In addition, we sought out and examined official government publications such as Criminal Justice Statistics, United States Congressional Reports, Prison Population Statistics and Building Programs, together with sworn affidavits, trial transcripts, and numerous court case documents and newspaper reports. Wherever possible, we sought to raise with prison administration authorities all matters of serious complaint.

Finally, we have drawn to the attention of the Federal Departments responsible for the various categories of complaint those matters which appear to us to be principal concerns. A copy of this report is being sent to all appropriate departments.

Findings

Our detailed inquiry has satisfied us individually and collectively that the Petitioners have made out a credible, reasoned, and temperately-presented case. From our knowledge of and discussions with petitioners we believe them to be motivated solely by sincere concern for minority groups of the United States on whose behalf they are well qualified to speak.

We find that a *prima-facie* case has been made out that there exists in the United States today a consistent pattern of gross and reliably attested violations of the human and legal rights of minorities, including policies of racial discrimination and segregation.

In reaching these findings we have at all times been conscious that individual cases of injustice occur in all systems of criminal justice. However, we find that, based upon all of the evidence we have examined, the number of factors shared commonly between individual cases and reliably attested documentary materials demonstrates a clear *prima-facie* case that patterns of violations exist which call for an immediate full inquiry under the authority of the Commission on Human Rights. We have set out below the specific human rights violation we have found and situations we have personally investigated that exemplify the violations enumerated. We are not suggesting, however, that the persons named are the only ones so effected or that our list is exhaustive but only that they are the specific members of the class of persons about whom we have had personal experience and who are suffering in the ways alleged in the Petition and in our findings. It seems fair to assume that many others can and should be added to our lists.

Finally, it should also be noted that during our tours we met prisoners who are not specifically enumerated by name in the petition but whom we believe to be properly included in the class as indicated. We have supplied the Sub-Committee specific information on these persons, not described in the Petition, for their use and consideration.

Our findings are presented in the remainder of this report under seven headings as follows:

Finding I: Four Categories of Political Prisoners;
Finding II: Abuse of Criminal Processes;
Finding III: Sentencing;
Finding IV: Prison Conditions;
Finding V: Appellate Remedies;
Finding VI: Native American; and
Finding VII: "Olympic Prison".

Finding I: Four Categories of Political Prisoners

We find a *prima-facie* case exists, supported by clear and convincing evidence, in respect to the violations of human rights of prisoners who can be truly classified as political prisoners and who may be categorized in the four ways which follow.

Political Prisoners: Category A

A class of victims of FBI misconduct through the COINTELPRO strategy and other forms of illegal governmental conduct who as political activists have been selectively targeted for provocation, false arrests, entrapment, fabrication of evidence, and spurious criminal prosecutions. This class is exemplified by at least: the Wilmington Ten, the Charlotte Three, Assata Shakur, Sundiata Acoli*, Imari Obadele and other Republic of New Afrika Defendants, David Rice, Ed Poindexter, Elmer 'Geronimo" Pratt*, Richard Marshall*, Russell Means, Ted Means*, and other American Indian Movement defendants. (* indicates names of prisoners not specifically named in the Petition but visited by the Jurists.)

Wilmington Ten

The Reverend Benjamin Chavis (Hillsborough Correctional Center, North Carolina), eight other Black men and one white woman, all politically active in relation to school segregation and other similar issues in Wilmington, North Carolina, were arrested over thirteen months after racist-provoked shootings and burnings there in February, 1972. Charged and convicted of conspiracy to burn property and to assault emergency personnel, they were sentenced to a total of 282 years. One witness, Allen Hall, testified to the participation of each defendant in the offences and he was partly corroborated by two others, Jerome Mitchell and Eric Junious. All three subsequently changed their testimony. Such was the international outcry at the injustices in this case that Amnesty International declared the Wilmington Ten "prisoners of conscience", and the United States Department of Justice took the unusual step of filing an amicus curiae brief on their appeal to the U.S. District Court for the Eastern District of North Carolina, Raleigh Division on 19th April, 1979. This appeal has been denied.

We respectfully adopt the conclusions of the United States Justice Department that Allen Hall was "simply not a reliable witness," and "the reliability of petitioners' convictions must be questioned."

Further apparently gross irregularities will be touched on later. (Findings II, III, IV, and V.)

Charlotte Three

Three Black activists, Dr. James Earl Grant, Jr., Thomas James Reddy, and Charles Parker were charged and convicted of unlawful burning of a stable three years after the occurrence of the incident. They were sentenced to 25, 20, and 10 years respectively.

At post-conviction hearings, it was established that the Justice Department and the Treasury Department had paid a total of $4,000 to two highly unreliable witnesses, Theodore Alfred Hood and Walter David Washington, and had dropped serious felony charges against them in exchange for their incriminating testimony. These two witnesses were the only persons able to place the defendants at the scene of the fire, and they testified at the post-conviction hearing that their testimony at the trial had been untrue.

The evidence in relation to Rev. Chavis and the Charlotte Three indicates FBI surveillance from 1968 onwards. During this period, Mr. Chavis recalls, "I was arrested over 30 times and charged with over 30 different charges and I have been convicted on one occasion—The Wilmington Ten." Armed raids were carried out on the defendants' houses, and they were subject to constant harassment.

We find it significant that in November, 1968, FBI Director Hoover was instructing field officers in Southern California to "fully capitalize" on differences between the Black Panther Party (BPP) and the United Slaves (U.S.) and to "submit imaginative and hard-hitting counterintelligence measures aimed at crippling the BPP." (See Appendix IV-23 of the Petition submitted to the U.N.) In that same month, Rev. Chavis was forced to expel Mr. Hood and Mr. Washington from the Charlotte Black Panther organization for bringing guns to meetings, urging violent activities, and behaving provocatively. Mr. Hood and Mr. Washington responded by setting up another organization called United Souls (U.S.)

The fact that two such men could subsequently bargain with prosecuting authorities for their freedom and financial advantage causes us the deepest concern. The fact that both men also testified in another trial against Rev. Ben Chavis and Dr. James Grant provides a vital link in the use by government agencies of these unreliable witnesses to discredit the leading political activists in the minority population of North Carolna.

We note that Amnesty International has, in our view with full justification, also proclaimed the Charlotte Three "prisoners of conscience." The above and other evidence we have examined satisfy us that there is good reason to believe that governmental agencies, both State and Federal, were engaged in a protracted conspiracy to defame and politically discredit the above defendants between at least 1968 and 1972.

Assata Shakur and Sundiata Acoli

Ms. Shakur (Clinton Reformatory for Women, New Jersey) and Mr. Acoli (Trenton State Prison, New Jersey) are both political activists and former Black Panthers who were convicted of the murder of a New Jersey State Police Officer and sentenced to life plus 24 to 32 years and life plus 40 years respectively. The police officer died in a shoot-out which occurred on the New Jersey Turnpike on Mary 3, 1973. A companion of Ms. Shakur and Mr. Acoli was also killed. The evidence showed that Ms. Shakur was shot three times and could not have fired the fatal shot and that Mr. Acoli was standing outside the car unarmed when the shooting started.

In their cases, the FBI, by use of widely disseminated photographs, reports and television broadcasts, made known that Assata Shakur could be shot on sight as she had been declared a dangerous criminal political activists. During the jurists' tour, all jurists received abundant evidence of the many occasions when the right of law enforcement officers to shoot to kill has been exercised wit alarming lack of restraint. (It should be noted that during the jurists' tour, it was announced that the United States Justice Department had filed a suit against the Mayor and Police Department of the City of Philadelphia for long standing "patterns and practices of brutality" against the community and most especially against minority people. See also Appendix XII of the Petition to the U.N.)

When arrested, Ms. Shakur was shot three times. We understand that uncontested medical evidence showed her arms were raised in the air in a gesture of surrender at that time. No single crime of which she was accused except in New Jersey was ever proved against her.

In lights of the declared aims of the FBI COINTELPRO, it appears to us that these cases were probably set up to provide the FBI with an excuse to eliminate them and those who might share their political views.

The Republic of New Afrika Defendants

One of the political responses by Black people in the 1960's to what seemed to them as racist and oppressive government policies and practices was the formation of organizations that advocated the establishment of a separate Black nation within the United States. Among such groups was the Republic of New Afrika (RNA). This organization became almost from its inception a target of COINTELPRO activities. In August of 1971, the police and FBI agents conducted a raid on the official residence of the provisional Government of the RNA in Jackson, Mississippi. A policeman lost his life in the attack and an FBI agent and policeman were wounded. An office of the RNA was also raided where the president of its government, Imari Abubakari Obadele I, two men, and the female national minister of information were staying.

Imari Obadele (RNA)

Imari Obadele is a prisoner in the Control Unit of Marion Federal Penitentiary in Marion, Illinois. The Republic of New Afrika (RNA) which laid territorial claims to six states located in the southern part of the United States was also a target of FBI outrages under the Hoover COINTELPRO plan.

Imari Obadele, as President of RNA, was the subject of innumerable documents and directives dispatched between field offices and FBI headquarters. Attempts were made to discredit him and create dissension among RNA members by suggesting in an "anonymous" letter circulated to the "Brothers and Sisters" that Mr. Obadele was putting RNA funds to personal use.

In August, 1971, a pre-dawn attack on two RNA locations by Mississippi police and agents of the FBI under the pretext of serving a warrant on two fugitives alleged to be in the RNA residence, resulted in the death of a policeman and injuries to an FBI agent and another policemen. The eleven persons arrested at the two locations included Mr. Obadele who was not present at the scene of the shooting. All were charged and subsequently convicted for murder and waging war against the State of Mississippi.

Ed Poindexter and David Rice

Ed Poindexter is in prison at Stillwater, Minnesota and David Rice is in prison in Lincoln, Nebraska. Both men were convicted of first-degree murder and are serving life sentences. Their names appear on the FBI COINTELPRO documents as targets for surveillance because of their association with the Black Panther Party and their leadership roles in the National Committee to Combat Fascism (NCCF). At the time of the bombing death of a policeman, whom Mr. Rice and Mr. Poindexter have been convicted of killing in August 1970, police-Black community relations were strained because of the former's unrestrained lawlessness directed against the latter.

On the basis of the inadequate testimony connecting Mr. Rice and Mr. Poindexter with the crime and the illegal methods used in obtaining the evidence, it is unquestionable that both men were singled out and framed because of their political beliefs and involvement with an unpopular political group.

Elmer "Geronimo" Pratt

Mr. Pratt has been a prisoner at San Quentin Prison in California serving a life sentence for murder since December, 1970. In the climax of attacks on the Black Panthers in Los Angeles, California in 1968, directed in part by FBI agents under COINTELPRO, Geronimo Pratt as a BPP leader was arrested on numerous occasions as part of a pattern of police harassment. Today he finds it hard to remember whether he was arrested for murder on six, seven, or eight occasions but each time he was released shortly after for "insufficiency of proof." He was the first person picked up by the police in their search for the Manson "family" and again he was released.

In the case for which he was sentenced, Mr. Pratt was accused of murdering a woman. Her husband described the assailant two months after the murder as being a tall, dark-skinned Black man. Mr. Pratt is short and light-skinned but approximately two years after the killing, the husband identified him as the murderer. His attorneys are investigating the possible psychological manipulation of the husband by the FBI in this matter and Mr. Pratt believes his case is one in which the CIA also played an active role.

Ted and Russell Means

The Means brothers, acknowledged American Indian Movement (see Finding VI), were convicted in 1976 of rioting to obstruct justice because of an incident arising out of Native Americans' refusal to stand when a judge entered a South Dakota courtroom and the ensuing encounter with the police riot squad which was summoned to remove them from the courtroom. Ted Means was sentenced to 2-1/2 years and Russell Means to 4 years imprisonment at Sioux Falls, South Dakota.

The statute which was invoked was over 100 years old and had never been utilized by the State of South Dakota. It has since been repealed by the state legislature and thus the Means brothers have been the first and the last persons to be convicted under this statute.

Political Prisoners: Category B

Persons convicted of crimes purportedly committed to advance their political beliefs in the need for the liberation of Puerto Rico from colonial status and who have been subjected to extraordinarily protracted sentences and unusually brutal conditions of confinement. (The jurists note that in 1972, the Colonization Committee of the United Nations recognized the inalienable rights of the people of Puerto Rico to self-determination and independence.) This class is exemplified by Lolita Lebron, Oscar Collazo, Irvin Flores Rodriguez, and Rafael Cancel Miranda.

The Puerto Rican Nationalists

The surviving imprison Puerto Rican Nationalists are:

- *Oscar Collazo*, Fort Leavenworth, Kansas; serving a life sentence; 29 years already served.
- *Irvin Flores Rodriguez*, Springfield, Missouri; serving 25-75 years; 25 years already served.
- *Lolita Lebron*, Alderson, West Virginia; serving 16-50 years; 25 years already served.
- *Rafael Cancel Miranda*, Marion, Illinois; serving 25-75 years; 25 years already served.

Leaders of their people claiming independence for Puerto Rico, these prisoners participated in an armed action to demonstrate their political beliefs. For over a quarter of a century, in United States; prisons, despite being consistently denied their rights to freedom of thought, expression, and communication, and suffering all kinds of degradations and violations of their human rights, they have held steadfast to their principles.

Oscar Collazo and Irvin Flores Rodriguez are two Puerto Rican Nationalists who have served 29 and 25 years in prison respectively. On interview, they appear undaunted in their convictions. Their solidarity and commitment are expressed by their decision not to accept the conditional parole that has been offered to them. The condition was that they no longer act as free citizens for the independence of Puerto Rico. They steadfastly maintain that Puerto Rico has the right to self-determination as recognized by the united Nations General Assembly Resolution 1514 (xv). They view the U.S. judicial system as a violation of international law in that they are prisoners of a battle for liberation.

Over the last quarter of a century, these political activists have been subjected to the hardest forms of imprisonment. They have endured protracted periods of isolation, based not on any infraction of prison rules, but solely on their political beliefs. They are viewed by the prison authorities as political activists and therefore their mail and visitation rights have been severely limited and at times completely suspended.

These arbitrary actions by prison officials are in clear violation of their human rights as guaranteed by the United Nations Standards of Minimum Rules on the treatment of prisoners. (Rule 6: Basic Principles; Rules 30 and 31: Discipline and Punishment; Rule 39: Contact with the Outside World.)

They point out that the level of their treatment and their dedication to their struggle was exemplified by Andres Figueroa Cordero, the fifth imprisoned Puerto Rican Nationalist who was released from prison on October 6, 1977. At the time of his release, Sr. Figueroa was terminally ill with cancer. The doctors estimated that he had but two weeks to live after he was finally diagnosed following years of complaining of his illness. Sr. Fugueroa did live however, for fourteen months after his release. During this time all of his energies and efforts were committed to the struggle for Puerto Rican independence.

Oscar Collazo and Irvin Flores Rodriguez remain confident of their ultimate success and conduct themselves with the dignity and courageous determination of national leaders.

Rafael Cancel Miranda, who was seventeen years old at his conviction, has completed 26 years of imprisonment, six of which have been spent at Alcatraz and ten at Leavenworth. He was placed in the Marion Control Unit from its very inception because of his participation in two work stoppages as a means of protesting guard brutality visited upon a Chicano prisoner.

In his two years in the Control Unit, Sr. Miranda witnessed beatings of prisoners, tear gas attacks upon prisoners, the throwing of urine on prisoners by guards, suicides, denials of medical treatment, and innumerable other atrocities carried out by the prison authorities.

On three occasions when his wife visited him at Marion she was made to strip naked in the presence of male guards who were allegedly in search of contraband. Sr. Miranda's visitation list is restricted to those persons who knew him prior to his incarceration in 1954.

Lolita Lebron, incarcerated at the Federal Women's Prison at Alderson, West Virginia, concluded her interview to the jurists with the following remarks:

> "We are a colonized people, oppressed and captive of the United States of America. Puerto Rican political prisoners are labeled terrorists.
>
> "I would like to state to mankind that on the first of March, 1954, as Puerto Rico defended itself with small armaments (pistols), the United States was shooting the greatest gun there is in the whole world. Yet for the United States there has never been a court of justice or judgment. There was no other alternative to bring to the attention of the world that Puerto Rico in reality is a colony of the United States of America.
>
> "Yet the USA committed one of the greatest crimes by using on the first of March, 1954, an attack on mankind with an H bomb, contaminating 7,000 miles with radiation....

"Because the USA will never learn of its efforts, the Puerto Rican freedom fighters will never cease to fight for freedom....There will not be a 51st state of the united States in Puerto Rico. We have decided to die rather than to become slaves of the United States' empire....

"I am for a change in the systems of mankind. We can be free without bloodshed and I wish that may be so. Puerto Rico can become free by peaceful means—parliamentary ways and protest—but we must know the United States is at least opening its ears to the fact that Puerto Rico is going to be free.

"We don't want another Cambodia in Puerto Rico, but we are willing to have anything that must happen in order to be free."

Special Note on the Puerto Rican Nationalists

A number of us have come from countries where people have gained independence from their colonial rulers and where national leaders who were kept in prisons yesterday are the leaders of their governments today. We must note that such casual treatment given to political leaders in prisons may prove to be not only myopic but ultimately costly to the United States.

The surviving Puerto Rican Nationalists have submitted a petition to the Secretary General of the United Nations. The petition entitled "Charges and Documentation of 25 Years of Human Rights Violations Against the Imprisoned Puerto Rican Nationalists, Prisoners of War," was prepared for presentation to the United Nations' Commission on Human Rights. The jurists who visited the Puerto Rican Nationalists were presented with and have examined a copy of this petition.

The standing of these petitioners to present their case to the U.N. Commission on Human Rights can clearly be supported by the fact that all legal remedies available to them in the United States have been exhausted and that their prolonged imprisonment at this time is clearly excessive, punitive, and violative of Human Rights. Also to be considered is U.N. General Assembly Resolution No. 1514 (XV) and subsequent resolutions which guarantee all countries the right to true self-determination.

The Puerto Rican Nationalists have been subjected to unprecedented treatment by the U.S. criminal justice system. They have spent in excess of 125 years in prisons, and therefore should be immediately released.

POLITICAL PRISONERS: CATEGORY C

Persons who because of their racial and economic status are arbitrarily selected for arrest, indictment, and conviction and especially during periods of social unrest, e.g., Tommy Lee Hines*, George Merritt, Gail Madden*, and Gary Tyler. (* Indicates names of prisoners not specifically named in the Petition but were visited by the jurists.)

Tommy Lee Hines

Serving a 30-year sentence for the alleged rape of a white woman in Decatur, Alabama, this 27-year-old, retarded Black man weighs 100 pounds and has an IQ of 36 and a mental age of six years or less. He is to be tried on two further charges of abduction and rape. In each case, although the alleged victim was larger than Hines, the victim was forcibly abducted and driven by car to a secluded place where she was raped.

At Hines' first trial in Cullman, Alabama, the judge refused to declare Mr. Hines incompetent and, after Ku Klux Klansmen had paraded through the town calling for his conviction, the all-white jury convicted him. We understand the court proposed to proceed with his second trial despite the fact that his pending appeal raises serious doubts as to his competence to plead and to understand other important factors which will bear on the remaining charges.

The racist atmosphere surrounding his conviction can be gaged from the fact that a Black minister who spoke against the conviction from the courthouse steps after the trial was himself abducted by KKK members and the Alabama Klan's second-in-command publicly boasted that the Klansmen took the Reverend Whitfield into some woods and whipped him. Rev. Whitfield declines to press charges saying, "It isn't the Christian thing to do."

During a thirty-minute visit with the jurists, Mr. Hines spoke a total of ten monosyllables in response to questions and he bore marks testifying to a recent sexual assault by other inmates about which the jurists were informed. His cell is next door to that of the white power fanatic who threw a bomb into a church in Birmingham, Alabama, killing four young girls in 1964.

Having regard to all of the improbabilities and apparent irregularities of this case, we must record our profound concern about the real opportunity for a fair trial under the miasma of racism and persecution in search of a scapegoat. We feel this case only serves as an extreme example of what is an all-too-common pattern.

George Merritt and Gail Madden

In the facially tense summer of 1967 at Plainfield, New Jersey, a policeman, John V. Gleason, was beaten to death after having pursued and critically wounded an unarmed Black youth.

Two months later, George Merritt and Gail Madden together with dozens of others were charged with the murder of the officer. Eventually forced into a group trial, they alone, of twelve defendants, were convicted.

After three years in prison, the Appellate Division of the Superior Court of New Jersey unanimously reversed their convictions, ordering a re-trial on the basis that the "pressure to convict someone" was inherent in a mass trial. The court also held that the only "eye-witness" to testify against George Merritt was "unreliable" and his testimony "flimsy and questionable."

The number of public demonstrations by the local Police Benevolent Association and frequency with which George Merritt has been characterized as a "cop-killer" suggest that he, facing his first criminal charge, was made a scapegoat. Neither Mr. Merritt nor Ms. Madden had any prior political involvement but their trial became political because of the prosecuting authority's desire to find a culprit however inadequate the evidence.

Mr. Merritt's second trial conviction was unanimously reversed due to error at the trial court level violating the rules of evidence. A third trial, with an all-white jury, again resulted in conviction. This time the appellate court refused to interfere although the same prejudicial evidence had again been admitted.

A petition for writ of habeas corpus has been filed in the united States District Court of New Jersey alleging substantial violations of federal constitutional rights by both prosecutor and trial court and refusal by the state appeal courts to make any articulated determination with respect to those violations.

In our view, having discussed the matters alleged in detail with Mr. Merritt and his highly experienced trial attorney, thre are substantial grounds for believing that he and Gail Madden were arbitrarily selected because of their racial and economic status.

Gary Tyler

This young Black man was convicted of murder on charges stemming from an incident associated with school integration. In October, 1974, a school bus carrying Black students was surrounded by a brick-and-bottle-throwing mob of white youths and adults. A shot rang out and a 13-year-old white youth was killed. The police searched the bus and no weapon was found. Gary Tyler subsequently was arrested for disturbing the peace and later, at the age of 17, was charged and convicted of first degree murder. The only witness against Mr. Tyler, a very young student, later admitted she lied under coercion by the prosecution.

An all-white jury deliberated only two hours before finding Gary Tyler guilty. He was given the mandatory death penalty and sent to death row. The Louisiana death penalty was found unconstitutional and Tyler's sentence has been reduced to life.

In each of the above cases, people who had no political background appear to have been selected for prosecution on the basis of race and economic status. All-white juries predominate and racist political pressure is applied to insure the conviction of a scapegoat out of a desire to placate the appetite for vengeance in the white community. We find that these cases represent a class of people who have no hope of justice at the first instance and little or no prospect of speedy or effective remedy on appeal and we urge the United Nations to investigate the institutionalized racism which produces this sad state of affairs.

Political Prisoners: Category D

Persons who after conviction and incarceration, because they become advocates for prison reform and spokespersons for grievances of prisoners as a class, are selected for additional criminal prosecutions and unusually brutal conditions of confinement. This class is exemplified by the Napanoch Defendants*, Reidsville Brothers*, the Eddyville Defendants*, Johnny (Imani) Harris, Oscar (Gamba) Johnson*, Ernest Graham and Eugent Allen*, John Rust*, the Marion Brothers, Albert Jackson*, Ike Taylor*, David McConnell*, and other Pontiac Brothers*. (* Indicates names of prisoners not specifically named in the Petition but visited by the jurists.)

The Napanoch Defendants

The Napanoch Defendants, currently housed in Sing Sing Prison, New York State, spent 3-1/2 years combating the brutality and racial persecution inflicted by self-confessed Ku Klux Klan (KKK) members in Napanoch Prison. Typical KKK activities outside prisons were repeatedly enacted insider, with fire bombings of cells and cross burnings by Klansmen in uniform.

As a result of their constant petitions and public exposure of fifteen KKK prison employees, including State Grand Dragon Earl J. Schoonmaker, certain defendants were thrown into the "hole" and had visiting privileges revoked. Protests against other prison conditions, including overcrowding, vermin-infested food, and racially selective enforcements of prison rules consistently went unheeded.

On August 8, 1977, mounting pressure culminated in a rebellion in which several wings of the prison were seized together with 15 hostages. Despite provocative attacks by the prison's special assault squad (CERT), no deaths or significant injuries resulted and the state regained its prison on the promise of satisfying certain grievances, including a full investigation of conditions at Napanoch. These promises have been abrogated and instead members of the prisoners' negotiating team, responsible for maintaining discipline and insuring hostages' safety during the rebellion, were shipped to Sing Sing, the only New York State prison with a higher percentage of Black guards than white. They see this as a deliberate attempt to muzzle their exposure of KKK activities.

Ten of the defendants have been selected for indictment on charges ranging from contraband to riot in the first degree with the possible additional sentence of life imprisonment. The selection appears to them to have been based on their degree of political articulateness rather than any direct acts.

On May 3, 1979, the first of them, Felix Castro, was tried and convicted by an all-white jury, one of whom had been a campaign organizer for the prosecuting District Attorney. We find it particularly unusual that the judge permitted the District Attorney to interrupt defense counsel's closing speech on sixty occasions and to have sustained his objections fifty-seven times.

Most disturbing of all is the recent New York State Court of Appeals ruling in *Curle v. Ward*, June, 1979, holding that a member of the KKK should be allowed to hold a position as sensitive as that of a prison guard. With all respect to the American Civil Liberties Union and the Court, it appears to us that this cannot safeguard a prisoner's right under Rule 6 of the United Nations' Standard Minimum Rules for the Treatment of Prisoners.

The Eddyville Defendants

The Eddyville Defendants find themselves in a situation similar to that of the Napanoch Defendants. They, too, are prisoners who were singled out for harsh treatment because they became politically active while in prison campaigning against cruel and unusual punishment. (See also Finding IV, The Eddyville Defendants.)

Reidsville Brothers

Prior to 1978, Reidsville Prison was scene of continual racial strife. The facilities were segregated and the living conditions of Blacks were inferior to those of white prisoners. Tension was created between the Black and white prisoners by the racist attitudes and activities of the guards. These activities included the placing a white prisoner in a cell with several Black prisoners to be raped and communicating the occurrence of the rape to the white prisoners. Subsequently, ten Black unarmed prisoners and forty white armed prisoners were placed in the yard and three Black prisoners were killed. Terror was so rampant that prisoners had to institute a twenty-four watch for their own protection.

Finding these circumstances unbearable, some Black prisoners formed the Inmate Unity Committee. The invited white prisoners to a meeting and a coalition of Black and white prisoners was organized. Some of the Reidsville Brothers were elected as representatives. After the forming of this coalition, the rate of incidents dropped dramatically. Terror subsided and the twenty-four hour prison watch was no longer necessary. The Committee then began to organize around prison conditions.

From its inception, the guards protested the organizing of the Inmate Unity Committee (IUC). The warden, however, favored it as he could see the decrease in violence. The guards continued their resistance, threatened to strike and hired a lawyer to block the development of the IUC. Under heavy pressure, the warden retracted his position of supporting the IUC. The guards made a concerted effort to destroy the IUC and to isolate its leaders. On July 23, 1978, the Black prisoners rose up in rebellion demanding an end to:

1. Guard brutality,
2. The arming of white inmates by the guards,
3. The degrading living conditions, and
4. The non-nutritious food.

The prisoners presenting these demands were unarmed and there were no hostages involved. The administrative answer to these demonstrations was the calling in of State Troopers. As prisoners were lining up to present their demands, the guards and troopers opened fire, leaving one guard and two white prisoners dead. Two Black prisoners were later killed by white prisoners. After the rebellion, the prison was "locked down." This lock-down lasted five weeks. Prisoners were only allowed out of their cells for meals, a few at a time. Exercise, visitation rights, showers, and work details were suspended.

The prisoners that we talked to stated that for five days after the rebellion Black prisoners were beaten day and night to get them to incriminate someone in the deaths. Six indictments against the group of Black prisoners who became known at the "Reidsville Brothers" were filed. No white prisoners were indicted. The Reidsville Brothers have been locked in administrative segregation in one-man cells for the past 2-1/2 years. They are allowed out of their tiny cells for only 30 minutes a day.

We were able to interview five of the six prisoners:

- *Dwight Lindsey:* Mr. Lindsey is currently serving a 15-year sentence for robbery and kidnapping a drug dealer in his community. He is a Vietnam Veteran who returned to the U.S. with a drug problem. He was an elected leader o fthe Reidsvill Prison Inmate Unity Committee that was organized to stop the racial violence among the inmates. To date, Mr. Lindsey is the only one of the Reidsville Brothers who has gong to trial and he has been convicted of murder.
- *Forest Jordan:* Mr. Jordan is currently on trial for the murder of the white prison guard and two prisoners that occurred during the Reidsville rebellion. He was a leader in the Inmate Unity Committee and is greatly respected by prisoners for his refusal to be intimidated from protesting prison conditions.
- *Moses Evans:* Mr. Evans has also been indicted for the deaths that occurred during the Reidsville rebellion. He had filed a successful lawsuit that resulted in desegregation of the inmates. He was also a leader in the Inmate Unity Committee and received beatings because he spoke up about prison conditions.
- *James Collins:* Mr. Collins' original conviction is still the

subject of legal proceedings which he has pursued vigorously on the grounds that he and two other Black men were forced to give a burglary confession at gunpoint by police. That activity resulted in prison officials singling him out as a trouble-maker. At the time of the Reidsville rebellion, he had been I Reidsville Prison for three weeks. He is under indictment for the deaths that occurred during the rebellion. On March 8, 1979, he was stabbed in the chest by a white prisoner while in his cell. He has received little or not treatment for his wound. The jurist noted during his August 7, 1979, visit that Collins' wound was not completely healed and appeared to be infected.

- *James Andrew Johnson:* Mr. Johnson is currently under indictment for the deaths at Reidsville. He was a leader in the Inmate Unity Committee. He spoke of the atmosphere of terror that exists at Reidsville.

The conditions in which the Reidsville Brothers find themselves illuminates the pattern and practice of singling out leaders and potential leaders and subjecting them to cruel and unusual punishment due to their political activities. Their treatment and conditions echo that of the Attica defendants described in the Petition. The substandard physical conditions and brutality of Reidsville and the treatment of prisoners who protest against them are unfortunately commonplace according to our observations.

Johnny "Imani" Harris

In 1970, Johnny Harris moved with his family into an all-white neighborhood in Birmingham, Alabama and was treated to garbage on their doorstep, paint and acid on their car and Ku Klux Klan literature slipped under their door. When the family refused to be intimidated, the police became involved and Harris was arrested for four robberies and rape. His court appointed lawyer, who never once visited him before the trial, convinced Harris to plead guilty because of the allegedly overwhelming evidence the state had. Harris thought he was pleading guilty to one charge and found he had pleaded "to all of them." He received five consecutive life sentences.

While in Atmore Prison, where prisoners faced inhuman conditions,

Harris became active in the Inmates for Action (IFA) and participated in a partially successful strike. Harris, like other prisoners, continued to protest conditions and in 1973 he was charged with attempted escape and placed in the segregation (isolation) unit. On January 18, 1974, guards from the nearby Holman Prison entered the segregation unit with bloody uniforms, beat an IFA member, and stated, "We ought to kill these revolutionary niggers the way we killed Clancy." Fearing attack, the prisoners too two guards hostage and freed other segregation unit prisoners. When the warden arrived, George "Chagina" Dobbins, IFA chairman, informed him that their sole demand was to see members of the press, clergy, legislative and prison administration to expose the beatings and conditions. The warden's response to Chagina was, "You area a dead man," and a few minutes later, he lead a shooting attack against the unarmed prisoners, in which a guard/hostage died. Harris and several other prisoners were indicted for the murder. Subsequent to the attack, three Black inmates, including Chagina were either "found dead or murdered." No one was ever charged with their deaths.

Harris was convicted of participating in the rebellion and, under an old pre-Civil War aiding-and-abetting statute, sentenced to death row.

Oscar "Gamba" Johnson

Mr. Johnson is twenty-eight years old. He is presently serving a 148-year prison sentence in Atmore Prison in Montgomery, Alabama. He was originally convicted of attempt to rob at the age of sixteen. It was his first felony conviction and he received a seventeen year sentence. He was a leader in the IFA at Atmore and is one of the Atmore-Holman Brothers. The length of the sentence he is now serving is a result of the January 18, 1974 demonstration at Atmore Prison. Mr. Johnson has been subjected to continual isolation. He is in a small cell without light, there is no bed, and no sanitary facilities. He is forced to urinate and defecate on the floor.

Ernest Graham and Eugene Allen

Mr. Graham and Mr. Allen began working together in prison for amelioration of prison conditions. Graham was serving an indeterminate sentence for a minor robbery. Allen had been convicted of a first-degree murder in the California Youth Authority where he was committed following the death of his parents; he was given a seven-year-to-life sentence. Three months after the two joined forces in August 1973, a white guard was found dead and Graham and Allen, both Black, were blamed. Prison guards warned they would eliminate the two if the courts failed to impose the death penalty. In reviewing their case, the California Supreme Court overturned the death sentence imposed by the lower court, basing its decision on the blatant exclusion of Black jurors from the trial. The two men, 25 and 23 years old, have been in solitary confinement for 5-1/2 years.

John Rust

At Nebraska Penal Complex in isolation on death row for offenses of murder and robbery, John Rust has filed suit against conditions under which death row prisoners are held. Because he has challenged the denial of medical treatment, deprivation of access to law books, as well as general conditions in the isolation units, all death row prisoners have now been deprived of the possibility of spending any of their sentence in less restrictive cells as had previously been the case.

Pontiac (Illinois) Brothers

The jurists visited Albert Jackson, David McConnell, and Ike Taylor, three of seventeen prisoners who have been indicted in connection with an uprising at the Pontiac Correctional Facility which occurred on July 22, 1978. The "Pontiac 17" defendants each face fifteen counts of murder for the deaths of three white prison guards, and fourteen assorted counts which include attempted murder, aggravated battery and mob action. The rebellion, according to the prisoners, was the culmination of sustained racist and brutal administrative practices by prison authorities, the overcrowding of the facility, the unsanitary conditions which prevailed, and the failure of the prison officials to alleviate these unbearable conditions even after they were brought to their attention on innumerable occasions.

Our observations from our visits with Category D political prisoners force us to conclude that the circumstances of the above class of prisoners illuminate a pattern and practice of singling out leaders who attempt to organize for prison reform and subjecting them to cruel and unusual punishment solely because of their political activity while in prisons. Many of the physical conditions violate the U.N. Standard Minimum Rules for the Treatment of Prisoners, and the persistent pattern of brutalization and denial of due process is in clear violation of human rights.

Finding II: Abuse of Criminal Process

We find that racism and abuse of political power have, in many instances, so trained criminal proceedings that the minimum internationally recognized standard of due process has bee denied certain accused. This class is exemplified by: Assata Shakur, The Wilmington Ten, The Charlotte Three, J. B. Johnson, Gail Madden*, George Merritt, Felix Castro*, Gary Tyler, and Johnny (Imani) Harris. (* Indicates names of prisoners not specifically named in the U.N. Petition but visited by the jurists.)

Jury Selection

The famous maxim that justice must not only be done but most also appear to be done cannot be emphasized enough. Looked at in this light, the trial of Blacks by all-white juries is hardly a circumstance which can inspire belief in the possibility of obtaining justice. This is all the more so when experience shows that all-white juries often, if not invariably, return the verdict "guilty" when trying Blacks.

The composition of juries is an important area where discrimination against Blacks and other minorities can be practiced and a statement made at a Panel on July 18, 1973 by Gene McNary, St. Louis County Attorney dealing with the J.B. Johnson case, may well be symptomatic of the practices of this kind of discrimination. We quote him:

> "Maybe Blacks are eliminated because they are Black, because most clients are citizens of St. Louis County where almost all Black citizens live. *If we have a Black victim, on the one hand, then we will keep a Black as a juror.* If we believe a man, as prospective juror, because he's Black will side with a Black defendant, we will take him off the jury."

In almost every case of political prisoners investigated under FINDING I: Categories A and C, the prosecuting attorney consistently used the power of peremptory challenges to exclude all Blacks from the jury. In many instances judges acceded to a prosecutor's challenge "for cause" when the juror was Black but denied defense challenges to white jurors even where some admitted membership in the Ku Klux Klan (the Charlotte Three and Wilmington Ten trials).

At the trial of Assata Shakur in Middlesex County, New Jersey, a National Jury Project survey showed 70% of the potential jurors thought her guilty before the trial, 90% had heard of the FBI publicity on her case; nevertheless, 50% still said they thought they could give her a fair trial. The judge refused to order a change of venue and prohibited questions about what jurors had heard and read of the case. By contrast, the prosecutor successfully challenged for cause any Black juror who was even related to any person recorded on his files of having ever been arrested.

During Felix Castro's trial (Napanoch defendant, see Finding I), the prosecuting attorney told the press he had challenged Black jurors, "Because obviously the KKK is going to be a key defense issue and I wouldn't want to see minority jurors subjected to undue pressure from their own ethnic group." The hollowness of this reasoning is echoed by the judge's refusal to allow the defense to raise the issue of provocation from Klan prison guards.

In the trial of Johnny (Imani) Harris (Atmore-Holman defendant, see Finding I), while Blacks made up 15.2% of Baldwin County's population, they made up only 7.7% of the jury "pool" for selection purposes. It appears that the pool is filled with the names of persons "known" to the jury commissioners. The commissioners have testified that they knew very few Black people apart from their own and their white friends' domestic workers and employees.

George Merritt, tried three times in relation to the death of a police officer(see Finding I: Category C), has had two Black jurors as compared to thirty-four whites.

The first Wilmington Ten jury was impaneled in June 1972, and the judge allowed any juror who admitted bias to leave the court. The prosecutor, James T. Stroud, had exhausted his peremptory challenges and the panel comprised ten Blacks and two whites. Mysteriously the prosecutor became ill during the night before the jury were to be sworn in and his immediate superior declined the judge's request to take over the case. Reluctantly the judge dismissed the jury and declared a mistrial. The prosecutor then requested a special judge and Judge Robert Martin, a man wit a reputation in the community as a racist, was appointed to the case in September 1972, and he permitted whites to remain on the panel after stating that they believed the accused to be guilty. He also refused to unseat a Klan member who said he would be sure to give them a fair trial. The prosecutor used thirty-nine peremptory challenges to remove Blacks, and the impaneled jury comprised ten whites and two Blacks, the latter elderly and economically dependent on whites. Asked what reason he knew of for James T. Stroud's illness, Rev. Ben Chavis replied, "What made Stroud sick was seeing ten Black people on the jury. He was seen walking the streets of Wilmington the next day."

Prosecutorial Misconduct

In a disturbing number of cases, the jurists received evidence of conduct falling so far below what are generally recognized standards of fair prosecution as to be highly reprehensible. One of the most flagrant is the purchase of testimony with cash, presents, and grants of immunity; this occurred in the cases of the Charlotte Three and the Wilmington Ten. In the context of the dubious character of the witnesses concerned and an admission that the prosecution had "coached" them intensively, their subsequent recantation, such conduct appears to us little short of bribery. (See Appendix A1-25 through 53 of the Petition to the U.N.)

Charlotte Three: Prosecution in this case took place three years after the incident had occurred. From the time of its occurrence, there had been no indication that the parties brought to trial were under investigation. This fact made it virtually impossible for the accused to gather alibi witnesses. There was also no actual physical evidence presented at the trial. Testimony was given that the investigators went the next day and took a photograph of the incendiary device. This photograph was taken in 1968 and even at that time was only an approximation of actual occurrence, as the incendiary device was placed back in position by the investigation team after having been moved by them the previous day. When the trial took place in 1972, this "evidence" had been lost. The prosecution withheld evidence by refusing to disclose in full to the defense the details of the deal made with prosecution witnesses despite the prosecutor undertaking to the court that he would do so.

Wilmington Ten: Here the prosecution failed to make known the fact that there were deals made with the chief state's witnesses. The witnesses with whom deals were made were the only witnesses to place defendants near the scene of the fire. In view of the fact that the deal was not known to the jury, this would amount to the withholding of evidence.

George Merritt: The sole state witness insisted on the stand that he had given the police an oral statement on July 24, 1967 identifying the defendant as one of the assailants. The officers with whom the witness allegedly spoke never made a record of the interview. The prosecutor indicated in the presence of the jury that he was unable to find the documentation in his file; however, he suggested that it did exist. It was only after close of testimony that the prosecutor admitted that a record of this interview did not exist, and it was clear that he had know this throughout.

J. B. Johnson: Mr. Johnson's first conviction was overruled on appeal due to the deliberate withholding of exculpatory evidence from the defense.

I Mirrouri State Prison we met J. B. Johnson. He had been arrested in 1970 and charged as an accomplice in a jewelry store robbery which resulted in the death of a policeman. Mr. Johnson denied any involvement in the crime but was sentenced to 99 years and a day for his supposed participation in the robbery and murder.

An examination of Johnson's case is illuminating on the discriminatory application of the law. The sole eyewitness to the crime was unable to identify Mr. Johnson in the police line-up. He identified another man. The man who already had been convicted of the murder stated in a sworn affidavit that he did not know Mr. Johnson. Other facts that are suggestive of injustice are that several days after his arrest, according to police testimony, they had found two rings from the jewelry store in his shoe. A fingerprint which was said to be J. B.'s was found on a jewelry box which Mr. Johnson said the police had given him to look at.

J. B. Johnson was tried twice. During the first trial, while on bail, he was a constant subject of harassment from the police. He says that the police threatened to shoot him if he was acquitted. He was arrested seven consecutive times and was told by the police that, whenever they say him on the street, he would be arrested and held for twenty-four hours.

Each time J. B. Johnson was tried and convicted by an all-white jury. The eye-witness, who could not identify Mr. Johnson, said that "All colored people look alike." During his summation to the jury in the first trial, the prosecutor justified this wrong identification by saying, "Let's face it, to many of us, they do look alike." During the second trial the prosecutor made the following remark, "J. B. Johnson must be guilty since the jury in the first trial found him guilty."

Exclusion of Evidence

In at least two cases which the jurists examined we were surprised by the apparent denial of the right to call relevant and available evidence.

During the trial of Assata Shakur at Middlesex County in 1977 her original counsel was granted court funds to obtain ballistic and other forensic evidence. The attorney died suddenly during the trial and, after a month's delay, new counsel was briefed. At this point it appears the judge rescinded his decision on the grounds that her defense had delayed obtaining the evidence. When the defendant's friends raised funds to pay for a ballistics expert, the trial judge ruled, before the closing of all the evidence, that it was too late for this witness to testify.

In the trial of Felix Castro, the judge refused to admit any evidence of events within Napanoch Prison such as might tend to show Mr. Castro's preparedness to use reason rather than force to remedy prison injustices and held that all evidence prior to the actual days of the prison rebellion was inadmissible. Mr. Castro's legal advisors were unable to obtain the basis of this ruling.

We find these allegations disturbing since, if true, they may have deprived the jury of evidence which may have materially affected their considerations.

Prejudicial Publicity

It is a matter for concern that the prejudicial atmosphere generated by media coverage of cases appears to have had adverse consequences and we received several instances of jurors stating that, from what they had read in the press, they believed the accused to be guilty. Upon assuring the judge that they could put such prejudice out of their minds and give the accused a fair trial they were allowed to hear the case.

The principle that justice must be even to be done seems to have been seriously damaged in the cases of Sundiata Acoli, Assata Shakur, George Merritt, Gail Madden*, the Napanoch Defendants*, the Charlotte Three, the Wilmington Ten, and Tommy Lee Hines*. (* Indicates names of prisoners not specifically named in the Petition to the U.N. but visited by the jurists.)

Cases were also encountered where the conduct of the court appointed trial lawyer at first instance may well have prejudiced the accused's right to a fair and full hearing. We wish to state a principle that where the offense alleged is of a serious nature it is part of the right of an accused person to be granted the best legal assistance.

Finding III: Sentencing

We find that, when defendants belong to the racial minority groups, there is a *prima-facie* case that the pattern of sentencing is so unconscionably punitive as to violate the internationally accepted human rights of all prisoners to an opportunity for rehabilitation and reintegration into their communities;

and/or

that the sanction of imprisonment is imposed so disproportionately that minority groups in the community become the majority groups in prisons. Cases considered in Johnny (Imani) Harris, Walter Chapman*, Barbette Williams*, Oscar (Gamba) Johnson*, Sundiata Acoli*, Assata Shakur, and

Rev. Benjamin Chavis. (* Indicates names of prisoners not specifically named in the Petition to the U.N. but visited by the jurists.)

Under the first heading we would include the following prisoners serving sentences in excel of life imprisonments:

- Johnny (Imani) Harris, Atmore-Holman Prison, sentenced to death plus five life sentences consecutive upon one another;
- Walter Chapman, Angola Prison, 205 years;
- Barbette Williams, Angola Prison, 150 years;
- Sundiata Acoli, Trenton Prison, life plus 24-30 years; and
- Assata Shakur, Clinton Prison life plus 28-33 years.

Any such sentence appears to us to violate human rights since it denies the right to all prospect of re-integration into society to many people who have become politically undesirable to the government. In these circumstances we have been repeatedly struck by the moral courage with which many of those we have seen are facing the most oppressive sentences. We cannot believe these people to be incapable of rehabilitation.

Many other cases came to our attention where heavy sentences had been passed and two extremes were related to us by Rev. Ben Chavis, who said, "In my time in prison, I have met a boy of 14 and a man of 100, just sentenced to 15 years.

In a country where a boy of 14 can be given a 48-year sentence for armed robbery and where the ratio of prisoners is 250 to every 100,000 people on any day (as opposed to Great Britain, with the highest West European incarceration rate of approximately 82 per 100,000), we found the element of racism in the generally heavy sentencing pattern to be strongly marked.

The most recently available analysis of incarceration ratios between Blacks and whites, published in *Prison Law Monitor* (Volume 1, Number 9, March 1979) by Frank Dunbough, indicates that while whites are incarcerated at a rate of 43.5 per 100,000, the rate for Blacks is 367.5 per 100,000. Every state in the United States imprisons at least three Blacks for every one white, and in 13 states ten Blacks are imprisoned for every one white. We also received evidence that, overall, Blacks receive sentences 20% longer than whites so the problem is increasing annually.

As lawyers and judges concerned with sentencing processes, we are aware of the dangers of comparing one sentence with another, but the analysis of comparative sentences at page I-56 of the Appendix of the Petition to the United Nations demonstrates how selective the Court's approach was in sentencing the Charlotte Three. The general severity of sentences in political cases was very noticeable, particularly when the judge who sentenced Rev. Chavis to 29-34 years claimed he was being merciful.

Another aspect of the racism inherent in sentencing was highlighted by the Assistant Warden of Trenton State Prison, New Jersey. He confirmed that police and court discretion in prosecution sentencing were significant factors in producing the disproportion of minorities in prison. This and the setting of unreasonably high bail bonds for poor and minority prisoners are supported by statistics from the Department of Justice Census of Jails and Survey of Jail Inmates 1978. (See also Petition Appendices III-1, 2 and IX-1 through 12.)

Perhaps the clearest example of judicial evaluation of the relative importance of Black and white lives is reflected in the "Death Row" population of the prisons: 54% are white and 41% Black. However, the taking of a Black life, even by another Black is statistically one-tenth as likely to be punished by death as the taking of a white life. Yet a Black who took a white life is five times as likely to receive the death penalty as a white doing the same thing. No white has ever been sentenced to death for murdering a Black person, and no white has ever received the death sentence for rape—again a great contrast to sentencing of Blacks.

Conclusion

We are driven to the conclusion that racist criteria play a significant role in the pattern of sentencing in the United States and that no judicial or other remedy appears likely to reverse this worsening process. We therefore urge the Untied Nations to inquire fully into this evidence.

Finding IV: Prison Conditions

We find that there is clear and convincing evidence which we have observed that the treatment and conditions of prisoners in the United States are in violation of the U. N. Standard Minimum Rules on the Treatment of Prisoners to an extent warranting and requiring a united Nations investigation. We are particularly concerned with violations of Rule 6, Basic Principle; Rules 10-14, Accommodations; Rule 15, Personal Hygiene; Rule 20, Food; Rule 21, Exercise and Sport; Rule 22, Medical Services; Rule 30 and 31, Discipline and Punishment; Rule 33, Instruments of Restraint; Rule 35, Information to and Complaints by Prisoners; Rule 39, Contact with the Outside World; Rule 41, Religion; Rules 77 and 78, Education and Recreation; Rules 79-81, Social Relations and After Care.

We conclude that the pattern of these violations is such that in many prisons they amount to a systematic policy of repression with few, if any, rehabilitative features. Some examples of specific violations are listed below.

Racial Segregation

Evidence was provided to the jurists from sources in the United States Justice Department that at least eight pending United States federal cases filed in the courts since 1977 allege a continuing pattern and practice of racial segregation. In six of these cases, the United States Justice Department appeared as Plaintiff and in one other as amicus curiae.

Defendant prison authorities from the states of Oklahoma, Mississippi, Texas (two cases), Louisiana (two cases), Ohio and Illinois do not appear to have denied the evidence of such segregation.

We find it highly disturbing that the most recent court order had to be made on 13th July, 1979, enjoining the administration of the Columbus Correctional Facility, Ohio, from continuing the practice of racial segregation and from the use of cruel and unusual punishment. (*Stewart et al. v. Rhodes et al.*, U.S. District Court, Southern District Ohio, East Div. Columbus.)

The continuation of such a manifest violation of human rights until so recently causes us concern that, despite the efforts of the U.S. Justice Department, those responsible for prison administration must be continuing these illegalities, and we would urge the United Nations to investigate this possibility.

Solitary Confinement

One of the worst cases is that of Assata Shakur, who spent over twenty months in solitary confinement in two separate men's prisons subject to conditions totally un-befitting any prisoners. Many more months were spent in solitary confinement in mixed or all-women's prisons.

Presently, after protracted litigation, she is confined dat Clinton Reformatory for Women in maximum security. She has never on any occasion been punished for any infraction of prison rules which might in any way justify such cruel or unusual punishment. (Petition Appendix VIII 1-83 refers to this and further abuses.)

Oscar (Gamba) Johnson: Serving a 148-year sentence in Atmore Prison, Montgomery, Alabama, he states he has spent five years in continuous and indefinite isolation in a small cell without light, bedding, or sanitary conditions. He is forced to urinate and defecate on the cell floor. For participating in a prison rebellion, his original sentence of 16 years was increased so excessively. Because he organized a prisoners' protest against jail conditions, he has been further punished by this isolation torture.

Fred Bustillo: He has been subjected for the last thirteen months to the tortures of the "Control Unit" at Marion, Illinois. Held *incommunicado* in an 8 x 20 foot cell for all but one-half hour of each day, this leading figure in the struggle for human rights for prisoners is deprived of all but the "privilegc" of clean clothes twice each week. His correspondence is restricted, and only non-contact visits are permitted him. He must, however, submit himself to degrading rectal searches in order to avail himself of visitation rights. Fred Bustillo has been committed to the control unit because he allegedly conspired to kill prison authorities. The Disciplinary Committee, before which he appeared, refused to state the source of the allegation on the grounds that prison security might be affected. His appeals to the regional and national Federal authorities have been fruitless.

"Behavior Modification Units"

This and similar euphemisms for indefinite isolation (sometimes total, at others in small groups) of a class of prisoners with whom disciplinary problems are anticipated, but have not actually occurred, constitutes a widespread pattern of violations of the rights of poor and minority prisoners on political and other grounds.

Marion County Federal Penitentiary, Illinois: The Federal government started the experiment in "behavior modification" in 1972 in order to break a work stoppage, and the jurists who visited found the unit used as a catchment center for state and federal prisoners outspoken in their criticisms of the American government and the repressive practices which abound within the prison system.

Marion is a maximum security Federal Prison built in 1963 and with its mechanized towers and repeated layers of barbed wires gives the appearance of a concentration camp. It houses four to five hundred prisoners, half of whom are Black and a quarter of whom are Chicanos. The prison has a notorious wing called the "Control Unit" which specializes in exceptionally harsh treatment of prisoners. More than the prison itself, the Control Unit is impenetrable because outside access to it is denied almost as a rule. We were denied access to it in spite of the Bureau of Prisons at Washington having been consulted. Earlier, a group of clergymen tried to visit it, but in vain.

Numerous complaints about the demeaning, degrading, and dehumanizing treatment given to prisoners at this prison and particularly those committed to the "Control Unit" were made to us. These included solitary confinement for 23 hours a day, frequent beating by the guards, slave camp conditions of work, shake-ups and searches including those of visitors covering every part of the body, the nus included, often leading the inmates either to commit suicide or to resort to desperate steps like being killed in seeking to escape.

In the absence of a full statement of facts from the other side we would have refrained from coming to any definite conclusions, but the following additional material was placed before us:

1. Report of official investigation of alleged incidents of beatings and throwing urine by guards at the inmates, etc., made in August 1976.
2. Resolution adopted at the 12th General Synod of the United Church of Christ in Indianapolis in June 1979. We quote from one of the findings of the official report:

"On March 1, 1976, while officers W.L. Ford and E.L. Middleton were serving the evening meal, emotionally disturbed prisoner LcCount Bly, Reg. No. 87076-132, confined in H Unit, threw liquid appearing to be urine and feces on Ford, and partially on Middleton. Ford reacted by obtaining a cup of urine and throwing the same on LaCount Bly. A disciplinary report had been prepared by both Officers and Middleton.

"However, the report did not indicate the action of Ford. On interview Ford readily admitted the action and his opinion that an Officer should not be subject to such abuse. Middleton's statements confirmed that of Ford. Both officers advised the investigators that a container or containers of urine were then kept in a cabinet in the office on the range for such purposes. However, neither officer had utilized it in this manner previously or subsequent to this incident."

We further quote from the above Resolution:

"WHEREAS Federal Judge James Foreman has stated, in part, in his 1978 Bono v. Saxbe decision that this control unit has been used to 'silence prison critics...and religious leaders...and economic and philosophical dissidents," and

"WHEREAS a group of prisoners who have been held in this solitary confinement unit (hereafter called the control unit) at the Marion Federal Prison, have filed a class action suit challenging the constitutionality of the control unit, and

"WHEREAS the Marion control unit represents an experimental model for similar units being opened in both state and federal prisons, and

"WHEREAS the class action suit against the control unit is on appeal in the Seventh Circuit Court of Appeals, and

"WHEREAS a national inter-faith religious delegation, including representatives from the United Church of Christ, the Disciples of Christ, the Roman Catholic Church, the African Methodist Episcopal Church, the United Methodist Church, and other denominations and faiths, wish to visit the prisoners in the control unit but have been refused by the prison authorities,

"THEREFORE the Twelfth General Synod, acting out of strong biblical, ethical, and historical concern for the rights and humanity of prisoners, reaffirms its support for the efforts of the Marion prisoners to close the control unit and end thc practice of indefinite solitary confinement at the Marion Federal Penitentiary, and

"The prison has been described as 'the end of the line of the end of the line' and wc have no hesitation in saying that it appears to be the embodiment of a systematic pacification if not elimination of its inmates and deserves immediate fuller investigations."

Angola State Penitentiary, Louisiana

Further examples of such inhumane forms of isolation were found at Angola Prison where, despite a court order restraining the prison from using light-excluding doors, these doors remain attached to the cells at "Camp J," and the jurist who visited found credible evidence to suggest that the court order was not being complied with. Total isolation in total darkness can only be considered a cruel and unusual punishment.

Johnny (Imani) Harris and Gary Tyler

Both men have spent five years in cells 5 x 8 feet for 23-1/2 hours a day with no determination how long this isolation will last.

Eddyville Penitentiary, Kentucky

At Eddyville State Penitentiary, Louisville, Kentucky, the administrative segregation unit has been the subject of a report in 1975 to the Kentucky State Governor's Select Advisory Committee on Prisons. The report stated in part:

> "Long term segregation in the special control unit contributes to the incidence of suicide. Better procedures must be established to ensure that punishments are never unfair or excessive or detrimental to the mental, emotional or physical health of the inmates."

Our interviews with prisoners Narvel Tinsley and Gary Daily suggest little or no improvement since 1975.

The jurists were provided with a file of 27 affidavits filed in cases of prisoners' actions against the prison authorities. In the principle action, Kendrick v. Carroll, the United States Justice Department is acting as amicus curiae. The affidavits and the Eddyville inmates interviewed by the jurists testify to a catalogue of gross unwarranted shacklings, gassings, beatings, abuse, denial of medical facilities, threats, and other numerous allegations.

Elmer "Geronimo" Pratt (See Finding I: Category A above)

After seven and a half years in isolation in San Quentin Prison, California, Mr. Pratt's attorneys finally succeeded in their petition for a court order to release him into the general population. Mr. Pratt says he won the issue because:

> "The officials had no other basis with the exception of political reasons. We are arguing that I have been kept in isolation because they don't want me to maintain contact with the Black community and the officials want to prevent me from politicizing the other prisoners."

He testified further to the institutional racism and political victimization used to generate tension where violence explodes occasionally into killings.

Trenton State Prison, New Jersey

The philosophy underlying Trenton State Prison's Management Control Unit (MCU) is in part "to neutralize the more violently oriented revolutionary and terrorist factions which regularly find their way into our correctional system." (Trenton State Prison Superintendent's Annual Report for year ending June 30, 1978.) The report further indicates that the "Vroom Readjustment Unit" on the grounds of Trenton Psychiatric Hospital is used for incarceration for "serious breaches of institutional discipline."

Neither unit offers prisoners a set of rules of behavior by which they may hope to regain admission to the general population, although the Assistant Warden, when asked, "Would a prisoner be told there is never a question of his being released from the MCU?" replied, "I'm not sure such language would be used." In contrast with this statement, the jurists examined the affidavit of an attorney for Sundiata Acoli (a/k/a Clark Squire) dated May 21, 1979 in which she swore that Trenton Prison's Superintendent told her, "He will never get out of MCU. I have nightmares about Clark Squire getting out of MCU." Given the sentence he is serving, Mr. Acoli could, therefore, be condemned to spend the rest of his life in conditions of severe physical and psychological privation, despite the fact that, when he was housed in the general population, he was never found guilty of any infraction.

The prisoners held in maximum security units gave evidence which tends to support the view that such units, whose populations are almost exclusively Black, are designed to break the prisoner physically and psychologically rather than to channel his or energies along construction paths such as those presently prevailing in Rahway Prison, New Jersey. All the indications are that prisoners are victimized on a racially and politically selective basis to prevent the articulation of legitimate grievances.

In our view the extent and consistent pattern of these violations demand an immediate full scale inquiry by the United Nations into the policy and practice of Behavior Modifications Units bearing in mind in particular U.N. Standard Minimum Rules 6, 10-15, 20, 22, 30, 31, 33, 35, 39, 41, 77-81.

Medical Maltreatment

Between her frequent periods of isolation, Assata Shakur became pregnant while in prison. That this should have embarrassed the authorities is understandable, but she testified that on three occasions the medical treatment accorded to her seriously endangered that pregnancy. First, in Morris County Jail, New Jersey, when she started to bleed and vomit at the second month of her term, the prison doctor told her, "If you see a lump in the toilet, that will be your baby." She was transferred to a hospital only after her attorneys produced medical testimony in court.

At Middlesex County Jail, New Jersey, she was given a tablet different in appearance from her daily vitamin tablet. When she insisted on finding out is purpose, she discovered it was a laxative strong enough to cause an abortion.

While on Rikers Island, New York, and suffering from hay-fever, she was prescribed an antihistamine. A prison medical book she consulted listed the drug as contra-indicated for pregnant women. When she pointed this out to the prison doctor who had told her it was safe, the book was withdrawn from circulation.

These allegations are not directly corroborated and so can only be judged on the basis of the temperate way in which they were related. The baby was born healthy and there appears no other reason for fabricating such charges. When weighed together with the substantial number of allegations of over-prescription of heavy sedatives and psychotropic drugs, we can only observe that a most disturbing pattern of medical abuse is suggested and that we feel these are matters which should receive close and urgent investigation. Petition Appendix VII-1-7 refers to medical maltreatment in the case of Rev. Benjamin Chavis.

The frequency with which the jurists encountered allegations not only of medical incompetence and denial of facilities but also of experimentation with and over-prescription of psychotropic or heavily sedative drugs disturbs us greatly. We are unable to pronounce reliably on these allegations since we lack the qualifications and opportunity to investigate and observe fully. Nevertheless, we were impressed that an inquiry across the whole range of federal and state prisons should examine quantitatively and qualitatively the drug and other treatment afforded in the lights of Rule 22: Medical Services; Rules 30 and 31: Discipline and Punishment; and Rule 33: Instruments of Restraint of the U.N. Standard Minimum Rules.

Racist Persecution

Both Sundiata and Assata Shakur testified to having been incarcerated in maximum security together with white supporters of fascist views, in what appears to have been an attempt to provoke racist violence. Prison authorities can hardly be unaware of the dangers inherent in such practices.

Statesville (Illinois) prisoners testified to numerous instances of persecution of the 85% Black population and even more disturbing was the case of Napanoch Prison, New York, where some of the overwhelming majority of white guards were self-admitted members of the Ku Klux Klan. The toleration of provocative and brutal behavior by such persons towards the prisoners appears to us to contravene the non-discrimination guarantees of Rule 6 of the United Nations Standard Minimum Rules.

Systematic Brutalities

Behavior, such as is evidenced by Appendix XIV-1 of the Petition, was testified to as occurring on a widespread and racially and politically selective scale by Sundiata Acoli, Assata Shakur, the Napanoch Defendants, Lolita Lebron, Rev. Ben Chavis, and the Eddyville Defendants. Cruel and unusual punishments are evidenced by the case of Stewart v. Rhodes (see above under Segregation) in a manner which the jurists consider most disturbing and which calls for full and immediate investigation.

Food

Rules 210 and 41 of the U.N. Standards seem frequently to have been infringed by the repeated serving of pork to persons known by the authorities to be Muslims.

Education and Recreation

While recording that few prisons appear to be giving sufficiently serious attention to these vital rehabilitative functions, we record two specific instances which appear to typify the lack of administrative concern in many establishments. Assata Shakur, previously housed in Alderson Women's Prison, West Virginia, a prison with a "progressive" reputation, related that the maximum security unit gave classes in "office skills." The material value of this training is limited by the complete absence of typewriters or business machines.

The Assistant Warden at Trenton State Prison, New Jersey, when asked about educational facilities replied, "There is one teacher who comes on a regular basis." Sensing that this sounded somewhat evasive, the jurist asked, "What does 'regular' mean—one lesson for one hour each week?" "Conceivably shorter," came the reply.

Prisoners' Complaints

We forcibly struck by either the absence or ineffectiveness of grievance procedures for inmates, particularly those in maximum security conditions. The federal and state prison administrations in many instances to not seem to have learned anything from the events at Attica and, indeed, it appears that many seem to regard the mere articulation of a complaint as a disciplinary offense. This has already in our view led to the creation of a new category of political prisoner and we have presented our findings in relation to them above. We could only mention here, in the interests of fairness and objectivity, the important and progressive developments at Rahway Prison where George Merritt and other prisoners work from offices with telephones to the outside world running educational and advisory programs for youths in trouble in the outside community. This contrasted totally with most of the other institutions we visited in providing prisoners with reasonable channels to air and resolve grievances.

Forced and Slave Labor

In concluding this section of our report, we must refer to an extraordinary statement which was made in the hearing of all the jurists by a legislative aide to a U.S. Congressman that, "Prisons are a large industry in the United States. The business of holding people in prison is a business." In view of this statement, it must be concluded that arrests, trials, length of incarceration, and appeals would all be clouded and colored by such a philosophy. Indeed, every action would be based on and calculated to obtain more and more prisons and prisoners to make that business profitable. This we found to be exemplified in the prisons in Georgia, Alabama, Louisiana, and Mississippi, where it was the boast of the prison authorities that prison labor, exploited as it was, is extraordinarily cheap, plentiful and long-lasting. In the case of one prison, it brought profits in excess of one million dollars in one year from cotton, animal husbandry and soybeans.

In our view, this type of labor is tantamount to a slave condition which borders on a contravention of the13th Amendment, Section I, of the United States Constitution. We strongly advocate that the Sub-Commission give its earnest and most serious consideration to the Petition.

The North Carolina roads, reputed to be the best in the United States, are kept in such good repair by prisoners earning forty cents a day. The days of the chain gang are scarcely over.

Conclusion

Coming, as we did, from diverse countries to one of the most economically developed countries in the world, it is a shock to all of us to have to report on the gross nature and widespread extent of the violations of human rights which we have examined. Having perused a multitude of prisoners' petitions, affidavits, and court decisions, we can only conclude that the difficulties put in the way of a prisoner's right to humane treatment are only very occasionally removed by the intervention of the Justice Department or the courts. Behind the few cases where prisoners manage to get their grievances heard by a court must lie hundreds and probably thousands who lack the ability, knowledge or facilities to obtain redress.

We therefore urge the United Nations to act on their behalf and to investigate the violations evidenced to us by the representatives of this class of poor and minority prisoners who form the overwhelming proportion of inmates.

Finding V: Appellate Remedies

We find that there have been instances where legal remedies, while ostensibly available to politically unpopular and racial minority prisoners, have been so tainted with racism and political abuse of the law and/or so unreasonably delayed, that they are rendered illusory and ineffective as avenues of redress. This class is exemplified by the Wilmington Ten, the Charlotte Three, and George Merritt.

Only a procedure which does not impose an excessive burden and can be rapidly determined can furnish an effective remedy to the appellant suffering a violation of human rights committed within the limits of the criminal case. If the putting into action of a certain proceeding is too financially burdensome to be within reach of the victim or if its duration can be considerably lengthened by procedural initiatives taken by the state respondents, it will be difficult to consider that the judicial system offers an effective remedy.

In this regard, two cases are particularly significant:

1. The case of the Wilmington Ten whose provisional freedom bail depended upon an exorbitant cash payment of $500,000.00
2. The case of George Merritt whose conviction was twice declared invalid by the Appellate Courts of New Jersey, who was twice bailed, and twice re-convicted, and who is still imprisoned awaiting the outcome of his third appeal, twelve years after he was first arrest.

If the victim is refused without just reason the opportunity to review pertinent documents, circumstances or facts which supply him information which is indispensable or particularly useful to intervene directly in the proceeding whose issue is or could be a determinant in the success of failure of his own appeal, it would be difficult to admit that he had an effective remedy. The Wilmington Ten were condemned on the basis of allegations of witnesses who had negotiated their testimonies and had received rewards that had been promised them. After sentencing, these witnesses affirmed under oath that their original testimony was false. In spite of this and the strong argument on their behalf in the Department of Justice's *amicus* brief, the Wilmington Ten could not obtain a favorable review of their trial or their appearance in court at the time of the re-hearing.

The Charlotte Three faced similar injustices and similarly delayed refusals to redress. The appeal judge in the Wilmington Ten case, having spent two and one half years considering the appeal, has taken a virtually unprecedented step of himself filing a motion to strike out their appellate petition to a higher court.

In this case and that of the Charlotte Three it is most surprising that no measures were taken either to prosecute the witnesses who committed perjury or, at least in the case of James Stroud, prosecutor in the Wilmington Ten, to investigate his questionable conduct. Quite the reverse happened, since the then president of the United States, Richard M. Nixon, elevated Stroud to the position of U.S. Attorney for the Eastern District of North Carolina, a position he lost after that president's resignation.

The Puerto Rican Nationalists, Sundiata Acoli, Johnny (Imani) Harris and all those mentioned under the heading of excessive sentences (Finding III) are without meaningful recourse to the appellate courts to reduce their sentences and, in many cases, it is recognized that the courts present no avenue of hope to the political prisoner. Accordingly, political channels are more frequently being pursued by way of petitions for pardon to state governors or to the United States President in frank recognition that the issue may be one on which only a politician has the ability to pronounce. A token reduction in sentence followed the Wilmington Ten's petition to North Carolina Governor Hunt.

Conclusion

We present the above examples of this class of case fully recognizing that appeal procedures in many countries take longer to be concluded than the original trial. However, a significant number o f other prisoners we interviewed testified not only to manifest injustices during their trials (see Finding II) or excessive sentences (see Finding III) but have also presented strong evidence to suggest a degree of political and/or race bias governing the consideration of their appeals.

In this latter regard we note with considerable surprise that, in the State of North Carolina at least, a Supreme Court judge is appointed through political channels and need have no legal or judicial training whatsoever. The office is frequently a political reward and holders include, *inter alia*, a former used-car salesman. This identity between judiciary and politics appears to be highly regrettable in the context of cases such as the Wilmington Ten.

These conditions appear without remedy within the United States and we accordingly request the United Nations to investigate and report on these findings.

Finding VI: Native Americans

We find that sufficient evidence exists to establish a *prima-facie* case that the United States government has, throughout its history, pursued a policy of systematic extermination of the Native American peoples. Most recently, these acts of aggression have been focused on the leaders and members of the American Indian Movement (AIM) who oppose these policies. We, therefore, urge that the United Nations institute a full investigation into these allegations of the crime of genocide.

While the attacks on the leaders of the American Indian Movement could well have been listed under Finding I, Category A-II, III, and V, and while many Native Americans could be considered under Finding I, Category C, we feel it necessary to set a section apart in this Report to express the depth of our concern for the plight of these peoples.

Having regard to the fact that the U.N. Sub-Commission is already apprised of this issue by virtue of the Petition lodged on behalf of the International Indian Treaty Council, we would respectfully adopt the allegations and recommendations contained therein. We will, therefore, limit our own observations on this most serious human rights issue to the following brief report from the jurists who visited the Pine Ridge

Reservation and Sioux Falls, South Dakota. Further substantiating evidence is to be found in Appendix X to the present Petition.

Native Americans, who constitute less than 1% of the population and who are the original inhabitants of America, who were colonized by the Europeans coming to the shores of America, have established a case of genocide against them reminiscent of the 1951 U.N. petition filed by Paul Robeson and William Patterson under the title, "We Charge Genocide." The Native Americans' experiences with the United States government further demonstrate the violation, indeed abrogation, of at least 400 treaties by the government of the U.S., and a failure on its part to settle disputes by negotiation. The leaders of the Native Americans and of the American Indian Movement have thus posed the most far-reaching challenge to the legal validity of the United States of America as now constituted and to its ownership of vast tracts of land acquired in violation of treaties duly negotiated and executed. They have established a sufficient claim to justify payment of reparations to reduce the legal injury arriving out of such violations and other equitable and legal remedies. Nevertheless, an estimated 75% suffer from malnutrition, 75-80% unemployment and a 44-year life expectancy where whites expect 74 years.

We were informed that the government of the U.S.A. has not only ignored demands made by Native Americans but has continued a policy of systematic extermination of the Native Americans which may well result in a permanent solution to this problem.

We visited the Indian Reservation in South Dakota and found a whole people living so completely in isolation as if condemned to perpetual solitary confinement. We heard accounts of daily harassment of Native Americans by the FBI from numerous people we met and found a painful sense of despondency among ordinary people whose grievances were not only ignored but whose harassment was officially and governmentally encouraged.

It is with this background in mind that it is necessary to see the cases and convictions of Richard Marshall, Russell Means, Ted Means, Leonard Peltier, and many, many other leaders of the American Indian Movement (AIM). Without going into the details of their cases, we consider it necessary to take the prosecution and conviction of the Means Brothers as an example and to point out certain features of it.

The prosecution of the Means Brothers and several others arose out of an incident where, during a court trial, the persons sitting in the courtroom did not pay their respect by standing when the judge entered the courtroom. This angered the judge and he returned to his chamber. On the second occasion when this "insolence" was repeated, the judge ordered the courtroom cleared by the riot-squad of the police. A melee ensued and some window panes were broken. Thereupon the Means Brothers were prosecuted under an act against rioting to obstruct justice.

We were informed that in nearly 150 years since this act was placed on the statute books this was the first instance of its application. The act was repealed in 1976. The prosecution of the Means Brothers is, therefore, not only the first prosecution, but also the last under it. Upon conviction, sentences of 2-1/2 years and 4 years were imposed on Ted and Russell Means respectively based on police witnesses in preference to the testimony of five Bishops who were eye-witnesses. After Ted Means was sentenced, he was offered a reduction of sentence from 30 months to 18 months if he complied with conditions, one of which was that he agree not to participate in the activities of the American Indian Movement. He refused the condition.

Quite apart from the serious doubts raised in our minds about the real purpose of prosecuting the leaders of AIM (particularly in view of 12 trials previously directed unsuccessfully against Russell Means), we cannot but express surprise at the aforesaid conditional offer made by the court which seeks to take away the fundamental rights guaranteed by the First Amendment of the U.S. Constitution.

We were also made aware of the plans for uranium mining in the Native American territory of the Black Hills which Native Americans are opposed to and which constitutes a serious hazard to health and life in the entire area.

Conclusion

We urge the United Nations to investigate speedily and thoroughly these well-attested allegations since there is not possible channel of remedies for the Native Americans to pursue in the United States given present governmental attitudes.

Finding VII: "Olympic Prison"

We are particularly disturbed to find that the United States Olympic Committee, the United States Bureau of Prisons, and other governmental agencies are intending to house Winter Games 1980 Olympic athletes in a newly constructed prison in Lake Placid. It is not our purpose to investigate the suitability of such accommodations for athletes (the jurists take note that many responsible organizations have called on U.N. member states to boycott the games if the prison is so used), however, our visit to this site has satisfied us that the site is totally inappropriate for a prison duc to the isolation, hostile climatic environment, and the great distance of the site from any urban center from which its poor minority prisoners may be expected to come, thus causing excessive hardships to them and their families.

The locale of this Lake Placid Prison, in upstate New York, is far removed from any sizable city and with poor communication facilities rendering almost impossible any contact by prisoners with the outside world. It is significant that this prison, 300 miles away from New York City, will serve as a huge corrective prison for young offenders eighteen to twenty-five years of age from the New York City, New York, and Boston, Massachusetts, areas convicted of federal crimes. Blacks, Hispanics, and other minorities from large urban areas who comprise a disproportionate percentage of the prison population can be expected to be the majority of prisoners confined there. Lake Placid, by reason of its being situated in a remote, white, rural area, will typically be staffed by white guards—a situation which will inevitably exacerbate racial tensions within the prison.

Thousands of Americans have protested this decision of the Federal Bureau of Prisons and the United States Congress on this after-use of the Olympic Village to no avail.

Indeed, when the jurists met the Chief Counsel to the House of Representatives Judiciary Committee's Sub-Committee on Courts, Civil Liberties and the Administration of Justice, he confirmed that the local Congressman who had arranged the financial appropriation for building the prison had been constitutionally enabled to do so without any consultation with the Sub-Committee of the Judiciary which would have overall responsibility for the prison's administration.

The Chief Counsel said that it was "a bureaucratic rather than a democratic decision" since once the finance had been organized there was effectively no constitutional means of reversing the decision.

Sixty-two Northern New York State Protestant, Roman Catholic, and Jewish clergy have issued a "Statement of Conscience" which articulates the objections to this plan very well and which we reproduce here in its entirety for the Commission's consideration.

> "As persons who have worked for years with prison inmates and their families back home we, the undersigned North Country clergy, wish to take our stand against the use of the Winter Olympic dormitories near Lake Placid as a medium security federal prison for youths 18-25 when the Olympic games conclude in 1980.
>
> "Even the Federal Bureau of Prisons admits that the location, 300 mines from New York City, the chief source of inmates, violates its own requirement for putting such facilities near the inmates' homes, social resources, families, and clergy. It admits that it would never have chosen Lake Placid, so far away from New York City, but that arrangements in Congress were made and it accepted them.
>
> We protest the inhuman location. Forty percent of federal prisoners are non-white; most are not sentenced for crimes of violence; most are from poor families, and Lake Placid is hard to reach even for the well to do. For the mothers, fathers, wives, ministers, and priests who will try to visit the inmates, it will be virtually impossible, given their weekly

income, the expense of getting to the prison and remaining overnight, and even giving up work time to go.

We know that policies which are morally wrong are usually financially expensive in the long run. The grotesque after-use of the Lake Placid Olympic dormitories makes a mockery of the games themselves, which are supposed to exemplify fair play, brotherhood, and good will. Even the Russians are building 1980 Summer Olympic dormitories which will be converted into a housing project after the games in Moscow, and event America's Olympic Committee Secretary-General, F. Don Miller, declared the Moscow facilities "the best village I have ever seen."

Could not the Lake Placid dormitories have been used for some fine purpose such as a sports training center, housing, or some health building purpose? These, too, would provide jobs for the North Country. It is not too late now to change our governmental policy and we ask that it be done. It is never too late to do the right thing.

When all Americans learn about the Lake Placid Olympic prison arrangement, and they will, they will not be proud. As North Country Clergy, we call upon the Lake Placid community, our Congress, and the Carter administration to reverse this inhumane decision. We ask that hearings be held in Congress to determine just how this arrangement came to be and how it can be changed. We ask our members of our congregations to sensitize themselves to the inhumane implications of this issue.

In the Scriptures, we read, "I was in prison and you visited me." These words will seldom be fulfilled at Lake Placid. We abhor the corruption of the high ideals toward which the Olympics and this nation strive.

All domestic remedies have failed to deter U.S. Authorities from this use of the Olympic Village and we have been asked to raise it before the International Community.

THEREFORE, we respectfully recommend that the Sub-Commission on Prevention of Discrimination and Protection of Minorities refer the Petition on HUMAN RIGHTS VIOLATIONS IN THE UNITED STATES and our Report to the Commission on Human Rights so that an ad-hoc committee may be immediately appointed to investigate these well-attested human rights violations.

August 18, 1979

MR. JUSTICE HARISH CHANDRA:
INDIA

CHIEF JUDGE PER EKLUND:
SWEDEN

RICHARD HARVEY:
GREAT BRITAIN

IFEANYI IFEBIGH:
NIGERIA

SERGIO INSUNZA BARRIOS:
CHILE (In Exile)

THE HON. SIR ARTHUR HUGH MCSHINE:
T.C., TRINIDAD-TOBAGO

BABACAR NIANG:
SENEGAL
INTERNATIONAL JURISTS OBSERVERS

Appendix 2
International Standards Relevant to the Death Penalty

Articles of the International Covenant on Civil and Political Rights
(Signed by the US Government on 5 October 1977)

Article 6

1. Every human being has the inherent right to life. This right shall be protected by law. No one shall be arbitrarily deprived of his life.

2. In countries which have not abolished the death penalty, sentence of death may be imposed only for the most serious crimes in accordance with the law in force at the time of the commission of the crime and not contrary to the provisions of the present Covenant and to the Convention on the Prevention and Punishment of the Crime of Genocide. This penalty can only be carried out pursuant to a final judgment rendered by a competent court.

3. When deprivation of life constitutes the crime of genocide, it is understood that nothing in this article shall authorize any State Party to the present Covenant to derogate in any way from any obligation assumed under thc provisions of the Convention on the Prevention and Punishment of the Crime of Genocide.

4. Anyone sentenced to death shall have the right to seek pardon or commutation of the sentence. Amnesty, pardon or commutation of the sentence of death may be granted in all cases.

5. Sentence of death shall not be imposed for crimes committed by persons below eighteen years of age and shall not be carried out on pregnant women.

6. Nothing in this article shall be invoked to delay or to prevent the abolition of capital punishment by any State Party to the present Covenant.

General Comment on Article 6 of the International Covenant on Civil and Political Rights

Adopted at Its 378th Meeting (16th Session) on 27 July 1982 by the Human Rights Committee Set Up under the International Covenant on Civil and Political Rights

1. The right to life enunciated in article 6 of the Covenant has been dealt with in all state reports. It is the supreme right from which no derogation is permitted even in time of public emergency which threatens the life of the nation (article 4). However, the Committee has noted that quite often the information given concerning article 6 was limited to only one or other aspect of this right. It is a right which should not be interpreted narrowly.

Articles of the American Convention on Human Rights

(Signed by the US Government on 1 June 1977)

Article 4. Right to Life

1. Every person has the right to have his life respected. This right shall be protected by law and, in general, from the moment of conception. No one shall be arbitrarily deprived of his life.
2. In countries that have not abolished the death penalty, it may be imposed only for the most serious crimes and pursuant to a final judgment rendered by a competent court and in accordance with a law establishing such punishment, enacted prior to the commission of the crime. The application of such punishment shall not be extended to crimes to which it does not presently apply.
3. The death penalty shall not be reestablished in states that have abolished it.
4. In no case shall capital punishment be inflicted for political offenses or related common crimes.
5. Capital punishment shall not be imposed upon persons who, at the time the crime was committed, were under 18 years of age or over 70 years of age; nor shall it be applied to pregnant women.
6. Every person condemned to death shall have the right to apply for amnesty, pardon, or commutation of sentence, which may be granted in all cases. Capital punishment shall not be imposed while such a petition is pending decision by the competent authority.

Resolution 1984/50 on Safeguards Guaranteeing Protection of the Rights of Those Facing the Death Penalty

Adopted by the United Nations Economic and Social Council at Its 1984 Spring Session on 25 May 1984

1. In countries which have not abolished the death penalty, capital punishment may be imposed only for the most serious crimes, it being understood that their scope should not go beyond intentional crimes with lethal or other extremely grave consequences.

2. Capital punishment may be imposed only for a crime for which the death penalty is prescribed by law at the time of its commission, it being understood that if, subsequent to the commission of the crime, provision is made by law for the imposition of a lighter penalty, the offender shall benefit thereby.

3. Persons below 18 years of age at the time of the commission of the crime shall not be sentenced to death, nor shall the death sentence be carried out on pregnant women, or on new mothers, or on persons who have become insane.

4. Capital punishment may be imposed only when the guilt of the person charged is based upon clear and convincing evidence leaving no room for an alternative explanation of the facts.

5. Capital punishment may only be carried out pursuant to a final judgment rendered by a competent court after legal process which gives all possible safeguards to ensure a fair trial, at least equal to those contained in article 14 of the International Covenant on Civil and Political Rights, including the right of anyone suspected of or charged with a crime for which capital punishment may be imposed to adequate legal assistance at all stages of the proceedings.

6. Anyone sentenced to death shall have the right to appeal to a court of higher jurisdiction, and steps should be taken to ensure that such appeals shall become mandatory.

7. Anyone sentenced to death shall have the right to seek pardon or commutation of sentence; pardon or commutation of sentence may be granted in all cases of capital punishment.

8. Capital punishment shall not be carried out pending any appeal or other recourse procedure or other proceeding relating to pardon or commutation of the sentence.

9. Where capital punishment occurs, it shall be carried out so as to inflict the minimum possible suffering.

Resolution on Safeguards Guaranteeing the Rights of Those Facing the Death Penalty

Adopted by the Seventh United Nations Congress on the Prevention of Crime and the Treatment of Offenders
Milan, 26 August-6 September 1985

(Extract Only)

"The Seventh United Nations Congress on the Prevention of Crime and the Treatment of Offenders...

1. *Endorses* the safeguards approved by the Economic and Social Council in its resolution 1984/50;

2. *Invites* all States retaining the death penalty and whose present standards fall short of the safeguards to adopt the safeguards and to take the necessary steps to implement them by

(a) Incorporating or making provision for the safeguards in national legislation and regulations;

(b) Ensuring that judges, lawyers, police officers, prison officials, and other persons, including military personnel who may be concerned with the administration of criminal justice, are familiar with the safeguards and any corresponding provisions in national legislation and regulations, by including them in all courses of instruction, by disseminating and publicizing them and by other appropriate means;

(c) Drawing the attention of persons facing the death penalty, and their representatives, to the safeguards and to any corresponding provisions in national legislation and regulations, and disseminating to the public those safeguards by all appropriate means..."

Resolution 1986/10 on Implementation of the Conclusions and Recommendations of the Seventh United Nations Congress on the Prevention of Crime and the Treatment of Offenders

Adopted by the United Nations Economic and Social Council at its 1986 Spring Session on 21 May 1986

(Extract Only)

"*Economic and Social Council, ...*

X. *Safeguards guaranteeing protection of the rights of those facing the death penalty...*

1. *Urges* Member States that have not abolished the death penalty to adopt the safeguards guaranteeing protection of the rights of those facing the death penalty approved by the Economic and Social Council in its resolution 1984/50 of 25 May 1984 and the measures for implementation of the safeguards approved by the Seventh United Nations Congress on the Prevention of Crime and the Treatment of Offenders..."

United Nations General Assembly Resolution 32.61 of 8 December 1977 on Capital Punishment

"*General Assembly,...*

Reaffirms that, as established by the General Assembly in resolution 2857 (XXVI) and by the Economic and Social Council in resolutions 1574 (L), 1745 (LIV) and 1930 (L VIII), the main objective to be pursued in the field of capital punishment is that of progressively restricting the number of offenders for which the death penalty may be imposed with a view to the desirability of abolishing this punishment."

World Medical Association Resolution on Physician Participation in Capital Punishment
(WMA, 1981)

Following concerns about the introduction of an execution method (lethal injection) which threatened to involve doctors directly in the process of execution, the WMA Secretary-General issued a press statement opposing any involvement of doctors in capital punishment. The 34th Assembly statement, endorsed the Secretary-General's statement in the following terms:

RESOLVED, that the Assembly of the World Medical Association endorses the action of the Secretary General in issuing the attached press release on behalf of the World Medical Association condemning physician participation in capital punishment.

FURTHER RESOLVED, that it is unethical for physicians to participate in capital punishment, although this does not preclude physicians certifying death.

FURTHER RESOLVED, that the Medical Ethics Committee keep this matter under active consideration.

Secretary General's Press Release
Ferney-Voltaire, France - September 11, 1981

The first capital punishment by intravenous injection of lethal dose of drugs was decided to bc carried out next week by the Court of the State of Oklahoma, USA.

Regardless of the method of capital punishment a State imposes, no physician should be required to be an active participant. Physicians are dedicated to preserving life.

Acting as an executioner is not the practice of medicine and physician services are not required to carry out capital punishment even if the methodology utilized pharmacological agents or equipment that might otherwise be used in the practice of medicine.

A physician's only role would be to certify death once the State had carried out the capital punishment.

Dr André Wynen
Secretary General

Principles of Medical Ethics Relevant to the Role of Health Personnel, Particularly Physicians, in the Protection of Prisoners and Detainees against Torture and Other Cruel, Inhuman, or Degrading Treatment or Punishment
Adopted by the 34th World Medical Assembly, Lisbon, Portugal, September 28 - October 2, 1981.

Principle 1

Health personnel, particularly physicians, charged with the medical care of prisoners and detainees have a duty to provide them with protection of their physical and mental health and treatment of disease of the same quality and standard as is afforded to those who are not imprisoned or detained.

Principle 2

It is a gross contravention of medical ethics, as well as an offence under applicable international instruments, for health personnel, particularly physicians, to engage, actively or passively, in acts which constitute participation in, complicity in, incitement to or attempts to commit torture or other cruel, inhuman, or degrading treatment or punishment.

Principle 3

It is a contravention of medical ethics for health personnel, particularly physicians, to be involved in any professional relationship with prisoners or detainees the purpose of which is not solely to evaluate, protect, or improve their physical and mental health.

BIBLIOGRAPHY

Articles and Books

American Correctional Association, *Annual Congress of Correction: Proceedings*, held in Pittsburgh, Pennsylvania, August 20-26, 1972, College Park, MD.

Amnesty International, *Children and the Death Penalty: Executions Worldwide Since 1990*, 2002.

Amnesty International, *Facts and Figures on the Death Penalty 2005.*

Amnesty International Report 1977-1978, London, England: Amnesty International Publications, 1978.

Aptheker, Bettina, *The Morning Breaks: The Trial of Angela Davis*, New York, NY: International Publishers, 1975.

Baldus, David C., Charles Pulaski and George Woodworth, "Comparative Review of Death Sentences: An Empirical Study of the Georgia Experience," *Journal of Criminal Law and Criminology,* 74 (3), Chicago, IL: Northwestern Univ. School of Law, 1983.

Bedau, Hugo, "The Death Penalty and State Constitutional Rights in the U.S." in *U.N. Crime Prevention and Criminal Justice Newsletter*, Nov. 1986.

Bell, Derrick, *Race, Racism, and American Law*, Boston, MA: Little, Brown, and Co., 1973.

Belknap, Michael R., Federal Law and Southern Order: Racial Violence and Constitutional Conflict in the Post-Brown South, Athens, GA: University of Georgia Press, 1987.

Black, Donald J. and Albert J. Reiss, "Patterns of Behavior in Police and Citizen Transactions," in Charles E. Reasons and Jack L. Kuykendall (eds.), *Race, Crime, and Society* (Pacific Palisade, CA: Goodyear, 1972).

Blackstone, Nelson, *COINTELPRO: The FBI's Secret War on Political Freedom,* New York, NY: Vintage Books, 1976.

Beer, Todd, "Police Killing of Blacks: Data for 2015, 2016, 2017, and First Half of 2018," *TheSocietyPages.org: Sociology Toolbox*, March, 2018, https://thesocietypages.org/toolbox/police-killing-of-blacks/, (May 9, 2019).

Borden, P., "Found Cumbering the Soil: Manifest Destiny and the Indian in the Nineteenth Century," *The Great Fear: Race in the Mind of America*, Nash, Gary and Richard Weiss, eds., New York, NY: Holt, Rinehart & Winston, 1970.

Bowers, William J., *Executions in America* Lexington, MA: Lexington Books, 1974.

Bowers, William J., Glenn L. Pierce, and John F. McDevitt, *Legal Homicide: Death as Punishment in America 1864-1982*, Chicago, IL: Northwestern Univ. Press, 1984.

Brody, Stuart A., "The Political Prisoner Syndrome: Latest Problem of the American Penal System," *Crime and Delinquency,* Vol. 20, No. 2, April 1974.

Buck, Rinker, "Corrections: Prisoner of Inertia," *Empire State Report,* New York, NY: May 1978.

Bulletin of Capital Punishment, 1988.

Burns, Haywood, "Racism and American Law," *Law Against the People.* Robert Lefcourt, ed., New York, NY: Vintage Books, 1971.

Chadbourn, James H., "Lynching and the Law," Southern Commission on the Study of Lynching, 1933, reprinted by the Lawbook Exchange, Ltd., 2008.

Chambliss, William J., *Whose Law? What Order?* New York, NY: John Wiley and Sons, 1976.

"Chicago Police Methods Exposed," *Ms. Magazine*, June 1979.

Child, Robert, "Concepts of Political Prisonerhood," *New England Journal on Prison Law,* Vol. 1, No. 1, Boston, MA: Spring 1974.

Clark, Ramsey, *Crime in America,* New York, NY: Penguin Books, 1971.

Conrad, Maisie and Richard, *Executive Order 9066,* San Francisco, CA: California Historical Society, 1972.

Crenlinsten, Robert, ed., *Terrorism and Criminal Justice: An International Perspective,* Lexington, MA: Lexington Books, 1978.

Cutler, J.E., "Capital Punishment and Lynching," *The Annals of the American Academy of Political and Social Science*, 1907.

Davis, Angela, *If They Come in the Morning,* New York, NY: New American Library, 1971.

Days, Drew, Statement at consultation on "Police Practices and the Preservation of Civil Rights," U. S. Commission on Civil Rights, Washington, DC: December 1978.

"Death at an Early Age: International Law Argument Against the Death Penalty for Juveniles," *Criminal Law Review*, Vol. 57, 245, 1988.

"The Domestic Effects of International Norms Restricting the Application of the Death Penalty," *University of Cincinnati Law Review,* Vol. 52, Cincinnati, OH, 1983.

Dworkin, Ronald, *Taking Rights Seriously,* Cambridge, MA: Harvard University Press, 1977.

Engquist, Virginia and Frances Coles, "'Political' Criminals in America." O'Hare, 1923; Cantine and Ranier, 1950; *Issues in Criminology,* Vol. 5, No. 2, Summer 1970, Berkeley, CA: University of California.

Ervin, Frank, "Biological Intervention Technologies and Social Control," *American Behavioral Scientist,* Vol. 18, No. 5, May/June 1975, New York, NY: Sage Publishing.

Flanigan, Daniel J., *The Criminal Law of Slavery and Freedom 1800-1868*, Taylor & Francis, 1987.

Flynn, Edith, "Political Prisoners and Terrorists in American Correctional Institutions," *Terrorism and Criminal Justice: An International Perspective,* Ronald Crenlinsten, ed., Lexington, MA: Lexington Books, 1978.

Franklin, John Hope, *From Slavery to Freedom: A History of African Americans,* 9th Ed., New York, NY: McGraw-Hill Education, 2010.

Genovese, E., *Roll Jordan Roll: The World the Slaves Made*, New York, NY: Vintage Books, 1976.

Gilchrist, Irvin, *Medical Experimentation on Prisoners Must Stop: Documents Generated during the Course of a Struggle*, College Park, MD: Urban Information Interpreters, 1974.

Glazer, Daniel, "Politicalization of Prisoners: A New Challenge to American Penology," *American Journal of Corrections,* November-December, 1971.

Goodell, Charles, *Political Prisoners in America,* New York, NY: Random House, 1973.

Goodell, William, *The American Slave Code in Theory and Practice*, New York, NY: American and Foreign Anti-Slavery Society, 1853; reprint on Amazon, 2018.

"Gordon Police Told Not to Stop Couple, Ex-Officer Testifies," *North Platte Telegraph*, North Platte, NE, July 2, 1979.

Greenberg, David F. and Fay Stender, "The Prison as a Lawless Agency," *Buffalo Law Review*, Buffalo, NY: 1972

Griswold, H. Jack, Mike Misenheimer, Art Powers and Ed Tromanhauser, *An Eye for an Eye,* New York, NY: Holt, Reinhart and Winston, 1970.

Groder, Martin, M.D., "Psychological, Behavioral and/or Social Research Involving Prisoners vs. Voluntary Subjects," *Research Involving Prisoners*, National Commission for the Protection of Human Subjects of Biomedical and Behavioral Research, Washington, DC: Government Printing Office, 1976.

Gross, Samuel R. and Robert Mauro – "Patterns of Death: An Analysis of Disparities in Capital Sentencing and Homicide Victimization," 37 *Stanford Law Review*, 27, 39, 1984.

Halperin, Morton H., Jerry J. Berman, Robert L. Borosage, and Christine M. Marwich, *The Lawless State: The Crimes of the U.S. Intelligence Agencies,* New York, NY: Penguin Books, 1976.

Harvard Civil Rights – Civil Liberties Law Review, Vol. 24, Cambridge, MA: 1989.

"The Death Penalty Revisited," *Harvard Law Review* 101, May 1988.

Hastings Constitutional Law Quarterly 16:1, Garrison, NY: Fall 1988.

Hayden, Tom, *TRIAL,* New York, NY: Holt, Rinehart and Winston, 1970.

Higginbotham, A. Leon, *In the Matter of Color: Race and the American Legal Process: The Colonial Experience* 1978.

Hill Witt, Shirley, "The Brave-Hearted Women: The Struggle at Wounded Knee," *The Civil Rights Digest,* Vol. 8, No. 4, Washington, DC: U.S. Government Printing Office, Summer 1976.

Hinds, Lennox S., "The Death Penalty: Continuing Threat to America's Poor" in *Freedomways*, First Quarter 1976.

Hinds, Lennox S., "Police Use of Excessive and Deadly Force: Racial Implications," *A Community Concern: Police Use of Deadly Force,* compiled by Robert N. Brenner and Marjorie Kravitz, Law Enforcement Assistance Administration, US Dept. of Justice, January 1979.

Hinds, Lennox S., "Political Prisoners in the U.S.," *Africa,* No. 85, September 1978.

Hirschfield, Sarina B., *Abuses of Police Authority,* Bureau of Social Science Research, Inc., 1970 (Pamphlet).

Hooks, Bell, *Ain't I a Woman: Black Women and Feminism,* Boston, MA: 1981.

Hudson, Brian, "Police Abuse and National Unrest," *The Guardian*, June 25, 1980.

Ingraham, B.L. and Kazuhiko Tokoro, "Political Crime in the United States and Japan: A Comparative Study," *Issues in Criminology,* Vol. 4, No. 2, Berkeley, CA: University of California, Fall 1969.

Instead of Prisons, Prison Research Action Project, Syracuse, NY, 1976.

Jackson, Anthony, "Director's Statement: April 19, 1979," available from Public Interest Law Center of Philadelphia, Philadelphia, PA.

Jacobs, Paul, Saul Landau with Eve Pell, *To Serve the Devil, Vol. 1: Natives and Slaves,* New York, NY: Vintage Books, 1971.

Johnson, Guy B., "The Negro and Crime," 271 *The Annals of the American Academy of Political and Social Science* 93, 1941.

Johnson, Sheri, "Black Innocence and the White Jury," 83 *Michigan Law Review*, 1611

Kercheimer, Otto, *Political Justice,* Princeton, NJ: Princeton University Press, 1961.

Kobler, Arthur, "Figures (and Perhaps Some Facts on Police Killings of Civilians in the United States, 1965-1969," from a synopsis found in *A Community Cancer: Police Use of Deadly Force*, Washington, DC: National Institute of Law Enforcement and Criminal Justice, 1978.

Kobler, Arthur, "Police Homicide in a Democracy," *Journal of Social Issues*, Vol. 31, No. 1, 1975.

"L.A. Cops Use of Deadly Force Rises," *The Guardian*, July 23, 1980.

Laffin, John, *The Anatomy of Captivity,* New York, NY: Abeland-Schuman, 1968.

Lefcourt, Robert, ed., *Law against the People,* New York, NY: Vintage Books, 1971.

Levy, Howard, MD, and David Miller, *Going to Jail: The Political Prisoner,* New York, NY: Grove Press, 1971.

Magnum, Charles Staples, *The Legal Status of the Negro*, Chapel Hill, NC: University of North Carolina Press, 1940.

Minor, W. William, "Political Crime, Political Justice and Political Prisoners," *Criminology,* Vol. 12, No. 4, February 1975.

Mitford, Jessica, *Kind and Usual Punishment,* New York, NY: Alfred A. Knopf, 1973.

Myerson, Michael, *Nothing Could Be Finer,* New York, NY: International Publishers, 1978.

Nagle, William, *The New Red Barn: A Critical Look at the Modern Prison,* New York, NY: Walker and Co., 1973.

National Urban League Inc., *The State of Black America 1990*, N.Y. Jan 1990.

Newman, Jon O., "Swing the Lawbreakers: Proposals to Strengthen the Section 1983 Damage Remedy for Law Enforcers' Misconduct," *Yale Law Review*, Vol. 87, No. 3, New Haven, CT: January, 1978.

Orwell, George, *1984,* New York, NY: Harcourt, Brace Jovanovich, Inc., 1949.

Oswald, Russell G., *Attica: My Story*, New York, NY: Doubleday, 1972.

Pappworth, M. H., *Human Guinea Pigs: Experimentation on Man*, New York, NY: Beacon Press, 1968.

Payne, Ethel L., "The Judge Said 'No,'" *The Chicago Defender*, Chicago, IL, October 14, 1977.

Peck, Richard, Testimony in August 1983 at the Evidentiary hearing on the Constitutionality of the application of the Death Penalty in *McClesky v Kemp*, 580 F. Supp 338.

Piliavin, Irvin and Scott Briar, "Police Encounters with Juveniles" in Donald Cressey and David Ward (eds.), *Delinquency, Crime, and Social Process,* New York, NY: Harper and Row, 1969.

Prison Research Education Action Project, ed., *Instead of Prison: A Handbook for Activists*, Syracuse, NY: Critical Resistance Publisher, 1976.

"Project: Suing the Police in Federal Court," *Yale Law Journal*, New Haven, CT: Vol. 88, No. 4, March 1979.

Quinney, Richard, *Critique of Legal Order,* Boston, MA: Little, Brown and Company, 1973.

"Race & the Death Penalty," American Civil Liberties Union (On Line) 2/26/2003.

Report of the National Advisory Commission on Civil Disorders, New York, NY: Bantam Books, 1968.

Richards, O'Hare, Kate, *In Prison: Sometime Federal Prisoner #21669,* Seattle, WA: University of Washington Press, 1976. Reprint of 1923 Knopf edition.

Rollins, Thomas M., "Mean Beats: Police Brutality in America," *Politics Today*, December 1978.

Rosenblum, Victor G., *Law as a Political Instrument,* New York, NY: Random House, 1955.

Rothman, David, "Behavioral Modification in Total Institutions, *Hastings Center Report*, 5 February 1975, Garrison, NY.

Schafer, Stephen, "Criminology: The Concept of the Political Criminal," *The Journal of Criminal Law, Criminology, and Police Science,* Vol. 62, No. 3, September 1971.

Schwartz, Louis B., "Complaints against the Police: Experience of the Community Rights Division of the Philadelphia District Attorney's Office," *University of Pennsylvania Law Review*, Vol. 118:1023, 1970.

Seale, Bobby, *Seize the Time*, New York, NY: Vintage Books, 1970.

"Sexual Assaults and Forced Homosexual Relationships: Cruel and Unusual Punishment," 36 *Albany Law Review*, 428, 1972.

Shelton, Dinah, "Improving Human Rights Protections: Recommendations for Enhancing the Effectiveness of the Inter-American Commission and Inter-American Court on Human Rights," *American University Law Review*, Vol. 3, 323-337, 1988.

Sherman, Lawrence W. and Robert H. Langworthy, "Measuring Homicide by Police Officers," *The Journal of Criminal Law and Criminology*, Vol. 70, No. 4; December 1979, p. 546-560.

Sherman, Lawrence, "The Breakdown of the Police Code of Silence," *Criminal Law Bulletin*, Mar./Apr. 1978.

Singer, Linda R. and Ronald L. Goldfarb, *After Conviction,* New York, NY: Simon and Schuster, 1973.

Skolnick, Jerome H., *The Politics of Protest,* New York, NY: Ballantine Books, 1969.

Smead, Howard, *Blood Justice Blood Justice: The Lynching of Mack Charles Parker*, New York, NY: Oxford University Press, USA (1984).

Sobell, Morton, *On Doing Time,* New York, NY: Bantam Books, May 1976.

Spear, C., *Essays on the Punishment of Death,* 220-31, Appendix 1, 1845.

Stampp, Kenneth, "Chattels Personal" in *Slavery in America*, 1976.

Stampp, Kenneth, "*The Peculiar Institution: Slavery in the Ante Bellum South*, New York, NY: Alfred A. Knopf, 1956.

Stephenson, Gilbert Thomas, "Actual Jury Service by Negroes in the South" in *Race Distinctions and American Law*, 1910; now available digitally through Google.

Streib, Victor L., "Capital Punishment of Children in Ohio," 18 *Akron Law Review,* 1984.

Swoffard, Stan, "How Due Process Died in North Carolina," *Greensboro Daily News,* 1977.

Takagi, Paul, "Death by 'Police Intervention,'" *A Community Concern: Police Use of Deadly Force*, National Institute of Law Enforcement and Criminal Justice, Washington, DC: Government Printing Office.

Takagi, Paul, Statement at consultation "Police Practices and the Preservation of Civil Rights," U. S. Commission on Civil Rights, Washington, DC: Government Printing Office, December 1978.

"Up Against the Law," *Equal Times: Boston's Newspaper for Working Women*, Vol. 5, No. 80, February 3, 1980.

Valdez, Luis and Stan Steiner, *Aztlan: An Anthology of Mexican American Literature,* New York, NY: Vintage Books, 1972.

Weiss, Carl and David Friar, *Terror in the Prisons,* Indianapolis, IN: Bobbs-Merrill, 1974.

White, Walter F., *Rope and Faggot: A Biography of Judge Lynch,* (19-39) New York, NY: Alfred Knopf, 1929.

Wicker, Tom, *A Time to Die*, New York, NY: Ballantine, 1975.

Wicker, Tom, "Attica Is Termed as Bad as before 1971 Rebellion," *The New York Times,* July 21, 1976.

Wilson, Theodore B., *Black Codes of the South,* Tuscaloosa, AL: Univ. of Alabama Press, 1965.

Woodson, Robert L., ed., *Black Perspectives on Crime and the Criminal Justice System,* a symposium sponsored by the National Urban League. Boston, MA: G.K. Hall and Company, 1977.

Woodward, C. Vann, *The Strange Career of Jim Crow,* 3rd Ed., New York, NY: Oxford Univ. Press, 1974.

Zangrando, Robert, NAACP Crusade Against Lynching 1909-1950, Philadelphia, PA: Temple Univ. Press, 1980.

Government Reports

Arizona Advisory Committee to the U.S. Commission on Civil Rights, *Justice in Flagstaff: Are These Rights Inalienable?* Washington, DC: U.S. Government Printing Office, 1977.

Attica: The Official Report of the New York Commission on Attica, New York, NY: Bantam, 1972.

Bureau of Statistics, National Prison Statistics, U.S. Department of Justice, *Capital Punishment,* Washington, D.C.: Government Printing Office, 1979.

Current Population Reports, Census Bureau, US Commerce Dept., Washington, DC: Government Printing Office, 1977.

"The Death of John Wesley Thompson," *New York City Board of Corrections Report*, Jan. 26, 1976.

Employment and Earnings, Bureau of Labor Statistics, US Dept. of Labor, Washington, DC: Government Printing Office, January 1978.

Final Report of the Select Committee to Study Governmental Operations with Respect to Intelligence Activities, Book III, U.S. Senate, Washington, DC: Government Printing Office, 1976.

Job Training and Placement for Offenders and Ex-Offenders, U.S. Dept. of Justice, Washington, DC: Government Printing Office, 1975.

Montana—North Dakota—South Dakota Joint Advisory Committee to the U.S. Commission on Civil Rights, *Indian Civil Rights Issues in Montana, North Dakota, and South Dakota,* Washington, DC: U.S. Government Printing Office, August 1974.

National Prisoner Statistics Bulletin, SD-NPS-CP-5, *Capital Punishment 1976,* U.S. Department of Justice, Law Enforcement Assistance Administration, National Criminal Justice Information and Statistics Service, Washington, DC: U.S. Government Printing Office, November 1977.

North Dakota Advisory Committee to the U.S. Commission on Civil Rights, *Native American Justice Issues in North Dakota,* Washington, DC: U.S. Government Printing Office, August 1978.

Oklahoma Advisory Committee to the U.S. Commission on Civil Rights, *Native American Justice Issues in Oklahoma,* Washington, DC: U.S. Government Printing Office, January 1974.

Oklahoma State Advisory Committee to the U.S. Commission on Civil Rights, "Indian Civil Rights Issues" in *Report of the National Advisory Commission on Civil Disorders*, Washington, D.C.: Government Printing Office, 1968.

Police Use of Deadly Force, preliminary report of the National Minority Advisory Council on Criminal Justice, Dr. Gwynne W. Pierson, senior researcher, Law Enforcement Assistance Administration, Washington, DC: U.S. Dept. of Justice. 1978.

Snell, Tracy L. (BJS Statistician), *Capital Punishment, 2006-Statistical Tables*, US Bureau of Justice, Washington, DC: U.S. Government Printing office, 2007.

Sourcebook of Criminal Justice Statistics, U.S. Department of Justice, Law Enforcement Assistance Administration, National Criminal Justice Information and Statistics Service, Washington, DC: U.S. Government Printing Office, 1975, 1976, 1978.

Statistical Abstract of the United States: 1977, U.S. Census Bureau, US Commerce Dept., Washington, DC: U.S. Government Printing Office.

Tennessee Advisory Committee to the U.S. Commission on Civil Rights, *Civic Crisis-Civic Challenge: Police-Community Relations in Memphis,* Washington, DC: U.S. Government Printing Office, August 1978.

Uniform Crime Reform, Crime in the United States, 1976, Federal Bureau of Investigation, Washington, DC: U.S. Government Printing Office, September 1977.

U.S. Commission on Civil Rights, *Mexican-Americans and the Administration of Justice in the Southwest,* Washington, DC: U.S. Government Printing Office, March 1970.

U.S. Commission on Civil Rights Report, Vol. 5, Washington, D.C.: Government Printing Office, 1961.

U.S. Commission on Civil Rights, *Racism in America,* Washington, DC: U.S. Government Printing Office, January 1970.

U.S. Commission on Civil Rights, *Stranger in One's Land,* Washington, DC: U.S. Government Printing Office, May 1970.

U.S. Commission on Civil Rights, *The Mexican-American,* Washington, DC: U.S. Government Printing Office, 1968.

U.S. Commission on Civil Rights, *The Navajo Nation: An American Colony,* Washington, DC: U.S. Government Printing Office, September 1975.

U.S. Commission on Civil Rights, *The Southwest Indian Report,* Washington, DC: U.S. Government Printing Office, May 1973.

U.S. Department of Justice, *The Federal Death Penalty System: A Statistical Survey, 1988-2000, Washington, DC: U.S. Government Printing Office, September 2000..*

Youth Advocate Program International (Online) Evidence of Bias – Juvenile Death Penalty

International Human Rights Law

American Convention on Human Rights Nov. 22, 1969.

American Declaration of the Rights and Duties of Man, Adopted May 2, 1948.

Article 18, Vienna Convention on the Laws of Treaties.

Article 3 of the Universal Declaration on Human Rights.

Article 4(2) of the American Convention on Human Rights (ACHR).

Article 6(5) of the International Covenant on Civil and Political Rights (ICC PR).

Buergenthal, "Implementation in the Inter-American Human Rights System" in *International Enforcement of Human Rights* 75, R. Berghardt & J. Jolowisz, Eds., 1987.

Charter of the Organization of American States April 30, 1948, Amend. Protocol, Feb. 3, 1967.

ECOSOC Resolution 1503 (XXLII) May 27, 1970 Sub-Commission for Prevention of Discrimination and Protection of Minorities.

ECOSOC Resolutions 1984/50, May 25, 1984.

Handbook of Existing Rules Pertaining to Human Rights in the Inter-American System, July 26, 1983.

Inter-American Commission on Human Rights, OEA/see L/V/11.69 Doc. 17.27 March 1987, Inter-American Decision § 58 Discussing the Execution of Jay Pinkerton and James Roach.

International Law Association, "Draft Minimal Rules of Procedure for International Human Rights Fact Finding Missions," Belgrade Conference 1980.

Resolution No. 3/87 Case No 9647 Inter-American Commission on Human Rights, March 1987

Shelton, Dinah "Implementation Procedures of the American Convention on Human Rights," 26 GERM. Y.B. Int'l L. 238, 251-61, 1983.

U.N. General Assembly Resolution 2857 (XXVI), 1971.

U.N. General Assembly Resolution 32/61, Dec 8, 1977.

U.N. General Assembly Resolution 35/172, Dec 15, 1980.

UNGAOR, Protection of Human Rights in Chile: Report of the Economic and Social Council Annex VII, U.N. Doc A/33/331 (1978).

University of Cincinnati Law Review, Vol. 52, 1983,

Cases Cited

Adams v. Carlson, 352 F.Supp. 882 (E.D. Ill., 1972).

Allec v. Medrano, 416 U.S. 802, 94 S.Ct. 2191, 40 L.Ed.2d 566.

Atkins v. Virginia, 536 U.S. 304 (2002) 260 VA 375, 534 S.E. 2d 312.

Batson v. Kentucky, 476 U.S. 79, 103 (1986).

Bono v. Saxbe, 450 F. Supp. 934 (E.D.Ill., 1978).

Boone v. Paderick, 541 F.2d 447 (4th Cir. 1976).

Brady v. Maryland, 373 U.S. 83, 10 L.Ed. 2d 215 (1963).

Brief of European Union as Amicus Curiae in *McCarver v. North Carolina*, O.T. 2001.

Brown v. Board of Education, 347 US 483 (1954).

Cherokee Nation v. Georgia, 30 U.S. (5 Pet.) I (1831).

Civil Rights Act of 1964, 42 USC §§2000b-3 (1982).

Civil Rights Act of 1964, 42 USC §§2000e-17 (1982).

Civil Rights Act of 1968, 42 USC §§3601-3631 (1982).

Coker v. Georgia, 433 US 584 (1977).

Damico v. California, 389 U.S. 416, 88 S.Ct. 526, 19 L.Ed.2d 647.

District of Columbia v. Carter, 409 U.S. 418, 93 S.Ct. 602, 34 L.Ed.2d 613.

Domingues v. U.S., (2002).

Edmund v. Florida, 458 US 782 (1982).

Ellis v. Dyson, 421 U.S. 426, 95 S.Ct. 1691, 44L.Ed.2d 274.
ExParte Virginia 100 US 339 (1879).
Filartiga v. Pena-Irala, 630 F2d 876 (2nd Cir. 1980).
Flowers v. Mississippi, US____, 2019; argued March 28, 2019; decided June 21, 2019.
Franklin v. South Carolina, 218 US 161 (1910).
Gibson v. Berryhill, 411 U.S. 564, 93 S.Ct. 1689, 36 L.Ed.2d 488.
Giglio v. United States, 405 U.S. 150, 31 L.Ed 2d 104 (1972).
Gregg v. Georgia, 428 U.S. 153 (1976).
Haitian Refugee Center v. Civilette, 503 F Supp. 442 (S.D. Fla 1980).
Houghton v. Shafer, 392 U.S. 639, 88 S.Ct. 2119, 20 L.Ed.2d 1319.
King v. Smith, 392 U.S. 309, 88 S.Ct. 2128, 20 L.Ed.2d 1118.
Lockhart v. McCree, (1986).
Mapp v. Ohio, 367 U.S. 643 (1961).
McClesky v. Kemp 481 US 279 (1987).
McNeese v. Board of Education, 373 U.S. 668, 83 S.Ct. 1433, 10 L.Ed.2d 622 (1963).
Monroe v. Pape, 365 U.S. 176, 81 S.Ct. 473, 5 L.Ed.2d 492 (1961)
Plessy v. Ferguson, 163 U.S. 537, (1896).
Prieser v. Rodriguez, 411 U.S. 475, 93S.Ct. 1827, 36 L.Ed.2d 439.
Rizzo v. Goode, 423 U.S. 362 (1976).
Roper v. Simmons, 545 U.S. 551 (2005).
Ruffin v. Commonwealth, 62 Da 790 (1871).
Stone v. Powell, 428 U.S. 465 (1976).
Strauder v. West Virginia, 100 US 303 (1879).
The Civil Rights Act of 1875, Ch 114 §4, 18 Stat. 336 (Codified as 18 USC § 243 (1982).
The Civil Rights Cases, 109 U.S. 3 (1883).
The Paquette Habana, 175 US 677 (1900).
The Restatement of the Foreign Relations Law of the United States (1985).
Thompson v. Oklahoma, 107 S.Ct 1284 (1957) 56 US LW 4892, June 29, 1988.
Trop v. Dullest, 356 US 86 (1958).
United States v. Agurs, 427 U.S. 97, 49 L.Ed 2d 342 (1976).
United States v. City of Philadelphia et al., Civil Action No. 79-2937, Eastern District Court of Pennsylvania.
United States v. Sutton, 542 F.2d 1239 (4th Cir. 1976).
Virginia v. Rives, 100 US 313 (1879)

Voting Rights Act of 1965 42 USC §§ 1971 to 173aa-3 (1982) & (1986).
Williams v. Mississippi, 170 US 213 (1898)
Wilwerding v. Swanson, 404 U.S. 249, 92 S.Ct. 407, 30 L.Ed.2d 418.
Woodson v. North Carolina, 428 U.S. 280 (1976)

LENNOX S. HINDS, J.D.

Lennox S. Hinds, a Professor Emeritus of Law and former Chair of the Administration of Justice Program, Rutgers University, drafted and presented the original Petition on Human Rights Violations in the United States to the United Nations (UN) on behalf of the sponsoring organizations on December 11, 1978. In addition to his practice as a criminal defense and international human rights lawyer, he was Counsel to Nelson Mandela, the African National Congress (ANC), and the Southwest African Peoples Organization (SWAPO) in the US. He is the permanent Representative to the UN for the International Association of Democratic Lawyers (IADL) and formerly served as IADL's vice president.

Before joining Stevens, Hinds and White, PC, as its senior partner, with law offices in New York and New Jersey, Hinds served for many years as National Director of the National Conference of Black Lawyers of the US and Canada. He has represented a number of politically unpopular clients, including Assata Shakur, the New York 8 and victims of police brutality and other governmental lawlessness including the FBI's Counter-intelligence Program (COINTELPRO).

Hinds has traveled, written, and lectured extensively in Africa, Europe, Asia and North America on international human rights issues and the impact of racism on the operation of the law, particularly on the criminal justice systems of the US. He is admitted to practice before the US Supreme Court, the International Criminal Court for Rwanda, the International Criminal Court for Yugoslavia, the Permanent International Criminal Court in The Hague and the Special Court for Sierra Leone. He has served on International Commissions of Inquiries and worked for the release of political prisoners in Asia, Africa, Europe and the Americas. He assisted in drafting the Luanda Convention on Mercenaries in Luanda, Angola in 1976.

Made in United States
North Haven, CT
25 January 2024

47839703R00313